CIMA

S T U D Y   T E X T

STRATEGIC

PAPER P6

MANAGEMENT ACCOUNTING – BUSINESS STRATEGY

In this edition we:

- **Highlight** the **most important elements** in the syllabus and the **key skills** you will need

- **Signpost** how each chapter links to the syllabus and the learning outcomes

- **Provide** lots of **exam focus points** demonstrating what the examiner will want you to do

- **Emphasise key points** in regular **fast forward** summaries

- **Test your knowledge** of what you've studied in **quick quizzes**

- **Examine your understanding** in our **exam question bank**

- **Reference** all the important topics in our **full index**

BPP Learning Media's **i-Learn** and **i-Pass** products also support this paper.

FOR EXAMS IN NOVEMBER 2008, MAY 2009 AND NOVEMBER 2009

LEARNING MEDIA

First edition 2004

Fifth edition May 2008

ISBN 9780 7517 5289 2
(previous edition 9780 7517 4216 9)

British Library Cataloguing-in-Publication Data
A catalogue record for this book
is available from the British Library

Published by

BPP Learning Media Ltd
BPP House, Aldine Place
London W12 8AA

www.bpp.com/learningmedia

Printed in Great Britain by

CPI William Clowes
Beccles
NR34 7TL

Your learning materials, published by BPP
Learning Media Ltd, are printed on paper sourced
from sustainable, managed forests.

We are grateful to the Chartered Institute of Management
Accountants for permission to reproduce past
examination questions. The suggested solutions in the
exam answer bank have been prepared by BPP Learning
Media Ltd.

Contents

Distance Learning from BPP Professional Education

You can access our exam-focused interactive e-learning materials over the **Internet**, via BPP Learn Online, hosted by BPP Professional Education.

BPP Learn Online offers **comprehensive tutor support**, **revision guidance** and **exam tips**.

Visit www.bpp.com/cima/learnonline for further details.

Learning to Learn Accountancy

BPP Learning Media's **Learning to Learn Accountancy** book is designed to be used both at the outset of your CIMA studies and throughout the process of learning accountancy. It can help you **focus your studies on the subject and exam**, enabling you to **acquire knowledge**, **practise and revise efficiently and effectively**.

How the BPP Learning Media Study Text can help you pass

Tackling studying

We know that studying for a number of exams can seem daunting, particularly when you have other commitments as well.

- We provide guidance on how to cover chapters **quickly.**

- We explain the **purposes** of the **different features** in the Study Text, demonstrating how they help you and improve your chances of passing.

Developing exam awareness

We never forget that you're aiming to pass your exams, and our Texts are completely focused on helping you do this.

- In the section **Studying P6** we introduce the key themes of the syllabus, describe the skills you need and summarise how to succeed.

- The **Introduction** to each chapter sets the chapter in the context of the syllabus and exam.

- We provide specific tips, **Exam focus points**, on what you can expect in the exam and what to do (and not to do!) when answering questions.

And our Study Text is **comprehensive**. It covers the syllabus content. No more, no less.

Using the Learning outcomes and Syllabus

CIMA's website sets out the Learning outcomes and Syllabus in full:
http://www.cimaglobal.com/cps/rde/xchg/SID-0AAAC564-1C631D43/live/root.xsl/1377.htm.

The **Learning outcomes** will show you what **capabilities** (skills) you'll have to demonstrate. The topics listed in the **Syllabus** are the **key topics** in this exam. By quickly looking through the Syllabus, you can see the breadth of the paper.

- Don't worry if the Syllabus seems large when you look through it; the Study Text will **carefully guide you** through it all.

- Remember the Study Text shows, at the start of every chapter, which **Learning outcomes** and **Syllabus areas** are covered in the chapter.

Testing what you can do

Testing yourself helps you develop the skills you need to pass the exam and also confirms that you can recall what you have learnt.

- We include **Questions** within chapters, and the **Exam Question Bank** provides lots more practice.

- Our **Quick Quizzes** test whether you have enough knowledge of the contents of each chapter.

Skim study technique

If you have limited time to cover a chapter, follow the **Skim study** technique below.

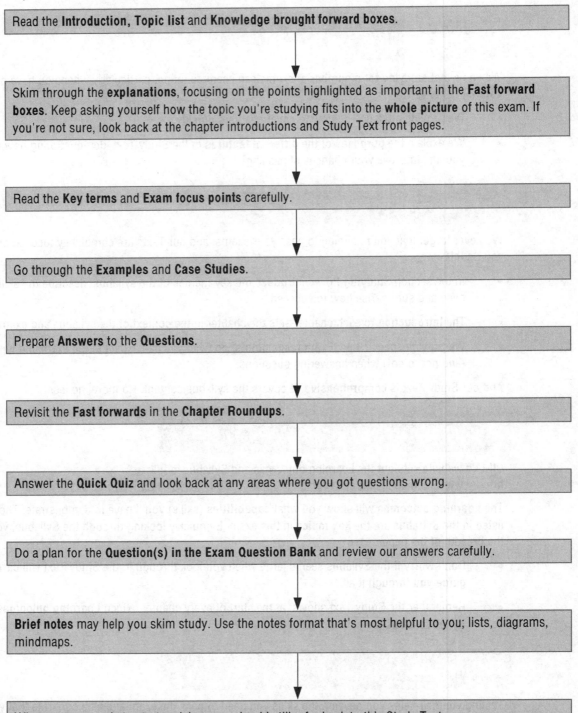

Read the **Introduction, Topic list** and **Knowledge brought forward boxes**.

Skim through the **explanations**, focusing on the points highlighted as important in the **Fast forward boxes**. Keep asking yourself how the topic you're studying fits into the **whole picture** of this exam. If you're not sure, look back at the chapter introductions and Study Text front pages.

Read the **Key terms** and **Exam focus points** carefully.

Go through the **Examples** and **Case Studies**.

Prepare **Answers** to the **Questions**.

Revisit the **Fast forwards** in the **Chapter Roundups**.

Answer the **Quick Quiz** and look back at any areas where you got questions wrong.

Do a plan for the **Question(s) in the Exam Question Bank** and review our answers carefully.

Brief notes may help you skim study. Use the notes format that's most helpful to you; lists, diagrams, mindmaps.

When you are ready to start revising, you should still refer back to this Study Text.
- As a source of **reference** (you should find the index particularly helpful for this)
- As a way to **review** (the Fast forwards, Exam focus points, Chapter Roundups and Quick Quizzes help you here)

Example chapter

Introduction

The Introduction sets the chapter in the context of the whole syllabus.

Topic list

The Topic list gives an overview of the chapter.

How the BPP Learning Media Study Text can help you pass

Introduction

This sample chapter will help you tackle the Study Text when you start studying the syllabus content in detail.

The chapter introduction explains **why** the topics in each chapter need to be studied. It links in with the **overall themes** of the Syllabus and exam, and signposts how the chapter relates to previous and future chapters. It also **highlights the main points** you should be looking out for as you go through the chapter.

Topic list	Learning outcomes	Syllabus reference	Ability required
1 The topic list helps you navigate each chapter	The Learning outcomes indicate what you will be expected to do as a result of studying this section	The Syllabus references show you how each topic fits into the Syllabus	The ability required references show you the depth of understanding you are expected to have
2 Each numbered topic is a numbered section within each chapter			
3 The topic list therefore emphasises the most important topics within each chapter			

Knowledge brought forward from earlier studies

Knowledge brought forward boxes summarise information and techniques that you are **assumed to know** from your earlier studies. As the exam may test your knowledge of these areas, you should **revise** your previous study material if you are unsure about them.

1 Key topic which has a section devoted to it

FAST FORWARD

Fast forwards give you a **summary** of the content of each of the main chapter sections. They are listed together in the roundup at the end of each chapter to allow you to review each chapter quickly.

1.1 Important topic within section

The headings within chapters give you a good idea of the **importance** of the topics covered. The larger the header, the more important the topic is. The headers will help you navigate through the chapter and locate the areas that have been highlighted as important in the front pages or in the chapter introduction.

Knowledge brought forward

Knowledge brought forward shows you what you need to remember from previous exams.

Fast forward

Fast forwards allow you to preview and review each section easily.

Example

Examples show you how theory is put into practice.

Key term

Key terms are the core vocabulary.

Exam focus point

Exam focus points provide specific links to the exam.

Formula to learn

You must remember these formulae in the exam.

Question

Questions provide vital practice of what you've learnt.

Case Study

Case Studies link what you've learnt with the business environment.

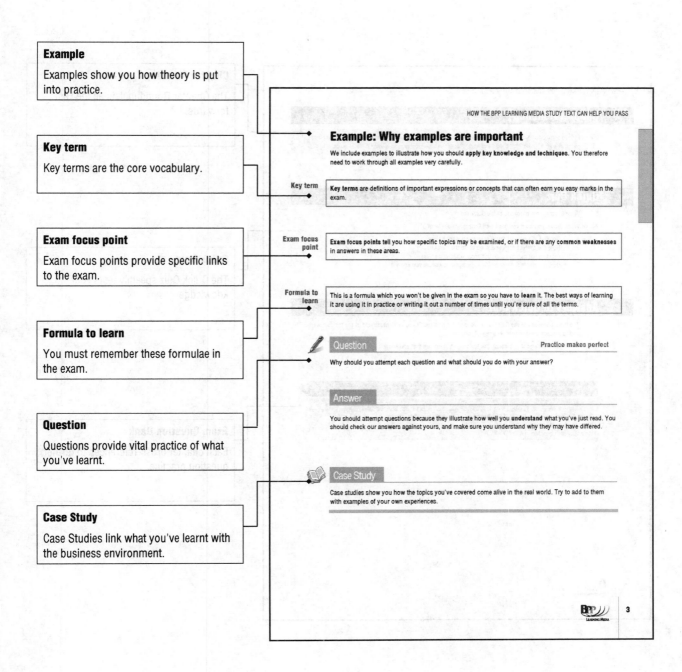

Example: Why examples are important

We include examples to illustrate how you should **apply key knowledge and techniques**. You therefore need to work through all examples very carefully.

Key term

Key terms are definitions of important expressions or concepts that can often earn you easy marks in the exam.

Exam focus point

Exam focus points tell you how specific topics may be examined, or if there are any common weaknesses in answers in these areas.

Formula to learn

This is a formula which you won't be given in the exam so you have to **learn** it. The best ways of learning it are using it in practice or writing it out a number of times until you're sure of all the terms.

Question — Practice makes perfect

Why should you attempt each question and what should you do with your answer?

Answer

You should attempt questions because they illustrate how well you **understand** what you've just read. You should check our answers against yours, and make sure you understand why they may have differed.

Case Study

Case studies show you how the topics you've covered come alive in the real world. Try to add to them with examples of your own experiences.

Chapter Roundup

• Fast forwards give you a **summary** of the content of each of the main chapter sections. They are listed together in the roundup at the end of each chapter to allow you to review each chapter quickly.

Quick Quiz

1 What are the main purposes of the Quick Quiz?

2 What should you do if you get Quick Quiz questions wrong?

A Nothing as you now know where you went wrong
B Note the correct answer and go on to the next chapter
C Practise full questions on this topic when you revise
D Go back and look through the topic again to ensure you know it

Answers to Quick Quiz

1 The main purposes of the Quick Quiz are to check how much you've remembered of the topics covered and to practise questions in a variety of formats.

2 D Go back and look through the topic again to ensure that you know it.

Now try the questions below from the Exam Question Bank

Number	Level	Marks	Time
Questions that give you practice of what you've learnt in each chapter	Examination	25	45 mins

---

Chapter Roundup

The Chapter Roundup lists all the Fast forwards.

Quick Quiz

The Quick Quiz speedily tests your knowledge.

Exam Question Bank

Each chapter cross-references to further question practice.

Approaching Strategic level exams

When students start studying Strategic level subjects they are often puzzled about how these exams differ from Managerial level papers. What are the implications of having an exam consisting of scenario questions worth 25 or 50 marks, with no short questions? This section explains the key features of Strategic level exams.

1 Strategic level fundamentals

1.1 Knowledge and application

Even at Managerial level, passing didn't only mean reproducing knowledge; you also had to **apply** what you knew. At Strategic level, the balance is tilted much more towards application. You will need a sound basis of technical knowledge; the exams will detect whether you have the necessary knowledge. However you won't pass if you just spend your time acquiring knowledge; developing application skills is vital.

1.2 Application skills

What application skills do you need? Most Strategic level questions will include detail in a scenario about a specific organisation. The following skills are particularly important when you're dealing with scenarios.

- **Identifying the most important features** of the organisation and its environment; clues to these will be scattered throughout the scenario. The technical knowledge that you have should help you do this, but you will also need business awareness and imagination
- **Using analysis techniques** that will give you more insight into the data that you're given
- **Selecting real-life examples** that are relevant to the scenario
- **Making informed judgements** that follow from your analysis about what the organisation is doing and should be doing
- **Communicating clearly and concisely** your analysis and recommendations.

1.3 Answering selectively

Examiners at Strategic level expect you to consider carefully what is relevant and significant enough to include in your answers. There are various signs that students are not making the necessary judgements:

- **Stating theories and concepts** rather than applying them
- **Quoting chunks of detail** from the question that don't add any value
- **Forcing irrelevancies into answers**, for example irrelevant theories or examples that don't relate to the scenario
- **Giving long lists or writing down all that's known** about a broad subject area, and not caring whether it's relevant or not
- **Failing to question the assumptions** made in the scenario or in the methods used to analyse the scenario
- **Focusing too narrowly on one area** – for example in P6 *Business Strategy* only covering financial strategies when non-financial strategies are also important

One aim of Strategic level papers is to prepare you for TOPCIMA; a number of marks will be available in TOPCIMA for distinguishing the relevant from the irrelevant and identifying the most important issues.

2 Knowledge brought forward

The examiners regard everything you studied at Managerial and Certificate level as knowledge that could be tested at Strategic level. It doesn't matter that this knowledge is not mentioned specifically in Strategic level syllabuses or learning outcomes; if it's relevant to the paper it could be tested.

3 Interaction of Strategic syllabuses

CIMA expects you to make links between the various papers and not see the three subjects in isolation.

- **Business strategy decisions** will **impact** upon the financial objectives, sources of finance chosen, the investment decisions, the risks the organisation faces and the controls necessary to counter those risks
- **Financial and risk and control strategies** must therefore fulfil the same criteria as business strategy; for example they should be **acceptable, suitable and feasible**
- At the same time **business strategy** will be **constrained** by the finance available and the level of risks the organisation is prepared to bear
- **Financial strategy decisions** will **impact** upon the **risks** the organisation bears and perhaps impose limitations on the controls the organisation can implement. Financial strategy will also be determined by the **financial risks** (some sources of finance may be thought too risky, the benefits of investment decisions too uncertain, risk may impact upon investment appraisal calculations)
- Remember that all three papers are management accounting papers. **Performance measurement** techniques such as ratio analysis may be useful in any paper. The **effectiveness of management accounting systems**, particularly the information provided and how useful they are as control mechanisms, could impact upon any of the papers

4 Helping yourself

4.1 Reading

Any reading you can do to develop your understanding of how businesses make strategic decisions, obtain finance and deal with risks will help. The business pages of quality newspapers can help give you the insights you need and provide some practical examples that you can use.

4.2 Post-exam guidance

Although Study Texts and Practice and Revision Kits refer to examiner's guidance, you should read all the post-exam guidance on CIMA's website for all the papers to see what questions are aiming to test, what receives credit, and the common mistakes students make. Post-exam guidance is **essential** reading.

4.3 Practice

The more practice you have, the more you will develop your application skills. The Study Text gives you questions within chapters and in the Exam Question Bank. You will also significantly improve your chances of passing by leaving yourself enough time to **attempt questions in full** from all areas of the syllabus from the BPP Learning Media Practice and Revision Kits.

Studying P6

1 What P6 is about

1.1 Introducing strategy

In Chapters 1 to 3, we are concerned with how **business strategies** are developed, and the role management information plays in strategic planning. Although we largely follow the rational model of strategic planning in P6, we acknowledge that there are a range of different perspectives on how strategies emerge, reflecting the complexity and variety of 'the real world'.

We also look at the importance of **information** (IS and IT) in business strategies, and how technological developments are influencing corporate strategy. Chapter 2 underlines the importance of knowledge and information to businesses, in both planning and control processes.

In Chapter 3 we look at the objectives and goals of organisations, and how stakeholders affect them. The P6 exam often includes a question on **stakeholders** and how they can affect an organisation and its strategy. It is important to remember the range of objectives an organisation may have, and we reflect this by looking at the themes of social responsibility and sustainability.

1.2 Strategic analysis

Considerations relating to the business environment account for 40% of the syllabus for P6, and we review them in Part B of this book, starting with a look at the general environmental factors in the macroenvironment (Chapter 4). We then move on to look the **competitive environment** in which firms operate, considering both the competitive forces affecting a particular industry and also the competitive advantage of nations(Chapter 5). In Chapter 6 we turn to look more specifically at the way organisations deal with two key stakeholders - customers and suppliers.

In Chapter 7 we move from an external focus to an internal focus, and look at some of the key aspects of an organisation's **current position** – including its value chain, and product portfolio.

The final chapter in this part of the book (Chapter 8) draws external and internal factors together, as we look at **corporate appraisal** (SWOT analysis). Corporate appraisal should indicate appropriate strategies which organisations can pursue to exploit their core competences, and achieve their financial objectives.

1.3 Strategic options

Part C of this book is concerned with the **strategic choices** organisations make. The most important issues here are how they **compete**, and what methods they employ to **grow** (Chapter 9). With respect to growth, we consider both the direction (new products and markets) and the method of growth – acquisition or organic growth (Chapter 10).

We finish this section by looking at the way management accountants can apply decision techniques to assist strategic decision making (Chapter 11).

1.4 Implementing strategy

The final part of this book covers issues which require strategic management attention – project management, change management, strategic marketing, business process re-engineering and organisational structure.

However, for an organisation to know whether a strategy has been successful it also needs to be able to **measure performance**. This is an area where the management accountant's role will be vital, although it is important that non-financial performance is considered as well as purely financial performance.

2 What's required

You need to show an understanding of, and an ability to use, business strategy ideas, and set your answers in context. At the heart of P6 is the ability to **apply your knowledge** to analyse and resolve practical problems. Key higher level skills being tested are analysis, evaluation and advice. The examiners are looking for:

- Well planned answers that are relevant and complete
- Understanding of the key issues and tools
- Ability to analyse data and information (going beyond a description of the issues)
- Answers focussed on the scenarios
- Business application to generate sensible, practical answers.

3 Passing P6

3.1 Study the whole syllabus

You need to be comfortable with **all areas of the syllabus** as questions, particularly compulsory Question 1, will often span a number of syllabus areas.

3.2 Lots of question practice

You can **develop application skills** by attempting questions in the Exam Question Bank and later on questions in the BPP Learning Media Practice and Revision Kit.

3.3 Analysing questions

For P6 it's particularly important to focus on **how long** to spend on each part of the question and not spend too much time doing any calculations at the expense of the written parts. Your primary focus in P6 should be using numerical data to support your written arguments, not simply doing calculations for their own sake.

Make sure you **read the scenario carefully to** pick up all the details given so that your answer is practical in the context (for example, how easy will it be to the organisation to raise funds to make an acquisition?)

3.4 Answering questions

You need to show understanding and ability to use relevant techniques, but most importantly make sure that you set your answers in context and don't make recommendations which are unsuitable for the organisation in question.

3.5 Exam technique

The following points of exam technique are particularly relevant to this paper.

- Analyse questions during the 20 minute reading time – for example by putting notes in the question margin

- Be aware of the verbs used in exam questions – for example, if you are asked to 'evaluate' a course of action you have to appraise and assess the value of that course of action, indicating whether it is beneficial or not.

- Identify all the question's requirements in your answer plan. The requirements of a question often contain a number of sub-requirements. Candidates often fail to answer the whole question because they do not address these sub-requirements.

- Knowledge alone is not enough to pass P6 - you have to be able to **apply** your knowledge to the scenario given in the question. A mistake which a lot of students make is to over-emphasise the theories in this paper, but fail to apply their knowledge as required. Remember, the vast majority of the marks available in this paper are for your ability to provide practical solutions to problems.

- Within each question in Paper P6 you will be presented with scenarios that detail the problems that organisations face. As such, the examiners want you to provide practical advice to these organisations as to how their problems can be overcome. Consequently your answer must relate to the organisation in question and its specific issues. General discussions with little or no application to the scenario will earn few marks. Refer to the person or organisation in the question by name in each point that you make in your answer.

4 Brought forward knowledge

The examiner may test knowledge or techniques you've learnt at Certificate or Managerial level. Paper P6 sits at the top of the Business Management Accounting Pillar in the exam structure. It will therefore draw on the materials from Paper P5 (Integrated Management) and Paper P4 (Organisational Management and Information Systems). It is essential that you have a good understanding of the syllabus areas covered by these Managerial level papers. Paper P6 requires the ability to apply such knowledge in the context of scenario organisations.

Remember, however, that brought forward knowledge will only be useful if it is linked to the particular organisation in the question.

5 Links with other Strategic level papers

Paper P6 and Paper P3 both cover Information technology/Information systems. The emphasis in P6 is how IT/IS could be used strategically for competitive advantage, whilst P3 emphasises the control aspects of IT/IS.

Business strategy decisions will impact upon the financial objectives, and investment decisions of an organisation. At the same time business strategy will be constrained by the finance available and the level of risks the organisation is prepared to bear. Therefore you should be aware of the possibility of links between P6 and P9.

The exam paper

Format of the paper

		Number of marks
Section A:	A compulsory scenario-based question, typically with 4 or 5 parts	50
Section B:	2 out of 4 scenario-based questions, 25 marks each	50
		100

Time allowed: 3 hours

Examiner guidance

The examiners have indicated that, as a general principle, there will be no marks available for knowledge itself. Instead, marks will be given for applying the correct theories or knowledge and making practical evaluations and recommendations in a variety of different business scenarios.

A likely weakness of answers is that they are too general, and are not applied closely enough to the scenario given in the question.

Plausible alternative answers could be given to many questions, so model answers should not be regarded as all-inclusive.

Numerical content

The paper is likely to have up to about 20 marks available for computations and analysis of numerical data. These have, historically, been in the compulsory Section A question. However, the examiners are under no obligation to restrict the numerical elements to Section A.

Breadth of question coverage

Questions in *both* sections of the paper may cover more than one syllabus area. Again, this reinforces the importance of reading the requirements of each question carefully to make sure you are aware of all the syllabus areas being tested before starting to answer a question.

Knowledge from other syllabuses

Where relevant, candidates should bring in their knowledge from other Strategic level papers. One aim of this paper is to prepare candidates for the TOPCIMA exam.

Analysis of past papers – Strategic level

Covered in Text chapter		Nov 2007	May 2007	Nov 2006	May 2006	Nov 2005	May 2005	Pilot paper
	INTRODUCING STRATEGY							
1	Strategic ideas & strategic planning models			O		O		
2	Information strategy & information systems					O		
2	Information technology				O			
	→ Outsourcing						O	
2	Knowledge management			C				
2	Sources of information	O				O		
3	Goals and objectives			O				
3	Stakeholders		O	O	O			O
3	Corporate social responsibility	O			O	O		
	STRATEGIC ANALYSIS							
4	PEST analysis		O			C	C, O	C
5	Porter's Five forces			O	C	O	O	O
5	Competitive advantage of nations	O				O	O	
5	Competitor analysis			O				
6	Supply chain		O					
	→ Outsourcing		O					
6	Customer profitability analysis	C						
7	Value chain				O			
7	Product portfolio & product life cycle		C		O			C
7	Benchmarking			C			O	
8	SWOT analysis							
8	Gap analysis	C						
8	Scenario planning			O				
	STRATEGIC OPTIONS							
9	Generic competitive strategies							
9	Ansoff's matrix	C, O		O		C		
10	Methods of growth (acquisition, joint venture, organic)							
11	Evaluating strategic options	O						
	IMPLEMENTING STRATEGY							
12	Change management	O						
12	Organisation structure	O						
12	Marketing / relationship marketing						C	
12	Business process re-engineering				O			
12	e-commerce and internet strategy							O
13	Performance measures		C			C		
13	Performance measurement		O					
13	Critical success factors							
13	Balanced scorecard			C				O
14	ROI & RI							
15	Transfer pricing						O	
15	Reward systems							
15	Strategic management styles	O						

C: Examined in compulsory Section A question
O: Examined in optional Section B question

Introducing strategy

Strategic ideas

Introduction

This is a scene-setting chapter, providing a framework for the content of the remainder of this Study Text. In it we first set out the general principles and practice of business strategy and then discuss the strategic role of the management accountant. With minor exceptions, this material does not form part of our coverage of your examination syllabus. However, we think it is worthwhile to cover this ground so that you may place the syllabus material in its proper context.

This Chapter builds on knowledge gained in paper P5 where you first saw different approaches to strategy.

Topic list	Learning outcomes	Syllabus references	Ability required
1 Strategic planning	–	–	–
2 Strategic planning: the rational model	–	–	–
3 Less formal strategic planning	–	–	–
4 Flexibility in strategic planning	–	–	–
5 Management accounting and business strategy	–	–	–
6 Management accounting systems	–	–	–

1 Strategic planning

All organisations need to plan if they are not to drift.

FAST FORWARD

> Strategic decisions relate to the scope of a firm's activities, the long-term direction of the organisation, and allocation of resources.

Managing business strategy involves the entire cycle of **planning and control**, at a **strategic** level.

- Strategic analysis
- Strategic choice
- Implementation of chosen strategies
- Review and control

Key term

> **Planning** is the 'establishment of objectives and the formulation, evaluation and selection of the policies, strategies, tactics and action required to achieve them. Planning comprises long-term/strategic planning, and short-term/operational planning'.
>
> *CIMA Official Terminology*

How does this relate to the management of business strategy?

Key term

> A **strategy** is a 'course of action, including the specification of resources required, to achieve a specific objective'.
>
> A **strategic plan** is a 'statement of long-term goals along with a definition of the strategies and policies which will ensure achievement of these goals'.
>
> *CIMA Official Terminology*

Keep in mind that there are a **number of approaches** to strategic decision-making: you do not need to have a formal planning process to have a strategy.

A strategic thinker should have a **vision** of:

- What the business is now
- What it could be in an ideal world
- What the ideal world would be like

2 Strategic planning: the rational model

FAST FORWARD

> The **rational model** is a comprehensive approach to strategy. It suggests a logical sequence which involves analysing the current situation, generating choices (relating to competitors, products and markets) strategies and implementing the chosen strategies.

To develop a business strategy, an organisation has to decide the following.

- What it is **good at**
- How the market might **change**
- How **customer satisfaction** can be delivered
- What might **constrain** realisation of the plan
- What should be done to **minimise risk**
- What **actions** should be put in place

Exam focus point

> To quote an article on strategy in the June 1998 issue of *Accountancy*, 'the real test of a good strategy is whether it enables the business to **use its capabilities successfully in circumstances it cannot confidently predict'**. There is no right or wrong answer. Remember this point as you tackle the case studies in the exam.

2.1 Characteristics of strategic decisions

Johnson, Scholes and Whittington (in *Exploring Corporate Strategy*) have summarised the characteristics of strategic decisions for an organisation as follows.

- Concerned with the **scope** of the organisation's activities
- Achieving **advantages** for the organisation over its competitors
- Matching of an organisation's activities to its **capabilities** and the **environment** in which it operates
- Likely to be complex in nature
- Major decisions about the allocation of **resources**
- Affect **operational** decisions, because they will set off a chain of 'lesser' decisions
- Shaped by the **values** and expectations of senior management, and other key stakeholders
- The long-term **direction** that the organisation takes
- Usually involve **change** in the organisation

2.2 The rational model   (05/06)

Strategic planning divides into a number of different stages: strategic **analysis**, strategic **choice** and **implementation**.

2.2.1 Strategic analysis

	Stage	Comment	Key tools, models, techniques
Step 1	Mission and/or vision	Mission denotes values, the business's rationale for existing; vision refers to where the organisation intends to be in a few years time	• Mission statement
Step 2	Goals	Interpret the mission to different stakeholders	• Stakeholder analysis
Step 3	Objectives	Quantified embodiments of mission	• Measures such as profitability, time scale, deadlines
Step 4	Environmental analysis	Identify opportunities and threats	• PEST analysis • Porter's 5 force analysis; 'diamond' (competitive advantage of nations) • Scenario building
Step 5	Position audit or situation analysis	Identify strengths and weaknesses Firm's current resources, products, customers, systems, structure, results, efficiency, effectiveness	• Resource audit • Distinctive competence • Value chain • Product life cycle • BCG matrix • Marketing audit
Step 6	Corporate appraisal	Combines Steps 4 and 5	• SWOT analysis charts
Step 7	Gap analysis	Compares outcomes of Step 6 with Step 3	• Gap analysis

2.2.2 Strategic choice

Stage	Comment	Key tools, models, techniques
Strategic options generation	Come up with new ideas: • How to compete (competitive advantage) • Where to compete • Method of growth	• Value chain analysis • Scenario building • Porter's generic strategic choices • Ansoff's growth vector matrix • Acquisition vs organic growth
Strategic options evaluation	Normally, each strategy has to be evaluated on the basis of • Acceptability • Suitability • Feasibility	• Stakeholder analysis • Risk analysis • Decision-making tools such as decision trees, matrices, ranking and scoring methods • Financial measures (eg ROCE, DCF)

Strategy selection involves choosing between the alternative strategies.

The **competitive strategies** are the generic strategies for competitive advantage an organisation will pursue. They determine **how you compete**.

Product-market strategies (which markets you should enter or leave) determine **where you compete** and the direction of growth.

Institutional strategies (ie relationships with other organisations) determine the **method of growth**.

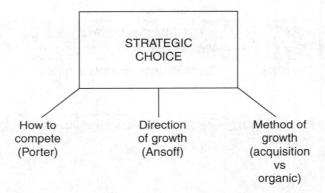

2.2.3 Strategy implementation

Strategy implementation is the **conversion** of the strategy into detailed plans or objectives for operating units.

The planning of implementation has several aspects.

• **Resource** planning
• **Operations** planning
• **Organisation** structure and control systems

2.3 Types of strategy

Corporate strategy is the most general level of strategy in an organisation, identifying the strategy for the business as a whole.

Business strategy. This relates to how an organisation approaches a particular market, or the activity of a particular business unit.

Operational and functional strategies involve decisions which are made at operational level. These decisions include product pricing, investment in plant, personnel policy and so forth. The contributions of these different functions determine the success of the strategy.

Ganymede Ltd is a company selling widgets. The finance director says: 'We plan to issue more shares to raise money for new plant capacity – we don't want loan finance – which will enable us to compete better in the vital and growing widget markets of Latin America. After all, we've promised the shareholders 5% profit growth this year, and trading is tough'.

Identify the corporate, business and functional strategies in the above quotation.

Answer

The corporate objective is profit growth. The corporate strategy is the decision that this will be achieved by entering new markets, rather than producing new products. The business strategy suggests that those markets include Latin America. The operational or functional strategy involves the decision to invest in new plant (the production function) which is to be financed by shares rather than loans (the finance function).

Exam focus point

Do not be too sequential and inflexible in your approach to answering a question on evaluating strategy. You may want to establish objectives and analyse the environment before you make choices, but allow yourself some flexibility in your thinking in case circumstances change beyond all recognition!

3 Less formal strategic planning

FAST FORWARD

A formal approach to strategy has identifiable advantages, but it has problems also. Alternative models include **incrementalism**, **freewheeling opportunism** and **crafting emergent strategies**. The management accountant's role differs in each case.

3.1 Advantages of formal planning

These are the advantages of a formal system of strategic planning.

Advantages	Comment
Identifies risks	Strategic planning helps in managing these risks.
Forces managers to think	Strategic planning can encourage creativity and initiative by tapping the ideas of the management team.
Forces decision-making	Companies cannot remain static – they have to cope with changes in the environment. A strategic plan draws attention to the need to change and adapt, not just to 'stand still' and survive.
Better control	Management control can be better exercised if targets are explicit.
Enforces consistency at all levels	Long-term, medium-term and short-term objectives, plans and controls can be made consistent with one another. Otherwise, strategies can be rendered ineffective by budgeting systems and performance measures which have no strategic content.

Advantages	Comment
Public knowledge	Drucker has argued that an entrepreneur who builds a long-lasting business has 'a theory of the business' which informs his or her business decisions. In large organisations, that theory of the business has to become public knowledge, as decisions cannot be taken only by one person.
Time horizon	Some plans are needed for the long term.
Co-ordinates	Activities of different business functions need to be directed towards a common goal.
Clarifies objectives	Managers are forced to define what they want to achieve.
Allocates responsibility	A plan shows people where they fit in.

 Case Study

UK defence firms

The UK *defence industry* faces lower government spending and greater competition as contracts are put out to open tender. There is greater competition in export markets. Having failed to diversify into civil areas, companies are changing the way they work.

Planning

A number of assumptions can be made about the environment and customer demands.

(a)   Military needs are for mobile and flexible forces.

(b)   For economic reasons, reliability and maintainability are desired.

(c)   There should be military applications of civilian technology.

(d)   The Ministry of Defence has also tightened up on procurement, replacing cost-plus contracts with competitive tenders.

European defence is likely to consolidate, and defence firms are undertaking strategic management, perhaps for the first time. All firms are concerned with cash flow and productivity. Strategic planning departments have been set up to provide necessary inputs and analyses. The planners emphasise the threat from arms manufacturers in Russia, Germany and Japan. Analysts have identified that improvements in productivity and quality, to ensure the systems work, is of key importance.

3.2 Criticisms of strategic planning in practice (Mintzberg)

The very notion that strategy-making can be reduced to planning processes has come under attack from Henry Mintzberg, in his book *The Rise and Fall of Strategic Planning.*

Problem	Comments
Practical failure	Empirical studies have not proved that formal planning processes contribute to success.
Routine and regular	Strategic planning occurs often in an annual cycle. But a firm 'cannot allow itself to wait every year for the month of February to address its problems'.
Reduces initiative	Formal planning discourages strategic thinking. Once a plan is locked in place, people are unwilling to question it.
Internal politics	The assumption of 'objectivity' in evaluation ignores political battles between different managers and departments.
Exaggerates power	Managers are not all-knowing, and there are limits to the extent to which they can control the behaviour of the organisation.

3.3 General limitations of planning models

Plans are made so that sensible attempts may be made to guide and control future developments. All planning methods are limited in their ability to help in doing this, simply because of the **unknowability of the future**.

(a) It is very common to assume that **the future will resemble the past**. Unfortunately, discontinuities or shocks occur and these are, by definition, impossible to predict with accuracy.

(b) All models require **assumptions** to be made. This has two important implications.

    (i) The assumptions used should be optimised to the industry and organisation in question. For example, industry price inflation rates may be different from the national rate.

    (ii) The further into the future one looks, the less likely it is that assumptions will **remain valid**. Predictions of more distant future events become less reliable. For some industries with extremely distant time horizons, forecasting on any basis may be quite impractical.

3.4 No strategic planning: 'freewheeling opportunism'

> An **opportunistic strategy** can seize fleeting opportunities, but may also fail to identify them.

The **freewheeling opportunism approach** suggests firms should not bother with strategic plans and should exploit opportunities as they arise.

Advantages

(a) Good opportunities are not lost.

(b) A freewheeling opportunistic approach would **adapt to change** (eg a very steep rise in the price of a key commodity) more quickly.

(c) It might encourage a more **flexible, creative attitude**.

Disadvantages

(a) **No co-ordinating framework** for the organisation, so that some opportunities get missed anyway.

(b) It emphasises the **profit motive** to the exclusion of all other considerations.

(c) The firm ends up **reacting** all the time rather than acting purposively.

3.4.1 Management accounting and freewheeling opportunism

A **freewheeling opportunism** approach eschews the careful routine of planning, and instead seizes such opportunities that arise. Not all 'opportunities' will work out, and there may be problems sustaining this policy.

The management accountant's role will be **investigative**.

(a) What are the financial characteristics of the proposed strategy? For example, in an acquisition, what is the effect on **cash flow**?

(b) How does the proposed strategy affect the firm's **risk profile**?

(c) What **new markets** will the firm be entering by pursuing this strategy? If so, what is the likely response of competitors?

3.4.2 Incrementalism

Herbert Simon suggested that managers muddle through with a solution which is reasonable, if not ideal. Managers are limited by **time**, by the **information** they have and by their own skills, habits and reflexes.

This has the following implications.

(a) Strategic managers do not evaluate all the possible options but choose between relatively few alternatives.

(b) Strategy making tends to involve small scale extensions of past policy – **incrementalism** – rather than radical shifts.

Incrementalism is an approach to strategy and decision making highlighting small and slow changes rather than one-off changes in direction. The danger is that such small scale adjustments may not be enough to move with customers and their needs.

Quinn coined the term **logical incrementalism** to mean that strategies might not be formulated by planning, but using an incremental process with an underlying logic. Top managers guide internal activities (as with the rational approach) while at the same time responding to external events, and develop their conscious strategies this way.

 Case Study

Tesco.com and Webvan

Tesco.com, the online shopping operation set up by the UK supermarket giant is an excellent example of successful incrementalism. In 1996, Tesco decided to test the potential for online grocery shopping with a website based on a single store at Osterley in West London. Over the next two years the business model was refined and the crucial decision to impose a delivery charge was made. This had the beneficial effect of leading customers to place fewer, larger orders so as to obtain the greatest benefit from the flat-rate charge. Tesco.com has grown successfully each year since its launch, partly because costs have been held down by making deliveries from existing stores. Tesco is now involved in a joint venture in the USA to create a similar home shopping operation.

Tesco's approach was markedly different from that of Webvan which set out to completely remodel the US grocery retailing industry in 1997. It aimed to create a chain of highly automated warehouses in order to increase worker productivity and offered free delivery. Unfortunately, Webvan was never really in control of its costs and it was estimated that the company lost US$130 on every order. By July 2001, the company was declared insolvent after burning its way through US$1.2bn.

3.5 No strategic planning: crafting emergent strategies

FAST FORWARD

Henry Mintzberg suggests a credible alternative to the rather clumsy rational model in the form of **emergent strategy**.

Some strategies emerge 'from below'. They can result from a number of **ad hoc choices**, perhaps made lower down the hierarchy.

Key term

An **emergent strategy** is one developed out of a pattern of behaviour not consciously imposed by senior management.

The diagram below should help to explain the point.

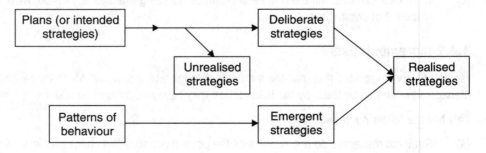

There are dangers in following an emergent strategy. It may involve **risks**, or it may **interfere** with other strategies. It will need to be **managed** if it commits the organisation to using resources.

3.5.1 Crafting strategy

Mintzberg uses the metaphor of **crafting strategy** to help understand the idea.

 Case Study

Honda

Honda is now one of the leading manufacturers of motorbikes. The company is credited with identifying and targeting an untapped market for small 50cc bikes in the US, which enabled it to expand, trounce European competition and severely damage indigenous US bike manufacturers. By 1965, Honda had 63% of the US market. But this occurred by accident.

On entering the US market, Honda had wanted to compete with the larger European and US bikes of 250ccs and over. These bikes had a defined market, and were sold through dedicated motorbike dealerships. Disaster struck when Honda's larger machines developed faults – they had not been designed for the hard wear and tear imposed by US motorcyclists. Honda had to recall the larger machines.

Honda had made little effort to sell its small 50 cc motorbikes – its staff rode them on errands around Los Angeles. Sports goods shops, ordinary bicycle and department stores had expressed an interest, but Honda did not want to confuse its image in its 'target' market of men who bought the larger bikes.

The faults in Honda's larger machines meant that *reluctantly*, Honda *had* to sell the small 50cc bikes just to raise money. They proved very popular with people who would never have bought motorbikes before. *Eventually* the company adopted this new market with enthusiasm with the slogan: 'You meet the nicest people on a Honda'. The strategy had emerged, *against* managers' conscious intentions, but they eventually responded to the new situation.

3.5.2 How to craft strategy

Mintzberg mentions the following essential activities in strategic management.

(a)   **Manage stability**.

(b)   **Detect discontinuity**. Environments do not change regularly, nor are they always turbulent. Some changes are more important than others.

(c)   **Know the business**. This has to include an awareness and understanding of operations.

(d)   **Manage patterns**. Detect emerging patterns and help them take shape if appropriate.

(e)   **Reconcile change and continuity**. Avoid concentrating on one or the other.

Following these, **crafting strategy** might involve the following roles for management accounting.

(a)   **Managing stability**. Standard management accounting information in stable environments enables the business to **control its activities** and use its resources effectively.

(b)   **Detecting discontinuity**. Management accountants are probably not the best source of information for detecting **environmental change**. Concerns such as the failure of a major customer may be picked up through debtors' age analysis.

(c)   **Know the business**

(i)   Management accounting information can model the operations of the business in financial terms.

(ii)   Many of a business's **critical success factors**, such as customer confidence, are not easily susceptible to management accounting analysis.

(d)   **Managing patterns**. The management accounting system must enable 'patterns' to be detected. All this would suggest an aggregation of financial and non-financial information in a **relational database**, with a variety of tools and techniques (eg graphical systems).

(e)   **Reconciling change and continuity**. The inflexibility of management accounting information makes it inappropriate for this purpose.

How do you think strategy is made in your organisation? Do you think that, in practice, strategy is a deliberate process, determined by senior management in a full scale planning exercise, or does it 'emerge' from the decisions made by more junior staff, which senior managers simply endorse?

Point to note

While the rational approach may mean that there is no room for **learning** in the strategy formulation process, the emergent approach could mean that there is no overall **control** over the strategy. Perhaps the best strategy is one that combines elements of both.

3.6 Chaos theory, strategy and organisations

FAST FORWARD ▶▶

The business can be seen as a self-organising complex entity that responds to its dynamic and complex environment in ways determined and promoted by its pattern of human relationships.

Organisations can be seen as structures to be made as **automatic and machine-like** as possible, but alternative (and more recent) views recognise the challenge presented by a **dynamic and complex environment**. *Stacey* discerns a further layer of complication in the way that organisations work, which he explores in terms of **chaos theory**. He proposes a radical theory of how strategy emerges, based on a view of the organisation as a **self-organising complex process, formed by human relationships**. This view contrasts sharply with what Stacey sees as orthodox theory built around **cybernetic** systems.

Stacey suggests that modern thinking about complexity can offer us a useful insight into the way organisations actually work, and how they move towards learning, innovation and adaptation to a complex and unstable global environment. Very complex systems, such as organisations, can (and do) undergo **unpredictable changes in their behaviour**, such as the adoption of a radical new strategy. **Organisations are chaotic systems**. Chaos theory holds that, although it is true that the environment is vast and is hard to model, behaviour is not random, nor is it totally unpredictable.

 Case Study

Consumer credit and banking strategies in China

The weather system is enormously complex and so, indeed, are human societies. A possible example of a small scale event or innovation, causing significant change and shifts in cultural preference, is perhaps the market for credit. According to The Economist (April 20th 2002), the market for consumer credit in East Asia is growing, and is evidenced in demand for credit cards, mortgages and so forth.

'It adds up to a seismic shift in the region's economies, banks and consumer patterns. For decades, the 'Asian' model of export-led development was based on high rates of saving and investment, with consumption suppressed. China's saving rate, at about 40 percent, is one of the highest in the world, and other East and South-east Asian countries are not far behind.'

Banks used to lend money to business conglomerates, but many loans are bad, hence the banks' wish to shift attention **from** firms **to** consumers (who are more profitable and less risky). Cultural barriers to borrowing have fallen. The main obstacles are poor payment infrastructures and limited information available to banks to assess consumers' credit risks. So, having changed strategy from lending to firms to targeting consumers – facilitated by changes in the law – the banks may still suffer from making imprudent lending decisions.

This example of self-organising change is a **collective response** of the whole system. Environmental change on the part of Asia's banks seems to have led to strategic change in their lending policies.

3.6.1 Complex adaptive systems

Below the level of the collective response, it should be remembered that organisations rely heavily on the individual **people** they contain. Those people interact according to common rules that are laid down in various ways.

- The formal organisation structure
- The organisation's culture
- The informal organisation
- Legal presumptions
- Cultural norms of the industry/national origin

Stacey sees the behaviour of the organisation as taking place both at the level of its people, and the collective level, simultaneously. He suggests that organisations that are capable of learning and adapting do so because, as systems, they are operating in the **chaotic region between stability and instability**. They will be poised in a state of '**bounded instability**', or chaos, and as a result, a new preferred state will be spontaneously created within it, allowing it to adapt and evolve through a process of self-organisation.

Matrix structure

We may observe features in organisations that are tending to operate in this way, usually as results of failures in the structured mechanistic approach. These features will often be informal, temporary, experimental and possibly unofficial ways of dealing with new problems. We might put the original introduction of progress chasers into this category; this idea subsequently developed into the **matrix structure**, as you will recall from your studies for P5.

Here are some other symptoms.

- *Ad hoc* committees and working parties
- The use of consultants
- A tendency among staff to short-circuit standard procedures in order to get things done
- The frequent introduction of new structures, reports, targets, checks and incentives

Note that all of these developments can (and often do) turn out to be of little value: the test is whether they succeed in making the organisation work in a more satisfactory manner.

Importance of management

Stacey pays considerable attention to the **position of the manager** in all this, and particularly the manager or managers at the strategic apex. Management has a very important role to play. They are in a position to see how things are going and to interact with many more other agents than most members of the organisation.

In the second edition (1996) of his book *Strategic Management and Organisational Dynamics*, Stacey discusses **ordinary management** and **extraordinary management**.

Ordinary management is just what most of us would mean by that term: it is bureaucratic, procedural, hierarchical, rational and largely consists of controlling resources and operations in order to achieve the objects of a stated plan.

Extraordinary management, on the other hand, is about the emergence of new paradigms from a free-form process of persuasion, intuition and group-based organisational learning. It exists alongside ordinary management and is the means by which the problems and anomalies that ordinary management finds it difficult to deal with are integrated and resolved.

3.6.2 Complex responsive processes

Stacey completely rewrote his book for the third (1999) edition, removing his discussion of these two aspects of management, since his views on the nature of organisations had changed. In the third edition, he was at pains to **move away from the idea of the manager as an observer**, outside the organisation and able to influence it in a rational manner. Instead, he emphasised that **managers cannot avoid being part of the systems they are trying to run** and must accept that the 'self-organising conversational life of an organisation' is fundamental to the way they (both managers and organisations) work.

This adjustment to his ideas about management and his dissatisfaction with the idea of the manager as an autonomous, objective observer, led Stacey to cease to use the term **complex adaptive system** of organisations and to see them more as the product of **complex responsive processes**: such processes operate without reference to the standard control model based on feedback and corrective action, producing new paradigms in a revolutionary fashion.

3.7 Resource-based strategy

FAST FORWARD

The resource-based approach to strategy starts from a consideration of strengths and weaknesses and, in particular, of **distinctive competences**.

All the approaches to strategy we have discussed so far are examples of what is known as the positioning approach to strategy. This is because they seek to develop competitive advantage in a way that responds to the **nature of the competitive environment**: the firm positions its offering in response to the opportunities or threats it discerns.

A fundamentally different approach is **resource-based strategy**. This was developed in response to two problems with the positioning method.

(a)   Many environments are too complex and dynamic to permit continuing effective analysis and response.

(b)   Once an opportunity is discerned and an offering made, it is very easy for competitors to make similar offerings, thus rapidly eroding competitive advantage.

The resource-based view is that sustainable competitive advantage is only attained as a result of the possession of distinctive resources. These may be physical **assets or resources**, such as the effective monopolisation of diamonds by *De Beers*, or, more typically in today's service economies, they may be capabilities or **competences**.

Competences develop in a variety of ways. Here are some examples.

- **Experience** in making and marketing a product or service
- The talents and potential of **individuals** in the organisation
- The **quality of co-ordination.**

3.7.1 Johnson, Scholes and Whittington

As is so often the case, the terminology used in the literature of resource-based strategy is not yet formalised. *Johnson, Scholes and Whittington* use their own very clear and specific set of terms when discussing resources and competences and your syllabus requires that you should understand and use these terms also.

Key terms

Strategic capability is the adequacy and suitability of the resources and competences of an organisation for it to survive and prosper.

Tangible resources are the physical assets of an organisation, such as plant, labour and finance.

Intangible resources are non-physical assets such as information, reputation and knowledge.

Competences are the activities and processes through which an organisation deploys its resources effectively.

Threshold capabilities are essential for the organisation to be able to compete in a given market.

Threshold resources and **threshold competences** are needed to meet customers' minimum requirements and therefore for the organisation to continue to exist.

Unique resources and **core competences** underpin competitive advantage and are difficult for competitors to imitate or obtain.

This analysis requires some discussion.

(a) Note the way that Johnson, Scholes and Whittington use the word **capabilities** to denote a useful overall category that contains both resources and competences.

(b) Look carefully at the definitions of **tangible** and **intangible resources**. These are not the tangible and intangible *assets* you are familiar with as an accountant: the inclusion of labour and finance under tangible resources, for example, demonstrates this.

(c) **Competences**. A connected point is the definition of **competences;** make sure you appreciate the difference between a **competence** and an **intangible resource**. We might say that the relationship between the two is that a competence might well create, use or exploit an intangible resource (or a tangible one, for that matter). Thus, information is an **intangible resource**; the ability to make good use of it is a **competence**.

(d) **Capabilities**. We have said that capabilities consist of **resources** and **competences**. As you can see, this means that Johnson, Scholes and Whittington effectively give a choice of definition for **threshold resources** and **threshold competences**. Each has its own specific definition, but since each qualifies as a **threshold capability**, we could, presumably, also use that definition.

(e) Johnson, Scholes and Whittington do not provide a term to mean **unique resources** and **core competences** taken together as a class: we might speculate that **unique capabilities** or **core capabilities** could be used in this way, but it would probably be unwise to do this in the exam.

3.7.2 Hamel and Prahalad

Hamel and Prahalad suggest that an important aspect of strategic management is the determination of the competences the company will require **in the future** in order to be able to provide new benefits to customers. They say a **core competence** must have three qualities.

- It must make a **disproportionate** contribution to the **value** the customer perceives
- It must be '**competitively unique**', which means one of three things: actually unique; superior to competitors; or capable of dramatic improvement
- It must be **extendable**, in that it must allow for the development of an array of new products and services

In many cases, a company might choose to combine competences.

Bear in mind that **relying on a competence is no substitute for a strategy**. However, a core competence can form a basis for a strategy. Here it is important to reiterate that a core competence must be difficult to imitate if it is to confer lasting competitive advantage. In particular, skills that can be bought in are unlikely to form the basis of core competences, since competitors would be able to buy them in just as easily. Core competences are more about what the organisation is than about what it does. So it is possible to regard a strong brand as a kind of core competence: it is a unique resource that confers a distinct competitive advantage.

3.8 Whittington's analysis

Whittington offers an analysis of approaches to strategy making.

(a) The **Classical School** lays down rules on the basis that both environment and firm are rational structures that can be analysed and a route to profit maximisation established.

(b) The **Evolutionary School** proposes a more organic approach based on survival because neither organisation nor environment can be completely analysed, nor can their behaviour be completely predicted.

(c) The **Processual School** emphasises internal processes of bargaining and learning and the gradual emergence of objectives.

(d) The **Systemic School** emphasises the need for awareness of the cultural and social environment.

Whittington's analysis is important because it highlights that there is not a single, right approach to strategy. However, it also highlights that while strategists can justifiably differ on their philosophical perspectives, their strategies must be coherent to be effective.

There may well not be a single correct answer to the exam questions you answer in P6. However, to score well you need to ensure that your answers are logical and coherent and relate exactly to the detail given in the question scenario.

4 Flexibility in strategic planning

FAST FORWARD

The business environment demands **flexibility** in strategy.

All companies must make allowances for the possible need to make changes. Planning must therefore have the following characteristics.

- It must be **flexible**.
- It must establish **controls** for measuring performance.

Thus, an objective of increasing turnover from £5 million in the past year to £10 million in five years' time, and raising profits from £1 million to £1.5 million, contains sufficient flexibility to permit growth by various options.

4.1 Example of flexibility in planning

Suppose that XYZ plc has been asked to tender for a contract. The estimated cost of the contract is £2,000,000 although there is a 10% probability that costs will exceed this amount by up to £200,000. The average amount of capital tied up in the project would be one half of the total cost – ie £1,000,000. The company's directors have set a minimum target return of 30% on capital for all contracts of this type. In this case, however, the directors are aware that a competitor is keen to win the contract, and could put in a tender price as low as £2,100,000. What should XYZ plc's tender price be?

If the company's price objective of a 30% return on capital is regarded as rigid, the tender price should be as follows.

	£
Cost – most likely estimate	2,000,000
Minimum return (30% of £1,000,000)	300,000
Price	2,300,000

At this price, however, XYZ plc might fail to win the contract since the rival bidder might put in a tender of £2,100,000.

XYZ plc should therefore consider the following options.

(a) Put in a tender of £2,300,000 and try to justify the higher price with the promise of a better quality product or service to the customer.

(b) Depending on how important the contract is to XYZ plc, the directors may agree to compromise on the target return of 30% and put in a tender below £2,300,000.

    (i) A tender of £2,200,000 should be sufficient to provide a return of 20%, and if costs do overrun, the contract would still just break even.

    (ii) A tender in the region of £2,100,000, the expected rival bid, would provide a return of only 10% and the possibility of making a loss if costs overrun.

5 Management accounting and business strategy

FAST FORWARD

Strategic management accounting information should have an **external and future orientation** and should provide **decision-relevant** information on issues such as product profitability, competition costs, the value of market share and so on.

5.1 Management accounting and planned strategies

The role of the **management accountant in strategic planning** is to provide management information in order that strategic planning and control decisions can be made. Particular examples of the role of the management accountant are found throughout this text.

> **Management accounting** is 'the application of the principles of accounting and financial management to create, protect, preserve and increase value for the stakeholders of for profit and not-for-profit enterprises in the public and private sectors.
>
> Management accounting is an integral part of management. It requires the identification, generation, presentation, interpretation and use of information relevant to:
>
> - Inform strategic decisions and formulate business strategy
> - Plan long, medium and short-run operations
> - Determine capital structure and fund that structure
> - Design reward strategies for executives and shareholders
> - Inform operational decisions
> - Control operations and ensure the efficient use of resources
> - Measure and report financial and non-financial performances to management and other stakeholders
> - Safeguard tangible and intangible assets
> - Implement corporate governance procedures, risk management and internal controls'.
>
> *CIMA Official Terminology*

5.1.1 Future uncertainty

It is worth emphasising the **uncertainty** in much strategic planning.

(a)   Strategic plans may cover a **long period** into the future.

(b)   Many strategic plans involve big changes and **new ventures**, such as capacity expansion decisions or decisions to develop into new product areas and new markets.

Inevitably, management accounting information for strategic planning will be based on incomplete data and will use **forecasts** and **estimates.**

(a)   It follows that strategic management accounting information is unlikely to give clear guidelines for management decisions and should incorporate some **risk and uncertainty analysis** (eg sensitivity analysis).

(b)   For longer term plans, DCF techniques ought to be used in financial evaluation.

(c)   The management accountant will be involved in the following.
- Project evaluation
- Managing cash and operational matters
- Reviewing the outcome of the project (post implementation review)

5.1.2 External and competitor orientation

Much management accounting information has been devised for internal consumption.

However, it is important to balance this with a consideration of external factors.

- Strategic management involves **environmental considerations**
- A strategy is pursued in relation to **competitors**

5.2 The challenge for management accountants

The challenge lies in providing more relevant information for decision making. Traditional management accounting systems may not always provide this.

(a) **Historical costs** are not necessarily the best guide to decision-making. One of the criticisms of management accounting in a strategic context is that management accounting information is biased towards the **past rather than the future.**

(b) **Strategic issues** are not easily detected by management accounting systems.

(c) **Financial models** of some sophistication are needed to enable management accountants to provide useful information.

The characteristics of a strategic management accounting system are discussed in some detail later in this chapter.

5.3 What is strategy?

Strategy is a concept that has many shades of meaning.

A **strategy** is a 'course of action, including the specification of resources required, to achieve a specific objective'.
CIMA *Official Terminology*

A basic premise is that strategy is concerned with **long-term direction**. Johnson, Scholes and Whittington (in *Exploring Corporate* Strategy) develop this idea.

'Strategy is the **direction** and **scope** of an organisation over the **long term** which achieves **advantage** in a changing **environment**, through its configuration of **resources** and **competences** with the aims of fulfilling **stakeholder expectations**.'

We can take the highlighted phrases out of this definition, and expand them to indicate that there is general agreement on what constitutes the key elements of strategy.

Phrase	Comment
Direction and scope	Strategy gives at least an **initial deliberate direction**, range of **activities** and **future** for the company to aim at, even if environmental circumstances conspire to send it off course and demand management action.
Long term	Most organisations are 'in it' for the **achievement of objectives** that will go beyond short-term profit targets. What constitutes 'long term' in business strategy is open to debate; Stacey (2000) claims that the average lifespan of commercial organisations in Western countries is about 40 years. Bear in mind that: • Time horizons are culturally determined; the 'long-term' means different things in different cultures. • The 'long-term' varies from industry to industry: compare fashion retailing with mining. A turnround strategy for a fashion retailer depends on success in one or two seasons.
Achieves advantage	Strategy affects the overall **welfare** of the organisation and its **position against competitors**.
Changing environment	It is a tenet of business strategy that an organisation is inextricably linked with its environment, and strategy can help the organisation to cope with **changes** and **complexity**.
Configuration of resources and competences	Strategies require **processes** to guide the **effective utilisation** of resources and competences.
Stakeholder expectations	Stakeholders (in particular **shareholders**) have their own interests in the organisation. Should the pursuit of shareholder wealth be the main concern of management? What about customer expectations and satisfying market demand?

Mintzberg argues that five definitions of strategy are needed. These are represented on the diagram which we have developed below.

Point to note

The diagram goes beyond giving a definition of strategy; it indicates some of the issues in the development of strategic thinking that we will be examining in the next chapter. The basic distinction is between planning a strategy (being 'rational'), and allowing it to emerge ('crafting' and learning).

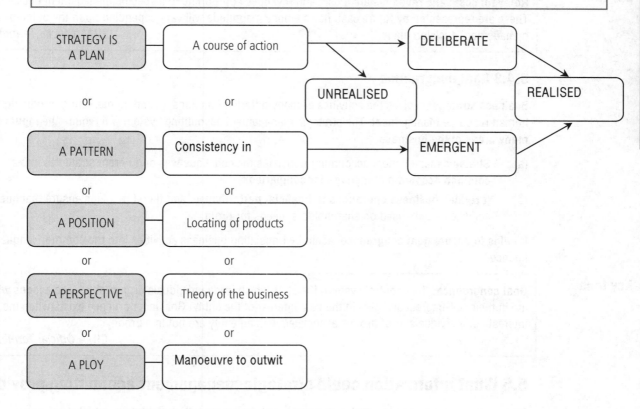

5.4 What is strategic management accounting?

Key term

Strategic management accounting is a 'form of management accounting in which emphasis is placed on information which relates to factors external to the entity, as well as non-financial information and internally generated information'.   CIMA *Official Terminology*

Ward suggests that the role of the strategic management accountant can be analysed as follows.

(a)   **Financial analysis** indicates the **current position** of a business and its financial performance in comparison with competitors, as well as breaking it down into product and customer profitability analyses. (These are discussed in later chapters.)

(b)   **Financial planning** quantifies the goals and objectives of the business, normally in a budget.

(c)   **Financial control**. Financial information is an essential part of the **feedback** mechanism comparing planned with actual performance.

5.4.1 External orientation

The important fact which distinguishes strategic management accounting from other management accounting activities is its **external orientation**, towards customers and competitors, suppliers and perhaps other stakeholders.

(a)   **Competitive advantage is relative**. Understanding competitors is therefore of prime importance.

(b)   **Customers** determine if a firm has competitive advantage.

5.4.2 Future orientation

Another criticism of traditional management accounts is that they are **backward-looking**. Decision-making is a forward and outward looking process.

Strategic management accountants will use **relevant costs** and revenues (ie **incremental** costs and revenues and **opportunity** costs) for decision-making.

> **Relevant costs and revenues** are 'costs and revenues appropriate to a specific management decision. These are represented by future cash flows whose magnitude will vary depending upon the outcome of the management decision made.'
> CIMA *Official Terminology*

5.4.3 Goal congruence

Business strategy involves the activities of many different functions, including marketing, production and human resource management. The strategic management accounting system will require the **inputs of many areas of the business**.

(a) Strategic management accounting translates the consequences of different strategies into a **common accounting language for comparison**.

(b) It **relates business operations to financial performance**, and therefore helps ensure that business activities are focused on shareholders' needs for profit.

It **helps to ensure goal congruence**, again by translating business activities into the common language of finance.

> **Goal congruence.** 'In a control system, the state which leads individuals or groups to take actions which are in their self-interest and also in the best interest of the entity. Goal incongruence exists when the interests of individuals or of groups associated with an entity are not in harmony.'
> CIMA *Official Terminology*

5.5 What information could strategic management accounting provide?

Bearing in mind the need for **goal congruence**, **external orientation** and **future orientation**, some **examples** of strategic management accounting are provided below.

(a) **Competitors' costs**. What are they? How do they compare with ours? Can we beat them? Are competitors vulnerable because of their cost structure?

(b) **Financial effect of competitor response**.

(c) **Product profitability**. A firm should want to know what profits or losses are being made by each of its products, and why.

(d) **Customer profitability**. Some customers or groups of customers are worth more than others.

(e) **Pricing decisions**. Accounting information can help to analyse how profits and cash flows will vary according to price and prospective demand.

(f) The **value of market share**. A firm ought to be aware of what it is worth to increase the market share of one of its products.

(g) **Capacity expansion**. Should the firm expand its capacity, and if so by how much?

(h) **Brand valuation**. What are the costs and benefits of investing in building brands?

(i) **Shareholder wealth**. Future profitability determines the value of a business.

(j) **Cash-flow**. A loss-making company can survive if it has adequate cash resources, but a profitable company cannot survive unless it has sufficient liquidity.

(k) Effect of **acquisitions** and **mergers**.

(l) Decisions to **enter or leave a business area**.

(m) Introduction of **new technology**.

> **Most strategic decisions are unique**, so the information needed to support them is likely to be ad hoc and specially tailored. This is also true for your exam. Make sure any strategic decisions you recommend are supported by the detail given in the scenario.

5.5.1 Useful cost categories for strategic management accounting

Some cost classifications are particularly relevant.

Key term

> **Differential/incremental cost**. This is the 'difference in total cost between alternatives'. For strategic decision making this can be considered as the extra cost that would be incurred by a decision.
>
> **Avoidable cost**. This is the 'specific cost of an activity or sector of a business which would be avoided if the activity or sector did not exist'.
>
> **Committed cost**. A 'cost arising from prior decisions, which cannot, in the short run, be changed'.
>
> **Controllable cost**. A 'cost that can be controlled, typically by a cost, profit or investment centre manager'.
>
> **Opportunity cost** is 'the value of the benefit sacrificed when one course of action is chosen in preference to an alternative'.
>
> CIMA *Official Terminology*

5.6 Success factors for a strategic management accounting system (SMAS)

Strategic management accounting has to bridge a gap between financial reporting on the one hand and the uncertainties of the future on the other. We can now go on to identify the success factors of a strategic management accounting system (as outlined by Ward). It should:

- Aid strategic decisions
- Close the communication gap between accountants and managers
- Identify the type of decision
- Offer appropriate financial performance indicators
- Distinguish between economic and managerial performance
- Provide relevant information
- Separate committed from discretionary costs
- Distinguish discretionary from engineered costs
- Use standard costs strategically
- Allow for changes over time

These are now discussed in more detail.

5.6.1 Aid strategic decisions

As part of a strategic management system, the SMAS will provide one-off information to support and evaluate particular strategic decisions and information for strategic management, in order to monitor strategies and the firm's overall competitive position. Changes in the external environment and competitor responses should be easily incorporated into the system.

5.6.2 Close the communication gap

The SMAS converts financial data into information for strategic decision-making. Financial data is off-putting to many people. Consequently, the preparer of such information should make sure that it is tailored.

- Ask the recipient how he or she would like the **format** of the report
- Provide only the **relevant** supporting financial data
- Identify the **key assumptions** on which the information is prepared

5.6.3 Identify the types of decision

Ward states that, despite the one-off nature of many strategic decisions, it is possible to identify the following types of financial decision.

(a) **Changing the balance of resource allocation** between different business areas, for example by increasing spending in one area.

(b) **Entering a new business area** (eg new product development, new markets). Some account will have to be taken of the timescale in which the strategy is expected to consume resources, as benefits may be some time in coming.

(c) **Exit decisions** which come in two forms.

    (i) **Closing down** part of the business and selling off the assets

    (ii) Selling the business as a **going concern**

To support such decisions, the SMAS should:

- Incorporate **future cash flows** rather than historic costs
- Include only those items which will be **changed** by the particular decision

5.6.4 Offer suitable financial performance measures

Two general points can be made.

(a) **Financial data is not enough**. Customers drive a business, and competitors can ruin it, so performance measures which ignore key variables of customer satisfaction or competitor activity ignore critical strategic issues.

(b) **The financial information must suit the competitive strategies**. A report complaining about the expense of an advertising campaign ignores the fact that failing to advertise could lead to loss of market share.

5.6.5 Distinguish economic versus managerial performance

A business's **overall economic performance** results from both controllable factors and uncontrollable factors.

(a) **Risk**. Shareholders may be happy with the risk, if it is balanced by suitable return, but a manager may be unhappy if his or her career is at risk from pursuing a strategy whose success is outside his or her control.

(b) **Performance**. Judging a manager's contribution on the basis of the overall economic performance of the business may not reflect his or her contribution at all. Managers should therefore be judged on their contribution in areas over which they have control.

5.6.6 Provide relevant information

Relevant financial information should be provided, which presents strategic decisions from the organisation's viewpoint. Specific, tailored reports should support individual decisions and activities, perhaps with **profitability analyses** for each market segment.

5.6.7 Separate committed from discretionary costs

Ignore sunk costs. This has a number of ramifications for the making of business strategies.

- A cost may be **committed** even though it has not actually been incurred.
- **Discretionary costs** are those over which the decision-maker still has choice.

5.6.8 Distinguish between discretionary and engineered costs

Engineered costs are those which derive from a relatively predictable relationship between input materials and output units of production.

5.6.9 Use standard costs strategically

Standard costs consist of a physical usage element (eg volume of materials) and a price element. The split between the **price** and **usage** elements is indicative.

- The extent to which the firm is **vulnerable** to suppliers raising prices
- The possible impact of **trade-offs** between, say, labour and materials

Trade-offs. If the relationships between the input material and output quantities are known, or variable, then standard costing can show the financial effects of different mixes.

(a) For example, if there is a trade off between labour and raw materials, changes in the relative costs of these factors can indicate a suitable mix: more expensive labour would result in less of a valued raw material being used.

(b) If the price of a raw material escalates suddenly, the standard costing system can be amended with the new price, and a new mix analysis calculated which takes it into account.

Absorbing indirect/fixed overheads into products can lead to poor pricing decisions, in the short term. If a factory is working at 60% capacity utilisation, this could lead to higher indirect costs being absorbed per unit. This information, if wrongly interpreted, could be used to suggest a price rise, rather than a reduction to encourage more sales and hence an increased utilisation of capacity.

6 Management accounting systems

FAST FORWARD

Management accounting information can be used to support **strategic decision making**.

6.1 What is a management accounting information?

Management accounting information is used by managers for a variety of purposes.

(a) To **make decisions**. Managers are faced with several types of decision.

    (i) **Strategic decisions** (which relate to the longer term objectives of a business) require information which tends to relate to the organisation as a whole, is in summary form and is derived from both internal and external sources.

    (ii) **Tactical and operational decisions** (which relate to the short or medium term and to a department, product or division rather than the organisation as a whole) require information which is more detailed and more restricted in its sources.

(b) To **plan** for the future. Managers have to plan and they need information to do this, much of it management accounting information.

(c) To **monitor the performance** of the business. Managers need to know what they want the business to achieve (targets or standards) and what the business is actually achieving. By comparing the actual achievements with targeted performance, management can decide whether control action is needed.

(d) To **measure profits** and put a **value to inventories**. Management accounting systems can be used to analyse the profitability of the business as a whole, and of the individual divisions, departments or products within the business. Putting a value to closing inventories is an element in the measurement of profits in a period (as well as for valuation purposes in the balance sheet) and costing systems are used to derive inventory values.

6.2 Strategic planning, management control and operational control

Another way of looking at the information that a management accounting system may be required to produce is to consider the question under three headings put forward by *Anthony:* strategic planning, management control and operational control.

6.2.1 Strategic planning information

Key term

Strategic plan. 'Statement of long-term goals along with a definition of the strategies and policies which will ensure achievement of these goals.'
CIMA Official Terminology

Strategic plans include such matters as the selection of products and markets, the required levels of company profitability and the purchase and disposal of subsidiary companies or major fixed assets.

Strategic planning information is generally **external data** about competitors, customers, suppliers, new technology, the state of markets and the economy, government legislation, political unrest and so on.

Such information includes overall profitability, the profitability of different segments of the business, future market prospects, the availability and cost of raising new funds, total manning levels and capital equipment needs. Much of this information must come from **environmental sources,** although internally generated information will always be used.

Point to note

Strategic information is prepared on an **ad hoc basis**. It also tends to be more **approximate** and **imprecise** than management control information.

6.2.2 Management control information

Key term

Management control. 'All of the processes used by managers to ensure that organisational goals are achieved and procedures adhered to, and that the organisation responds appropriately to changes in its environment.

Closed loop system

Control system that includes provision for corrective action, taken on either a feedforward or a feedback basis.

Feedback control

Measurement of differences between planned outputs and actual outputs achieved, and the modification of subsequent action and/or plans to achieve future required results.

Feedforward control

Forecasting of differences between actual and planned outcomes, and the implementation of action, before the event, to avoid such differences.

Open loop system

Control system that includes no provision for corrective action to be applied to the sequence of activities.'
CIMA *Official Terminology*

The information required for management control **embraces the entire organisation** and **provides a comparison between actual results and the plan**. The information is often **quantitative** (labour hours, quantities of materials consumed, volumes of sales and production) and is commonly **expressed in money terms**.

Such information includes productivity measurements, budgetary control or variance analysis reports, cash flow forecasts, profit results within a particular department of the organisation, labour turnover statistics within a department and so on. A large proportion of this information will be **generated from within the organisation** and it will often have an **accounting emphasis**.

6.2.3 Operational control information

Operational information is information which is **needed for the conduct of day-to-day implementation of plans**. It will include much **'transaction data'** such as data about customer orders, purchase orders, cash receipts and payments.

The amount of **detail** provided in information is likely to vary with the purpose for which it is needed, and operational information is likely to go into much more detail than management control information. Operational information is often **expressed in terms of units, hours, quantities of material and so on**.

Chapter Roundup

- Strategic decisions relate to the scope of a firm's activities, the long-term direction of the organisation, and allocation of resources.

- The **rational model** is a comprehensive approach to strategy. It suggests a logical sequence which involves analysing the current situation, generating choices (relating to competitors, products and markets) strategies and implementing the chosen strategies.

- A formal approach to strategy has identifiable advantages, but it has problems also. Alternative models include **incrementalism**, **freewheeling opportunism** and **crafting emergent strategies**. The management accountant's role differs in each case.

- An **opportunistic strategy** can seize fleeting opportunities, but may also fail to identify them.

- *Henry Mintzberg* suggests a credible alternative to the rather clumsy rational model in the form of **emergent strategy**.

- The business can be seen as a self-organising complex entity that responds to its dynamic and complex environment in ways determined and promoted by its pattern of human relationships.

- The resource-based approach to strategy starts from a consideration of strengths and weaknesses and, in particular, of **distinctive competences**.

- The business environment demands **flexibility** in strategy.

- Strategic management accounting information should have an **external and future orientation** and should provide **decision-relevant** information on issues such as product profitability, competition costs, the value of market share and so on.

- Management accounting information can be used to support **strategic decision making**.

Quick Quiz

1   What is a strategy?

2   Which of these terms does Stacey believe best describes the way organisations should be seen as working:

    A   Cybernetic control system
    B   Complex responsive processes

3   What is the basic principle of resource-based strategy?

4   What is strategic management accounting?

5   What are the three criteria which are usually used to evaluate strategy?

6   Decision making is a

    A   forward and inward looking process
    B   backward and outward looking process
    C   forward and outward looking process
    D   backward and inward looking process

7   What are the three stages of strategic planning?

8   Management accounting system information, including to Anthony's three headings, can assist with

    (1)   ....
    (2)   ....
    (3)   ....

9   What is an emergent strategy?

10   What does Ward suggest are the three aspects of a strategic management accountant's role?

1   A strategy is a course of action, including the specification of resources required, to achieve a specific objective.

2   B

3   Competitive advantage can only be sustained by the possession of distinctive resources or competences.

4   CIMA has defined strategic management accounting as follows: 'Form of management accounting in which emphasis is placed on information which relates to factors external to the entity, as well as non-financial information and internally generated information'.

5   Suitability, acceptability and feasibility.

6   C

7   Strategic analysis, strategic choice, and strategic implementation.

8   (1)   Strategic planning
    (2)   Management control
    (3)   Operational control

9   An emergent strategy is one developed out of a pattern of behaviour, not consciously imposed by senior management.

10 Financial analysis; financial planning; financial control.

Now try the question below from the Exam Question Bank

Number	Level	Marks	Time
Q1	Introductory	n/a	30 mins

Information and strategy

2

Introduction

In this chapter we examine some aspects of information management that have strategic significance. It is obvious that the rational model is highly dependent on information from both outside the organisation and from within it. It is not perhaps quite so obvious that other methods of making strategy are equally information-dependent. However, consider the famous Honda motorcycle instance of emergent strategy: this could not have occurred if the Honda management had not analysed the sales data to learn what was happening.

Information is also essential for strategic control, a topic dealt with later in this Study Text.

Topic list	Learning outcomes	Syllabus references	Ability required
1 Strategic information systems	B(vi)	B9	Evaluation
2 Information strategy	B(vi)	B9	Evaluation
3 Information sources and management	A(iii), A(iv)	A10	Evaluation
4 Information for planning and control	A(iii), A(iv)	A10	Evaluation
5 Knowledge management	B(vi), D(vi)	B7, B10	Evaluation
6 Databases and models	B(vi)	B7	Evaluation
7 Data warehousing and data mining	B(vi)	B7	Evaluation
8 The IT department	D(iv), D(v)	D9	Evaluation

1 Strategic information systems

Key terms

Data is the raw material for data processing. Data consists of numbers, letters and symbols and relates to facts, events, and transactions.

Information is data that has been processed in such a way as to be meaningful to the person who receives it.

1.1 Strategic information

FAST FORWARD

Strategic information is used to **plan** the **objectives** of the organisation, and to **assess** whether the objectives are being met in practice.

Strategic planning, management control and operational control may be seen as a hierarchy of planning and control decisions. (This is sometimes called the Anthony hierarchy, after the writer *Robert Anthony*.)

Strategic information is used to **plan** the **objectives** of the organisation, and to **assess** whether the objectives are being met in practice. Such information includes overall profitability, the profitability of different segments of the business, future market prospects, the availability and cost of raising new funds, total cash needs, total manning levels and capital equipment needs.

Strategic information is:

- Derived from both **internal and external** sources
- **Summarised** at a high level
- Relevant to the **long term**
- Concerned with the **whole organisation**
- Both **quantitative** (numerical) and **qualitative** (descriptive, based on qualities)
- **Uncertain**, as the future cannot be accurately predicted

1.2 Strategic information systems

FAST FORWARD

Strategic IT systems include **EIS**, **MIS** and **DSS**. **Value added networks** facilitate the strategic use of information in order to add value.

1.2.1 Executive Information Systems (EIS)

Key term

> An **Executive Information System (EIS)** pools data from internal and external sources and makes information available to senior managers in an easy-to-use form. EIS help senior managers make strategic, unstructured decisions.

An EIS should provide senior managers with easy access to key **internal and external** information. The system summarises and tracks strategically critical information, possibly drawn from internal MIS and DSS, but also including data from external sources eg competitors, legislation, external databases such as Reuters.

An EIS is likely to have the following **features**.

- Flexibility
- Quick response time
- Sophisticated data analysis and modelling tools

A model of a typical EIS is shown below.

An Executive Information System (EIS)

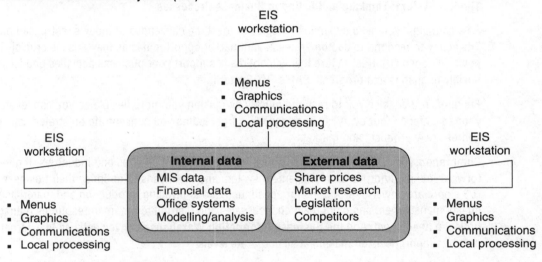

1.2.2 Management Information Systems (MIS)

Key term

> **Management Information Systems (MIS)** convert data from mainly internal sources into information (eg summary reports, exception reports). This information enables managers to make timely and effective decisions for planning, directing and controlling the activities for which they are responsible.

An MIS provides regular reports and (usually) on-line access to the organisation's current and historical performance.

MIS usually transform data from underlying transaction processing systems into summarised files that are used as the basis for management reports.

MIS have the following characteristics:

- Support **structured** decisions at operational and management control levels
- Designed to report on **existing** operations
- Have little analytical capability
- Relatively **inflexible**
- Have an **internal** focus

1.2.3 Decision support systems (DSS)

> **Decision support systems (DSS)** combine data and analytical models or data analysis tools to support semi-structured and unstructured decision making.

DSS are used by management to assist in making decisions on issues which are subject to high levels of uncertainty about the problem, the various **responses** which management could undertake or the likely **impact** of those actions.

Decision support systems are intended to provide a wide range of alternative information gathering and analytical tools with a major emphasis upon **flexibility** and **user-friendliness**.

DSS have more analytical power than other systems enabling them to analyse and condense large volumes of data into a form that helps managers make decisions. The objective is to allow the manager to consider a number of **alternatives** and evaluate them under a variety of potential conditions.

Case Study

The R/3 System: Thinking and Acting in Business Processes

As a company, you need dynamic strategies to meet the challenges of today's fast-paced business world. The ability to respond to customer needs and market opportunities as they arise is crucial. The answer? A powerful, open IT infrastructure that will optimally support your business activities and let you adjust flexibly to change and progress: **SAP's R/3 System**.

Flexible. R/3 enables you to respond quickly by making you more flexible so you can leverage changes to your advantage. Your everyday business will surge, letting you concentrate on strategically expanding to address new products and markets.

Comprehensive. SAP's R/3 System is ideal for companies of all sizes and industries. It gives them both a forward-looking information management system and the means to optimise their business processes. At R/3's core are powerful programs for accounting and controlling, production and materials management, quality management and plant maintenance, sales and distribution, human resources management, and project management. And the **Business Information Warehouse** conveniently edits external and internal data to support decision making at all corporate levels.

Integrated. Sales and materials planning, production planning, warehouse management, financial accounting, and human resources management are all integrated into a workflow of business events and processes across departments and functional areas. Employees receive the right information and documents at the right time at their desktops.

Beyond the company. But R/3 does more than open up completely new IT solutions within your company. Its applications also link your business processes with those of customers and suppliers to create complete logistical chains covering the entire route from supply to delivery. R/3 lets you integrate banks and other business partners into inter-company communications.

Best business practices. R/3 software lets you integrate all your business operations in an overall system for planning, controlling and monitoring. They include **best business practices that reflect the experiences, suggestions and requirements of leading companies in a host of industries**. R/3 lets you profit directly from this wealth of business and organisational know-how.

1.2.4 Value added networks

Value added networks (VANs) are networks that facilitate the adding of value to products and (particularly) to services by the strategic use of information. Typically, VANs will link separate organisations together, contributing to the development of **business networks**.

Also, they are often business ventures in their own right, with companies subscribing to the services available. Good examples are the SABRE, Amadeus and Galileo airline flight booking system. A simpler example is the electronic data interchange systems between manufacturers and their suppliers that facilitate the operation of JIT logistics.

VANs give mutual competitive advantage to all their subscribers, but only so long as some competitors are left outside of the system. As soon as membership of the VAN (or a competing VAN) becomes a standard feature of the industry, the original competitive advantage is lost. Competitive advantage based on VAN membership can then only exist if there is more than one VAN and each VAN in the industry offers a different degree of benefit in terms of cost reduction or differentiation.

The term 'value added network' is to some extent being replaced by 'extranet'.

2 Information strategy 05/06

FAST FORWARD

Information strategy can be divided into **information systems strategy, information technology strategy** and **information management strategy**. The strategic significance of information requires that it be itself managed strategically so that the systems, the technology and the information itself support the overall strategic policy.

As with so many other aspects of business strategy, the terminology used in the world of information strategy is not clearly defined. Terms such as 'information management' are used in slightly different ways by different groups of professionals. In this chapter we will provide you with information that will help you to gain a fuller understanding of the ways in which various terms are used and some of the range of meanings and connotations they possess.

2.1 Information and information systems

To begin with, let us consider the difference between **information** itself and the **means by which it is collected, processed, moved around and stored**. Information is intangible and in its most basic form exists in people's minds. However, there is a limit to the amount of information any one person can remember and make effective use of; as a result, **physical records** of information have been with us for thousands of years. So, right from the beginning, we have a **distinction between information itself and the means by which it is handled**. The clay tablet that survives from ancient Sumeria is an example of information technology; we can hold it in our hands, but the information it stores is lost to us unless we can decipher the symbols used by the person who inscribed it.

Today we have a huge array of means in which we can store and manipulate information; many of these are electronic, but paper records are still fundamental to many aspects of information handling. We would not necessarily think of a hand-written memo as an example of information technology, such is its simplicity, but, in principle, it is.

Generally, today, information technology means **computers**: electronically-based processing and storage systems and all the **peripherals**, **communication links** and **software** that go with them. The extreme complexity of these systems leads to the creation of large amounts of information relating specifically to their design, maintenance and operation, but this information is not their purpose: it is part of the technology itself. The information technology systems we use in business exist to help us to make use of **information that is external to the overall system itself**, information that we need to carry on our business operations.

The immense potential of computer-based systems provides an increasingly wide range of ways in which we can exploit information in business. We need to decide how we are going to use the information we have, how we are going to obtain more information and how we are going to exploit the information technology that we use to handle it. The decisions we make about these problems constitute our **information strategy**.

2.2 Information strategy

Earl's analysis of information strategy into three elements is useful.

The first distinction he made was between the strategies for **information technology** and **information systems**.

2.2.1 Information systems strategy

The **information systems (IS) strategy** is concerned with specifying the systems (in the widest meaning of the word) that will best **enable the use of information to support the overall business strategy**. In this context, a 'system' will include all the **activities, procedures, records** and **people** involved in a particular aspect of the organisation's work, as well as the **technology** used. The information systems strategy is focussed on **business requirements**, the demands they make for information of all kinds and the nature of the benefits that information systems are expected to provide. This strategy is very much **demand-led** and **business-driven**: each SBU in a large organisation is likely to have its own information systems strategy.

Information technology strategy (IT)

The information technology strategy, by contrast is (unsurprisingly) technology focussed, technically driven and concerned with supplying technical solutions to the demands made by the information systems strategy. This strategy is likely to be concerned with such matters as standardisation, integration, economies of scale, good practice and architectural coherence. It is likely to be formulated at the corporate apex.

Information management strategy (IM)

Subsequently, Earl discerned a need for an information management strategy. The emphasis here is on management: this strategy is oriented towards **roles and relationships** and covers such matters as the responsibilities and organisation of the IT staff; control and accounting requirements for IT assets; and the 'design of the management processes required across all the IT activities in an organisation'.

We might sum this up in very simple terms by saying that IS strategy defines what is to be achieved; IT strategy determines how hardware, software and telecommunications can achieve it; and the IM strategy describes who controls and uses the technology provided.

This model of information strategy has the advantage of being **internally consistent** and quite **simple** to understand. Unfortunately, the picture is spoiled by a different use of the term information management. You may come across a rather narrow use of this term to mean 'the approach taken to storing and accessing data'. Since this is really just an aspect of the information technology strategy as defined above, we do not recommend the use of the term in this way.

Key terms

> The **information systems (IS) strategy** is the long-term plan for systems to exploit information in order to support business strategies or create new strategic options.
>
> The **information technology (IT) strategy** is concerned with selecting, operating and managing the technological element of the IS strategy.
>
> The **information management (IM) strategy** deals with the roles of the people involved in the use of IT assets, the relationships between them and design of the management processes needed to exploit IT.
>
> **Strategic information systems** are systems at any level of an organisation that change goals, processes, products, services or environmental relationships with the aim of gaining competitive advantage.

Exam focus point

> The May 2006 exam required students to recommend the IT hardware and software an organisation would need in order to implement an Intranet upgrade project. The examiner noted that although IS and IT are core topics students displayed poor knowledge of them. The examiner stressed that the IS/IT/IM section of the syllabus should not be ignored.

2.3 The need for a strategic approach

Earl says that a strategy for information systems and information technology is **justified** on the grounds that IS/IT:

- Involves **high costs**
- Is **critical to the success** of many organisations
- Is now used as part of the commercial strategy in the battle for **competitive advantage**

- Impacts on **customer service**
- Affects **all levels of management**
- Affects the way **management information** is created and presented
- **Requires effective management** to obtain the maximum benefit
- Involves many **stakeholders** inside and outside the organisation

2.3.1 IS/IT is a high cost activity

Many organisations invest large amounts of money in IS, but not always wisely. The unmanaged proliferation of IT is likely to lead to expensive mistakes. Two key benefits of IT, the ability to **share** information and the **avoidance of duplication**, are likely to be lost. All IT expenditure should therefore require approval to ensure that it enhances rather than detracts from the overall information strategy. There is also the possibility that the failure of a very large IT investment might have strategic negative impact on the organisation concerned, possibly even leading to business failure.

2.3.2 IS/IT is critical to the success of many organisations

When developing an IS/IT strategy a firm should assess **how important IT is** in the provision of products and services. The role that IT fills in an organisation will vary depending on the type of organisations. IS/IT could be:

- A **support** activity
- A **key** operational activity
- **Potentially** very important
- A **strategic** activity (without IT the firm could not function at all)
- A source of **competitive advantage**

2.3.3 Information and competitive advantage

It is now recognised that information can be used as a source of competitive advantage. Many organisations have recognised the importance of information and developed an **information strategy**, covering both IS and IT.

Information systems should be tied in some way to **business objectives**.

(a) The **corporate strategy** is used to plan functional **business plans** which provide guidelines for information-based activities.

(b) On a year-by-year basis, the **annual plan** would try to tie in business plans with information systems projects for particular applications, perhaps through the functioning of a steering committee.

2.3.4 IT can impact significantly on the business context

IT is an **enabling** technology, and can produce dramatic changes in individual businesses and whole industries. For example, the deregulation of the airline industry encouraged the growth of computerised seat-reservation systems. IT can be both a **cause** of major changes in doing business and a **response** to them.

2.3.5 IT affects all levels of management

IT has become a routine feature of office life, **a facility for everyone to use**. IT is no longer used solely by specialist staff.

2.3.6 IT and its effect on management information

The use of IT has permitted the design of a range of information systems. Executive Information Systems (EIS), Management Information Systems (MIS), Decision Support Systems (DSS), Knowledge Work Systems (KWS) and Office Automation Systems (OAS) can be used to improve the quality of management information.

IT has also had an effect on **production processes**. For example, Computer Integrated Manufacturing (CIM) changed the methods and cost profiles of many manufacturing processes. The techniques used to **measure and record costs** have also adapted to the use of IT.

2.3.7 IT and stakeholders

Parties interested in an organisation's use of IT are as follows.

(a)   **Other business users** – for example to facilitate Electronic Data Interchange (EDI).

(b)   **Governments** – eg telecommunications regulation, regulation of electronic commerce.

(c)   **IT manufacturers** looking for new markets and product development. User-groups may be able to influence software producers.

(d)   **Consumers** – for example as reassurance that product quality is high, consumers may also be interested if information is provided via the Internet.

(e)   **Employees** – as IT affects work practices.

2.3.8 Other aspects

In addition to these arguments we might also identify the reasons below.

(a)   IS are by their nature open to external influences, particularly improvements and updates. A strategic view should be taken in order to obtain optimum benefit from these influences and prevent the proliferation of incompatible developments.

(b)   Environmental dynamism means that the need for information is constantly recreated in new ways.

(c)   Information is fundamental to strategic planning and so it should be managed strategically.

2.3.9 Advantages of a strategic approach

(a)   Competitive advantage is more easily attained.

(b)   There is **congruence** between the goal structure of the IS strategy and the overall corporate strategy.

(c)   Technical developments can be monitored and assessed with a view to introduction at a suitable time, rather than being ignored or introduced before they are properly developed.

(d)   Expenditure can be controlled strategically.

Question	Babbage and Newman

Learning outcome B(vi)

Babbage and Newman plc is a company with an established base of IT applications. The finance department has a fully computerised accounting system. The marketing department has developed a primitive customer modelling package. The production department 'does not need IT'.

The Finance Director is in charge of IT at Babbage and Newman. He proposes in the annual corporate budget a 10% increase in IT expenditure based on last year, for the relevant departments. This will enable system upgrades.

Comment briefly on the information strategy at Babbage and Newman.

Answer

There is no strategy at all. The Finance Director regards IT as a cost. Moreover the IT 'strategy' is directed to enhancing its existing base (eg in the accounts department) rather than areas where it might prove competitively valuable (eg in marketing).

2.4 How IT is changing corporate strategy

Porter and Millar say that IT changes corporate strategy since products and business activities have both **physical** and **informational** aspects. The rapid rate of change in IT is having drastic effects on the informational aspects of both products and activities. Also, IT has the potential to **transform competition** in three ways: its effect on the **five competitive forces**; its potential for implementing the **generic strategies**; and its contribution to the **emergence of completely new businesses**.

It should be obvious that information systems and information technology should **support** corporate strategy, but there are also a number of ways IS/IT can **influence** corporate strategy.

In 1985, the Harvard Business Review published an article by *Michael Porter* and *Victor Millar*. aimed at general managers facing the changes resulting from the rapid and extensive development of information technology. Although it is now over twenty years old, the article still has great relevance to the **strategic employment of information systems** and the use of information technology. It dealt with three main interlinked topics.

- The ways in which IT had become **strategically significant**
- How the **nature of competition** had changed
- **How to compete** in the new, IT influenced environment

2.4.1 The strategic significance of IT

IT transforms the **value chain**. This model of business activity is dealt with in detail later in this Study Text; for now it will be sufficient to say that it analyses the ways in which businesses **add value** to their inputs into nine activities: five primary, and four support. The article remarks that each of these activities has both **physical** and **information** aspects and points out that, while until quite recently, technical advances were concentrated in the physical aspects, **current improvements tend to be IT driven**. Simple improvements are made by faster and more accurate processing of existing forms of data; more dramatic ones by creating new flows of previously unavailable information. This has a particular effect on the linkages between the various activities and extends the company's **competitive scope**, which is the range of activities it can efficiently undertake.

Porter and Millar provide a diagram of the value chain in which they give examples of the ways in which IT was influencing the various activities at the time the article was written. These are still very relevant.

Support activities	Firm infrastructure	Planning models				
	Human resource management	Automated personnel scheduling				
	Technology development	Computer aided design	Electronic market research			
	Procurement	Online procurement of parts				
		Automated warehouse	Flexible manufacturing	Automated order processing	Telemarketing Remote terminals for salespersons	Remote servicing of equipment Computer scheduling and routing of repair trucks
		Inbound logistics	Operations	Outbound logistics	Marketing and sales	Service
		Primary activities				**Margin**

IT transforms the **product**. It is possible to view products as having physical and informational content, with the mix varying from product to product. **Diesel fuel**, for example, is an almost **entirely physical** product, though it is necessary to be aware that it will not work with petrol-engined vehicles. This Study

Text, on the other hand, consists almost entirely of information, though, obviously, it has a physical aspect. An intermediate case would be an aircraft, which has a very obvious physical existence, but which cannot be used without a great deal of information on servicing, handling characteristics and the operation of its systems. Porter and Millar make the point that there is an unmistakeable trend towards **supplying increasing amounts of information with products** as, for instance, in the case of freight and courier services that provide on-line tracking of consignments.

2.4.2 How IT changes the nature of competition

IT changes the **structure of industry** through its effect on the **five competitive forces**. This model of the market environment is also dealt with in depth later in this Study Text. Here we may simply give some examples of the way in which structural change is induced.

(a)   Supermarket loyalty card schemes and Internet marketing systems have the potential to allow a precise customisation of sales offerings to potential buyers.

(b)   Computer-aided design and manufacturing systems can be used to introduce new and reconfigured products rapidly enough to fend off any threat from substitutes.

(c)   Improved levels of service based on expensive IT systems have erected major cost barriers to new entrants.

IT **enhances competitive advantage** in two principal ways:

- by **reducing costs**
- by making it easier to **differentiate products**.

Good examples of IT-driven cost reductions appear in the automation of much clerical work that has apparent since the introduction of mainframe computers in the middle of the twentieth century. The incorporation of increasing amounts of information into basic products mentioned above is an example of how differentiation can be achieved.

IT forms the basis of complete **new businesses**. It makes new businesses technically feasible; it creates derived demand for new products; and it creates new businesses inside old ones. The impact of *Apple's iPod* gives examples of all three effects. The device itself is based on the MP3 file format; a large **iPod ecosystem** of accessories has been created; and the product itself represents a departure from Apple's previous hardware and software strategies.

2.4.3 Competing in the information age

Porter and Millar propose a five step process to take advantage of new information-based opportunities.

Step 1   **Assess information intensity**. A high level of information content in either products or processes indicates that IT can play a strategic role.

Step 2   **Determine the role of IT in industry structure**. IT may have the potential to radically change the way in which the industry operates, including changing the basis of competition and moving its boundaries.

Step 3   **Identify and rank the ways in which IT might create competitive advantage**. Possible value chain-based applications include opportunities for reducing cost or enhancing differentiation and establishing new links between activities. There may also be opportunities to enter new market segments and to introduce new products.

Step 4   **Investigate how IT might spawn new businesses**. These might be based on the exploitation of new categories of information and the sale of information-processing capacity.

Step 5   **Develop a plan to exploit IT**. Effectively, this is the creation of a comprehensive strategy and has implications for most parts of the organisation.

An important role of the information technology and finance functions is to help ensure the agreed strategy is proceeding according to plan. The table below outlines the rationale behind this view.

	Traditional view	Strategic implications
Cost	The finance and information technology functions can be relatively expensive	Shared services and outsourcing could be used to capture cost savings
IT	IT has traditionally been transaction based	IT/IS should be integrated with business strategy
Value	The finance and IT functions do not add value	Redesign the functions
Strategy	Accountants and IT managers are seen as scorekeepers and administrators rather than as a business partner during the strategic planning process	Change from cost-orientated to market-orientated ie development of more effective strategic planning systems

2.4.4 The importance of managing technology

The success of an organisation's use of technology depends largely on how technology is selected, implemented and **managed**. For example, **information systems** may **fail to deliver the benefits expected** for any of the following reasons.

(a)   They are used to tackle the **wrong problem** (ie the use of IT has not been thought through in the context of the wider organisation).

(b)   Senior management are not interested.

(c)   Users are ignored in design and development.

(d)   No attention is given to behavioural factors in design and operation.

If an organisation develops and follows a realistic information strategy and information systems plan for information systems and technology then there is less chance that these problems will arise.

Organisations have typically gone through a process of evolution in the development and management of their IS strategy. *Nolan* identified six stages based on the level of expenditure involved.

Initiation: computers are introduced, usually by financial staff, in order to make cost savings.

Contagion: computers are introduced into other areas in an uncontrolled fashion, with varying degrees of success.

Control: Senior managers, concerned about expenditure, create a central IT staff and concentrate control in its hands.

Integration: a need for innovative joint development by users and specialists is accepted and controls are loosened.

Data administration: the value of information is recognised and drives development; databases are set up.

Maturity: a strategic view is taken and IS strategy is incorporated into overall organisational strategy.

Obviously, factors other than the progression outlined in this model will affect expenditure, including the rapid fall in the cost of IT and the development of completely new technologies, such as video conferencing. The value of Nolan's model is the guidance it gives on how the **management of IT resources** might reasonably proceed and evolve.

Organisations typically go through a process of evolution in their IT strategy, moving from **simple automation of processes** such as bookkeeping to fully-fledged **information-based business strategy**. Along the way they may pass through stages of expansion, centralised control of IT and wider dispersion of IT development. Different management techniques tend to be used as the process continues.

Exam focus point

> You should look out for question scenarios in which the management of IS and IT strategies appears to be deficient and be prepared to offer sensible advice. The aim should be to achieve strategic objectives while controlling costs: this will require the input of user needs and practical experience to be combined with the IT specialist's knowledge of the available technology and how to make the best use of it.

2.5 Developing strategy

FAST FORWARD

A strategy for IT is developed from the strategy for information, which in turn supports overall strategy. Earl suggests such a strategy may be **top down/business objective** led; **bottom up/business system led** or **inside out/innovative/exploitative**. Other approaches include **enterprise analysis** and the use of **critical success factors**.

Just as business strategy should be subject to continuing review and development, it would be inappropriate to consider an information strategy as a fixed and immutable. Developments both within the organisation and in the environment will inevitably require that the **information strategy be developed and subject to change**. Obvious potential influences include technical developments in hardware and software and changes in the business strategy itself. A simple guide to the continuing development of an information strategy might include the features outlined below.

(a)   There should be **constant reference to the overall business strategy**. This will shape the demand for information and thence the IS, IT and IM strategies. There may be companies in which the overall strategy is driven by the appearance of new technology, but it is important to be aware that, generally, this will not be the case and it will be **inappropriate to seek to adopt new technology for its own sake**.

(b)   **Compatibility of technologies** should be carefully considered.

(c)   Similarly, the **wider implications** of proposed developments must be thoroughly considered. Each part of the organisation should be able to make appropriate inputs into plans for change.

(d)   Where significant change is envisaged, it must be **properly planned**, possibly using a methodology such as Structured Systems Analysis and Design Methodology (SSADM). Hardware and software choices must be made; decisions must be taken about the extent to which work should be outsourced, if at all, and costs and benefits should be considered.

A successfully developed strategy will contribute to the success of the organisation. Its success may also be judged by the extent to which it performs three specific functions.

(a)   Prediction and definition of major areas of strategic choice

(b)   Indication of the degree of common ground between business and information managers on such matters as strategic assumptions, objectives and policies

(c)   Timely identification of the information resources required to implement the business strategy

2.5.1 Information needs

The identification of organisational **information needs** and the information systems framework to satisfy them is at the heart of a strategy for information systems and information technology.

The IS and IT strategies should complement the overall strategy for the organisation. It follows therefore that the IS/IT strategy should be considered whenever the organisation prepares other long-term strategies such as marketing or production.

2.5.2 Earl's three leg analysis

The writer Earl devised a method for the development of IS strategies. His method identified three legs of IS strategy development:

- Business led (top down emphasis, focuses on **business plans and goals**)
- Infrastructure led (bottom up emphasis, focuses on **current systems**)
- Mixed (inside out emphasis, focuses on **IT/IS opportunities**)

A diagrammatic representation of the three legs follows.

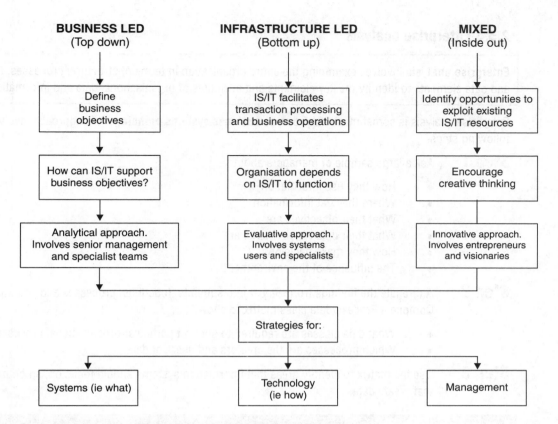

Earl's three leg analysis is explained in the following table.

Leg or approach	Comment
Business led (top down)	The **overall objectives** of an organisation are identified and then IS/IT systems are implemented to enable these objectives to be met. This approach relies on the ability to break down the organisation and its objectives to a series of business objectives and processes and to be able to identify the information needs of these. This is an analytical approach. The people usually involved are senior management and specialist teams.
Infrastructure led (bottom up)	Computer based **transaction systems** are critical to business operations. The organisation focuses on systems that facilitate transactions and other basic operations. This is an evaluative approach. The people usually involved are system users and specialists.
Mixed (inside out)	The organisation encourages ideas that will **exploit existing IT and IS resources**. Innovations may come from entrepreneurial managers or individuals outside the formal planning process. This is an innovative/creative approach. The people involved are entrepreneurs and/or visionaries.

We will now look at a number of other methodologies and frameworks that may be used as part of the information systems strategy development process.

2.5.3 Enterprise analysis

Key term

> **Enterprise analysis** involves examining the entire organisation in terms of structure, processes, functions and data elements to identify the key elements and attributes of organisational data and information.

Enterprise analysis is sometimes referred to as **business systems planning**. This approach involves the following steps.

Step 1   Ask a large sample of managers about:

- How they use information
- Where they get information
- What their objectives are
- What their data requirements are
- How they make decisions
- The influence of the environment

Step 2   Aggregate the findings from *Step 1* into subunits, functions, processes and data matrices. Compile a Process/data class matrix to show:

- What data classes are required to support particular organisational processes
- Which processes are the creators and users of data

Step 3   Use the matrix to identify areas that information systems should focus on, eg on processes that create data.

Enterprise analysis approach – strength	Comment
Comprehensive	The enterprise analysis approach gives a comprehensive view of the organisation and its use of data and systems.

Enterprise analysis approach – weaknesses	Comment
Unwieldy	The enterprise analysis approach results in a mountain of data that is expensive to collect and difficult to analyse.
Focussed on existing information	Survey questions tend to focus on how systems and information are currently used, rather than on how information that is needed could be provided. The analysis has tended to result in existing systems being automated rather than looking at the wider picture.

2.5.4 Critical success factors

The use of **critical success factors (CSFs)** can help to determine the information requirements of an organisation. CSFs are operational goals. If operational goals are achieved the organisation should be successful.

We will return to CSFs later in this Study Text; for now we may define CSFs as the small number of key operational goals vital to the success of an organisation.

The CSF approach is sometimes referred to as the **strategic analysis** approach. The philosophy behind this approach is that managers should focus on a small number of objectives, and information systems should be focussed on providing information to enable managers to monitor these objectives.

Where measures use quantitative data, performance can be measured in a number of ways.

- In **physical quantities**, for example units produced or units sold
- In **money terms**, for example profit, revenues, costs or variances
- In **ratios** and **percentages**

2.5.5 Data sources for CSFs

In general terms *Rockart* identifies four **general sources** of CSFs.

(a)   The **industry** that the business is in.

(b)   The **company** itself and its situation within the industry.

(c)   The **environment**, for example consumer trends, the economy, and political factors of the country in which the company operates.

(d)   Temporal organisational factors, which are **areas of corporate activity** which are currently **unacceptable** and represent a cause of concern, for example, high stock levels.

More specifically, possible internal and external data sources for CSFs include the following.

(a)   **The existing system**. The existing system can be used to generate reports showing **failures to meet CSFs.**

(b)   **Customer service department**. This department will maintain details of **complaints** received, **refunds** handled, **customer enquiries** etc. These should be reviewed to ensure all failure types have been identified.

(c)   **Customers**. A survey of customers, provided that it is properly designed and introduced, would reveal (or confirm) those areas where **satisfaction** is high or low.

(d)   **Competitors**. Competitors' operations, pricing structures and publicity should be closely monitored.

(e)   **Accounting system**. The **profitability** of various aspects of the operation is probably a key factor in any review of CSFs.

(f)   **Consultants**. A specialist consultancy might be able to perform a detailed review of the system in order to identify ways of satisfying CSFs.

2.5.6 CSF approach: strengths and weaknesses

CSF approach – strengths	Comment
Takes into account environmental changes	The CSF approach requires managers to examine the environment and consider how it influences their information requirements.
Focuses on information	The approach doesn't just aim to establish organisational objectives. It also looks at the information and information systems required to establish and monitor progress towards these objectives.
Facilitates top management participation in system development	The clear link between information requirements and individual and organisational objectives encourages top management involvement in system (DSS, ESS) design.
CSF approach – weaknesses	Comment
Aggregation of individual CSFs	Wide-ranging individual CSFs need to be aggregated into a clear organisational plan. This process relies heavily on judgement. Managers who feel their input has been neglected may be alienated.
Bias towards top management	When gathering information to establish CSFs it is usually top management who are interviewed. These managers may lack knowledge of operational activities.
CSFs change often	The business environment, managers and information systems technology are subject to constant change. CSFs and systems must be updated to account for change.

Question

Learning outcome B(vi)

Here is the first paragraph of an exam question scenario.

'HJK Ltd is a light engineering company which produces a range of components, machine tools and electronic devices for the motor and aircraft industry. It employs about 1,000 people in 12 main divisions.'

Identify some CSFs for HJK Ltd.

Answer

CSFs might include technological excellence to keep pace with the industries served, and co-ordination of divisional activities. You may have thought of others.

2.6 Information audit

FAST FORWARD

An **information audit** aims to establish the information needs of users **and** how these needs could be met.

The audit has three stages.

Stage		Comment
1	Information needs assessment	This stage involves **gathering information**, usually through interviews and questionnaires.
		Information users are asked what information they require, why they require it, when they require it and the preferred format.
		People should be encouraged to think laterally about what information would help them do their job, rather than simply listing the information they currently receive.
		To encourage wide-ranging thought, users should be asked to state the information they would like in an 'ideal world'. Unrealistic and uneconomic needs can be rejected (tactfully) at a later stage.
2	Information analysis	This stage **examines the information** provided by the existing information system. Both the quantity and the quality of the information are analysed. For example, the timing of information may reduce the quality of otherwise excellent information as it is provided too late to influence decision-making. Slightly less accurate information, provided earlier, may be more desirable.
3	Gap analysis	This stage **compares** the information needs identified in stage 1 with the information identified as being provided in stage 2. Gaps between what is required and what is currently provided are identified.
		'Information gaps' are analysed to evaluate the costs and benefits of closing the gap.

An information system **resource analysis** involves a review of **all** information systems and information technology used within an organisation. The review includes all aspects of hardware, software, communications devices, network topologies, systems development methodologies, maintenance procedures, contingency plans and IS/IT personnel. The review looks at all of these aspects in the context of the organisation's overall strategy and the IS/IT strategy.

Resource analysis is sometimes called **Current Situation Analysis (CSA)**. The analysis establishes the current status of IS/IT within the organisation. The CSA has similar problems to that of a cost-benefit analysis in that it relies on the **subjective judgements** of information users. A group of people using the same system for the same purpose may come up with different ratings for system efficiency and user-friendliness.

Two techniques that could be useful when conducting a CSA are **Earl's grid** and the **applications portfolio**.

2.6.1 Earl's grid

Earl suggests a grid to analyse an organisation's current use of information systems. Current systems are plotted on the following grid.

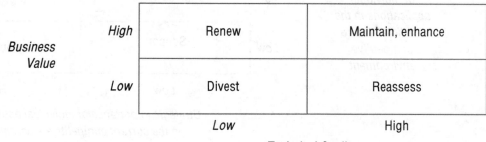

(a) A system of poor quality and little value should be **disposed of** (divest).

(b) A system of high business value and low technical quality should be **renewed** (invested in). An important system of low quality carries a high business risk.

(c) A system of high quality but low business value should be **reassessed**. Is the system meeting an information need? Why is it under-utilised?

(d) High quality systems with a high business value should be **maintained** to preserve the high quality, and if possible **enhanced** in the quest for competitive advantage.

Establishing where to place systems on the grid is the difficult part. Consultation with system users and those for formulating and implementing information system strategy would be undertaken to form an opinion of each system. Again, judgements are subjective.

2.6.2 The strategic grid

The importance of IS/IT to an organisation was studied by *McFarlan and McKenney* in 1983.

They devised a matrix designed to show the level of dependence on IS/IT within an organisation. The grid classifies four levels of dependence.

Strategic importance of planned information systems		Turnaround	Strategic
	High	Turnaround	Strategic
	Low	Support	Factory
		Low	*High*

*Strategic importance of **current** information systems*

(a) Organisations in the **strategic** quadrant currently depend on IS/IT for competitive advantage, and expect to continue to do so.

(b) Organisations in the **turnaround** quadrant do not currently view IS/IT as having strategic importance, but expect IS/IT will be strategically important in the future.

(c) Organisations in the **support** quadrant see no strategic value in IS/IT.

(d) Organisations in the **factory** quadrant sees IS/IT as strategically significant at the moment, but predict this will not be the case in the future.

2.6.3 Applications portfolio

The strategic grid is interesting, but of limited use for detailed planning. *Peppard* developed it into the **applications portfolio**. This is used to analyse the strategic impact of **individual applications** within an organisation. It therefore is intended to offer more detailed analysis.

*Strategic importance of individual applications in the predicted **future** competitive environment*	High	High potential	Strategic
	Low	Support	Key operational
		Low	High

*Strategic importance of individual applications in the **current** competitive environment*

(a) **Support applications** are not critical to business success, but are designed to improve the productivity and efficiency of the internal activities of an organisation. Examples include an accounting system, or a payroll package.

(b) **Key operational applications** support established core business activities. A production planning system is a good example, inventory control is another example. These are critical for a business to maintain its performance relative to its competitors.

(c) **Strategic applications** are vital to the organisation's future success. They seek to gain competitive advantage through innovation in support of business strategies. Finance/service companies are becoming increasingly dependent on information systems and technology.

(d) **High potential applications** are applications likely to have a significant impact in the future environment. They are often innovative. However, a business must be careful not to invest too much too quickly in these systems in case there is no market acceptance. A supermarket on-line ordering application is an example, an expert system is another example.

3 Information sources and management

FAST FORWARD

> An information system should be designed to obtain information from **all relevant sources** – both internal and external.

Data and information come from sources both inside and outside an organisation. An organisation's information systems should be designed so as to obtain – or **capture** – all the relevant data and information required.

3.1 Internal information

Capturing data and information from **inside** the organisation involves designing a system for collecting or measuring data and information which sets out procedures for:

- What data and information is collected
- How frequently
- By whom
- By what methods
- How data and information is processed, filed and communicated

The accounting records

The accounting ledgers provide an excellent source of information regarding what has happened in the past. This information may be used as a basis for predicting future events.

3.2 External information

Formal collection of data from outside sources includes the following.

(a)   A company's **tax specialists** will be expected to gather information about changes in tax law and how this will affect the company.

(b)   Obtaining information about any new legislation on health and safety at work, or employment regulations, must be the responsibility of a particular person – for example the company's **legal expert** or **company secretary** – who must then pass on the information to other managers affected by it.

(c)   Research and development (R & D) work often relies on information about other R & D work being done by another company or by government institutions. An **R & D official** might be made responsible for finding out about R & D work in the company.

(d)   **Marketing managers** need to know about the opinions and buying attitudes of potential customers. To obtain this information, they might carry out market research exercises.

Informal gathering of information from the environment occurs naturally, consciously or unconsciously, as people learn what is going on in the world around them – perhaps from newspapers, television reports, meetings with business associates or the trade press.

Organisations hold external information such as invoices, letters, advertisements and so on **received from customers and suppliers**. But there are many occasions when an active search outside the organisation is necessary.

Key term

> The phrase **environmental scanning** is often used to describe the process of gathering external information, which is available from a wide range of sources.

Sources of external information include:

(a)   The government.

(b)   Annual reports and press statements of competitors or other firms.

(c)   Advice or information bureaux.

(d)   Consultants.

(e)   Newspaper and magazine publishers.

(f)   Market research and other report, for example from Mintel or the Economist Intelligence Unit.

(f)   Libraries and information services.

(g)   Increasingly businesses can use each other's systems as sources of information, for instance via extranets or electronic data interchange (EDI).

(h)   **Electronic sources** of information are becoming increasingly important.

    (i)   For some time there have been 'viewdata' services such as **Prestel** offering a very large bank of information gathered from organisations such as the Office for National Statistics, newspapers and the British Library. **Topic** offers information on the stock market. Companies like **Reuters** operate primarily in the field of provision of information.

    (ii)   The **Internet** is a vast source of information. A number of journals and articles are now published on line, and many organisations now also display information about themselves on their home pages.

 Question

Decisions

Learning out come A(iii)

Information is often required by people **outside** the organisation for making judgements and decisions relating to an organisation. Give four examples of decisions which may be taken by outsiders.

Answer

There are many possible suggestions, including those given below.

(a)   The organisation's **bankers** take decisions affecting the amount of money they are prepared to lend.

(b)   The **public** might have an interest in information relating to an organisation's products or services.

(c)   The **media** (press, television etc) use information generated by organisations in news stories, and such information can adversely or favourably affect an organisation's relationship with its environment.

(d)   The **government** (for example the Department of Trade and Industry) regularly requires organisational information.

(e)   The **Inland Revenue** and **HM Customs and Excise** authorities require information for taxation and VAT assessments.

(f)   An organisation's **suppliers** and **customers** take decisions whether or not to trade with the organisation.

Exam focus point

One of the optional questions in the November 2007 exam asked students to recommend the nature and sources of information a company should use when evaluating potential countries to invest in. if you are faced with a similar question, make sure the sources of information you recommend are practical and relevant to the context of the scenario.

4 Information for planning and control

FAST FORWARD

Control information, to be useful, must aid the decision-making process.

Key term

Strategic planning is a process of deciding on objectives of the organisation, on changes in these objectives, on the resources used to attain these objectives and on the policies that are to govern the acquisition, use and disposition of these resources.

Strategic decision making:

- Is medium– to **long-term**
- Involves high levels of **uncertainty** and risk (the future is unpredictable)
- Involves situations that **may not recur**
- Deals with **complex** issues

Key term

Operational control ensures that specific tasks are carried out effectively and efficiently. It focuses on individual tasks, and is carried out within the strictly defined guidelines issued by strategic planning and tactical control decisions.

4.1 The decision-making process

The stages in making a decision are as follows.

Step 1   Problem recognition.

Step 2   Problem definition and structuring.

Step 3   Identifying alternative courses of action.

Step 4   Making and communicating the decision.

Step 5   Implementation of the decision.

Step 6 Monitoring the effects of the decision.

Information and decision-making

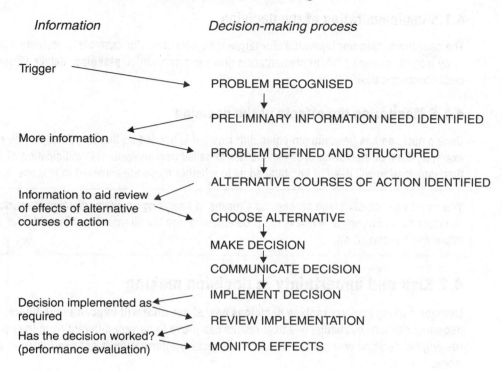

Information   *Decision-making process*

Trigger → PROBLEM RECOGNISED

↓

PRELIMINARY INFORMATION NEED IDENTIFIED

More information → PROBLEM DEFINED AND STRUCTURED

ALTERNATIVE COURSES OF ACTION IDENTIFIED

Information to aid review of effects of alternative courses of action → CHOOSE ALTERNATIVE

↓

MAKE DECISION

COMMUNICATE DECISION

↓

IMPLEMENT DECISION

Decision implemented as required → REVIEW IMPLEMENTATION

Has the decision worked? (performance evaluation) → MONITOR EFFECTS

4.1.1 Problem recognition

Decisions are not made without **information**. The decision-maker needs to be informed of a problem in the first place. This is sometimes referred to as the **decision trigger**.

4.1.2 Problem definition and structuring

Normally **further information** is then required. This further information is **analysed** so that the problem can be **defined** precisely.

Consider, for example, a company with falling sales. The fall in sales would be the **trigger**. **Further information** would be needed to identify where the deficiencies were occurring. The company might discover that sales of product X in area Y are falling, and the problem can be **defined** as:

'Decline of sales of product X in area Y due to new competitor: how can the decline be reversed?'

One of the purposes of **defining** the problem is to identify the **relationships** between the **various factors** in it, especially if the problem is complex.

4.1.3 Identifying alternative courses of action

Where alternative courses of action are identified, **information** is needed about the likely effect of each, so they can be assessed.

As a simple example, if our company wishes to review the price of product X in area Y, information will be needed as to the effect of particular price levels on demand for the product. Such information can include external information such as market research (demand at a particular price) and the cost of the product, which can be provided internally.

4.1.4 Making and communicating the decision

The decision is **made** after review of the information relating to alternatives. However, the decision is useless if it is not **communicated**. So, in our example, if the **marketing director** decides to lower the price of product X and institute an intensive **advertising** campaign, nothing will happen unless the advertising department is informed, and also the **manufacturing** department, who will have to prepare new packaging showing the lower price.

4.1.5 Implementation of the decision

The decision is then **implemented**. For large-scale decisions (for example to relocate a factory 100 miles away from its current site), implementation may need substantial **planning**, detailed information and very clear communication.

4.1.6 Monitoring the effects of the decision

Once a decision has been implemented, information is needed so that its effects can be **reviewed**. For example, if a manufacturing organisation has installed new equipment in anticipation of savings in costs, then information will need to be obtained as to whether these are achieved in practice.

4.2 Risk and uncertainty in decision making   11/05

Decision making involves **making decisions now about what will happen in the future**. Obviously, decisions can turn out badly, or actual results can prove to be very different from the estimates on which the original decision was made because the necessary **information is not available** when the decision is made.

The management accountant, who must present relevant cost and revenue data to assist a manager who is about to make a decision, should consider two things.

(a)   If the figures are **only slightly in doubt** or the amounts themselves are not material, a **best estimate** with a note that the figures are not certain may be good enough.

(b)   If the amount or the **degree of uncertainty was large**, to present just one set of forecast figures would be unwise. For example, if a forecast of sales demand is 'anywhere between 1,000 and 10,000 units', it would be naive and unhelpful to prepare a **single point estimate** of sales – just one forecast figure – of, say, 5,000 units.

If the uncertainty in a situation does warrant special attention in the figures, the next problem is **how the uncertainty** in the figures should be presented.

There are various methods of bringing uncertainty and risk analysis into the evaluation of decisions. They include the following.

(a)   **Conservative estimates:** estimating outcomes in a conservative manner in order to provide a built-in safety factor.

(b)   Looking at the **worst possible** and **best possible** outcomes, as well as the most likely outcome, and reaching a decision which takes these into account.

(c)   **Sensitivity analysis:** any technique that tests decision options for their vulnerability to changes in a 'variable' such as expected sales volume.

(d)   Assessing **probabilities** and calculating, for each decision alternative, either the **expected value** of costs or benefits with, possibly, the standard deviation of the possible outcomes, or a probability distribution of the possible outcomes. **Decision trees** might be used to illustrate in a 'pictorial' or 'graphical' form the alternatives facing the decision-maker.

4.3 Perfect information

Obtaining more information first about what is likely to happen can sometimes reduce the uncertainty about the future outcome from taking a decision. We can categorise information depending upon **how reliable** it is likely to be for predicting what will happen in the future and hence for helping managers to make better decisions.

Perfect information is information that predicts the future with perfect accuracy.

Imperfect information is information which cannot be guaranteed to be completely accurate. Almost all information is therefore imperfect – but may still be very useful.

5 Knowledge management   11/06

The aim of **knowledge management** is to capture, organise and make widely available all the knowledge the organisation possesses, whether in recorded form or in people's heads.

Knowledge management is the systematic process of finding, selecting, organising, distilling and presenting information so as to improve comprehension of a specific areas of interest. Specific activities help focus the organisation on acquiring storing and utilising knowledge for such things as problem solving, dynamic learning, strategic planning and decision making.   *CIMA Official Terminology*

Organisational knowledge is the collective and shared experience accumulated through systems, routines and activities of sharing across the organisation.   *Johnson, Scholes and Whittington*

Knowledge management is a relatively new concept in business theory. It is connected with the theory of the **learning organisation** and founded on the idea that knowledge is a major source of competitive advantage in business.

Studies have indicated that 20 to 30 percent of company resources are wasted because organisations are not aware of what knowledge they already possess. *Lew Platt,* Ex-Chief Executive of *Hewlett Packard,* has articulated this, saying 'If only HP knew what HP knows, we would be three times as profitable'.

Knowledge is thus seen as an important **resource** and may in itself constitute a **competence**: it can certainly **underpin** many competences, and knowledge management should be seen as a strategy to achieve competitive advantage, for example, through the sharing of cost reduction ideas across divisions, or through the diffusion of innovation.

In a knowledge management system, an organisation will appoint **knowledge managers** who are responsible for collecting and categorising knowledge, and encouraging other people in the organisation to use the available knowledge. The knowledge managers also monitor the use of knowledge in their organisation.

5.1 Organisational learning

Organisational learning is particularly important in the increasing number of task environments that are both complex and dynamic. It becomes necessary for strategic managers to promote and foster a **culture that values intuition, argument from conflicting views and experimentation**. A willingness to back ideas that are not guaranteed to succeed is another aspect of this culture: there must be freedom to make mistakes.

The aim of **knowledge management** is to exploit existing knowledge and to create new knowledge so that it may be exploited in turn. This is not easy. All organisations possess a great deal of data, but it tends to be unorganised and inaccessible. It is often locked up inside the memories of people who do not realise the value of what they know. This is what *Nonaka* calls **tacit knowledge**. Even when it is made **explicit**, (available to the organisation) by being recorded in some way, it may be difficult and time consuming to get at, as is the case with most paper archives. This is where knowledge management technology (discussed below) can be useful. Another important consideration is that tacit knowledge is inherently more **robust** (in the sense explained in the previous Section) than explicit knowledge.

From 'tacit' to 'explicit' knowledge

Nonaka and Takeuchi describe four ways in which knowledge moves within and between the tacit and explicit categories.

(a)   **Socialisation** is the informal process by which individuals share and transmit their tacit knowledge.

(b)   **Externalisation** converts tacit knowledge into explicit knowledge; this is a very difficult process to organise and control.

(c)   **Internalisation** is the learning process by which individuals acquire explicit knowledge and turn it into their own tacit knowledge.

(d)   **Combination** brings together separate elements of explicit knowledge into larger, more coherent systems; this is the arena for meetings, reports and computerised knowledge management systems.

5.2 The learning organisation

Continuing challenge to assumptions and search for improvement are typical of a **learning organisation**.

Key term

A **learning organisation** is capable of continual regeneration from the variety of knowledge, experience and skills of individuals within a culture that encourages mutual questioning and challenge around a shared purpose or vision.   *Johnson, Scholes and Whittington*

A learning organisation emphasises the **sharing of information and knowledge** both up and down the normal communication channels and horizontally through **social networks** and **interest groups**. It challenges notions of hierarchy and managers are facilitators rather than controllers. Such an organisation is inherently capable of change, because behaviours are adapted to reflect new knowledge. The concept has much in common with that of **logical incrementalism**. The challenge is to combine the advantages of rational planning with the resilience and adaptability provided by the learning approach.

5.3 Data, information and knowledge

FAST FORWARD

Data are simple facts that can be organised in a way that creates **information**. **Knowledge** is patterns of information that are strategically useful and context independent.

There is an important conceptual hierarchy underpinning knowledge management. This distinguishes between **data, information** and **knowledge**. The distinctions are not clear-cut and, to some extent, are differences of degree rather than kind. An understanding of the terms is best approached by considering the relationships between them.

5.3.1 Data

We start with **data**. Data typically consists of individual facts, but in a business context may include more complex items such as opinions, reactions and beliefs. It is important to realise that a quantity of data, no matter how large, does not constitute **information**.

5.3.2 Information

Information is data that is **organised** in some useful way. For instance, an individual credit sale will produce a single invoice identifying the goods, the price, the customer, the date of the sale and so on. These things are data: their usefulness does not extend beyond the purpose of the invoice, which is to collect the sum due. Even if we possess a copy of every invoice raised during a financial year, we still only have data. However, if we **process** that data we start to create information. For instance, a simple combination of analysis and arithmetic enables us to state total sales for the year, to break that down into sales for each product and to each customer, to identify major customers and so on. These are pieces of information: they are useful for the **management** of the business, rather than just inputs into its administrative systems.

5.3.3 Knowledge

Nevertheless, we still have not really produced any knowledge. Information may be said to consist of the relationships **between items of data**, as when we combine turnover with customer details to discover which accounts are currently important and which are not. We need to go beyond this in order to create knowledge.

The conceptual difference between data and information is fairly easy to grasp: it lies chiefly in the **processes** that produce the one from the other. The difference between information and knowledge is more complex and varies from setting to setting. This is not surprising, since knowledge itself is more complex than the information it derives from.

5.3.4 Differences between data, information and knowledge

A good starting point for understanding the difference is an appreciation of the importance of pattern: knowledge tends to originate in the **discovery of trends or patterns in information**. To return to our invoicing example, suppose we found that certain combinations of goods purchased were typical of certain customers. We could then build up some interesting customer profiles that would enhance our market segmentation and this in turn might influence our overall strategy, since we could identify likely prospects for cross-selling effort.

Another important aspect of the differences between data, information and knowledge is the relevance of **context**. Our sales invoice is meaningless outside its context; if you, as a marketing person, found an invoice in the office corridor, it would be little more than waste paper to you, though no doubt, the accounts people would like it back. However, if you found a list of customers in order of annual turnover, that would be rather more interesting from a marketing point of view. The information is **useful outside of its original context** of the accounts office.

This idea also applies to the difference between information and knowledge. If you were a visitor to a company and found a copy of the turnover listing, it would really only be useful to you if you were trying to sell the same sort of thing to the same customers. Its value outside its context would be small. However, if you found a marketing report that suggested, based on evidence, that customers were becoming more interested in quality and less interested in price, that would be applicable to a wide range of businesses, and possibly of strategic importance. This highlights another characteristic of knowledge: that it is a key **source of comparative advantage**.

Here is a table that summarises the progression from data to knowledge.

	Data	Information	Knowledge
Nature	Facts	Relationships between processed facts	Patterns discerned in information
Importance of context	Total	Some	Context independent
Importance to business	Mundane	Probably useful for management	May be strategically useful: Source of comparative advantage.

There is one final important point to note here and that is that the **progression** from data to knowledge is not the same in all circumstances. The scale is moveable and depends on the general complexity of the setting. Something may be **information** within its own context. Something similar may be **knowledge** in a different context. The difference will often be associated with the scale of operations. Take the example of a customer going into insolvent liquidation with £200,000 outstanding on its account. For a small supplier with an annual turnover of, say, £10 million, a bad debt of this size would be of strategic importance and might constitute a threat to its continued existence. Advance notice of the possibility would be valuable **knowledge**. However, for a company operating on a global scale, the bad debt write-off would be annoying but still only one item in a list of bad debts – **data**, in other words.

5.4 Other ideas about knowledge

Individuals acquire knowledge in a variety of ways including those listed below.

- Education and training
- Experience of work
- Observation of others
- Informal exchanges such as coaching and brain storming

Davenport and Prusak echo our earlier description of the relationship between data, information and knowledge and suggest that people **create knowledge from information by four processes**.

- **Comparison** with earlier experience
- **Consequences**: the implication of information
- **Connections**: relationships between items
- **Conversation**: discussion with others

5.5 Knowledge management (KM) systems   11/05

FAST FORWARD

Knowledge must be managed in a way that makes it easily available. IT systems and techniques such as **groupware**, **data warehousing** and **datamining** can help.

Recognition of the value of knowledge and understanding of the need to organise data and make it accessible have provoked the development of sophisticated IT systems. Such systems deal, by definition with **explicit knowledge**: that is, knowledge that is widely distributed.

Office automation systems are IT applications that improve productivity in an office. These include word processing and voice messaging systems.

Groupware, such as **Lotus Notes** provides functions for collaborative work groups. In a sales context, for instance, it would provide a facility for recording and retrieving all the information relevant to individual customers, including notes of visits, notes of telephone calls and basic data like address, credit terms and contact name. These items could be updated by anyone who had contact with a customer and would then be available to all sales people.

Groupware also provides such facilities as messaging, appointment scheduling, to-do lists, and jotters.

Intranet

An intranet is an internal network used to share information using Internet technology and protocols. The **firewall** surrounding an intranet fends off unauthorised access from outside the organisation. Each employee has a browser, used to access a server computer that holds corporate information on a wide variety of topics, and in some cases also offers access to the Internet. Applications include company newspapers, induction material, procedure and policy manuals and internal databases.

(a) Savings accrue from the **elimination of storage**, **printing** and **distribution of documents** that can be made available to employees online.

(b) Documents online are often **more widely used** than those that are kept filed away, especially if the document is bulky (eg manuals) and needs to be searched. This means that there are improvements in productivity and efficiency.

(c) It is much easier to **update information in electronic form**.

Extranet

An extranet is a collaborative network which uses internet technology to join organisations: extranets may be divided into **intronets** and **supranets**.

Intronet

When access to an intronet is extended to trusted external agencies, such as suppliers and customers, it becomes an **intronet**. The intronet's system content and functionality are under the control of the organisation that provides it. Intronets allow suppliers and customers to again privileged access to data held by the host. This may form the basis of a long-term relationship if the external user becomes dependent on the system's information content

Supranet

A **supranet** differs from an intronet in that it is set up in a co-operative fashion and control is not exercised by a single host. The aim is to insure the overall efficiency of the consortium of entities concerned.

Security is a major issue for extranets and may require firewalls, server management, encryption and the issue of digital certificates.

Expert system

An **expert system** is a computer program that captures **human expertise** in a limited domain of knowledge. Such software uses a knowledge base that consists of facts, concepts and the relationships between them and uses pattern-matching techniques to solve problems. For example, many financial institutions now use expert systems to process straightforward loan applications. The user enters certain key facts into the system such as the loan applicant's name and most recent addresses, their income and monthly outgoings, and details of other loans. The system will then:

(a)   Check the facts given against its **database** to see whether the applicant has a good previous credit record.

(b)   Perform **calculations** to see whether the applicant can afford to repay the loan.

(c)   Make a **judgement** as to what extent the loan applicant fits the lender's profile of a good risk (based on the lender's previous experience).

(d)   **A decision is then suggested**, based on the results of this processing.

IT systems can be used to store vast amounts of data in accessible form. A **data warehouse** receives data from operational systems, such as a sales order processing system, and stores it in its most fundamental form, without any summarisation of transactions. Analytical and query software is provided so that reports can be produced at any level of summarisation and incorporating any comparisons or relationships desired.

The value of a data warehouse is enhanced when **datamining** software is used. True datamining software **discovers previously unknown relationships** and provides insights that cannot be obtained through ordinary summary reports. These hidden patterns and relationships constitute **knowledge**, as defined above, and can be used to guide decision making and to predict future behaviour. Datamining is thus a contribution to organisational learning.

 Case Study

Wal-Mart

The American retailer Wal-Mart discovered an unexpected relationship between the sale of nappies and beer! Wal-Mart found that both tended to sell at the same time, just after working hours, and concluded that men with small children stopped off to buy nappies on their way home, and bought beer at the same time. Logically, therefore, if the two items were put in the same shopping aisle, sales of both should increase. Wal-Mart tried this and it worked.

Here is an amended version of our earlier table. This one includes the relevant IT systems.

	Data	Information	Knowledge
Nature	Facts	Relationships between processed facts	Patterns discerned in information
Importance of context	Total	Some	Context independent

	Data	Information	Knowledge
Importance to business	Mundane	Probably useful for management	May be strategically useful
Relevant IT systems	Office automation Data warehouse	Groupware Expert systems Report writing software Intranet	Datamining Intranet Expert systems

We will conclude this section with an example of the modern approach to knowledge management. You will notice that the IT system eventually developed looks like something half way between groupware and a database. However, the strategic impact of the system and its ability to create new corporate knowledge mean that it is properly described as a knowledge management system.

Notice also that the knowledge originates with people who are fairly low down in the hierarchy and who would not normally be described as knowledge workers. This illustrates the very important principle that valuable knowledge can be found at all levels and is not the prerogative of an elite.

 Case Study

Servicing *Xerox* copiers

Our story begins with researchers working on artificial intelligence who wanted to see if they could replace the paper documentation that Xerox technicians used on the road with an expert system.

The team found that it was indeed possible to build software that could do just that. But when they showed their first efforts to technicians, the response was underwhelming.

What kept technicians from finding fixes was not that the documentation was paper-based but that it didn't address all the potential problems. And not all problems were predictable. Machines in certain regions could react to extreme temperatures in different ways. A can of Mountain Dew overturned in one part of a machine could wreak havoc in another seemingly unconnected part. Technicians could handle these mishaps quickly only if they had seen them before or if another technician had run into a similar problem and shared the results.

Once the conversations with technicians revealed this gap in information sharing, the researchers realised that AI was the wrong approach. What Xerox needed instead was knowledge management. It wasn't a smart computer program that was going to fix these things, it was sharing the best ways to make these repairs.

When the researchers realised they needed to look at the way technicians work, they spent time in the field, following the technicians from call to call. What they observed proved invaluable – knowledge sharing was already unofficially ingrained in the organisation. Most striking was not how technicians solved common problems, but what they did when they came up against a tricky, intermittent one. Often they called one another on radios provided by the company. And in informal gatherings they shared vexing problems and their fixes.

Meanwhile, another researcher was busy comparing the way French and U.S. technicians worked. He discovered that, while French technicians appeared to work from immaculate, uniform documentation put out by headquarters, their real solutions also came from a second set of documentation – notes they carried with them detailing what they'd learned. It was from that database that researchers started building the first laptop-based knowledge-sharing system.

The researchers took the first iteration to France and began a series of exhaustive sessions with the French experts in the Xerox headquarters outside Paris. In those sessions, something magical happened: The system took on the shape of the people working on it, evolving with each suggestion from the actual users.

But the worldwide customer service group didn't take the project seriously. Nobody believed that the knowledge of the technicians was really valuable. So, working stealthily, outside the realm of worldwide management, the research team gave laptops and the fledging program to 40 technician and matched them with a control group of technicians who relied solely on their own knowledge when fixing machines. After two months, the group with the laptops had 10 percent lower costs and 10 percent lower service time than those without – and the control group was jealous of those with the system.

By 1998, the system was officially deployed in the United States and began to make its way around the globe. Today it has more than 15,000 user tips, with more being added every day. The hope is that by 2002 it will be distributed worldwide to the company's 25,000 technicians. And already success stories abound. One technician in Montreal authored a tip about a 50-cent fuse-holder replacement that caused a chronic problem with a high-speed colour copier. A Brazilian technician had the same problem, and his customer wanted the $40,000 machine replaced. When he found the tip from Montreal, he fixed the machine in minutes. Current estimates have the system saving Xerox at least $7 million in time and replacement costs. It's tales like those that make senior management happy.

Adapted from Meg Mitchell, *www.darwinmag.com* February 2001.

5.6 A strategy for knowledge management

An organisation that wishes to exploit its knowledge resource strategically should take a strategic approach.

(a) A **top-down** strategy uses the **overall strategic plan** to identify the areas in which knowledge can be best exploited.

(b) A **bottom-up** strategy is based on **research into existing key business processes** in order to determine important needs and issues.

(c) Knowledge is widely known to represent **power** and staff will hoard it. A culture of **knowledge sharing** must be developed.

(d) **IT** may have a role to play, especially in matters such as **capturing, communicating and storing knowledge**. However, the KM strategy need not be IT-driven. IT should support rather than dominate.

(e) **Support from the strategic apex** is essential, to provide the necessary **resources** and to lead the development of a **knowledge-based culture**.

5.7 The benefits of knowledge management

As well as increasing an organisation's ability to compete by virtue of its greater knowledge base, knowledge management may also improve productivity through higher workforce motivation, and staff using knowledge to improve efficiency.

6 Databases and models

FAST FORWARD

A database is a collection of data organised to service many applications. The database provides convenient access to data for a wide variety of users and user needs. **Advantages of a database system** include the avoidance of data duplication, management is encouraged to manage data as a valuable resource, data consistency across the organisation, and the flexibility for answering ad-hoc queries. **Disadvantages of a database system** include initial development costs and the potential problems of data security.

The way in which data is held on a system affects the ease by which the data is able to be accessed and manipulated. Many modern software packages are built around a database. A database provides a comprehensive set of data for a number of different users.

A **database** is a collection of data organised to service many applications. The database provides convenient access to data for a wide variety of users and user needs.

A **database management system** (**DBMS**) is the software that centralises data and manages access to the database. It is a system which allows numerous applications to extract the data they need without the need for separate files.

6.1 The characteristics of a database system

(a) **Shared**. Different users are able to access the same data for their own processing applications. This removes the need for duplicating data on different files.

(b) **Controls** to preserve the **integrity** of the database. Users should not be able to alter the data on file so as to **spoil** the database records for other users. However, users must be able to make **valid** alterations to the data.

(c) **Flexibility.** The database system should provide for the **needs of different users**, who each have their own processing requirements and data access methods. The database should be capable of **evolving** to meet **future** needs.

6.2 Advantages and disadvantages

The **advantages** of a database system are as follows.

(a) **Avoidance of unnecessary duplication of data**

It recognises that data can be used for many purposes but only needs to be input and stored once.

(b) **Multi-purpose data**

From (a), it follows that although data is input once, it can be used for several purposes.

(c) **Data for the organisation as a whole, not just for individual departments**

The database concept encourages management to regard data as a resource that must be properly managed just as any other resource. Database systems encourage management to analyse data, relationships between data items, and how data is used in different applications.

(d) **Consistency**

Because data is only held once, it is easier to ensure that it is up-to-date and consistent across departments.

(e) **New uses for data**

Data is held independently of the programs that access the data. This allows greater flexibility in the ways that data can be used. New programs can be easily introduced to make use of existing data in a different way.

(f) **New applications**

Developing new application programs with a database system is easier as a central pool of data is already available to be drawn upon.

(g) **Flexibility**

Relational systems are extremely flexible, allowing information from several different sources to be combined and providing answers to ad-hoc queries.

The **disadvantages** of a database systems relate mainly to security and control.

(a) There are potential problems of **data security** and **data privacy**. Administrative procedures for data security should supplement software controls.

(b) Since there is only one set of data, it is essential that the data should be **accurate** and free from corruption. A back-up routine is essential.

(c) Initial **development costs** may be high.

(d)   For hierarchical and network structures, the access paths through the data must be **specified in advance**.

(e)   Both hierarchical and network systems require intensive **programming** and are **inflexible**.

6.3 Using databases for planning

Planning will always involve an element of risk – as it deals with the **future**. Databases can at least ensure that information we have about the present and the past is available to aid planning. Organised data retrieval techniques make the data available in an effective way. In a world in which decisions must be ever more rapid, it is crucial to be able to access diverse, complex, multiple data bits and to analyse them to rapidly and correctly extract the knowledge they contain.

Databases can be used in conjunction with a variety of tools and techniques, eg Decision Support Systems, Executive Information Systems, data warehousing, and data mining.

An **object model**, as described below, has characteristics of both a database and a **planning model**. The article explains how models can assist the strategic planning process.

 Case Study

Using models for strategic planning

Financial and business planning is probably the most important activity that an organisation will undertake. However, traditional tools like spreadsheets were never designed for planning and have inherited the task. This article will demonstrate the **strategic value of objects** over traditional spreadsheets.

So what are 'objects'?

Objects are based on **models organised around real-world concepts**. Essentially **they consist of data and a program held together in a single entity**.

Although 'objects' are a technology that were developed more than ten years ago it is only now that they have reached a stage where they can be **considered of strategic importance** for organisations. This is because, unlike traditional tools, they can **capture knowledge** and guarantee integrity. This means that managers are equipped to become strategic planners rather than spreadsheet programmers.

It is easy to see why spreadsheets are so popular—they can be efficient, cost-effective and flexible. However, the explosive growth in their use has far outpaced the understanding of the associated risks or the application of best practice. In an investigation into blue-chip companies using large spreadsheets, KPMG Management Consulting reported that up to 95% of models were found to contain major errors (ie those that could affect decisions).

In 1995 Commercial and General Systems undertook some research, talking to management consultancies, accountants, venture capitalists and banks about the main **problems in financial and business planning**. Those identified were:

Consolidation: Time is incurred in agreeing a common standard for each model, as there are many different accounting formats and standards that need to be applied. Figures to be consolidated tend to come from a variety of sources and those from colleagues are often looked upon with distrust. This means that with revisions or new sets of figures being consolidated there is constant checking and re-checking for errors which means increased time and costs.

Sharing: The business plan should reflect the plan of the business but very often it is difficult for different departments to contribute successfully. Planning 'knowledge' is not shared, with users ending up speaking different languages. This can lead to bad assumptions being incorporated into financial models which are inevitably carried through to the final plan.

Re-invention: PC stands for 'personal computer' and that is exactly what it is – personal. Using spreadsheets, users tend to work on their own models, which are developed in isolation of each other. This leads to duplication of effort and substantial time is wasted in reinventing similar models.

Re-scheduling: Business planning involves conducting 'what if' scenario analysis and spreadsheets prove to be inflexible in this—try moving all of the costs for a new project out, say, three months on your spreadsheet models and watch the formulas 'fall over'. This inflexibility means that managers are not really planning.

Hidden mistakes: With spreadsheets, mistakes are made unknowingly and these are often amplified when refinements are made to the plan. The revenue and cost drivers are not always fully understood and are buried deep inside the spreadsheet. Models are therefore inherently incorrect, leading to bad decision-making.

Managers become programmers: The skills now required to be competent with spreadsheets are fairly significant and many business models are being compromised by lack of programming skills. Managers become frustrated and end up doing the wrong job. They are technically programming instead of financial and business planning.

Limited audit trail: Audit-trails in spreadsheets are very limited at best, and you can't review what you did very easily, let alone tracking someone else's changes! Managers **cannot therefore learn from mistakes** and capture or evolve organisational best practice.

How can object type models be of strategic value?

The appeal of an object-orientated approach is that the **information in each object can be re-used** repeatedly in a variety of applications. As can be seen, the common tasks that are performed in financial and business planning are much more effectively done by the use of objects. The value of this re-usability **facilitates the capture of knowledge and organisational learning**. With guaranteed integrity, managers are secure about the figures they use, whether self-generated or from colleagues. Taking all these factors into account it is easy to see how objects can be of strategic value.

It is important to recognise that objects will not replace spreadsheets, just as spreadsheets didn't replace paper. They do, however, represent a new set of tools for managers that complement existing ones. Using objects can confer competitive advantage for organisations and offer the benefits of **knowledge capture and guaranteed integrity**.

Adapted from an article by L Porter, J Oakland and K Gadd, CIMA articles database September 1999

7 Data warehousing and datamining

Two techniques designed to utilise the ever-increasing amounts of data held by organisations are **data warehousing** and **datamining**.

7.1 Data warehousing

A **data warehouse** consists of a database, containing data from various operational systems, and reporting and query tools.

Organisations may build a single central data warehouse to serve the entire organisation or may create a series of smaller **data marts**.

Key term

A **data warehouse** consists of a database, containing data from various operational systems, and reporting and query tools.

A data warehouse contains data from a range of internal (eg sales order processing system, nominal ledger) and external sources. One reason for including individual transaction data in a data warehouse is that if necessary the user can drill-down to access transaction level detail. Data is increasingly obtained from newer channels such as customer care systems, outside agencies or websites.

Maintenance of a data warehouse is an iterative process that continually refines its content. Data is copied to the data warehouse as often as required – usually either daily, weekly or monthly. The process of making any required changes to the format of data and copying it to the warehouse is usually automated.

The result should be a coherent set of information available to be used across the organisation for management analysis and decision making. The reporting and query tools available within the warehouse should facilitate management reporting and analysis.

The reporting and query tools should be flexible enough to allow multidimensional data analysis, also known as **on-line analytical processing** (OLAP). Each aspect of information (eg product, region, price, budgeted sales, actual sales, time period etc) represents a different dimension. OLAP enables data to be viewed from each dimension, allowing each aspect to be viewed and in relation to the other aspects.

7.1.1 Features of data warehouses

A data warehouse is subject-oriented, integrated, time-variant, and non-volatile.

(a)   **Subject-oriented**

A data warehouse is focussed on data groups not application boundaries. Whereas the operational world is designed around applications and functions such as sales and purchases, a data warehouse world is organised around major **subjects** such as customers, supplier, product and activity.

(b)   **Integrated**

Data within the data warehouse must be consistent in format and codes used – this is referred to as **integrated** in the context of data warehouses.

For example, one operational application feeding the warehouse may represent **sex** as an 'M' and an 'F' while another represents **sex** as '1' and '0'.

While it does not matter how **sex** is represented in the data warehouse (let us say that 'M' and 'F' is chosen), it **must** arrive in the data warehouse in a **consistent integrated** state. The data import routine should cleanse any inconsistencies.

(c)   **Time-variant**

Data is organised by time and stored in time-slices.

Data warehouse data may cover **a long time horizon**, perhaps from five to ten years. Data warehouse data tends to deal with **trends** rather than single points in time. As a result, each data element in the data warehouse environment must carry with it the time for which it applies.

(d)   **Non-volatile**

Data **cannot be changed** within the warehouse. Only load and retrieval operations are made.

Organisations may build a single central data warehouse to serve the entire organisation or may create a series of smaller **data marts**. A data mart holds a selection of the organisation's data for a specific purpose.

A data mart can be constructed more quickly and cheaply than a data warehouse. However, if too many individual data marts are built, organisations may find it is more efficient to have a single data warehouse serving all areas.

The components of a data warehouse are shown in the following diagram.

Components of a data warehouse

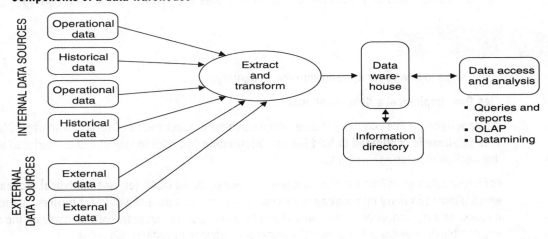

7.1.2 Advantages of data warehouses

Advantages of setting up a data warehouse system include the following.

(a) Supports strategic decision making: The warehouse provides a single source of authoritative data which can be analysed using data making techniques to support strategic decision making.

(b) Decision makers can access data without affecting the use of operational systems.

(c) Data quality. Having a single source of data available will reduce the risk of inconsistent data being used by different people during the decision making process.

(d) Having a wide range of data available to be queried easily encourages the taking of a wide perspective on organisational activities.

(c) Data warehouses have proved successful in some businesses for:

    (i)   Quantifying the effect of marketing initiatives.

    (ii)   Improving knowledge of customers.

    (iii) Identifying and understanding an enterprise's most profitable revenues streams.

7.1.3 Limitations of data warehouses

Some organisations have found they have invested considerable resources implementing a data warehouse for little return. To benefit from the information a data warehouse can provide, organisations need to be flexible and prepared to act on what they find. If a warehouse system is implemented simply to follow current practice it will be of little value.

Other limitations exist, particularly if a data warehouse is intended to be used as an operational system rather than as an analytical tool. For example:

(a) The data held may be outdated.

(b) An efficient regular routine must be established to transfer data into the warehouse.

(c) A warehouse may be implemented and then, as it is not required on a day-to-day basis, be ignored.

There is also an issue of **security**. The management aim of making data available widely and in an easily understood form can be at variance with the need to maintain confidentiality of, for example, payroll data. This conflict can be managed by **encrypting** data at the point of capture and **restricting access** by a system of authorisations entitling different users to different levels of access. For this to work, the data held must be classified according to the degree of protection it requires: users can then be given access limited to a given class or classes of data. Encryption at the point of capture also exerts control over the **unauthorised uploading** of data to the data warehouse.

7.1.4 Metadata

Metadata is data about data. A software information model can create metadata for a data warehouse. This can describe the way the data is structured and assist access, merge and combine data from disparate sources and verify the quality of data held. It can also attend to housekeeping issues such as the update schedule, who is responsible for each type of data and how information was derived.

 Case Study

Seven steps to bring your systems into the 21 Century.

Step One. Implement a data warehouse

A data warehouse is a computer loaded with a database product such as Oracle or Microsoft SQL server. **This database is configured to hold the key information** you want to look at and is interfaced with the 'transaction processing' systems.

For larger volumes of data a toolset has been developed called **OLAP (on-line analytical processing)** which allows **summary information** to be created and stored across the different business performance metrics. As a consequence of this, on-line and instant enquiries can potentially be made on the balances of any combination of customer/product/regional performance by date/period range.

The performance of the transaction-processing systems will not be affected by heavy use of the data warehouse for a complex set of enquiries, as you will not be working with the live information.

Once this warehouse has been set up, information can be combined from the different operations systems into a consistent format and can be accessed by a wide variety of reporting/analysis/web tools.

Step Two. Reporting tools

Time and time again finance directors say that their key IT issue is lack of reporting capabilities in the systems they are using. Reporting problems tend to fall into three categories.

First, the **inability to access the source data**. This is either because it is in a format that cannot be accessed by PC technology or it is held in so many places that its structure is incomprehensible to a member of the finance team.

Second, the **tools to make the enquiries** or produce the reports are often **difficult to use** and do not produce the reports in a 'user friendly' format with 'drill down' capabilities.

Third, there is the issue of **consistency of information** across systems. In order to get an overall picture of your organisation's performance you will usually need to access data from different operation applications. All too often the data is not the same across these systems.

The argument for replacing what you have is well rehearsed. New systems promise the latest technology for reporting and enquiries. **Enterprise Resource Planning (ERP)** packages promise to integrate your different applications smoothly and give you a single point of access to all data. **Customer Relationship Management (CRM)** software has been added to this recipe to give this approach a better chance of happening.

There are a myriad of reporting tools costing from a few pounds to hundreds of thousands of pounds. One that is regularly overlooked is the **spreadsheet**. Excel is the product most commonly used by accountants. With the advent of Microsoft Office 2000 there is a bewildering array of features to present information on your desktop or paper. **Pivot tables** are starting to be used more widely for multi-dimensional analysis and can be combined with the increasingly powerful **graphical capabilities** of Excel. Spreadsheets are much underrated and it is surprising how many organisations go out and buy expensive new knowledge-management tools when they already have a product on their computer that will deliver all the reporting/enquiry performance they require.

So, see how far your spreadsheet will take you and see if you can avoid the cost of another new IT tool.

Step Three. Intranet-enabled-reporting/enquiries

Larger companies have by now started to implement a **corporate intranet**. This typically holds information on employee phone and contact details, standard forms for holiday requests, terms and conditions of employment and so on.

It is possible now to integrate financial reporting into an intranet. The leading web page development tools allow the display of information from a data warehouse. Excel has facilities to post spreadsheets and pivot table information straight to a web page and for users to drill down to the detail from a summary level. There are a number of **benefits** to this.

First, the information is presented in a **user-friendly** format and can be made 'idiot proof' for non-IT literate staff.

Second, the benefit of using a web browser is that it allows for **remote access** to the information quickly and easily. This means that people working at different parts of the organisation or away from the office can access this data rapidly.

Third, the web browser technology is becoming an **industry standard** and as such is well supported and increasingly reliable.

So start to use a web browser to access your reports and **publish these to your intranet** server rather than printing them out.

Step Four. Client/supplier access to information

So you have implemented the above and have your core business data from your different systems in **a single data warehouse**. You will be using PC tools like Excel to access this and will have developed part of your intranet so that staff can access key information quickly and easily wherever they are.

Why not consider making **some of this information available to your business partners**? For example, if you have customer sales order information in your data warehouse, why not make it available to your customers and even suppliers? If you have internal information on the products and services that you sell, why not do likewise?

This is where the Internet can really start to bite and give your organisation real commercial benefit.

Step Five. Streamlined transaction processing

The next step is to look at the possibility of **streamlining your business processes**. How many times are you capturing your transactions in your organisation?

Why not allow customers to generate their own orders via the web? If the data warehouse holds information on the clients, the products and services you sell, it could be relatively straightforward to create an order front-end with a web browser to this information.

You could populate the data warehouse with these incoming orders and use this to upload your core transaction processing systems. Most packages now have data import modules and this process may be more straightforward than you think and a lot cheaper and easier than replacing your core business systems. Why not extend this to allowing your employees and even customers to 'self service' the information in your systems and keep it up-to-date themselves.

Clearly there are lots of caveats to this option. **Security** is always a concern, as is the resilience of the IT infrastructure necessary to support on-line order processing by clients. However, a number of forward-thinking businesses have achieved this without replacing all their systems.

Step Six. Train staff in what you already have

Do your staff really understand the features of your accounting and business systems? Are they familiar with what the web can offer your organisation? Put together a **comprehensive training programme**.

Step Seven. Get board buy-in

A note of caution to conclude on: **you MUST get board and senior management buy-in to what you are planning**.

Source: Adapted from an article by John Tate, Management Accounting, April 2000

7.2 Datamining

FAST FORWARD

> **Datamining** software looks for **hidden** patterns and relationships in large pools of data. Datamining uses **statistical analysis tools** as well as **neural networks**, **fuzzy logic** and other **intelligent techniques**.

Key term

> **Datamining** software looks for hidden patterns and relationships in large pools of data.

True datamining software discovers **previously unknown relationships**. The hidden patterns and relationships the software identifies can be used to guide decision making and to **predict future behaviour**, as with the Wal-Mart beer and nappies example given earlier.

Datamining uses statistical analysis tools as well as neural networks, fuzzy logic and other **intelligent techniques**.

The types of relationships or patterns that datamining may uncover may be classified as follows.

Relationship/ Discovery	Comment
Classification or cluster	These terms refer to the identification of patterns within the database between a range of data items. For example, datamining may find that unmarried males aged between 20 and 30, who have an income above £50,000 are more likely to purchase a high performance sports car than people from other demographic groups. This group could then be targeted when marketing material is produced/distributed.
Association	One event can be linked or correlated to another event – such as in Wal-Mart example.
Forecasting	Trends are identified within the data that can be extrapolated into the future.

8 The IT department

FAST FORWARD

The main choice about organising the IT specialists is whether they should be centralised or decentralised. There is a tension between **control** and **relevance to local conditions**. An **information centre** is an important aspect of the IT department, providing rapid support to users together with an element of supervision.

Key terms

A **centralised** IS/IT department involves all IS/IT staff and functions being based out at a single central location, such as head office.

A **decentralised** IS/IT department involves IS/IT staff and functions being spread out throughout the organisation.

There is no single 'best' structure for an IS/IT department – an organisation should consider its IS/IT requirements and the merits of each structure.

8.1 Centralisation

Advantages of a centralised IS/IT department

(a) Assuming centralised processing is used, there is only one set of files so everyone uses the same data and information.

(b) It gives better security/control over data and files so it is easier to enforce standards.

(c) Head office is in a better position to know what is going on.

(d) There may be economies of scale available in purchasing computer equipment and supplies.

(e) Computer staff are in a single location, more expert staff are likely to be employed and career paths may be more clearly defined.

Disadvantages of a centralised IS/IT department

(a) Local offices might have to wait for IS/IT services and assistance.

(b) Reliance on head office, so local offices are less self-sufficient.

(c) A system fault at head office will impact across the organisation.

Centralisation is appropriate in a coherent integrated organisation where all locations or departments are doing much the same thing and there is no equivalent for specialised systems. A chain of supermarkets would be a good example. This is sometimes called the 'star organisations' approach.

A degree of decentralisation or **partial distribution** may be appropriate where departments or sites are doing similar things but with different data: there can be commonality of systems but local processing may be appropriate. An example would be a manufacturer operating on several sites and using the same production control system at each installation: different products, manufacturing processes and stock levels might make distributed systems appropriate.

8.2 Decentralisation

Advantages of a decentralised IS/IT department

(a) Each office can introduce an information system specially **tailored** for its individual needs so local changes in business requirements can be taken into account.

(b) Each office is more self-sufficient.

(c) Offices are likely to have quicker access to IS/IT support/advice.

(d) A decentralised structure is more likely to facilitate accurate IS/IT cost/overhead allocations.

Disadvantages of a decentralised IS/IT department

(a) Control may be more difficult – different and uncoordinated information systems may be introduced.

(b) Self-sufficiency may encourage a lack of co-ordination between departments.

(c) Increased risk of data duplication, with different offices holding the same data on their own separate files.

Full decentralisation may be seen in a **network organisation**, especially where there are incompatible legacy systems. There is unlikely to be any central IT management function; though there will probably be co-ordination by agreement. Information sharing and integration will be a priority, but may be difficult to achieve.

8.3 The information centre

Key term

> An **Information Centre (IC)** is a small unit of staff with a good technical awareness of computer systems, whose task is to provide a support function to computer users within the organisation.

Information centres, sometimes referred to as **support centres**, are particularly useful in organisations which use distributed systems and so are likely to have hardware, data and software scattered throughout the organisation.

8.3.1 Help

An IC usually offers a **Help Desk** to solve IT problems. Help may be via the telephone, e-mail, through a searchable knowledge base or in person. **Remote diagnostic software** may be used which enables staff in the IC to take control of a computer and sort out the problem without leaving their desk. The help desk needs sufficient staff and technical expertise to respond quickly and effectively to requests for help. IC staff should also maintain good relationships with hardware and software suppliers to ensure their maintenance staff are quickly on site when needed.

8.3.2 Problem solving

The IC will maintain a **record of problems** and identify those that occur most often. If the problem is that users do not know how to use the system, training is provided. Training applications often contain analysis software, drawing attention to trainee progress and common problems. This information enables the IC to identify and address specific training needs more closely. If the problem is with the system itself, a solution is found, either by modifying the system or by investment in new hardware or software.

8.3.3 Improvements

The IC may also be required to consider the viability of suggestions for improving the system, and to bring these improvements into effect.

8.3.4 Standards

The IC is also likely to be responsible for setting, and encouraging users to conform to, common **standards**.

(a) Hardware standards ensure that all of the equipment used in the organisation is compatible and can be put into use in different departments as needed.

(b) Software standards ensure that information generated by one department can easily be shared with and worked upon by other departments.

(c) Programming standards ensure that applications developed by individual end-users (for example complex spreadsheet macros) follow best practice and are easy to modify.

(d) Data processing standards ensure that certain conventions such as the format of file names are followed throughout the organisation. This facilitates sharing, storage and retrieval of information.

8.3.5 Security

The IC may help to preserve the security of data in various ways.

(a) It may develop utility programs and procedures to ensure that back-ups are made at regular intervals.

(b) The IC may help to preserve the company's systems from attack by computer viruses, for instance by ensuring that the latest versions of anti-virus software are available to all users, by reminding users regularly about the dangers of viruses, and by setting up and maintaining 'firewalls', which deny access to sensitive parts of the company's systems.

8.3.6 End-user applications development

An IC can help applications development by providing technical guidance to end-user developers and to encourage comprehensible and well-documented programs. Understandable programs can be maintained or modified more easily. Documentation provides a means of teaching others how the programs work. These efforts can greatly extend the usefulness and life of the programs that are developed.

8.4 Outsourcing IT/IS services   5/05

Key term

> **Outsourcing** is the contracting out of specified operations or services to an external vendor.

The arrangement varies according to the circumstances of both organisations.

Feature	Outsourcing arrangement		
	Timeshare	Service	Facilities Management (FM)
What is it?	Access to an external processing system on a time-used basis	Focus on specific function, eg payroll	A outside agency manages the organisation's IS/IT facilities. The client retains equipment but all services provided by FM company
Management responsibility	Mostly retained	Some retained	Very little retained
Focus	Operational	A function	Strategic
Timescale	Short-term	Medium-term	Long-term
Justification	Cost savings	More efficient	Access to expertise; better service; management can focus on core business activities

Managing such arrangements involves deciding **what** will be outsourced, choosing a supplier and the supplier **relationship**.

8.4.1 How to determine what will be outsourced?

(a)   What is the system's **strategic importance**? A third party IT specialist cannot be expected to possess specific business knowledge.

(b)   Functions with only **limited interfaces** are most easily outsourced, eg payroll.

(c)   Do we know enough about the system to manage the arrangement?

(d)   Are our requirements likely to **change**?

The arrangement is incorporated in a contract sometimes referred to as the **Service Level Contract** (SLC) or **Service Level Agreement** (SLA).

Element	Comment
Service level	Minimum levels of service with penalties for example: • Response time to requests for assistance/information • System 'uptime' percentage • Deadlines for performing relevant tasks
Exit route	Arrangements for an exit route, transfer to another supplier or move back in-house.
Timescale	When does the contract expire? Is the timescale suitable for the organisation's needs or should it be renegotiated?
Software ownership	This covers software licensing, security and copyright (if new software is to be developed)?
Dependencies	If related services are outsourced, the level of service quality agreed should group these services together.
Employment issues	If the organisation's IT staff to move to the third party, employer responsibilities must be specified clearly.

8.4.2 Advantages of outsourcing arrangements

(a)   Outsourcing can remove uncertainty about **cost**, as there is often a long-term contract where services are specified in advance for a **fixed price**.

(b)   Long-term contracts (maybe up to ten years) encourage **planning** for the future.

(c)   Outsourcing can bring the benefits of **economies of scale**. For example, an IT company's research into new software may benefit several of their clients.

(d)   A specialist organisation is able to **retain skills and knowledge**. Many organisations' IT departments are too small to develop good people.

(e)   New skills and knowledge become available. A specialist company can **share** staff with **specific expertise** between several clients.

(f)   **Flexibility**. Resources may be scaled up or down depending upon demand.

8.4.3 Disadvantages of outsourcing arrangements

(a)   Information and its provision is **an inherent part of business and management**. If the information system is outsourced, the organisation will have less control over the system. If controls are subsequently relaxed, or the quality of information falls, this could damage the organisation's competitive position.

(b)   Information strategy can be used to gain **competitive advantage**. Opportunities may be missed if a third party is handling IS services.

(c)   The organisation will lose the knowledge of key staff, which again may weaken its competitive position.

(d)   An organisation may have highly **confidential information** and to let outsiders handle it could be seen as **risky** in commercial and/or legal terms.

(e)   An organisation may find itself **locked in** to an unsatisfactory contract.

 Case Study

In October 2005 *Sainsburys* brought its contract with *Accenture* to a premature end and took the management of its IT systems back in-house after encountering problems. Independent analyst Douglas Hayward suggested that there had been poor decision-making by Sainsbury's executives, weak outsourcing governance, political in-fighting and a risky 'big-bang' approach that made too many assumptions and took too many risks.

Chapter Roundup

- **Strategic information** is used to **plan** the **objectives** of the organisation, and to **assess** whether the objectives are being met in practice.

- Strategic IT systems include **EIS**, **MIS** and **DSS**. **Value added networks** facilitate the strategic use of information in order to add value.

- Information strategy can be divided into **information systems strategy, information technology strategy** and **information management strategy**. The strategic significance of information requires that it be itself managed strategically so that the systems, the technology and the information itself support the overall strategic policy.

- Porter and Millar say that IT changes corporate strategy since products and business activities have both **physical** and **informational** aspects. The rapid rate of change in IT is having drastic effects on the informational aspects of both products and activities. Also, IT has the potential to **transform competition** in three ways: its effect on the **five competitive forces**; its potential for implementing the **generic strategies**; and its contribution to the **emergence of completely new businesses**.

- A strategy for IT is developed from the strategy for information, which in turn supports overall strategy. Earl suggests such a strategy may be **top down/business objective led; bottom up/business system led** or **inside out/innovative/exploitative**. Other approaches include **enterprise analysis** and the use of **critical success factors**.

- An **information audit** aims to establish the information needs of users **and** how these needs could be met.

- An information system should be designed to obtain information from **all relevant sources** – both internal and external.

- Control information, to be useful, must aid the decision-making process.

- The aim of **knowledge management** is to capture, organise and make widely available all the knowledge the organisation possesses, whether in recorded form or in people's heads.

- **Data** are simple facts that can be organised in a way that creates **information**. **Knowledge** is patterns of information that are strategically useful and context independent.

- Knowledge must be managed in a way that makes it easily available. IT systems and techniques such as **groupware**, **data warehousing** and **datamining** can help.

- A database is a collection of data organised to service many applications. The database provides convenient access to data for a wide variety of users and user needs. **Advantages of a database system** include the avoidance of data duplication, management is encouraged to manage data as a valuable resource, data consistency across the organisation, and the flexibility for answering ad-hoc queries. **Disadvantages of a database system** include initial development costs and the potential problems of data security.

- A **data warehouse** consists of a database, containing data from various operational systems, and reporting and query tools.

- Organisations may build a single central data warehouse to serve the entire organisation or may create a series of smaller **data marts**.

- **Datamining** software looks for **hidden** patterns and relationships in large pools of data. Datamining uses **statistical analysis tools** as well as **neural networks**, **fuzzy logic** and other **intelligent techniques**.

- The main choice about organising the IT specialists is whether they should be centralised or decentralised. There is a tension between **control** and relevance to local conditions. An **information centre** is an important aspect of the IT department, providing rapid support to users together with an element of supervision.

Quick Quiz

1   Strategically useful information will rarely be obtained from sources internal to the organisation.

☐   True

☐   False

2   The decision making process may be said to commence with

A   Identifying courses of action
B   Problem definition
C   Problem recognition
D   None of the above

3   What are the three 'legs' of IS strategy development which Earl identified?

4   What is the difference between data and information?

5   An IT system that holds a selection of the organisation's data for a specific purpose is called a:

A   Data warehouse
B   Intranet
C   Groupware
D   Data mart

6   List three advantages of outsourcing.

7   What is environmental scanning?

Answers to Quick Quiz

1   False. Many organisations possess large amounts of strategically useful information in their internal records.

2   C. The need for a decision must first be recognised; defining the problem comes next.

3   Business led; infrastructure led; mixed.

4   Information is data that is organised in some useful way.

5   D. A data warehouse holds all the data. An intranet and groupware are systems for accessing and sharing data, information and knowledge.

6   Any three of: removes uncertainty about cost; benefit from economies of scale; benefit from specialist knowledge: scalability of resources.

7   Environmental scanning is the process of gathering external information from a wide range of sources.

Now try the question below from the Exam Question Bank

Number	Level	Marks	Time
Q2	Examination	25	45 mins

Strategic objectives

Introduction

In this chapter we consider the **objectives and goals** of an organisation. A **mission** (Section 1) describes what the organisation is for and how it relates to the wider society. Many organisations, especially public sector ones, have to juggle a number of conflicting objectives, and so developing a mission may be difficult. Businesses (Section 2) generally pursue some kind of **financial return**, although a number of measures can be used. **Secondary objectives** support this return. Trade-offs have to be made between goals.

Various groups of **stakeholders** (Section 3) have their own expectations of the organisation. Different stakeholder groups exercise different degrees of power.

Allied to a consideration of stakeholders is the question of **short versus long term perspectives** on business performance (Section 4).

The theme of **social responsibility and sustainability** (Section 5) is the question of how far a business is accountable to the wider community for the effects of its operations, and the fact that resources are finite and need to be replaced.

The chapter closes with a look at the specific issues relating to the **not-for-profit** and **public sector** objectives.

Topic list	Learning outcomes	Syllabus references	Ability required
1 Mission, goals and strategy	A(i), C(i)	A3, C1	Evaluation
2 Business goals and objectives	A(i), C(i)	A3, C1	Evaluation
3 Stakeholder goals and objectives	A(i), B(iii), C(i)	A3, B3, C1	Evaluation
4 The short term and long term	A(i), C(i)	A3, C1	Evaluation
5 Corporate social responsibility and sustainability	B(ii), B(iii)	B3	Evaluation
6 Not-for-profit organisations	B(ii), B(iii)	B3	Evaluation
7 The public sector	B(iii)	B3	Analysis

1 Mission, goals and strategy

Strategies are developed in order to achieve desired outcomes. These are inherent in the organisation's mission or defining purpose. Whether stated or not, the **mission** of a business always includes return to investors. Mission guides strategic decisions and provides values and a sense of direction.

Key term

When we introduced the rational model of strategy we said that it takes **mission** (or vision) as its starting point. In this chapter we will use the word 'mission' to denote the overall purpose for which the organisation exists.

The *Ashridge College* model of mission **links business strategy to culture and ethics** by including four separate elements in an expanded definition of **mission**.

(a) **Purpose**. Why does the company exist? Who does it exist for?

    (i)   To create wealth for shareholders, who take priority over all other stakeholders?

    (ii)   To satisfy the needs of all stakeholders, including employees, for example?

    (iii)   To reach some higher goal such as the advancement of society?

(b) **Values** are the beliefs and moral principles that underlie the organisation's culture.

(c) **Strategy** provides the commercial logic for the company, and so addresses the following question: 'What is our business? What should it be?'

(d) **Policies and standards of behaviour** provide guidance on how the organisation's business should be conducted. For example, a service industry that wishes to be the best in its market must aim for standards of service, in all its operations, which are at least as good as those found in its competitors.

1.1 The importance of mission for corporate strategy

Mission and values are taken seriously by many businesses, though some managers think the idea is no more than a consultant-driven fad. There are several reasons why a business should give serious consideration to establishing a clear concept of its corporate mission.

(a) Values are acknowledged as integral elements of consumers' buying decisions; this is shown by the attention paid to them in advertising, brand building and market research. Customers ask not only 'What do you sell?' but 'What do you stand for?'

(b) Studies into organisational behaviour show that people are motivated by many things other than money: employees are likely to be both more productive and more satisfied with their work when they feel that what they are doing has significance beyond the mere pursuit of a living.

(c) Some writers believe there is an empirical relationship between strong corporate values and profitability.

 Case Study

The *Financial Times* reported the result of research by the Digital Equipment Corporation into a sample of 429 company executives.

- 80% of the sample have a formal mission statement
- 80% believed mission contributes to profitability
- 75% believe they have a responsibility to implement the mission statement

1.2 Mission statements

Key term

> A mission statement is a published statement, apparently of the entity's fundamental objective(s). This may or may not summarise the true mission of the entity.　　　　CIMA *Official Terminology*

Mission statements are formal documents that state the organisation's mission. There is no standard format, but the four element Ashridge model of mission is a good basis for writing a mission statement. Mission statements are published within organisations in order to promote desired behaviour: support for strategy and purpose, adherence to values and adoption of policies and standards of behaviour.

Lynch (in *Corporate Strategy*)has provided the following criteria by which to judge the effectiveness of a corporate mission statement:

(a)　Is it specific enough to impact upon individuals' behaviour?

(b)　Does it reflect the distinctive advantage of the organisation?

(c)　Is it realistic and attainable?

(d)　Is it flexible to the demands of a changing environment?

 Case Study

Evaluate the following mission statements.

(a)　**Glaxo** 'is an integrated research-based group of companies whose corporate purpose is to create, discover, develop, manufacture and market throughout the world, safe, effective medicines of the highest quality which will bring benefit to patients through improved longevity and quality of life, and to society through economic value.'

(b)　**IBM (UK)**: 'We shall increase the pace of change. Market-driven quality is our aim. It means listening and responding more sensitively to our customers. It means eliminating defects and errors, speeding up all our processes, measuring everything we do against a common standard, and it means involving employees totally in our aims'.

(c)　**Matsushita**: 'the duty of the manufacturer is to serve the foundation of man's happiness by making man's life affluent with an inexpensive and inexhaustible supply of life's necessities.'

Some are suspicious of mission statements.

(a)　They are often **public relations** exercises rather than an accurate portrayal of the organisation's actual values.

(b)　They can often be full of **generalisations** which are impossible to tie down to specific strategic implications, and practical objectives.

(c)　They may be ignored by the people responsible for formulating or implementing strategy.

(d)　They become obsolete, as they fail to evolve over time with the organisation.

1.3 Mission and planning

The mission statement can play an important role in the strategic planning process.

(a)　**Inspires and informs planning**. Plans should further the organisation's goals and be consistent with its values. In this way, the mission statement provides a focus for consistent strategic planning decisions.

(b)　**Screening**. Mission acts as a yardstick by which plans are judged.

(c)　Mission also affects the **implementation** of a planned strategy in terms of the ways in which the firm carries out its business and the culture of the organisation. A mission statement often establishes an ethics framework.

The Co-op has explicit social objectives. In some cases it will retain stores which, although too small to be as profitable as a large supermarket, fulfil an important social role in the communities which host them.

2 Business goals and objectives

FAST FORWARD

Goals and **objectives** derive from mission and support it. For a business, a primary corporate objective will be the return offered to shareholders, however this is measured. There may be other primary objectives and there will certainly be supporting objectives for costs, innovation, markets, products and so on.

2.1 Goals, objectives and targets

An understanding of the organisation's mission is invaluable for setting and controlling the overall **functioning and progress** of the organisation. However, it is possible for an organisation to operate reasonably effectively even if most of the people within it have only an vague or intuitive understanding of its purpose. Most people's work is defined in terms of far more specific and immediate **things to be achieved**: if these things are related in some way to the wider purpose, the organisation will function. Loosely speaking, these 'things to be achieved' are the goals, objectives and targets of the various departments, functions, and individuals that make up the organisation. In more effective organisations **goal congruence** will be achieved: all these disparate goals, objectives and targets will be **consistent** with one another and will **operate together** to support progress with the mission.

2.1.1 A hierarchy of objectives

A simple model of the relationship between the various goals, objectives and targets is a **pyramid** analogous to the traditional organisational hierarchy. At the top is the **overall mission**; this is supported by a **small number of wide ranging goals**, which may correspond to overall departmental or functional responsibilities. Each of these goals is supported in turn by **more detailed, subordinate goals** that correspond, perhaps, to the responsibilities of the senior managers in the function concerned. This pattern is continued downwards until we reach the work targets of individual members of the organisation.

As we work our way down this pyramid of goals we will find that they will typically become **more detailed** and will relate to **shorter timeframes**. So, the mission might be very general and specify no time scale at all, but an individual worker is likely to have very specific things to achieve every day, or even every few minutes.

Note that this description is very basic and that the structure of objectives in a modern organisation may be much more complex than this, with the pursuit of some goals involving input from several functions. Also, some goals may be defined in very general terms, so as not to stifle innovation, co-operation and informal ways of doing things.

An important feature of any structure of goals is that there should be **goal congruence**; that is to say, goals that are related to one another should be **mutually supportive**. Goals can be related in several ways:

- **Hierarchically**, as in the pyramid structure outlined above
- **Functionally**, as when colleagues collaborate on a project
- **Logistically**, as when resources must be shared or used in sequence
- In **wider organisational senses**, as when senior executives make decisions about their operational priorities

A good example of the last category is the tension between long– and short-term priorities in such matters as the need to contain costs while at the same time increasing productivity by investing in improved plant.

The words *goal*, *objective* and *target* are used somewhat imprecisely and, to some extent, interchangeably. The suggestions we make below about the usage of these words are only tentative and you should read as widely as you can in order to make your own mind up about how to employ them.

A **goal** is often a longer term overall aspiration: Mintzberg defines **goals** as 'the intentions behind decisions or actions, the states of mind that drive individuals or collectives of individuals called organisations to do what they do.' Goals may be difficult to quantify and it may not be very helpful to attempt to do so. An example of a goal might be to raise productivity in a manufacturing department.

Objectives are often quite specific and well-defined, though they can also embody comprehensive purposes.

Targets are generally expressed in concrete numerical terms and are therefore easily used to measure progress and performance.

2.1.2 Management by objectives

We owe the concept of a hierarchy or cascade of objectives to the great management thinker and writer *Peter Drucker*, who outlined the system now known as **management by objectives** (MbO) in the middle of the twentieth century. MbO is still in use as a management tool, though no longer promoted as a universal solution. It forms part of the syllabus for Paper P5 and so is something you should have some familiarity with. Its importance for this discussion of goals and objectives is that Drucker was the first to suggest that objectives should be SMART, thereby contrasting objectives with mission statements which tend to be more open-ended. This acronym originally stood for the qualities listed below.

Specific   **M**easurable   **A**chievable   **R**ealistic   **T**ime-related

Today, *realistic* is often replaced with *results–focussed*, for two reasons.

(a)   The current pursuit of innovation as a route to competitive advantage makes it very important that managerial attention is directed towards **achieving results** rather than just **administering established processes.**

(b)   Realistic means much the same thing as achievable, anyway.

There are other variants: *achievable* may be replaced with *attainable*, which has an almost identical meaning, and *relevant* (meaning appropriate to the group or individual concerned) has been proposed as a third option for *R*. Notice that whichever version you prefer, a SMART objective corresponds very closely with our description of the way the word *target* is commonly used.

Functions of objectives

(a)   **Planning**: objectives define what the plan is about.

(b)   **Responsibility**: objectives define the responsibilities of managers and departments.

(c)   **Integration**: objectives should support one another and be consistent; this integrates the efforts of different departments.

(d)   **Motivation**: the first step in motivation is knowing what is to be done. Objectives must be created for all areas of performance.

(e)   **Evaluation**: performance is assessed against objectives and control exercised.

2.2 Primary and secondary objectives

Some objectives are more important than others. In the hierarchy of objectives, there is a **primary corporate objective** and other **secondary objectives** which should combine to ensure the achievement of the overall corporate objective.

For example, if a company sets itself an objective of growth in profits, as its primary aim, it will then have to develop strategies by which this primary objective can be achieved. An objective must then be set for each individual strategy. Secondary objectives might then be concerned with sales growth, continual technological innovation, customer service, product quality, efficient resource management or reducing the company's reliance on debt capital.

Corporate objectives should relate to the business as a whole.

- Profitability
- Market share
- Growth
- Cash flow

- Customer satisfaction
- The quality of the firm's products
- Human resources
- Innovation

Note, objectives can be both financial and non-financial, and we look more closely at the importance of non-financial objectives in Chapter 13, when we discuss multi-dimensional measures of performance, such as the **balanced scorecard**.

 Case Study

British Airways publicity once indicated the following corporate goals. What do you think of them? Which is most important? Will they have changed since the events of September 11 2001 and the subsequent turmoil in the airline industry?

- Safety and security
- Strong and consistent financial performance
- Global reach
- Superior services

- Good value for money
- Healthy working environment
- Good neighbourliness

'Overall, our aim is to be the best and most successful company in the airline industry.'

2.3 Time horizons: long-term objectives and short-term objectives

Objectives may be long-term and short-term. A company that is suffering from a recession in its core industries and making losses in the short term might continue to have a long term primary objective of achieving a growth in profits, but in the short term its primary objective might be survival.

We return to this topic later in the chapter.

 Case Study

McDonnell Douglas

With $14bn in sales, McDonnell Douglas was one of the nation's largest defence companies. It had done a good job of turning around the C-17 transport plane program, which a few years earlier was nearly cancelled by the Air Force over technical flaws and delays. But its commercial aircraft arm, Douglas Aircraft, was a disaster, caught in the tailwinds of Boeing and Airbus. In 1994, McDonnell Douglas's board shocked investors by bringing in an outsider – a brash, controversial former GE executive, Harry Stonecipher – as CEO.

At first Stonecipher insisted that the firm was committed to building passenger airplanes. At one point he said the business was so good that if Douglas wasn't in it already, 'we would be looking for a way to get in'. But years of under-investment had resulted in planes with little imagination, and Douglas would need to spend billions to catch up. Ultimately Stonecipher wasn't willing to make that investment, preferring to focus on short-term stock performance.

During his tenure as CEO, McDonnell Douglas's stock quadrupled (Stonecipher carries a laminated copy of the stock chart in his briefcase), but critics say the failure to invest in R&D would have been disastrous eventually. 'This is a company that would have gone out of business in five years', says Richard Aboulafia, an analyst at Teal Group, an aviation research firm. 'It was headed to oblivion.'

Eventually, McDonnell Douglas merged with Boeing.

Fortunes, 9 April 2004

2.4 Financial objectives

For businesses in the UK, the primary objective is concerned with the **return to shareholders**.

(a) A satisfactory return for a company must be sufficient to **reward shareholders adequately** in the long run for the risks they take. The reward will take the form of **profits**, which can lead to **dividends** or to **increases in the market value** of the shares.

(b) The size of return which is adequate for ordinary shareholders will vary according to the risk involved.

There are different ways of expressing a financial objective in quantitative terms. Financial objectives would include the following.

- Profitability
- Return on investment (ROI) or return on capital employed (ROCE)
- Share price, earnings per share, dividends
- Growth

We will look at performance measurement in more detail in Chapters 13 and 14.

Growth

There are some difficulties in accepting growth as an overall objective.

(a) **Growth of what?** In the long run, some elements must be expected to grow faster than others because of the dynamics of the business environment.

(b) In the long run, growth might lead to **diseconomies of scale** so that inefficiencies will occur.

Smaller companies will usually have a greater potential for significant rates of growth, especially in new industries, and growth will be a prime objective. Larger companies grow to achieve a size which will enable them to compete with other multinationals in world markets.

2.5 Multiple objectives

A firm might identify several financial objectives.

- Scope for growth and enhanced **corporate wealth**
- Maintaining a policy of paying attractive but not over-generous **dividends**
- Maintaining an acceptable **gearing ratio**

2.6 Subsidiary or secondary objectives

Whatever primary objective or objectives are set, **subsidiary objectives** will then be developed beneath them.

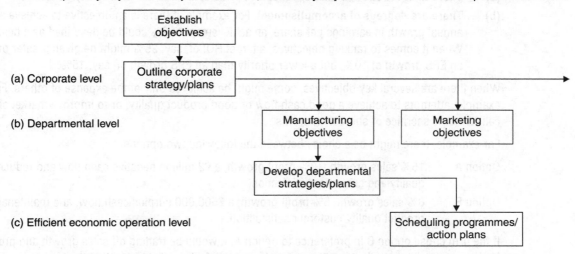

The overall objectives of the organisation will indicate different requirements for different functions.

2.6.1 Unit objectives

Unit objectives relate either to strategic business units or functions of the business.

(a)   From the private sector:

    (i)   Increasing the number of customers by 10%

    (ii)   Reducing the number of rejects by 50%

    (iii)   Producing monthly reports more quickly, within five working days of the end of each month

(b)   From the public sector:

    (i)   Responding more quickly to emergency calls

    (ii)   Reducing the length of time a patient has to wait for an operation

2.6.2 Goals for markets and marketing

Goals for **markets** will involve the following type of decisions.

(a)   **Market leadership**. Whether the organisation wants to be the market leader, or number two in the market, what rate of growth it desires and so on.

(b)   **Coverage**. Whether the product range needs to be expanded.

(c)   **Positioning**. Whether there should be an objective to shift position in the market – eg from producing low-cost for the mass market to higher-cost specialist products.

(d)   **Expansion**. Whether there should be an objective of broadening the product range or extending the organisation's markets.

2.6.3 Goals for products and services

Labour productivity objectives are often quantified as targets to reduce unit costs **and increase output per employee** by a certain percentage each year. **Capital productivity** is measured less often, but it can denote how efficiently a firm is using its equipment.

Quality objectives might be measured in low rejects (eg 'six sigma'). In some environments, targets may be set for service delivery, such as speed in answering the telephone, customer satisfaction and service quality.

Goals for products include **technology**.

2.7 Ranking objectives and trade-offs

Where there are multiple objectives a problem of ranking can arise.

(a)   **There is never enough time or resources** to achieve all of the desired objectives.

(b)   **There are degrees of accomplishment**. For example, if there is an objective to achieve a 10% annual growth in earnings per share, an achievement of 9% could be described as a near-success. When it comes to ranking objectives, a target ROI of, say, 25% might be given greater priority than an EPS growth of 10%, but a lower priority than an EPS growth of, say, 15%.

When there are several key objectives, some might be achieved only at the expense of others. For example, attempts to achieve a good cash flow or good product quality, or to improve market share, might call for some sacrifice of short term profits.

For example, there might be a choice between the following two options.

Option A   15% sales growth, 10% profit growth, a £2 million negative cash flow and reduced product quality and customer satisfaction.

Option B   8% sales growth, 5% profit growth, a £500,000 surplus cash flow, and maintenance of high product quality/customer satisfaction.

If the firm chose option B in preference to option A, it would be trading off sales growth and profit growth for better cash flow, product quality and customer satisfaction. It may feel that the long-term effect of reduced quality would negate the benefits under Option A.

One of the tasks of strategic management is to ensure **goal congruence**. Some objectives may not be in line with each other, and different **stakeholders** have different sets of priorities.

2.7.1 Conflict between goals

Dealing with conflicts between different types of goals

(a)   **Rational evaluation** according to financial criteria.

(b)   **Bargaining**. Managers with different goals will compete and will form alliances with other managers to achieve their goals.

(c)   **Satisficing**. Organisations do not aim to maximise performance in one area if this leads to poor performance elsewhere. Rather they will accept satisfactory, as opposed to excellent, performance in a number of areas.

(d)   **Sequential attention**. Goals are dealt with one by one in a sequence.

(e)   **Priority setting**. Certain goals get priority over others. This is determined by senior managers, but there are quite complicated systems to link goals and strategies according to certain criteria.

(f)   **Exercise of power**.

2.8 Critical success factors

When we were considering information strategy in Chapter 2, we examined the **critical success factor** approach. This approach can be used as an alternative to the cascade or pyramid structure of objectives discussed above. The aim is to identify a small number of performance areas in which satisfactory results will result in satisfactory competitive performance overall. This idea is linked to the resource-based approach to strategy and the importance of core competences discussed in Chapter 1.

Key term

> **Critical success factors** (CSFs) are those product features that are particularly valued by a group of customers and, therefore, where the organisation must excel to outperform competitors.
>
> *Johnson, Scholes and Whittington*

Johnson and Scholes describe a six stage process for using CSFs.

(a)   **Identify the CSFs** for the process under review. (Try to restrict the number of CSFs to six or less.)

(b)   **Identify the underlying competences** required to gain a competitive advantage in each of the CSFs.

(c)   Ensure the list of competences is sufficient to generate competitive advantage.

(d)   **Develop performance standards** – key performance indicators (KPIs).

(e)   Ensure these standards cannot be matched by competitors. (If they can be matched by competitors they will not form the basis of competitive advantage.)

(f)   **Monitor competitors** and assess the impact on the CSFs of any response competitors may make.

We will look again at CSFs and their related performance indicators when we consider performance measurement later in this Study Text.

3 Stakeholder goals and objectives   05/06, 11/06, 05/07

FAST FORWARD

> **Stakeholders** are those individuals or groups that, potentially, have an interest in what the organisation does. Different stakeholder groups have different degrees of power and interest, and management must respond to each in a different way.

Key term

> **Stakeholders** are 'those persons and organisations that have an interest in the strategy of an organisation. Stakeholders normally include shareholders, customers, staff and the local community.'
>
> (CIMA *Official Terminology*)

There are three broad types of stakeholder in an organisation, as follows.

- **Internal** stakeholders (employees, management)
- **Connected** stakeholders (shareholders, customers, suppliers, financiers)
- **External** stakeholders (the community, government, pressure groups)

3.1 Internal stakeholders: employees and management

Because **employees and management** are so intimately connected with the company, their objectives are likely to have a strong influence on how it is run. They are interested in the following issues.

(a) The **organisation's continuation and growth**. Management and employees have a special interest in the organisation's continued existence.

(b) Managers and employees have **individual interests** and goals which can be harnessed to the goals of the organisation.

Internal stakeholder	Interests to defend	Response risk
Managers and employees	<ul><li>Jobs/careers</li><li>Money</li><li>Promotion</li><li>Benefits</li><li>Satisfaction</li></ul>	<ul><li>Pursuit of 'systems goals' rather than shareholder interests</li><li>Industrial action</li><li>Negative power to impede implementation</li><li>Refusal to relocate</li><li>Resignation</li></ul>

3.2 Connected stakeholders

Writing in *Management Accounting* (November 1997) Malcolm Smith stated that increasing shareholder value should assume a core role in the strategic management of a business. If management performance is measured and rewarded by reference to changes in **shareholder value** then shareholders will be happy, because managers are likely to encourage long-term share price growth.

Connected stakeholder	Interests to defend	Response risk
Shareholders (corporate strategy)	<ul><li>Increase in shareholder wealth, measured by profitability, P/E ratios, market capitalisation, dividends and yield</li><li>Risk</li></ul>	<ul><li>Sell shares (eg to predator) or boot out management</li></ul>
Bankers (cash flows)	<ul><li>Security of loan</li><li>Adherence to loan agreements</li></ul>	<ul><li>Denial of credit</li><li>Higher interest charges</li><li>Receivership</li></ul>
Suppliers (purchase strategy)	<ul><li>Profitable sales</li><li>Payment for goods</li><li>Long-term relationship</li></ul>	<ul><li>Refusal of credit</li><li>Court action</li><li>Wind down relationships</li></ul>
Customers (product market strategy)	<ul><li>Goods as promised</li><li>Future benefits</li></ul>	<ul><li>Buy elsewhere</li><li>Sue</li></ul>

 Case Study

A survey of FTSE 100 companies conducted by the *Financial Times* asked what part leading shareholders play in the running of companies and what top directors think of their investors.

Almost half of those surveyed felt that their main shareholders 'rarely or never' offered any useful comments about their business. 69% of respondents however felt that their major investors understood their business well or very well. 89% did not feel hampered by shareholders in taking the correct long term strategy.

Almost all directors felt their biggest shareholders were in it for the long term. This latter point probably reflects the fact that the top ten fund managers own 36 per cent of the FTSE 100 – few fund managers can afford to move out of a FTSE 100 company altogether and therefore remain long term shareholders whether the investment is liked or not.

There is a perceived trend towards greater involvement and communication. To quote one director: 'Investors are much more sensitive to their responsibilities than in the past because they are looked on as the guardians of the corporate conscience.'

3.3 External stakeholders

External stakeholder groups – the government, local authorities, pressure groups, the community at large, professional bodies – are likely to have quite diverse objectives.

External stakeholder	Interests to defend	Response risk
Government	• Jobs, training, tax	• Tax increases • Regulation • Legal action
Interest/pressure groups	• Pollution • Rights • Other	• Publicity • Direct action • Sabotage • Pressure on government

3.4 The nature of stakes

Stakes may be analysed in several ways.

(a)   Local, national or international

(b)   Single or multiple issues

(c)   Economic or social (ie financial– or concern-based: the latter would include interests such as equal opportunities)

(d)   Concrete or symbolic: symbolic stakes are hard to define but important to the persons concerned and include general concern, anxiety and the need for respect

3.5 Primary and secondary stakeholders

Stakeholders may also be analysed by reference to whether they have a **contractual relationship** with the organisation. Stakeholders who have such a relationship are called **primary stakeholders**, while those who do not are known as **secondary stakeholders**. The primary stakeholder category thus includes **internal** and **connected** stakeholders, while the secondary stakeholders category equates to **external** stakeholder status.

3.6 Stakeholder conflicts

The analysis above demonstrates that conflict is likely between stakeholder groups simply because of the divergence of their interests. The picture is complicated when individuals are members of more than one stakeholder group and when members of the same stakeholder group do not share the same principal interest. Both cases are illustrated by considering a workforce, some of whose members are also shareholders and some of whom are not.

3.7 Dependency

A firm might depend on a stakeholder group at any particular time.

(a) A firm with persistent cash flow problems might depend on its bankers to provide it with money to stay in business at all.

(b) In the long term, any firm depends on its customers.

The degree of dependence or reliance can be analysed according to these criteria.

(a) **Disruption**. Can the stakeholder disrupt the organisation's plans (eg a bank withdrawing overdraft facilities)?

(b) **Replacement**. Can the firm replace the relationship?

(c) **Uncertainty**. Does the stakeholder cause uncertainty in the firm's plans? A firm with healthy positive cash flows and large cash balances need not worry about its bank's attitude to a proposed investment.

The way in which the relationship between company and stakeholders is conducted is a function of the parties' **relative bargaining strength** and the philosophy underlying **each party's objectives**. This can be shown by means of a spectrum.

		Weak			Stakeholders' bargaining strength			Strong
Company's conduct of relation- ship	Command/ dictated by company	Consultation and consideration of stakeholders' views	Negotiation	Participation and acceptance of stakeholders' views	Democratic voting by stakeholders	Command/ dictated by stakeholders

3.8 Stakeholder mapping: power and interest

Mendelow suggests that stakeholders may be positioned on a matrix whose axes are **power** held and likelihood of showing an **interest** in the organisation's activities. These factors will help define the type of relationship the organisation should seek with its stakeholders.

Level of interest

	Low	High
Low	A	B
High	C	D

(Power)

(a) **Key players** are found in segment D: strategy must be *acceptable* to them, at least. An example would be a major customer.

(b) Stakeholders in segment C must be treated with care. While often passive, they are capable of moving to segment D. They should, therefore be **kept satisfied.** Large institutional shareholders might fall into segment C.

(c) Stakeholders in segment B do not have great ability to influence strategy, but their views can be important in influencing more powerful stakeholders, perhaps by lobbying. They should therefore be **kept informed.** Community representatives and charities might fall into segment B.

(d) Minimal effort is expended on segment A.

A single stakeholder map is unlikely to be appropriate for all circumstances. In particular, stakeholders may move from quadrant to quadrant when different potential future strategies are considered.

Stakeholder mapping is used to assess the **significance** of stakeholder groups. This in turn has implications for the organisation.

(a)   The framework of **corporate governance** should recognise stakeholders' levels of interest and power.

(b)   It may be appropriate to seek to **reposition** certain stakeholders and discourage others from repositioning themselves, depending on their attitudes.

(c)   Key **blockers** and **facilitators** of change must be identified.

Stakeholder mapping can also be used to establish political priorities. A map of the current position can be compared with a map of a desired future state. This will indicate critical shifts that must be pursued.

In *Power In and Around Organisations*, *Mintzberg* identifies groups that not only have an interest in an organisation but power over it.

The external coalition	The internal coalition
• Owners (who hold legal title) • Associates (suppliers, customers, trading partners) • Employee associations (unions, professional bodies) • Public (government, media)	• The chief executive and board at the strategic apex • Line managers • Operators • The technostructure • Support staff

Each of these groups has three basic choices.

•   **Loyalty**. They can do as they are told.

•   **Exit**. For example by selling their shares, or getting a new job.

•   **Voice**. They can stay and try to change the system. Those who choose **voice** are those who can, to varying degrees, influence the organisation. Influence implies a degree of power and willingness to exercise it.

Existing structures and systems can channel stakeholder influence.

(a)   They are the **location of power**, giving groups of people varying degrees of influence over strategic choices.

(b)   They are **conduits of information**, which shape strategic decisions.

(c)   They **limit choices** or give some options priority over others. These may be physical or ethical constraints over what is possible.

(d)   They **embody culture**.

(e)   They **determine the successful implementation** of strategy.

(f)   The **firm has different degrees of dependency** on various stakeholder groups. A company with a cash flow crisis will be more beholden to its bankers than one with regular cash surpluses.

Question   Stakeholder influences

Learning outcome B(iii)

Ticket and Budget International is a large multinational firm of accountants. The firm provides audit services, tax services, and consultancy services for its many clients. The firm has a strong Technical Department which designs standardised audit procedures. The firm has just employed a marketing manager. The marketing manager regards an audit as a 'product', part of the entire marketing mix including price (audit fees), place (usually on the client's premises) and promotion (advertising in professional journals) The marketing manager is held in high regard by the firm's senior partner. The marketing director and the senior partner have unveiled a new strategic plan, drawn up in conditions of secrecy, which involves a tie-up with an advertising agency. The firm will be a 'one-stop shop' for business services and advice to management on any subject. Each client, or 'customer' will have a dedicated team of auditors, consultants and advertising executives. Obviously, a member of staff will be a member of a number of different teams.

The firm has recently settled a number of expensive law suits for negligence (which it has, of course, 'contested vigorously') out of court, without admitting liability. The Technical Department is conducting a thorough review of the firm's audit procedures.

In the light of what we have covered in this section, what do you think will be the organisational and stakeholder influences on the proposed strategy?

Answer

Accountants have divided loyalties – to their firm, and to their profession.

The Technical Department will almost certainly resist such a change, as the proposals devalue audit to being one of many business services to management. An audit is undertaken for the benefit of shareholders, not the company management. The Technical Department (the firm's technostructure) is also powerful as enforcement of the standards it will suggest should reduce professional negligence costs. The technostructure will thus exert a powerful influence over the strategy and business practices. External influences include *professional associations* which have a technostructural influence on the profession as a whole. The marketing manager may also be misled as to the degree to which *customers* want a 'one-stop shop' for accounting and advertising services. Perhaps he is overestimating the power of this factor in the external coalition.

So, different stakeholders will have their own views as to strategy. As some stakeholders have **negative power**, in other words power to impede or disrupt the decision, their likely response might be considered.

Exam focus point

Every exam is likely to have at least one question on stakeholders.

In an exam question, you will usually have to:

- Identify the stakeholders in the situation
- Identify what their particular interests are

You may also have to:

- Explain the importance of developing and maintaining relationships with them
- Explain how their varying interests may be reconciled

3.9 The strategic value of stakeholders

The firm can make strategic gains from managing stakeholder relationships. Studies have revealed the following correlations.

(a) A correlation between **employee** and **customer loyalty** (eg reduced staff turnover in service firms generally results in more repeat business).

(b) **Continuity** and **stability** in relationships with employees, customers and suppliers is important in enabling organisations to respond to certain types of change, necessary for business as a sustained activity.

Responsibilities towards customers are mainly those of providing a product or service of a quality that customers expect, and of dealing honestly and fairly with customers.

Responsibilities towards suppliers are expressed mainly in terms of trading relationships.

(a) The organisation's size could give it considerable power as a buyer. One ethical guideline might be that the organisation should not use its power unscrupulously.

(b) Suppliers might rely on getting prompt payment in accordance with the terms of trade negotiated with its customers.

(c) All information obtained from suppliers and potential suppliers should be kept confidential.

3.10 Measuring stakeholder satisfaction

If it is accepted that stakeholders other than shareholders have a legitimate interest in what the firm does, it is appropriate to consider measuring the degree of success it achieves in satisfying those interests. We deal with performance measurement generally in Part D of this Study Text, but we will consider **stakeholder measures** here for convenience.

We have already considered ways in which stakeholders may be classified and given some instances of their probable interests. Measuring the satisfaction of stakeholder interests is likely to be difficult, since many of their expectations relate to **qualitative** rather than **quantitative** matters. It is, for example, difficult to measure good corporate citizenship. On the other hand, some of the more important stakeholder groups do have fairly specific interests, the satisfaction of which should be fairly amenable to measurement. Here are some examples of possible measures.

Stakeholder group	Measure
Employees	Staff turnover; pay and benefits relative to market rate; job vacancies
Government	Pollution measures; promptness of filing annual returns; accident rate; energy efficiency
Distributors	Share of joint promotions paid for; rate of stock-outs

4 The short term and the long term

FAST FORWARD

Objectives are set for varying time horizons. There is a **trade-off** between long and short term objectives when they are in conflict or resources are scarce. For example, capital expenditure projects may be postponed or abandoned in order to protect short term cash flow and profits.

Key term

Short-termism is 'bias towards paying particular attention to short-term performance with a corresponding relative disregard to the long run'.   (CIMA *Official Terminology*)

4.1 Long-term and short-term objectives

Objectives may be long-term or short-term.

(a) For example, a company's primary objective might be to increase its earnings per share from 30p to 50p in the next five years. Strategies for achieving the objective might be selected to include the following.

    (i) Increasing profitability in the next twelve months by cutting expenditure.

    (ii) Increasing export sales over the next three years.

    (iii) Developing a successful new product for the domestic market within five years.

(b) Secondary objectives might then be re-assessed to include the following.

    (i) The objective of improving manpower productivity by 10% within twelve months.

    (ii) Improving customer service in export markets with the objective of doubling the number of overseas sales outlets in selected countries within the next three years.

    (iii) Investing more in product-market research and development, with the objective of bringing at least three new products to the market within five years.

Targets cannot be set without an awareness of what is realistic. Quantified targets for achieving the primary objective, and targets for secondary objectives, must therefore emerge from a realistic 'position audit'.

4.2 Trade-offs between short-term and long-term objectives

Just as there may have to be a trade-off between different objectives, so too might there be a need to make trade-offs between short-term objectives and long-term objectives. This is referred to as **S/L trade-off**.

Decisions which involve the **sacrifice of longer-term objectives** include the following.

(a) Postponing or abandoning capital expenditure projects, which would eventually contribute to growth and profits, in order to protect short term cash flow and profits.

(b) Cutting R&D expenditure to save operating costs, and so reducing the prospects for future product development. Ultimately, cost leadership as a whole is a short term strategy.

(c) Reducing quality control, to save operating costs (but also adversely affecting reputation and goodwill).

(d) Reducing the level of customer service, to save operating costs (but sacrificing goodwill).

(e) Cutting training costs or recruitment (so the company might be faced with skills shortages).

5 Corporate social responsibility and sustainability

Some argue that a business has a **social responsibility** for the cost of its activities, while others argue that businesses already contribute enough to society via the taxes on their profits.

The **sustainability** of business activity is becoming a major concern as business moves into the 21st century. This considers both environmental and social pressures. The '**triple bottom line**' refers to a whole new way of measuring business performance using not only economic prosperity, but environmental quality and social equality.

5.1 Corporate social responsibility   05/06, 11/07

If it is accepted that businesses do not bear the total **social cost** of their activities, it could be suggested that **corporate social responsibility** might be a way of recognising this.

Key terms

> **Social cost.** 'Tangible and intangible costs and losses sustained by third parties or the general public as a result of economic activity, for example pollution by industrial effluent'.
>
> **Social responsibility accounting.** 'Identification, measurement and reporting of the social costs and benefits resulting from economic activities.'   CIMA *Official Terminology*

Businesses, particularly large ones, are subject to increasing expectations that they will exercise **social responsibility**. This is an ill-defined concept, but appears to focus on the provision of specific benefits to society in general, such as charitable donations, the creation or preservation of employment, and spending on environmental improvement or maintenance. A great deal of the pressure is created by the activity of minority action groups and is aimed at businesses because they are perceived to possess extensive resources. The momentum of such arguments is now so great that the notion of social responsibility has become almost inextricably confused with the matter of ethics. It is important to remember the distinction.

Social responsibility and ethical behaviour are not the same thing although they are related. Business ethics is concerned with the standards of behaviour in the conduct of business. Corporate social responsibility (CSR) is an organisation's obligation to maximise positive stakeholder benefits while minimising the negative effects of its actions. CSR includes economic and legal issues, as well as ethical ones: reflecting the whole range of stakeholders who have an interest in an organisation. In this respect, CSR requires an organisation to go beyond simply adhering to minimum ethical standards. Ethics concerns issues such as justice, fairness and honesty, which are fundamental, unchanging values that have implications for business.

CSR is more closely associated with contemporary business issues, and concerns organisations giving something back to society, and being good citizens. Therefore, in contrast to ethics, CSR is socially mediated and likely to be specific to the time and culture in which it is considered.

However, in this context, you should also remember that a business managed with the sole objective of maximising shareholder wealth can be run in just as ethical a fashion as one in which far wider stakeholder responsibility is assumed. On the other hand, there is no doubt that many large businesses have behaved irresponsibly in the past and some continue to do so.

Exam focus point

The November 2007 exam included a question on corporate social responsibility in relation to a logging company. The nature of the industry means that the company faces a number of environmental issues. However, you must remember that P6 is a business strategy paper so you need to consider business issues as well as environmental ones.

5.1.1 Against corporate social responsibility

Milton Friedman argued against corporate social responsibility along the following lines.

(a) Businesses do not have responsibilities, only people have responsibilities. Managers in charge of corporations are responsible to the owners of the business, by whom they are employed.

(b) These employers may have charity as their aim, but 'generally [their aim] will be to make as much money as possible while conforming to the basic rules of the society, both those embodied in law and those embodied in ethical custom.'

(c) If the statement that a manager has social responsibilities is to have any meaning, 'it must mean that he is to act in some way that is not in the interest of his employers.'

(d) If managers do this they are, generally speaking, spending the owners' money for purposes other than those they have authorised; sometimes it is the money of customers or suppliers that is spent and, on occasion, the money of employees. By doing this, the manager is, in effect, both raising taxes and deciding how they should be spent, which are functions of government, not of business. There are two objections to this.

   (i) Managers have not been democratically elected (or selected in any other way) to exercise government power.

   (ii) Managers are not experts in government policy and cannot foresee the detailed effect of such social responsibility spending.

Friedman argues that the social responsibility model is politically collectivist in nature and deplores the possibility that collectivism should be extended any further than absolutely necessary in a free society. A second argument against the assumption of corporate social responsibility is that the **maximisation of wealth is the best way that society can benefit from a business's activities**.

(a) Maximising wealth has the effect of increasing the tax revenues available to the state to disburse on socially desirable objectives.

(b) Maximising shareholder value has a 'trickle down' effect on other disadvantaged members of society.

(c) Many company shares are owned by pension funds, whose ultimate beneficiaries may not be the wealthy anyway.

5.1.2 The stakeholder view

The **stakeholder view** is that many groups have a stake in what the organisation does. This is particularly important in the business context, where shareholders own the business but employees, customers and government also have particularly strong claims to having their interests considered. This is fundamentally an argument derived from **natural law theory** and is based on the notion of individual and collective **rights**.

It is suggested that modern corporations are so powerful, socially, economically and politically, that unrestrained use of their power will inevitably damage other people's rights. For example, they may blight an entire community by closing a major facility, thus enforcing long term unemployment on a large proportion of the local workforce. Similarly, they may damage people's quality of life by polluting the environment. They may use their purchasing power or market share to impose unequal contracts on suppliers and customers alike. And they may exercise undesirable influence over government through their investment decisions. Under this approach, the exercise of corporate social responsibility constrains the corporation to act at all times as a good citizen.

Another argument points out that corporations exist within society and are dependent upon it for the resources they use. Some of these resources are obtained by direct contracts with suppliers but others are not, being provided by government expenditure. Examples are such things as transport infrastructure, technical research and education for the workforce. Clearly, corporations contribute to the taxes that pay for these things, but the relationship is rather tenuous and the tax burden can be minimised by careful management. The implication is that corporations should recognise and pay for the facilities that society provides by means of socially responsible policies and actions.

Henry Mintzberg (in *Power In and Around Organisations*) suggests that simply viewing organisations as vehicles for shareholder investment is inadequate.

(a) In practice, he says, organisations are rarely controlled effectively by shareholders. Most shareholders are passive investors.

(b) Large corporations can manipulate markets. Social responsibility, forced or voluntary, is a way of recognising this.

(c) Moreover, as mentioned above, businesses do receive a lot of government support. The public pays for roads, infrastructure, education and health, all of which benefits businesses. Although businesses pay tax, the public ultimately pays, perhaps through higher prices.

(d) Strategic decisions by businesses always have wider social consequences. In other words, says Mintzberg, the firm produces two kinds of outputs: **goods and services** and the **social consequences of its activities** (eg pollution).

5.1.3 The social audit

Firms sometimes carry out **social audits**. This generally involves:

- Recognising a firm's rationale for engaging in socially responsible activity
- Identifying of programmes which are congruent with the mission of the company
- Setting of objectives and priorities related to this programme
- Specifying of the nature and range of resources required
- Evaluating of company involvement in such programmes (past, present and future)

Whether or not a social audit is used depends on the degree to which social responsibility is part of the **corporate philosophy**. A cultural awareness must be achieved within an organisation in order to implement environmental policy, which requires Board and staff support.

In the USA, social audits on environmental issues have increased since the *Exxon Valdez* catastrophe in which millions of gallons of crude oil were released into Alaskan waters. The **Valdez principles** were drafted by the Coalition for Environmentally Responsible Economics to focus attention on environmental concerns and corporate responsibility.

- Eliminate pollutants and hazardous waste
- Conserve non-renewable resources
- Market environmentally safe products and services
- Prepare for accidents and restore damaged environments
- Provide protection for employees who report environmental hazards
- Companies should appoint an environmentalist to the board of directors, name an executive for environmental affairs and develop an environmental audit of global operations

There are many contrasting views about the responsibilities of the corporation.

(a) If the company creates a social problem, it must fix it (eg Exxon).

(b)   Companies already discharge their social responsibility, simply by increasing their profits and thereby contributing more in taxes. If a company was expected to divert more resources to solve society's problems, this would represent a double tax.

(c)   The multinational corporation has the resources to fight poverty, illiteracy, malnutrition, illness and so on. This approach disregards who actually creates the problems.

5.2 Strategies for social responsibility

Proactive strategy	A strategy which a business follows where it is prepared to take full responsibility for its actions. A company which discovers a fault in a product and recalls the product without being forced to, before any injury or damage is caused, acts in a proactive way.
Reactive strategy	This involves allowing a situation to continue unresolved until the public, government or consumer groups find out about it.
Defence strategy	This involves minimising or attempting to avoid additional obligations arising from a particular problem.
Accommodation strategy	This approach involves taking responsibility for actions, probably when one of the following happens. • Encouragement from special interest groups • Perception that a failure to act will result in government intervention

5.3 Environmental and green concerns

Business activities in general were formerly regarded as problems for the environmental movement, but the two are now increasingly complementary. There has been an increase in the use of the green approach to market products. 'Dolphin friendly' tuna and paper products from managed forests are examples.

Environmental impacts on business may be direct.

•   Changes affecting costs or resource availability
•   Impact on demand
•   Effect on power balances between competitors in a market

They may also be **indirect**. Pressure for better environmental performance is coming from many quarters.

(a)   **Green pressure groups** have increased their membership and influence dramatically.

(b)   **Employees** are increasing pressure on the businesses in which they work for a number of reasons – partly for their own safety, partly in order to improve the public image of the company.

(c)   **Legislation** is increasing almost by the day. Growing pressure from the green or green-influenced vote has led to mainstream political parties taking these issues into their programmes, and most countries now have laws to cover land use planning, smoke emission, water pollution and the destruction of animals and natural habitats.

(d)   **Environmental risk screening** has become increasingly important. Companies in the future will become responsible for the environmental impact of their activities.

5.4 Strategic planning

Physical environmental conditions are important for strategic planning.

(a)   **Resource inputs**. Managing physical resources successfully (eg oil companies, mining companies) is a good source of profits.

(b)   **Logistics.** The physical environment presents logistical problems or opportunities to organisations. Proximity to road and rail links can be a reason for siting a warehouse in a particular area.

(c)   **Government.** The physical environment is under the control of other organisations.

(i)   Local authority town planning departments can influence where a building and necessary infrastructure can be sited.

(ii)   Governments can set regulations about some of the organisation's environmental interactions.

(d)   **Disasters.** In some countries, the physical environment can pose a major 'threat' to organisations.

Issues relating to the effect of an organisation's activities on the physical environment have come to the fore in recent years.

5.4.1 How green issues will impinge on business

Possible issues to consider are these.

- **Consumer demand** for products which appear to be environmentally friendly
- Demand for **less pollution** from industry
- Greater **regulation** by government and the EU (eg recycling targets)
- Demand that **businesses be charged** with the external cost of their activities
- Possible requirements to conduct **environmental audits**
- Opportunities to develop **products and technologies** which are environmentally friendly
- Taxes (eg landfill tax)

The consumer demand for products which claim environmental soundness has waxed and waned, with initial enthusiasm replaced by cynicism as to 'green' claims.

(a)   **Marketing.** Companies such as Body Shop have exploited environmental friendliness as a marketing tool.

(b)   **Publicity.** Perhaps companies have more to fear from the impact of bad publicity (relating to their environmental practices) than they have to benefit from positive ecological messages as such. Public relations is a vital competitive weapon.

(c)   **Lifestyles.** There may be a limit to which consumers are prepared to alter their lifestyles for the sake of ecological correctness.

(d)   Consumers may be **imperfectly educated** about green issues. (For example, much recycled paper has simply replaced paper produced from trees from properly managed (ie sustainably developed) forests.) In short, some companies may have to 'educate' consumers as to the relative ecological impact of their products.

5.4.2 Renewable and non-renewable resources

Key term

> **Sustainability** involves developing strategies so that the company only uses resources at a rate that allows them to be replenished. At the same time, emissions of waste are confined to levels that do not exceed the capacity of the environment to absorb them.

Sustainability means that resources consumed are **replaced** in some way: for every tree cut down another is planted. Some resources, however, are inherently non-renewable. For example, oil will eventually run out, even though governments and oil firms have consistently underestimated reserves.

(a)   Metals can be recycled. Some car manufacturers are building cars with recyclable components.

(b)   An argument is that as the price of resources rise, market forces will operate to make more efficient use of them or to develop alternatives. When oil becomes too expensive, solar power will become economic.

 Case Study

Motor manufacturers are looking to a future without oil. Hydrogen power is one option, using **fuel cell** technology.

John Elkington, chairman of the think-tank SustainAbility Ltd, has said that **sustainability** now embraces not only environmental and economic questions, but also social and ethical dimensions. He writes about the **triple bottom line**, which means 'business people must increasingly recognise that the challenge now is to help deliver simultaneously:

- Economic prosperity
- Environmental quality
- Social equity

Elkington quotes the example of Kvaerner, the Norwegian construction company. An environmental report compiled by the company listed the following.

- A 1% reduction in absence due to sick leave is worth $30 million
- A 1% reduction in material and energy consumption is worth $60 million
- A 20% cut in insurance premiums would be worth $15 million

A full consideration of sustainability in company reports is hampered by several difficulties.

- Lack of a standard methodology
- Accountants/auditors lack environmental expertise
- Difficulties in determining environmental costs
- Identification and valuation of potential liabilities is problematic

Elkington considers there to be three main forms of capital that businesses need to value.

- **Economic capital** (physical, financial and human skills and knowledge)
- **Natural capital** (replaceable and irreplaceable)
- **Social capital** (the ability of people to work together)

Environmental and social accounting is still embryonic, but Elkington believes that it will eventually develop our ability to see whether or not a particular company or industry is 'moving in the right direction'.

Exam focus point

A number of articles have appeared in *Management Accounting* (now *Financial Management*) on environmental topics, which all conclude that the management accountant has a lot to contribute. It ties neatly in with this examiner's preoccupation with short– and long –termism, in that some decisions that could be taken from a sustainability standpoint may have an adverse impact on short-term performance.

6 Not-for-profit organisations

FAST FORWARD

Not-for-profit organisations have their own objectives, generally concerned with **efficient use of resources** in the light of specified targets.

6.1 Voluntary and not-for-profit sectors

Although most people would know one if they saw it, there is a surprising problem in clearly defining what counts as a **not-for-profit (NFP) organisation**. Local authority services, for example, would not be setting objectives in order to arrive at a profit for shareholders, but nowadays they are being increasingly required to apply the same disciplines and processes as companies which are oriented towards straightforward profit goals.

Oxfam operates more shops than any commercial organisation in Britain, and these operate at a profit. The Royal Society for the Protection of Birds operates a mail order trading company which provides a 25% return on capital, operating very profitably and effectively.

Bois proposes that a **not-for-profit organisation** be defined as:' ... an organisation whose attainment of its prime goal is not assessed by economic measures. However, in pursuit of that goal it may undertake profit-making activities.'

This may involve a number of different kinds of organisation with, for example, differing legal status – charities, statutory bodies offering public transport or the provision of services such as leisure, health or public utilities such as water or road maintenance.

Business strategy issues are just as relevant to a not-for-profit organisation as they are to a business operating with a profit motive. The tasks of setting objectives, developing strategies and controls for their implementation can all help in improving the performance of charities and NFP organisations. Whilst the basic principles are appropriate for this sector, differences in how they can be applied should not be forgotten.

6.2 Objectives

Objectives will not be based on profit achievement but rather on achieving a **particular response** from various target markets. This has implications for reporting of results. The organisation will need to be open and honest in showing how it has managed its budget and allocated funds raised. **Efficiency and effectiveness** are particularly important in the use of donated funds, but there is a danger that resource efficiency becomes more important than the service effectiveness.

Here are some possible objectives for a NFP organisation.

(a) Surplus maximisation (equivalent to profit maximisation)
(b) Revenue maximisation (as for a commercial business)
(c) Usage maximisation (as in leisure centre swimming pool usage)
(d) Usage targeting (matching the capacity available, as in the NHS)
(e) Full/partial cost recovery (minimising subsidy)
(f) Budget maximisation (maximising what is offered)
(g) Producer satisfaction maximisation (satisfying the wants of staff and volunteers)
(h) Client satisfaction maximisation (the police generating the support of the public)

There are no buyers in the NFP sector, but rather a number of different **audiences**.

(a) A **target public** is a group of individuals who have an interest or concern about the charity.
(b) Those benefiting from the organisation's activities are known as the **client public**.
(c) Relationships are also vital with **donors and volunteers** from the general public.
(d) There may also be a need to lobby **local and national government** and businesses for support.

The objective setting process must **balance** the interests and concerns of these audiences, which may result in a range of objectives, rather than a single over-riding one. In order to allow for this balance to be achieved, NFPs may allow wide **participation** in the objective setting process, or, indeed, may have it enforced upon them by, for example, legal requirements for consultation with interested parties, or constitutional provision for a range of constituencies to be heard.

NFP objective-setting has other complications.

(a) Providers of funds have potentially greater influence than members or beneficiaries and may have different objectives.
(b) There is no overall profit motive.
(c) Priorities may change rapidly as circumstances change, as for instance when a natural disaster occurs or a government changes.
(d) All the factors above make it easier for powerful insiders to pursue their personal objectives for power or recognition.

Charities and NFP organisations often deal more with **services and ideas** than products.

(a) **Appearance** needs to be business-like rather than appearing extravagant.
(b) **Process** is increasingly important, for example, the use of direct debit to pay for council tax, reduces administration costs leaving more budget for community services.

(c)   **People** need to offer good service and be caring in their dealings with their clients.

(d)   **Distribution channels** are often shorter with fewer intermediaries than in the profit making sector. Wholesalers and distributors available to a business organisations do not exist in most non-business contexts.

(e)   **Promotion is usually dominated by personal selling**. Advertising is often limited to public service announcements due to limited budgets. Direct marketing is growing due to the ease of developing databases. Sponsorship, competitions and special events are also widely used.

(f)   **Pricing** is probably the most different element in this sector. Financial price is often not a relevant concept. Rather, opportunity cost, where an individual is persuaded of the value of donating time or funds, is more relevant.

Controlling activities is complicated by the difficulty of judging whether **non-quantitative objectives** have been met. For example assessing whether the charity has improved the situation of client publics is difficult to research. Statistics related to product mix, financial resources, size of budgets, number of employees, number of volunteers, number of customers serviced and number and location of facilities, are all useful for this task.

7 The public sector

FAST FORWARD

In the public sector, resources (not sales) are the limiting factor. The rationing of health care typifies the problems faced.

In a business, the level of sales often indicates the level of activity (number of goods produced). Effectively, sales are a limiting factor, and once the level of activity has been determined, resources are obtained to satisfy this demand.

While sales of services can be used in some public sector organisations as the starting point of the budgeting process, this cannot be the case when the services are not sold but are provided to meet social needs. Instead **resources are the limiting factor**, since demand is potentially limitless. Many of the concerns about rationing health care suggest precisely this problem.

7.1 'Care in the Community'

The Audit Commission in the UK published some guidelines for budgeting, in situations where levels of service provision must be matched to available resources. An example is a guideline for budgeting for local authority support for community care. Rather than look after the elderly, disabled or mentally ill in institutions, care is delivered at the patient's home. How do authorities deal with the delivery of services to dependent elderly people?

A basic problem with this sort of budget in the public sector is to find the starting point.

(a)   Planners can **budget for a set level of service provision**. The budget is based upon the number of home helps currently available and the number of day care centres to be run.

(b)   Planners can identify the **needs of service recipients**. These can be classified and ranked to establish various levels of possible demand for the service.

Relevant factors need to be identified.

•   The **needs** of the local dependent elderly population
•   The various **alternative policies** by which these needs can be met
•   The **resources actually available**
•   The amount of those resources which are already **committed**

Identifying the needs means that the level of service can be tailored more accurately to the requirements of the clients.

7.2 Responsibility accounting in health care

An example of the problems in introducing management accounting techniques to achieve the objectives of public sector stakeholders is offered by the extension since the 1970s of **responsibility accounting** to the UK National Health Service (outlined by Irvine Lapsey in an article in *Management Accounting Research*). Responsibility accounting aims to devolve budget and expenditure control to decision-makers, such as doctors.

The NHS internal market is now in place with purchasers arranging contracts with hospitals. Trust hospitals now work autonomously.

In the NHS, the introduction of management accounting techniques based on private sector practice is problematic for the following reasons.

(a)   Although NHS self-governing hospital trusts are financially autonomous, they are not profit-making businesses. The purpose of the internal market is to **allocate resources efficiently**, not to make a profit.

(b)   Many doctors resent managerial and financial involvement in medical decisions. NHS managers may seek the cheapest option rather than what the doctor considers most effective.

(c)   The level of paperwork involved in implementing the system causes a lot of resentment.

(d)   The budgetary system is often conducted on an annual basis. Strategic planning, as we have seen, should be a long-term process.

(e)   There is political interference – after all, the NHS survives on tax-payers' money and NHS funding decisions are a matter of public policy.

What is undeniably true is that there is an increased emphasis on **performance**. Schools and hospitals publicise **league tables** on certain key criteria.

(a)   Critics argue these ignore the real differences in the schools' environments (eg a school's exam success might depend on the quality of its pupils and the relative social deprivation of its catchment area).

(b)   Supporters argue that league tables give clients of services a better choice and concentrate managers' minds on improving performance.

Chapter Roundup

- Strategies are developed in order to achieve desired outcomes. These are inherent in the organisation's mission or defining purpose. Whether stated or not, the **mission** of a business always includes return to investors. Mission guides strategic decisions and provides values and a sense of direction.

- **Goals** and **objectives** derive from mission and support it. For a business, a primary corporate objective will be the return offered to shareholders, however this is measured. There may be other primary objectives and there will certainly be supporting objectives for costs, innovation, markets, products and so on.

- **Stakeholders** are those individuals or groups that potentially have an interest in what the organisation does. Different stakeholder groups have different degrees of power and interest and so management must respond to each in a different way.

- Objectives are set for varying time horizons. There is a **trade-off** between long and short term objectives when they are in conflict or resources are scarce. For example, capital expenditure projects may be postponed or abandoned in order to protect short term cash flow and profits.

- Some argue that a business has a **social responsibility** for the cost of its activities, while others argue that businesses already contribute enough to society via the taxes on their profits.

- The **sustainability** of business activity is becoming a major concern as business moves into the 21st century. This considers both environmental and social pressures. The '**triple bottom line**' refers to a whole new way of measuring business performance using not only economic prosperity, but environmental quality and social equality.

- Not-for-profit organisations have their own objectives, generally concerned with **efficient use of resources**, in the light of specified targets.

- In the public sector, resources (not sales) are the limiting factor. The rationing of health care typifies the problems faced.

Quick Quiz

1   What are the four elements in a definition of 'mission'?

    P ....
    S ....
    P ....
    V ....

2   Mission statements have a standard format.

    ☐ True
    ☐ False

3   Distinguish between critical success factors, key tasks and priorities.

4   Fill in the gaps: 'Most organisations set themselves quantified (1) .... in order to enact the corporate (2) .... Many objectives are:

    (3)   S ....
    (4)   M ....
    (5)   A ....
    (6)   R ....
    (7)   T ....

5   What are the two axes of Mendelow's matrix?

6   What is corporate social responsibility?

7   There are three broad types of stakeholder

        (1)   ....
        (2)   ....
        (3)   ....

8   How do questions of sustainability tie in with the long/short term debate?

9   Define a not-for-profit organisation.

10   What is usually the limiting factor for a public sector organisation?

Answers to Quick Quiz

1   Purpose
        Strategy
        Policies and standards of behaviour
        Values

2   False

3   Critical success factors (CSFs) 'are those factors on which the strategy is fundamentally dependent for its success', and at which an organisation must excel to outperform its competitors.
        Key tasks are what must be done to ensure each critical success factor is achieved.
        Priorities indicate the order in which tasks are achieved.

4   (1) objectives (2) mission (3) specific (4) measurable (5) attainable (6) results-orientated (or realistic) (7) time bounded

5   Level of interest; power

6   Corporate social responsibility is an organisation's obligation to maximise positive stakeholder benefits while minimising the negative effects of its actions.

7   (1)   internal
        (2)   connected
        (3)   external

8   For example, some decisions that are taken from an ecological sustainability standpoint may impact short term performance, such as the decision to invest in a new recycling process.

9   An organisation whose attainment of its prime goal is not assessed by economic measures. Their first objective is to be a non-loss operation in order to cover costs. Profits are made only as a means to an end, such as providing a service.

10   Availability/supply of resources

Now try the question below from the Exam Question Bank

Number	Level	Marks	Time
Q3	Examination	25	45 mins

As this is the first exam-level question you have encountered so far in the text, and because it is fairly tricky, we have analysed the question and its requirements in detail.

Strategic analysis

The changing environment

Introduction

Considerations relating to the business environment make up 40% of the syllabus for this paper.

(a) You should note the **influences of the environment** on an organisation. Some factors are more directly relevant than others. You should remember that information about the environment is often uncertain, incomplete and even ambiguous. This makes some of the tasks of business strategy quite difficult for the management accountant.

(b) You should appreciate how **environmental changes**, in any given situation, might have an impact on **corporate appraisal**, particularly in terms of opportunities and threats.

Gathering **strategic intelligence** is an important task. The **Internet** and **databases** are increasingly being used as sources of strategic intelligence.

Topic list	Learning outcomes	Syllabus references	Ability required
1 Relating the organisation to its environment	A(iii), A(iv), B(i)	A1, B1	Evaluation
2 The political and legal environment	A(iii), A(iv), B(i), B(ii)	A1, B2	Evaluation
3 The economic environment	A(iii), A(iv), B(i)	A1	Evaluation
4 The social and cultural environment	A(iii), A(iv), B(i)	A1	Evaluation
5 The technological environment	A(iii), A(iv), B(i)	A1	Evaluation
6 Interest and pressure groups	B(i), B(ii), B(iii)	B3	Evaluation
7 Environmental information and analysis	A(iii), A(iv), B(i)	A10	Evaluation

1 Relating the organisation to its environment 5/07, 11/05

The environment exists outside an organisation's boundaries, and organisations survive and prosper in this context. To secure **environmental fit**, an analysis of the environment therefore is required. PEST is a useful mnemonic to discuss these issues. Uncertainty in the environment arises from complexity and dynamism.

It is usual to consider the organisation as having boundaries that separate it from its environment. You must remember that it can be useful to regard organisation and environment as inextricably linked, interpenetrating one another in a wide range of ways. This is consistent with the modern emphasis on stakeholders, organisational networks and the strategic importance of human resource management.

Exam focus point

This feature of interrelatedness is also relevant to the way you should use models and theories in your P6 exam. Questions may well require you to use more than one model to interpret a scenario. Therefore when looking at models such as PEST (this chapter) and Porter's Five Forces (Chapter 5) do not simply think of them in isolation: rather think what impact the features or changes identified in one model could have on a range of other models.

1.1 Environmental factors

Organisations exist within an environment which strongly influences what they do and whether they survive and develop. Strategic planners must take account of potential environmental impacts in order to produce plans that are realistic and achievable. Where international or even global operations are undertaken, it is important to understand that there may be important differences between the environments present in the various regions and countries involved.

The environment of an organisation is everything outside its boundaries. It may be segmented according to the diagram below.

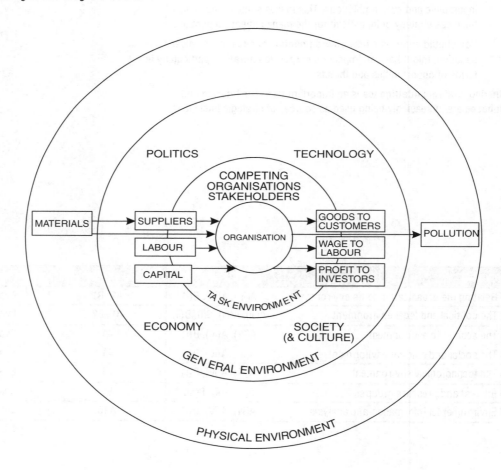

The **general environment** covers all the political/legal, economic, social/cultural and technological (**PEST**) influences in the countries an organisation operates in.

The **task environment** relates to factors of particular relevance to a firm, such as its competitors, customers and suppliers of resources.

In the rest of this chapter we will be concerned with the **general environment**. We consider the **task environment** in Chapter 5.

The mnemonic PEST is often used in environmental analysis. **PEST** stands for political, economic, social and technical; legal matters are considered under the political heading and cultural matters under the social heading. Increasing public concern for the natural environment and corporate sensitivity about protest groups has led in recent years to the inclusion of a second 'E' in the mnemonic, to stand for environment. This has given rise to new arrangements such as **STEEPLE** and **PESTEL**.

An even more exotic analysis is DEEPLIST: demographic, environment, economics, politics, law, information, society, technology.

The PEST model is a useful checklist for general environmental factors – remember that in the real world they are **interlinked** and any given environment(al) development is likely to qualify under two or more of the PEST or PESTEL headings.

1.2 Environmental fit

One approach to strategy is to seek **environmental fit**, relating a company to its environment.

Any strategy is made in conditions of **partial ignorance**. The environment is a major cause of such 'ignorance'.

(a) It contains **opportunities and threats** which may influence the organisation's activities and may even threaten its existence.

(b) The environment is sometimes so **varied** that many organisations will find it difficult to discern its effects on them. We cover complexity in Section 7.

(c) Firms can conduct **audits** to identify which of the many different sorts of environmental factors have had a significant influence.

(d) Environmental conditions change: see Section 7.

1.3 Complexity and dynamism

Johnson and Scholes contrast the concepts of **environmental complexity** (how many influences and the inter-relationships between them) and **environmental dynamism** (the rate of change).

Together, complexity and dynamism create **uncertainty**.

1.3.1 The strategic impact of uncertainty

A high degree of uncertainty can have an important impact on the strategic management of a business.

(a) There is likely to be a wish for **more and better information** in order to enhance the likelihood of making useful forecasts. The difficulty of achieving this is likely to lead to a **close planning time horizon**.

(b) Decisive moves to new strategies are unlikely: strategy is likely to be **conservative** and new ideas may only appear as **emergent strategies**.

1.4 Time horizon

You should bear in mind which environmental issues are of:

• **Long-term impact**, which can be dealt with in advance
• **Short-term impact**, which require crisis management

Text messages

In many countries, text messaging is growing rapidly as a significant use of mobile phones. In the UK and Germany, for example, almost 40 text messages are sent by each mobile subscriber per month. The big operators make $50bn in annual revenues.

However, in France and the USA, sending text messages is far less popular. Both are wealthy, technologically advanced, IT-literate societies. What environmental factors might cause the difference?

The USA

In the USA, there are several incompatible technologies still in place. Voice calls on mobile phones are cheaper than in other countries so there is less incentive to save money by texting. Also, texting is an extra paid-for service. To summarise, the business model is different.

France

In France, only 65% of the population have a mobile phone compared to 90% in the UK, Spain or Italy. Some people explain this as a result of lack of competition, as Orange, the main mobile phone operator, is part of France Telecom which benefits from Orange's revenues and cash flows. French operators were slow to introduce texting, but even so, texting is still not so attractive. *The Economist* (7/10/2004) suggested that 'it is difficult to avoid the conclusion that cultural factors also play a role: perhaps mobile phones simply do not fit in with the relaxed French lifestyle'.

1.5 Environmental interactions

We have mentioned the various mnemonics used to help in making a comprehensive analysis and assessment of the general environment and, indeed, we will use the PEST approach to give structure to much of the rest of this chapter. It is very important that you understand that **this framework is merely one of convenience**. Environmental influences on business do not appear in neatly packaged groups: they interact and take effect in complex ways. A good example is the way in which **government policy affects economic factors**. Policy is by definition a political matter, but it is inevitable that economic conditions and developments will be heavily influenced by policy developments. Similarly, policy itself is likely to evolve in the face of demographic change or the development of opinion in society. Advanced nations are currently very concerned about the aging of their populations, for example, while the growth of concern over green issues has led to subsidy for power generation that does not produce carbon dioxide.

2 The political and legal environment

FAST FORWARD

Government policy influences the economic environment, the framework of laws, industry structure and certain operational issues. Political instability is a cause of risk. Different approaches to the political environment apply in different countries. International trade is subject to a further layer of international law and regulation.

The **political environment** affects the firm in a number of ways.

* A basic legal framework generally exists
* The government can take a particular stance on an issue of direct relevance to a business or industry
* The government's overall conduct of its economic policy is relevant to business

PEST analysis is a useful tool to employ in the case study as an initial survey of conditions and options. But remember the real world doesn't have neatly defined categories like a model does; for example, political and economic factors often overlap. Use the model to generate ideas, but do not be too concerned with attributing factors to a specific category: identifying relevant factors is more important.

2.1 The political and legal environment

Laws come from common law, parliamentary legislation and government regulations derived from it, and obligations under treaties such as those establishing the European Union.

Some legal factors affect all companies, for example tax law (corporation tax, sales tax, income tax); employment law; health and safety law; and company law which governs directors and their duties, reporting requirements, takeover proceedings and shareholders rights.

Other legal and regulatory factors affect **particular industries**, where the public interest is served by doing so. For example, electricity, gas, telecommunications, water and rail transport are subject to **regulators** (Ofgem, Oftel, Ofwat, Ofrail) who have influence over market access, competition and pricing policy (can restrict price increase)

This is because either:

- The industries are, effectively, monopolies
- Large sums of public money are involved (eg in subsidies to rail companies)

 Case Study

The National Lottery in the UK is one of the most highly regulated lotteries in the world. Under the terms of its licence, Camelot (the operator) is required to operate the lottery in an efficient and socially responsible way, protecting players and the integrity of the lottery, and to ensure that it generates the maximum amount of money for the 'Good Causes' which are designated by Parliament:

- The Community Fund
- The Millennium Commission
- The Sports Council
- The Heritage Lottery Fund
- The Arts Council
- New Opportunities Fund

The National Lottery Commission regulates the operation of the lottery. It has the right to award and revoke the operating licence, determine the number of games that can be offered and to carry out compliance audits (such as making sure there are no sales to under 16s).

Camelot's strategic objectives are clear:

(i) Deliver target returns to Good Causes in a socially responsible way
(ii) Increase the number of players and total sales
(iii) Maximise player and retailer satisfaction
(iv) Retain the trust and support of the general public
(v) Deliver healthy returns for shareholders

However, it sees the regulatory regime in which it operates (there are over 2,000 regulations) as a barrier to a rapid response to an increasingly competitive market. Unequal tax regimes are a prime concern. The tax on bingo has been abolished, and it seems likely that regulation over competitors to the Lottery will be further reduced. Camelot believes that the only way to achieve a more effective balance between its own commercial requirements and the needs of customers is to allow it greater self regulation. It believes that its 8 years of running the Lottery are testament to its integrity and ability.

2.2 The impact of government

Porter notes several ways whereby the **government** can directly affect the **economic structure** of an industry. They are explained below.

Capacity expansion	Government policy can encourage firms to increase or cut their capacity.
	(a) The UK tax system offers 'capital allowances' to encourage investment in equipment
	(b) A variety of incentives, funded by the EU and national governments, exist for locating capacity in a particular area
	(c) **Incentives** are used to encourage investment by overseas firms. Different countries in the EU have 'competed' for investment from Japan, for example
Demand	(a) The government is a major customer
	(b) Government can also influence demand by legislation, tax reliefs or subsidies
Divestment and rationalisation	In some European countries, the state takes many decisions regarding the selling off or closure of businesses, especially in sensitive areas such as defence.
Emerging industries	can be promoted by the government or damaged by it.
Entry barriers	Government policy can discourage firms from entering an industry, by restricting investment or competition or by making it harder, by use of quotas and tariffs, for overseas firms to compete in the domestic market.
Competition	(a) The government's **purchasing decisions** will have a strong influence on the strength of one firm relative to another in the market (eg armaments).
	(b) **Regulations and controls** in an industry will affect the growth and profits of the industry – eg minimum product quality standards.
	(c) As a supplier of **infrastructure** (eg roads), the government is also in a position to influence competition in an industry.
	(d) Governments and supra-national institutions such as the EU might impose policies which keep an industry **fragmented**, and prevent the concentration of too much market share in the hands of one or two producers.

In some industries, governments regulate the adoption of **new products**. This is well illustrated by the pharmaceuticals industry, where new drugs or medicines must in many countries undergo stringent testing and obtain government approval before they can be marketed.

National and EU institutions also affect the operating activities of some organisations, for example:

- Anti-discrimination legislation
- Health and safety legislation
- Product safety and standardisation (especially EU standards)
- Workers' rights (eg unfair dismissal, maternity leave)
- Training and education policies can determine the 'standard' of recruits

 Question   **Government impact**

Learning outcome A(iii)

How do you think government policy affects the pharmaceutical industry in your country?

Using the example of the UK.

(a)   The government must authorise most new drugs (eg for safety before they can be sold).

(b)   The UK government is a major purchaser of pharmaceuticals, for the national health service, and so has significant buying power.

(c)   Health education policies affect consumer demand.

(d)   Funding of universities affects the science base for recruitment.

(e)   Employment practices, such as working hours, are influenced by EU employment directives.

2.3 Influencing government   11/05

Businesses are able to influence government policies in a number of ways.

(a)   They can employ **lobbyists** to put their case to individual ministers or civil servants.

(b)   They can give MPs **non-executive directorships**, in the hope that the MP will take an interest in all legislation that affects them.

(c)   They can try to **influence public opinion**, and hence the legislative agenda, by advertising.

Of particular importance is the need to influence the decision making processes of the European Commission. EU regulations, for practical purposes, take priority over national law. They are arrived at after a great deal of negotiation, and for this reason alone, are difficult to change. It is therefore much better to influence the **drafting process** of new regulations than to try and get them changed once they have been implemented.

The EU will have an increasing role in the conduct of **European businesses** in:

- Product standards
- Environmental protection
- Monetary policy (a European Central Bank might set interest rates)
- Research and development
- Regional policy
- Labour costs (wages, pensions)

2.4 Political risk and political change

Changes in UK law are often predictable. A government will publish a **green paper** discussing a proposed change in the law, before issuing a **white paper** and passing a bill through Parliament. Plans should be formulated about what to do if the change takes place.

The political environment is not simply limited to legal factors. Government policy affects the whole **economy**, and governments are responsible for enforcing and creating a **stable framework** in which business can be done. A report by the World Bank indicated that the quality of **government policy is important in providing the right**:

- Physical infrastructure (eg transport)
- Social infrastructure (education, a welfare safety net, law enforcement)
- Market infrastructure (enforceable contracts, policing corruption)

However, it is **political change** which complicates the planning activities of many firms. Many economic forecasts ignore the implications of a change in government policy.

(a)   At **national level**, political influence is significant and includes legislation on trading, pricing, dividends, tax, employment as well as health and safety (to list but a few).

(b)   Politics at **international level** also has a direct bearing on organisations. EU directives affect all countries in the EU.

The **political risk** in a decision is the risk that political factors will invalidate the strategy and perhaps severely damage the firm. Examples are wars, political chaos and regime change, social unrest, corruption and nationalism.

Political risk checklist

A political risk checklist was outlined by Jeannet and Hennessey. Companies should ask the following six questions.

1	How stable is the host country's political system?
2	How strong is the host government's commitment to specific rules of the game, such as ownership or contractual rights, given its ideology and power position?
3	How long is the government likely to remain in power?
4	If the present government is succeeded, how would the specific rules of the game change?
5	What would be the effects of any expected changes in the specific rules of the game?
6	In light of those effects, what decisions and actions should be taken now?

It is also important to remember that there are many countries that do not conform to the Western model of the **rule of law**. Political power may well be extra legal, with the legal system being manipulated or even ignored by government or by other powerful groups such as political parties.

Question	Political risk

Learning outcome B(ii)

For a business of your choice, identify the most significant areas of political risk.

2.5 International trade

The political environment is of particular importance in **international trade**. Such trade is governed by an extra layer of legislation contained in treaties and agreements and is potentially subject to a **higher level of political risk**. This may be manifested in a variety of ways, such as taxation law, labour regulation and economic policy on such matters as ownership. At worst, there is a threat of expropriation or nationalisation. Failure to repress lawlessness and corruption are further complicating factors, as is open or covert refusal to consider international bidders for government contracts.

2.6 Global business regulation

The wider political and legal environment interacts with the immediate task environment in the sphere of business regulation. Here, industry-specific rules are laid down and enforced.

Braithwaite and Drahos, in their book *Global Business Regulation*, discuss the way that the development of globally effective regulation has taken place. They argue that, while laws are passed by national legislatures, the rules they embody are actually created by discussion, negotiation and agreement among a **variety of expert bodies** including states, corporations and international bodies.

The emergence of global regulation does not necessarily march in step with the globalisation of either markets or business organisations. Gambling, for example, *via* the Internet, is a global market, but it is regulated in different ways by different states. By contrast, regulations relating to prescription drugs are now largely global in effect, but national markets are kept isolated from one another by differences in government policy on medicine as a welfare benefit. Pharmaceutical firms, however, are among the best established of global businesses.

Common features in global regulation

The processes that result in developments in global regulation are complex and vary from industry to industry. But some common features emerge.

(a) **Power of individual countries**. The **USA** has huge influence over the globalisation of regulation; the **EU** is beginning to have similar influence. Among individual countries, the **UK** is second to the US in influence.

(b) **International organisations** such as the WTO, IMF and International Chamber of Commerce also have extensive power to influence the development of regulations.

(c) **US corporations** are very effective at enrolling the power of their own government and international bodies to promote their interests. For example, at one time, the technical committees of the International Telecommunications Union nearly all had chairmen and vice-chairmen that had been nominated by US companies. As a result, US patented systems become global standards.

(d) Change in global regulatory regimes often results from two contrasting sequences: the proactive and the reactive.

    (i) The **proactive** sequence involves the promotion of regulatory innovation to one or more early mover organisations: these organisations will initially suffer a cost disadvantage but if the new standard is globalised, they will enjoy early mover benefits.

    (ii) The **reactive** sequence starts with a disaster, followed by media hypes and public unrest: subsequent adoption of regulation placates the public.

However, despite any changes in the level at which regulation is made, it remains in the interests of businesses to **remain alert to the general thrust of regulation** as it affects their industries, and to participate in the processes of lobbying and representation in order to preserve their self-interest.

3 The economic environment

FAST FORWARD

Economic factors include the overall level of growth, the business cycle, official monetary and fiscal policy, exchange rates and inflation.

3.1 The importance of the economic environment

The economic environment is an important influence at local and national level. Here are some factors that firms must attend to.

Factor	Impact
Overall growth or fall in Gross Domestic Product	Increased/decreased demand for goods (eg dishwashers) and services (holidays).
Local economic trends	Type of industry in the area. Office/factory rents. Labour rates House prices.
National economic trends:	
Inflation	Low in most countries; distorts business decisions; wage inflation compensates for price inflation
Interest rates	How much it costs to borrow money affects **cash flow**. Some businesses carry a high level of debt. How much customers can afford to spend is also affected as rises in interest rates affect people's mortgage payments.
Tax levels	Corporation tax affects how much firms can invest or return to shareholders. Income tax and VAT affect how much consumers have to spend, hence demand.
Government spending	Suppliers to the government (eg construction firms) are affected by spending.

Factor	Impact
The business cycle	Economic activity is always punctuated by periods of growth followed by decline, simply because of the nature of trade. The UK economy has been characterised by periods of 'boom' and 'bust'. Government policy can cause, exacerbate or mitigate such trends, but cannot abolish the business cycle. (Industries which prosper when others are declining are called counter-cyclical industries.)
Productivity	An economy cannot grow faster than the underlying growth in productivity, without risking inflation. UK manufacturing productivity is still lower than that of its main competitors, but in services, the UK is relatively efficient.

The **forecast state of the economy** will influence the planning process for organisations which operate within it. In times of boom and increased demand and consumption, the overall planning problem will be to **identify** the demand. Conversely, in times of recession, the emphasis will be on cost-effectiveness, continuing profitability, survival and competition.

3.1.1 Growth of the service sector

There is a trend in many developed economies, such as the UK, the US and so on, for **services** to account for a growing proportion of national economic activity and employment. The **service sector** accounts for most output. Services include activities such as restaurants, tourism, nursing, education, management consultancy, computer consulting, banking and finance. Manufacturing is still important, especially in exports, but it employs fewer and fewer people.

Key term

> **Services** are value creating activities which in themselves do not involve the supply of physical product. Service provision may be subdivided into:
>
> (a) *Pure services*, where there is no physical product, such as consultancy
> (b) *Service with a product attached*, such as the design and installation of a computer network
> (c) *Products with services attached*, such as the purchase of a computer with a maintenance contract

3.1.2 Impact of international factors on a country's economy

Factor	Impact
Exchange rates	Cost of imports, selling prices and value of exports; cost of hedging against fluctuations
Characteristics of overseas markets. Different rates of economic growth and prosperity, tax etc	Desirable overseas markets (demand) or sources of supply
Capital flows and trade	Investment opportunities, free trade, cost of exporting
Globalisation	Increased competition, increasing prosperity

3.2 Government economic policy

Governments generally accept that they have a role to play in the management of the macroeconomy. Their objectives are generally to achieve satisfactory and stable **growth**, while controlling **inflation** and avoiding significant changes in the value of their **currencies**. Growth is required since it enhances general economic **well-being** and provides for high levels of **employment**.

A government can use various policy tools as follows.

Fiscal policy	• Taxation and other sources of income
	• Government spending
	• Borrowing whenever spending exceeds income
	• Repaying debt when income exceeds expenditure

Monetary policy	• Interest rates • Exchange rates or exchange controls • Control of the money supply • Controls over bank lending and credit (rarely used) nowadays

Businesses are affected by a government's tax policy (eg corporation tax rates), and monetary policy (high interest rates increase the cost of investment, or depress consumer demand).

In practice, governments are making use of these tools in different ways.

In the UK, the USA and the Euro-zone, control of **monetary policy** (interest rates) is set by independent bodies (the Bank of England, the Federal Reserve, the European Central Bank), over which governments have little direct influence. In other countries, this is not the case.

Some countries use exchange rate policy and exchange controls to affect economic activity. Not all currencies are fully convertible into others. The government of Malaysia used this approach, by restricting the import and export of Malaysian *ringgit*, in the financial crises of Asia in the late 1990s.

Finally, there is pressure in some jurisdictions for co-ordination of fiscal policies.

3.2.1 Government spending

Governments nationally and locally spend money on the following.

- Payments of wages and salaries to employees, and of pensions to old age pensioners
- Payments for materials, supplies and services
- Purchases of capital equipment
- Payments of interest on borrowings and repayments of capital

Tax and spending decisions have the effect of increasing or decreasing the amount that consumers have to spend generally and **re-allocating resources** in the economy to the public sector activities.

3.2.2 Involvement of the private sector

In many countries, various areas of the public sector have been delivered to the private sector in a process of **privatisation**. Where these were utilities, these organisations are regulated by bodies such as Ofcom. This process has had a number of sometimes conflicting objectives.

(a) **Reductions in public sector borrowing** and expenditure to finance tax cuts and/or spending.

(b) **Greater investment** which the government is unwilling or unable to fund from its own resources. Privatised utilities are then **free to borrow**.

(c) **New management practices** are introduced.

(d) Privatisation can encourage **competition**, but some utilities have been sold off as **monopolies**, subject to a regulator.

Privatisation is now relatively uncontroversial in the UK, but still causes political hostility in the developing world.

The blurring of boundaries between public and private sector continues.

(a) **Contracting out**. Some work which was previously done by government employees has been contracted out to firms in the private sector.

(b) **Welfare spending**. Government policy has been to shift some welfare spending to individuals, such as in personal pensions.

(c) **Private finance initiative**. In the UK, the private sector is involved in financing public projects, such as roads and hospitals.

In some countries, therefore, government policy has been to purchase welfare services from private sector suppliers rather than manage them directly.

3.2.3 Inflation and interest rates

Inflation can be a deterrent to real economic growth, creating expectations of further inflation and undermining business confidence. The consequences include the following.

(a)   A demand for **higher money wages** to be paid to employees to compensate for the fall in value of their wages.

(b)   A demand for **high interest rates**, so that investors can be compensated for inflation and borrowers are deterred.

3.2.4 The housing market

An important feature of the UK and other countries is the **housing market.**

(a)   The **housing market** is a key factor for people in the UK and many other countries. Most houses are owner-occupied, and most people's wealth is tied up in their homes. UK borrowers generally borrow at variable rates of interest, so are vulnerable to changes in interest rates.

(b)   **Rising prices** encourage people to take out extra loans to spend on other things. This was held to lead to inflation.

(c)   Most of the debt owed by UK borrowers is at **variable rate**. Changes in interest rates have an immediate effect on people's pockets. This is not necessarily the case elsewhere.

3.3 International trade and exchange rates

International trade and finance consists of:

- Trade in goods and services, forming the **balance of trade**
- Long-term and short-term **investments** from other countries and into other countries
- Movements in a government's **official reserves** of foreign currency, gold etc

Faced with a **trade deficit**, a government might once have considered **protectionist measures** and, in the case of developing countries, **exchange controls**.

However, a government's long-term strategy for a balance of trade deficit should be to improve conditions in the domestic economy.

(a)   The improvements required could include bringing inflation under control, encouraging investment in domestic industries and depressing consumer demand.

(b)   The **quality** of the deficit is an important consideration. If capital goods are imported, this might mean only a short-term deficit, as the machinery enhances the productivity and export capacity of domestic firms in the long term. If consumer goods are imported, this might not be as sustainable in the long run.

Question   Single currency

Learning outcome A(iv)

What might be the implications of the single European currency, for the following UK businesses?

(a)   A package holiday firm, mainly selling holidays to France and Germany.

(b)   An exporter of power station generating equipment to developing countries in Asia.

(c)   An importer of wine from Australia.

Do this exercise twice, firstly on the assumption that the UK adopts the Euro, swapping sterling for the Euro, and secondly on the assumption that it keeps sterling as its currency.

Answer

We can offer no definitive solution, but here are some points to consider.

(a)   For companies trading primarily within the EU, such as the package holiday firm, adopting the Euro will mean a reduction in exchange rate volatility – businesses will be able to compete on the essentials of cost and productivity. An analogy is the USA – although there are many 'states' there is only one currency. Most British trade is with EU countries.

(b) and (c)

Companies trading outside the Euro-zone would remain subject to exchange rate risk, based on the Euro rather than sterling. It all depends on how the European Central Bank manages the currency - if the Euro becomes a 'hard' currency, with a high value, then exports will cost more to overseas customers, but imports from overseas suppliers might be cheaper. Many internationally traded goods, such as oil or aircraft, are priced in US dollars anyhow, so the impact will be indirect.

Of course, if the UK stays out of the Economic and Monetary Union (EMU) and does not adopt the Euro it will not be in a position to influence the monetary policies of countries which use the Euro, although these policies will undoubtedly affect the UK economy and British businesses.

3.4 Economic factors and the management accountant

The management accountant may be asked to estimate the effect of particular economic factors on the firm's operations.

(a)   **Interest rates**

(i)   A rise might increase the cost of any borrowing the company has undertaken, thereby reducing its profitability. It also has the possible effect of raising a firm's cost of capital. An investment project therefore has a higher hurdle to overcome to be accepted. If, on the other hand, a firm has surplus cash, this can be invested for a higher return.

(ii)   Interest rates also have a general effect on consumer confidence and liquidity, and hence demand, especially in relation to the housing markets.

(b)   **Inflation**. For an economy has a whole, inflation works as a 'tax on savers' given that it reduces the value of financial assets and the income of those on fixed incomes.

(i)   It requires high **nominal interest rates** to offer investors a real return.

(ii)   Inflation makes it hard for businesses to plan, owing to the uncertainty of future financial returns. Inflation and expectations of it help explain 'short-termism'.

(iii)   Inflation has a number of effects on how firms report their performance and how they plan.

Exchange rate volatility affects the cost of imports from overseas, and the prices that can be charged to overseas customers. A high value to the pound means that customers must be charged more in their local currencies – and imports are cheaper.

Exchange rates do not only affect imports and exports. Many firms invest large sums of money in factories in overseas markets.

(a)   The **purchasing power parity** theory of exchange rate suggests that, in the long term, differences in exchange rates caused by inflation or higher interest rates will even out. It looks at what people can buy in their own country and uses this to compare economic performance. The Chinese economy is, measured in US $, much smaller than the US economy: the difference in size is not so marked when purchasing power parity is used for comparisons.

(b)   Firms are very vulnerable to changes in exchange rates over the short to medium term, especially as a subsidiary's reported profit can affect the reported profit of the holding company and hence, by implication, its share price. Firms can guard against the risk of exchange rates by a number of financial instruments such as **hedges**.

4 The social and cultural environment

FAST FORWARD

Social and cultural factors relate to two main issues. **Demography** is the study of the population as a whole: its overall size, whether it is growing, stable, or falling; the proportion of people of different age groups – in industrial countries the proportion of elderly people is increasing; where people live and work; ethnic origin. **Culture** includes customs, attitudes, characteristic ways of viewing the world and behaviour: most countries contain several subcultures.

4.1 Social change and social trends

Social change involves changes in the nature, attitudes and habits of society. Social changes are continually happening, and trends can be identified, which may or may not be relevant to a business.

 Case Study

In January 2006, *Canterbury Foods*, a manufacturer of food products such as pastries, sausages and hamburgers, collapsed into insolvency with debts of £15m. The Chief Executive, Paul Ainsworth, had said in September 2005 that the TV campaign by celebrity chef Jamie Oliver to drive up the quality of school meals had helped to undermine the company's position, though commentators noted that it had been heavily indebted and trading at a loss for some time. Britain's largest catering firm, *Compass*, said that sales of several food companies had been hit by the school meals campaign: 'there has been a move away from Turkey Twizzlers'.

4.2 Demography

Key term

Demography is the study of populations and communities. It provides analysis of statistics on birth and death rates, age structures of populations, ethnic groups within communities and so on.

Demography is important for these reasons.

- Labour is a factor of production
- People create demand for goods, services and resources
- It has a long-term impact on government policies
- There is a relationship between population growth and living standards

Here are some statistics, which might help to explain the importance many businesses are placing on overseas markets. The figures are taken from *Social Trends*.

	1994 Population (millions)	2025 Population (millions)	% increase 1994-2025
World population	5,665.5	8,472.4	49%
Europe (including Baltic states)	512.0	541.9	5%
Former USSR (excluding Baltic states)	284.5	344.5	21%
Canada and USA	282.7	360.5	27%
Africa	681.7	1,582.5	32%
Asia	3,233.0	4,900.3	65%
Latin America	457.7	701.6	53%
Oceania (including Australia)	27.5	41.3	50%

The following demographic factors are important to organisational planners.

Factor	Comment
Growth	The rate of growth or decline in a national population and in regional populations.
Age	Changes in the age distribution of the population. In the UK, there will be an increasing proportion of the national population over retirement age. In developing countries there are very large numbers of young people.
Geography	The concentration of population into certain geographical areas.
Ethnicity	A population might contain groups with different ethnic origins from the majority. In the UK, about 5% come from ethnic minorities, although most of these live in London and the South East.
Household and family structure	A household is the basic social unit and its size might be determined by the number of children, whether elderly parents live at home etc. In the UK, there has been an increase in single-person households and lone parent families.
Social structure	The population of a society can be broken down into a number of subgroups, with different attitudes and access to economic resources. Social class, however, is hard to measure (as people's subjective perceptions vary).
Employment	In part, this is related to changes in the workplace. Many people believe that there is a move to a casual flexible workforce; factories will have a group of core employees, supplemented by a group of insecure peripheral employees, on part time or temporary contracts, working as and when required. Some research indicates a 'two-tier' society split between 'work-rich' (with two wage-earners) and 'work-poor'. However, despite some claims, most employees are in permanent, full-time employment.
Wealth	Rising standards of living lead to increased demand for certain types of consumer good. This is why developing countries are attractive as markets.

4.2.1 Implications of demographic change

(a)   **Changes in patterns of demand**: an ageing population suggests increased demand for health care services: a 'young' growing population has a growing demand for schools, housing and work.

 Case Study

The UK disposable nappy market turnover fell by 18% to £344m between 1999 and 2003, according to *Mintel*, a market research company. This fall echoes a 15% fall in live births between 1998 and 2004.

(b)   **Location of demand**: people are moving to the suburbs and small towns.

(c)   **Recruitment policies**: there are relatively fewer young people so firms will have to recruit from less familiar sources of labour.

(d)   **Wealth and tax**.

4.3 Culture

Key term

Culture is used by sociologists and anthropologists to encompass 'the sum total of the beliefs, knowledge, attitudes of mind and customs to which people are exposed in their social conditioning.'

Through contact with a particular culture, individuals learn a language, acquire values and learn habits of behaviour and thought. Culture has the following characteristics.

(a)   **Beliefs and values**. Beliefs are what we feel to be the case on the basis of objective and subjective information (eg people can believe the world is round or flat). Values are beliefs which are relatively enduring, relatively general and fairly widely accepted as a guide to culturally appropriate behaviour.

(b) **Customs:** modes of behaviour which represent culturally accepted ways of behaving in response to given situations.

(c) **Artefacts:** all the physical tools designed by human beings for their physical and psychological well-being: works of art, technology, products.

(d) **Rituals.** A ritual is a type of activity which takes on symbolic meaning, consisting of a fixed sequence of behaviour repeated over time.

The learning and sharing of culture is made possible by language (both written and spoken, verbal and non-verbal).

 Case Study

Islamic banking

Islamic banking is a powerful example of the importance of culture in an economy. The Koran abjures the charging of interest, which is usury. However whilst interest is banned, profits are allowed. A problem is that there is no standard interpretation of the sharia law regarding this. Products promoted by Islamic banks include:

(a) Leasing (the Islamic Bank TII arranged leases for seven Kuwait Airways aircraft)
(b) Trade finance
(c) Commodities trading

The earlier Islamic banks offered current accounts only, but depositors now ask for shares in the bank profits. To tap this market, Citibank, the US bank, opened an Islamic banking subsidiary in Bahrain.

4.3.1 Importance of culture for business

Knowledge of the culture of a society is clearly of value to businesses in a number of ways.

(a) **Marketers** can adapt their products accordingly, and be fairly sure of a sizeable market. This is particularly important in export markets.

(b) **Human resource managers** may need to tackle cultural differences in recruitment. For example, some ethnic minorities have a different body language from the majority, which may be hard for some interviewers to interpret.

Culture in a society can be divided into **subcultures** reflecting social differences. Most people participate in several of them.

Subculture	Comment
Class	People from different social classes might have different values reflecting their position of society.
Ethnic background	Some ethnic groups can still be considered a distinct cultural group.
Religion	Religion and ethnicity are related.
Geography or region	Distinct regional differences might be brought about by the past effects of physical geography (socio-economic differences etc). Speech accents most noticeably differ.
Age	Age subcultures vary according to the period in which individuals were socialised to an extent, because of the great shifts in social values and customs in this century. ('Youth culture'; the 'generation gap' etc.)
Sex	Some products are targeted directly to women or to men.
Work	Different organisations have different corporate cultures, in that the shared values of one workplace may be different from another.

Cultural change might have to be planned for. There has been a revolution in attitudes to female employment, despite the well-publicised problems of discrimination that still remain.

Question
Social trends

Learning outcome B(i)

Club Fun is a UK company which sells packaged holidays. It offers a standard 'cheap and cheerful' package to resorts in Spain and the Greek islands. It was particularly successful at providing holidays for the 18-30 age group.

What do you think the implications are for Club Fun of the following developments?

- A fall in the number of school leavers
- The fact that young people are more likely now than in the 1960s to go into higher education
- Holiday programmes on TV which feature a much greater variety of locations
- Greater disposable income among the 18-30 age group
- Increasing levels of Internet access

Answer

The firm's market is shrinking. There is an absolute fall in the number of school leavers. Moreover, it is possible that the increasing proportion of school leavers going to higher education will mean there will be fewer who can afford Club Fun's packages. That said, a higher disposable income in the population at large might compensate for this trend. People might be encouraged to try destinations other than Club Fun's traditional resorts if these other destinations are publicised on television. Growing access to the Internet makes it easier for other suppliers to compete.

5 The technological environment

FAST FORWARD

Technological factors have implications for economic growth overall, and offer opportunities and threats to many businesses. Meta-technologies are technologies that are applicable to many applications.

The strategic importance of technology relates to all these aspects. In the most general senses, technology contributes to overall **economic growth**. Consider the **production possibility curve** which describes the total production in an economy. Technology can shift this curve, increasing total output, by enabling:

- Gains in productivity (more output per units of input)
- Reduced costs (eg transportation technology, preservatives)
- New types of product

Technological change is rapid, and organisations must adapt themselves to it. Technological change can affect the activities of organisations as follows.

(a)   **The type of products or services that are made and sold**. For example, consumer markets have seen the emergence of personal computers, DVDs, digital cameras and digital TV; industrial markets have seen the emergence of custom-built microchips, robots and local area networks for office information systems.

Case Study

The development of the transistor made valve radios obsolete. Japanese firms were thus able easily to enter the consumer electronics market, where they are now key competitors. Japanese firms had no previous investment in valve radio production.

(b) **The way in which products are made.**

      (i)   Modern production equipment reduces the need for labour.

      (ii)   Technology can also develop new raw materials.

(c) The way in which services are provided, for example travel agencies over the internet.

(d) The way in which markets are identified. Database systems make it much easier to analyse the market place.

(e) The way in which firms are managed. IT has helped in the 'delayering' of organisational hierarchies (in other words, the reduction of management layers between the senior managers and the workforce), but requires greater workforce skills. Using technology often requires changes in working methods. Information technology, in particular, requires skills at manipulating and interpreting abstract data.

(f) The means and extent of communications with external clients.

Impact of technological change

The impact of technological change also has potentially important social consequences.

(a) Whereas people were once collected together to work in factories, **home working** will become more important.

(b) Certain sorts of skill, related to **interpretation** of data and information processes, are likely to become more valued than manual or physical skills.

(c) Technology increases manufacturing productivity, so that more people will be involved in **service** jobs.

It is extremely difficult to **forecast** developments beyond more than a few years. For example, many of the current developments in information technology would have seemed almost impossible not much more than a decade ago.

(a) **Futurology** is the science and study of sociological and technological developments, values and trends with a view to planning for the future.

(b) The **Delphi model** involves a panel of experts providing views on various events to be forecast such as inventions and breakthroughs, or even regulations or changes over a time period in to the future.

(c) In some cases, instead of technical developments being used to predict future technologies, future social developments can be predicted, in order to predict future **customer needs**.

It is also possible that one particular invention or technique will have wide ranging applications. Such a technology might be called a **meta-technology**.

 Case Study

An example of a meta-technology might be the technology behind lasers. Lasers are used for a huge variety of jobs.

- Eye surgery (eg on the cornea, as it is more precise than a scalpel, and the heat effectively seals the wound)
- Industrial cutting
- Illuminating public monuments at night
- Reading data from compact disks or DVDs (for recorded music, interactive video games, interactive encyclopaedias, publishing)
- Discotheques

 Case Study

Ethanol in Brazil

The need to consider the general environment as an integrated whole and not as a group of separate influences is illustrated by the history of the ethanol fuel industry in Brazil.

Ethanol as an alternative or supplement to petroleum products for motor vehicle fuel came back into prominence in 2005 because of major demand-driven rises in the global price of oil. In January 2006, *The Financial Times* reported that the Brazilian ethanol industry had been established in response to the oil crises of the 1970s. Subsidies for cane mills and price controls had helped to create a major industry. Here we see a problem that combines politics and economics being solved with a combination of politics, economics and technology.

During the 1980s, nearly all cars in Brazil were running on ethanol, so there was clearly a significant social effect in terms of acceptance. Unfortunately, in 1989, world sugar prices spiked and ethanol producers shifted their raw material (sugar cane) to the production of sugar. The price of ethanol was still controlled, so the inevitable result was a major shortage of the fuel, which prejudiced consumers against it for a decade. Once again, politics, economics and social factors interact. A prejudice was created against ethanol fuelled cars, focussing on their inferior performance. This has only recently been overcome by the introduction of higher technology 'flex fuel' cars that adjust a mix of ethanol and petrol to boost performance.

6 Interest and pressure groups

6.1 Pressure groups

FAST FORWARD

> The members of **pressure groups** come together to promote an issue or cause.

Stakeholders may be unable to exercise any power over an organisation, whether as consumers, employees or members of the public at large. In these circumstances, individuals may seek to influence an organisation by joining a **pressure group**.

Pressure groups arise for two reasons.

- Political representatives fail to air important concerns
- Different groups in society have different interests

Pressure groups have an interest in matters of public policy, but do not aspire to control the machinery of government. There are many thousands of groups ranging from major umbrella groups to small purely local groups, often established for a specific purpose.

(a) **Cause** groups (or **promotional** groups) promote a distinct cause or issue (eg CND, Greenpeace, Howard League for Penal Reform).

(b) **Interest groups** (or **defensive** or **sectional** groups) defend the wide interests of groups in society such as mineworkers (NUM), business firms (CBI) or consumers.

Some of these groups have other activities than trying to influence government and might regard political activity as only one of their many roles. Some of the major charities, such as Oxfam, do good work and also try to influence government policy. A group can have one of two sorts of relationship with government.

(a) **Insider groups** are regularly consulted by government as a matter of routine in areas of policy. In fact, some insider groups *expect* to be consulted. Note that insider groups do not necessarily support the government of the day. The British Medical Association, for example, although not always supporting government policy on the NHS, is still regularly consulted.

(b) **Outsider groups** do not have a direct link to government. Some of their activities are to **promote interest** in their cause outside government (eg in the media) so that the issue is raised in the public arena and to **gain credibility** in the eyes of the public and recognition of their importance by the government, so that their pronouncements are taken seriously.

The role of pressure groups is controversial.

(a) Some argue that the existence of a pressure group means that **power** is **diffused widely**, and that they are an informal check on ever-increasing power of the state. They also help protect minorities.

(b)   Others argue that some pressure groups (eg business interests) are far **more influential** than others (eg some supporters of rail transport believe that 'the road lobby' has undue influence on UK transport policy) and that this is anti-democratic.

Pressure groups may either encourage or try to discourage a policy.

 Case Study

Examples of two contrasting pressure groups in Britain are the Countryside Alliance and the Hunt Saboteurs Association. The main press focus on the Countryside Alliance has been on its opposition to the ban on hunting. As well as marches, the Association also tried to increase understanding and support for hunting with dogs by campaigns and information packs. The Alliance also investigated legal challenges to any proposed ban on hunting, including challenges under human rights legislation and problems over contract law.

Over time the Alliance's remit widened, to cover 'the real rural agenda'. This included other country sports, such as angling and fishing. As well as campaigns, the Alliance provided members with advice on recent legislation and practical skills, for example shotgun technique courses.

Wider rural concerns of the Alliance include the production of food; the concern is that smaller businesses are being edged out due to inappropriate regulations and failure by businesses and consumers to buy local products. ' (We) believe that food production in Britain does not need special exemptions or subsidies. It needs sensible regulation and an ability to compete in the marketplace. Consumers who demand higher standards, in terms of food safety, environmental protection and animal welfare must be willing to pay for the true cost of this food production.'

The Hunt Saboteurs Association's website is rather more narrowly-focused. It is designed to arouse strong reactions from users by including graphic pictures of animal suffering. It also includes quotes allegedly made by leading huntsmen that do not portray them in a good light. Apart from these the site is focused on sabotage operations, covering not just hunts, but also dealing with traps and snares and angling. The main support service offered is legal advice, with details of how saboteurs have fared when charged with offences under public order legislation, and also contact details should saboteurs find themselves in difficulty.

6.2 Interest groups

The main pressure groups reflecting economic interests are as follows.

(a)   **Businesses**: Employers' organisations. These can be supplemented by smaller more specified trade associations in particular industries, which gang together to promote common interests (eg newspapers to oppose tax on the press).

(b)   **Professional associations** are groups of people who do the same type of job or use similar skills such as accountants and doctors. Professional associations are generally involved in setting standards of skill and enforcing adherence to good practice (for example, through disciplinary schemes) on the part of members who do the same type of job or use similar skills.

(c)   **Trade unions** are similar to professional associations, in that they represent people who work.

(d)   **Consumers' associations** represent people as consumers, in other words, campaigning for the interests of consumers on issues such as product pricing, safety, quality and information. Consumer associations have campaigned for labelling on food, for example.

Exam focus point

You may have to suggest a strategy for dealing with pressure groups in your exam. A plan might identify the following:

(a)   Which pressure groups are likely to have an impact or an interest

(b)   How these impacts can be addressed:
  (i)   Provide information to correct misapprehensions.
  (ii)   Use public relations in crisis management.

7 Environmental information and analysis

A company's response to the environment is influenced by its complexity and its dynamism. The value of forecasts varies according to these factors.

7.1 Environmental analysis and uncertainty

Johnson and Scholes suggest that a firm should conduct an **audit of environmental influences**. This will identify the environmental factors which have had a significant influence on the organisation's development or performance in the past.

Strategic decisions are made in partial ignorance, as we have seen, because the environment is **uncertain**. As we mentioned earlier, uncertainty arises from the **complexity and dynamism** of the environment.

(a) **Complexity** arises from:

    (i) The **variety of influences** faced by the organisation. The more open an organisation is, the greater the variety of influences. The greater the number of markets the organisation operates in, the greater the number of influences to which it is subject.

    (ii) The amount of **knowledge** necessary. All businesses need to have knowledge of the tax system, for example, but only pharmaceuticals businesses need to know about mandatory testing procedures for new drugs.

    (iii) The **interconnectedness** of environmental influences. Importing and exporting companies are sensitive to exchange rates, which themselves are sensitive to interest rates. Interest rates then influence a company's borrowing costs.

(b) **Dynamism**. Stable environments are unchanging. Dynamic environments are in a state of change. The computer market is a dynamic market because of the rate of technological change, for example.

Question
Contrasting environment

Learning outcome A(iii)

Analyse the environments of the two situations below according to the criteria given above.

(a) A new product has just been introduced to a market segment. It is proving popular. As it is based on a unique technology, barriers to entry are high. The product will not be sold outside this market segment.

(b) A group of scientists has recently been guaranteed, by an EU research sponsoring body, funds for the next ten years to investigate new technologies in the construction industry, such as 'smart materials' (which respond automatically to weather and light conditions). This is a multi-disciplinary project with possible benefits for the construction industry. A number of building firms have also guaranteed funds.

Answer

(a) The environment is simple, as the product is only being sold in one market. The environment is dynamic, as the product is still at the introduction stage and demand might be predicted to increase dramatically.

(b) The environment is complex, but stable. The knowledge required is uncertain, but funds are guaranteed for ten years.

The implication is that the type of business strategy adopted, and indeed the approach to making business strategy, will depend on the type of environment the firm inhabits.

7.2 Impact of uncertainty

If an organisation is operating in a highly uncertain environment this will affect its strategy.

- **The planning horizon will be shortened** because the uncertainty will mean that management will not dare plan too far ahead.

- **Strategies may be more conservative** because management are unlikely to risk anything new. However, the counter argument to this is that management may want to try something new, because the uncertainty could mean that the existing strategies will no longer work.

- **Emergent strategies may be encouraged**, instead of planned strategies. Advocates of emergent strategies argue they are more appropriate to periods of uncertainty because of their adaptability to changing circumstances.

- **Increased information requirements**. Management will require more regular information to allow them to monitor and assess the changing conditions. Uncertainty will make forecasting harder, so management will need more information to gauge their strategic position.

- **Firms may follow multiple strategies**. Firms may respond to risk and uncertainty by trying to develop a number of alternative options. For example, in the current climate of uncertainty surrounding oil reserves and production, oil firms may try to develop multiple sources of oil around the world, to avoid being dependent on a particular region or a particular extraction technology.

7.3 Forecasts

Key term

> A **forecast** is 'a prediction of future events and their quantification for planning purposes'.
>
> (CIMA *Official Terminology*)

Forecasting attempts to reduce the uncertainty managers face. In **simple/static conditions the past is a relatively good guide** to the future. Techniques are:

(a) **Time series analysis.** Data for a number of months/years is obtained and analysed. The aim of time series analysis is to identify:

    (i) Seasonal and other cyclical fluctuations

    (ii) Long term underlying trends

    An example of the use of this approach is the UK's monthly unemployment statistics which show a 'headline figure' and the 'underlying trend'.

(b) **Regression analysis** is a quantitative technique to check any underlying correlations between two variables (eg sales of ice cream and the weather). Remember that the relationship between two variables may only hold between certain values.

(c) Econometrics is the study of economic variables and their interrelationships.

    (i) **Leading indicators** are indicators which change before market demand changes. For example, a sudden increase in the birth rate would be an indicator of future demand for children's clothes.

    (ii) The ability to predict the span of time between a change in the indicator and a change in market demand. Change in an indicator is especially useful for demand forecasting when they reach their highest or lowest points (when an increase turns into a decline or vice versa).

In **dynamic/complex conditions**, the picture is different.

- **Future developments:** the past is not a reliable guide.

- Techniques such as **scenario building** are useful as they can propose a number of possible futures.

- **Complex environments** require techniques to reduce the effects of complexity on organisational structure and decision-making.

Some firms aim to deal with planning in complex environments by techniques such as scenario building.

7.4 Strategic intelligence

An organisation should plan to obtain **strategic intelligence** as a basis for future strategies. Internal and external databases should be maintained and the data they contain assessed and applied.

If a key task of strategic management is to ensure environmental fit, managers need a willingness and an ability to understand the environment and to anticipate future trends.

- A separate strategic planning department collects data on trends
- The marketing department identifies customer needs
- The R&D department identifies new technology
- The production department suggests process innovation

Arguably, as strategy is about the whole organisation, there are dangers in restricting the gathering of strategic information to functional departments. The whole firm needs to be aware of **strategic intelligence**.

Key term

> **Strategic intelligence**, according to Donald Marchand, is defined as 'what a company needs to know about its business environment to enable it to anticipate change and design appropriate strategies that will create business value for customers and be profitable in new markets and new industries in the future'.

A model of the process of creating strategic intelligence is outlined below.

Sensing	Identify appropriate external indicators of change
↓	↓
Collecting	Gather information in ways that ensure it is relevant and meaningful
↓	↓
Organising	Structure the information in the right format
↓	↓
Processing	Analyse information for implications
↓	↓
Communicating	Package and simplify information for users
↓	↓
Using	Apply strategic intelligence

Key dimensions of strategic intelligence

Information culture	What is the role of information in the organisation? Is it only distributed on a 'need to know basis' or do people have to give specific reasons for secrecy?
Future orientation	Is the focus on specific decisions and trade-offs, or a general attitude of enquiry?
The structure of information flows	Is communication vertical, up and down the hierarchy, or lateral?
Processing strategic intelligence	Are 'professional' strategists delegated to this task or is it everybody's concern?
Scope	Is strategic intelligence dealt with by senior management only, or is intelligence built throughout the organisation?
Time horizon	Short-termist or orientated towards the long term?
The role of IT	Some firms are developing sophisticated knowledge management systems to capture the ?
Organisational 'memory'	In other words, do managers keep in mind the lessons of past successes or failures?

There are many **sources** of strategic intelligence.

(a)   **Internal sources** or sources relatively close to the company.

(i) The **sales force** deals with customers, and so is in a position to obtain customer and competitor information.

(ii) Many companies conduct **market research**. Although generally this deals with specific issues, it can indicate general environmental concerns (eg consumers' worries).

(iii) The management information system may generate information about the environment, although its main focus is internal.

(b) **External sources** of environmental data are various.

(i) **Media**. Newspapers, periodicals and television offer environmental information.

(ii) Sometimes, more detailed country information is needed than that supplied by the press. **Export consultants** might specialise in dealing with particular countries, and so can be a valuable source of information. The **Economist Intelligence Unit** offers reports into particular countries.

(iii) Academic or **trade journals** might give information about a wide variety of relevant issues to a particular industry.

(iv) **Trade associations** also offer industry information.

(v) The government can be a source of statistical data relating to money supply, the trade balance and so forth, which is often summarised in newspapers. The DTI also publishes **Overseas Trade**, concentrating on export opportunities for UK firms.

(vi) Sources of technological environmental information can include the Patent Office.

(vii) Stockbrokers produce investment reports for the clients which involve analysis into particular industries.

(viii) Specialist consultancy firms (eg CACI census data) provide information.

(ix) The Internet.

7.5 Database information

A **management information system** or **database** should provide managers with a useful flow of relevant information which is easy to use and easy to access. Information is an important corporate resource. Managed and used effectively, it can provide considerable competitive advantage and so it is a worthwhile investment. Large scale databases are created and stored on **computer systems,** using **database application packages** such as **Microsoft Access**.

It is now possible to access large volumes of generally available information through databases held by public bodies and businesses.

(a) Some **newspapers** offer free or paid-for access on the web to both current and archived editions, with search facilities looking for information on particular companies or issues.

(b) Public databases are also available for inspection. **Dun and Bradstreet** provide general business information. **AC Nielsen** operate on-line information regarding products and market share.

(c) Developments in information technology allow businesses to have access to the databases of **external organisations**. Reuters, for example, provides an on-line information system about money market interest rates and foreign exchange rates to firms involved in money market and foreign exchange dealings, and to the treasury departments of a large number of companies. The growing adoption of technology at **point of sale** provides a potentially invaluable source of data to both retailer and manufacturer.

 Case Study

CACI is a company which provides market analysis, information systems and other data products to clients. It advertises itself as 'the winning combination of marketing and technology'.

As an illustration of the information available to the marketing manager through today's technology, here is an overview of some of their products.

Paycheck:	this provides income data for all 1.6 million individual post codes across the UK. This enables companies to see how mean income distribution varies from area to area.
People UK:	this is a mix of geodemographics, life stage and lifestyle data. It is person rather than household specific and is designed for those companies requiring highly targeted campaigns.
InSite:	this is a geographic information system (GIS). It is designed to assist with local market planning, customers and product segmentation, direct marketing and service distribution.
Acorn:	this stands for A Classification of Residential Neighbourhoods, and has been used to profile residential neighbourhoods by post code since 1976. ACORN classifies people in any trading area or on any customer database into 54 types.
Lifestyles UK:	this database offers over 300 lifestyle selections on 44 million consumers in the UK. It helps with cross selling and customer retention strategies.
Monica:	this can help a company to identify the age of people on its database by giving the likely age profile of their first names. It uses a combination of census data and real birth registrations.

Legislation and regulation exists to protect consumers form misuse of **personal details** held on computer, unsolicited mail and invasion of privacy.

(a)   There are now stringent trading practices and regulations in the direct mail industry, administered by the Direct Mail Services Standards Board (DMSSB) and Mail Order Protection Scheme (for display advertisements in national newspapers that ask for money in advance).

(b)   The **Mailing Preference Service** allows customers to state whether they would – and more often, would not – be willing to receive direct mail on a range of specific areas.

(c)   The **Data Protection Acts 1984 and 1998** provide that data users (organisations or individuals who control the contents of files of personal data and the use of personal data) must register with the Data Protection Registrar. They must limit their use of personal data (defined as any information about an identifiable living individual) to the uses registered.

 Case Study

Retailers have been collecting data about their customers, through loyalty card schemes, for a number of years, in order to target their marketing more effectively.

7.5.1 Environmental data

Nine areas of environmental data that ought to be included in a database for strategic planners could be as follows.

(a)   **Competitive data.** This would include information derived from an application of Porter's Five Forces analysis (see Chapter 5)

(b)   **Economic data.** Details of past growth and predictions of future growth in GDP and disposable income, the pattern of interest rates, predictions of the rate of inflation, unemployment levels and tax rates, developments in international trade and so on

(c)   **Political data.** The influence that the government is having on the industry

(d)   **Legal data.** The likely implications of recent legislation, legislation likely to be introduced in the future and its implications

(e)   **Social data.** Changing habits, attitudes, cultures and educational standards of the population as a whole, and customers in particular

(f) **Technological data**. Technological changes that have occurred or will occur, and the implications that these will have for the organisation

(g) **Geographical data**. Data about individual regions or countries, each of them potentially segments of the market with their own unique characteristics

(h) **Energy suppliers data**. Energy sources, availability and price of sources of supply generally

(i) **Data about stakeholders in the business**. Employees, management and shareholders, the influence of each group, and what each group wants from the organisation

In other words data which covers the key elements of the general and market environment should be included in a database for strategic and marketing planners.

As well as obtaining data from its own internal database system an organisation can obtain it from an **external database** operated by another organisation.

7.5.2 A word of caution

Most external databases are on-line databases, which are very large computer files of information, supplied by **database providers** and managed by **host** companies whose business revenue is generated through charges made to **users**.

Information sources have to be used with caution. The Internet, in particular, has made data more available: but this data is unvetted and often unmediated.

Chapter Roundup

- The environment exists outside an organisation's boundaries, and organisations survive and prosper in this context. To secure **environmental fit**, an analysis of the environment therefore is required. PEST is a useful mnemonic to discuss these issues. Uncertainty in the environment arises from complexity and dynamism.

- Government policy influences the economic environment, the framework of laws, industry structure and certain operational issues. Political instability is a cause of risk. Different approaches to the political environment apply in different countries. International trade is subject to a further layer of international law and regulation.

- Economic factors include the overall level of growth, the business cycle, official monetary and fiscal policy, exchange rates and inflation.

- Social and cultural factors relate to two main issues. **Demography** is the study of the population as a whole: its overall size, whether it is growing, stable, or falling; the proportion of people of different age groups – in industrial countries the proportion of elderly people is increasing; where people live and work; ethnic origin. **Culture** includes customs, attitudes, characteristic ways of viewing the world and behaviour: most countries contain several subcultures.

- Technological factors have implications for economic growth overall, and offer opportunities and threats to many businesses. Meta-technologies are technologies that are applicable to many applications.

- The members of **pressure groups** come together to promote an issue or cause.

- A company's response to the environment is influenced by its complexity and its dynamism. The value of forecasts varies according to these factors.

- An organisation should plan to obtain **strategic intelligence** as a basis for future strategies. Internal and external databases should be maintained and the data they contain assessed and applied.

1   What does PEST stand for?

2   Distinguish between the general environment and the task environment.

3   What is political risk?

4   Are the following related to government fiscal or monetary policy?

    (a)   taxation

    (b)   borrowing

    (c)   interest rates

    (d)   control of the money supply

    (e)   exchange rates

    (f)   government spending

5   Give an example showing why knowledge of culture is useful to a business.

6   How can technological change affect the activities of organisations? (List 4 ways).

Answers to Quick Quiz

1   Political, economic, social, technological – factors which shape an organisations environment.

2   The general environment covers all the political/legal, economic, social/cultural and technological (PEST) influences in the countries an organisation operates in.

   The task environment relates to factors of particular relevance to a firm, such as its competitors, customers and suppliers of resources.

3   The political risk in a decision is the risk that political factors will invalidate the strategy and perhaps severely damage the firm. Examples are wars, political chaos, corruption and nationalisation.

4   (a)   fiscal
   (b)   fiscal
   (c)   monetary
   (d)   monetary
   (e)   monetary
   (f)   fiscal

5   Marketers can adapt their products accordingly, and be fairly sure of a sizeable market. This is particularly important in export markets. Human resource managers may need to tackle cultural differences in recruitment.

6   Any 4 from:

   –   it can affect the type of products or services that are made and sold
   –   it can affect the way in which products are made
   –   it can affect the way in which services are provided (especially with the growth of the internet)
   –   it can affect the way in which markets are identified
   –   it can affect organisational strucutre and the way firms are managed
   –   it can affect the way organisations communicate with their customers or suppliers

Now try the question below from the Exam Question Bank

Number	Level	Marks	Time
Q4	Examination	25	45 mins

The global competitive environment

Introduction

Chapter 4 dealt with **general environmental factors** in the **macroenvironment**, identifying some trends which affect most organisations to a greater or lesser degree. In this chapter we narrow the focus significantly, and deal with a number of aspects of the **micro environment**.

Most businesses compete with other firms, but they do not compete with every firm. **Competitors** are a vital influence on decision-making. So Section 1 discusses the **five competitive forces** underlying a particular industry.

Section 2, on **globalisation**, indicates how the competitive environment of many industries might be fundamentally changed by much freer international trade - but we also warn against some of the hype surrounding notions of a 'borderless world'. Section 3, on the **competitive advantage of nations**, indicates how the domestic origins of an industry can affect its competitive success.

Finally, we narrow the focus still further, and analyse individual competitors. It is here that you might find your management accounting techniques most useful.

Topic list	Learning outcomes	Syllabus references	Ability required
1 The competitive environment: the five forces	A(iii), A(iv)	A7, B5	Evaluation
2 The impact of globalisation on competition	A(iii), A(iv)	A4, A5	Evaluation
3 The competitive advantage of a nation's industries	A(iii), A(iv)	A6	Evaluation
4 Competitor analysis	A(iii), A(iv)	A8, A9	Evaluation
5 Accounting for competitors	A(iii), A(iv)	A8, A9	Evaluation
6 E-commerce and the Internet	B(v)	B6	Evaluation

1 The competitive environment: the five forces

A market is a group of customers with needs to satisfy. An industry is the companies that use similar technologies to satisfy those needs. For any industry, **five forces** determine its profitability: 'threat of new entrants, substitute products, customers, suppliers and the intensity of competition'.

We must make a basic distinction between the **market** and the **industry**.

Key terms

A **market** comprises the customers or potential customers who have needs which are satisfied by a product or service.

An **industry** comprises those firms which use a particular competence, technology, product or service to satisfy customer needs.

Question

Industries and markets

Learning outcome A(iii), A(iv)

Assume that you are based in London and that you need to attend a meeting in Glasgow. Which industries can satisfy your need to attend the meeting?

Answer

(a)   The airline industry: a number of airlines will compete to fly you from London to Glasgow.

(b)   The railways: it is possible that two railway companies will compete to take you there.

(c)   The car industry, if you have purchased a car.

(d)   The bus industry: several bus firms will compete to drive you to Glasgow.

(e)   The telecommunications industry. You may not need to travel at all, if the conference can be held via a video-conferencing system or even something simpler like a 'conference call'. Telecommunications firms might compete to provide this service.

Key term

Competitive forces/five forces. CIMA defines these as 'external influences upon the extent of actual and potential competition within any industry which in aggregate determine the ability of firms within that industry to earn a profit'. Porter argues that a firm must adopt a strategy that combats these forces better than its rivals' strategies if it is to enhance shareholder value.

In discussing competition, *Porter* (*Competitive Strategy*) distinguishes between factors which characterise the nature of competition:

(a)   **In one industry compared with another** (eg in the chemicals industry compared with the clothing retail industry) and make one industry as a whole potentially more profitable than another (ie yielding a bigger return on investment).

(b)   **Within a particular industry.** These relate to the competitive strategies that individual firms might select.

Porter suggests that five **competitive forces** influence the state of competition in an industry, which collectively determine the profit (ie long-run return on capital) potential of the industry as a whole. **Learn them.**

- The threat of **new entrants** to the industry
- The threat of **substitute** products or services
- The bargaining power of **customers**
- The bargaining power of **suppliers**
- The **rivalry** amongst current competitors in the industry

Source: adapted from Porter *(Competitive Strategy)*

Exam focus point

This model is fundamental to business strategy. You must know it and be able to apply it to circumstances as set out in questions. Not all five forces will necessarily be represented in a scenario and so it may not provide an exhaustive answer. However, it should provide a good framework to build on.

1.1 The threat of new entrants (and barriers to entry to keep them out)

A new entrant into an industry will bring extra capacity and more competition. The strength of this threat is likely to vary from industry to industry, depending on:

- The strength of the **barriers to entry**. Barriers to entry discourage new entrants.
- The likely response of existing competitors to the new entrant.

Barriers to entry	Comment
Scale economies	As scale of operations increases, unit costs tend to fall. This means that new entrants must start their operations on a large scale or suffer a vast disadvantage. A high level of fixed costs, with a consequent high breakeven point also requires entry on a large scale. If the market as a whole is not growing, the new entrant has to capture a large slice of the market from existing competitors.
Product differentiation	Existing firms in an industry may have built up a good brand image and strong customer loyalty over a long period of time. A few firms may promote a large number of brands to crowd out the competition.
Capital requirements	When capital investment requirements are high, the barrier against new entrants will be strong, particularly when the investment would possibly be high-risk.
Switching costs	Switching costs refer to the costs (time, money, convenience) that a customer would have to incur by switching from one supplier's products to another's. Although it might cost a consumer nothing to switch from one brand of frozen peas to another, the potential costs for the retailer or distributor might be high.
Access to distribution channels	Distribution channels carry a manufacturer's products to the end-buyer. New distribution channels are difficult to establish, and existing distribution channels hard to gain access to.
Cost advantages of existing producers, independent of economies of scale	Include: • Patent rights • Experience and know-how (the learning curve) • Government subsidies and regulations • Favoured access to raw materials

Japanese firms

A little while ago, it was assumed that, following the success of Japanese firms worldwide in motor vehicles (Nissan, Honda, Toyota) and consumer electronics (eg Sony, JVC, Matsushita), no Western companies were safe from Japanese competition. Kao (household goods), Suntory (drinks), Nomura (banking and securities) were seen as successors to firms such as Procter and Gamble, Heineken etc.

This has not happened: for example, Japanese pharmaceutical firms, such as Green Cross, have not achieved world domination. US and European firms are still dominant in this industry.

Perhaps cars and consumer electronics were the exception rather than the rule. The reason for this might be distribution. Normally, outsiders do not find it easy to break into established distribution patterns. However, distribution channels in cars and consumer electronics offered outsiders an easy way in.

(a) The car industry is vertically integrated, with a network of exclusive dealerships. Given time and money, the Japanese firms could simply build their own dealerships and run them as they liked, with the help of local partners. This barrier to entry was not inherently complex.

(b) **Consumer electronics**

  (i) In the early years, the consumer electronics market was driven by technology, so innovative firms such as Sony and Matsushita could overcome distribution weaknesses with innovative products, as they had plenty to invest. This lowered entry barriers.

  (ii) Falling prices changed the distribution of hifi goods from small specialist shops to large cut-price outlets, such as Comet. Newcomers to a market are the natural allies of such new outlets: existing suppliers prefer to shun 'discount' retailers to protect margins in their current distribution networks.

Japanese firms have *not* established dominant positions in:

(a) Healthcare, where national pharmaceuticals wholesalers are active as 'gatekeepers'.
(b) Household products, where there are strong supermarket chains.
(c) Cosmetics, where department stores and specialist shops offer a wide choice.

Entry barriers might be **lowered** by:

- Changes in the environment
- Technological changes
- Novel distribution channels for products or services

1.2 The threat from substitute products

A **substitute product** is a good/service produced by **another industry** which satisfies the same customer needs.

The Channel Tunnel

Passengers have several ways of getting from London to Paris, and the pricing policies of the various industries transporting them there reflects this.

(a) 'Le Shuttle' carries cars in the Channel Tunnel. Its main competitors come from the *ferry* companies, offering a substitute service. Therefore, you will find that Le Shuttle sets its prices with reference to ferry company prices, and vice versa.

(b) Eurostar is the rail service from London to Paris/Brussels. Its main competitors are not the ferry companies but the *airlines*. Initially, prices on the London-Paris air routes fell with the commencement of Eurostar services, and some airlines curtailed the number of flights they offer. Low-cost airlines have changed this equation by offering a cheaper alternative.

1.3 The bargaining power of customers

Customers include both the **ultimate consumer** and the buyers forming the **distribution channel**. Customers want better quality products and services at a lower price. Satisfying this want might force down the profitability of suppliers in the industry. Just how strong the position of customers is dependent on several factors.

- How much the **customer buys**
- How **critical** the product is to the customer's own business
- **Switching costs (ie the cost of switching supplier)**
- Whether the products are **standard items** (hence easily copied) or specialised
- The **customer's own profitability**
- Customer's **ability to bypass** the supplier or might take over the supplier
- The **skills** of the customer **purchasing staff**, or the price-awareness of consumers
- The importance of **product quality** to the customer

Case Study

Although the Ministry of Defence may wish to keep control over defence spending, it is likely as a customer to be as concerned that the products it purchases perform satisfactorily than with getting the lowest price possible for everything it buys.

1.4 The bargaining power of suppliers

Suppliers can exert pressure for higher prices but this is dependent on several factors.

(a) Whether there are just **one or two dominant suppliers** to the industry, able to charge monopoly or oligopoly prices

(b) The threat of **new entrants** or substitute products to the **supplier's industry**

(c) Whether the suppliers have **other customers** outside the industry, and do not rely on the industry for the majority of their sales

(d) The **importance of the supplier's product** to the customer's business

(e) Whether the supplier has a **differentiated product** which buyers need to obtain

(f) Whether **switching costs** for customers would be high

Exam focus point

The November 2005 exam contained a rather off-beat question based on the five forces model. It asked how the forces exerted in a customer-supplier relationship led Porter to conclude that firms 'compete with their customers and suppliers'. This unusual phraseology had the potential to confuse a large number of candidates and emphasises the very important principle that you must be prepared to **think** about the questions you are presented with.

1.5 The rivalry amongst current competitors in the industry

The **intensity of competitive rivalry** within an industry will affect the profitability of the industry as a whole. Competitive actions might take the form of price competition, advertising battles, sales promotion campaigns, introducing new products for the market, improving after sales service or providing guarantees or warranties.

The intensity of competition will depend on the following factors.

Factor	Comment
Market growth	Rivalry is intensified when firms are competing for a greater market share in a total market where growth is slow or stagnant.
Cost structure	High fixed costs are a temptation for to compete on price, as in the short run any contribution from sales is better than none at all.
Switching	Suppliers will compete if buyers switch easily (eg Coke vs Pepsi).
Capacity	A supplier might need to achieve a substantial increase in output *capacity*, in order to obtain reductions in unit costs.
Uncertainty	When one firm is not sure what another is up to, there is a tendency to respond to the uncertainty by formulating a more competitive strategy.
Strategic importance	If success is a prime strategic objective, firms will be likely to act very competitively to meet their targets.
Exit barriers	Make it difficult for an existing supplier to leave the industry. • Fixed assets with a low break-up value (eg there may be no other use for them, or they may be old). • The cost of redundancy payments to employees. • If the firm is a division or subsidiary of a larger enterprise, the effect of withdrawal on the other operations within the group.

 Case Study

Low cost airlines

Low cost airlines first appeared in Europe in 1997 after aviation liberalisation. Firms such as *Ryanair* and *EasyJet* copied American companies. They undercut the major carriers on price. The business model included:

- a single-type fleet of planes
- fast turnaround at airports
- no frills
- low fares, which only rose when seats were filled
- cost advantages such as non-unionised labour

Things have changed.

In the US, the budget carriers are moving up market, offering well-defined service, not only low prices. The bigger they grow, the less easy they are to distinguish from their more upmarket rivals.

In Europe, the market for low cost flights is still young. There is overcapacity as new entrants spring up and disappear rapidly. EasyJet and Ryanair have issued profit warnings in 2004. In Europe the low-cost airline faces several threats.

- An all out price war between airlines.
- Low barriers to entry with a glut of second hand aircraft, off the shelf software and low interest rates.
- Established competitors such as BA have adopted some of the innovations of the low-cost airlines, cut their prices and offer better service. Also they have a dominating presence in the most central and attractive airports.

New capacity is being added, as EasyJet and Ryanair buy more planes. Finally, most of the low cost trade is VFR – visiting friends and relatives. The danger is that the 'low-cost' airlines will end up attracting some higher costs in their pursuit of growth.

1.6 Complements

An important aspect of industries is the existence of **complements**. This is a concept you should recall from your basic economics studies: a complement is a product that is consumed at the same time as another one and both are, therefore, required. For example, a CD player is useless without CDs. In modern high technology industries, the existence of such complements is very important and fundamental to growth. The existence or otherwise of complements may almost be regarded as another competitive force, in that the more of them there are, the better for all concerned. Thus, the growth of IT based industries requires a kind of mutual support between telecomms companies, mobile phone manufacturers, chip manufacturers, software houses and so on. This implies that **collaboration** and **co-operation** are important aspects of strategy in these industries.

1.7 The impact of information technology on the competitive forces

Case Study

The Internet has had a variety of impacts.

The *Financial Times* reported that German companies were losing lucrative niche markets because the Internet made it easier for customers to compare prices from other suppliers by obtaining other information over the Internet. High prices made German retailers vulnerable in an age when 'a shopper with a credit card and computer could sit at home and could order from around the world'.

The Internet is a competitive weapon. Supermarket home shopping service are supported by Internet technology.

1.7.1 Barriers to entry and IT

(a) **IT can raise entry barriers** by increasing economies of scale, raising the capital cost of entry or effectively colonising distribution channels by tying customers and suppliers into the supply chain or distribution chain.

(b) **IT can surmount entry barriers**. An example is the use of telephone banking.

1.7.2 Bargaining power of suppliers and IT

(a) **Increasing the number of** accessible **suppliers.** IT enhances supplier information available to customers.

(b) **Closer supplier relationships.** Suppliers' power can be shared. CAD can be used to design components in tandem with suppliers. Such relationships might be developed with a few key suppliers.

(c) **Switching costs.** Suppliers can be integrated with the firm's administrative operations, by a system of electronic data interchange.

1.7.3 Bargaining power of customers

IT can 'lock customers in'.

(a) IT can raise switching costs.

(b) Customer information systems can enable a thorough analysis of marketing information so that products and services can be tailored to the needs of certain segments.

1.7.4 Substitutes

In many respects, **IT itself is 'the substitute product'**. Here are some examples.

(a) Video-conferencing systems might substitute for air transport in providing a means by which managers from all over the world can get together in a meeting.

(b) IT is the basis for leisure activities (eg games) which substitute for TV, cinema, music or other pursuits.

(c) E-mail might substitute for some postal deliveries and phone calls. Mobile text messages can substitute for email.

(d) Digital cameras, with output via computer, can substitute for traditional film and film processing labs.

1.7.5 IT and the state of competitive rivalry

(a) IT can be used in support of a firm's **competitive** strategy of cost leadership, differentiation or focus. These are discussed later in this text.

(b) IT can be used in a **collaborative** venture, perhaps to set up new communications networks. Competitors in the financial services industry share the same ATM network.

1.8 Evaluation of the five forces model

The five forces model offers a comprehensive framework into which appropriate aspects of economic theory, such as scale economies, may be fitted alongside elements of commercial practice, such as price negotiations. **Segmental analysis models** such as the five forces and PEST and its variants have much to offer the business strategist.

(a) They point out **key strategic uses**.
(b) They permit strategic analysis to be **divided up** among staff.
(c) Their wide acceptance provides a **clear basis for discussion**.
(d) They provide for **comprehensive analysis**.

Nevertheless, Porter's five forces model has come in for criticism.

(a) The model relies on a **static picture of the competition** and therefore plays down the role of innovation.

(b) It overemphasises the importance of the **wider environment** and therefore ignores the significance of possible individual company advantages with regard to resources, capabilities and competence.

(c) Its model of government is essentially passive – as a referee in the competitive battle – rather than an active agent and shaper of the competitive environment.

Exam focus point

It is very important to learn Porter's five forces; the examiner has sometimes expressed surprise at candidates' lack of familiarity with them. He has also suggested that you should consider **government** as a **sixth force** with a significant impact on the dynamics of industry.

1.9 Negotiation with customers and suppliers

FAST FORWARD

Trading relationships have strategic impact and, while mutual benefit may be desirable, they must be firmly managed.

To survive and prosper, a business must **create value** on a long term basis; this ultimately boils down to operating profitably. Costs and revenues have obvious impact on profitability and, therefore, purchasing and selling prices must be managed appropriately. While it is tempting to see trade with suppliers and customers as mutually beneficial and the prosperity of trading partners as a continuing desirable outcome, the strategic control of a business requires a firm control of trading relationships. This can only be achieved through **negotiation**, unless the business is in a position simply to accept the terms it is offered: this will anyway be impracticable for firms selling to the general public.

(a) Terms of business are usually drafted to confer maximum advantage on the drafting organisation: they will often clash with those of trading partners and when this cannot be resolved by simple insistence, **mutually agreeable terms** must be arranged. This is particularly important when considering payment terms and the passing of property and risk in goods.

(b)   Trading relationships between unequal partners are frequently one-sided. The weaker partner must be sure that the terms and their impact are understood in detail.

(c)   Price structures can be made deliberately complex and difficult to understand: **quantity and settlement discounts** must be managed with care.

(d)   Price is an important aspect of the marketing mix and, especially in consumer markets, can send important messages about **quality**.

(e)   Weaker partners can gain advantage from membership of **purchasing and selling consortia**.

1.10 The industry life cycle

FAST FORWARD   Industries may display a **lifecycle**: this will affect and interact with the five forces.

We have already defined an industry, earlier in this section. Later we will discuss the concept of the **product life cycle**: this is a well established strategic and marketing tool. It may be possible to discern an **industry life cycle**, which will have wider implication for the nature of competition and competitive advantage. This cycle reflects changes in demand and the spread of technical knowledge among producers. Innovation creates the new industry, and this is normally product innovation. Later, innovation shifts to processes in order to maintain margins. The overall progress of the industry lifecycle is illustrated below.

	Inception	Growth	Maturity/shakeout	Decline
Products	Basic, no standards established	Better, more sophisticated, differentiated	Superior, standardised	Varied quality but fairly undifferentiated
Competitors	None to few	Many entrants Little concentration in industry	Competition increases, weaker players leave	Few remain. Competition may be on price
Buyers	Early adopters, prosperous, curious must be induced	More customers attracted and aware	Mass market, brand switching common	Enthusiasts, traditionalists, sophisticates
Profits	Negative – high first mover advantage	Good, possibly starting to decline	Eroding under pressure of competition	Variable
Strategy	Dominate market, build quality	React to competitors with marketing spend	Cost reductions sought	Control costs

1.11 Survival and success factors

We have already made reference to critical success factors (CSFs). **Survival and success factors** (SSFs) are rather different. While CSFs are vital aspects of an individual organisation's activity, SSFs relate to a **complete industry**. If an organisation wishes to operate in an industry at all, it must deploy survival factors; if it wishes to succeed, it must deploy success factors. Generally, survival and success will represent two different degrees of achievement in similar fields. Thus, in a technically complex manufacturing industry, a survival factor would be technical competence with existing technology, while the equivalent success factor might be the ability to introduce technical innovations on a continuing basis.

The identification of survival and success factors should be one of the outcomes of environmental analysis.

2 The impact of globalisation on competition

> The continuing process of **globalisation** is driven by the convergence of markets and the lifting of trade restrictions. It brings both increased opportunities and increased threats. Global corporations aspire to transcend national loyalties, but they tend to have identifiable national bases.

Harvard Business School professor Ted Levitt predicted the development of a '**global village**' in which consumers around the world would have the same needs and attitudes and use the same products.

Key term

> '**Globalisation** of markets' (Levitt 1983) is an expression which relates first to demand: tastes, preferences and price-mindedness are becoming increasingly universal.
>
> Second, it relates to the supply side: profits and services tend to become more standardised and competition within industries reaches a world-wide scale.
>
> Third, it relates to the way firms, mainly multinational corporations (ie those with operations in more than one country), try to design their marketing policies and control systems appropriately so as to remain winners in the global competition of global products for global consumers.

Other writers have developed the globalisation debate and the factors defining **global competitiveness**. They include Michael Porter (see Section 3).

Some would say that **global organisations** are rare. Industry structures change, foreign markets are culturally diverse, and the transformations brought about by developments in information technology mean that the world market is in a state of **turbulence**.

Here are some of the changes that have happened in the world market place.

- **Globalisation of business** – increased competition and global customers
- **Science and technology** developments
- Mergers, acquisitions and **strategic alliances**
- Changing **customer values** and behaviour
- Increased **scrutiny** of business decisions by government and the public
- Increased **deregulation** and co-operation between business and government
- Changes in **business practices** – downsizing, outsourcing and re-engineering
- Changes in the **social and business** relationships between companies and their employees, customers and other stakeholders

While more and more companies are competing in the world market place, most of them tend to focus on the developed markets of North America, Europe and Japan. A vast majority of the world's population resides in countries where GDP is less than $10,000 per head. Such countries offer tremendous marketing opportunities.

This leads on to the question of **market convergence** – how likely is it that consumers' tastes and preferences may converge? On the face of it, there is no reason why they should not, and **convergence theories** do have strong anecdotal support. The average French high school student appears very similar to American students of the same age (clothing, eating and entertainment preferences). Take a student from Nigeria and compare him to one from Finland, however, and the story is likely to be different.

Global drivers (factors encouraging the globalisation of world trade) include the following.

(a) **Financial factors** eg Third world debt. Often the lenders require the initiation of economic reforms as a condition of the loan.

(b) **Country/continent** alliances, such as that between the UK and USA (foster trade and tourism).

(c) **Legal factors**, such as patents and trade marks, encourage the development of technology and design.

(d) **Stock markets** facilitate trading in international commodities.

(e) The level of **protectionist** measures is under downward pressure from the World Trade Organisation.

Despite the real gains in liberalisation 'globalisation' in its full-blooded form is **not an accurate description** of the reality facing many businesses.

(a)   **Depends on the industry.** Some services are still subject to **managed trade** (eg some countries prohibit firms from other countries from selling insurance) and there are some services which by their very nature can never be exported (eg haircuts are resolutely 'local').

(b)   There is **unlikely ever to be a global market for labour**, given the disparity in skills between different countries, and restrictions on immigration. Even so, some services, as well as manufactures can be exported.

(c)   **Depends on the market**

(i)   **Upmarket luxury goods** may not be required or afforded by people in developing nations: whilst there is competition, it is limited to certain locations.

(ii)   Some goods can be sold almost anywhere, but to limited degrees. Television sets are consumer durables in some countries, but still luxury or relatively expensive items in other ones. Goods, such as oil, are needed almost everywhere: arguably, the oil industry is truly global.

Effect of 'globalisation' on the firm

- Opportunities to compete abroad via exports
- Opportunities to invest abroad
- Opportunities to raise finance from overseas sources of capital

 Case Study

In January 2006 the Financial Times reported on three small UK firms that it saw as typical of a new trend: the **need to sell globally from the inception of the business** because the UK market for their very specialised products simply is not big enough to be viable. All three companies are clear that their future success **depends** on export sales, perhaps to the extent of having no UK sales at all.

Point to note

Bear in mind that 'protectionist' measures are not the only barrier to entry. Differences in:

- Tax regimes   • Language and culture
- Wage levels   • Skills levels
- Infrastructure   • Prosperity

still exist.

2.1 Global or boundary-less corporations

Some argue there is an increasing number of 'stateless corporations', whose activities transcend national boundaries, and whose personnel come from any country.

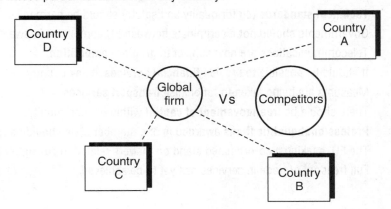

Many firms are setting up global alliances and firms such as BT see their ambitions as being worldwide.

Do these stateless corporations really exist? The following objections have been raised.

(a) **Workforce.** Most multinationals, other than those based in small nations, have less than half of their employees abroad.

(b) **Ownership and control of multinationals remain restricted.** Few so-called global companies are currently quoted on more than two stock markets, but more and more are seeking a listing in a number of financial markets.

(c) **Top management is rarely as multinational in composition** as the firm's activities. (A foreigner is rarely seen on the Tokyo-based board of a Japanese multinational.)

(d) National residence and status is important for **tax reasons**.

(e) **R&D.** The bulk of a typical multinational's research and development is generally done in the home country, where strategic decisions are made. But this is changing, especially as R&D is sometimes subcontracted.

(f) Where **capital is limited**, 'global' companies stick to the home market rather than developing overseas ones.

(g) Profits from a global company must be **remitted somewhere.**

It is important to acknowledge that the internationalisation of a business does not remove cultural and political boundaries. While there has been an increasing internationalisation of production through the expansion of multinational companies and foreign direct investment, the extent to which the economy can be seen as truly global is still debatable.

2.2 Regional trading organisations

FAST FORWARD

The **EU** is the most integrated of the regional trading organisations, aspiring to a single market in goods, services and factors of production.

Countries in various regions have entered into closer economic arrangements such as NAFTA (USA, Canada, Mexico), the EU, Mercosur (Brazil, Argentina, Uruguay, Paraguay and now Chile). The **EU** is the world's largest single market, but is unusual in that it features a common political decision-making process (Council of Ministers, Commission, Parliament) and a single currency.

The EU single market programme has involved areas as diverse as harmonising technical standards, opening up areas such as telecommunications to competition, consumer protection, mutual recognition of professional qualifications and so on. Much work remains to be done.

2.2.1 The European Union

The European Union operates a single European market, allowing for the free movement of labour, goods and services, and free competition.

- **Physical barriers** (eg customs inspection) on goods and service have been removed for most products.
- **Technical standards** (eg for quality and safety) should be harmonised.
- Governments should not discriminate between EU companies in awarding public works contracts.
- Telecommunications are now subject to **greater competition.**
- It should be possible to provide **financial services** in any country.
- Measures are being taken to rationalise **transport services.**
- There should be **free movement of capital** within the community.
- **Professional qualifications** awarded in one member state should be recognised in the others.
- The EU is taking a co-ordinated stand on matters related to **consumer protection.**
- Full freedom of trade in services has yet to be achieved.

- A common currency, the Euro, has been widely adopted within the EU. The refusal of the European Central Bank to use interest rates as an instrument of counter-cyclical policy is widely believed to be largely responsible for high unemployment in France and Germany.

There are many areas where harmonisation is some way from being achieved.

(a) **Taxation**. Tax rates, which can affect the viability of investment plans, vary from country to country within the EU. Similarly, with **indirect taxation (VAT)**, whilst there have been moves to harmonisation, there are still differences between rates imposed by member states.

(b) **Differences in prosperity**. There are considerable differences in prosperity between the wealthier EU economies and the poorest.

    (i)   Grants are sometimes available to depressed regions, which might affect investment decisions

    (ii)   Different marketing strategies are appropriate for different markets

(c) **Differences in workforce skills**. Again, this can have a significant effect on investment decisions. The workforce in Germany is perhaps the most highly trained, but also the most highly paid, and so might be suitable for products of a high added value.

(d) **Infrastructure.** Some countries are better provided with road and rail than others. Where accessibility to a market is an important issue, infrastructure can mean significant variations in distribution costs.

On April 2 1997, the European Union completed the liberalisation of its **aviation market**. From that day, European airlines saw the removal of the last restrictions on their operations, leaving them free to operate domestic services in countries other than their own. In the past, air transport (including level of fares and services) had been heavily regulated, as many governments chose to support the 'national' airline. The UK was one of the first to privatise air transport. The final stage allows airlines to set their own fares or services within the EU, subject to predatory pricing restrictions.

Small airlines such as Ryanair and EasyJet have proliferated, and have introduced low cost flights between a range of EU countries. However, fares for many European routes are still higher than the equivalent distances in the US. In part this is because airports are still publicly owned, in the main, and landing 'slots' (periods of time available for take off and landing) are hard to come by.

Before getting carried away by notions that the world is splitting into trading blocks, remember that:

- There is increasingly free movement of capital
- Global trade is becoming liberalised
- Some of the world's markets offering the greatest potential for growth (eg India and China) are not part of a regional trading organisation
- New technology, such as the Internet, makes it harder to police trade barriers in some areas

2.2.2 The North American Free Trade Agreement (NAFTA)

In 1993 Mexico joined the existing free trade arrangements between Canada and the USA, thus forming the NAFTA area. The agreement covered free trade in 99% of goods and most services, while providing for the observance of environmental protection standards and legislation on health and safety and labour standards. Most restrictions on foreign direct investment were removed, but with protection for certain prized national interests such as US airlines and the Canadian media.

2.2.3 MERCOSUR

Mercosur joins Argentina, Brazil, Paraguay and Uruguay in a free trade agreement.

2.2.4 Other regional trade agreements

Economic integration has not progressed far outside Europe and the Americas. There are two schemes in Asia: ASEAN and APEC but neither has achieved much.

2.3 International trade liberalisation: the World Trade Organisation (WTO)

The **World Trade Organisation** was set up to promote free trade and resolve disputes between trading partners.

The theory of **comparative advantage** suggests that **free trade** is the best way to promote global economic growth and, by implication, domestic prosperity. In other words, people should be free to buy and sell goods and services anywhere in the world.

Many countries have limited or controlled their trading activities, with varying success. **Protectionist measures to restrict competition** from overseas include:

- **Quotas** on the number of items that can be imported (eg Japanese cars)
- **Import bans** (eg Brazil prohibited the import of cheap US-made computers)
- **Restrictions** on foreign ownership of certain industries (eg defence)
- **Tariffs**

Business people and politicians have had an ambivalent attitude in the past towards this issue. Free trade is favoured by importers or multinationals, but protectionism gives businesses the benefit of a cosy domestic market. Their inefficiencies are not penalised and customers pay higher prices.

Since 1945, the major industrial, and now the developing, countries have sought to increase trade. Efforts to liberalise trade culminated in the founding of the World Trade Organisation (WTO) in 1995 as successor to the former General Agreement on Tariffs and Trade (GATT).

Most countries in the developed world are signatories and the WTO is an important influence over the trading environment, although it also attracts a lot of criticism from activists and commentators who claim that it can have too much power (and too little accountability) over the lives of people in economically disadvantaged countries. Important facts to keep in mind about the WTO are these.

(a) **The WTO has dispute resolution powers**. Aggrieved countries can take matters up with the WTO if they cannot be resolved bilaterally.

(b) **Membership** of the WTO requires **adherence to certain conditions** regarding competition in the home market and protection of intellectual property.

(c) **Membership rules are slightly less onerous for 'developing countries'**, which can maintain some protectionist measures.

3 The competitive advantage of a nation's industries
11/07, 11/05, 5/05

Four factors support **competitive success** in a nation's industries: factor conditions, demand conditions, related and supporting industries, and firm strategy, structure and rivalry.

Michael Porter's *The Competitive Advantage of Nations,* suggests that some nations' industries succeed more than others in terms of international competition. UK leadership in some industries (eg ship-building) has been overtaken (by Japan and Korea).

Porter does not believe that countries or nations as such are competitive, but he asks:

(a) 'Why does a **nation become the home base** for successful international competitors in an industry?'

(b) 'Why are firms based in a particular nation able to create and **sustain competitive advantage** against the world's best competitors in a particular field?'

(c) 'Why is **one nation** often the home for **so many of an industry's world leaders**?'

The original explanation for **national** success was the theory of **comparative advantage**. This held that relative **factor opportunity costs** in countries determined the appropriateness of particular economic activities in relation to other countries. (In other words, countries should concentrate on what they are best at in relation to other countries.)

Porter argues that **industries that require high technology and highly skilled employees are less affected** than low technology industries by the relative costs of their inputs of raw materials and basic labour as determined by the national endowment of factors.

Comparative advantage is too **general a concept** to explain the success of **individual companies and industries**. If high technology and global markets allow firms to circumvent (or ignore) the constraints (or advantages) of their home country's endowment of raw materials, cheap labour, access to capital and so forth, how can they be successful internationally?

Porter identifies determinants of national competitive advantage which are outlined in the diagram below. Porter refers to this as the **diamond.**

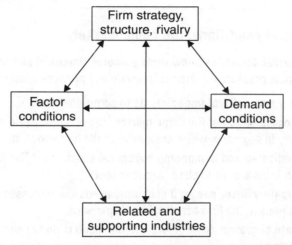

Each element of the diamond is capable of enhancing national competitive advantage. Conversely, a nation that enjoys competitive advantage will find it diminishes if the elements cease to work positively.

3.1 Analysing the diamond

Exam focus point

The diamond, like Porter's 'five forces' is an important model. However, you need to be prepared to apply it in your exam. The May 2005 exam took an unusual approach to the topic. In a 25-mark question, you had to use Porter's diamond from the perspective of a **government** trying to attract inward investment. 7 marks were available for knowledge alone. In November 2005 you were asked if a company might gain competitive advantage as a result of being based in a certain country. The November 2007 exam took a more straightforward approach and asked what characteristics and factors a company would look for in a country when deciding where to open an overseas operation. Remember, however, to make sure that the factors you suggest are relevant to the type of organisation described in the scenario.

3.1.1 Factor conditions

Factor conditions are a country's endowment of inputs to production.

- Human resources (skills, motivation, industrial relations)
- Physical resources (land, minerals, climate, location relative to other nations)
- Knowledge (scientific and technical know-how, educational institutions)
- Capital (amounts available for investment, how it is deployed)
- Infrastructure (transport, communications, housing)

Porter distinguishes between:

(a) **Basic factors:** natural resources, climate, semiskilled and unskilled labour. Basic factors are inherited, or at best their creation involves little investment.

(b) **Advanced factors** include modern digital communications, highly educated personnel research laboratories and so forth. They are necessary to achieve high order competitive advantages such as differentiated products and proprietary production technology.

Inappropriate decisions and economic policy, in particular, can lead to erosion of advantageous factor conditions. This is particularly true of advanced factor conditions, which require significant investment, but even the advantage provided by basic physical factors can be eroded if markets change significantly. For example, there is plenty of coal left under England but it is difficult to work underground and open-cast extraction is politically unacceptable because of its environmental effects.

Point to note

> An abundance of factors is not enough. It is the efficiency with which they are deployed that matters. The former USSR had an abundance of natural resources and a fairly well educated workforce, but was an economic catastrophe.

3.1.2 Demand conditions: the home market

The **home market determines how firms perceive, interpret and respond to buyer needs.** This information puts pressure on firms to innovate and provides a launch pad for global ambitions.

(a) There are **no cultural impediments** to communication.

(b) The **segmentation** of the home market shapes a firm's priorities: companies will be successful globally in segments which are similar to the home market.

(c) **Sophisticated and demanding buyers** set standards. ('The British are known for gardening, and British firms are world class in garden tools.')

(d) **Anticipatory buyer needs:** if consumer needs are expressed in the home market earlier than in the world market, the firm benefits from experience.

(e) The **rate of growth**. Slow growing home markets do not encourage the adoption of state of the art technology.

(f) **Early saturation** of the home market will encourage a firm to export.

(g) Serving a substantial home market allows the attainment of economies of scale.

Advantage here can be eroded if a gap emerges between local and foreign demand.

3.1.3 Related and supporting industries

Competitive success in one industry is linked to success in related industries. Domestic suppliers are preferable to foreign suppliers, as 'proximity of managerial and technical personnel, along with cultural similarity, tends to facilitate free and open information flow' at an early stage. However, it is easy for this aspect of the diamond to lose its advantage if individual companies do not remain competitive or mutually supportive. See below for a case study on the situation in Italy.

3.1.4 Firm strategy, structure and rivalry

Structure. National cultural factors create certain tendencies to orientate business people to certain industries. German firms, according to Porter, have a strong showing in 'industries with a high technical content'.

Strategy. Industries in different countries have different **time horizons**, funding needs and so forth.

(a) **National capital markets** set different goals for performance. In some countries, banks are the main source of capital, not equity shareholders.

(b) When an industry faces difficult times, it **can either innovate within the industry**, to sustain competitive position or **shift resources from one industry to another** (eg diversification).

Domestic rivalry is important because:

- With little domestic rivalry, firms are happy to rely on the home market
- Tough domestic rivals teach a firm about competitive success
- Each rival can try a different strategic approach

If rivalry collapses, perhaps because of consolidation, standards are likely to slip, reducing competitiveness.

3.1.5 Losing competitive advantage

It is important to remember that the factors which create competitive advantage are dynamic, and so over time they may deteriorate eroding a nation's competitive advantage.

- Factor conditions may deteriorate due to a lack of investment in technology or education.
- Demand conditions may deteriorate due to a recession or deflationary government policies.
- Supporting clusters may collapse as firms diversify and therefore stop concentrating on their own business.

3.2 Influencing the diamond

3.2.1 Interactions between the determinants

The factors in the diamond are interrelated. Competitive advantage rarely rests on only one element of the diamond.

(a) **Related industries** affect **demand conditions** for an industry. An example from the context of international marketing is piggy-back exporting in which an exporting company also exports some of the products of related industries.

(b) **Domestic rivalry** can encourage the **creation of more specialised supplier industries.**

Porter says that a nation's competitive industries are **clustered**. Porter believes clustering to be a key to national competitive advantage. A cluster is a linking of industries through relationships which are either vertical (buyer-supplier) or horizontal (common customers, technology, skills). For example, the UK financial services industry is clustered in London.

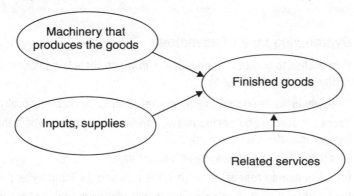

The **individual** firm will be more likely to succeed internationally if there is a **supporting cluster.** Such a cluster can lead to lower costs or the achievement of differentiation; the presence of advanced factors such as skilled labour and digital infrastructure; the transfer of expertise; and a degree of vertical integration through the development of network relationships among the organisations concerned.

3.2.2 Government policy

Porter also points out the importance of **government policy** in nurturing all four of the diamond factors by means of education, subsidy and the provision of services. He also reminds us that **chance** plays an important part.

 Case Study

Lack-lustre clusters

Time was when the only thing more fashionable than an Italian suit was the cluster that made it.

The small companies that both competed and co-operated with each other in industrial districts all over Italy – some making shoes, some clothing and others machine tools – were regarded as an example to the rest of the world. Their flexibility contrasted with slow-moving manufacturers that depended on mass production and suffered heavily in the recession of the early 1990s.

The pendulum always swings back and it has done so viciously in the case of Italy's clusters. The country faces an industrial crisis caused by the high euro and competition from low-wage countries. Companies making footwear, textiles and leather goods – specialisms of some northern regions – struggle to compete against China.

The problem goes deeper than labour costs and an expensive currency. The clusters are showing their age as a way to organise businesses in a mature economy. Some have become conservative and inward-looking, more focused on finding outlets for goods they have traditionally made locally than designing and marketing innovative products.

While the Lira could be devalued and competition with China was restrained by trade barriers, any structural weaknesses among the 500,000 companies in Italy employing fewer than 20 people remained hidden.

Italy is trying to adjust. Many industrial companies outsource some production to eastern European countries such as Romania and Slovakia and to China. Some industrial districts have taken similar steps. The Montebelluna cluster of companies producing sports shoes set up an industrial park in Romania. But clusters that do everything from weaving cloth to making clothes can find it harder to discard local jobs and craft skills in favour of production abroad than bigger manufacturers which have less at stake.

Small companies that mainly interact with others in their district may also lack the expertise to manage a global supply network, a comparative advantage of big companies.

Above all, clusters face the problem of being rooted in craft industries rather than value-added services such as design and marketing. In the days when consumers were less demanding, if was sufficient to buy in such services from agencies in Milan and Rome. But they must now compete with rivals that focus all their efforts on services instead of manufacturing.

(John Gapper, *Financial Times*, 26 May 2005)

3.2.3 Overcoming lack of advantage

If a UK firm wishes to compete in an industry in which there is no national competitive advantage, it can take a number of steps to succeed.

(a)   **Compete in the most challenging market,** to emulate domestic rivalry and to obtain information.

(b)   **Spread research and development** activities to countries where there is an established research base or industry cluster already.

(c)   Be prepared to **invest heavily in innovation**.

(d)   **Invest in human resources**, both in the firm and the industry as a whole.

(e)   **Look out for new technologies** which will change the rules of the industry.

(f)   **Collaborate with foreign companies.** American motor companies successfully learned Japanese production techniques.

(g)   **Supply overseas companies**. Japanese car plants in the UK have encouraged greater quality in UK components suppliers.

(h)   **Source components from overseas**. In the UK crystal glass industry, many firms buy crystal glass from the Czech Republic, and do the cutting and design work themselves.

(i)   **Exert pressure on politicians** and opinion formers to create better conditions for the diamond to develop (eg in education).

 Question

National advantage

Learning outcome A(iii), A(iv)

The Republic of Albion, an island in the North East Atlantic inhabited by about 40m people, has a climate which is plagued by fog, damp and rain. Life is a battle to keep dry. In this battle, the Republic has set up 20 research institutes into 'Water and Aridity Studies'. A variety of companies compete in devising new ways of keeping houses (and their owners!) dry, involving advanced technology. A recent innovation is the ionising umbrella, with an electric field that drives away water particles. The country imports most of its raw materials. The water problem is so bad that the country has a network of canals taking surplus water to the sea, through a network of hydroelectric turbines.

What do you think are the possible competitive advantages of the industries of the Republic of Albion?

Answer

The only *basic* factor endowment appears to be rain. Advanced factors include the research institutes. The country also has very sophisticated demand conditions for umbrellas and water-proof items. There seems to be domestic competition in the industry. In addition to umbrellas, you would expect related industries (such as high-technology waterproof raincoats) to appear. The country's firms could compete successfully in global markets for waterproof materials.

It is possible that the country's inhabitants would also have certain expertise in building technologies (eg damp proofing) which could be exported to the construction industry. Finally hydro-electric turbines *might* be a source of advantage: but the amount of water-for-energy is so plentiful that only the simplest technology need be used to harness it.

3.3 The diamond and competitive strategy

Porter's description of the diamond is more a piece of positive economic theory than a useful strategic tool. Individual companies cannot rely on favourable diamond conditions to provide them with competitive advantage. Countries with extremely favourable national conditions still have their share of poor companies.

- In international trade it is essential to study and analyse environmental conditions within the **target nation**, as discussed earlier.

- The theory of the diamond is largely based on exporting manufacturing industry: it is less relevant to service industries and any industry that expands internationally by setting up local production or provision of services.

4 Competitor analysis   11/06

FAST FORWARD

> Firms should **analyse their competitors** and build models of how they might react based on their future goals, assumptions, capability and current situation.

Exam focus point

The November 2006 exam included a question on competitor analysis. The two requirements boiled down to explaining **why** it should be carried out and **how** it should be done. This structure is quite common and has wider applicability outside the exam. It is quite a good idea to approach any topic with these two question words in the forefront of your mind. This could form a useful basis for your revision, for example.

4.1 Who are competitors?

Key term

Competitive position is the market share, costs, prices, quality and accumulated experience of an entity or a product relative to competition.

In any market where there are significant competitors, the strategic decisions and marketing decisions made by a firm will often be partly a response to what a competitor has done. This is because competitors' autonomous policies and reactions to market developments have great influence on each firm's freedom of action and ultimately on its profitability. In its simplest form, competitor analysis will be concerned with the extent to which competition exists: this is clearly bound up with the relevance of product and industry life cycles.

Firms must be on the lookout for **potential competitors**, and the potential impact of competitor actions on their profits: for example, a competitor may introduce price cuts or aggressive advertising campaigns to increase market share, or launch a new product. Firms must be alert to these threats so that they can respond to them.

 Case Study

(a) The convergence of the technologies underlying imaging and communication is leading to a battle between computer manufacturers, games manufacturers and TV manufacturers to supply the environment of digital entertainment. Is the TV or the PC going to be the hub of the home entertainment system?

(b) In the UK, petrol companies have been wrong-footed by supermarkets, who now sell petrol.

A firm must **define who its current competitors actually are**. This group may be larger than is immediately apparent. *Coca-Cola*, for example, competes against the following.

- *Pepsi* in the Cola market, retailers' own brands.
- All other soft drinks.
- Tea and coffee.
- Coca-Cola's chief executive has declared that 'the main competitor is tap water: any other definition is too narrow'.

4.1.1 Types of competitor

Kotler lists four kinds of competition.

(a) **Brand competitors** are similar firms offering similar products: for example, *McDonald's* and *Burger King*.

(b) **Industry competitors** have similar products but are different in other ways, such as geographical market or range of products: for example, *Amazon* and *HMV*, or *British Airways* and *American Airways*.

(c) **Generic competitors** compete for the same disposable income with different products: for example, home improvements versus foreign vacations.

(d) **Form competitors** offer products which are technically significantly different, but satisfy the same needs: for example, manufacturers of matches and cigarette lighters.

4.2 Analysing competitors: the main issues

Key term

> **Competitor analysis** is the 'identification and quantification of the relative strengths and weaknesses (compared with competitors or potential competitors), which could be of significance in the development of a successful competitive strategy'.
>
> (CIMA *Official Terminology*)

An important initial variable is **industry structure**. A fragmented industry with many small players is unlikely to be highly competitive overall, since most firms will seek to pursue a **niche strategy**. The situation is the opposite in a consolidated industry, where a small number of firms are striving for a dominating market share and **cost leadership**. When a condition of **oligopoly** is reached, with just a few major players, competition will be restructured to anything but price, because of the well-known oligopolists' **kinked demand curve** phenomenon.

Some industries cannot easily be consolidated and the niche structure may continue indefinitely.

An organisation should look at four key factors when undertaking competitor analysis:

Factor	Comment
Competitor's goals (the firm as a whole and the business unit)	• What are the business's **stated financial goals**? What trade-offs are made between long-term and short-term objectives? • What is the competitor's attitude to **risk**? • Do **managerial beliefs** (eg that the firm should be a market leader) affect its goals? • **Organisation structure**: what is the relative status of functional areas? • What **incentive systems** are in place? • What are the **managers** like? Do they favour one particular type of strategy? • To what extent does the business **cross-subsidise** others in the group if the business is part of a group? What is the purpose of the business: to raise money for the group?
The **competitor's assumptions** about the industry	• What does a competitor believe to be its **relative position** in the industry (in terms of cost, product quality)? • Are there any **cultural or regional differences** that indicate the way managers are likely to respond? • What does the competitor believe about the future for the industry? • Does the competitor accept the industry's **'conventional wisdom'**?
The **competitor's current and potential situation and strategy**	• Distribution • Organisation • Operations • Research and engineering • Overall costs • Managerial ability • Marketing and selling • Products • Financial strengths
Competitor's capability	• The **competitor's core competences**. In other words, what does the competitor do distinctively well? • Does the competitor have the **ability to expand** in a particular market? • What competitive advantages and disadvantages does the competitor possess?

4.2.1 Competitor response profiles

All these are combined in a **competitor response profile**. This indicates the competitor's vulnerability and the right 'battleground' on which to fight.

Kotler lists four response profiles.

- The **laid back** competitor does not respond
- The **tiger** responds aggressively to all opposing moves
- The **selective** competitor reacts to some threats in some markets but not to all
- The **stochastic** competitor is unpredictable

The reasons for these observed profiles may be complex. An effort should be made to understand them and how they fit into the competitor's overall strategy.

The **strategic intelligence system** can collect information from the following sources.

- Financial statements
- Information from common customers and suppliers
- Inspection of a competitor's products
- Information from former employees
- Job advertisements

4.2.2 Competitive significance

Competition is likely to be intense when firms have strategic similarities in such matters as those below.

- Technology used
- Management skills
- Distribution channels
- Products offered
- Geographic coverage

Given when current products are dissimilar, similarities in other areas may well see new competition emerging, as for instance when *Marks & Spencer*, an own brand clothes retailer, started selling own brand food.

4.2.3 Exit barriers

Exit barriers are those which **prevent a firm from leaving an industry**, or increase the cost of so doing. Cost-related exit barriers include the following.

(a) **Vertically integrated companies** producing products for many markets. Exiting one market would not significantly alter its cost structure. In global commodity markets, inability to buy cheaply on spot markets can be a severe hindrance to competitive pricing, as is seen for example in the UK petrol market, where supermarkets have greater flexibility than the major integrated companies who are committed to selling their own oil through their own filling stations.

(b) **Common administrative costs** might be shared over a number of different businesses. This might result in a high overhead charge, but whilst the apportionment might turn one of the businesses into a loss, closing the business down might save little of the overhead expenditure.

Question

Competitor analysis

Learning outcome A(v)

Jot down a list of items of information that might be obtained from an environmental analysis of competitors. The list can be a long one!

Answer

(a) Who are the existing competitors? How much of the market do they hold in each segment of the markets (eg in each particular region or country?)

(b) Who are potential competitors? How soon might they enter the market?

(c) How profitable are existing competitors? What is their EPS, dividend yield, ROCE etc?

(d) What do the goals of each competitor appear to be, and what strategies have they adopted so far?

(e) What products/services do they sell? How do they compare with the organisation's own products or services?

(f) How broad is their product line? (eg Are they 'up-market high quality, or down-market low quality, low price and high volume producers?)

(g) What is their distribution network?

(h) What are their skills and weakness in direct selling, advertising, sales promotions, product design etc.

(i) What are their design skills or R&D skills? do they innovate or follow the market leader with new product ideas?

(j) What are their costs of sale and operational capabilities? With respect to equipment, technology, intellectual property etc?

(k) What are their general managerial capabilities? How do these compare with those of the organisation?

(l) Financial strengths and weaknesses. What is the debt position and financial gearing of each competitor? Do they have easy access to sources of new finance? What proportion of profits do they return in the business in order to finance growth?

(m) How is each competitor organised? How much decentralisation of authority do they allow to operating divisions, and so how flexible or independent can each of the operating divisions be?

(n) Does the competitor have a good spread or portfolio of activities? What is the risk profile of each competitor?

(o) Does any competitor have a special competitive advantage – eg a unique government contract or special access to government authorities?

(p) Does any competitor show signs of changing strategy to increase competition to the market?

5 Accounting for competitors

> The **management accountant's techniques** are useful in competitor analysis (eg by analysing how a competitor's cost structure influence the options available to it) and by modelling the impact of different strategies.

Competitive strategies can be analysed in financial terms, as we know, using simple techniques such as NPV. However, simple models really require a consideration of likely competitive response if they are to be useful in forecasting the likely return on a strategic investment.

5.1 Competitor response

In practice, anticipated **competitor actions** are dealt with indirectly in the planning process. The management accounting system may not be able to identify those deficiencies in performance arising from competitors' activities **after** the plan has been implemented.

A few detergent companies own many of the brands offered to the market. This deters competitors. How do you evaluate, financially, a strategy such as this?

(a) The expenditure to **maintain market share** and sustain brands is a known cost. However the benefit is not known exactly.

(b) There might be a variety of **assumptions** about market size, market shares and the profit assumptions of a number of the scenarios identified.

(c) There are problems with forecasting the future cash flows of market share estimates.

A useful approach to take is to **analyse the anticipated loss** caused by **not** undertaking a particular course of action: the present value of this loss becomes, effectively, the maximum size of the investment. For example, A Ltd is worried that a competitor will shift the market dynamics from I to II.

	Market state	
	I	*II*
A Ltd's market share	20%	15%
Present value of future cash flows	£1m	£800,000

(a) There is a present value loss of £200,000. If a marketing manager suggested that spending £100,000 would see off the competitor, this action would be worth taking.

(b) There is still the problem of estimating the difference between market states I and II: after all, the marketing campaign might deter **other** competitors, or create an increase in demand. It is also impossible to be certain that the competitor will in fact be deterred by an advertising campaign.

5.2 Competitor modelling

5.2.1 Sources of information

Data sources include: published accounts and annual reports, market research reviews and reports (eg Economist Intelligence Unit); investment analysts' notes; industry experts and consultants; suppliers, shared customers, the competitor's marketing strategy; public communications (magazines, journals and newsletters) and the internet.

A great deal can be gleaned from using one's own company as a model, and adjusting it for significant differences in competitors' businesses. For example, a firm might make some sub-components in-house, whereas a competitor might buy them on the open market.

5.2.2 Cost structures

Important differences between firms include the following.

- Absolute cost levels
- The proportion of fixed to variable costs
- The strategic impact of outsourcing decisions on competitive flexibility
- The sales price in relation to costs, and unit costs. (This will affect a firm's ability to respond to a competitors' price cut.)
- Not all businesses require the same rate of return
- Exit costs. (If a firm has high exit costs, it is likely to stay in an industry and compete aggressively, rather than leaving the industry.)

5.2.3 Barriers to entry

Competitor analysis should also consider the costs that any potential new entrant to the industry will incur to overcome barriers to entry. (We discussed the nature of barriers to entry earlier in this chapter when we were considering Porter's five forces model.)

Comparing entry costs with the present value of the returns the entrant could achieve will indicate the likelihood of new entrants. If revenues exceed costs the market is financially attractive to new entrants; if costs exceed revenues the threat of new entrants is reduced.

Exam focus point

It is important to remember competitor analysis does not simply involve finding out information about competitors. An organisation should also consider how it can use the information it has gained to shape its own strategies.

If the market appears attractive to new entrants, an organisation should compare the cost of raising new barriers (for example, by spending on a brand) to the potential loss of revenue if a new competitor does enter the market. If the potential loss of revenue from a new competitor entering the market exceeds the cost of raising new barriers, the organisation should look at raising new barriers to entry.

6 E-commerce and the Internet

 FAST FORWARD

> The **Internet** is transforming much of the way business is conducted. This is especially true of business-to-business commerce.

6.1 Electronic commerce

Electronic commerce is the latest example of the impact of technology on global markets.

Key terms

Electronic commerce can be defined as using a computer network to speed up all stages of the business process, from design to buying, selling and delivery. The process is fairly familiar between companies, but less so between retailer and customer.

The **Internet** is the sum of all the separate networks (or stand-alone computers) run by organisations and individuals alike. (It has been described as an **international telephone service** for computers.)

We deal with e-commerce in detail later in this Study Text.

6.2 Growth of the Internet

60% of households in the USA and 50% of households in the UK had Internet access by the end of 2002. A critical factor in the long-run expansion of the Internet is its use today by children, the adult consumers of tomorrow. The Internet is not expanding at the same rate in every sphere of business. The rate of growth is influenced by a number of factors.

(a)   The degree to which the customer can be persuaded to believe that using the Internet will **deliver some added-value** – in terms of quickness, simplicity and price.

(b)   Whether there are 'costs' which the **customer** has to bear – not exclusively 'costs' in the financial sense, but also such psychological 'costs' as the isolated online shopping experience.

(c)   The **market segment** to which the individual belongs. The Internet is largely the preserve of younger, more affluent, more technologically competent individuals with above-average amounts of disposable income.

(d)   The frequency of supplier/customer **contact** required.

(e)   The availability of **incentives** which might stimulate Internet acceptance. For example, interest rates on bank accounts which are higher than those available through conventional banks (Egg), the absence of any charges (Freeserve), the creation of penalties for over-the-counter transactions (Abbey National), and the expectations of important customers (IBM's relationships with its suppliers).

 Case Study

In many areas, users are proactively switching to the Internet. When *Lloyds TSB* first developed Internet banking facilities, they were not publicised but customers were seeking it out and joining at the rate of 380 accounts per day. At the same time, customers are not yet ready to abandon the channels they used in the past: even with Internet and telephone banking, many still visit their bank branches regularly.

Arguably, the most profitable pure Internet companies, as well as the most influential, will be **business-to-business 'infomediaries'** (the term coined by John Hagel of McKinsey), because they can exploit the Internet's most salient characteristics.

(a)   **The Internet shifts power from sellers to buyers by reducing switching costs.** Buyers may feel overwhelmed by this power, but they typically want one-stop shopping, with information they believe and advice they can trust.

(b)   **The Internet reduces transaction costs and thus stimulates economic activity.** According to one US calculation, a banking transaction via the Internet costs 1 cent, 27 cents at an ATM (automated teller machine) and 52 cents over the telephone. Infomediaries can enable significant savings to be enjoyed by small-scale or even single customers.

(c)   **The speed, range and accessibility of information on the Internet, and the low cost of capturing and distributing it, create new commercial possibilities.** Infomediaries can focus on particular product/service supply issues; by doing so, they attract specialised buyers and sellers; in turn they acquire more expertise which generates continued customer loyalty and participation.

The major growth so far in the field of e-commerce has concentrated on the **Business-to-Business** (B2B) sector.

(a)   **Major companies** are setting themselves up as e-businesses. In November 1999, both Ford and General Motors announced that they were switching a major portion of their procurement and supply chain management to the web.

(b)   IBM now requires **all its suppliers to quote and invoice electronically** – no paper documentation is permitted.

(c)   Many firms are using the Internet to exploit the **transparency of supplier prices**, and to maximise their purchasing benefits from the availability of world-wide sourcing. Robert Bosch, the German kitchen appliance manufacturer, **requires all its suppliers to have web-based catalogues** and prices.

(d)   Companies are also increasing their customer service through the web. Dell, the computer company, has created **extranets for its major business customers**, enabling them to receive personalised customer support, their own price lists, and some free value-added services.

The Internet has the potential to turn business upside down and inside out, to fundamentally change the way companies operate, whether in high-tech or metal-bashing. This goes far beyond buying and selling over the Internet, or e-commerce, and deep into the processes and culture of an enterprise.

Some companies are using the Internet to make direct connections with their customers for the first time. Others are using secure Internet connections to intensify relations with some of their trading partners, and using the Internet's reach and ubiquity to request quotes or sell off perishable stocks of goods or services by auction.

The Internet is helping companies to lower costs dramatically across their supply and demand chains, take their customer service into a different league, enter new markets, create additional revenue streams and redefine their business relationships.

Some writers argue that companies can be either 'brick' or 'click' businesses, but they can't be both: if they are a 'brick' operation – ie they have real premises, real shops, real factories and warehouses – then their culture will make it impossible for them fully to assimilate the drastic changes required in order to operate successfully in a 'click' environment. It is no accident, therefore, that companies like Prudential Assurance have initiated their Internet activities through stand-alone enterprises, using newly-recruited people situated in geographically-distinctive locations.

The Internet provides opportunities to automate tasks which would previously have required more costly interaction with the organisation. These have often been called low-touch or zero-touch approaches.

Chapter Roundup

- A market is a group of customers with needs to satisfy. An industry is the companies that use similar technologies to satisfy those needs. For any industry, **five forces** determine its profitability: 'threat of new entrants, substitute products, customers, suppliers and the intensity of competition'.

- **Trading relationships** have strategic impact and, while mutual benefit may be desirable, they must be firmly managed.

- Industries may display a **lifecycle**: this will affect and interact with the five forces.

- The continuing process of **globalisation** is driven by the convergence of markets and the lifting of trade restrictions. It brings both increased opportunities and increased threats. Global corporations aspire to transcend national loyalties, but they tend to have identifiable national bases.

- The **EU** is the most integrated of the regional trading organisations, aspiring to a single market in goods, services and factors of production.

- The **World Trade Organisation** was set up to promote free trade and resolve disputes between trading partners.

- Four factors support **competitive success** in a nation's industries: factor conditions, demand conditions, related and supporting industries, and firm strategy, structure and rivalry.

- Firms should **analyse their competitors** and build models of how they might react based on their future goals, assumptions, capability and current situation.

- The **management accountant's techniques** are useful in competitor analysis (eg by analysing how a competitor's cost structure influence the options available to it) and by modelling the impact of different strategies.

- The **Internet** is transforming much of the way business is conducted. This is especially true of business-to-business commerce.

1   Distinguish 'market' from 'industry'

2   **Fill in the blanks** in the statement below, using the words in the box.

(1) .... competitive forces influence the state of competition in an (2) .... , which collectively determine the (3) .... of the industry as a whole:

- the threat of (4) .... to the industry
- the threat of (5) ....
- the (6) .... power of (7) ....
- the bargaining power of (8) ....
- the (9) .... amongst current (10) ....

•	industry	•	five	•	profit	•	new entrants
•	bargaining	•	competitors	•	substitutes	•	rivalry
•	customers	•	suppliers				

3   Define a switching cost.

4   List three factors encouraging the globalisation of world trade

....

....

....

5   The theory of .... suggests that .... is the best way to promote global economic growth and domestic prosperity.

6   Fill in the diagram of Porter's diamond

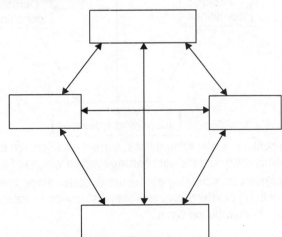

7   What would you find in a competitor response profile?

8   How can IT raise entry barriers?

1   The market comprises the customers or potential customers who have needs which are satisfied by a product or service.

   The industry comprises those firms which use a particular competence, technology, product or service to satisfy customer needs.

2   (1) five (2) industry (3) profit (4) new entrants (5) substitutes (6) bargaining (7) customers (8) suppliers (9) rivalry (10) competitors

3   Switching costs refer to the costs (time, money, convenience) that a customer would have to incur by switching from one supplier's products to another's.

4   Financial factors eg Third world debt. Often the lenders require the initiation of economic reforms as a condition of the loan.

   Country/continent alliances, such as that between the UK and USA, which fosters trade and other phenomena such as tourism.

   Legal factors such as patents and trade marks, which encourage the development of technology and design.

   Stock markets trading in international commodities.

   The level of protectionist measures.

5   Comparative advantage, free trade

6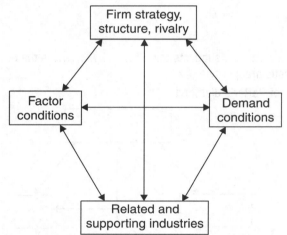

7   An analysis of competitors' goals, assumptions, current situation, strategy and capabilities. This indicates the competitors' vulnerability and the right battleground on which to fight

8   IT can raise entry barriers by increasing economies of scale, raising the capital cost of entry (by requiring a similar investment in IT) or effectively colonising distribution channels by tying customers and suppliers into the supply chain or distribution chain.

Now try the question below from the Exam Question Bank			
Number	**Level**	**Marks**	**Time**
Q5	Examination	25	45 mins

Customers and suppliers

Introduction

In order to fulfil the company's mission and maximise long-term owner value, management activities will be influenced to a greater or lesser extent by **customers** and **suppliers**, some of the key **stakeholders** in the organisation.

Customers' demands will dictate decisions for investment in new products, development of existing ones and setting-up of new outlets. They will also affect the standards adopted for quality control, and the extent to which they can be enticed away by competitors' products will affect the planned advertising spend.

Suppliers' and distributors' demands will affect the timing and amount of production.

In this chapter we have included an overview of some key **marketing** issues. Detailed knowledge of marketing concepts and techniques is not required by the *Business Strategy* syllabus, but it is worth presenting some background to the syllabus material.

Topic list	Learning outcomes	Syllabus references	Ability required
1 The supply chain	B(iv)	B4	Analysis
2 Marketing	B(iv)	B4	Analysis
3 Marketing: products, customers and segmentation	B(iv)	B4	Analysis
4 Reviewing the customer portfolio	B(iv)	B4	Analysis

1 The supply chain

FAST FORWARD

Whatever the exact nature of supplier bargaining power, many firms aim to build closer relationships for the sake of efficiency.

A firm can make strategic gains from managing **stakeholder relationships**, such as those with customers and suppliers.

Supply chain management is about optimising the activities of companies working together to produce goods and services. Supply chain relationships are becoming increasingly more co-operative rather than adversarial.

Many multinational enterprises (MNEs) have been getting larger. Some writers are arguing that the trend will continue – so that for many sectors there will be relatively few players of world class. In the car industry there have been a number of mergers and takeovers. Some have been successful, such as Renault's takeover of Japan's Nissan. Others have been less successful, such as the merger between Daimler of Germany and Chrysler of the US to form Daimler Chrysler.

There have been, at the same time, much **closer links** with companies in the supply chain in order to extract best value for money and reduce stockholdings. This has had major consequences on the distribution methods of companies in these supply chains, delivering to their customers on a **just in time** (JIT) basis. The **adversarial,** arms length relationship with a supplier has been replaced by one which is characterised by closer co-operation.

The change in supply chain linkage is demonstrated in the following model (taken from *Monczka*).

1.1 Supply chain model

The supply chain is the network of organisations involved in the different processes and activities that are necessary to transform goods from their original raw materials into finished goods and services in order to produce value for the ultimate customer.

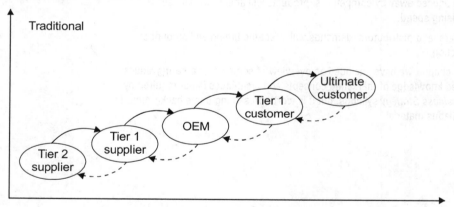

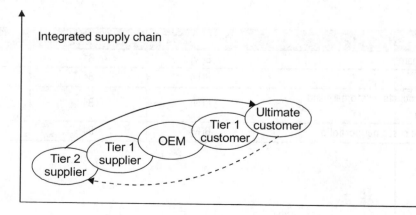

Historically, businesses in the supply chain operated relatively independently of one another to create value for an ultimate customer. Independence was maintained by buffers of material, capacity and lead-times. This is represented in the 'Traditional' model shown above.

Market and competitive demands are now, however, **compressing lead times** and businesses are reducing inventories and excess capacity. Linkages between businesses in the supply chain must therefore become much tighter. This new condition is shown in the 'Integrated supply chain' model.

Monczka further claims that there seems to be increasing recognition that, in the future, it will be **whole supply chains** which will compete and not just individual firms. This will continue to have a great impact upon distribution methods.

Key term

> **Supply chain management** is about optimising the activities of companies working together to produce goods and services, to be responsive to customers demands and reliable in the delivery of them.

1.2 Supply chain management

Supply chain management (SCM) is a means by which the firm aims to manage the chain from input resources to the consumer. It involves the following.

(a)   Reduction in the number of suppliers

(b)   Reduction in customers served, in some cases, for the sake of focus, and concentration of the company's resources on customers of high potential value

(c)   Price and inventory co-ordination. Firms co-ordinate their price and inventory policies to avoid problems and bottlenecks caused by short-term surges in demand, such as promotions

(d)   Linked computer systems – electronic data interchange saves on paperwork and warehousing expense

(e)   Early supplier involvement in product development and component design

(f)   Logistics design. Hewlett-Packard restructured its distribution system by enabling certain product components to be added at the distribution warehouse rather than at the central factory, for example user-manuals which are specific to the market (ie user manuals in French would be added at the French distribution centre)

(g)   Joint problem solving

(h)   Supplier representative on site

Point to note

> The aim is to co-ordinate the whole chain, from raw material suppliers to end customers. The chain should be considered as a **network** rather than a **pipeline** – a network of vendors support a network of customers, with third parties such as transport firms helping to link the companies.

Lean supply chain

The idea of supply chain management can be extended to the concept of the lean supply chain. The objective of developing a lean supply chain is to completely remove waste from the process in order to achieve a competitive advantage.

Advantages	Counter arguments
– Reduced cost	Leanness focuses on reducing cost rather than improving quality. Too much concentration on cost reduction may actually worsen quality.
– Improved quality (and lower costs of re-working and quality problems)	
– Reduced inventories	There may be insufficient slack in the system to deal with fluctuations in damage.

Advantages	Counter arguments
– Shorter lead times	Lean supply chain consists of a series of preferred supplier relationships. These may be akin to monopolies, so good for firms involved but not for the consumer, because the market operates most efficiently under perfect competition.

 Case Study

The Hong Kong based export trading company, *Li & Fung*, takes the following approach to its manufacturing supply chain.

'Say we get an order from a European retailer to produce 10,000 garments. It's not a simple matter of our Korean office sourcing Korean products or our Indonesian office sourcing Indonesian products. For the customer we might decide to buy yarn from a Korean producer but have it woven and dyed in Taiwan. So we pick the yarn and ship it to Taiwan. The Japanese have the best zippers and buttons, but they manufacture them mostly in China. Okay, so we go to *YKK*, a big Japanese zipper manufacturer and we order the right zippers from their Chinese plants. Then we determine that, because of quotas and labour conditions, the best place to make the garments is Thailand. So we ship everything there. And because the customer needs quick delivery, we may divide the order across five factories in Thailand. Effectively, we are customising the value chain to best meet the customer's needs.

'Five weeks after we have received the order, 10,000 garments arrive on the shelves in Europe, all looking like they came from one factory with colours, for example, perfectly matched. Just think about the logistics and the co-ordination.

'This is a new type of value added, a truly global product that has never been seen before. The label may say "Made in Thailand", but it's not a Thai product. We dissect the manufacturing process and look for the best solution to each step. We're not asking which country can do the best job overall. Instead, we're pulling apart the value chain and optimising each step – and we're doing it globally…. The classic supply-chain manager in retailing is *Marks & Spencer*. They don't own any factories, but they have a huge team that goes into the factories and works with the management.'

(Harvard Business Review)

The importance of context

Managing the supply chain **varies from company to company**. A company such as Unilever will provide the same margarine to both Tesco and Sainsbury. The way in which the product is delivered, transactions are processed and other parts of the relationship are managed will be different since these competing supermarket chains have their own ways of operating. The focus will need to be on customer interaction, account management, after sales service and order processing.

A supplier that 'knows' what his customers want does not have to guess or wait until the customer places an order. It will be able to better plan its own delivery systems. The potential for using the **Internet** to allow customers and suppliers to acquire up to date information about forecast needs and delivery schedules is a very recent development, but one which is being used by an increasing number of companies.

The greatest changes in supply chain management have taken place in the implementation of **software applications**. Managers today have a wider choice of systems with quick implementation times – important in a competitive market where a new supply chain system is required. Supply chains at local, regional and global level are often managed simultaneously, via a standardised infrastructure that nevertheless allows for local adaptation where this is important.

- A leading European manufacturer has said: 'We must localise those part of our supply chain that face the customer and regionalise all other parts of our supply chain to lower costs and improve speed of operations'.

- *PricewaterhouseCoopers* ran full page newspaper advertisements promoting its supply chain consultancy services, which indicates the importance of supply chain management to most companies. The text of one such advertisement reads: 'When it comes to supply chain management, there's one universal truth: every customer is unique. What may be right for one, may not be for another…. We're working on some of the toughest supply chain problems all around the world. Reinventing strategy, optimising processes and applying new technologies intelligently. All to help companies improve their ability to operate globally and serve customers locally. With 150,000 people working in 50 different countries, we can make the world seem like a pretty small place'.

  This may contain more than its fair share of buzzwords, but it does illustrate the issues involved: the importance of individual customers, strategy and technology, and the ability of a large company to deliver services on a global basis because it has the resources.

As well as tactical issues, what might be the underlying strategic concerns?

(a) Close partnerships are needed with suppliers whose components are essential for the business unit.

(b) A firm should choose suppliers with a distinctive competence similar to its own. A firm selling 'cheap and cheerful' goods will want suppliers who are able to supply 'cheap and cheerful' subcomponents.

Problems with the **partnership approach** to supply chain management are these.

- Each partner needs to remain competitive in the long term
- There is a possible **loss of flexibility**
- The **relative bargaining power** may make partnership unnecessary
- Arguments about sharing profits

2 Marketing

FAST FORWARD

Marketing as a concept of the way business should be done must be distinguished from marketing as a business function. Operational marketing is the best developed form of the latter.

2.1 The nature of marketing

You may have noticed that in the world of corporate strategy, the terminology used is sometimes rather imprecise. An important area of potential confusion arises in the relationship between 'strategic management' and 'marketing'. A number of ideas and models are shared between the two activities (to the extent that they are, in fact, separate activities), and many marketing authors write as though 'marketing' encompasses all of 'strategic management'. We reject this view: for our purposes, 'marketing' is an important area of business activity that makes a particular contribution to strategic management, but is ultimately subordinate to it.

What is marketing?

Marketing is the management process responsible for identifying, anticipating and satisfying customer requirements profitably. *(Chartered Institute of Marketing)*

While useful in its way, the CIM definition is not the only one we might consider; in fact there are many. Here is what *Dibb, Simkin, Pride and Ferrel* have to say:

Marketing consists of individual and organisational activities that facilitate and expedite satisfying exchange relationships in a dynamic environment through the creation, distribution, promotion and pricing of goods, services and ideas.

This is a more detailed definition and has the advantage of being very specific about the activities it includes under the umbrella term 'marketing'.

Finally, let us consider what Philip Kotler says

'The marketing concept holds that the key to achieving organisational goals lies in determining the needs and wants of target markets and delivering the desired satisfactions more efficiently and effectively than the competition.

Kotler's statement is very important because it identifies four key concepts in marketing:

(a)   Identifying **target markets**.
(b)   Determining the **needs and wants** of those markets.
(c)   Delivering a **product offering** which meets the needs and wants of those markets.
(d)   Meeting the needs of the market **profitability**.

2.2 Models of marketing

The material below is taken from the introduction to the syllabus for the Chartered Institute of Marketing (CIM) qualification. It therefore represents an authoritative view of just what marketing is.

'The type, or model, of marketing practised in any organisation depends on a number of factors, not least of which are the activities to be performed according to the nature of the business and the organisation's dominant orientation. Marketing activities in organisations can be grouped broadly into four roles.

(a)   **Sales support**: the emphasis in this role is essentially reactive: marketing supports the direct sales force. It may include activities such as telesales or telemarketing, responding to inquiries, co-ordinating diaries, customer database management, organising exhibitions or other sales promotions, and administering agents. These activities usually come under a sales and marketing director or manager.

(b)   **Marketing communications**: the emphasis in this role is more proactive: marketing promotes the organisation and its product or service at a tactical level. It typically includes activities such as providing brochures and catalogues to support the sales force.

(c)   **Operational marketing**: the emphasis in this role is for marketing to support the organisation with a co-ordinated range of marketing activities including marketing research; brand management; product development and management; corporate and marketing communications; and customer relationship management. Given this breadth of activities, planning is also a function usually performed in this role but at an operational or functional level.

(d)   **Strategic marketing**: the emphasis in this role is for marketing to contribute to the creation of competitive strategy. As such, it is practised in customer-focused and larger organisations. In a large or diversified organisation, it may also be responsible for the coordination of marketing departments or activities in separate business units.

Operational marketing activities.

- Research and analysis
- Contributing to strategy and marketing planning
- Managing brands
- Implementing marketing programmes
- Measuring effectiveness
- Managing marketing teams

The operational marketing role, where it exists, will be performed by a marketing function in a business.'

So, what is the relationship between marketing and strategic management? The two are closely linked since there can be no corporate plan which does not involve products/services and customers.

Corporate strategic plans aim to guide the overall development of an organisation. Marketing planning is subordinate to corporate planning but makes a significant contribution to it and is concerned with many of the same issues. The marketing department is probably the most important source of information for the development of corporate strategy. The corporate audit of product/market strengths and weaknesses, and much of its external environmental analysis is directly informed by the **marketing audit**.

Specific marketing strategies will be determined within the overall corporate strategy. To be effective, these plans will be interdependent with those for other functions of the organisation.

(a) The **strategic** component of marketing planning focuses on the direction which an organisation will take in relation to a specific market, or set of markets, in order to achieve a specified set of objectives.

(b) Marketing planning also requires an **operational** component that defines tasks and activities to be undertaken in order to achieve the desired strategy. The **marketing plan** is concerned uniquely with **products** and **markets**.

Marketing management aims to ensure the company is pursuing effective policies to promote its products, markets and distribution channels. This involves exercising strategic control of marketing, and the means to apply strategic control is known as the **marketing audit**. Not only is the marketing audit an important aspect of **marketing control**, it can be used to provide much information and analysis for the **corporate planning process**.

2.3 Marketing audit

Key term

> The CIM defines a **marketing audit** as 'a systematic assessment of the organisation's marketing objectives, strategies, organisation and performance'.

The CIM definition goes on to say that the first aspect of the marketing audit is an audit of the environment. We know this as the **environmental analysis** stage of the rational model. However, the rest of the CIM's discussion is uncontentious, focussing, as it does, on purely marketing matters: strategy, organisation, systems, productivity and functions.

Cannon uses the phrase 'marketing audit' in an obscure and entirely different way, mostly focussing on competitor analysis. He suggests five steps.

(a) **Define the market** in terms of products, benefits, size, growth, successful strategies and requirements for success.

(b) **Determine performance differentials** in terms of competitors, products and customers, to identify subsectors of the market which might provide an entry point for new entrants, or an area to expand into.

(c) **Determine differences in competitive programmes** by examining competitors' existing products and markets and their likely future moves.

(d) **Profile competitors' strategies** and compare them with the firm to identify the main threats to the firm.

(e) **Determine the strategic planning structure**; that is, organise the internal strategic planning effort.

3 Marketing: products, customers and segmentation

The strategy of a business is often orientated towards its customers, it source of revenue. Marketing, as a business function, seeks to identify customers and their needs, and to encourage them to buy. Segments are groups of customers with similar needs that can be **targeted** with a distinctively **positioned** marketing **mix**.

3.1 Products and customers

Key term

> A **product** *(goods or services)* is anything that satisfies a need or want. It is not a 'thing' with 'features' but a package of benefits. For example a CD and hifi system provide recorded music, and other benefits. From most customers' point of view, the electronics inside are not important as long as they are reliable and deliver a certain quality of sound.

The immediate task of a marketing manager with respect to the **products** of the organisation may be any of the following.

- To create demand (where none exists)
- To develop a latent demand
- To revitalise a sagging demand
- To attempt to smooth out (synchronise) uneven demand
- To sustain a buoyant demand (maintenance marketing)
- To reduce excess demand

Many products might satisfy the same customer need. On what basis might a customer choose?

(a) **Customer value** is the customer's estimate of how far a product or service goes towards satisfying his or her need(s).

(b) Every product has a cost, and so the customer makes a trade-off between the expenditure and the value offered.

(c) According to Kotler a customer must feel he or she gets a better deal from buying an item than by any of the alternatives.

Companies must make a distinction between the **customer** and the **consumer**.

(a) The **customer** is the person or organisation buying the product or service. For example, a cat's owner will buy food for the cat.

(b) The **consumer** is the person who uses the product or receives the benefit of the service. In the case of cat food, the cat is the consumer, not the purchaser.

Marketing has a role in the organisation's **value chain**. The end result of a value chain is a product or service, whose price must in some way equate with the **customer's perception of value**, but whose cost allows the producer a **margin or profit**.

3.2 The importance of developing a market orientation in strategic planning

The importance of developing a market orientation to strategic planning is implicit in the marketing concept. An organisation commits itself to supplying what customers need. As those needs change, so too must the goods or services which are produced. In other words, **marketing orientation enables a firm to adapt to the environment**.

(a) By applying the marketing concept to product design the company might hope to make more attractive products, hence to achieve sustained sales growth and so make higher profits.

(b) Profits do not only come from individual transactions with customers, but also from the customer's propensity to deal with the firm rather than its competitors.

Strategic planning involves making decisions about the choice of **product-market strategies** – developing new products and new markets that will fill the '**profit gap**'. A marketing orientation should help planners to identify more successfully what products or markets would earn good profits for the organisation.

Having decided on a competitive strategy a firm must then decide on the following.

- Which target markets should be selected for development.
- How the firm should offer its product or service in comparison with the offerings of competitors.
- How to establish a **marketing system** and organisation for the firm.
- How to develop a **marketing plan** and then implement and control it.

3.3 Buyer behaviour

FAST FORWARD

The decision to make a purchase can be very simple, very complex or somewhere between the two. Buyers do not always proceed rationally, thought the motivation of industrial buyers may be more logical than that of consumers.

In marketing, a market is defined in terms of its **buyers** or **potential buyers**.

- **Consumer markets** (eg for soap powder, washing machines, TV sets, clothes)
- **Industrial markets** (eg for machine tools, construction equipment)
- **Government markets** (eg for armaments, and, in the UK, medical equipment)
- **Reseller markets**
- **Export markets**

3.3.1 Consumer goods

Consumer goods are in such a form that they can be used by the consumer without the need for any further commercial processing. Consumer goods are further classified according to the method by which they are purchased.

- **Convenience goods**
- **Shopping goods**
- **Speciality goods**

If an article has close substitutes, is purchased regularly in small amounts of low unit value, and the customer insists on buying it with the minimum of inconvenience, the article is called a **convenience good**. Convenience goods are everyday purchases such as toothpaste, bread, coffee, chocolate etc, and are likely to be produced by several manufacturers. Promoting a unique image for the product, for example by **branding**, is therefore important.

Shopping goods are goods for which customers are more discriminating. They usually have a higher unit value than convenience goods and are bought less frequently, usually from a specialist outlet with a wider range on offer. **Examples** of shopping goods are cars, furniture, hi-fi equipment, many clothes, household appliances such as washing machines and cookers.

When a manufacturer, either by product design or advertising, has become associated in the public mind with a particular product (eg Rolls Royce cars, Wedgwood pottery) the article produced is no longer a shopping good, but a **speciality good**, possessing a unique character which will make a customer go out of his way to ask for it by name and find a dealer who sells it.

3.3.2 Industrial or business-to-business markets

In industrial markets, the customer is another firm, such as for the sale of machine tools or consultancy advice. The industrial market, more than the consumer market, is influenced by the general state of the economy and the government's economic policy (see Chapter 4).

The demand for industrial goods and services is derived from the demand for the product or service to which they contribute. For example, the demand for aluminium is in part derived from the demand for cans, which might itself be derived from demand for the beer with which the cans will be filled.

Industrial buyers are more **rationally motivated** than consumers in deciding which goods to buy. Sales policy decisions by a supplier are therefore more important than sales promotion activities in an industrial market. Special attention should be given in selling to quality, price, credit, delivery dates, after-sales service, etc, and it is the importance of these rational motivations which make it difficult for an untried newcomer to break into an industrial goods market.

3.3.3 Organisational buying behaviour

The organisational buying behaviour process has some similarities with consumer buyer behaviour, but is supposedly more rational.

- How are needs recognised in a company?
- What is the type of buying situation?
- How is a supplier selected?
- How will performance be reviewed after purchase?

3.3.4 The decision-making unit

The **decision-making unit (DMU)** is a term used to describe the person or people who actually take the decision to buy a good or service. The marketing manager needs to know who in each organisation makes the effective buying decisions and how decisions are made: the DMU might act with formal authority, or as an informal group reaching a joint decision. Many large organisations employ specialist purchasing departments or 'buyers' – but the independence of the buyers will vary from situation to situation.

The *American Marketing Association* identifies **six buying roles** that might be played by one or more people involved in a purchase:

- The **Initiator** first suggests buying a particular product.
- The **Influencer's** views carry weight in the consideration of the purchase: typically this role will be played a technical expert such as an engineer.
- The **Decider** makes the final decision: this may be a committee role.
- The **User** consumes or utilises the purchase: this role may be combined with that of the initiator.
- The **Buyer** deals with the administration of the purchase.
- The **Gatekeeper** controls communication with deciders and influencers.

3.3.5 Factors in the motivation mix of business or government buyers

Business or government buyers are motivated as follows.

(a) **Quality**.
(b) **Price**. Where profit margins in the final market are under pressure, the buyer of industrial goods will probably make price the main purchasing motivation.
(c) **Budgetary control** may encourage the buying department to look further afield for potential suppliers to obtain a better price or quality of goods.
(d) **Fear of breakdown**. Where a customer has a highly organised and costly production system, he will clearly want to avoid a breakdown in the system, due to a faulty machine or running out of stocks of materials.
(e) **Credit**. The importance of credit could vary with the financial size of the buyer.
(f) **Delivery**. Generally, buyers want delivery without delay.

3.4 Market segmentation

FAST FORWARD

> Both consumer and industrial markets can usefully be segmented and several bases exist for the process. The aim is to identify a coherent segment that is both valid and attractive.

Much marketing planning is based on the concepts of **segmentation and product positioning.** The purpose of segmentation is to identify target markets in which the firm can take a position. A market is not a mass, homogeneous group of customers, each wanting an identical product. Market segmentation is based on the recognition that every market consists of potential buyers with different needs, and different buying behaviour. It is relevant to a **focus strategy**.

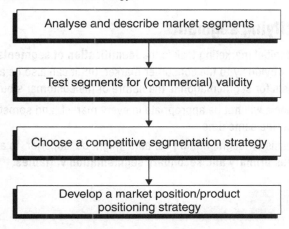

Analyse and describe market segments

Test segments for (commercial) validity

Choose a competitive segmentation strategy

Develop a market position/product positioning strategy

Key term

> **Market segmentation** is 'the subdividing of a market into distinct and increasingly homogeneous subgroups of customers, where any subgroup can conceivably be selected as a target market to be met with a distinct marketing mix'.
> (Kotler)

There are two important elements in this definition of market segmentation.

(a) Although the total market consists of widely different groups of consumers, each group consists of people (or organisations) with **common needs and preferences**, who perhaps react to 'market stimuli' in much the same way.

(b) Each market segment can become a **target market for a firm**, and would require a unique marketing mix if the firm is to exploit it successfully.

Reasons for segmenting markets

Reason	Comment
Better satisfaction of customer needs	One solution will not satisfy all customers
Growth in profits	Some customers will pay more for certain benefits
Revenue growth	Segmentation means that more customers may be attracted by what is on offer, in preference to competing products
Customer retention	By targeting customers, a number of different products can be offered to them
Targeted communications	Segmentation enables clear communications as people in the target audience share common needs
Innovation	By identifying unmet needs, companies can innovate to satisfy them
Segment share	Segmentation enables a firm to implement a focus strategy successfully

Steps in segmentation, targeting and positioning identified by Kotler

Step 1	Identify **segmentation** variables and segment the market	Segmentation
Step 2	Develop segment profiles	
Step 3	Evaluate the attractiveness of each segment	Targeting
Step 4	Select the **target** segment(s)	
Step 5	Identify **positioning** concepts for each target segment	Positioning
Step 6	Select, develop and communicate the chosen concept	

3.5 Identifying segments

An important initial marketing task is the **identification of segments** within the market. Segmentation applies more obviously to the consumer market, but it can also be applied to an **industrial market**. An important basis for segmentation is the nature of the customer's business.

(a) One basis will not be appropriate in every market, and sometimes two or more bases might be valid at the same time.

(b) One basis or 'segmentation variable' might be 'superior' to another in a hierarchy of variables. Here are thus **primary and secondary segmentation variables.**

 Case Study

An airport cafe conducted a segmentation exercise of its customers. It identified a number of possible segments.

- Business travellers
- Airport employees
- Groups
- Single tourists

However, further analysis revealed that running through each of these categories was the same fault line.

- Those 'in a hurry'
- Those with time to spare

For marketing purposes, this latter segmentation exercise was more useful, and the firm was able to develop an 'express menu' for those in a hurry.

3.5.1 Geography

At its simplest, this involves dividing the market into regions and tailoring the marketing mix accordingly.

(a) An example is **commercial radio stations**, which broadcast local news.

(b) The market for educational material in the UK segments geographically: Scotland has a different system to England.

 Case Study

The Australian Tourist Commission (ATC) was established in 1967 to promote Australia as an international tourism destination. Two of its principal objectives are to increase the number of visitors to Australia from overseas, and to maximise the benefits to Australia from overseas visitors. ATC has maximised the efficiency of its marketing by breaking up the travel market into the following segments:

- Independent adventurers aged 25-34
- Young independent travellers aged 18-24
- Independent travellers aged 45-65

With young travellers, the marketing approach was to communicate the aspects of Australia that would most appeal to them:

- Young, vibrant, dynamic (city life)
- Innovative (lifestyle, food and wine, culture)
- Active and sporty (beaches and sport facilities)
- Fun loving (parties, festivals, events)

3.5.2 Geodemographic segmentation

The ACORN system divides the UK into 17 groups which together comprise a total of 54 different types of areas, which share common socio-economic characteristics. Unlike geographical segmentation, which is fairly crude by area, geodemographics enables similar groups of people to be targeted, even though they might exist in different areas of the country. These various classifications share certain characteristics, including:

- Car ownership
- Unemployment rates
- Purchase of financial service products
- Number of holidays
- Age profile

The **family life cycle** (FLC) is a summary demographic variable. It brings together factors of age, marital status, career status (income) and the presence or absence of children. As a consequence, it is able to characterise the various stages through which households progress, with each stage involving **different needs and resources**.

Age and sex present few problems but **social class** has always been one of the most dubious areas of marketing research investigation. 'Class' is a highly personal and subjective phenomenon, to the extent that some people are 'class conscious' or class aware and have a sense of belonging to a particular group.

From 2001 the UK Office for National Statistics used a new categorisation system, which reflects recent changes in the UK population.

New social class	Occupations	Example
1	Higher managerial and professional occupations	
1.1	Employers and managers in larger organisations	Bank managers, company directors
1.2	Higher professional	Doctors, lawyers
2	Lower managerial and professional occupations	Police officers
3	Intermediate occupations	Secretaries, clerical workers
4	Small employers and own-account workers	
5	Lower supervisory, craft and related occupations	Electricians
6	Semi-routine occupations	Drivers, hairdressers, bricklayers
7	Routine occupations	Car park attendants, cleaners

3.5.3 Behavioural segmentation

Behavioural segmentation segments buyers into groups based on their attitudes to and use of the product, and the **benefits** they expect to receive.

Benefit segmentation of the toothpaste market						
Segment name	Principal benefit sought	Demographic strengths	Special behavioural characteristics	Brands disproportionately favoured	Personality characteristics	Lifestyle characteristics
The sensory segment	Flavour, product appearance	Children	Users of spearmint flavoured toothpaste	Colgate, Stripe	High self-involvement	Hedonistic
The Sociables	Brightness of teeth	Teens, young people	Smokers	Macleans, Ultra-Brite	High sociability	Active
The Worriers	Decay prevention	Large families	Heavy users	Crest	High hypochondriasis	Conservative
The Independent Segment	Price	Men	Heavy users	Brands on sale	High autonomy	Value oriented

3.6 Segmentation of the industrial market

Industrial markets can be segmented with many of the bases used in consumer markets such as geography, usage rate and benefits sought. Additional, more traditional bases include customer type, product/technology, customer size and purchasing procedures.

(a) **Geographic location.** Some industries and related industries are clustered in particular areas. Firms selling services to the banking sector might be interested in the City of London.

(b) **Type of business** (eg service, manufacturing)

    (i) **Nature of the customers' business.** Accountants or lawyers, for example, might choose to specialise in serving customers in a particular type of business. An accountant may choose to specialise in the accounts of retail businesses, and a firm of solicitors may specialise in conveyancing work for property development companies.

    (ii) **Components manufacturers specialise in the industries of the firms to which they supply components.**

(c) **Use of the product.** In the UK, many new cars are sold to businesses, as benefit cars. Although this practice is changing with the viability of a 'cash alternative' to a company car, the varying levels of specification are developed with the business buyer in mind (eg junior salesperson gets an Escort, Regional Manager gets a Ford Mondeo).

(d) **Type of organisation.** Organisations in an industry as a whole may have certain needs in common. Employment agencies offering business services to publishers, say, must offer their clients personnel with experience in particular desk top publishing packages. Suitable temporary staff offered to legal firms can be more effective if used to legal jargon. Each different type of firm can be offered a tailored product or service.

(e) **Size of organisation.** Large organisations may have elaborate purchasing procedures, and may do many things in-house. Small organisations may be more likely to subcontract certain specialist services.

3.7 Segment validity

A market segment will only **be valid if it is worth designing and developing a unique** marketing mix for that specific segment. The following questions are commonly asked to decide whether or not the segment can be used for developing marketing plans.

Criteria	Comment
Can the segment be measured?	It might be possible to conceive of a market segment, but it is not necessarily easy to measure it. For example, for a segment based on people with a conservative outlook to life, can conservatism of outlook be measured by market research?
Is the segment big enough?	There has to be a large enough potential market to be profitable.
Can the segment be reached?	There has to be a way of getting to the potential customers via the organisation's promotion and distribution channels.
Do segments respond differently?	If two or more segments are identified by marketing planners but each segment responds in the same way to a marketing mix, the segments are effectively one and the same and there is no point in distinguishing them from each other.
Can the segment be reached profitably?	Do the identified customer needs cost less to satisfy than the revenue they earn?
Is the segment suitably stable?	The stability of the segment is important, if the organisation is to commit huge production and marketing resources to serve it. The firm does not want the segment to 'disappear' next year. Of course, this may not matter in some industries.

Steps in the analysis of segmentation

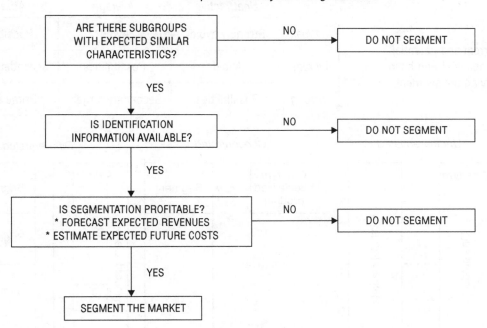

3.8 Segment attractiveness

A segment might be valid and potentially profitable, but is it potentially **attractive?**

(a)   A segment which has **high barriers to entry** might cost more to enter but will be less **vulnerable to competitors.**

(b)   For firms involved in **relationship marketing**, the segment should be one in which a **viable relationship** between the firm and the customer can be established.

Segments which are most attractive will be those whose needs can be met by building on the company's strengths and where forecasts for demand, sales profitability and **growth** are favourable.

3.9 Target markets

Because of limited resources, competition and large markets, organisations are not usually able to sell with equal efficiency and success to the entire market, ie to every market segment. It is necessary for the sake of efficiency to select **target markets**. A target market is a market or segment selected for special attention by an organisation, possibly to be served with a distinct marketing mix. The marketing management of a company may choose one of the following policy options.

Key terms

> **Undifferentiated marketing**: this policy is to produce a single product and hope to get as many customers as possible to buy it; that is, ignore segmentation entirely.
>
> **Concentrated marketing**: the company attempts to produce the ideal product for a single segment of the market (eg Rolls Royce cars for the wealthy).
>
> **Differentiated marketing**: the company attempts to introduce several product versions, each aimed at a different market segment. For example, manufacturers of soap powder make a number of different brands, marketed to different segments.

It is important to assess company strengths when evaluating attractiveness and targeting a market. This can help determine the appropriate strategy, because once the attractiveness of each identified segment has been assessed it can be considered along with relative strengths to determine the potential advantages the organisation would have. In this way preferred segments can be targeted.

Market segment attractiveness

Current and potential company strengths in serving the segment	Unattractive	Average	Attractive
Weak	Strongly avoid	Avoid	Possibilities
Average	Avoid	Possibilities	Secondary targets
Strong	Possibilities	Secondary targets	Prime targets

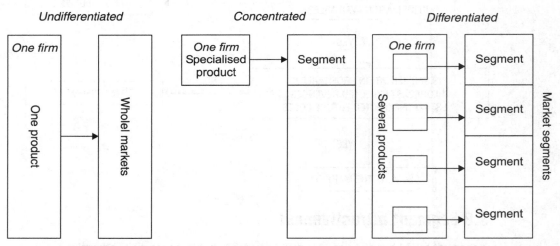

The major **disadvantage of differentiated marketing** is the additional costs of marketing and production (more product design and development costs, the loss of economies of scale in production and storage, additional promotion costs and administrative costs etc). When the **costs of further differentiation of the market exceed the benefits** from further segmentation and **target marketing**, a firm is said to have **over-differentiated**.

The major **disadvantage of concentrated marketing** is the business risk of relying on a single segment of a single market. On the other hand, specialisation in a particular market segment can give a firm a profitable, although perhaps temporary, competitive edge over rival firms.

The choice between undifferentiated, differentiated or concentrated marketing as a marketing strategy will depend on the following factors.

(a)   The extent to which the product and/or the market may be considered **homogeneous**. **Mass marketing** may be 'sufficient' if the market is largely homogeneous (for example, for safety matches).

(b)   The **company's resources** must not be over extended by differentiated marketing. Small firms may succeed better by concentrating on one segment only.

(c)   The product must be sufficiently **advanced in its life cycle** to have attracted a substantial total market; otherwise segmentation and target marketing is unlikely to be profitable, because each segment would be too small in size.

Remember

> The ideal mix for a convenience good (requiring a heavy emphasis on distribution and sales promotion) will be different from that for an industrial good (where price, design, quality and after-sales service are more important).

4 Reviewing the customer portfolio

FAST FORWARD

> The **customer base** is an asset to be invested in, as future benefits will come from existing customers, but not all customers are as important as others. It will help you in evaluating the customer portfolio if you consider the customer base as an asset worth 'investing' in.

Case Study

(a)   Coca-Cola paid $200m to Pernod of France, which, under contract, had effectively built a customer base for Coca-Cola, as well as building up a distribution network. Coca-Cola wanted to take charge of the marketing of Coke in France.

(b)   Supermarket loyalty cards reward customers with bonus points, saving them money, or allowing them to redeem points for products according to how much they spend.

(c)   Many banks lose money on student accounts, in the hope that they will earn it back later in the customer's life cycle.

A **marketing audit** involves a review of an organisation's products and markets, the marketing environment, and its marketing system and operations. The profitability of each product and each market should be assessed, and the costs of different marketing activities established.

Information obtained about markets

(a)   **Size of the customer base**. Does the organisation sell to a large number of small customers or a small number of big customers?

(b)   **Size of individual orders**. The organisation might sell its products in many small orders, or it might have large individual orders. Delivery costs can be compared with order sizes.

(c)   **Sales revenue and profitability.** The performance of individual products can be compared, perhaps as follows:

Product group	Sales revenue		Contribution to profits	
	£'000	% of total	£'000	% of total
B	7,500	35.7	2,500	55.6
E	2,000	9.5	1,200	26.7
C	4,500	21.4	450	10.0
A	5,000	23.8	250	5.6
D	2,000	9.5	100	2.2
	21,000	100.0	4,500	100.0

An imbalance between sales and profits over various product ranges can be potentially dangerous. In the figures above, product group A accounts for 23.8% of turnover but only 5.6% of total contribution, and product group D accounts for 9.5% of turnover but only 2.2% of total contribution.

(d) **Segments.** An analysis of sales and profitability into export markets and domestic markets.

(e) **Market share.** Estimated share of the market obtained by each product group.

(f) **Growth.** Sales growth and contribution growth over the previous four years or so, for each product group.

(g) Whether the **demand** for certain products is **growing, stable or likely to decline.**

(h) Whether **demand is price sensitive** or not.

(i) Whether there is a growing tendency for the market to become **fragmented**, with more specialist and 'custom-made' products.

Information about current marketing activities

- Comparative pricing
- Advertising effectiveness
- Effectiveness of distribution network
- Attitudes to the product, in comparison with competitors

4.1 Customers

Key customer analysis calls for six main areas of investigation in to customers, in order to identify which customers offer most profit.

Many firms – especially in business-to-business markets – sell to a relatively small number of customers. **Not all customers are as important as others.** The checklist below can help identify the most important.

Strategic importance evaluation guide	High	Medium	Low	N/A
1 Fit between customer's needs and our capabilities, at present and potentially.				
2 Ability to serve customer compared with our major competitors, at present and potentially.				
3 'Health' of customer's industry, current and forecast.				
4 'Health' of the customer, current and forecast.				
5 Customer's growth prospects, current and forecast.				
6 What can we learn from this customer?				
7 Can the customer help us attract others?				
8 Relative *significance:* how important is the customer compared *with other* customers?				
9 What is the *profitability* of serving the customer?				

4.2 Customer analysis

Key customer analysis calls for six main areas of investigation into customers. A firm might wish to identify which customers offer most profit. Small businesses are especially prone to overtrading.

Area	Detail
Key customer identity	• Name of each key customer • Location • Status in market • Products they make and sell • Size of firm (capital employed, turnover, number of employees)
Customer history	• First purchase date. • Who makes the buying decision in the customer's organisation? • What is the average order size, by product? • What is the regularity/ periodicity of the order, by product? • What is the trend in size of orders? • What is the motive in purchasing? • What does the customer know about the firm's and competitors' products? • On what basis does the customer reorder? • How is the useful life of the product judged? • Were there any lost or cancelled orders? For what reason?
Relationship of customer to product	• What does the customer use the product for? • Do the products form part of the customer's own service/product?
Relationship of customer to potential market	• What is the size of the customer in relation to the total end-market? • Is the customer likely to expand, or not? Diversify? Integrate?
Customer attitudes and behaviour	• What interpersonal factors exist which could affect sales by the firm and by competitors? • Does the customer also buy competitors' products? • To what extent may purchases be postponed?
The financial performance of the customer	How successful is the customer?

4.3 Customer profitability analysis (customer account profitability)

11/07

Customer profitability analysis is an analysis of the total sales revenue generated from a customer or customer group, less all the costs that are incurred in servicing that customer group.

Key term

Customer profitability analysis (CPA). 'Analysis of the revenue streams and service costs associated with specific customers or customer groups.' (CIMA *Official Terminology*)

'An immediate impact of introducing any level of strategic management accounting into virtually every organisation is to destroy totally any illusion that the same level of profit is derived from all customers'.
(Ward, *Strategic Management Accounting*)

The total costs of servicing customers can vary depending on how customers are serviced.

(a) **Volume discounts**. A customer who places one large order is given a discount, presumably because it benefits the supplier to do so (eg savings on administrative overhead in processing the orders – as identified by an ABC system).

(b) **Different rates** charged by power companies to domestic as opposed to business users. This in part reflects the administrative overhead of dealing with individual customers. In practice, many domestic consumers benefit from cross-subsidy.

> Customer profitability is the 'total sales revenue generated from a customer or customer group, less all the costs that are incurred in servicing that customer or customer group.'

It is possible to analyse customer profitability over a single period but more useful to look at a longer time scale. Such a multi period approach fits in with the idea of **relationship marketing** discussed later in this Text, with its emphasis on customer retention for the longer term.

Question

Profitable customers

Learning outcome B(iv)

Seth Ltd supplies shoes to Narayan Ltd and Kipling Ltd. Each pair of shoes has a list price of £50 each; as Kipling buys in bulk, Kipling receives a 10% trade discount for every order over 100 shoes. it costs £1,000 to deliver each order. In the year so far, Kipling has made five orders of 100 shoes each. Narayan Ltd receives a 15% discount irrespective of order size, because Narayan Ltd collects the shoes, thereby saving Seth Ltd any distribution costs. The cost of administering each order is £50. Narayan makes ten orders in the year, totalling 420 pairs of shoes. Which relationship is the most profitable for Seth?

Answer

You can see below that the profit earned by Seth in servicing Narayan is greater, despite the increased discount.

	Kipling	Narayan
Number of shoes	500	420
	£	£
Revenue (after discount)	22,500	17,850
Transport	(5,000)	
Administration	(250)	(500)
Net profit	17,250	17,350

Customer profitability analysis (CPA) focuses on profits generated by customers and suggests that **profit does not automatically increase with sales revenue**. CPA can benefit a company in the following ways.

- It enables a company to **focus resources** on the most profitable areas
- It identifies unexpected **differences in profitability** between customers
- It helps quantify the **financial impact** of proposed changes
- It helps highlight the **cost** of obtaining **new** customers and the **benefit** of retaining existing customers
- It helps to highlight whether **product** development or **market** development is to be preferred
- An appreciation of the costs of servicing clients assists in **negotiations** with customers

4.3.1 Limitations of CPA

However, there are also some limitations of CPA.

- Practical calculations can be very difficult – in particular assigning indirect costs to different activities or customers. If costs are wrongly apportioned then customer profitability will be distorted.
- CPA tends to be used on single products, but in practice customers may buy a range of products. Although a customer may not be profitable on the single product being assessed they may be across the range of products they buy. CPA could overlook this leading to flawed decision-making.

4.4 Identifying profitable customers/segments

> **FAST FORWARD**
>
> To analyse customer profitability successfully it may be necessary to structure **accounting information systems** to take account of the many factors by which customers can be analysed.

An important area in marketing strategy is **retaining** customers, so as to generate new business from them. But how do you identify which customers, or customer groups generate the most profit?

- First divide the customer base into segments (for example, by purchase value, by geographic region or by payment method)
- Then calculate the annual revenues earned (net of direct production costs) from each of the segments.
- Finally, calculate the annual costs of serving each of the segments (for example, delivery costs, promotional costs, cost of processing orders, sales returns or warranty costs, and any special costs due to last minute orders. This will involve the adoption of Activity Based Costing techniques).
- By comparing revenues with costs it is possible to identify which segments are profitable.

Remember

> This is a consideration that must be brought into the design of management information and administration systems. The firm's existing customer groupings, as reported in management accounts, may reflect administrative measures rather than their strategic value.

Question

Choosing data

Learning outcome B(iv)

Busqueros Ltd has 1,000 business customers spread fairly evenly over the UK. The sales force is organised into ten regions, each with 100 customers to be serviced. There are sales force offices at the heart of each region. Information is collected on a regional basis. The marketing director has recently carried out an analysis of the major customers by sales revenue. There are five significant customers, who between them account for 20% of the sales revenue of the firm. They do not get special treatment. What does this say about customer profitability analysis in Busqueros Ltd?

Answer

The information reflects sales force administration and convenience. However, it might obscure an analysis of customer profitability, in which case presenting information by customer size might be more important than geography.

4.4.1 Accounting systems

To analyse customer profitability successfully it may be necessary to structure accounting information systems to take account of the many factors by which customers can be analysed. A **relational database**, whereby information can be structured in many different ways, offers a useful approach.

How do you apportion costs to customer segments? Assume you have a customer base of 15,000 people. You have just spent £20,000 on an advertising campaign and 5,000 new customers have been found. How do you allocate the cost of the campaign? You do not know whether each new customer was attracted by the campaign, or by word-of-mouth.

Different customer costs can arise out of the following.

- Order size
- Sales mix
- Order processing

- Transport costs (eg if JIT requires frequent deliveries)
- Management time
- Cash flow problems (eg increased overdraft interest) caused by slow payers
- Order complexity (eg if the order has to be sent out in several stages)
- Stockholding costs can relate to specify customers
- The customer's negotiating strength

4.4.2 Product attributes

A further complication is that the nature of the product (its **attributes**) may be a compromise between the varying requirements of different customers. Under these circumstances it is inevitable that some customers will be offered greater value than they need and at a price they are unwilling to pay; thus the actual sales volume to this segment of the market may be depressed and profit be less than it might be with a simpler product. Against this must be set the potential extra cost and complication of offering a special product.

4.4.3 Example

Here is a possible layout for a **customer profitability analysis.**

	£'000
Gross sales	1,072
Less discounts	45
Net sales	1,027
Production	
Less production costs	510
	517
Marketing	
Less specific marketing costs:	
sales calls	10
in-store promotions	5
customer bonuses	5
Less share of other marketing costs:	
sales force management	10
customer service	10
	477
Distribution	
Less specific distribution costs:	
Transportation	5
Packaging	17
Refusals	2
outstanding debts	30
	423
Less shares of distribution costs:	
order processing	4
stock holding	24
Warehousing	20
collecting debts	10
Customer Contribution	365

Such a report can highlight the differences between the cost of servicing different individuals or firms which can then be applied as follows.

(a) **Directing effort to cutting customer specific costs**. Installing an electronic data interchange system (EDI) can save the costs of paperwork and data input.

(b) **Identifying those customers who are expensive to service**, thereby suggesting action to increase profitability.

(c) **Using CPA as part of a comparison with competitors' costs**. A firm which services a customer more cheaply than a competitor can use this cost advantage to offer extra benefits to the customer.

(d)   Indicating cases where **profitability might be endangered**, for example by servicing customers for whom the firm's core competence is not especially relevant.

CPA might provide answers to the following questions. Obviously a firm doing work for one major customer will find it easier to answer these questions than one which works for many customers.

- What **profit/contribution** is the organisation making on sales to the customer, after discounts and selling and delivery costs?
- What would be the **financial consequences** of losing the customer?
- Is the customer buying in order sizes that are **unprofitable** to supply?
- What is **return on investment** on plant used?
- What is the level of **inventory** required specifically to supply these customers?
- Are there any other **specific costs** involved in supplying this customer, eg technical and test facilities, R&D facilities, special design staff?
- What is the ratio of net contribution per customer to total investment?

4.5 The customer lifecycle

We mentioned earlier that it is probably appropriate to think in terms of customer revenues and costs over more than one period. We can refine our financial analysis by working in terms of the PV of customer costs and revenues, and by incorporating the concept of the **customer lifecycle**. This is less developed than the equivalent product and industry lifecycle models, but it can be useful to consider the following matters.

(a)   **Promotional expense** relating to a single customer is likely to be heavily **front-loaded**: it is much cheaper to retain a customer than to attract one.

(b)   It is likely that **sales** to a customer will start at a low level and increase to a higher level as the customer gains confidence, though this is not certain and will vary from industry to industry.

(c)   A customer who purchases a basic or commodity product initially may move on to **more differentiated products** later.

(d)   In consumer markets, career progression is likely to provide the individual with steadily increasing amounts of disposable income, while the **family lifecycle** will indicate the ranging nature of likely purchases as time passes.

Any attempt to estimate lifecycle costs and revenues should also consider existing and potential **environmental impacts**, including, in particular, the likely actions of competitors and the potential for product and process innovation.

Chapter Roundup

- Whatever the exact nature of supplier bargaining power, many firms aim to build closer relationships for the sake of efficiency.

- A firm can make strategic gains from managing **stakeholder relationships**, such as those with customers and suppliers.

- **Supply chain management** is about optimising the activities of companies working together to produce goods and services. Supply chain relationships are becoming increasingly more co-operative rather than adversarial.

- **Marketing** as a concept of the way business should be done must be distinguished from marketing as a business function. Operational marketing is the best developed form of the latter.

- The strategy of a business is often orientated towards its customers, it source of revenue. Marketing, as a business function, seeks to identify customers and their needs, and to encourage them to buy. Segments are groups of customers with similar needs that can be **targeted** with a distinctively **positioned** marketing **mix**.

- The decision to make a purchase can be very simple, very complex or somewhere between the two. Buyers do not always proceed rationally, thought the motivation of industrial buyers may be more logical than that of consumers.

- Both consumer and industrial markets can usefully be segmented and several bases exist for the process. The aim is to identify a coherent segment that is both valid and attractive.

- The **customer base** is an asset to be invested in, as future benefits will come from existing customers, but not all customers are as important as others. It will help you in evaluating the customer portfolio if you consider the customer base as an asset worth 'investing' in.

- **Key customer analysis** calls for six main areas of investigation in to customers, in order to identify which customers offer most profit.

- **Customer profitability analysis** is an analysis of the total sales revenue generated from a customer or customer group, less all the costs that are incurred in servicing that customer group.

- To analyse customer profitability successfully it may be necessary to structure **accounting information systems** to take account of the many factors by which customers can be analysed.

Quick Quiz

1   Give an example showing why there should be a correlation between employee and customer loyalty.

2   What is the difference between the 'traditional' and the 'integrated' supply chain?

3   Which of the statements below describes differentiated marketing?

   (a)   The company attempts to produce the ideal product for a single segment of the market (eg Rolls Royce cars for the wealthy).

   (b)   This policy is to produce a single product and hope to get as many customers as possible to buy it, ignoring segmentation entirely.

   (c)   The company attempts to introduce several product versions, each aimed at a different market segment. For example, manufacturers of soap powder make a number of different brands, marketed to different segments.

4   How can different costs arise with different customers? Give five examples.

5   What are the three categories of consumer goods?

Answers to Quick Quiz

1   Reduced staff turnover in service firms can result in more repeat business because of improved service quality due to more knowledgeable staff.

2   With the 'traditional' model, businesses in the supply chain operated relatively independently of one another, with independence maintained by factors such as capacity limitations and lead times. Linkages are now much tighter, business pressures have compressed lead times and reduced stock holding and excess capacity. This new situation is shown by the 'integrated' model.

3   (c)

4   • Order size
    • Sales mix
    • Order processing
    • Transport costs (eg if JIT requires frequent deliveries)
    • Management time
    • Cash flow problems (eg increased overdraft interest) caused by slow payers
    • Order complexity (eg if the order has to be sent out in several stages)
    • Stockholding costs can relate to specify customers
    • The customer's negotiating strength

5   Convenience, shopping and speciality

Now try the question below from the Exam Question Bank

Number	Level	Marks	Time
Q6	Examination	25	45 mins

Resource analysis

Introduction

In earlier chapters we reviewed both the general and competitive environments. In this chapter we examine some of the key aspects of the organisation's current **position**.

A **resource audit** (Sections 1 and 2) identifies any gaps in resources and limiting factors on organisational activity.

Value chain analysis (Section 3) identifies how the business adds value to the resources it obtains, and how it deploys these resources to satisfy customers.

We then review the organisation's current outputs, its **product portfolio**, in Section 4. A review of its current portfolio may encourage an organisation to develop new products (Section 5).

An organisation's resources and competences are difficult to assess in isolation, so some form of comparison is needed. **Benchmarking** (Section 6) is now common, and involves comparing an organisation's processes with those of best practice, such as those employed by an exemplar organisation, which may be an organisation in a different industry. Such an exercise will highlight areas where improvements can be made, notably in the value chain.

Topic list	Learning outcomes	Syllabus references	Ability required
1 The position audit	C(vi)	A2, A8, C5	Analysis
2 Resources and limiting factors	C(vi)	C5	Analysis
3 Converting resources: the value chain	C(vi)	C8	Comprehension
4 Outputs: the product portfolio	C(vi)	C6	Evaluation
5 New products and innovation	C(ii)	C6, D12	Evaluation
6 Benchmarking	C(iii)	C7	Analysis

1 The position audit

To develop a strategic plan, an organisation's management must be aware of the current position of the organisation.

Key term

> **Position audit** is 'part of the planning process which examines the current state of the entity in respect of:
>
> - Resources of tangible and intangible assets and finance
> - Products, brands and markets
> - Operating systems such as production and distribution
> - Internal organisation
> - Current results
> - Returns to stockholders'.
>
> (CIMA *Official Terminology*)

The rest of this chapter is concerned with how this vital task may be successfully carried out.

2 Resources and limiting factors

FAST FORWARD

For many companies this might involve a broader review of the firm's:

- Effectiveness in meeting the needs of its chosen client or stakeholder groups.
- Efficiency in the use of resources (the maximum output for a given level of input).

Firms do not have unlimited resources, and so have to do the best they can from limiting factors.

A resource audit is an internal review. The **Ms model** categorises the factors as follows.

Resource	Example
Machinery	Age. Condition. Utilisation rate. Value. Replacement. Technologically up-to-date? Cost.
Make-up	Culture and structure. Patents. Goodwill. Brands.
Management	Size. Skills. Loyalty. Career progression. Structure.
Management information	Ability to generate and disseminate ideas. Innovation. Information systems.
Markets	Products and customers.
Materials	Source. Suppliers and partnering. Waste. New materials. Cost. Availability. Future provision.
Men and women	Number. Skills. Wage costs. Proportion of total costs. Efficiency. Labour turnover. Industrial relations.
Methods	How are activities carried out? Capital-intensive or labour-intensive, outsourcing, JIT.
Money	Credit and turnover periods. Cash surpluses/ deficits. Short term and long term finance. Gearing levels.

Resources are of no value unless they are organised into systems, and so a resource audit should go on to consider how well or how badly resources have been utilised, and whether the organisation's systems are effective and efficient. This includes the quality and timeliness of information available to managers.

2.1 Limiting factors

Every organisation operates under resource **constraints**.

A **limiting factor** or **key factor** is 'anything which limits the activity of an entity. An entity seeks to optimise the benefit it obtains from the limiting factor.

Examples are a shortage of supply of a resource or a restriction on sales demand at a particular price'.

(CIMA *Official Terminology*)

Examples of limiting factors are:

- A shortage of production capacity
- A limited number of key personnel, such as salespeople with technical knowledge
- A restricted distribution network
- Too few managers with knowledge about finance, or overseas markets
- Inadequate research design resources to develop new products or services
- A poor system of strategic intelligence
- Lack of money
- A lack of staff who are adequately trained

Once the limiting factor has been identified, the planners should:

- In the short term, make best use of the resources available.
- Try to reduce the limitation in the long term.

Case Study

In February 2006, The Financial Times reported that the North Sea oil exploration was being constrained by a shortage of the mobile drilling rigs used for exploration. The number of yards building rigs fell in the late 1990s as oil prices fell and there has been significant attrition of numbers from storm and operational damage. As a result, rigs built in the 1970s and laid-up are being brought back into service.

2.2 Resource use

Resource use is concerned with the **efficiency** with which resources are used, and the **effectiveness** of their use in achieving the planning objectives of the business. Remember that in Chapter 1 we identified that resources can be a source of competitive advantage (resource-based strategy) but in order to take full advantage of its resources an organisation must use them with efficiently and effectively.

Efficiency is 'how well the resources have been utilised irrespective of the purpose for which they have been employed'.

Effectiveness is 'whether the resources have been deployed in the best possible way'.

3 Converting resources: the value chain 5/06

The **value chain** models all the activities of a business and the linkages between them. It shows how value is created, how costs are caused and how competitive advantage can be gained.

The **value chain** model of corporate activities, developed by Michael Porter, offers a bird's eye view of the firm and what it does. Competitive advantage, says Porter, arises out of the way in which firms organise and perform **activities**. This reminds us that businesses are made up of value-creating activities, and so it is important to consider the structure of an organisation in terms of these activities rather then simply by looking at an organisation chart.

> **Activities** are the means by which a firm creates value in its products. (They are sometimes referred to as **value activities**.)

Activities incur costs, and, in combination with other activities, provide a product or service which earns revenue.

3.1 Example of the value chain

Let us explain this point by using the example of a **restaurant**. A restaurant's activities can be divided into buying food, cooking it, and serving it (to customers). There is no reason, in theory, why the customers should not do all these things themselves, at home. The customer however, is not only prepared to **pay for someone else** to do all this but also **pays more than the cost of** the resources (food, wages etc). The ultimate value a firm creates is measured by the amount customers are willing to pay for its products or services above the cost of carrying out value activities. A firm is profitable if the realised value to customers exceeds the collective cost of performing the activities.

(a)   Customers **purchase value**, which they measure by comparing a firm's products and services with similar offerings by competitors.

(b)   The business **creates value** by carrying out its activities either more efficiently than other businesses, or combine them in such a way as to provide a unique product or service.

Question

Creating value

Learning outcome C(vi)

Outline different ways in which the restaurant can 'create' value.

Answer

Here are some ideas. Each of these options is a way of organising the activities of buying, cooking and serving food in a way that customers will value.

(a)   It can become more efficient, by automating the production of food, as in a fast food chain.

(b)   The chef can develop commercial relationships with growers, so he or she can obtain the best quality fresh produce.

(c)   The chef can specialise in a particular type of cuisine (eg Nepalese, Korean).

(d)   The restaurant can be sumptuously decorated for those customers who value 'atmosphere' and a sense of occasion, in addition to a restaurant's purely gastronomic pleasures.

(e)   The restaurant can serve a particular type of customer (eg celebrities).

Porter (in *Competitive Advantage*) grouped the various activities of an organisation into a value chain.

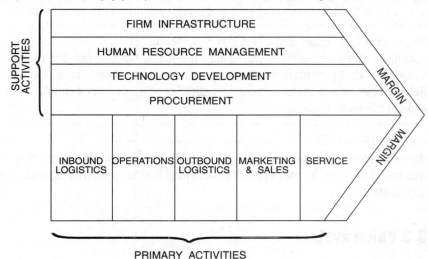

The **margin** is the excess the customer is prepared to **pay** over the **cost** to the firm of obtaining resource inputs and providing value activities.

3.2 Activities

Primary activities are directly related to production, sales, marketing, delivery and service.

	Comment
Inbound logistics	Receiving, handling and storing inputs to the production system (ie warehousing, transport, stock control etc).
Operations	Convert resource inputs into a final product. Resource inputs are not only materials. 'People' are a 'resource' especially in service industries.
Outbound logistics	Storing the product and its distribution to customers: packaging, warehousing, testing etc.
Marketing and sales	Informing customers about the product, persuading them to buy it, and enabling them to do so: advertising, promotion etc.
After sales service	Installing products, repairing them, upgrading them, providing spare parts and so forth.

Support activities provide purchased inputs, human resources, technology and infrastructural functions to support the primary activities.

Activity	Comment
Procurement	Acquire the resource inputs to the primary activities (eg purchase of materials, subcomponents equipment).
Technology development	Product design, improving processes and/or resource utilisation.
Human resource management	Recruiting, training, developing and rewarding people.
Firm infrastructure	Planning, finance, quality control: Porter believes these are crucially important to an organisation's strategic capability in all primary activities.

Linkages connect the activities of the value chain.

(a)　**Activities in the value chain affect one another**. For example, more costly product design or better quality production might reduce the need for after-sales service.

(b)   **Linkages require co-ordination**. For example, Just In Time requires smooth functioning of operations, outbound logistics and service activities such as installation.

3.3 Value system

Activities that add value do not stop at the organisation's **boundaries**. For example, when a restaurant serves a meal, the quality of the ingredients – although they are chosen by the cook – is determined by the grower. The grower has added value, and the grower's success in growing produce of good quality is as important to the customer's ultimate satisfaction as the skills of the chef. A firm's value chain is connected to what Porter calls a **value system**.

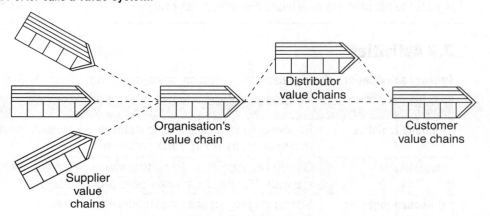

It may be possible to capture the benefit of some of the value generated both upstream and downstream in the value system. An obvious way to do this is by **vertical integration** through the acquisition of supplies and customers. This aspect of strategy is dealt with in more detail later in this Study Text.

It is possible for large and powerful companies to exercise less formal power over supplies and customers by using their **bargaining power** to achieve purchase and selling prices that are biased in their favour.

A more subtle advantage is gained by fostering good relationships that can promote **innovation** and the **creation of knowledge**.

 Case Study

Toyota is well-known for close involvement with its suppliers. The company works with suppliers to improve their methods and the quality of their output; and to develop new, improved materials and components for input into its own operations. The relationship has benefits for all parties, but tends to be unequal, with Toyota dominating the operations of a large number of semi-captive suppliers.

Li & Fung, to whom we have already referred, aim for more equal relationships with the large number of clothing manufacturers it deals with. It guarantees to take at least 30% of a supplier's output in order to build a close relationship that can be built on to improve innovation and learning. But it also tries to limit its purchases to no more than 70% of a supplier's output in order to avoid creating a dependent organisation whose managers are influenced more by fear than by trust.

3.4 Using the value chain

A firm can secure competitive advantage by:

- Inventing new or better ways to do activities, perhaps by taking a **BPR approach** (see Chapter 12)
- Combining activities in new or better ways
- Managing the linkages in its own value chain to increase efficiency and reduce cost
- Managing the linkages in the value system. This links back to the ideas of **supply chain management** and creating beneficial relationships between suppliers.

The **value system** may be particularly fruitful, since it offers the potential for achieving great improvements in efficiency and reductions in cost through negotiation, bargaining, collaboration and even vertical integration. The last option holds out the possibility of **migrating** to that part of the value system that offers the greatest potential for adding value and thus enhancing profitability.

Question	Value chain and value system

Learning outcome C(vi)

Sana Sounds is a small record company. Representatives from Sana Sounds scour music clubs for new bands to promote. Once a band has signed a contract (with Sana Sounds) it makes a recording. The recording process is subcontracted to one of a number of recording studio firms which Sana Sounds uses regularly. (At the moment Sana Sounds is not large enough to invest in its own equipment and studios.) Sana Sounds also subcontracts the production of records and CDs to a number of manufacturing companies. Sana Sounds then distributes the disks to selected stores, and engages in any promotional activities required.

What would you say were the activities in Sana Sounds' value chain?

Answer

Sana Sounds is involved in the record industry from start to finish. Although recording and CD manufacture are contracted out to external suppliers, this makes no difference to the fact that these activities are part of Sana Sounds' own value chain. Sana Sounds earns its money by managing the whole set of activities. If the company grows then perhaps it will acquire its own recording studios.

The value chain is an important analytical tool because it helps management:

- To see the business as a whole
- To identify potential sources of competitive advantage
- To suggest strategies
- To analyse competitors
- To implement activities such as benchmarking, outsourcing, business process re-engineering, performance measurement and activity based costing and management

The value chain models the process by which organisations convert inputs into outputs. If the purpose of this process is the creation of value, then the accountant should be able to contribute to the **strategic analysis of costs**.

Case Study

The Department of Trade and Industry in the UK produced a 'Value Added Scoreboard' in May 2002, focusing on a particular measure of company output. A company's basic 'value added' is calculated by taking its sales and subtracting the cost of buying materials, components and services. When this is divided by the number of employees (or their hours worked), this indicates how good a company is at turning ideas and goods into services and products that customers will buy.

The 300 businesses in the report have an average annual added value per employee of £49,900, but value added ratios differ widely between different sectors. Oil and gas, for example, score very highly (average value added per employee of £191,500) for the following reasons.

- Cheap raw materials
- Uses more capital equipment than labour
- Workers are highly skilled
- Tight control over distribution, and therefore pricing

Retailing, by contrast, is a low scorer, with £21,300 per employee.

- Virtually all goods sold are bought-in from suppliers
- Employees are numerous but low-skilled
- Little intellectual capital

3.5 The value chain and management accounting

There is a clear link between the concept of value activities that cut across departments and the principles of activity-based costing.

A summary of the failure of traditional costing systems, and a contrast based on the value chain, is outlined in the table below.

	Traditional costing systems	Value chain cost analysis: an alternative
Focus	Manufacturing operations	Customers Value perceptions
Cost objects	Products Functions Expense heads	Value-creating activities Product attributes
Organisational focus	Cost and responsibility centres	Strategic business units (SBUs) Value-creating activities
Linkages	1 Largely ignored 2 Cost allocations and transfer prices used to reflect interdependencies	Recognised and maximised
Cost drivers	Simple volume measures	Strategic decisions
Accuracy	High apparent precision	Low precision Indicative answers

The practical application of value chain cost analysis can be seen with the following illustration which relates each element to the example of a supermarket's operations.

	Value chain cost analysis	Practical example
Focus	Customers	The supermarket is keenly focused on the customers as the key source of value. Specific customers are targeted through marketing campaigns and 'customer delight' is sought.
		All retailers are being forced by competition to invest more in customer service, systems and price.
Cost objects	Value-creating activities and profit attributes	Activities which promote customer loyalty and bigger spend are investigated and developed. For example, giving a 10% discount to new mothers could increase sales and profit margin above the cost of the discounts given. Self-scanning technology increases sales in the stores where it is introduced.
Linkages	Recognised and maximised	Supplier and customer relationships are nurtured. Suppliers are ranked for their ability to meet the supermarket's demand and customers are constantly reminded via instore promotions of the supermarket's commitment to giving them value.
Cost drivers	Strategic decisions	These are prompted either by competitor activity (eg price cuts) or new business initiatives such as investment in new technology or development of overseas markets.
		Target rates of return are required, often also measured in terms of the required sales uplift and related margin to justify an activity.
Accuracy	Indicative answers	A wealth of detail on sales and margin by product is collected and individual customer spends are analysed.
		Much importance is also attached to less quantifiable measures such as customer surveys, and level of customer complaints. They may highlight areas where the business is falling down and losing customers to rivals.

3.5.1 How the value chain drives costs

What might influence the costs of the value chain?

(a) **Structural cost drivers** are major 'strategic choices made by the firm which determine its underlying cost base'.

    (i)   **Scale** of operations, capacity etc, giving rise to economies or diseconomies of scale

    (ii)   **Scope**: to what extent is the firm vertically integrated?

    (iii)   **Experience**: has the firm climbed the learning curve?

    (iv)   **Technology** used in the value chain

    (v)   **Complexity** and breadth of product range

(b) **Management** influences how well a firm manages the value chain in operational terms.

    (i)   Capacity utilisation

    (ii)   Product and process design

    (iii)   Learning opportunities offered by continuous improvement programmes

    (iv)   How well external linkages (eg liaison with suppliers) are exploited

Firms might create a more **outward-looking focus** in their costing systems as follows.

(a) Most products are a collection of benefits, which is why customers buy them. Ultimately, the provision of customer benefits is the real cost driver of the business, and it should be possible to work backwards, as it were, from these customer benefits to the underlying costs.

$$
\begin{array}{l}
\text{Input} \\
\text{costs}
\end{array}
\longrightarrow
\textit{Activities}
\begin{array}{l}
\longleftarrow \text{Cost driver A} \longleftarrow \quad \text{A} \\
\longleftarrow \text{Cost driver B} \longleftarrow \quad \text{B} \\
\longleftarrow \text{Cost driver C} \longleftarrow \quad \text{C}
\end{array}
\begin{array}{l}
\text{Customer} \\
\text{benefit} \\
\text{sought}
\end{array}
$$

(b) For different products, it should be possible to identify the customer's perception of the value of the benefit and the cost of providing it.

For the accountant, a problem with this approach is:

- A lack of precision in the data
- The inevitable subjectivity in deciding what customers value as a benefit

3.6 Limitations of the value chain

(a) It is not designed for use with **service businesses**.

(b) The idea of the value system is difficult to apply to **network organisations**.

(c) Making the best use of the value chain idea is dependent on adopting at least some part of **activity-based costing**, in order to establish the costs of value activities. This can be a time consuming and expensive move.

(d) The costs of the analysis may exceed the potential benefits.

(e) The value chain takes little account of the increasing role of IT in business. It was in response to this criticism that Porter and Millar revisited the model and stressed the importance of using technology to increase linkages (see Chapter 2.4.1 – The strategic importance of IT)

3.7 Alternative approaches

Stabell and Fjeldstad address the first two limitations listed in Section 3.6 above by proposing **new lists of primary activities** that relate better to service and network organisations respectively.

3.7.1 Service organisations

The service organisation model is based on the solution of customer problems, so is perhaps seen most clearly in revelation to a professional practise such as a firm of accountants or lawyers. Expertise is the principal asset, and is built by experience.

Primary activities include:

- **Problem acquisition and diagnosis**: marketing effort and professional expertise are required
- **Finding solutions**: more extensive professional expertise must be deployed
- **Choice between solutions**: choosing consultation with the client
- **Solution implementation**
- **Control and feedback**: to ensure effectiveness

3.7.2 Network organisations

The emphasis here is on the wider network of unrelated stakeholders, not the network approach to internal structure.

Primary activities include:

- **Network promotion and contract management**: this combines marketing with administration
- **Service provisioning**: day to day liaison, communication and decision making
- **Infrastructure operation**: physical and intangible resources must be maintained and exploited; this is perhaps clearest in the context of IT systems

4 Outputs: the product portfolio

Many firms make a number of different products or services. Each product or service has its own financial, marketing and risk characteristics. The combination of products or services influences the attractiveness and profitability of the firm.

4.1 The product life cycle

5/06

 FAST FORWARD

The **product life cycle** concept holds that products have a life cycle, and that a product demonstrates different characteristics of profit and investment at each stage in its life cycle. The life cycle concept is a model, not a prediction. (Not all products pass through each stage of the life cycle.) It enables a firm to examine its portfolio of goods and services as a whole.

Case Study

Glaxo has for many years produced *Zantac* an anti-ulcer drug. Patents expire after a defined period. Glaxo has been anticipating this development for a while and has invested in new drugs to provide income when returns from Zantac fall.

The profitability and sales of a product can be expected to change over time. The **product life cycle** is an attempt to recognise distinct stages in a product's sales history. Marketing managers distinguish between different aspects of the product.

(a) **Product class:** this is a broad category of product, such as cars, washing machines, newspapers' also referred to as the **generic product**.

(b) **Product form:** within a product class there are different forms that the product can take, for example five-door hatchback cars or two-seater sports cars; twin tub or front loading automatic washing machines; national daily newspapers or weekly local papers and so on.

(c) **Brand:** the particular type of the product form (eg *Ford Focus*).

The product life cycle applies in differing degrees to each of the three cases. A product-class (eg cars) may have a long maturity stage, and a particular make or brand *might* have an erratic life cycle (eg Rolls Royce) or not. Product forms however tend to conform to the classic life cycle pattern.

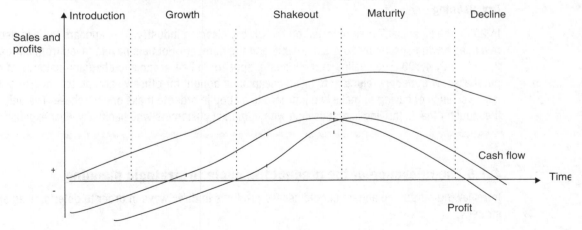

4.1.1 Introduction

- A new product takes time to find acceptance by would-be purchasers and there is a slow growth in sales. Unit costs are high because of low output and expensive sales promotion.
- There may be early teething troubles with production technology.
- The product for the time being is a loss-maker, and has negative cash flows.

- The product is high risk because it has not yet been accepted by the market.
- Few competitors.

4.1.2 Growth

- If the new product gains market acceptance, sales will eventually rise more sharply and the product will start to make profits. However, capital investments needed to fulfil levels of demand means cash flow remains lower than profit.
- Competitors are attracted and as sales and production rise, unit costs fall.
- Need to add additional features to differentiate from competitors, or to lower price and compete on price grounds.

4.1.3 Shakeout

- Market becomes saturated, as supply begins to exceed demand. Excess supply can possibly be addressed through price cuts.
- Number of producers reduces either as a result of business failures or takeovers.
- Maximum profitability is reached, but will start to fall as supply exceeds demand.

4.1.4 Maturity

The rate of sales growth slows down and the product reaches a period of maturity which is probably the longest period of a successful product's life as customers buy to replace existing products when they reach the end of their useful lives. Most products on the market will be at the mature stage of their life. Profits remain good, and levels of investment are low, meaning cash flow is also positive.

4.1.5 Decline

Eventually, the product is superceded by technically superior substitutes. Sales will begin to decline so that there is over-capacity of production in the industry. Severe competition occurs, profits fall and some producers leave the market. The remaining producers seek means of prolonging the product life by modifying it and searching for new (niche) market segments. Although some producers are reluctant to leave the market, many inevitably do because of falling profits.

 Case Study

Dry cleaning

In 2005, the Financial Times reported on the UK dry cleaning industry. This appears to be in decline, with revenues having shrunk by 10% since 1999 and the number of outlets having fallen from almost 5,300 in 2000 to only 4,500. The decline of the industry appears to be traceable to changing patterns of clothes purchases, with people reluctant to clean cheap suits bought for office wear, and to a dislike of the inconvenience of having to make two journeys to a shop in order to make one purchase. The only segment of the industry that is thriving is that dealing with upmarket customers who habitually wear expensive clothes.

4.1.6 The relevance of the product life cycle to strategic planning

In reviewing outputs, planners should assess products in three ways in order to determine an appropriate strategy.

(a)   The **stage of its life cycle** that any product has reached.
(b)   The **product's remaining life**, ie how much longer the product will contribute to profits.
(c)   How **urgent is the need to innovate**, to develop new and improved products?

4.1.7 Difficulties of the product life cycle concept

(a) **Recognition**. How can managers recognise where a product stands in its life cycle?

(b) **Not always true**. The theoretical curve of a product life cycle does not always occur in practice. Some products have no maturity phase, and go straight from growth to decline. Some never decline if they are marketed competitively.

(c) **Changeable**. Strategic decisions can change or extend a product's life cycle.

(d) **Competition varies** in different industries. The financial markets are an example of markets where there is a tendency for competitors to copy the leader very quickly, so that competition has built up well *ahead* of demand.

(e) **Focus on the product**. Sometimes a customer group or market is a better unit of strategic analysis than a single product. A product may be at different stages of its life cycle in different markets.

4.2 Portfolio planning

FAST FORWARD

Portfolio analysis examines the current status of the organisation's products and their markets. Portfolio analysis is the first stage of **portfolio planning**, which aims to create a balance among the organisation's market offerings in order to maximise competitive advantage. The same approach is equally applicable to products, market segments and even SBUs.

Four **major strategies** can be pursued with respect to products, market segments and, indeed, SBUs.

(a) **Build**. A build strategy forgoes short term earnings and profits in order to increase market share.

(b) **Hold**. A hold strategy seeks to maintain the current position.

(c) **Harvest**. A harvesting strategy seeks short-term earning and profits at the expense of long-term development.

(d) **Divest**. Divestment reduces negative cash flow and releases resources for use elsewhere.

4.2.1 Market share, market growth and cash generation: the Boston classification

5/07

FAST FORWARD

The **Boston classification** classifies products in terms of their capacity for growth within the market and the market's capacity for growth as a whole. A firm should have a balanced **portfolio of products**. The GE Business Screen and the Shell matrix are similar tools.

The **Boston Consulting Group** (BCG) developed a matrix based on empirical research that assesses a company's products in terms of potential cash generation and cash expenditure requirements. Products or SBUs are categorised in terms of **market growth rate** and **relative market share**.

Key term

Market share: 'One entity's sale of a product or service in a specified market expressed as a percentage of total sales by all entities offering that product or service.'

(a) Assessing rate of **market growth** as high or low depends on the conditions in the market. No single percentage rate can be set, since new markets may grow explosively while mature ones grow hardly at all. High market growth rate can indicate good opportunities for profitable operations. However, intense competition in a high growth market can erode profit, while a slowly growing market with high barriers to entry can be very profitable.

(b) **Relative market share** is assessed as a ratio: it is market share compared with the market share of the **largest competitor**. Thus a relative market share greater than unity indicates that the product or SBU is the market leader. BGG settled on market share as a way of estimating the costs associated with given products. This was chosen because both costs and market share are connected with **production experience**: as experience in satisfying a particular market demand for value increases, market share can be expected to increase also, and costs to fall. The connection between lower costs and higher market share was independently confirmed by PIMS studies, as discussed in Chapter 9. However, it is important to understand that, as in other contexts, **correlation does not**

prove causation. We would normally expect the cost-reducing effect of the experience curve to assist a company to expand, but there may be occasions when low cost comes first and leads to market expansion without there necessarily being any experience effects.

(c)   Note that there is an unspoken assumption that the **market** itself is easily defined. This may not be the case and it is likely that much thought will have to be given to this problem, even if only to decide whether the analysis should be in terms of brand, generic product or product form.

(d)   Be aware also that the matrix ignores potential links between products. However, it is important to consider such links: for example, if a firm stops producing one product will it have a knock on effect on say other products?

		Market share	
		High	Low
Market growth	High	Stars	Question marks/ Problem children
	Low	Cash cows	Dogs

The product portfolio should be balanced, with cash cows providing finance for stars and question marks; and a minimum of dogs.

(a)   **Stars**. In the short term, these require capital expenditure in excess of the cash they generate, in order to maintain their market position, but promise high returns in the future. Strategy: **build**.

(b)   In due course, stars will become **cash cows**. Cash cows need very little capital expenditure and generate high levels of cash income. However, it is important to remember that apparently mature products can be invigorated, possibly by competitors, who could thus come to dominate the market. Cash cows can be used to finance the stars. Strategy: **hold** or **harvest** if weak.

(c)   **Question marks**. Do the products justify considerable capital expenditure in the hope of increasing their market share, or should they be allowed to die quietly as they are squeezed out of the expanding market by rival products? Strategy: **build** or **harvest**.

(d)   **Dogs**. They may be ex-cash cows that have now fallen on hard times. Although they will show only a modest net cash outflow, or even a modest net cash inflow, they are cash traps which tie up funds and provide a poor return on investment. However, they may have a useful role, either to complete a product range or to keep competitors out. There are also many smaller niche businesses in market that are difficult to consolidate that would count as dogs but which are quite successful. Strategy: **divest** or **hold**.

Exam focus point

> If you are asked to recommend a strategy (as candidates were in the May 2007 exam) think critically about the model before doing so. For example, the May 2007 exam showed a 'dog' which contributed nearly 40% of a company's profits. With this level of profit, divesting would not be a sensible strategy.

Although developed for use with a *product* portfolio, the BCG matrix is also used in diversified conglomerates to assess the strategic position of subsidiary SBUs, using exactly the same reasoning, albeit at a more complex level, since an SBU may have a range of products of varying market characteristics. However, the BCG approach is still a useful way of assessing an SBU's overall position and prospects.

Note, however that critics argue the axes are two simplistic. A high market share is assumed to indicate competitive strength; but this is not necessarily true. A strong brand may yield competitive strength despite a relatively low market share. Similarly high market growth is deemed to indicate an attractive industry. But fast growing industries are likely to require significant investment, so they may not be attractive to a firm with limited available capital.

Learning outcome: C(vi)

The marketing manager of Juicy Drinks Ltd has invited you in for a chat. Juicy Drinks Ltd provides fruit juices to a number of supermarket chains, which sell them under their own label. 'We've got a large number of products, of course. Our freshly squeezed orange juice is doing fine – it sells in huge quantities. Although margins are low, we have sufficient economies of scale to do very nicely in this market. We've got advanced production and bottling equipment and long term contracts with some major growers. No problems there. We also sell freshly squeezed pomegranate juice: customers loved it in the tests, but producing the stuff at the right price is a major hassle: all the seeds get in the way. We hope it will be a winner, once we get the production right and start converting customers to it. After all the market for exotic fruit juices generally is expanding fast.'

What sort of products, according to the Boston classification, are described here?

Answer

(a) Orange juice is a cash cow
(b) Pomegranate juice is a question mark, which the company wants to turn into a star.

Case Study

Unilever

Unilever reappraised its strategies in 1996, to revive sales in sated markets of Europe and America.

Unilever's cash cow is margarine. Unilever intends to focus on core product categories. Unilever says it know what it wanted to do but did not always succeed. **'Star'** categories such as ice cream and cosmetics were identified, but sometimes they were denied sufficient financial and human resources.

Unilever has introduced a new analytical tool to assess its businesses. Unilever will reduce its huge portfolio by 'harvesting' some products (taking profits but reinvesting little), and selling or closing others. The group has already disposed of its processed meats and mass-market cosmetics businesses in the past 18 months.

With fewer businesses, Unilever can pour more financial, technical and human resources into those that remain. It can also concentrate its efforts on emerging markets. Two years ago Unilever said it planned to have 30% of its turnover from emerging markets by 2000. This goal has now been achieved.

4.2.2 The General Electric Business Screen

The approach of the GE Business Screen (GEBS) is similar to that of the BCG matrix. The GEBS includes a broader range of company and market factors. A typical example of the GE matrix is provided on the next page. This matrix **classifies products (or businesses)** according to **industry attractiveness** and **company strengths**. The approach aims to consider a variety of factors which contribute to both these variables.

	Attractive	Average	Unattractive
Strong	Invest for growth	Invest selectively for growth	Develop for income
Average	Invest selectively and build	Develop selectively for income	Harvest or Divest
Weak	Develop selectively Build on strengths	Harvest	Divest

Business Strength (vertical axis: Strong, Average, Weak)

Market attractiveness (horizontal axis: Attractive, Average, Unattractive)

The broader approach of the GE matrix emphasises the attempt to match competences within the company to conditions within the market place. Difficulties associated with measurement and classification mean that again the results of such an exercise must be interpreted with care.

4.2.3 The Shell directional policy matrix

There have been several other matrices designed as guides to strategy. The **Shell directional policy matrix** is similar to the GEBS in that its classifications depend upon **managerial judgement** rather than simple **numerical scores**, as in the BCG matrix. Its axes are **competitive capability** and **prospects for sector profitability**. Clearly, these measures are very similar to those used in the GEBS.

Prospects for sector profitability

	Unattractive	Average	Attractive
Weak	Disinvest	Phased withdrawal	Double or quit
Average	Phased withdrawal	Custodial Growth	Try harder
Strong	Cash generation	Growth Leader	Leader

Enterprise's competitive capabilities (vertical axis: Weak, Average, Strong)

4.2.4 Problems with portfolio planning

Exam focus point

Portfolio planning, whether by means of market growth/market share analysis or product life cycle analysis, is something that you might be called on to apply yourself in an examination question. It is a useful approach to the analysis of a firm's product-market mix.

In addition to the questionable assumptions that the market is easy to define and that low cost is a result of experience, there are other important criticisms of the portfolio matrix approach.

(a) Its recommendations are over-simplistic and, in particular, make no mention of **innovation**.

(b) There are often dynamic links between products that mean that a successful product can be damaged if a less successful one is discontinued or starved of funds. **Completeness of range** is important to both consumers and distributors, for example.

(c)   While it implicitly considers the position of the market leader, **it ignores other rivals** that may be growing more effectively.

Also, it is difficult to convert these analyses into a planning technique for deciding the following:

(a)   How the position of the company's products in its markets should be **improved** – ie how much extra or less market share to go for.

(b)   What the **mix** of question marks, stars and cash cows ought to be.

(c)   How a policy of developing question marks into stars and stars into cash cows can be implemented in **practice**.

4.3 Direct product profitability

> The profitability of individual products should be reviewed.

This can be done using direct product profitability analysis. The management accountant may be called upon to review the profitability of a product or a product line.

4.3.1 Direct product profitability (DPP)

An example of how management accounting techniques are used in practice is **direct product profitability**. This is a technique to analyse the profit on each individual product line, to arrive at relative profitabilities of different products.

Key term

> **Direct product profitability** is a measure 'used primarily within the retail sector, (and) involves the attribution of both the purchase price and other indirect costs (for example distribution, warehousing and retailing) to each product line. Thus a net profit, as opposed to a gross profit, can be identified for each product. The cost attribution process utilises a variety of measures (for example warehousing space and transport time) to reflect the resource consumption of individual products.'   (CIMA *Official Terminology*)

DPP has grown primarily from the need for manufacturers to encourage retailers to place new products onto their shelves. Supermarkets analyse the direct profitability of every branded and non-branded product they sell. This helps them decide on what ranges to present in store and also provides a focus for individual marketing initiatives. The profitability of entire commodity groups is presented after taking account of factors in addition to cost, such as supplier discounts and wastage levels.

It is useful to analyse how DPP can be used in practice. We can take the limiting factor to be shelf space in this example.

	Product		
	X	Y	Z
Selling price	£1.50	£1.25	£1.30
Purchase cost	£1.00	£0.80	£1.00
Gross profit	£0.50	£0.45	£0.30
Gross profit % of sales price	33%	36%	23%
Shelf space per unit	15 cm²	9 cm²	12 cm²
Gross profit per cm²	3.3p	5p	2.5p

This would imply that Y was the most profitable for the retailer: however this ignores stock turnover. In other words, if sales volumes of Y are higher than for X or Z, the product makes a higher profit in total. Let us add sales volumes into the calculation and estimate as to how much shelf space the product takes up.

	Product		
	X	Y	Z
Gross profit per product	£0.50	£0.45	£0.30
Total shelf space	750 cm²	600 cm²	1,200 cm²
Weekly sales volume	30	20	60
Gross profit per cm² per week	$\frac{50p \times 30}{750} = 2p$	$\frac{45p \times 20}{600} = 1.5p$	$\frac{30p \times 60}{1,200} = 1.5p$

This analysis, based on sales volume suggests that for the retailer X is the better bet. Why might this be so?

(a) **Inventory turnover**. The manufacturer of X might offer to replenish the shelves twice a week, thereby halving the amount of space needed to support the same sales volume. This increases the profit per unit of scarce resource.

(b) **Product size**, as indicated, is a reason why the unit profit might differ. This is why packaging decisions can, from the retailer's viewpoint, affect a product's attractiveness.

This example demonstrates how it is necessary for the management accountant to obtain sufficient information before a meaningful analysis can be carried out. Simple information on cm² occupied per unit was insufficient. Sales volumes, total shelf space required and probably in some cases additional direct costs (such as handling, administration) all need to be taken into account.

The problems with DPP are these.

(a) Expenditure supporting a brand can be spread over a number of different individual products, and from the **manufacturer's** point of view it might not be a simple matter to allocate this expenditure properly.

(b) **Cross-subsidisation** is a feature of many product strategies. An example is provided by computer games.

   (i) The hardware (eg the games console) may be priced relatively cheaply:
      – To deter competitors (raising entry barriers)
      – To encourage customers to buy

   (ii) The software, or games which are run, will be priced relatively expensively, to recoup some of the cost. Also, barriers to entry will exist as the manufacturer will own patents, have exclusive distribution deals etc, and there will be a switching cost, of course.

   However, DPP overlooks these interrelations between products.

5 New products and innovation

5.1 Innovation

FAST FORWARD

Innovation can be a major source of competitive advantage but brings a burden of cost and uncertainty. To avoid waste, there should be a programme of assessment for major product development.

5.1.1 Innovation and competitive advantage

For many organisations, product innovation and being the **first mover** may be a major source of competitive advantage.

(a) A reputation for innovation will attract **early adopters**, though it depends in part on promotional effort.

(b) Customers may find they are locked in to innovative suppliers by unacceptable **costs of switching** to competitors.

(c) The **learning** (or experience) **curve** effect may bring cost advantages.

(d) The first mover may be able to **define the industry standard**.

(e) A **price skimming** strategy can bring early profits that will be denied to later entrants.

(f) Legal protection, such as patents, for intellectual property may bring important revenue advantages. This is particularly important in the pharmaceutical industry.

However, the first mover also has particular problems.

- Gaining regulatory approval where required
- Uncertain demand
- High levels of R&D costs
- Lower cost imitators
- Costs of introduction such as training sales staff and educating customers

PIMS data indicate that there is a **negative correlation** between **profitability** and a high level of expenditure on **R&D**, perhaps because of the costs associated with these problems.

5.1.2 Technology and the value chain

Porter points out in *Competitive Advantage* that 'every value activity uses some technology to combine purchased inputs and human resources to produce some output.' He goes on to discuss the varied role of **information technology** and emphasises the often-overlooked importance of **administrative** or **office technology**. The significance of this for strategy lies in the area of **core competences**. Just as **R&D** is as much concerned with processes as with products, so improvement in the linkages of the value chain will enhance competitive advantage.

5.2 New product strategies

The development of new products might be considered an important aspect of a firm's competitive and marketing strategies.

(a)   New and innovative products can lower **entry barriers** to existing industries and markets, if new technology is involved.

(b)   The interests of the company are best met with a balanced product portfolio. Managers therefore must plan when to introduce new products, how best to extend the life of mature ones and when to abandon those in decline.

A strategic issue managers must consider is their approach to new product development.

(a)   **Leader strategy**. Do they intend to gain competitive advantage by operating at the leading edge of new developments? There are significant implications for the R&D activity and the likely length of product life cycles within the portfolio if this strategy is adopted. Also, **R&D costs** are likely to be heavy, with a significant reduction in potential profitability as a result.

(b)   **Follower strategy**. Alternatively they can be more pro-active, adopt a follower strategy, which involves lower costs and less emphasis on the R & D activity. It sacrifices early rewards of innovation, but avoids its risks. A follower might have to license certain technologies from a leader (as is the case with many consumer electronics companies). However, research indicates that this can be a **more profitable strategy** than being an innovator, especially when the follower is able to learn from the leader's mistakes.

A matrix of new product strategies and new market strategies can be set out as follows.

	Product		
	No technological change	*Improved technology*	*New technology*
Market unchanged	–	*Reformulation* A new balance between price/quality has to be formulated	*Replacement* The new technology replaces the old
Market strengthened (ie new demand from same customers)	*Remerchandising* The product is sold in a new way – eg by re-packaging	*Improved product* Sales growth to existing customers sought on the strength of product improvements	*Product line extension* The new product is added to the existing product line to increase total demand
New market	*New use* By finding a new use for the existing product, new customers are found	*Market extension* New customers sought on the strength of product improvements	*Diversification*

5.3 Types of 'new' products

Booz, Allen and Hamilton identified the following categories in a survey of 700 firms.

- New to the world   10%
- New product lines   20%
- Additions to product line   26%
- Repositionings   7%
- Improvements/revisions   26%
- Cost reductions   11%

5.4 Research and development

Research may be **pure, applied** or **development**. It may be intended to improve **products** or **processes**. New product development should be controlled by requiring strategic approval at key points of development.

R&D should support the organisation's strategy and be closely co-ordinated with marketing. There are distinct problems to managing R&D.

Here are some definitions culled from *Statement of Standard Accounting Practice 13*.

Key terms

Pure research is original research to obtain new scientific or technical knowledge or understanding. There is no obvious commercial or practical end in view.

Applied research is also original research work like (a) above, but it has a specific practical aim or application (eg research on improvements in the effectiveness of medicines etc).

Development is the use of existing scientific and technical knowledge to produce new (or substantially improved) products or systems, prior to starting commercial production operations.

Many organisations employ **specialist staff** to conduct research and development (R&D). They may be organised in a separate functional department of their own. In an organisation run on a product division basis, R&D staff may be employed by each division.

5.5 Product and process research

There are two categories of R&D.

Key terms

Product research is based on creating new products and developing existing ones, in other words the organisation's 'offer' to the market.

Process research is based on improving the way in which those products or services are made or delivered, or the efficiency with which they are made or delivered.

Product research – new product development

The new product development process must be carefully controlled; new products are a major source of competitive advantage but can cost a great deal of money to bring to market. A screening process is necessary to ensure that resources are concentrated on projects with a high probability of success and not wasted on those that have poor prospects.

Cooper describes a typical modern screening process that he calls **Stage-Gate™**. This emphasises a cross-functional, prioritised, quality managed, project management approach consisting, typically, of five stages. Each stage begins with a **gate**; that is, a review meeting of managers who have the power either to kill the project or to allocate the resources necessary for it to progress to the next gate. Each gate incorporates the same three management elements.

(a)   **Deliverables** are the results of the preceding stage's activity and are specified at its beginning.

(b)   **Criteria** are applied by the decision makers to judge the progress of the project and decide whether or not to continue with it.

(c)   **Outputs** are a **decision**, and such things as an **action plan**, a **budget** and a list of **deliverables** for the next gate.

A typical five stage process would look like this.

(a)   The new idea is subjected to an initial screening to check such things as basic feasibility, strategic fit and marketability. Financial criteria are not usually applied at this stage.
This is **Gate 1**.

(b)   **Stage 1. Preliminary investigation**.

Preliminary investigation is likely to take less than a month and concentrates on preliminary assessment of market potential, technical implications and financial viability. Quick legal and risk assessments will also take place. This stage leads to **Gate 2**, which is similar to gate 1 in nature, but more rigorous. Gates 1 and 2 are probably operated by middle level managers since, in each case, the resources required to progress to the next stage are only moderate.

(c)   **Stage 2. Business case**.

It is now appropriate to **build a business case** for the project. The product is defined in detail and a full **marketing analysis** is carried out, featuring such processes as competitor analysis, user needs-and-wants studies, and value-in-use studies. There are also full **technical** and **manufacturing appraisals** and a detailed **financial analysis**. **Gate 3** assesses this business case and is probably operated by the company's senior management team, since approval at this stage will lead to heavy expenditure.

(d)   **Stage 3. Physical development**.

The physical development of the product now proceeds, subject to a strict time schedule and budget of resources. Lengthy development phases may incorporate their own project management milestones to ensure control, but these are not formal gates in the Cooper sense. This stage leads to **Gate 4**, the **post development review**. The emphasis here is not on whether to proceed further but on ensuring that the project is on track and on reviewing the earlier work on feasibility using up to date information.

(e)   **Stage 4. Testing and validation**.

This is the **testing and validation** stage and validates the entire commercial viability of the project. It may include **pilot production**, **field trials** and **test marketing**. **Gate 5** is **precommercialisation business analysis**. This gives top management the opportunity to check the work done in the testing and validation stage and apply final financial return and launch planning criteria.

(f)   **Stage 5. Full production and market launch**.

Both full production and market launch must be carefully monitored and lead inexorably to the **post implementation review**, which considers the degree of success achieved by both the new product itself and the development process that led to its launch.

External to the **Stage-Gate™** management process are **idea generation** and **strategy formulation**.

(a)   **Idea generation**, to be effective requires a system to promote, and reward creativity and innovative ideas. You will find lots of ideas elsewhere in this Study Text about how this can be done. Cooper suggests a four point plan.

   (i)   Nominate one manager to be the **focal point for ideas**.
   (ii)   That manager establishes where ideas may **arise**.
   (iii) Those sources are **encouraged**.
   (iv)   The ideas they produce are **captured**.

(b)   **Strategy formulation**. A business should have a detailed new product strategy, specifying goals, priorities, funding and methods. This is a top management responsibility.

Product research is not confined to dealing with new products. It has an important role in connection with **existing products**.

(a) **Value engineering** may be used to continue the development of existing products so that they use less costly components or processes without compromising the perceived value of the market offer.

(b) As products near the end of their **life cycle**, it may be possible to develop them for launch in a different market, or simply to extend their lives.

(c) Where products are being replaced by new versions it may be advantageous to ensure that the new products are **backwards compatible** with the installed base. This is an important consideration in software engineering, for example.

5.6 Process research

Process research involves attention to how the goods/services are produced. Process research has these aspects.

(a) **Processes** are crucial in service industries (eg fast food), where processes are part of the services sold.

(b) **Productivity**. Efficient processes save money and time.

(c) **Planning**. If you know how long certain stages in a project are likely to take, you can plan the most efficient sequence.

(d) **Quality management** for enhanced quality.

An important aspect of process research is that advances are much more difficult to imitate then are product developments. Competitors can purchase and **reverse engineer** new products. With good physical security in place, they will find it much more difficult to imitate new processes.

The strategic role of R&D. R&D should support the organisation's chosen strategy. To take a simple example, if a strategy of **differentiation** has been adopted, it would be inappropriate to expend effort on researching ways of minimising costs. If the company has a competence in R&D, this may form the basis for a strategy of product innovation. Conversely, where product lifecycles are short, as in consumer electronics, product development is fundamental to strategy.

5.7 Problems with R&D

(a) **Organisational**. Problems of authority relationships and integration arise with the management of R&D. The function will have to liase closely with marketing and with production, as well as with senior management responsible for corporate planning: its role is both strategic and technical.

(b) **Financial**. R&D is by nature not easily planned in advance, and financial performance targets are not easily set. Budgeting for long-term, complex development projects with uncertain returns can be a nightmare for management accountants.

(c) **Evaluation and control**. Pure research or even applied research may not have an obvious pay off in the short term. Evaluation could be based on successful application of new ideas, such as patents obtained and the commercial viability of new products.

(d) **Staff problems**. Research staff are usually highly qualified and profession-orientated, with consequences for the style of supervision and level of remuneration offered to them.

(e) **Cultural problems**. Encouraging innovation means trial and error, flexibility, tolerance of mistakes in the interests of experimentation, high incentives etc. If this is merely a subculture in an essentially bureaucratic organisation, it will not only be difficult to sustain, but will become a source of immense 'political' conflict. The R&D department may have an 'academic' or university atmosphere, as opposed to a commercial one.

5.8 R&D and marketing

(a) Customer needs, as identified by marketers, should be a vital input to new product developments.

(b) The R&D department might identify possible changes to product specifications so that a variety of marketing mixes can be tried out and screened.

Case Study

An example of the relationship of R&D to marketing was described in an article in the *Financial Times* (14 July 1992) about the firm Nestlé, which invests £46m a year in research (and approximately £190m on development). Nestlé had a central R&D function, but also regional development centres. The central R&D function was involved in basic research. 'Much of the lab's work was only tenuously connected with the company's business... When scientists joined the lab, they were told "Just work in this or that area. If you work hard enough, we're sure you'll find something"'. The results of this approach were:

(a)   The research laboratory was largely cut off from development centres.

(b)   Much research never found commercial application.

As part of Nestlé's wider reorganisation, which restructured the business into strategic business units (SBU's), formal links have been established between R&D and the SBUs. This means that research procedures have been changed so that a commercial time horizon is established for some projects.

5.8.1 Intrapreneurship

FAST FORWARD

Intrapreneurship is entrepreneurship carried on within the organisation at a level below the strategic apex.

The encouragement of intrapreneurship is an important way of promoting innovation. Such encouragement has many aspects.

(a)   Encouragement for individuals to achieve results in their own way without the need for constant supervision

(b)   A culture of risk-taking and tolerance of mistakes

(c)   A flexible approach to organisation that facilitates the formation of project teams

(d)   Willingness and ability to devote resources to trying out new ideas

(e)   Incentives and rewards policy that support intrapreneurial activity

Case Study

Disney and Pixar

Organisational culture is an extremely important influence on innovation. A Financial Times report on **Disney's** purchase of **Pixar** in 2006 contrasted their distinct organisational styles.

> 'Disney has become a pathologically dysfunctional organisation. Like IBM of the 1970s or AT&T in the 1980s, Disney grew fat and bureaucratic in the 1990s, long after cementing its lucrative entertainment franchise. Some of Disney's problems are endemic to large corporations. When a company has 133,000 employees, it cannot be governed by human beings. Instead, it must rely on a culture to preserve its earlier entreprenuerialism, while focusing workers on the continuing mission.
>
> Unfortunately, Disney's culture, like that of IBM and AT&T, encouraged inefficiency and stifled creativity. Over the past five years, Disney's shares have lost a third of their value and the company has become a corporate governance pariah. Many thought the low point was the fiasco surrounding Michael Ovitz, who left Disney with $140m after just 14 months. But more troubling was the release of the abysmal *Treasure Planet*, a film that cost about as much as Mr Ovitz and avoided universal ignominy only because so few people saw it.
>
> To survive and prosper, large organisations must be divided into manageable pods, whose workers have independence and incentive. In contrast to Disney, Pixar was just such a free-standing, free-spirited group with a relaxed, open-plan office and no signs of managerial hierarchy. John Lasseter, Pixar's creative leader, wore Hawaiian shirts and rode a scooter inside. When Pixar won Oscars, employees displayed the statues proudly but dressed them in Barbie doll clothing. Whereas Disney executives micromanaged films, including those with Pixar, Mr Lasseter let his crew run free and encouraged ideas.'

5.8.2 Drivers for innovation

Market pull

Marketers would have us believe that the best way to competitive advantage is to find out what the market wants and give it to them. We might call this approach, when applied to innovation, **market pull**.

Technology push

Unfortunately, market pull innovation tends merely to produce better versions of products that already exist. A more fruitful approach may be the 'product orientation', disdained by the marketing fraternity: the world is full of products that no-one asked for, including post-it notes and mobile phones that are also cameras. This approach we might call **technology push**.

Collaboration

Perhaps the most fruitful approach would be a combination of the two, where technologists try to solve customers' problems and marketers try to find applications for new and emerging technologies. Many new developments are, in fact, the result of **collaboration between suppliers and customers**.

 Case Study

Microsoft and Sony

A company's policy on innovation will be linked to its assessment of how the product lifecycle concept applies to its portfolio.

Microsoft has generally followed a policy of fairly limited incremental upgrades. Writing in the *Financial Times* on 19 May 2005, *John Gapper* pointed out that it had used this approach to gradually outflank *Apple's* OS, developing a credible alternative by steadily updating its *Windows* operating system. It followed a similar policy in upgrading its *Xbox* games console, releasing the *Xbox 360* only four years after the first Xbox.

Sony, on the other hand, has taken a longer view, working on a 10 year life cycle for video games consoles. This has led it to give its new *PlayStation 3* far greater imaging power than the Xbox 360 possesses. PlayStation 3's potential can only be realised by coupling it to a high-definition TV: the planned life of the product will give time for such TVs to become affordable and widely purchased.

6 Benchmarking   11/06, 5/05

FAST FORWARD

Benchmarking enables a firm to meet industry standards by copying others, but it is perhaps less valuable as a source of innovation.

Key term

Benchmarking is the 'establishment, through data gathering, of targets and comparators, that permit relative levels of performance (and particularly areas of underperformance) to be identified. Adoption of identified best practices should improve performance.

- **Internal benchmarking**. Comparing one operating unit or function with another within the same industry.
- **Functional benchmarking**. Comparing internal functions with those of the best external practitioners, regardless of their industry (also known as operational benchmarking or generic benchmarking).
- **Competitive benchmarking**. In which information is gathered about direct competitors through techniques such as reverse engineering.
- **Strategic benchmarking**. Type of competitive benchmarking aimed at strategic action and organisational change.'   (CIMA *Official Terminology*)

Benchmarking can be divided into stages.

Stage 1   **Obtain management support**

The first stage is to **ensure senior management commitment** to the benchmarking process. This will only be genuinely available when the senior managers have a full appreciation of what is involved: the objectives of the project, its benefits and its costs. Senior management are quite capable of changing their minds when it becomes apparent that they did not anticipate the actual levels of cost or inconvenience a project may bring, for example. For the project to be a success it is essential that senior management endorse it.

Stage 2   **Determine the areas to be benchmarked and set objectives**

Determine areas to benchmark. The areas to be benchmarked should be determined by identifying the critical business processes or those which are the main drivers of revenues and costs.

Set objectives. Note that here, the objectives will not be in the form of aspirations for improvement to specific processes and practices, but more in the nature of stating the extent and depth of the **enquiry**.

Stage 3   **Understand processes and identify key performance measures**

Understand processes. Before any key performance measures can be set, the benchmarking team will need to understand the processes which drive them. This will require discussion with **key stakeholders** plus observation and documentation of the way work is carried out.

Identify key performance measures. Once the team understand the processes, then they can identify key performance measures for the processes (for example, the length of time between receiving a customer order and despatching the goods ordered).

Stage 4   **Choose organisations to benchmark against**

This can either be done **internally** (comparing one division against another) or through **external** competitive benchmarking (comparing performance with rival companies). Firms often want to compare their performance against the '**best in class**' external performer.

Stage 5   **Measure performance**

Measure own and others' performance. Negotiation should take place to establish just who does the measurement. Ideally, a joint team made up of people from both the organisations being benchmarked should do it, but there may be issues of **confidentiality** or **convenience** that mean each organisation does its own measuring.

Stage 6   **Compare performance and discuss results**

Raw data must be carefully analysed if appropriate conclusions are to be drawn.

Discuss results with management and staff. It will be appropriate to discuss initial findings with the **stakeholders** concerned: they are likely both to have useful comment to offer and also to be anxious about the possibility of adverse reflection upon them. It is important to remember that the purpose of benchmarking is not to apportion blame for poor performance, but to act as an opportunity to improve performance.

Stage 7   **Improvement programmes**

Design and implement improvement programmes. It may be possible to import complete systems; alternatively, it may be appropriate to move towards a synthesis that combines various elements of best practice. Sometimes, improvements require extensive **reorganisation** and **restructuring,** and may sometimes also involve **outsourcing**.

In many cases, there is likely to be a requirement for **training**. Improvements in administrative systems often call for investment in new equipment, particularly in IT systems.

Stage 8 Monitor improvements

The continuing effectiveness of improvements must be monitored. At the same time, it must be understood that **improvement is a continuous process rather than a one-off change** and so further adjustments (and follow-up benchmarking exercises) may be beneficial.

Johnson and Scholes and Whittington set out questions that should be asked when carrying out a benchmarking exercise as part of a wider strategic review.

- **Why** are these products or services provided at all?
- Why are they provided **in that particular way**?
- What are the examples of **best practice** elsewhere?
- How should activities be **reshaped** in the light of these comparisons?

They see three levels of benchmarking.

Level of benchmarking	Through	Examples of measures
Resources	Resource audit	Quantity of resources • revenue/employee • capital intensity Quality of resources • Qualifications of employees • Age of machinery • Uniqueness (eg patents)
Competences in separate activities	Analysing activities	Sales calls per salesperson Output per employee Materials wastage
Competences in linked activities	Analysing overall performances	Market share Profitability Productivity

Exam focus point

You could use the information above as the framework for an answer to a question about carrying out a benchmarking exercise. A May 2005 25-mark question covered benchmarking in a medical charity, and its potential impact on staff. The question was fairly straightforward: 8 marks for the advantages and disadvantages, 13 for the stages of conducting a benchmarking exercise and 4 for implementing the benchmarking plan.

When selecting an appropriate **benchmark basis**, companies should ask themselves the following questions.

(a) Is it possible and easy to obtain reliable competitor information?

(b) Is there any wide discrepancy between different internal divisions?

(c) Can similar processes be identified in non-competing environments and are these non competing companies willing to co-operate?

(d) Is best practice operating in a similar environmental setting?

(e) What is our timescale?

(f) Do the chosen companies have similar objectives and strategies?

6.1 Advantages of benchmarking

Benchmarking has the following advantages.

(a) **Position audit**. Benchmarking can assess a firm's existing position, and provide a basis for establishing standards of performance.

(b) The comparisons are **carried out by the managers** who have to live with any changes implemented as a result of the exercise.

(c) Benchmarking **focuses** on improvement in key areas and sets targets which are challenging but evidently achievable.

(d) The sharing of information can be a **spur to innovation**.

(e) The result should be **improved performance**, particularly in cost control and delivering value.

6.2 Dangers of benchmarking

Many companies have gained significant benefits from benchmarking but it is worth pointing out a number of possible dangers.

(a) It concentrates on **doing things right** rather than **doing the right thing**: the difference between **efficiency** and **effectiveness**. A process can be efficient but its output may not be useful. Other measures (such as amending the value chain) may be a better way of securing competitive advantage.

(b) The benchmark may be **yesterday's solution to tomorrow's problem**. For example, a cross-channel ferry company might benchmark its activities (eg speed of turnround at Dover and Calais, cleanliness on ship) against another ferry company, whereas the real competitor is the Channel Tunnel.

(c) It is a **catching-up exercise** rather than the development of anything distinctive. After the benchmarking exercise, the competitor might improve performance in a different way.

(d) It depends on **accurate** information about comparator companies.

(e) It is **not cost-free** and can divert **management attention**.

(f) It can become a hindrance and even a threat: **sharing information** with other companies can be a burden and a security risk.

(g) It may actually reduce managerial motivation, if the performance of the managers' areas is compared unfavourably to rival organisations.

 Case Study

A recent five year research programme by INSEAD business school identified the following five companies as likely to still be successful 10 or 20 years from now.

- American International Group (AIG), the US insurer
- Heineken, the Dutch brewer
- Hewlett-Packard, the US electronics manufacturer
- JP Morgan, the US bank
- SGS Thomson, the Franco-Italian semiconductor maker

The underlying premise of the study , as reported in the *Financial Times*, is that success or failure depends on a complex series of actions. Companies were compared on 12 capabilities – customer orientation, technical resources, market strategy and so forth. An overall score for effectiveness was calculated.

The study showed how the best companies go about their business, and allowed others to diagnose their shortcomings. To quote the project leader when talking about IBM: 'There was a time when it was the best at customer orientation. If we had had this tool 20 years ago, we could have seen it going wrong.'

Chapter Roundup

- To develop a strategic plan, an organisation's management must be aware of the current position of the organisation.

- For many companies this might involve a broader review of the firm's:
  - effectiveness in meeting the needs of its chosen client or stakeholder groups;
  - efficiency in the use of resources (the maximum output for a given level of input).

- Firms do not have unlimited resources, and so have to do the best they can from limiting factors.

- The **value chain** models all the activities of a business and the linkages between them. It shows how value is created, how costs are caused and how competitive advantage can be gained.

- The **product life cycle** concept holds that products have a life cycle, and that a product demonstrates different characteristics of profit and investment at each stage in its life cycle. The life cycle concept is a model, not a prediction. (Not all products pass through each stage of the life cycle.) It enables a firm to examine its portfolio of goods and services as a whole.

- **Portfolio analysis** examines the current status of the organisation's products and their markets. Portfolio analysis is the first stage of **portfolio planning**, which aims to create a balance among the organisation's market offerings in order to maximise competitive advantage. The same approach is equally applicable to products, market segments and even SBUs.

- The **Boston classification** classifies products in terms of their capacity for growth within the market and the market's capacity for growth as a whole. A firm should have a balanced **portfolio of products**. The GE Business Screen and the Shell matrix are similar tools.

- The profitability of individual products should be reviewed.

- **Innovation** can be a major source of competitive advantage but brings a burden of cost and uncertainty. To avoid waste, there should be a programme of assessment for major product development.

- Research may be **pure, applied** or **development**. It may be intended to improve **products** or **processes**. New product development should be controlled by requiring strategic approval at key points of development.

- R&D should support the organisation's strategy and be closely co-ordinated with marketing. There are distinct problems to managing R&D.

- **Intrapreneurship** is entrepreneurship carried on within the organisation at a level below the strategic apex.

- **Benchmarking** enables a firm to meet industry standards by copying others, but it is perhaps less valuable as a source of innovation.

1   Position audit is part of the planning process which examines the current state of the entity in respect of:

    R ....
    P ....
    O ....
    I ....
    C ....
    R ....

2   What are the 9 'Ms' categorised in the Ms model?

3   What is a limiting or key factor? Give an example.

4   Which of these describes 'efficiency', and which 'effectiveness'?

    (a)   Whether the resources have been deployed in the best possible way.

    (b)   How well the resources have been utilised irrespective of the purpose for which they have been employed.

5   Is logistics a primary or secondary activity in the value chain?

6   In Porter's value chain model, who is value ultimately created for?

7   What are the stages of the product life cycle?

8   Complete the BCG matrix below

Market ....

		High	Low
Market	High	....	....
	Low	....	....

9   Who are the chief users of direct product profitability?

10   What are Johnson, Scholes and Whittington's three levels of benchmarking?

1   • Resources of tangible and intangible assets and finance
    • Products, brands and markets
    • Operating systems (such as production and distribution)
    • Internal organisation
    • Current results
    • Returns to stockholders

2   Machinery; Make-up; Management; Management Information; Markets, Materials; Men and women; Methods; Money

3   A limiting factor or key factor is 'a factor which at any time or over a period may limit the activity of an entity, often one where there is shortage or difficulty of supply.' An example would be a shortage of production capacity.

4   (a)   effectiveness
    (b)   efficiency

5   Primary

6   The end-user consumer. The value chain expresses the way value is added to the products or services produced by an entity from the perspective of the end-user consumer (not from the perspective of the organisation.)

7   Introduction, growth, stakeout, maturity, decline.

8

| | Market share | |
	High	Low
Market growth — High	Stars	Question marks
Market growth — Low	Cash cows	Dogs

9   Retailers, because it takes into account factors such as inventory turnover and shelf space.

10 Resources, competences in separate activities, competences in linked activities.

Now try the question below from the Exam Question Bank

Number	Level	Marks	Time
Q7	Intermediate	n/a	30 mins

8

SWOT analysis and gap analysis

Introduction

In SWOT analysis (Section 1) we combine the results of the **environmental analysis** we covered in Chapters 4 and 5 with the internal appraisal covered in Chapter 6, to see how the organisation's strategy (specifically its strengths and weaknesses) is able to deal with changes in the environment.

The position audit identifies **strengths and weaknesses** (Section 2). The environmental analysis identifies **opportunities and threats** (Section 3). These are combined (Section 4) so that appropriate strategies can be suggested which will exploit core competences.

Gap analysis (Section 5) indicates the scale of the task to be achieved to reach the organisation's financial objectives, while **forecasting** and **scenario planning** are undertaken by firms to try and predict what the future will be.

These analyses indicate the type of strategic decisions that need to be addressed.

Topic list	Learning outcomes	Syllabus references	Ability required
1 Corporate appraisal: SWOT analysis	A(iii), A(iv)	A2	Evaluation
2 Strengths and weaknesses	A(iii), A(iv)	A2	Evaluation
3 Opportunities and threats	A(iii), A(iv)	A2	Evaluation
4 Combining the elements of the SWOT analysis	A(iii), A(iv)	A2	Evaluation
5 Analysing the planning gap	C(i)	C3	Evaluation
6 Forecasting	C(i)	C2	Evaluation
7 Scenario planning	C(i)	C3	Evaluation

1 Corporate appraisal: SWOT analysis

SWOT analysis or corporate appraisal is a quantitative and qualitative review of internal **strengths** and **weaknesses** and their relationship with external **threats** and **opportunities**.

Having gathered information about itself and its environment from a **position audit** and an **environmental analysis**, strategic planners can go on to make a **corporate appraisal**.

Key term

> **Corporate appraisal** is a 'critical assessment of the strengths and weaknesses, opportunities and threats (**SWOT analysis**) in relation to the internal and environmental factors affecting an entity in order to establish its condition prior to the preparation of the long term plan'. (CIMA *Official Terminology*)

(a) **Strengths and weaknesses** analysis involves looking at the particular strengths and weaknesses of the organisation itself and its product/service range. It is an **internal appraisal**.

(b) An analysis of **opportunities and threats** is concerned with profit-making opportunities in the business environment, and with identifiable threats. It is therefore an **external appraisal**.

It is important to remember the phrase 'critical assessment' used in the Key Term above. A simple listing of four types of factor is not likely to produce a robust and workable strategy. The managers involved must have a detailed and intimate understanding of the nature and implications of the factors. In particular, it is important to be **realistic**, erring neither towards optimism nor towards pessimism.

1.1 SWOT: positioning-based or resource-based?

In this Text, we have laid out our discussion of the strategy-making process in accordance with the traditional positioning-based approach: we therefore discuss SWOT at this stage as a kind of summary or synthesis of our prior examination of resources and environment in the light of our mission statement.

It is important to understand that the alternative, more recently developed resource-based approach to strategy would use SWOT as the first stage of the strategy making process, seeking to establish the nature of the organisation's core competences before deciding what the objectives of strategy should be.

2 Strengths and weaknesses

Strengths and weaknesses are internal matters. The management accountant's role is to appraise and measure them.

In essence, an internal appraisal seeks to identify the following.

- **Shortcomings** in the company's present skills and resources
- **Strengths** which the company should seek to exploit

The precise content of the SWOT analysis will depend on the company.

Area	Issues
Marketing	Fate of new product launches Use of advertising Market shares and market sizes Growth markets Success rate of the sales team Level of customer/client service
Products and brands	Analysis of sales Margin and contribution Product quality Reputation of brands Age and future life of products Price elasticity of demand

Area	Issues
Distribution	Service standards Delivery fleet facilities Geographical availability
Research and development	Relevance Costs Benefits Workload
Finance	Availability of funds Contribution Returns on investment Accounting ratios
Plant and equipment/ production	Production capacity Value of assets Land and buildings Economies of scale
Management and staff	Age Skills Industrial relations Training Recruitment Communications
Business management: organisation	Organisation structure Management style Communication links Information systems Strategic intelligence
Raw material and finished goods inventories	Sources of supply Turnover periods Storage capacity Obsolescence and deterioration

The appraisal should give particular attention to the following.

(a) **A study of past accounts and the use of ratios**. By looking at trends, or by comparing ratios with those of other firms in a similar industry, it might be possible to identify strengths and weaknesses.

(b) **Product position** and product-market portfolio.

(c) **Cash and financial structure**. If a company intends to expand or diversify, it will need cash or sufficient financial standing in order to acquire subsidiaries by issuing shares.

(d) **Cost structure**. If a company operates with high fixed costs and relatively low variable costs, it might be in a relatively weak position with regards to production capacity as this implies a high breakeven point.

(e) **Managerial ability**. Objective measurements should be sought.

2.1 The role of the management accountant in strengths and weaknesses analysis

The role of the management accountant will be to supply relevant information for this appraisal to be carried out successfully. Improving results within the existing business can take the form of cutting costs and/or improving product appeal.

(a) **Cost effectiveness programme**
  (i) Improvements to labour utilisation
  (ii) Reduction in systems costs and delays
  (iii) Implementation of a value analysis programme

(b) **Product analysis**
  (i) An analysis of competing products to see what features might be 'copied'
  (ii) Marketing appeal of competing products to see if improved products can be developed cost effectively
  (iii) An analysis of what customers require, and if these requirements can be supplied cheaply

(c) **Product attitude survey**
  (i) How do the customers see our products?
  (ii) Sales staff opinions
  (iii) Brand image in comparison with competitors

Specific areas of finance or accounting where weaknesses may exist include the following.

- The average debtors' payment period and credit taken from suppliers
- Liquidity
- Investments in stock
- Interest rates on current loans
- Earning interest on cash in hand
- Tax liability arrangements
- Under-utilised assets
- Overall utilisation of assets
- The interest burden and the gearing level

However, it is in the area of **product profitability** that the greatest opportunities are likely to exist.

- Changes in pricing policy, and the potential response from the competition or risks of a potential price war
- Increasing sales in existing markets
- Entering new markets with existing products
- Improving product sales appeal by, for example, market segmentation
- Improving distribution services
- Reducing overhead costs
- Reducing labour and material costs
- Rationalising the product range
- Standardising parts of a product or methods of manufacture

3 Opportunities and threats

 Opportunities and threats exist in the environment.

An **external appraisal** is required to identify profit-making opportunities which can be exploited by the company's strengths and also to anticipate environmental threats (a declining economy, competitors' actions, government legislation, industrial unrest etc) against which the company must protect itself.

An effective SWOT analysis needs to combine both *internal* and *external* factors, so internal strengths and weaknesses should be appraised alongside an environmental analysis. The PEST analysis will highlight the opportunities and threats an organisation faces.

For **opportunities**, it is necessary to decide the following.

- What opportunities exist in the business environment?
- What is the capability profile of competitors? Are they better placed to exploit these opportunities?
- What is the company's comparative performance potential in this field of opportunity?

For **threats**, it is necessary to decide the following.

- What threats might arise, to the company or its business environment?
- How will market players be affected?

Opportunities and threats might relate to any or all of the items covered in Chapters 4 and 5.

(a)   **Economic**: a recession might imply poor sales.

(b)   **Political**: legislation may affect a company's prospects through the threats/ opportunities of pollution control or a ban on certain products, for example.

(c)   **Competitors** can threaten to 'steal' customers with better and/or cheaper products or services.

(d)   **Technology**: if technological changes are anticipated, there is a possibility of new products appearing, or cheaper means of production or distribution being introduced.

(e)   **Social** attitudes can be a threat.

Exam focus point

The compulsory case study question may ask you for a corporate appraisal of the company outlined in the scenario.

4 Combining the elements of the SWOT analysis

FAST FORWARD

Strategies should be developed to remove weaknesses or develop strengths and to exploit opportunities and counter threats.

SWOT analysis indicates the **types of strategies** that appear to be available, both to exploit strengths and opportunities and to deal with weaknesses and defend against threats.

The internal and external appraisals of SWOT analysis will be brought together. It is likely that **alternative strategies** will emerge from the identification of strengths, weaknesses, opportunities and threats.

(a)   Major strengths and profitable opportunities can be exploited especially if strengths and opportunities are matched with each other.

(b)   Major weaknesses and threats should be countered, or a contingency strategy or corrective strategy developed.

4.1 The cruciform chart

A **cruciform chart** is a table summarising significant strengths, weaknesses, opportunities and threats. In the example below, the development of potential strategies from an analysis is illustrated.

Strengths	Weaknesses
£10 million of capital available.	Heavy reliance on a small number of customers.
Production expertise and appropriate marketing skills.	Limited product range, with no new products and expected market decline.
	Small marketing organisation.
Opportunities	**Threats**
Government tax incentives for new investment.	Major competitor has already entered the new market.
Growing demand in a new market, although customers so far relatively small in number.	

In this simple example, it might be possible to identify that the company is in imminent danger of losing its existing markets and must diversify. The new market opportunity exists to be exploited and since the number of customers is currently few, the relatively small size of the existing marketing force would not be an immediate hindrance.

In practice, **a combination of individual strategies** will be required with regard to product development, market development, diversification, resource planning, risk reduction etc. The following three steps are taken.

- The gap between the current position of the firm and its planned targets is estimated
- One or more courses of action are proposed
- These are tested for their 'gap-reducing properties'

It will help you to get used to the basic thinking that underlies strategic planning if you try a short exercise in SWOT analysis.

Question   Strengths and weaknesses

Learning outcome A(iii)

Hall Faull Downes Ltd has been in business for 25 years, during which time profits have risen by an average of 3% per annum, although there have been peaks and troughs in profitability due to the ups and downs of trade in the customers' industry. The increase in profits until five years ago was the result of increasing sales in a buoyant market, but more recently, the total market has become somewhat smaller and Hall Faull Downes has only increased sales and profits as a result of improving its market share.

The company produces components for manufacturers in the engineering industry.

In recent years, the company has developed many new products and currently has 40 items in its range compared to 24 only five years ago. Over the same five year period, the number of customers has fallen from 20 to nine, two of whom together account for 60% of the company's sales.

Give your appraisal of the company's future, and suggest what it is probably doing wrong.

Answer

A general interpretation of the facts as given might be sketched as follows.

(a)   Objectives: the company has no declared objectives. Profits have risen by 3% per annum in the past, which has failed to keep pace with inflation but may have been a satisfactory rate of increase in the current conditions of the industry. Even so, stronger growth is indicated in the future.

(b)

Strengths	Weaknesses
Many new products developed. Marketing success in increasing market share	Products may be reaching the end of their life and entering decline. New product life cycles may be shorter. Reduction in customers. Excessive reliance on a few customers. Doubtful whether profit record is satisfactory.
Threats	**Opportunities**
Possible decline in the end-product. Smaller end-product market will restrict future sales prospects for Hall Faull Downes.	None identified.

(c)   Strengths: the growth in company sales in the last five years has been as a result of increasing the market share in a declining market. This success may be the result of the following.

(i)   Research and development spending.
(ii)   Good product development programmes.
(iii)   Extending the product range to suit changing customer needs.
(iv)   Marketing skills.

(v)   Long-term supply contracts with customers.

(vi)   Cheap pricing policy.

(vii)   Product quality and reliable service.

(d)   Weaknesses:

    (i)   The products may be custom-made for customers so that they provide little or no opportunity for market development.

    (ii)   Products might have a shorter life cycle than in the past, in view of the declining total market demand.

    (iii) Excessive reliance on two major customers leaves the company exposed to the dangers of losing their custom.

(e)   Threats: there may be a decline in the end-market for the customers' product so that the customer demands for the company's own products will also fall.

(f)   Opportunities: no opportunities have been identified, but in view of the situation as described, new strategies for the longer term would appear to be essential.

(g)   Conclusions: the company does not appear to be planning beyond the short-term, or is reacting to the business environment in a piecemeal fashion. A strategic planning programme should be introduced.

(h)   Recommendations: the company must look for new opportunities in the longer-term.

    (i)   In the short term, current strengths must be exploited to continue to increase market share in existing markets and product development programmes should also continue.

    (ii)   In the longer term, the company must diversify into new markets or into new products and new markets. Diversification opportunities should be sought with a view to exploiting any competitive advantage or synergy that might be achievable.

    (iii) The company should use its strengths (whether in R&D, production skills or marketing expertise) in exploiting any identifiable opportunities.

    (iv)   Objectives need to be quantified in order to assess the extent to which new long-term strategies are required.

4.2 Using SWOT analysis to generate strategy

Having constructed a matrix of strengths, weaknesses, opportunities and threats with some evaluation attached to them, it then becomes feasible to make use of that matrix in guiding strategy formulation. The two major options are as follows.

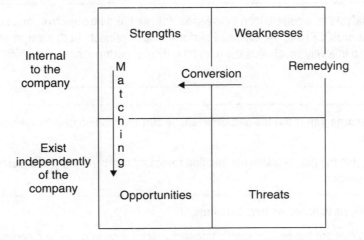

(a)   **Matching**

This entails finding, where possible, a match between the strengths of the organisation and the opportunities presented by the market.

(b)   **Conversion**

This requires the development of strategies which will convert weaknesses into strengths in order to take advantage of some particular opportunity.

A third possible option is to attempt to **remedy weaknesses** so as to reduce exposure to threats and increase the ability to grasp opportunities. However, this course does not in itself lead to a sustainable strategy and is best regarded as a preliminary phase to matching or conversion.

4.3 Weirich's TOWS matrix

Weirich, one of the earliest writers on corporate appraisal, originally spoke in terms of a TOWS matrix in order to emphasise the importance of threats and opportunities. Note that this is therefore an inherently **positioning** approach to strategy. A further important element of Weirich's discussion was his categorisation of strategic options.

- **SO strategies** employ strengths to seize opportunities.
- **ST strategies** employ strengths to counter or avoid threats.
- **WO strategies** address weaknesses so as to be able to exploit opportunities.
- **WT strategies** are defensive, aiming to avoid threats and the impact of weaknesses.

One useful impact of this analysis is that the four groups of strategies tend to relate well to different time horizons. SO strategies may be expected to produce good short-term results, while WO strategies are likely to take much longer to show results. ST and WT strategies are probably more relevant to the medium term.

This consideration of time horizon may be linked to the overall resource picture: SO strategies can be profitable in the short term, generating the cash needed for investment in WT strategies, improving current areas of weakness so that further opportunities may be seized. ST and WT strategies are likely to be more or less resource-neutral, but care must be taken to achieve an overall balance.

5 Analysing the planning gap   11/07

> **FAST FORWARD**
>
> **Gap analysis** quantifies the size of the gap between the objective for the planning period and the forecast based on the extrapolation of the current situation, and current prospects.

Having carried out a SWOT analysis, strategic planners must next think about the extent to which new strategies are needed to enable the organisation to achieve its objectives. One technique whereby this can be done is **gap analysis**.

Key term

> **Gap analysis** is 'a comparison between an entity's ultimate objective (most commonly expressed in terms of profit or ROCE) and the expected performance of projects both planned and underway. Differences are classified in a way which aids the understanding of performance, and which facilitates improvement.'
>
> (CIMA *Official Terminology*)

Point to note

> The **planning gap** is **not** the gap between the current position of the organisation and the desired future position.
>
> Rather, it is the gap between the position forecast from continuing with current activities, and the desired future position.

Gap analysis is based on two questions.

(a)   What are the organisation's targets for achievement over the planning period?

(b)   What would the organisation be expected to achieve if it 'did nothing' – ie did not develop any new strategies, but simply carried on in the current way with the same products and selling to the same markets?

This difference is the gap. New strategies will then have to be developed which will close this gap, so that the organisation can expect to achieve its targets over the planning period.

'Gap analysis' is a generic term and can be used to refer to more than one basis for analysis.

- CIMA *Official Terminology* describes an analysis of existing and potential sales.
- The term is more commonly used in connection with plans for eliminating a future gap in overall performance.

We examine these two versions below, before mentioning some other possible uses of the gap analysis idea.

5.1 A forecast or projection based on existing performance: F_0 forecasts

This is a **forecast** of the company's future results assuming that it does nothing. For example, if the company sells ten products in eight markets, produces them on a certain quantity and type of machinery in one factory, has a gearing structure of 30% and so on, a forecast will be prepared, covering the corporate planning period, on the assumption that none of these items are changed.

Argenti identified four stages in the preparation of such a forecast.

(a) **Review** past results and analyse.
    (i)   revenues into units of sale and price
    (ii) costs into variable, fixed, and semi-variable

(b) A **projection** into the future for each major item of revenue and cost should be made up to the end of the planning period.

(c) **Consider any other factors** which might significantly affect the projections. Examples are as follows.
    (i)   Internal factors such as machine breakdown, strikes and so on
    (ii) External PEST factors, such as new technology or changes in the law

(d) The forecast is then **finalised**. The forecast allows the company no new products or markets and no other new strategies: but the purpose of the forecast and gap analysis is to determine the size of the task facing the company if it wishes to achieve its target profits.

5.1.1 Errors in the forecast

A forecast cannot be expected to guarantee **accuracy** and there must inevitably be some **latitude for error**.

(a) By estimating **likely variations**. For example, 'in 20X8 the forecast profit is $5 million with possible variations of plus or minus $2 million'.

(b) By providing a **probability distribution** for profits. For example, 'in 20X8 there is a 20% chance that profits will exceed $7 million, a 50% chance that they will exceed $5 million and an 80% chance that they will exceed $2½ million. Minimum profits in 20X8 will be $2 million.'

5.2 Analysing an existing gap in sales

The diagram below is adapted from the CIMA *Official Terminology*.

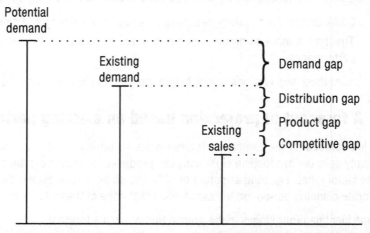

The **demand gap** is the difference between total market potential and current demand from users.

The **distribution gap**, **product gap** and **competitive gap** together make up the difference between current demand and actual sales achieved.

(a)   The **distribution gap** arises from lack of access to or utilisation of distribution channels.

(b)   The **product gap** arises from product failure or deliberate product decisions.

(c)   The **competitive gap** arises from failures of pricing or promotion.

This analysis is based on the 4Ps of the **marketing mix**, which is dealt with in detail later in Chapter 12 of this Study Text.

5.3 The profit gap

The **profit gap** is the difference between the target profits and the profits on the forecast.

(a)   First of all the firm can estimate the effects on the gap of any projects or strategies in the pipeline. Some of the gap might be filled by a new project.

(b)   Then, if a gap remains, new strategies have to be considered to close the gap.

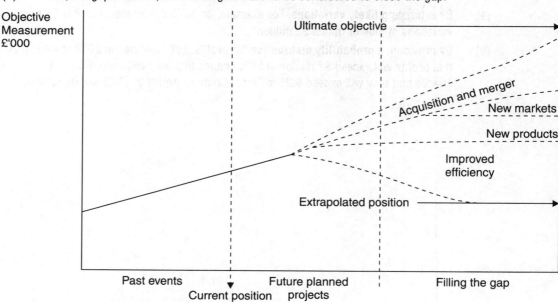

Some possible problems are these.

(a)   The financial propositions may be susceptible to **inflation** – there is no easy way of dealing with this problem.

(b)   More serious, however, is risk: remember that in many cases a higher return can equate to a higher risk. In seeking to develop strategies to give a higher return, the firm may, unwittingly, be raising its **risk profile**.

5.4 Other forms of gap analysis

The same basic technique can be used as a starting point for formulating any particular strategy.

(a)   In planning for **manpower**, gap analysis would be used to assess the difference over time between the following.

   (i)   What the organisation **needs** to have in terms of differing skills and seniority

   (ii)   What the organisation **is likely** to have

(b)   In planning facilities, a similar analysis can be made of the gap between the facilities which the organisation needs to have, and what it is likely to have if nothing is done about the situation.

(c)   A sales gap can be filled by diversification, product development and so on.

5.4.1 Continuous gap analysis

A gap analysis can be used as a means of strategic control. This means that the gap analysis is regularly updated.

(a)   Were the assumptions in the F_0 forecast justified?

(b)   A similar question can be asked of the other strategies which are supposed to fill the gap.

   (i)   Have they been implemented as planned?

   (ii)   Have they generated the expected level of sales and/or profit?

This **continuing gap analysis** can be allied to forecasting as it can be used to measure the extent to which it is likely a firm can fulfil its objectives. Gap analysis, in general, also relies on an organisation's ability to forecast its performance into the future.

6 Forecasting

FAST FORWARD

> **Forecasting** is an essential part of the process of strategic management. Methods include the use of statistical techniques based on extrapolation; modelling; and expert jury opinion. Sometimes individual judgement is used. The weakness of all these methods is that they are based on the assumption that the future will tend to resemble the past.

Some definitions can usefully be outlined at this stage.

Key terms

A **forecast** is 'a prediction of future events and their quantification for planning purposes'.

A **projection** is 'expected future trend pattern obtained by extrapolation. It is principally concerned with quantitative factors, whereas a forecast includes judgements.'   (CIMA *Official Terminology*)

Extrapolation is the technique of determining a projection by statistical means.

As you know, a variety of techniques is used in connection with forecasting, including DCF, expected values and sensitivity analysis. Different techniques are appropriate accordingly to the **degree of uncertainty** perceived in the relevant forecast.

(a)   We are used to employing a **NPV** approach when the amount and timing of future cash flows are assumed to be known with something **approaching certainty**.

(b)   Projects that are **repeated several times** lend themselves to the use of **expected values** and **decision trees**.

(c)   **Modelling** and **sensitivity analysis** are appropriate when there is **less confidence** about the range and distribution of potential outcomes: such techniques are employed in conjunction with decision rules that reflect the degree of risk aversion of the decision makers.

(d)   It is important to remember that **certainty cannot be attained in any forecast**. Major, rapid changes, such as the collapse of the dot com bubble and the oil shocks of the 1970s simply are not knowable in advance. This is perhaps the realm where **scenario planning** makes its greatest contribution.

6.1 Statistical projections

Statistical forecasts take past data and endeavour to direct it to the future, by **assuming** that **patterns or relationships which held in the past will continue to do so**. Many statistical techniques aim to reduce the uncertainty managers face. In **simple/static conditions the past is a relatively good guide** to the future.

Statistical forecasting techniques for static conditions

(a)   **Time series analysis**. Data for a number of months/years is obtained and analysed. The aim of time series analysis is to identify:

(i)   Seasonal and other cyclical fluctuations

(ii)   Long term underlying trends

For example, the UK's monthly unemployment statistics show a **headline figure** and the **underlying trend**.

(b)   **Regression analysis** is a quantitative technique to check any underlying correlations between two variables (eg sales of ice cream and the weather). Remember that the relationship between two variables may **only hold between certain values**. (You would expect ice cream consumption to rise as the temperature becomes hotter, but there is a maximum number of ice creams an individual can consume in a day, no matter how hot it is.)

(c)   **Econometrics** is the study of economic variables and their interrelationships, using computer models. Short-term or medium-term econometric models might be used for forecasting.

(i)   **Leading indicators** are indicators which change **before** market demand changes. For example, a sudden increase in the birth rate would be an indicator of future demand for children's clothes. Similarly, a fall in retail sales would be an indicator to manufacturers that demand from retailers for their products will soon fall.

(ii)   The firm needs the ability to **predict the span of time between a change in the indicator and a change in market demand**. Change in an indicator is especially useful for demand forecasting when they reach their highest or lowest points (when an increase turns into a decline or *vice versa*).

(d)   **Adaptive forecasts** change in response to **recent** data.

6.1.1 Problems with statistical projections

(a)   Past relationships do not necessarily hold for the future.

(b)   Data can be misinterpreted, and **relationships assumed where none exist**. For example, sales of ice cream rise in the summer, and sales of umbrellas fall – the link is the weather, not any correlation between them.

(c)   Forecasts do not account for special events (eg wars), the likely response of competitors and so on.

(d)   The variation and depth of business cycles fluctuate.

(e)   In practice statistical forecasters **underestimate uncertainty**.

6.2 Judgemental forecasts

Judgemental forecasts are used principally for the long term, covering several decades. However, because of the limitations of short-term forecasting they are used for the short term too. Effectively, they are based on **hunches or educated guesses**. Sometimes, these prove surprisingly accurate. At other times they are wide of the mark.

(a)   **Individual forecasting**. A company might forecast sales on the basis of the judgement of one or more executives.

(i) **Advantages** are that it is cheap and suitable if demand is stable or relatively simple.

(ii) The **disadvantage** is that it is swayed most heavily by **most recent** experience rather than trend.

(b) **Genius forecasting**

An individual with expert judgement might be asked for advice. This might be the case with the fashion industry; although demand might be hard to quantify, an ability to understand the mind of the customer will be very useful.

(c) In practice, forecasts might be prepared by an interested individual who has read the papers, say, and has promoted an item for management attention.

6.3 Modelling

At various points in this text, you have been given frameworks or models to structure your thinking.

Key term

A **model** is anything used to represent something else.

- *Descriptive*: describing real-world processes
- *Predictive*: attempting to predict future events
- *Control*: showing how action can be taken

A model is a simplified representation of reality, which enables complex data to be classified and analysed.

6.3.1 Examples of models

Type of model	Example
Descriptive	Value chain BCG analysis Five competitive forces Buyer behaviour
Predictive	Product life cycle Cost-volume profit analysis

Their relevance to building a future orientation depends on **how well they are used** and a **recognition of their limitations**.

6.4 Consensus forecasts

6.4.1 Jury forecasts

A panel of experts and/or executives prepare their own forecasts and a consensus forecast emerges from this.

(a) **Advantages**: expert opinions are sought and obtained.

(b) **Disadvantages**. The jury might **dilute** the best. The **group dynamics** will interfere with the decision. Each expert might differ and, in a face-to-face situation, the more forceful or confident would win the argument.

6.4.2 Delphi method

This was developed to overcome problems relying on **known** experts or personalities in the jury.

(a) Participants remain **anonymous**, known only to the organiser.

(b) Participants respond to a **questionnaire** containing tightly-defined questions. The Delphi technique **retains anonymity**. The results are collated and statistically analysed, and are returned by the organiser to each expert. The experts respond again, having seen the opinions of the other experts.

(c)   The Delphi technique is **time consuming**.

(d)   In practice, it seems to be the case that experts are **universally optimistic**.

6.5 Statistical versus judgemental and consensus forecasts

David Mercer identifies the relative advantages and disadvantages of each method.

Use of forecasts	Statistical	Judgement
Changes in established patterns	Past data is no guide	Can be predicted but could be ignored
Using available data	Not all past data is used	Personal biases and preferences obscure data
Objectivity	Based on specific criteria for selection	Personal propensity to optimism/pessimism
Uncertainty	Underestimated	Underestimated, with a tendency to over-optimism
Cost	Inexpensive	Expensive

6.5.1 Using both methods

Judgemental forecasting is **speculative**. However, speculation may be necessary to identify changing patterns in data or weak signals reflecting or presaging social changes.

 Case Study

Many small enterprises lack even the most basic marketing skills, with seven out of ten start-ups failing to identify their market and potential customers. But simple marketing techniques can make the difference between failure and runaway success.

Some of Britain's most innovative entrepreneurs started their businesses as little more than cottage industries. Richard Branson founded his business empire – which now stretches from air travel to personal equity plans – by selling records to his school friends, and Anita Roddick started *The Body Shop* by bottling potions and lotions on her kitchen table. Both have eschewed the text book marketing techniques and the jargon favoured by their competitors because they are intuitive marketers and, crucially, they carefully identified their target markets.

Inevitably, not all those starting up a new enterprise have the innate talent of a Branson or a Roddick and some fail to embrace even the most basic marketing principles. John Stubbs, chief executive of the Marketing Council, says: 'Marketing for some remains obscure and is perceived as an expensive luxury.' Research from *Barclays Bank* indicated that only three in ten start-up businesses carry out initial research to identify their market and potential customers, increasing the likelihood of one of the most common causes of business failure: loss of market and sales.

6.6 Market forecasts and sales forecasts

Market forecasts and sales forecasts complement each other. The market forecast should be carried out first of all and should cover a longer period of time.

Key term

Market forecast. This is a forecast for the market as a whole. It is mainly involved in the assessment of environmental factors, outside the organisation's control, which will affect the demand for its products/services.

(a) **Components of a market forecast**.

    (i)   The **economic review** (national economy, government policy, covering forecasts on investment, population, gross national product, and so on).

    (ii)   **Specific market research** (to obtain data about specific markets and forecasts concerning total market demand).

    (iii)   Evaluation of **total market demand** for the firm's and similar products (for example, profitability and market potential).

(b) **Sales forecasts** are estimates of sales (in volume, value and profit terms) of a product in a future period at a given marketing mix.

6.6.1 Research into potential sales

Key term

> **Sales potential** is an estimate of the part of the market that is within the possible reach of a product.

Factors governing sales potential

- The price of the product
- The amount of money spent on sales promotion
- How essential the product is to consumers
- Whether it is a durable commodity whose purchase is postponable
- The overall size of the possible market
- Competition

Whether sales potential is worth exploiting will depend on the cost which must be incurred to realise the potential.

6.7 Example

Market research has led a company to the opinion that the sales potential of product X is as follows.

	Sales value	Contribution earned before selling costs deducted	Cost of selling
either	£100,000	£40,000	£10,000
or	£110,000	£44,000	£15,000

In this example, it would not be worth spending an extra £5,000 on selling in order to realise an extra sales potential of £10,000, because the net effect would be a loss of £(5,000 − 4,000) = £1,000.

7 Scenario planning

FAST FORWARD

> **Industry scenarios** can be used to analyse the industry environment. They are more local than the global scenarios which analyse the effects of general environmental trends.
>
> Successful scenario building requires that the likely responses of **competitors** can be input into the model. **Competitor analysis** makes this possible.

Because the environment is so complex, it is easy to become overwhelmed by the many factors. Firms therefore try to model the future by constructing scenarios to assist them with setting their strategic direction.

Key term

> A **scenario** is 'an internally consistent view of what the future might turn out to be'.

In addition to their usefulness in providing some guidance in strategic planning, scenarios are also valuable in that preparing and updating them forces the managers at the strategic apex to **look carefully at the business environment** and to monitor developments within it.

7.1 Macro scenarios

Macro scenarios use macro-economic or political factors, creating alternative views of the future environment (eg global economic growth, political changes, interest rates). Macro scenarios were developed because the activities of oil and resource companies (which are global and at one time were heavily influenced by political factors) needed techniques to deal with uncertainties.

7.1.1 Steps in scenario planning

There is no one single way to construct a scenario. However, the ten steps which *Schoemaker* describes are a good illustration of how a scenario could be created.

Step 1   **Define the scope**

The scope should be defined with reference to time frame involved, products considered and markets considered.

Step 2   **Identify the major stakeholders** that drive change or affect the industry (within the scope of the scenario identified in step 1.)

Step 3   **Identify the basic trends** that affect the industry and the business environment.

Step 4   **Identify the key areas of uncertainty** and their drivers. Uncertainties in scenario planning should be viewed as future possibilities. They could be based upon the political/legal, economic, social/cultural and technological (PEST) factors identified through environmental analysis, and also an organisation's own competencies and capabilities.

Step 5   **Construct initial scenarios** based on the key areas of uncertainties. The scenarios should be created by shaping the key areas of uncertainty (step 4) into coherent themes.

Step 6   **Check for consistency** and plausibility. In other words, re-examine the scenarios to assess whether they make sense. For scenario planning to be useful, the scenarios presented must be able to happen, and in the timescale identified by the scope of the scenario.

Step 7   **Develop learning scenarios.** At this stage, the initial frameworks identified in step 5 should be expanded into full descriptions of the scenario as if it were actually occurring.

At this point, **senior management should become involved** in the process, and should start considering the implications of each scenario in terms of the potential impacts they could have on their business.

Step 8   **Identify research needs:** understand what additional information is required to fill in any gaps in the scenario, and obtain that information to improve the coverage given by the scenario.

Step 9   **Develop quantitative models.** This stage builds on step 7, to put together business models to forecast the effects of different scenarios on an organisation's activities and future profitability/cash flow.

Step 10   **Use scenarios to formulate competitive strategy.** The value of scenario planning process is that it assists an organisation's decision-making in times of uncertainty. The process should have exposed the key areas of uncertainty which face an organisation, and in this final stage, management should develop strategic courses of action which they can apply to each of the scenarios to deal with the uncertainties they may face.

7.2 Industry scenarios

Porter believes that the most appropriate use for scenario analysis is if it is restricted to an industry. An **industry scenario** is an internally consistent view of an **industry's** future structure. Different competitive strategies may be appropriate to different scenarios.

The **entire range**, not the most **likely** 'future', is used to design a competitive strategy. The process is as follows.

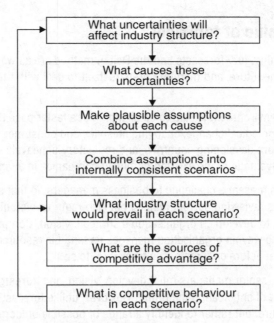

7.2.1 Using scenarios to formulate competitive strategy

(a) A strategy built in response to only **one scenario is risky**, whereas one supposed to cope with them **all might be expensive**.

(b) Choosing scenarios as a basis for decisions about competitive strategy.

Approach	Comment
Assume the most probable	This choice puts too much faith in the scenario process and guesswork. A less probable scenario may be one whose failure to occur would have the worst consequences for the firm.
Hope for the best	A firm designs a strategy based on the scenario most attractive to the firm: wishful thinking.
Hedge	The firm chooses the strategy that produces satisfactory results under all scenarios. Hedging, however, is not optimal. The low risk is paid for by a low reward.
Flexibility	A firm taking this approach plays a 'wait and see' game. It is safer, but sacrifices first-mover advantages.
Influence	A firm will try and influence the future, for example by influencing demand for related products in order that its favoured scenario will be realised in events as they unfold, or even by attempting to influence government and regulatory bodies.

7.2.2 Benefits of scenario planning

It is unusual for scenario planning to create an accurate prediction of what actually happens. Therefore it may be tempting to dismiss it as a worthless exercise. However, it does have some valuable benefits:

- It identifies the key uncertainties to which an organisation is exposed, allowing it to plan for how to deal with them and to know what warning signs to look for as time goes on.

- It forces management to look externally at the wider business environment rather then focus purely on the internal operations of an organisation.

- It may provide managers with useful insights into the future of their industry which can then help shape their strategy.

7.3 The value of foresight

Scenario planning, jury forecasts and the Delphi method are all ways management can attempt to get insights into the future, and therefore prepare itself to deal with the opportunities and threats the future holds for it.

The business environment is said to be changing at a faster pace than ever before. A number of factors - including technological change, changing lifestyles and consumer tastes, the rise of international competitors from developing countries, and regulatory upheavals - are presenting challenges to the competitive advantage of the existing dominant companies in an industry.

These changes present a challenge to business managers, in that successful management no longer simply involves reviewing current results, but also requires **visioning** the opportunities and threats that may lie ahead, to develop an organisation's strategic vision. Competitive advantage no longer simply comes from the way an organisation manages its tangible resources, but from the way it reinvents its business model before circumstances force it to do so.

In this context, senior managers must develop 'vision' and '**foresight**.' Foresight can be described as the art and science of anticipating the future. However, unlike forecasting, foresight does not attempt to predict the future, but rather to identify a range of possible outcomes based on an understanding and analysis of current trends.

Futurists argue that the future is continuous with the present, so by analysing the present we can learn a lot about what might happen in the future.

A foresight project can be divided into four stages:

- **Monitoring** – identifying relevant current trends
- **Analysis** – understanding the drivers of change
- **Projection** – anticipating the future
- **Transformation** – drawing implications for the business based on the projected futures (in terms of new product or new business development, and in terms of strategic management).

An organisation can use of number of techniques to improve its foresight. These include:

- **Scenario planning** - We have already discussed scenario planning as a way of generating a range of possible futures derived from the current environment and the uncertainties contained within it

- **Delphi technique** – where a number of experts are asked to independently and anonymously give their opinions and insights on a particular trend and how it may develop. These initial results are summarised and the summary is returned to the experts, who are then asked to respond again once they have seen the responses of the group. The process is repeated until a consensus is achieved.

- **Cross-impact analysis** - A basic limitation of many forecasting methods (including the Delphi technique) is that they produce only isolated forecasts. In other words, events and trends are projected one by one, without explicit reference to their possible influence on each other. However, most events and developments are connected to each other in some way, and so the interdependencies between them need to be considered to develop more consistent and accurate foresight. Cross-impact analysis addresses these interdependencies.

Cross-impact analysis involves recording events on a matrix, and at each matrix intersection questioning what impact the event in the row occurring would have on the likelihood of the event in the column occurring. In this way, cross-impact analysis provides a more systematic way of examining a range of possible future events and outcomes.

- **Morphological analysis** – All the attributes of a product or strategy are listed as column headings in a table and then as many variations of each attribute as possible are listed in each column. In effect, a matrix of components is created. One entry from each column is then chosen to create a new mixture of components. This new mixture could represent a new product or strategy.

Morphological analysis can be used to identify a range of opportunities for an organisation which would not otherwise be obvious. Also, if an organisation carried out a morphological analysis on its competitors it may be able to identify new products or strategies that they are considering.

- **Visioning** – Visioning requires an organisation's management to develop an image of a possible or desirable future state. This image may initially be quite vague, but then needs to be developed into a more definite goal, accompanied by a strategic plan for how to achieve that goal. However, for visioning to be a useful for an organisation, the image or goal articulated has to be a realistic and achievable alternative to the current state, and one which is preferable to the current state.

- **Opportunity mapping** - An opportunity map is a qualitative and experience-based analysis aimed at identifying gaps in the current user experience of an organisation's product portfolio. Opportunity maps allow an organisation to discover the desired qualities of its products, which may in turn prompt it to change its priorities and strategies in order to provide those desired qualities.

- **Trend extrapolation** - This is a projection technique based on the assumption that certain social, economic or technological trends or patterns identified in the past will manifest themselves in the future and that one can forecast future trends by observing how certain patterns have changed in the past and projecting or extrapolating those changes into the future.

- **Role-playing** – This is another technique where alternative options are generated by a group, but unlike the Delphi technique it does not use experts. A group of people are given a description of a hypothetical future situation, and told to act as they think they would if that situation was actually happening. Analysing their actions can give useful insights into what might happen if that hypothetical situation actually occurs.

One of the disadvantages of foresight is that it relies on the future being shaped by actions that can be imagined now. It cannot take account of sudden one-off events which could dramatically change the business environment. For example, a person at the start of the 20th century may not have been able to foresee that by the end of the century the world would be shaped by (among other things) television, computers, aeroplanes, the rise and the decline of communism, and atomic energy and weapons. Nevertheless, foresight can help organisations plan for the uncertainties which they will inevitably face in the future.

- **SWOT analysis** or **corporate appraisal** is a quantitative and qualitative review of internal **strengths** and **weaknesses** and their relationship with external **threats** and **opportunities**.

- Strengths and weaknesses are internal matters. The management accountant's role is to appraise and measure them.

- Opportunities and threats exist in the environment.

- Strategies should be developed to remove weaknesses or develop strengths and to exploit opportunities and counter threats.

- SWOT analysis indicates the **types of strategies** that appear to be available, both to exploit strengths and opportunities and to deal with weaknesses and defend against threats.

- **Gap analysis** quantifies the size of the gap between the objective for the planning period and the forecast based on the extrapolation of the current situation, and current prospects.

- **Forecasting** is an essential part of the process of strategic management. Methods include the use of statistical techniques based on extrapolation; modelling; and expert jury opinion. Sometimes individual judgement's used. The weakness of all these methods is that they are based on the assumption that the future will tend to resemble the past.

- **Industry scenarios** can be used to analyse the industry environment. They are more local than the global scenarios which analyse the effects of general environmental trends.

- Successful scenario building requires that the likely responses of **competitors** can be input into the model. **Competitor analysis** makes this possible.

Quick Quiz

1 A SWOT analysis is also known as a ....

2 (a) Strengths and weaknesses analysis offers an internal/external appraisal
   (b) Opportunities and threats analysis offers an internal/external appraisal

3 List some areas of finance or accounting where weaknesses may exist.

4 **Fill in the gaps** in the statement below, using the words in the box.

   For opportunities, it is necessary to decide the following.

   – What opportunities exist in the (1) ....?
   – What is the (2)............... of competitors? Are they better placed to (3) .... these opportunities?
   – What is the company's (4) .... performance potential in this field?

• comparative		• business environment	
• capability profile		• exploit	

5 What is a cruciform chart?

6 The planning gap is the gap between the current position of the organisation and the forecast desired position.

   ☐ True
   ☐ False

7 Distinguish a 'forecast' from a 'projection'.

8 What are the ten steps in scenario planning?

Answers to Quick Quiz

1. Corporate appraisal

2. (a) internal
   (b) external

3.
   - The average receivables payment period and credit taken from suppliers
   - Liquidity
   - Investments in inventory
   - Interest rates on current loans
   - Earning interest on cash in hand
   - Tax liability arrangements
   - Under-utilised assets
   - The interest burden and the gearing level

4. (1) business environment (2) capability profile (3) exploit (4) comparative

5. A cruciform chart is a table summarising the significant strengths, weaknesses, opportunities and threats.

6. False. It is the gap between the forecast position from continuing with current activities, compared to the desired future position.

7. A forecast is 'a prediction of future events and their quantification for planning purposes'. (CIMA)

   A projection is 'an expected future trend pattern obtained by extrapolation. It is principally concerned with quantitative factors, whereas a forecast includes judgements'. (CIMA)

8. Step 1 Define the scope
   Step 2 Identify the major stakeholders
   Step 3 Identify basic trends
   Step 4 Identify key areas of uncertainty
   Step 5 Construct initial scenarios
   Step 6 Check for consistency and plausibility
   Step 7 Develop learning scenarios
   Step 8 Identify research needs
   Step 9 Develop quantitative models
   Step 10 Use scenarios to formulate competitive strategy

Now try the question below from the Exam Question Bank

Number	Level	Marks	Time
Q8	Examination	25	45 mins

Strategic options

Competition, products and markets

Introduction

After the corporate appraisal, we come to **strategic choices** that firms make, the subject of Chapters 9 and 10.

Section 1 offers a brief overview of some strategic options, and includes a discussion of what firms consider to be their **core activity.** We need some understanding of what a firm competes with: what products and services does it offer? So we also discuss some key issues relating to **marketing**.

To respond to the environment, business have three choices.

(a) **How to compete.** Competitive strategies include cost leadership, differentiation or focus (Section 2). You should be aware of some of the problems with this approach.

(b) **Direction of growth.** Product/market strategy refers to the mix of product and markets (new or existing) and what the firm should do. This includes pricing strategy and is covered in Sections 3, 4 and 5.

(c) **Method of growth** (acquisition or organic growth) is covered in Chapter 10.

These decisions are not necessarily taken at the same time, of course, nor are they taken in the same way. The basic competitive strategy cannot be changed every year – but the decision to acquire a business is often taken suddenly.

Topic list	Learning outcomes	Syllabus references	Ability required
1 Strategic options and marketing issues	C(i), A(vi)	C4	Evaluation
2 Generic competitive strategies	C(i)	C4	Evaluation
3 Using the value chain in competitive strategy	C(iv)	C8	Evaluation
4 Pricing and competition	C(i)	C6	Evaluation
5 Product-market strategy: direction of growth	C(ii)	C4	Evaluation
6 The strategic role of directors	C(vii)	C11	Analysis

1 Strategic options and marketing issues

An organisation, having identified its strengths and weaknesses, and its opportunities and threats, must make choices about what **strategies** to pursue in order to achieve its targets and objectives.

1.1 Core businesses

A business should have a **common thread** running through all of its activities, which gives them a purpose or logic.

(a)   The aim of some businesses is to pursue **diversified activities**. The common thread in such businesses will usually be to earn a high return on investments, largely through acquisitions and disposals.

(b)   Many organisations, however, identify themselves with **certain products or markets**, to which most of their activities are devoted. These are the organisation's **core businesses**.

In seeking to define their core businesses, firms should not confuse the **market** with the **industry**.

(a)   **The market** is defined by consumer needs and reflects consumer demands.

(b)   **The industry** is defined by related firm capabilities and industries are based on supply technologies. Washing machines and refrigerators are products of the same industry, despite their wholly different purposes.

If a company recognises that it is in a declining business, or in one where future growth will be restricted, it should seek to expand in other areas or to exploit the remaining competitive advantages it has.

Case Study

Tobacco companies, for example, recognising that their markets in the West are declining because of the trend away from smoking, have opened up new markets for tobacco products in the Third World and have also diversified into paper, retailing and hotels.

1.2 Strategic choices

There are three categories of strategic choice.

*   **How** to compete
*   **Where** to compete
*   **Method** of growth

It is possible to analyse strategic choice into three categories.

(a)   Competitive strategies are the strategies an organisation will pursue for competitive advantage. They determine **how you compete**.

(b)   Product-market strategies determine **where you compete** and the direction of growth.

(c)   Institutional strategies determine the **method of growth**.

1.2.1 Horizontal boundaries

A firm's **horizontal boundaries** define the variety of products and services that it produces. The optimum horizontal boundary for a firm depends on **economies of scale**. In some industries, such as pharmaceuticals, company size is influenced by a preference for mergers ('bigger is better') and corporate giants emerge, such as *Du Pont*. A few large firms account for the vast proportion of industry sales.

Economies of scale occur when large scale processes, such as production and distribution, have cost advantages over smaller scale processes. Economies of scale affect both the size of firms and the structure of markets, and so consideration of them, and therefore where organisational boundaries should be, is vital in any business strategy decision about possible merger or expansion.

1.2.2 Vertical boundaries

The **vertical boundaries** of a firm define which activities the firm performs itself and which it purchases from independent firms. (We look at outsourcing in Chapter 12.) The concept of vertical boundaries is allied to the concept of the **value chain** (discussed in detail in Chapter 7) which describes the process beginning with the acquisition of raw materials and culminating in distribution and sale of the finished goods.

Horizontal and vertical integration are discussed later in this chapter in the context of **related diversification** as a product-market strategy.

1.2.3 Products and services

The right strategy depends on the type of product or service that the firm is producing.

(a) **Search products**. These are products whose attributes the consumer can discern, evaluate and compare fairly easily, eg size and colour.

(b) **Experience products**. These are products whose attributes cannot be discerned until the consumer has had experience of using the product – eg taste in the case of food.

(c) **Credence products**. These are products whose important attributes cannot be evaluated by the consumer either because the product's attributes might vary the next time (eg quality of service in a restaurant) or because the product's attributes cannot easily be evaluated (eg pet food).

Products may be categorised as follows.

(a) **Breakthrough products** offer either a radical performance advantage over competition, drastically lower price, or ideally, may offer both.

(b) **Improved products** are not radically different to their competition but are obviously superior in terms of better performance at a competitive price.

(c) **Competitive products** show no obvious advantage over others, but derive their appeal from a particular compromise of cost and performance.

1.2.4 Services

It will also be useful to identify the extent to which a product has a **service element**. We mentioned services briefly in Chapter 4, but here is a definition from the perspective of an influential marketing writer.

> '**Services** are any activity of benefit that one party can offer to another that is essentially intangible and does not result in the ownership of anything. Its production may or may not be tied to a physical product.'
>
> (P Kotler, *Social Marketing*)

There are five major characteristics of services.

(a) **Intangibility** refers to the lack of substance which is involved with service delivery. Unlike goods (physical products such as confectionery), there is no substantial material or physical aspects to a service: no taste, feel, visible presence and so on. Most 'offers' to customers combine product and service elements on a 'service continuum' as we show below.

(b) **Inseparability**. Many services are created at the same time as they are consumed. No service exists until it is actually being experienced/consumed by the person who has bought it.

(c) **Variability**. Many services face the problem of maintaining consistency in the standard of output. It may be hard to attain precise standardisation of the service offered.

(d) **Perishability.** Services are innately perishable.

(e) **Lack of ownership.** Services do not result in the transfer of property. The purchase of a service only confers on the customer access to or a right to use a facility.

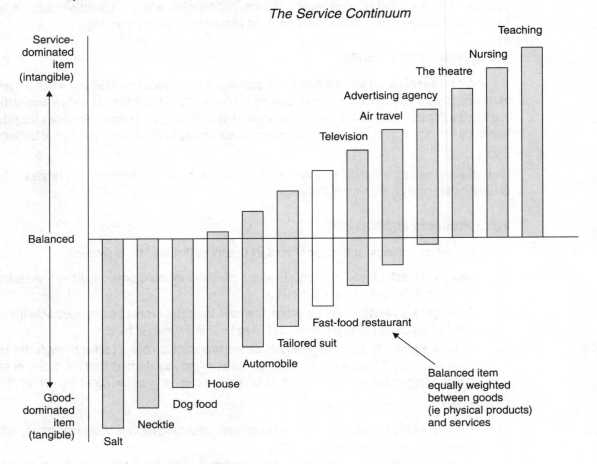

The Service Continuum

1.3 Strategic marketing issues

Strategic marketing issues include market share, which has implications for ROI.

A **standard** product might satisfy the needs of all customers in the market. On the other hand, **variations** in a product's design might appeal more strongly to some prospective customers than others.

Customers differ in various respects – according to age, sex, income, geographical area, buying attitudes, buying habits etc. Each of these differences can be used to **segment** a market.

By creating a new market segment or entering a growing market segment a company can hope to achieve the following.

(a) **Increase sales and profits**, by meeting customer needs in a number of different ways
(b) Extend the life cycle of the product
(c) Capture some of the overall market share from competitors
(d) Survive in the face of competition

1.3.1 Market share

The evaluation of market share has two purposes.

(a) It helps to identify who the **true competitor** is
(b) It serves as a basis for marketing strategy

There are four strategic options for market share.

(a) **Building market share**. This is usually easiest when the product is in the early stages of its life, and the market is growing (a rising star, or question mark in BCG terminology).

(b)   **Holding market share**. This strategy is appropriate in a situation where the products are mature, and in a mature market (cash cows). Competition will come from innovators, and competitive promotions.

Case Study

Xerox lost out, for example, by ignoring the lower end of the photocopier market, as Japanese competitors entered this part of the market and took most of Xerox's market share.

(c)   **Harvesting**. Harvesting means aiming for a lower market share which gives the company its best short-run returns, with a longer-term view of eventually pulling out of the market.

(d)   **Divestment/withdrawal**. In such circumstances, the market share is so low that the product is no longer viable.

Market share strategies for declining industries would include harvesting or divestment options.

1.3.2 Profit Impact of Marketing Strategies (PIMS)

The concepts behind **Profit Impact of Market Strategy** (PIMS) analysis were developed at General Electric in the 1960s. The PIMS database is now maintained by the Strategic Planning Institute, a consulting organisation. The database provides empirical evidence of the impact of various marketing strategies on corporate success.

Like some of the portfolio analysis tools we looked at earlier, the PIMS framework regards **competitive strength** and **market attractiveness** as important determinants of profitability. However, perhaps the single most significant factor to emerge from the PIMS data is the link between profitability and **relative market share**. You will recall that relative market share was one of the axes of the **BCG matrix.**

There is a definite, observable correlation between market share and return on investment. This is probably the result of **economies of scale.** Economies of scale linked to increasing market share are particularly evident in **purchasing** and the **utilisation of fixed assets.**

One source of economies of scale is the **experience curve.**

1.3.3 Use of experience curves

We mentioned the importance of the extent of production experience when we discussed the BCG matrix in Chapter 7. That portfolio model uses **relative market share** as an indicator of the extent to which production experience and improvements may be expected to have driven costs down. Relative market share is in fact being used as a way of estimating the company's position on the **experience curve**.

The **experience curve** can be used in strategic control of costs. It suggests that as output increases, the cost per unit of output falls. This results from the following.

(a)   **Economies of scale** – in other words an increased volume of production leads to lower unit costs, as the firm approaches full capacity.

(b)   A genuine **learning effect** as the workforce becomes familiar with the job and learns to carry out the task more efficiently. As a process is repeated, it is likely that costs will reduce due to **efficiency, discounts** and **reduced waste**.

(c)   **Technological improvements**.

The cost-reducing effects of movement along the experience curve do not just apply to production: the whole **value chain** is affected.

Strategic importance of experience curves

Experience curves are strategically important for the following reasons:

(a)   Businesses **can predict their likely future costs,** and plan more effectively in the project appraisal process.

(b) **Early mover advantages/disadvantages**. They can indicate the advantages of either being first in a market or following another firm. Being the first to enter a market is no guarantee of long-term success, of course, but if there is a very steep learning curve (ie learning benefits are obtained quickly), the first into the market may reap all the advantages and build up a commanding position by obtaining an early leadership in market share.

(c) **Life cycle**. On the other hand, a firm might be prepared to make losses in the short term, in order to build up volume and experience, so that the product is profitable over its life cycle.

(d) A policy of **reducing prices** as process costs fall can help a company to win a dominant market share. As costs fall, the company may find itself in a **cost leadership** position in terms of Porter's generic strategy model.

(e) Greater experience can also be used to **differentiate** a product, either via greater experience of the market or the ability to utilise technology in a unique way. Products may be **redesigned** to boost production efficiency.

Price/quantity. An experience curve which models production costs can be related to customer demand schedules.

(a) If the experience curve suggests increased quantities of production, then it is possible that the increased volume will have to be sold at a lower price.

(b) The management accountant might usefully relate experience curves to demand schedules, in particular price elasticity, to establish likely profitability of the product.

(c) Furthermore, the 'quantity sold' to the market as a whole needs to take the entry of competitors into account.

 Case Study

Vodafone

Mark Ritson, a marketing academic with a particular expertise in branding, discussed Vodafone in his weekly column in *Marketing* in March 2006. The company had been forced to write down its book value by £28bn and Professor Ritson analysed the pressures that had led to this evidence of strategic failure. After mentioning competitive pressure, failure to develop internet telephony and a fixation on 3G, he turned to the scale of Vodafone's operations.

'Perhaps most problematic of all is Vodafone's size. There are advantages in having 180m customers in 27 countries, but there is also a **crucial trade-off between scale economies and brand focus**. Many analysts now believe Vodafone is simply too big and too cumbersome to succeed.

For all the talk of global brands, there are two key caveats to remember. First, most customers usually prefer national or local brands to bland global offerings. Second, most marketing managers can't build a national brand successfully, let along a global one.'

(BPP emphasis)

1.3.4 Low market share

Low market share does not inevitably mean poor returns. Company strategy and/or market characteristics may lead to prosperity even with a low market share.

(a) **Company strategy**
   (i) **Market segmentation**. New market segments might be a small proportion of the total market, but profitable
   (ii) **Premium products**. Emphasising product quality, and charging higher prices
   (iii) Wanting to stay small, and consciously avoiding growth
   (iv) Cost control

(b)   **Market characteristics**

(i)   The market is stable
(ii)   Product innovations are rare
(iii)   Most products are standardised
(iv)   Companies produce supplies or components for industrial customers
(v)   Repeat-buying is frequent
(vi)   The value added is high

1.3.5 Trade-offs

Some firms are prepared to **sacrifice profitability for market share** over a period of time. Some Japanese firms were willing to charge low prices to buy market share and fatally weaken competitors.

2 Generic competitive strategies

> Porter suggests there are three generic strategies: **cost leadership**, **differentiation** and **focus**.

In any market where there are competitors, strategic and marketing decisions will often be in response to what a competitor has done.

Competitive advantage is anything which gives one organisation an edge over its rivals. Porter argues that a firm should adopt a competitive strategy which is intended to achieve some form of competitive advantage for the firm. A firm that possesses a **competitive advantage** will be able to make profit exceeding its cost of capital: in terms of economic theory, this is '**excess profit**' or '**economic rent**'. The existence of excess profit tends to be temporary because of the effect of the **five competitive forces**. When a company can continue to earn excess profit despite the effects of competition, it possesses a **sustainable competitive advantage**.

Key term

> **Competitive strategy** means 'taking offensive or defensive actions to create a dependable position in an industry, to cope successfully with ... competitive forces and thereby yield a superior return on investment for the firm. Firms have discovered many different approaches to this end, and the best strategy for a given firm is ultimately a unique construction reflecting its particular circumstances'.   (Porter)

2.1 The choice of competitive strategy

Porter believes there are three **generic strategies** for competitive advantage. To be successful, Porter argues, a company must follow only one of the strategies. If they try to combine more than one they risk losing their competitive advantage and becoming 'stuck in the middle.'

Key terms

> **Cost leadership** means being the lowest cost producer in the industry as a whole.
> **Differentiation** is the exploitation of a product or service which the **industry as a whole** believes to be unique.
> **Focus** involves a restriction of activities to only part of the market (a segment) through:
> - Providing goods and/or services at lower cost to that segment (**cost-focus**)
> - Providing a differentiated product or service to that segment (**differentiation-focus**)

Cost leadership and differentiation are industry-wide strategies. Focus involves segmentation but involves pursuing, within the segment only, a strategy of cost leadership or differentiation.

2.1.1 Cost leadership

A cost leadership strategy seeks to achieve the position of lowest-cost producer in the **industry as a whole**. By producing at the lowest cost, the manufacturer can compete on price with every other producer in the industry, and earn the higher unit profits, if the manufacturer so chooses.

How to achieve overall cost leadership

- Set up production facilities to obtain **economies of scale**
- Use the **latest technology** such as CAD/CAM and computerised stock and logistics control to reduce costs and/or enhance productivity
- Exploit the **learning curve effect**
- Concentrate on **improving productivity**
- **Minimise overhead costs**
- **Get favourable access to sources of supply**
- **Relocate to cheaper areas**
- Use **IT** to record and analyse costs

Classic examples of companies deliberately pursuing cost leadership are Black and Decker and South West Airlines.

 Case Study

Watermark is a supplier of catering and other services to airlines. It had a good six months in the first half of 2005, with turnover increasing from £30.5m to £35.2m and profits rising from £1.6m to £2.4m. John Caulcott, the CEO, declared that the company's business was, in essence, finding savings in the airlines' supply chain: 'we can sell the savings to our clients and keep some of it for ourselves'.

2.1.2 Differentiation

A differentiation strategy assumes that competitive advantage can be gained through **particular characteristics** of a firm's products. Products may be categorised as:

(a) **Breakthrough products** offer a radical performance advantage over competition, perhaps at a drastically lower price (eg float glass, developed by Pilkington).

(b) **Improved products** are not radically different from their competition but are obviously superior in terms of better performance at a competitive price (eg microchips).

(c) **Competitive products** derive their appeal from a particular compromise of cost and performance. For example, cars are not all sold at rock-bottom prices, nor do they all provide immaculate comfort and performance. They compete with each other by trying to offer a more attractive compromise than rival models.

How to differentiate

- **Build up a brand image**
- **Give the product special features** to make it stand out
- **Exploit other activities of the value chain** such as marketing and sales or service
- Use **IT** to create new **services** or **product features**

Advantages and disadvantages of industry-wide strategies

Competitive force	Advantages		Disdvantages	
	Cost leadership	Differentiation	Cost leadership	Differentiation
New entrants	Economies of scale raise entry barriers	Brand loyalty and perceived uniqueness are entry barriers		
Substitutes	Firm is not so vulnerable as its less cost effective competitors to the threat of substitutes	Customer loyalty is a weapon against substitutes		

Competitive force	Advantages		Disdvantages	
	Cost leadership	Differentiation	Cost leadership	Differentiation
Customers	Customers cannot drive down prices further than the next most efficient competitor	Customers have no comparable alternative Brand loyalty should lower price sensitivity		Customers may no longer need the differentiation factor Sooner or later, customers become price sensitive
Suppliers	Flexibility to deal with cost increases	Higher margins can offset vulnerability to supplier price rises	Increase in input costs can reduce price advantages	
Industry rivalry	Firm remains profitable when rivals go under through excessive price competition	Unique features reduce direct competition	Technological change will require capital investment, or make production cheaper for competitors Competitors learn via imitation Cost concerns ignore product design or marketing issues	Imitation narrows differentiation

2.1.3 Focus (or niche) strategy

In a focus strategy, a firm concentrates its attention on one or more particular segments or niches of the market, and does not try to serve the entire market with a single product. **IT** can be useful in establishing the exact determining characteristics of the chosen niche, using existing customer records.

(a)   A **cost-focus strategy:** aim to be a cost leader for a particular segment. This type of strategy is often found in the printing, clothes manufacture and car repair industries.

(b)   A **differentiation-focus strategy:** pursue differentiation for a chosen segment. Luxury goods suppliers are the prime exponents of such a strategy. *Ben and Jerry's* ice cream is a good example of a product offering based on differentiation-focus.

 Case Study

In 2005, the *Financial Times* reported on *Tyrrells' Potato Chips*, a niche manufacturer of crisps that uses potatoes produced on its own farm. William Chase, owner of the company, set it up in part to escape from dependence on the major supermarkets and in part to add extra value to his basic product, potatoes. A major feature of his strategy is to sell mainly though small retailers at the upper end of the grocery and catering markets. The Financial Times summarises the Tyrells' strategy under six headings.

- **Branding**. Tyrrells' marketing taps into the public's enthusiasm for 'authenticity' and 'provenance'. Its crisp packets tell the story of Tyrrells'. Pictures of employees growing potatoes on the Herefordshire farm and then cooking them illustrate the journey from 'seed to chip'.

- **Quality**. Tyrrells' chips are made from traditional varieties of potato and 'hand-fried' in small batches.

- **Distribution**. Tyrrells' sells directly to 80 per cent of its retail stockists. Students from a local agricultural college are employed to trawl through directories and identify fine-food shops to target with samples. After winning their business, Tyrrells' develops the relationship though personal contact.

- **Diffusion strategy**. Selling to the most exclusive shops creates a showcase for Tyrrells' to target consumers who are not sensitive to price, allowing it to grow profitably.

- **New product development**. Tyrrells' is constantly bringing out new flavours and products. Experimental recipes are produced in sample runs and given free to shops to test with customers.

Recent introductions include apple chips, honey glazed parsnips and Ludlow sausage with wholegrain mustard.

- **Exporting**. This has created a further sales channel through fine-food stores. Yet it has also forced greater dependency on distributors, introducing an unwelcome layer between itself and its customers.

Porter suggests that a focus strategy can achieve competitive advantage when '**broad-scope**' businesses fall into one of two errors.

(a) **Underperformance** occurs when a product does not fully meet the needs of a segment and offers the opportunity for a **differentiation focus** player.

(b) **Overperformance** gives a segment more than it really wants and provides an opportunity for a **cost focus** player.

Advantages of a focus strategy

- A niche is more secure and a firm can insulate itself from competition.
- The firm does not spread itself too thinly.

Drawbacks of a focus strategy

(a) The firm sacrifices economies of scale which would be gained by serving a wider market.

(b) Competitors can move into the segment, with increased resources (eg the Japanese moved into the US luxury car market, to compete with Mercedes and BMW).

(c) The segment's needs may eventually become less distinct from the main market.

2.2 Which strategy?

Although there is a risk with any of the generic strategies, Porter argues that a firm must pursue one of them. A **stuck-in-the-middle** strategy is almost certain to make only low profits. 'This firm lacks the market share, capital investment and resolve to play the low-cost game, the industry-wide differentiation necessary to obviate the need for a low-cost position, or the focus to create differentiation or a low-cost position in a more limited sphere.'

Question   Hermes

Learning outcome C(i)

The managing director of Hermes Telecommunications plc is interested in corporate strategy. Hermes has invested a great deal of money in establishing a network which competes with that of Telecom UK, a recently privatised utility. Initially Hermes concentrated its efforts on business customers in the South East of England, especially the City of London, where it offered a lower cost service to that supplied by Telecom UK. Recently, Hermes has approached the residential market (ie domestic telephone users) offering a lower cost service on long-distance calls. Technological developments have resulted in the possibility of a cheap mobile telecommunication network, using microwave radio links. The franchise for this service has been awarded to Gerbil phone, which is installing transmitters in town centres and stations etc.

What issues of competitive strategy have been raised in the above scenario, particularly in relation to Hermes Telecommunications plc?

Answer

(a) Arguably, Hermes initially pursued a cost-focus strategy, by targeting the business segment.

(b) It seems to be moving into a cost leadership strategy over the whole market although its competitive offer, in terms of lower costs for local calls, is incomplete.

(c)   The barriers to entry to the market have been lowered by the new technology. Gerbil phone might pick up a significant amount of business.

In practice, it is rarely simple to draw hard and fast distinctions between the generic strategies as there are conceptual problems underlying them.

(a)   **Problems with cost leadership**

   (i)   **Internal focus.** Cost refers to internal measures, rather than the market demand. It can be used to gain market share: but it is the **market share that is important,** not cost leadership as such. Economies of scale are an effective way to achieve low costs, but they depend on high volumes. In turn, high volumes may depend on low prices, which, in turn, require low costs. There is a circular argument here.

   (ii)   **Only one firm.** If cost leadership applies cross the whole industry, only one firm will pursue this strategy successfully.

   (iii)   **Higher margins can be used for differentiation.** Having low costs does not mean you have to charge lower prices or compete on price. A cost leader can choose to 'invest higher margins in R&D or marketing'. Being a cost leader arguably gives producers more freedom to choose other competitive strategies.

(b)   **Problems with differentiation**. Porter assumes that a differentiated product will always be sold at a higher price.

   (i)   However, a **differentiated product** may be sold at the same price as competing products in order to **increase market share.**

   (ii)   **Choice of competitor.** Differentiation from whom? Who are the competitors? Do they serve other market segments? Do they compete on the same basis?

   (iii)   **Source of differentiation**. This includes **all** aspects of the firm's offer, not only the product. However, it is difficult to achieve differentiation purely by **promotion**, though some managers think it can be done this way.

Focus probably has fewer conceptual difficulties, as it ties in very neatly with ideas of market segmentation. In practice most companies pursue this strategy to some extent, by designing products/services to meet the needs of particular target markets.

'Stuck-in-the-middle' is therefore what many companies actually pursue quite successfully. Any number of strategies can be pursued, with different approaches to **price** and the **perceived added value** (ie the differentiation factor) in the eyes of the customer.

2.3 Limitations of the generic strategy approach

Porter's model depends on clear notions of what the **industry** and **firm** in question are. However, this may not be clear, since many companies are part of larger organisations and many 'industries' have boundaries that are hard to define. Also, we are faced with the difficulty of determining whether strategies should be pursued at SBU or corporate level, and in relation to exactly which category of products. For example, *Proctor and Gamble* have a huge range of products and brands: are they to follow the same strategy with all of them?

There have been several criticisms of Porter's approach. One is that it does not allow for **expansion into new industries**, perhaps as the result of creative innovation, as was the case with *Apple's iPod*. This is not really valid: Porter may be silent on this topic, but his model does not preclude it.

A second erroneous criticism is to see the model as dividing products into basic goods and luxury goods. This is to over simplify the model. Cost leadership might well be pursued over a wide range of product quality, though it seems likely that the emphasis will shift to differentiation where the higher quality products are concerned.

A further questionable point that may be raised is that the model does not allow for technical obsolescence and the introduction of new products. This is simply incorrect, as shown by *Black and Decker's* regular new product launches. These, generally, are marketed on the basis of high volume and low price, economies of scale being the basis of the business model.

 Case Study

Petrol is a commodity product, so it is difficult for suppliers to base their strategies on factors such as brand image and product characteristics. Instead, they tend to concentrate on cost reduction and operational efficiencies.

Mobil took this one step further in the late 1990s. Because some competitors had access to low cost crude, it realised that a cost leadership strategy was unlikely to be sustainable in the long run. Mobil's strategy for growth therefore aimed to attract customers who bought more petrol than average, were willing to pay higher prices for Mobil petrol, and who would also provide non-petrol revenue (eg from the forecourt's convenience store). To help in this, they identified five distinct consumer segments in the gasoline buying public and targeted the top three.

3 Using the value chain in competitive strategy

FAST FORWARD

The **value chain** can be used to design a competitive strategy.

The value chain can be used to design a competitive strategy, by deploying the various activities strategically. The examples below are based on two supermarket chains, one concentrating on low prices, the other differentiated on quality and service. See if you can tell which is which.

(a)

Firm infrastructure	Minimum corporate HQ				
Human resource management		De-skilled store-ops	Dismissal for checkout error		
Technology development	Computerised warehousing		Checkouts simple		
Procurement	Branded goods only – big discounts	Low cost sites			Use of concessions
	Bulk warehousing	1,000 lines only		Low price promotion	Nil
		Price points		Local focus	
		Basic store design			
	INBOUND LOGISTICS	OPERATIONS	OUTBOUND LOGISTICS	MARKETING & SALES	SERVICE

(b)

Firm infrastructure	Central control of operations and credit control				
Human resource management	Recruitment of mature staff	Client care training	Flexible staff to help with packing		
Technology development		Recipe research	Electronic point of sale	Consumer research & tests	Itemised bills
Procurement	Own label products	Prime retail positions		Adverts in quality magazines & poster sites	
	Dedicated refrigerated transport	In store food halls Modern store design Open front refrigerators Tight control of sell-by dates	Collect by car service	No price discounts on food past sell-by dates	No quibble refunds

INBOUND LOGISTICS   OPERATIONS   OUTBOUND LOGISTICS   MARKETING & SALES   SERVICE

The two supermarkets represented are based on the following.

(a)   The value chain in (a) is the 'discount' supermarket (perhaps similar to *Lidl* in the UK) which sells on price, pursuing a cost leadership, or perhaps more accurately, a cost-focus strategy. This can be seen in the limited product range and its low-cost sites.

(b)   The value chain in (b) is for the supermarket which seeks to differentiate on quality and service (for example, *Waitrose* in the UK). Hence the 'no quibble' refunds, the use of prime retail sites, and customer care training.

You can probably think of other innovations, such as loyalty cards and Internet shopping.

4 Pricing and competition

FAST FORWARD

Pricing strategy is an important component, both as part of the marketing mix and as a company's competitive weapon.

Key terms

Pricing. 'Determination of a selling price for the product or service produced. A number of methodologies may be used.

Competitive pricing. Setting a price by reference to the prices of competitive products.

Cost plus pricing. Determination of price by adding a mark-up, which may incorporate a desired return on investment, to a measure of the cost of the product/service.

Dual pricing. Form of transfer pricing in which the two parties to a common transaction use different prices.

Historical pricing. Basing current prices on prior period prices, perhaps uplifted by a factor such as inflation.

Market-based pricing. Setting a price based on the value of the product in the perception of the customer. Also known as perceived value pricing.

Penetration pricing. Setting a low selling price in order to gain market share.

Predatory pricing. Setting a low selling price in order to damage competitors. May involve dumping, ie selling a product in a foreign market at below cost, or below the domestic market price (subject to, for example, adjustments for taxation differences, transportation costs, specification differences).

Price skimming. Setting a high price in order to maximise short-term profitability, often on the introduction of a novel product.

Range pricing. The pricing of individual products such that their prices fit logically within a range of connected products offered by one supplier, and differentiated by a factor such as weight of pack or number of product attributes offered.

Selective pricing. Setting different prices for the same product or service in different markets. Can be broken down as follows:

- **Category pricing.** Cosmetically modifying a product such that the variations allow it to sell in a number of price categories, as where a range of 'brands' are based on a common product.
- **Customer group pricing.** Modifying the price of a product or service so that different groups of consumers pay different prices.
- **Peak pricing.** Setting a price which varies according to level of demand.
- **Service level pricing.** Setting a price based on the particular level of service chosen from a range.
- **Time material pricing.** A form of cost plus pricing in which price is determined by reference to the cost of the labour and material inputs to the product/service.'

(CIMA *Official Terminology*)

4.1 Price

All profit organisations and many non-profit organisations face the task of **setting a price** on their products or services. Price can go by many names: fares, tuitions, rent, assessments and so on.

Price can be defined as a measure of the **value exchanged by the buyer for the value offered by the seller**. It might be expected, therefore, that the price would reflect the costs to the seller of producing the product and the benefit to the buyer of consuming it.

Unlike the other marketing mix elements, pricing decisions affect profits through their impact on **revenues** rather than costs. It also has an important role as a **competitive tool** to differentiate a product and an organisation and thereby exploit market opportunities.

Although pricing can be thought of as fulfilling a number of roles, in overall terms a price aims to produce the desired level of sales in order to meet the objectives of the business strategy.

Two broad categories of objectives may be specified for pricing decisions.

(a) **Maximising profits** is concerned with maximising the returns on assets or investments. This may be realised even with a comparatively small market share depending on the patterns of cost and demand.

(b) **Maintaining or increasing market share** involves increasing or maintaining the customer base which may require a different, more competitive approach to pricing, while the company with the largest market share may not necessarily earn the best profits.

4.2 Pricing and the customer

4.2.1 Elasticity of demand

Pricing policy is also crucial in matching production capacity with customer demand. The concept of price elasticity is important.

$$\frac{\% \text{ change in sales demand}}{\% \text{ change in sales price}}$$

(a) When elasticity is greater than 1 (ie **elastic**), a change in price will lead to a change in total revenue.

(i) If the price is lowered, total sales revenue would rise, because of the large increase in demand.

(ii) If the price is raised, total sales revenue would fall because of the large fall in demand.

(b)   When elasticity is less than 1 (ie **inelastic**) the following will happen.

    (i)   If the price is lowered, total sales revenue would fall, because the increase in sales volume would be too small to compensate for the price reduction.

    (ii)   If the price is raised, total sales revenue would go up in spite of the small drop in sales quantities.

4.2.2 Price sensitivity

Price sensitivity will vary amongst purchasers. Those that can pass on the cost of purchases will be the least sensitive and will therefore respond more to other elements of perceived value.

(a)   The family on holiday is likely to be very price sensitive when choosing an overnight stay.

(b)   In industrial marketing the purchasing manager is likely to be more price sensitive than the engineer who will use the new equipment that is being sourced.

4.2.3 Price perception and quality connotations

Price perception is an important factor in the ways customers react to prices. For example, customers may react to a price increase by buying more. This could be for a variety of reasons.

(a)   They expect further price increases to follow (they are 'stocking up')

(b)   Many customers appear to judge quality by price

    (i)   They assume the quality has increased, if there is a price rise

    (ii)   The brand takes on a 'snob appeal' because of the high price

4.2.4 Intermediaries' objectives

If an organisation distributes products or services to the market through independent **intermediaries**, the objectives of these intermediaries complicate the pricing decision. Such intermediaries are likely to deal with a range of suppliers and their aims concern their own profits rather than those of suppliers.

4.2.5 Suppliers

If an organisation's suppliers notice a price rise for the organisation's products, they may seek a rise in the price for their supplies to the organisation on the grounds that it is now able to pay a higher price.

4.2.6 Inflation

In periods of inflation the organisation may need to change prices to reflect increases in the prices of supplies, labour, rent and so on.

4.2.7 Exchange rates

Changes in the rate of exchange can lead to price rises or decreases, and are particularly relevant to importers and exporters.

4.2.8 Income effects

In times of rising incomes, price may become a less important marketing variable compared with product quality and convenience of access (distribution). When income levels are falling and/or unemployment levels rising, price will become a much more important marketing variable.

4.2.9 Multiple products and loss leaders

Most organisations sell a range of products. The management of the pricing function is likely to focus on the profit from the whole range rather than the profit on each single product. Take, for example, the use of **loss leaders**: a very low price for one product is intended to make consumers buy additional products in the range which carry higher profit margins.

4.2.10 Ethics

Ethical considerations are a further factor, for example whether or not to exploit short-term shortages through higher prices. The outcry surrounding the series of petrol price rises following the outbreak of the Gulf Crisis in 1990 was a good example of public sensitivity to pricing decisions.

4.3 New product pricing: market penetration and market skimming

There are three elements in the pricing decision for a new product.

- Getting the product **accepted**
- Maintaining a **market share** in the face of competition
- Making a **profit** from the product

4.3.1 Penetration

Market penetration pricing is a policy of low prices when the product is first launched in order to gain sufficient penetration into the market. It is therefore a policy of sacrificing short-term profits in the interests of long-term profits.

(a)   The firm wishes to **discourage rivals** from entering the market.

(b)   The firm wishes to **shorten the initial period of the product's life cycle**, in order to enter the growth and maturity stages as quickly as possible. (This would happen if there is high elasticity of demand for the product.)

4.3.2 Skimming

Market skimming. The aim of market skimming is to gain high unit profits very early on in the product's life.

(a)   The firm charges high prices when a product is first launched.

(b)   The firm spends heavily on advertising and sales promotion to win customers.

(c)   As the product moves into the later stages of its life cycle (growth, maturity and decline) progressively lower prices will be charged. The profitable 'cream' is thus 'skimmed' off in progressive stages until sales can only be sustained at lower prices.

(d)   The firm may lower its prices in order to attract more price-elastic segments of the market; however, these price reductions will be gradual. Alternatively, the entry of competitors into the market may make price reductions inevitable.

Introductory offers and temporary **discounts** may be used to attract an initial customer interest.

4.4 Other pricing decisions

Promotional prices are short-term price reductions or price offers which are intended to attract an increase in sales volume. (The increase is usually short-term for the duration of the offer, which does not appear to create any substantial new customer loyalty). Loss leaders and 'money off' coupons are a form of promotional pricing.

A temporary **price cut** may be preferable to a permanent reduction because it can be ended without unduly offending customers and can be reinstated later to give a repeated boost to sales.

4.5 Pricing and the management accountant

The decision about pricing is one which involves both the accountant and the marketing manager.

Short-term pricing. Marketing management should have the responsibility for estimating the price-demand inter-relationship for their organisation's products. The accountant should become involved in short-term pricing decisions because of cost.

(a)   The sales-revenue maximising price for a product and the profit-maximising price might not be the same.

(b)   Simple CVP analysis can be used to estimate the breakeven point of sales, and the sales volume needed to achieve a target profit figure.

(c)   Many organisations use a **cost-plus** approach to pricing. Accounting figures are needed for cost in order to establish a floor for making a cost-plus pricing decision.

By analysing **product profitability**, the accountant also provides information for pricing control, because profit statements indicate whether prices have been high enough, given the sales demand, to provide a satisfactory return.

4.6 Price and competition

In classical economic theory, price is the major determinant of demand and brings together supply and demand to form an equilibrium market price. However, economic theory can only determine the optimal price structure under the two extreme market conditions.

(a)   **Perfect competition**: many buyers and many sellers all dealing in an identical product. Neither producer nor user has any market power and both must accept the prevailing market price.

(b)   **Monopoly:** one seller who dominates many buyers. The monopolist can use his market power to set a profit maximising price.

However, in practice most of British industry can be described as an **oligopoly:** where relatively few competitive companies dominate the market.

4.6.1 Price leadership

Given that price competition can have disastrous consequences in conditions of oligopoly, it is not unusual to find that large corporations emerge as price leaders.

A price leader will have the dominant influence on price levels for a class of products. Price increases or decreases by the price leader provide a direction to market price patterns.

However, a danger with price leadership is that it might appear to limit the impact of competition. If firms actively collude to keep prices to a certain level, and to divide the 'spoils' between them, they are forming a cartel. Cartels are illegal under UK and European competition law.

Generally speaking, therefore, price cuts to increase market share will be matched by competitors in some way. If a rival firm cuts its prices in the expectation of increasing its market share, a firm has the following options.

(a)   **Maintain its existing prices**. This would be done if the expectation is that only a small market share would be lost, so that it is more profitable to keep prices at their existing level. Eventually, the rival firm may drop out of the market or be forced to raise its prices.

(b)   **Maintain prices but respond with a non-price counter-attack**. This is a more positive response, because the firm will be securing or justifying its current prices with a product change, advertising, or better back-up services, etc.

(c)   **Reduce prices**. This should protect the firm's market share so that the main beneficiary from the price reduction will be the consumer.

(d)   **Raise prices and respond with a non-price counter-attack**. A price increase would be based on a campaign to emphasise the quality difference between the rival products.

Predatory pricing is the use of price to drive a competitor out of business. It is a grey area, as competing on price is legitimate and economically efficient.

The intensely competitive supermarket sector in the UK and US provides a prime example of periodic price cutting activity, that can lead in extreme cases to all-out price 'wars' between the largest competitors. **Price competition** like this will undermine the value of the market that is being competed for.

Here are some questions that companies in such an environment might ask themselves.

•   What is the minimum potential **sales loss** that justifies meeting a **lower competitive price**?

- What is the minimum potential **sales gain** that justifies **not following** a competitive price **increase**?
- What is the minimum potential **sales loss** that justifies **not following** a competitive price **decrease**?

4.7 Example

Deere Ltd's largest competitor has reduced its prices by 15%. Deere currently enjoys a contribution margin of 45%. If Deere's customers are highly loyal there will of course be no need to respond, but what sales volume change would justify a response?

Solution

	@ Reduced price £85	@ Current price £100
	£	£
Sales revenue (3,000 units)	255,000	300,000
Variable cost (£55 per unit)	165,000	165,000
Contribution	90,000	135,000
Contribution margin	35.3%	45%

Deere Ltd needs to work out the level of sales at the current price (£100) which will yield the same contribution as current sales volume at the new reduced price. If sales decrease below that level, the company should match the price change. The relevant formula is below.

$$\frac{\% \text{ breakeven sales change}}{\text{for reactive price change}} = \frac{\text{Change in price}}{\text{Contribution margin}} = \frac{-15\%}{45\%} = -33^{1}/_{3}\%$$

If Deere Ltd is to generate £90,000 worth of contribution at current price levels, sales can drop by $33^{1}/_{3}$, or 1,000 units, as demonstrated below.

	£
Sales revenue (2,000 units)	200,000
Variable cost	110,000
Contribution	90,000

If sales fall any further, Deere should match the price change.

Note that in the formula, 'breakeven sales' refers to the **level of sales needed to generate the same contribution**.

For the purposes of this example, Deere Ltd has a choice between reducing its prices by 15% or maintaining them at current levels. If it does reduce its prices, contribution decreases (assuming sales volume stays the same). If it maintains its prices, it can expect sales volume to fall.

We can of course turn this on its head and, still applying the formula above, say that if Deere Ltd's competitors had **increased** their prices by 15%, a 33.3% **gain** in sales volume would have to be realised in order for 'doing nothing' to be more profitable than a reactive price increase. This is of course a simplistic analysis that assumes sales volumes will rise and fall exactly in line with any price changes, but it illustrates the issues involved.

4.8 Competitive pricing actions

Different competitive pricing actions can say a lot about a company's strategy and send signals to the market.

(a) **Reducing price below that of competitors** in order to win a contract gives certain messages.

    (i)   The company is desperate for sales volume

    (ii)   It believes it is the lowest cost supplier

    (iii)   The target customer is strategically important

(b) **Reducing price by the same amount as a competitor,** in order to win back business, demonstrates to that competitor that contracts cannot be won or lost on price considerations alone.

(c) **Substantial price reductions** and public announcements of new manufacturing facilities show the market that despite price reductions, sales are set to expand and revenues will not decrease in the long term.

(d) A **quick negotiation of lower prices** without alerting the competition indicates a belief that a gain can be made through the short term winning of a customer.

5 Product-market strategy: direction of growth

11/07, 11/06, 11/05

FAST FORWARD

Product-market strategy is the mix of products and markets. Segmentation is important in identifying new markets, and a firm will use a marketing mix to arrive at a particular market position. The Ansoff matrix identifies various options.

- **Market penetration**: current products, current markets
- **Market development**: current products, new markets
- **Product development**: new products, current markets
- **Diversification**: new products, new markets

All of these can secure growth. **Diversification** is often perceived to be most **risky**. Although justified by 'synergies' (common assets, expertise etc which can be applied in a number of different business areas), these are often more apparent than real.

Key term

> **Product-market mix** is a short hand term for the **products/services** a firm sells (or a service which a public sector organisation provides) and the **markets** it sells them to.

5.1 Product-market mix: Ansoff's growth vector matrix

Ansoff drew up a **growth vector matrix**, describing how a combination of a firm's activities in current and new markets, with existing and new products can lead to **growth**. Ansoff's original model was a 4 cell matrix based on product and market, shown as the first diagram below. *Lynch* has produced an enhanced model that he calls the **market options matrix**. This adds the external options shown in the second diagram.

	PRODUCT	
	Present	New
MARKET Present	Market penetration	Product development
MARKET New	Market development	Diversification • related • unrelated

Ansoff's matrix

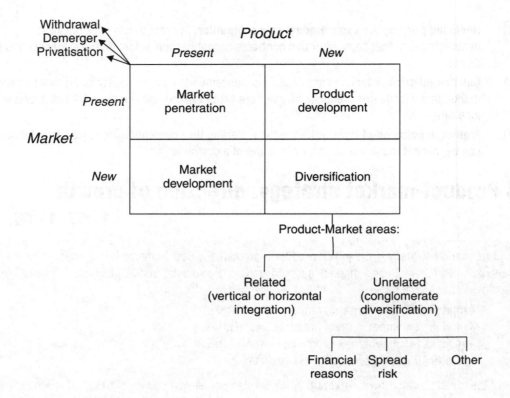

Lynch – Market options matrix

Exam focus point	Do not confuse Ansoff's matrix with the BCG matrix of market growth and share!

5.1.1 Current products and current markets: market penetration

Market penetration. The firm seeks to:

- **Maintain or to increase its share** of current markets with current products, eg through competitive pricing, advertising, sales promotion
- Secure dominance of growth markets
- Restructure a mature market by driving out **competitors**
- Increase usage by existing customers (eg airmiles, loyalty cards)

5.1.2 Present products and new markets: market development

- **New geographical areas** and export markets
- **Different package sizes** for food and other domestic items
- **New distribution channels** to attract new customers
- **Differential pricing policies** to attract different types of customer and create **new market segments**

5.1.3 New products and present markets: product development

Product development is the launch of new products to existing markets.

(a) **Advantages**
    (i)   Product development forces competitors to innovate
    (ii)   Newcomers to the market might be discouraged

(b) The **drawbacks** include the expense and the risk.

5.1.4 New products: new markets (diversification)

Diversification occurs when a company decides to make **new products for new markets**. It should have a clear idea about what it expects to gain from diversification.

(a) **Growth.** New products and new markets should be selected which offer prospects for growth which the existing product-market mix does not.

(b) **Investing surplus** funds not required for other expansion needs. (The funds could be returned to shareholders.)

 Case Study

Johnson Wax

When you think 'platform,' you probably think 'software' – with Microsoft Windows dominating the pack. But *any* product, not just software, can become a platform. What's required is imagination. Consider how *SC Johnson & Son*, the multibillion-dollar consumer products company, managed to 'platform' its way from floors to shaving cream to candles – and much, much more.

Samuel Curtis Johnson started the company in 1886 when he purchased the parquet flooring division of the Racine Hardware Company. After laying floors, Johnson would finish the wood with a special wax of his own creation, which became very popular with customers. Their repeated requests to buy extra wax led Johnson to develop *Johnson's Prepared Wax* and move into consumer products.

Another product – a paste blended with wax that created a spectacular sheen – also looked very promising, but there seemed to be no convenient way for customers to use it. Then the company discovered aerosol can technology (first patented by Erik Rotheim of Norway in 1927), put the wax and paste mix into pressurised cans, and launched *Pledge* – the first sprayable furniture polish for home use.

The company soon realized it could fill aerosol cans with anything sprayable: Scented liquid became *Glade*, an air freshener now available in more than a dozen fragrances; *DEET* was combined with other ingredients to create an insect repellent *Off!*, which is still the category leader. Later, company scientists working on shaving technologies discovered that gel was a better lubricant for skin than traditional shaving cream. But how to dispense gel from an aerosol can? They solved this dilemma by introducing an expandable bladder in the bottom of the can; when the company launched *Edge*, it found a whole new market.

Meanwhile, Off! led to plug-in insect repellents and, through another route, to DEET-infused candles. Lanterns based on the candle technology now use Off! cartridges as well. In short, SC Johnson advanced from indoor parquet floors to outdoor insect-repelling lanterns by thinking of aerosol technology as a platform rather than simply as a way to put wax on wood.

J Sviokla and A Paoni, *Harvard Business Review*, October 2005

Exam focus point

In November 2005, the Section A case study offered 10 marks for reasoned proposals that would allow the business in question to extend its operations beyond its current services. It was important to be realistic in making suggestions: this is where wider awareness acquired from reading the business press is rewarded.

5.2 Related diversification

Key term

Related diversification is 'development beyond the present product market, but still within the broad confines of the industry ... [it] ... therefore builds on the assets or activities which the firm has developed' (Johnson and Scholes). It takes the form of vertical or horizontal integration.

Horizontal integration is development into activities which are competitive with or directly **complementary** to a company's present activities; for example, a newspaper company moving into magazine production. The firm's advantage lies in using its technical and technological competences. This form of integration is also called **concentric diversification**.

Vertical integration occurs when a company becomes its own:

(a) **Supplier** of raw materials, components or services (**backward vertical integration**). For example, backward integration would occur where a milk producer acquires its own dairy farms rather than buying raw milk from independent farmers.

(b) **Distributor** or sales agent (**forward vertical integration**), for example: where a manufacturer of synthetic yarn begins to produce shirts from the yarn instead of selling it to other shirt manufacturers.

Advantages of vertical integration

- A **secure supply of components** or **materials,** thus lower supplier bargaining power
- **Stronger relationships** with the 'final consumer' of the product
- Win a share of the **higher profits** at all stages of the **value chain**
- Pursue a **differentiation strategy** more effectively
- Raise **barriers to entry**
- Improvements in **quality** and **innovation**

Disadvantages of vertical integration

(a) **Overconcentration.** A company places 'more eggs in the same end-market basket' (Ansoff). Such a policy is fairly inflexible, more sensitive to instabilities and increases the firm's dependence on a particular aspect of economic demand.

(b) The firm **fails to benefit from any economies of scale or technical advances** in the industry into which it has diversified. This is why, in the publishing industry, most printing is subcontracted to specialist printing firms, who can work machinery to capacity by doing work for many firms.

(c) **Risk.** Ward regards the benefits of vertical integration as 'one of the all-time great myths of the business world'. 'In most cases, vertical integration strategies take the business away from their previous areas of competitive strength and involve managers in new products with new technologies and processes'. Ward believes that vertical integration increases the risk to shareholders, without a corresponding return, thus leading to an erosion in value.

5.3 Unrelated diversification

Key term

> **Unrelated or conglomerate diversification** 'is development beyond the present industry into products/ markets which, at face value, may bear no close relation to the present product/market.'

Conglomerate diversification is now very unfashionable. However, it has been a key strategy for companies in Asia, particularly South Korea.

Advantages of conglomerate diversification

- **Risk-spreading** by entering new products into new markets
- An improvement of the **overall profitability and flexibility** of the firm through synergy
- **Escape** from the present business
- **Better access to capital** markets
- **Organisational learning by buying in expertise**
- **Use surplus cash**
- **Exploit under-utilised resources**
- **Obtain cash**, or other financial advantages (such as accumulated tax losses)
- **Use a company's image and reputation** in one market to develop into another

Disadvantages of conglomerate diversification

- The dilution of shareholders' earnings
- Lack of a common identity and purpose in a conglomerate organisation
- Failure in one of the businesses will drag down the rest
- Lack of management experience may reduce management's ability to run the new business properly

- Increased risk: the business is either entering a new market or producing a new product. Because they are new, they carry an increased risk that the venture may not be successful.

5.4 Trade-offs

Conglomerate diversification can lead to a wide rage of organisational characteristics. Generally there will be trade-offs to be made between elements such as those listed below.

- Economies of scale (increasing the utilisation of dedicated assts)
- Economies of scope (increasing the utilisation of general assets)
- Overhead cost structure and level
- Responsiveness to changing customer needs and wants
- Exploitation of resources and competences
- Organisational learning
- Competition reaction
- Management attention and capacity

5.5 Diversification and synergy

Synergy is the 2 + 2 = 5 effect, where a firm looks for **combined results** that reflect a better rate of return than would be achieved by the same resources used independently as separate operations. Synergy is used to justify diversification. Much of the benefit of synergy is derived from **economies of scale and scope**.

5.5.1 Obtaining synergy

(a) **Marketing synergy:** use of common marketing facilities such as distribution channels, sales staff and administration, and warehousing.

(b) **Operating synergy:** arises from the better use of operational facilities and personnel, bulk purchasing, a greater spread of fixed costs whereby the firm's competence can be transferred to making new products. For example, although there is very little in common between sausages and ice cream, both depend on a competence of refrigeration.

(c) **Investment synergy:** the joint use of plant, common raw material inputs, transfer of research and development from one product to another – ie from the wider use of a common investment in fixed assets, working capital or research.

(d) **Management synergy:** the advantage to be gained where management skills concerning current operations are easily transferred to new operations because of the similarity of problems in the two industries.

| Question | Road transport |

Learning outcome C(ii)

A large organisation in road transport operates nationwide in general haulage. This field has become very competitive and with the recent down-turn in trade, has become only marginally profitable. It has been suggested that the strategic structure of the company should be widened to include other aspects of physical distribution so that the maximum synergy would be obtained from that type of diversification.

Suggest two activities which might fit into the suggested new strategic structure, explaining each one briefly. Explain how each of these activities could be incorporated into the existing structure. State the advantages and disadvantages of such diversification.

Answer

The first step in a suggested solution is to think of how a company operating nationwide in general road haulage might diversify, with some synergistic benefits. Perhaps you thought of the following.

(a)   To move from nationwide to international haulage, the company might be able to use its existing contacts with customers to develop an international trade. Existing administration and depot facilities in the UK could be used. Drivers should be available who are willing to work abroad, and the scope for making reasonable profits should exist. However, international road haulage might involve the company in the purchase of new vehicles (eg road haulage in Europe often involves the carriage of containerised products on large purpose-built vehicles). Since international haulage takes longer, vehicles will be tied up in jobs for several days, and a substantial investment might be required to develop the business. In addition, in the event of breakdowns, a network of overseas garage service arrangements will have to be created. It might take some time before business builds up sufficiently to become profitable.

(b)   Moving from general haulage to 'speciality' types of haulage, perhaps haulage of large items of plant and machinery, or computer equipment. The same broad considerations apply to speciality types of haulage. Existing depot facilities could be used and existing customer contacts might be developed. However, expertise in specialist work will have to be 'brought in' as well as developed within the company and special vehicles might need to be bought. Business might take some time to build up and if the initial investment is high, there could be substantial early losses.

5.6 Withdrawal

It might be the right decision to cease producing a product and/or to pull out of a market completely. This is a hard decision for managers to take if they have invested time and money or if the decision involves redundancies.

Exit barriers make this difficult.

- Cost barriers include redundancy costs and the difficulty of selling assets
- Managers might fail to grasp opportunity costing
- Political barriers include government attitudes
- Marketing considerations may delay withdrawal
- Managers hate to admit failure
- People might wrongly assume that carrying on is a low risk strategy

Reasons for exit

- The company's business may be in buying and selling firms
- Resource limitations mean that less profitable businesses have to be abandoned
- A company may be forced to quit, because of insolvency
- Change of competitive strategy
- Decline in attractiveness of the market
- Funds can earn more elsewhere

5.7 Guidelines for a product-market strategy

Johnson and Scholes suggested the following principles and guidelines for product-market planning.

(a)   **The potential for improvement and growth**. It is one thing to eliminate unprofitable products but will there be sufficient growth potential among the products that remain in the product range?

(b)   **Cash generation**. New products require some initial capital expenditure. Retained profits are by far the most significant source of new funds for companies. A company investing in the medium to long term which does not have enough current income from existing products, will go into liquidation, in spite of its future prospects.

(c)   **The timing decision for killing off existing products**. There are some situations where existing products should be kept going for a while longer, to provide or maintain a necessary platform for launching new models.

(d)   **The long-term rationale of a product or market development**.

(e) **Diversification by acquisition**. It might pay to buy product ranges or brands in a takeover deal. If the product-market strategy includes a policy of diversification, then the products or services which the expanding company should seek to acquire should provide definite benefits. We discuss acquisitions in the next chapter.

5.7.1 Closing the profit gap and product-market strategy

The aim of product-market strategies is to **close the profit gap** that is found by gap analysis. A mixture of strategies may be needed to do this.

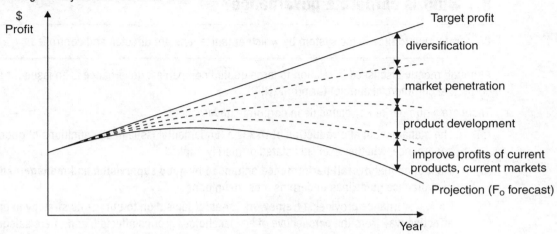

It is worth remembering that **divestment** is a product-market option to close the profit gap, if the business is creating losses.

A related question in what do you do with spare capacity – go for market penetration, or go into new markets. Many companies begin exporting into new overseas markets to use surplus capacity.

The strategies in the Ansoff matrix are not mutually exclusive. A firm can quite legitimately pursue a penetration strategy in some of its markets, while aiming to enter new markets.

5.8 Brand switching and competitive rivalry

A company may introduce measures to counteract **brand switching** by customers (and consequent loss of market share). One example is provided by the loyalty card schemes used by supermarkets to encourage repeat (and increased) spending by customers who may otherwise defect to the opposition.

6 The strategic role of directors

In most businesses, a few strategic decisions can make the difference between superior long-term performance and ordinary results, and these decisions frequently affect the whole organisation and its stakeholders. Consequently there is a lot of responsibility attached to these decisions, making it appropriate that they are taken by very senior management – usually the directors of a business.

In this section, we will consider directors' roles and responsibilities to an organisation.

FAST FORWARD

Good corporate governance involves **risk management** and **internal control, accountability** to stakeholders and other shareholders and conducting business in an **ethical and effective way.**

6.1 What is corporate governance?

Key term

Corporate governance is the system by which organisations are directed and controlled.

Although mostly discussed in relation to large quoted companies, governance is an issue for all bodies corporate; commercial and not for profit (NFP).

There are a number of key elements in corporate governance:

(a)   The management and **reduction of risk** is a fundamental issue in all definitions of good governance; whether explicitly stated or merely implied.

(b)   The notion that **overall performance enhanced** by **good supervision** and **management** within set best practice guidelines underpins most definitions.

(c)   Good governance provides a **framework** for an organisation to pursue its strategy in an **ethical and effective** way from the perspective of all stakeholder groups affected, and offers safeguards against misuse of resources, physical or intellectual.

(d)   Good governance is not just about externally established codes, it also requires a willingness to **apply the spirit** as well as the letter of the law.

(e)   **Accountability** is generally a major theme in all governance frameworks.

6.2 Role of the board

FAST FORWARD

*   The board should be responsible for taking major **policy** and **strategic** decisions.
*   Directors should have a **mix of skills** and their **performance** be assessed regularly.
*   Appointments should be conducted by formal procedures administered by a nomination committee.

6.3 Scope of role

The King report provides a good summary of the role of the **board of directors**.

> 'To define the purpose of the company and the values by which the company will perform its daily existence and to identify the stakeholders relevant to the business of the company. The board must then develop a strategy combining all three factors and ensure management implements that strategy.'

If the board is to act effectively, its role must be defined carefully. The Cadbury report suggests that the board should have a formal schedule of matters specifically reserved to it for decision. Some would be decisions such as mergers and takeovers that are fundamental to the business and hence should not be taken just by executive managers. Other decisions would include **acquisitions and disposals of assets of the company** or its subsidiaries that are material to the company and **investments, capital projects, bank borrowing** facilities, **loans** and their repayment, foreign currency transactions, all above a certain size (to be determined by the board).

Other tasks the board should perform include:

*   Monitoring the chief executive officer
*   Overseeing strategy
*   Monitoring risks and control systems
*   Monitoring the human capital aspects of the company in regard to succession, morale, training, remuneration and so on.
*   Ensuring that there is effective communication of its strategic plans, both internally and externally

6.4 Attributes of directors

In order to carry out effective scrutiny, directors need to have **relevant expertise** in industry, company, functional area and governance. The board as whole needs to contain a **mix of expertise** and a **balance** between **executive management** and independent non-executive directors. The King report stresses the importance also of having a good **demographic balance.**

New and existing directors should also have **appropriate training** to develop the knowledge and skills required.

6.5 Responsibilities of directors

The directors of a commercial enterprise are **collectively responsible** for the conduct of its affairs. There is a **scalar chain of authority and accountability** that runs hierarchically up and down the organisation. Junior managers are accountable to more senior ones and so on up the chain until the board of directors is reached. The question then arises: to whom are the directors accountable for the activities of the company as a whole?

As a matter of principle we can say that in any type of organisation there should be some external entity on whose behalf the managers at the strategic apex act and to whom they are accountable. In the case of an incorporated business in which ownership is separated from control, the answer is that the directors are ultimately accountable to the **shareholders** collectively, according to the internal rules of the company.

6.5.1 Fiduciary responsibility and due diligence

The essence of external accountability is that **organisations are not autonomous**: that is to say, they do not exist to serve their own purposes or those of their senior managers. They exist to serve some external purpose and their managers have a duty to run them in a way that serves that purpose, whether it be to relieve distress (a charity), to keep the peace and manage the economy (a government), to promote the interests of its members (a trade union) or to make a profit (a business). Managers have a **fiduciary responsibility** (or duty of faithful service) in this respect and their behaviour must always reflect it.

In addition to the requirement to act in good faith, directors are also expected not to be negligent or reckless and to bring a reasonable degree of competence to the discharge of their duties. There is thus a requirement to act with **due diligence**, a phrase you may be more familiar with in connection with business acquisitions; there, the phrase describes just one aspect of the directors' duty of care.

6.5.2 The objectives of commercial organisations

We implied above that the objective of a commercial organisation is to make a profit. It is possible to argue that **wider objectives** should be acknowledged and that the interests of people other than the owners should be served. This is the *stakeholder view* and is discussed elsewhere in this Study Text. Nevertheless, whatever an organisation's objectives may be, it is the duty of its managers to seek to attain them. Many senior figures in the world of business have given the impression that the organisations they run exist to serve their own personal purposes. This is not the case and managers at all levels must be aware of this.

6.5.3 Personal motivation and corruption

We must emphasise that managers need not be actually corrupt in order to fail in their fiduciary duty. The CEO who sets in motion a takeover bid that will enhance his prestige; the head of department who 'empire builds'; and the IT manager who buys an unnecessarily sophisticated system are all failing in their fiduciary duty even though they receive no material benefit themselves.

Shell

'I am becoming sick and tired about lying.' Those are not the words shareholders want to hear from a senior executive. They are certainly not words anybody ever expected from an heir-apparent at Royal Dutch/Shell, one of the world's largest – and until recently, one of its most admired – oil companies.

And yet, as a new report is revealed this week, those words of exasperation did indeed come from a senior Shell executive. Walter van de Vijver, until recently the firm's head of exploration and production (E&P), wrote them in an angry e-mail to Sir Phillip Watts, then the firm's chairman, in November 2003 – fuming that he was tired of covering up for shortfalls in the firm's reserves that resulted from 'far too aggressive/optimistic bookings'. Alas, the overzealous booker was none other than Sir Phillip, who preceded him as head of E&P.

The overbooking finally caught up with both men when, in January, Shell was forced to reclassify a whopping fifth of its 'proved' reserves. When preliminary investigations pointed the finger at the two men, both were forced out.

(The Economist, 24 April 2004)

Chapter Roundup

- An organisation, having identified its strengths and weaknesses, and its opportunities and threats, must make choices about what **strategies** to pursue in order to achieve its targets and objectives.

- There are three categories of strategic choice.

    - **How** to compete
    - **Where** to compete
    - **Method** of growth

- **Strategic marketing issues** include market share, which has implications for ROI.

- Porter suggests there are three generic strategies: **cost leadership**, **differentiation** and **focus**.

- The **value chain** can be used to design a competitive strategy.

- **Pricing strategy** is an important component, both as part of the marketing mix and as a company's competitive weapon.

- **Product-market strategy** is the mix of products and markets. Segmentation is important in identifying new markets, and a firm will use a marketing mix to arrive at a particular market position. The Ansoff matrix identifies various options.

    - **Market penetration**: current products, current markets
    - **Market development**: current products, new markets
    - **Product development**: new products, current markets
    - **Diversification**: new products, new markets

    All of these can secure growth. **Diversification** is often perceived to be most **risky**. Although justified by 'synergies' (common assets, expertise etc which can be applied in a number of different business areas), these are often more apparent than real.

- Good corporate governance involves **risk management** and **internal control, accountability** to stakeholders and other shareholders and conducting business in an **ethical and effective way.**

- The board should be responsible for taking major **policy** and **strategic** decisions.

- Directors should have a **mix of skills** and their **performance** be assessed regularly.

- Appointments should be conducted by formal procedures administered by a nomination committee.

Quick Quiz

1   What are the three categories of strategic choice?

    ....

    ....

    ....

2   What is the difference between horizontal boundaries and vertical boundaries?

3   **Fill in the blanks**.

In the context of Porter's three generic strategies:

(1) .... and (2) .... are industry wide strategies

(3) .... involves segmentation

4   A differentiation strategy assumes that competitive advantage can be gained through particular characteristics of a firm's products.

   ☐ True

   ☐ False

5   In a focus strategy a firm tries to serve the entire market with a single product.

   ☐ True

   ☐ False

6   Define 'price'.

7   Give the formula for price elasticity.

$$\frac{\%}{\%}$$

8   A pricing policy that aims to gain high unit profits very early in the product's life is known as

Market penetration
Market skimming

9   What is the 'product market mix'?

10 Fill in the Ansoff matrix

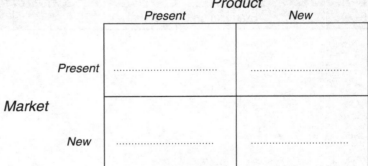

1   How you compete
    Where you compete
    Method of growth

2   A firm's horizontal boundary defines the variety of products and services it produces. The vertical boundary defines which activities (in the chain from production to distribution) the firm undertakes itself rather than outsourcing to other independent firms.

3   (1)   cost leadership
    (2)   differentiation
    (3)   focus

4   True

5   False

6   Price can be defined as a measure of the value exchanged by the buyer for the value offered by the seller.

7   $\dfrac{\%\ \text{change in sales demand}}{\%\ \text{change in sales price}}$

8   Market skimming

9   Product-market mix is a short hand term for the products/services a firm sells (or a service which a public sector organisation provides) and the markets it sells them to.

10

	Product	
	Present	*New*
Present	Market penetration; (for growth) or consolidation (to maintain position) or withdrawal	Product development
New	Market development	Diversification

Market (row label on left, between Present and New rows)

Now try the question below from the Exam Question Bank

Number	Level	Marks	Time
Q9	Examination	25	45 mins

Growth and divestment

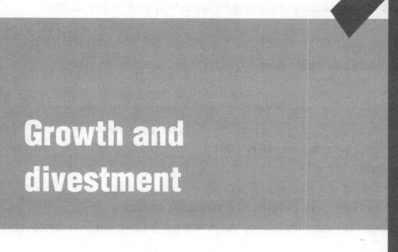

Introduction

This chapter discusses the organisational method by which companies pursue their competitive and product-market strategies (which we identified in Chapter 9). We look at international expansion as a topic in its own right in Section 3.

(a) **Organic growth**: effectively, any expansion is managed internally, with the firm's existing expertise and resources. A firm effectively builds the new business from scratch (Section 2).

(b) **Acquisition**: buy an already existing business (Section 4). Takeovers are often headline news. It might benefit your exam answers to quote an example. **Mergers** occur when businesses combine their operations.

(c) Many firms seek to combine or work together (Section 5). A variety of arrangements can be exploited.

Each method has its particular advantages and disadvantages, relating to a whole variety of factors, including risk, resources and corporate culture.

Try and be clear in your own mind, however, the difference between **product-market strategy** – the direction of growth – and **institutional strategy** – the method of growth. For example, a firm can use organic growth to diversify, but it can also diversify by takeover.

Topic list	Learning outcomes	Syllabus references	Ability required
1 Methods of growth	C(i)	C4	Evaluation
2 Organic growth and in-house innovation	C(i)	C4	Evaluation
3 International expansion	C(i)	C4	Evaluation
4 Mergers and acquisitions	C(i)	C9	Evaluation
5 Joint ventures, alliances and franchising	C(i)	C4, C9	Evaluation
6 Divestment	C(i)	C9	Evaluation
7 The public and not-for-profit sectors	C(i)	C4	Evaluation

1 Methods of growth

FAST FORWARD **Growth** may be achieved organically or through a link to another firm.

Once a firm has made its choice as to which strategies to pursue it needs to choose an appropriate **mechanism**.

- Develop the business from scratch
- Acquire or merge with an already existing business
- Co-operate in some way with another firm

The main issues involved in choosing a method of growth are these.

- A firm many not be able to go it alone, or it may have plenty of **resources** to invest
- Two different businesses might have **complementary skills**
- Does a firm need to **move fast**?
- A firm might wish to **retain control** of a product or process
- Combining businesses involves integrating **people and organisation culture**
- **Risk**. A firm may either increase or reduce the level of risk to which it is subject. Risk is discussed in Chapter 11.

The type of relationships between two or more firms can display differing degrees of intensity.

- **Formal integration**: acquisition and merger
- Formalised ownership/relationship, such as a joint venture
- Contractual relationships, such as franchising

1.1 Expansion method

Lynch summarised possible expansion methods in an expansion method matrix that analysed them on two axes: **internal-external** development, and **home country-international** location.

(a)　**Internal development** in the **home country** is simply organic growth

(b)　**Internal development internationally**

　　(i)　Exporting　　　　　　　　(iv)　Multi national operation
　　(ii)　Overseas office　　　　　(v)　Global operation
　　(iii)　Overseas manufacture

(c)　**External development** in the **home country** or **internationally**

　　(i)　Merger　　　　　　　　　(iii)　Joint venture or alliance
　　(ii)　Acquisition　　　　　　　(iv)　Franchising or licensing

Company

	Inside	Outside
Home country	Organic growth	Merger Acquisition Joint venture Alliance Franchise License
International	Exporting Overseas office Overseas manufacture Multi-national operation Global operation	Merger Acquisition Joint venture Alliance Franchise License

Location (vertical axis label)

Lynch – Expansion method matrix

2 Organic growth and in-house innovation

Organic growth is expansion by use of internal resources. The advantages are control, and the fact that managers can concentrate on product-market issues, rather than concerns of organisation structure.

Organic growth is the primary method of growth for many organisations. Organic growth is achieved through the development of internal resources.

Key term

> **Organic growth.** Expansion of a firm's size, profits, activities achieved without taking over other firms.

Why might a firm pursue organic growth?

- The **process of developing** a new product gives the firm the best understanding of the market and the product
- It might be the only sensible way to pursue **genuine technological innovations**
- There is **no suitable target for acquisition**
- It can be planned and financed easily from the company's **current resources**
- The same **style of management** and corporate culture can be maintained
- **Hidden or unforeseen losses** are less likely with organic growth

If we assume that existing products have a finite life, a strategy of organic growth must include plans for **innovation**.

- It provides the organisation with a **distinctive competence**, and with the ability to maintain such a competence
- It maintains the organisation's **competitive advantage** and market share

 Case Study

Organic growth by innovation is not always the guarantee of success. *The Economist* reported a research study into successful innovations.

(a) Pioneers often fail to conjure up a mass market. The first video recorder was developed in 1956 by *Ampex* – they sold for $50,000. The firm made no attempt to expand the market. *Sony, JVC* and *Matsushita* spent 20 years turning it into a mass market product.

(b) Another reason is financial strength. *Coca-Cola's Fruitopia* brand was positioned against firms such as Snapple which had pioneered the market in non-cola 'alternative beverages'.

Innovative companies are not necessarily the most successful. Success is based upon other factors such as distribution capability, technical expertise and marketing skills. The anti-ulcer drug *Zantac* from *Glaxo* was an imitative product, but it overtook *Tagamet* from *SmithKline* due to Glaxo's commercial skills in exploiting it.

2.1 Capacity issues: critical mass and economies of scale

For some firms, organic growth must result in a target **critical mass** being achieved, in order to achieve economies of scale. In an industry where fixed costs are high, and variable costs relatively small, significant reductions in unit costs can be achieved by producing on a larger scale.

For example, suppose that in the widget-manufacturing industry, the following costs are applicable.

Factory capacity (output in units pa)	Fixed costs £	Unit variable costs £
10,000	400,000	5.00
50,000	800,000	4.80
200,000	1,600,000	4.60

Unit costs of producing at maximum capacity in each size of factory would be as follows.

		Unit costs		
Capacity Units	Fixed £	Variable £	Total £	
10,000	40.0	5.0	45.00	Effect of
50,000	16.0	4.8	20.80	economies of
200,000	8.0	4.6	12.60	scale

If an organisation plans to achieve a certain capacity of output, it will not minimise its costs unless actual production volumes reach the capacity level. In the table above, the factory with 200,000 units capacity can achieve unit costs of £12.60 when operating at full capacity; but if actual production were only 50%, say, unit fixed costs would double to £16, and unit costs would be £20.60 (very nearly as high as in a factory with a 50,000 units capacity operating at full capacity).

3 International expansion

FAST FORWARD

International expansion is a big undertaking and firms must know their reasons for it, and be sure that they have the resources to manage it, both strategically and operationally. The decision about which overseas market to enter should be based upon assessment of **market attractiveness**, **competitive advantage**, and **risk**.

3.1 Some key decisions for international expansion

Firms must deal with three major issues.

- Whether to market abroad at all
- Which markets to enter
- The mode(s) of entry

3.2 Why expand overseas?

Firms may be **pushed** into international expansion by domestic adversity, or **pulled** into it by attractive opportunities abroad. More specifically, some of the reasons firms expand overseas are the following. They can be classified as either **internal** or **external** factors.

(a) **Chance.** Firms may enter a particular country or countries by chance. A company executive may recognise an opportunity while on a foreign trip or the firm may receive chance orders or requests for information from potential foreign customers.

(b) **Life cycle.** Home sales may be in the mature or decline stages of the product life cycle. International expansion may allow sales growth since products are often in different stages of the product life cycle in different countries.

(c) **Competition.** Intense competition in an overcrowded domestic market sometimes induces firms to seek markets overseas where rivalry is less keen. This was a major reason in Gillette's decision to begin marketing razor blades outside its US home markets.

(d) **Reduce dependence.** Many companies wish to diversify away from an over-dependence on a single domestic market. Increased geographic diversification can help to **spread risk**.

(e) **Economies of scale.** Technological factors may be such that a large volume is needed either to cover the high costs of plant, equipment, R&D and personnel or to exploit a large potential for economies of scale and experience. For these reasons firms in the aviation, ethical drugs, computer and automobile industries are often obliged to enter multiple countries.

(f) **Variable quality.** International expansion can facilitate the disposal of discontinued products and seconds since these can be sold abroad without spoiling the home market. Conversely, many companies, such as most UK pottery manufacturers, reserve their first quality outputs for sale in lucrative high income countries like the USA, selling only seconds in the home country.

(g) **Finance.** Many firms are attracted by favourable opportunities such as the following.

   (i) The development of lucrative emerging markets (such as China and India)

   (ii) Depreciation in their domestic currency values

   (iii) Corporate tax benefits offered by particular countries

   (iv) Lowering of import barriers abroad

(h) **Familial.** Many countries and companies trade because of family or cultural connections overseas. For example, the Kenyan horticultural industry exports to the UK.

(i) **Aid agencies.** Countries that benefit from bilateral or unilateral aid often purchase goods which normally they would not have the money for. Toyota vehicles have been bought for aid projects in Africa via United Nations development funds.

3.2.1 Involvement overseas

(a) **Reasons supporting involvement overseas**

   (i) **Profit margins** may be higher abroad.

   (ii) Increase in **sales volume** from foreign sales may allow large reductions in unit costs.

   (iii) The **product life cycle** may be extended if the product is at an earlier stage in the life cycle in other countries.

   (iv) **Seasonal fluctuations** may be levelled out (peak periods in some countries coinciding with troughs in others).

   (v) It offers an opportunity of **disposing of excess production** in times of low domestic demand.

   (vi) International activities **spread the risk** which exists in any single market (eg political and economic changes).

   (vii) **Obsolescent products** can be sold off overseas without damage to the domestic market.

   (viii) The firm's prestige may be enhanced by portraying a **global image**.

(b) **Reasons for avoiding involvement**

   (i) Profits may be unduly affected by factors outside the firm's **control** (eg due to fluctuation of exchange rates and foreign government actions).

   (ii) The **adaptations** to the product (or other marketing mix elements) needed for success overseas will diminish the effects of economies of scale.

   (iii) Extending the product life cycle is not always **cost effective**. It may be better to develop new products for the domestic market.

   (iv) The **opportunity costs** of investing abroad may be better utilised at home.

   (v) In the case of marginal cost pricing, **anti-dumping duties** are more quickly imposed now than in the past.

Before getting involved in overseas expansion, the company must consider both strategic and tactical issues.

(a) **Strategic issues**

   (i) Does the strategic decision fit with the company's overall mission and objectives? Or will 'going international' cause a mis-match between objectives on the one hand and strategic and tactical decisions on the other?

(ii) Does the organisation have (or can it raise) the resources necessary to exploit effectively the opportunities overseas?

(b) **Tactical issues**

(i) How can the company get to understand customers' needs and preferences in foreign markets?

(ii) Does the company know how to conduct business abroad, and deal effectively with foreign nationals?

(iii) Are there foreign regulations and associated hidden costs?

(iv) Does the company have the necessary management skills and experience?

In making a decision as to which market(s) to enter the firm must start by establishing its objectives. Here are some examples.

(a) What proportion of total sales will be overseas?

(b) What are the longer term objectives?

(c) Will it enter one, a few, or many markets? In most cases it is better to start by selling in countries with which there is some familiarity and then expand into other countries gradually as experience is gained. Reasons to enter fewer countries at first include the following.

(i) Market entry and market control costs are high

(ii) Product and market communications modification costs are high

(iii) There is a large market and potential growth in the initial countries chosen

(iv) Dominant competitors can establish high barriers to entry

(d) What types of country should it enter (in terms of environmental factors, economic development, language used, cultural similarities and so on)? Three major criteria should be as follows.

(i) Market attractiveness

(ii) Competitive advantage

(iii) Risk

The matrix below can be used to bring together these three major criteria and assist managers in their decisions.

Evaluating which markets to enter

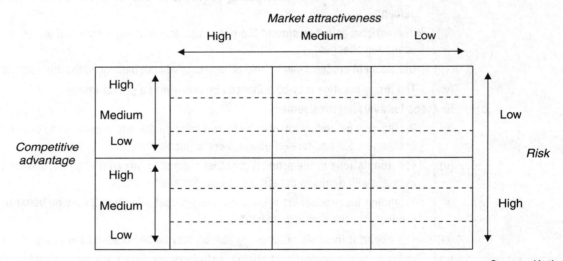

Source: Kotler

(a) **Market attractiveness**. This concerns such indicators as GNP/head and forecast demand, and market accessibility.

(b) **Competitive advantage**. This is principally dependent on prior experience in similar markets, language and cultural understanding.

(c) **Risk**. This involves an analysis of political stability, the possibility of government intervention and similar external influences.

The best markets to enter are those located at the top left of the diagram. The worst are those in the bottom right corner. Obtaining the information needed to reach this decision requires detailed and often costly international marketing research and analysis. Making these decisions is not easy, and a fairly elaborate screening process will be instituted.

In international business there are several categories of risk.

(a) **Political risk** relates to factors as diverse as wars, nationalisation, arguments between governments etc.

(b) **Business risk.** This arises from the possibility that the business idea itself might be flawed. As with political risk, it is not unique to international marketing, but firms might be exposed to more sources of risk arising from failures to understand the market.

(c) **Currency risk.** This arises out of the volatility of foreign exchange rates. Given that there is a possibility for speculation and that capital flows are free, such risks are increasing.

(d) **Profit repatriation risk.** Government actions may make it hard to repatriate profits.

3.3 Involvement in international markets

Firms develop through various stages of learning as commitment grows, and there are choices to be made along the way as to the extent to which a company commits itself to the international market. These stages are identified below.

(a) **Domestic marketing**. The firm is preoccupied with home marketing.

(b) **Pre-export stage**. A search is conducted and export opportunities are assessed.

(c) **Experimental involvement**. There is some limited involvement in exporting: unsolicited and easy-to-get orders are accepted.

(d) **Active involvement**. This indicates systematic analysis of export opportunities and expansion into foreign markets.

(e) **Committed involvement**. The firm allocates its resources according to opportunities in different countries.

Different levels of involvement are shown below.

LEVELS OF COMMITMENT TO INTERNATIONAL EXPANSION

Casual or accidental exporting	*Active exporting*	*Committed international business*
Occasional, unsolicited foreign orders are received. There is no real commitment to international business. →	The recognition that foreign markets exist. Attempts are made to cultivate sales across national boundaries. Little effort is made to consider foreign markets in the overall strategy. Minor adjustments may be made for foreign market product acceptance. →	Markets across national boundaries are a consideration in the strategy. International activities are an integral part of the overall strategy programme. Divisions or subsidiaries may be developed to serve the foreign target market.

Another model identifies **three** stages.

(a) **Domestic stage.** Firms are happy to concentrate on the home market. Exports are made, but without direction: overseas buyers may order products. Where domestic demand is weak, exporting is a 'second-best' means of getting rid of surplus stock. There is no particular relationship with organisation size. Many small, specialist organisations export. Many large companies do not (many of the UK's large utilities only began overseas activities after privatisation).

(b) **International stage.** The firm's exporting activities are taken more seriously, and an export department might be set up to develop export markets. At this stage a **multi-domestic** strategy is pursued, in which each country is regarded as a separate market. Arguably, this is sensible market segmentation. However, this relies mainly on exports; only a few activities are conducted overseas.

(c) At the **multinational** stage the company has a large number of activities in different countries, including both marketing and production facilities. However, the firm still has a recognisable 'home'.

4 Mergers and acquisitions

A **merger** is the integration of two or more businesses. An **acquisition** is where one business purchases another. This offers speedy access to new technologies and markets, but there are risks: only about half of acquisitions succeed.

Many companies consider growth through acquisitions or mergers.

Key terms

A **merger** is the joining of two separate companies to form a single company.
An **acquisition** is the purchase of a controlling interest in another company.

It is important for a company to understand its reasons for acquisition and that these reasons should be valid in terms of its strategic plan. The classic reasons for acquisition as a part of strategy are as follows.

Reason	Effect on operations
Marketing advantages	New (or extended) product range Market presence Rationalise distribution and advertising Eliminate competition Combine adjoining markets
Production advantages	Economies of scale: synergies Acquire technology and skills Greater production capacity Safeguard future supplies Bulk purchase opportunities
Finance and management	Management team improve running of the business Cash resources Gain assets, including intellectual property Tax advantages (eg losses bought) Asset stripping Turn round opportunities
Risk-spreading	Diversification
Retain independence	
Overcome barriers to entry	
Outplay rivals	

Acquisitions provide a means of entering a market, or building up a market share, more quickly and/or at a lower cost than would be incurred if the company tried to develop its own resources. Corporate planners must however consider the level of **risk** involved. Acquiring companies in overseas markets is more risky, for a number of reasons.

The acquirer should attempt an evaluation of the following.

- The prospects of technological change in the industry
- The size and strength of competitors
- The reaction of competitors to an acquisition
- The likelihood of government intervention and legislation
- The state of the industry and its long-term prospects
- The amount of synergy obtainable from the merger or acquisition

Whatever the reason for the merger or acquisition, it is unlikely to be successful unless it offers the company opportunities that cannot be found within the company itself and unless the new subsidiary fits closely into the strategic plan outlined for future growth.

Case Study

Rolls-Royce has a strong business in defence aerospace, and has won an average of 30% of the civil aerospace market over the past three years.

With aerospace a maturing market, Rolls-Royce has looked for new expansion opportunities. Since its acquisition of *Vickers* in 1999, it has built a strong presence in marine markets, which now accounts for about 15% of the Rolls-Royce group's turnover. More than 20,000 commercial and naval vehicles use Rolls-Royce equipment, and Rolls-Royce engines power 400 ships in 30 navies. Its global presence makes this possible: *Rolls-Royce Naval Marine Inc* deals with the US Navy as a US-registered company. The reasons for its expansion are:

(a)   The marine industry is looking to increase engine power for both passenger and freight ships
(b)   The marine industry is under pressure to meet demanding emissions regulations

The products acquired as a result of the Vickers takeover were market leading marine brands that expanded Rolls-Royce's route to market and made it a world leader in marine systems, from vessel design and control to winch manufacture and steering gear.

4.1 The mechanics of acquiring companies

As a management accountant you may be required to assess the value of an acquisition. A number of methods are available.

(a)   **Price/earnings ratio:** the markets expectations of future earnings. If it is high, it indicates expectations of high growth in earnings per share and/or low risk.

(b)   **Accounting rate of return**, whereby the company will be valued by estimated future profits over return on capital.

(c)   **Value of net assets** (including brands).

(d)   **Dividend yield**.

(e)   **Discounted cash flows**, if cash flows are generated by the acquisition. A suitable discount rate (eg the acquirer's cost of capital) should be applied.

(f)   **Market prices.** Shareholders may prefer to hang on for a better bid.

4.2 Takeovers or mergers financed by a share exchange arrangement

Many acquisitions are paid for by **issuing new shares** in the acquiring company, which are then used to buy the shares of the company to be taken over in a 'share exchange' arrangement. An enlarged company might then have the financial 'muscle' and borrowing power to invest further so as to gain access to markets closed to either company previously because they could not individually afford the investment.

Case Study

In the computer technology industry, where new business opportunities are continually presenting themselves, *Sinclair* proved itself to be a highly innovative company, but was restricted from greater expansion by lack of financial resources and inadequate profits, until it was eventually taken over by *Amstrad*.

4.3 Acquisitions and earnings per share

Growth in EPS will only occur after an acquisition in certain circumstances.

(a)   When the company that is acquired is bought on a lower P/E ratio or

(b)   When the company that is acquired is bought on a higher P/E ratio, but there is profit growth to offset this.

4.3.1 Buying companies on a lower P/E ratio

For example, suppose that Giant plc takes over Tiddler Ltd by offering two shares in Giant for one share in Tiddler. Details about each company are as follows.

	Giant plc	Tiddler Ltd
Number of shares	2,800,000	100,000
Market value per share	£4	–
Annual earnings	£560,000	£50,000
EPS	20p	50p
P/E ratio	20	–

By offering two shares in Giant worth £4 each for one share in Tiddler, the valuation placed on each Tiddler share is £8, and with Tiddler's EPS of 50p, this implies that Tiddler would be acquired on a P/E ratio of 16, which is lower than the P/E ratio of Giant, which is 20.

Now, suppose that the acquisition produces no synergy, and there is no growth in the earnings of either Giant or its new subsidiary Tiddler, the EPS of Giant would still be higher than before, because Tiddler was bought on a lower P/E ratio. The combined group's results would be as follows.

	Giant group
Number of shares (2,800,000 + 200,000)	3,000,000
Annual earnings (560,000 + 50,000)	£610,000
EPS	20.33p

If P/E ratio is still 20, the market value per share would be: £4.07

The opposite is true as well, so that if a subsidiary is acquired on a higher P/E ratio, and there is no profit growth, then the enlarged group would suffer a fall in EPS and probably also a fall in share price.

4.3.2 Buying companies on a higher P/E ratio, but with profit growth

Buying companies on a higher P/E ratio will result in a fall in EPS unless there is profit growth to offset this fall. For example, suppose that Starving plc acquires Bigmeal plc, by offering two shares in Starving for three shares in Bigmeal. Details of each company are as follows.

	Starving plc	Bigmeal plc
Number of shares	5,000,000	3,000,000
Value per share	£6	£4
Annual earnings		
Current	£2,000,000	£600,000
Next year	£2,200,000	£950,000
EPS (current)	40p	20p
P/E ratio	15	20

Starving plc is acquiring Bigmeal on a higher P/E ratio, and it is only the profit growth in the acquired subsidiary that gives the enlarged Starving group its growth in EPS.

	Starving group
Number of shares (5,000,000 + 2,000,000)	7,000,000
Earnings	
If no profit growth (2,000,000 + 600,000)	£2,600,000 – EPS would have been 37.14p
With profit growth (2,200,000 + 950,000)	£3,150,000 – EPS will be 45p

4.4 Debt finance

Another feature of takeover activities in the USA especially, but also in the UK, has been the **debt-financed takeover**. This is a takeover bid where most or all of the purchase finance is provided by a syndicate of banks for the acquisition. The acquiring company will become very highly geared and will normally sell off parts of the target company.

A **leveraged buy-out** (LBO) is a form of debt-financed takeover where the target company is bought up by a team of managers in the company.

4.5 Acquisitions and organic growth compared

Advantages of acquisition

Acquisitions are probably only desirable if organic growth alone cannot achieve the targets for growth that a company has set for itself.

- Acquisitions can be made to enter new product or geographical areas, or to expand in existing markets, much more **quickly**
- Acquisitions can be made **without cash**, if share exchange transactions are acceptable
- When an acquisition is made to diversify into new product areas, the company will be buying **technical expertise, goodwill and customer contracts**

Disadvantages of acquisitions

(a) **Cost**. They might be too expensive: some might be resisted by the directors of the target company.

(b) **Customers** of the target company might consider going to other suppliers for their goods.

(c) **Incompatibility**. In general, the problems of assimilating new products, customers, suppliers, markets, employees and different systems of operating might create 'indigestion' and management overload in the acquiring company.

(d) **Lack of information**. John Kay suggests that the 'acquisitions' market for companies is rarely efficient.

(e) **Cultural difference**. There may be clashes if the culture and management style of the acquired company is different to the acquiring one. There is potential for human relations problems to arise *after* the acquisition.

It is worth considering the **stakeholders** in the acquisition process.

(a) Some acquisitions are driven by the personal goals of the acquiring company's **managers**.

(b) **Corporate financiers and banks** also have a stake in the acquisitions process as they can charge fees for advice.

Takeovers often benefit the shareholders of the acquired company more than the acquirer. According to the Economist Intelligence Unit, there is a consensus that fewer than half all acquisitions are successful. One of the reasons for failure is that firms rarely take into account non-financial factors. A survey by London Business School examining 40 acquisitions (in the UK and USA) revealed some major flaws (supported by research by the Economist Intelligence Unit).

(a) All acquirers conducted financial audits, but only 37% conducted anything approaching a **management audit**.

(b) Some major problems of implementation relate to **human resources and personnel issues** such as morale, performance assessment and culture. If key managers or personnel leave, the business will suffer.

Case Study

Acquisitions research

Acquisitions are a financial disaster for shareholders, new research suggests.

A study of the performance of large takeovers completed between 1977 and 1994 has found that in the five years after a deal, the total return on investment underperformed by an average of 26 per cent, compared with shares in companies of similar size.

The research, by Alan Gregory and John Matako, of the University of Exeter's new Centre for Finance and Investment, showed that the effect of acquisitions on share price and dividends varied according to whether the bids were hostile or non-hostile and whether they were equity–financed or cash backed.

The underperformance on share-based deals is 36 per cent over five years, relative to unacquisitive companies.

Agreed bids also generated negative returns, with shareholders doing 27 per cent less well. Agreed share-based deals led to underperformance of 37 per cent.

Cash financing or bidder hostility were not enough on their own to make a profit likely, the report found However, bids that are cash-backed and hostile have a better chance of creating, rather than destroying, shareholder value.

On a low sample, the academics found that a successful hostile cash bids generated an average 50 per cent increase in the profitability of shares in the five years after the bid. Share-based bids perform poorly because shares in the acquiring companies are overvalued in the first place, Dr Gregory suggested.

He added that the process of gaining co-operation from the target board might also increase the cost, as executives might have to be persuaded to agree only if the acquirer offers over-generous terms. Unnecessary cost may be incurred if executives in an acquired company retain their jobs after completion of deals, he said.

Gabriel Rozenberg, The Times, 18 October 2004

5 Joint ventures, alliances and franchising

FAST FORWARD

There are other types of arrangement whereby businesses pool resources.

- **Joint ventures**, consortia and other alliances
- **Franchising**, where the franchiser provides expertise, a brand name etc, and the franchisee offers some of the capital

Short of mergers and takeovers, there are other ways by which companies can co-operate.

Consortia: organisations co-operate on specific business prospects. Airbus is an example, a consortium including British Aerospace, Dasa, Aerospatiale and Casa.

Joint ventures: two or more organisations set up a new, separate organisation in which they each hold an equity stake. This is very common in entering normally closed markets. For example, Jardine Matheson (historically based in Hong Kong, from where it derives much of its profits, but now registered in Bermuda with shares traded in Singapore) has a joint venture with Robert Fleming the UK merchant bank, in the firm Jardine Fleming, which amongst other things, is involved in securities trading.

Key term

> A **joint venture** is a 'contractual arrangement whereby two or more parties undertake an economic activity which is subject to joint control'.
> (CIMA *Official Terminology*)

Like any acquisition, joint ventures provide a way of building scale quickly. Joint ventures are especially attractive to **smaller or risk-averse firms**, or where very expensive new technologies are being researched and developed because they allow risks and capital commitment to be shared between the venture partners. Other advantages are these.

- Joint ventures permit coverage of a **larger number of countries** since each one requires less investment.
- A joint venture can reduce the risk of **government intervention.**
- Joint ventures can provide close **control** over operations.
- A joint venture with an indigenous firm provides **local knowledge.**
- Alliances offer several benefits in the **value chain.**
- Alliances can also be a **learning exercise.**
- Alliances provide funds for expensive **technology and research** projects.
- A joint venture is often an alternative to seeking to buy or build a wholly owned manufacturing operation abroad.

The major disadvantage of joint ventures is that there can be major **conflicts of interest**. Disagreements may arise over profit shares, amounts invested, the management of the joint venture, and the marketing strategy.

Other disadvantages are:

- The profits from the venture have to be shared among the venture partners, reducing the amount earned by each partner
- Partners can gain confidential information about each other which could subsequently be used competitively by one partner against the other.

5.1 Strategic alliances

Some firms enter long-term **strategic alliances** with others for a variety of reasons.

(a)   They share development costs of a particular technology, and share the risks associated with developing them.

(b)   The regulatory environment prohibits take-overs (eg most major airlines are in strategic alliances because in most countries – including the US – there are limits to the level of control an 'outsider' can have over an airline).

(c)   Complementary markets, technology, or competences.

(d)   Smaller firms can often work together in an alliance to act as more effective competition to a dominant player in the market then they could if they all acted independently.

Strategic alliances only go so far, as there may be disputes over control of strategic assets leading to a breakdown of trust and co-operation among the partners. Also, because the partners in an alliance remain separate entities they may fail to achieve the level of integration needed to deliver any significant competitive advantage or economies of scale.

5.1.1 Choosing alliance partners

Hooley et al suggest the following factors should be considered in choosing alliance partners.

Drivers	What benefits are offered by collaboration?
Partners	Which partners should be chosen?
Facilitators	Does the external environment favour a partnership?
Components	Activities and processes in the network.
Effectiveness	Does the previous history of alliances generate good results? Is the alliance just a temporary blip? For example, in the airline industry, there are many strategic alliances, but these arise in part because there are legal barriers to cross-border ownership.
Market-orientation	Alliance partners are harder to control and may not have the same commitment to the end-user.

In January 2006 *Siemens* and *General Electric* announced that they would co-operate in the launch of a new GE-developed security device for shipping containers. The two companies are the largest conglomerates in Europe and the USA respectively.

The product, called *Commerce Guard*, will have first mover advantage, but GE believes Siemens' strength in Europe makes co-operation necessary if the product is to achieve a high level of penetration globally.

Alliances have some **limitations**.

(a)   **Core competence**. Each organisation should be able to focus on its core competence. Alliances do not enable it to create new competences.

(b)   **Strategic priorities**. If a key aspect of strategic delivery is handed over to a partner, the firm loses flexibility. A core competence may not be enough to provide a comprehensive customer benefit.

5.1.2 IS based alliances

The cost of major IS based methods of working, combined with their inherent communications capability have made alliances based on IS a natural development. There are four common types.

(a)   **Single industry partnerships**: for example, UK insurance brokers can use a common system called IVANS to research the products offered by all of the major insurance companies.

(b)   **Multi-industry joint marketing partnerships**: some industries are so closely linked with others that it makes sense to establish IS linking their offerings. A well-known example is holiday bookings, where a flight reservation over the Internet is likely to lead to a seamless offer of hotel reservations and car hire.

(c)   **Supply chain partnerships**: as discussed in Chapter 6, greater and closer co-operation along the supply chain has led to the need for better and faster information flows. Electronic data interchange between customers and suppliers is one aspect of this improvement, perhaps seen most clearly in the car industry, where the big-name manufacturers effectively control the flow of inputs from their suppliers.

(d)   **IT supplier partnerships**: a slightly different kind of partnership is not uncommon in the IT industry itself, where physical products have their own major software content. The development of these products requires close co-operation between the hardware and software companies concerned.

5.2 Other arrangements

A **licensing agreement** is a commercial contract whereby the licenser gives something of value to the licensee in exchange for certain performances and payments.

(a)   The licenser may provide any of the following.

   (i)   Rights to produce a patented product or use a patented production process
   (ii)   Manufacturing know-how (unpatented)
   (iii)   Technical advice and assistance
   (iv)   Marketing advice and assistance
   (v)   Rights to use a trademark, brand etc

(b)   The licenser receives a royalty.

(c)   Production is higher with no investment.

(d)   The licensee might eventually become a competitor.

(e)   The supply of essential materials, components, plant.

Subcontracting is also a type of alliance. Co-operative arrangements also feature in supply chain management.

5.2.1 Franchising

Franchising is a method of expanding the business on less capital than would otherwise be possible. Franchisers include *Budget Rent-a-car*, *Dyno-rod*, *Express Dairy*, *Holiday Inn*, *Kall-Kwik Printing*, *KFC*, *Prontaprint*, *Sketchley Cleaners*, the *Body Shop* and even *McDonalds*.

(a) Offered by the franchiser.
  (i) The franchiser's name, and any goodwill associated with it
  (ii) The franchiser's system, business methods and support services (including central marketing support)
  (iii) The franchiser's product/service to self

(b) The franchisee pays the franchisers for being granted these rights.

(c) The franchisee has responsibility for the day-to-day running, and for the ultimate profitability, of his own franchise.

(d) The franchisee supplies capital, personal involvement (staff, and human resources management) and local market knowledge. As well as reducing costs for the franchiser, this can also allow barriers to entry to be overcome effectively.

5.2.2 Disadvantages of franchising (for the franchiser)

(a) The **search for competent candidates** is both costly and time consuming where the franchiser requires many outlets (eg McDonald's in the UK).

(b) Part of profit has to be paid to franchisee

(c) Danger that poor franchisee performance can harm the brand.

(d) Danger that franchises can gain confidential information about the franchiser and subsequently set up as competitor.

6 Divestment

FAST FORWARD

> **Divestment** and **demerger** have become more common, as firms seek to reverse the diversification strategies they once pursued.

Most strategies are designed to promote growth, but management should consider what rate of growth they want, whether they want to see any growth at all, or whether there should be a contraction of the business.

Key term

> **Divestment** is 'disposal of part of its activities by an entity'.   CIMA *Official Terminology*

Reasons for divestment are these.

(a) To **rationalise** a business as a result of a strategic appraisal, perhaps as a result of portfolio analysis. Another reason might be to concentrate on core competences and synergies.

(b) To sell off **subsidiary companies** at a profit, perhaps as an exit route after managing a turn-round.

(c) To allow market valuation to reflect growth and income prospects. Where a low growth, steady income operation exists alongside a potentially high growth new venture, the joint P/E is likely to be too high for the cash cow and too low for the star. The danger is that a predator will take over the whole operation and split the business in two, allowing each part to settle at its own level.

(d) Satisfy investors: diversified conglomerates are unfashionable. Modern investment thinking is that investors prefer to provide their own portfolio diversification.

(e) To **raise funds** to invest elsewhere or to reduce debt.

Philips, the Dutch manufacturer of consumer electronics, divested some non-core businesses in order to concentrate on core businesses as a strategy for improving profitability. It sold its production of white goods (large kitchen appliances) to an American firm, Whirlpool. There was overcapacity in the market. Philips was suffering from declining profitability and did not have the resources to invest in all its product ranges.

Methods of divestment

Methods of divestment are these.

- Sold as a going concern to another business (in return for cash and/or shares.)
- Assets are liquidated: the business is closed and its assets are sold.
- Demerger
- Management buyout

6.1 Demergers

One term that describes divestment is **demerger**. This is sometimes referred to as **unbundling**. The main feature of a demerger is that one corporate entity becomes two or more separate entities. The newly-separated businesses might have the same shareholders, but they will usually have different people on their board of directors. In other words the supposed synergies are negative (a '2 + 2 = 3' effect, rather than a '2 + 2 = 5' effect).

6.2 Management buyouts

Typically, a better price can be obtained by selling a business as a unit, and there might well be many other firms interested in buying. In recent years there have been a large number of **management buyouts**, whereby the subsidiary is sold off to its managers. The managers put in some of their own capital, but obtain the rest from venture capital organisations and hope to make a bigger success of the business than the company which is selling it off.

Key term

> A **management buy-out** is 'purchase of a business from its existing owners by members of the management team, generally in association with a financing institution. Where a large proportion of the new finance required to purchase the business is raised by external borrowing, the buy-out is described as *leveraged*'.
> (CIMA *Official Terminology*)

6.2.1 Strategic factors in a buyout decision

Particularly important questions are as follows.

(a) Can the buyout team **raise the finance** to pay for the buyout? Buyouts are well-favoured by venture capital organisations, which regard them as less risky than new start-up businesses.

(b) Can the bought-out operation generate enough **profits** to pay for the costs of the acquisition?

7 The public and not-for-profit sectors

FAST FORWARD

> **Public sector** and **not-for-profit organisations** will find some commercial strategic management techniques useful, particularly in the fields of marketing and innovation.

7.1 The public sector

Just as business organisations' objectives are set according to the priorities of their stakeholders, with owners having priority and managers great influence, so public sector organisations' objectives are set in theory for the benefit of the public in general and the defined client groups in particular, but are in fact subject to politicians' and civil servants' own personal and professional priorities. Political forces, in particular, can introduce **rapid policy changes**, while budgetary stringency or *largesse* can lead to the imposition of sudden spending cuts or the equally sudden availability of funds for which there are no planned applications. In the second case, actually spending the money can be more important than what it is spent on, so that an **underspend** need not be reported.

These considerations make much business strategy theory irrelevant to this sector. However, *Montanari and Bracker* proposed a matrix for the analysis of services provided by public sector bodies. This might be applied at the level of local or national government, or an executive agency with a portfolio of services. The axes are an assessment of service efficiency and public attractiveness: naturally, political support for a service or organisation depends to a great degree on the extent to which the public need and appreciate it.

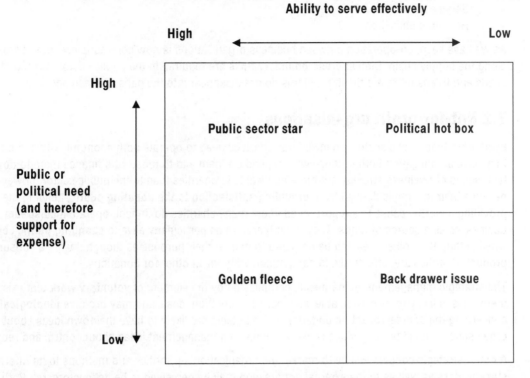

(a) A **public sector star** is something that the system is doing well and should not change. They are essential to the viability of the system.

(b) **Political hot boxes** are services that the public want, or which are mandated, but for which there are not adequate resources or competences.

(c) **Golden fleeces** are services that are done well but for which there is low demand. They may therefore be perceived to be undesirable uses for limited resources. They are potential targets for cost cutting.

(d) **Back drawer issues** are unappreciated and have low priority for funding. They are obvious candidates for cuts, but if managers perceive them as essential, they should attempt to increase support for them and move them into the **political hot box** category.

A similar concept, the Maslin Multidimensional matrix has been proposed. This is also a two-axis, four cell structure, with one axis dedicated to client group needs and wants and the other used for any dimension that might be seen as useful. The four cells are then defined by high and low levels of needs or wants and the extremes of the chosen second dimension. An example of the latter might be level of finance available.

Public servants are under an obligation to deliver certain services in an effective and economical fashion. This implies that certain problems and choices are likely to appear repeatedly.

(a) Plans must be made for the **delivery of services**. This may involve consideration of **core competences**, **transaction costs** and **outsourcing**.

(b)   Budgets must be managed to provide mandated services. Choices must be made about **investment in physical and human resources** of all kinds.

(c)   Some **marketing** activity will be required, certainly in the form of **communication** with politicians, departmental staff, client groups and the wider public; and possibly in the form of **market research**, particularly in relation to the design and effectiveness of services.

(d)   Just as in business, there will be a requirement for continuing **innovation** in products and methods in the search for increased effectiveness and economy. This will require the development of knowledge, assets and competences

A public sector organisation's strategy will have three major elements.

- Marketing
- Service delivery
- Resource utilisation

As we have seen, co-operation between business organisations is now commonplace, both across and along the supply chain. Similar **cross-boundary links** are required in the public sector, both to meet client needs and to ensure that difficult problems do not disappear into the gaps between agencies.

7.2 Not-for-profit organisations

Even more than public sector organisations, charities need to operate both **economically** and **effectively**: they have an obligation both to those who depend on them and to those who finance them to do so. The techniques of business strategy are more applicable to charities than to the public sector, however, because their income is derived from **providing satisfaction to the donating public**, albeit in the form of providing a worthy cause to support. In addition, many charities do, in fact, operate mainstream businesses as a source of funds. They must therefore be particularly alive to **changing public concerns** when setting their objectives and be prepared to market their purpose as though it were a consumer product. Charities are, effectively, in competition with one another for donations.

The strategic management of charities is complicated by the element of **voluntary work** that exists within them. This is likely to be driven, at least in part, by very high ideals and may produce **ideological pressure** concerning the courses of action undertaken. Volunteers are likely to have their own ideas about how the organisation should be run, which is likely to constrain management ideas about control and reporting.

A major strategic concern will be to market the organisation's priorities and methods to its **internal stakeholders** as well as to the external donors who may be perceived to be its 'customers'. Both groups must be satisfied that the organisation is making proper use of the resources entrusted to it.

Strategic concern for charities

Haberberg and Rieple recognise three strategic concerns for charities.

- Organise and manage internal structure and systems so as to achieve the mission
- Develop and manage fundraising to provide consistent and predictable levels of income
- Demonstrate good governance

Chapter Roundup

- **Growth** may be achieved organically or through a link to another firm.

- **Organic growth** is expansion by use of internal resources. The advantages are control, and the fact that managers can concentrate on product-market issues, rather than concerns of organisation structure.

- **International expansion** is a big undertaking and firms must know their reasons for it, and be sure that they have the resources to manage it, both strategically and operationally. The decision about which overseas market to enter should be based upon assessment of **market attractiveness**, **competitive advantage**, and **risk**.

- A **merger** is the integration of two or more businesses. An **acquisition** is where one business purchases another. This offers speedy access to new technologies and markets, but there are risks: only about half of acquisitions succeed.

- There are other types of arrangement whereby businesses pool resources.

    - **Joint ventures**, consortia and other alliances

    - **Franchising**, where the franchiser provides expertise, a brand name etc, and the franchisee offers some of the capital

- **Divestment** and **demerger** have become more common, as firms seek to reverse the diversification strategies they once pursued.

- **Public sector** and **not-for-profit organisations** will find some commercial strategic management techniques useful, particularly in the fields of marketing and innovation.

Quick Quiz

1   What is the primary method of growth for most organisations?

    A   acquisitions
    B   organic growth
    C   merger
    D   franchising

2   Why is innovation important in any organic growth strategy?

3   Distinguish a merger from an acquisition.

4   **Fill in the blanks** in the statement below, using the words in the box.

    (1) .... provide a means of entering a (2) .... or building up a (3) .... , more (4) .... than would be the case if the company tried to develop its own (5) .... Corporate planners must however consider the level of (6) .... involved.

• risk	• quickly	• market
• market share	• resources	• acquisitions

5   Define a joint venture. What is the chief disadvantage of joint ventures?

6   What three broad mechanisms can be considered by a company seeking growth?

7   What are the classic reasons for acquisition as a part of strategy?

8   What are the methods of divestment?

1   B

2   It provides the organisation with a distinctive competence, and with the ability to maintain such a competence. Also it maintains the organisation's competitive advantage and market share

3   A merger is the joining of two separate companies to form a single company.

     An acquisition is the purchase of a controlling interest in another company.

4   (1) Acquisitions (2) market (3) market share (4) quickly (5) resources (6) risk

5   A joint venture is an arrangement where two firms (or more) join forces for manufacturing, financial and marketing purposes and each has a share in both the equity and the management of the business. The major disadvantage of joint ventures is that there can be conflicts of interest.

6   Develop the business internally (organic growth)

     Acquire/merge with an existing business

     Co-operate in some way with another firm eg joint venture

7   Marketing advantages

     Production advantages

     Finance and management

     Risk-spreading

     Retain independence

     Overcome barriers to entry

     Outplay rivals

     Speed of growth

8   Sale as a going concern

     Sale of assets

     Demerger

     Management buyout

Now try the question below from the Exam Question Bank

Number	Level	Marks	Time
Q10	Examination	25	45 mins

Strategic decisions

Introduction

This chapter describes how management accountants can apply decision techniques to strategic issues such as investment appraisal, risk and operational gearing, and uncertainty. The basic theory and mathematics of such techniques as discounting and breakeven analysis should already be familiar to you. The aim of this chapter is to illustrate the way these methods can be used to support strategic decision making. Such decision-making is complicated by such factors as incompleteness of information and the need to apply more than one set of ideas to a problem in order to analyse it fully. Management accountants operating at a strategic level must, for example, appreciate the constraints applied by the marketing function and be prepared to incorporate them into their analyses.

Topic list	Learning outcomes	Syllabus references	Ability required
1 Evaluating strategic choices	C(vi)	C2	Analysis
2 Strategic management accounting, DCF and investment appraisal	C(vi)	C2	Analysis
3 Risk and cost behaviour	C(vi)	C2	Analysis
4 Decision techniques	C(vi)	C2	Analysis

1 Evaluating strategic choices

> Strategic choices are evaluated according to their **suitability** (to the organisation and its current situation), their **feasibility** (eg in terms of usefulness or competences) and their **acceptability** (eg to relevant stakeholder groups).

According to the rational model, individual strategies have to be **evaluated**, according to a number of criteria, before a strategy or a mixture of strategies is chosen. *Johnson and Scholes* narrow these down to **suitability**, **feasibility** and **acceptability**. Suitability differs from feasibility and acceptability in that **little can be done with an unsuitable strategy**. However, it may be possible **adjust the factors** that initially lead to the view that a strategy is not acceptable or not feasible. Suitability should, therefore, be the first evaluation criterion to be applied.

1.1 Suitability

Exam focus point

> If you are asked to evaluate a strategy you should always consider its suitability, acceptability and feasibility – relating these specifically back to the context given in the question scenario.

Suitability relates to the **strategic logic** of the strategy. The strategy must fit the company's operational circumstances.

- **Exploit** company strengths and distinctive **competences**?
- Rectify company **weaknesses**?
- **Neutralise** or deflect environmental **threats**?
- Help the firm to seize **opportunities**?
- **Satisfy the goals** of the organisation?
- **Fill the gap** identified by gap analysis?
- Generate/maintain **competitive advantage**?
- Involve an acceptable level of **risk**?
- Suit the **politics** and corporate **culture**?

1.2 Acceptability (to stakeholders)

The acceptability of a strategy relates to people's expectations of it. It is here that stakeholder analysis can be brought in.

(a) **Financial considerations**. Strategies will be evaluated by considering how far they contribute to meeting the dominant objective of increasing shareholder wealth.
   - (i)   Return on investment
   - (ii)   Profits
   - (iii) Growth
   - (iv) EPS
   - (v)   Cash flow
   - (vi) Price/Earnings
   - (vii) Market capitalisation

(b) **Customers** may object to a strategy if it means reducing service, but on the other hand they may have no choice.

(c) **Management** have to implement the strategy via their staff.

(d) **Staff** have to be committed to the strategy for it to be successful. If staff are unhappy with the strategy they could leave.

(e) **Suppliers** have to be willing and able to meet the input requirements of the strategy.

(f) **Banks** are interested in the implications for cash resources, debt levels etc.

(g) **Government**. A strategy involving a takeover may be prohibited under monopolies and mergers legislation. Similarly, the environmental impact may cause key stakeholders to withhold consent.

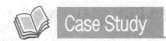 Case Study

The Irish government in 1998 imposed a temporary ban on superstores in excess of 32,000 square feet. Such constraints have led to interest in overseas development. *Tesco* has expanded into Thailand and South Korea in addition to its stores in Eastern Europe, in pursuit of an avowedly global strategy.

(h)　**The public**. The environmental impact may cause key stakeholders to protest.

(i)　**Risk**. Different shareholders have different attitudes to risk. A strategy which changed the risk/return profile, for whatever reason, may not be acceptable.

1.3 Feasibility

Feasibility asks whether the strategy can in fact be implemented.

- Is there enough **money**?
- Is there the **ability** to deliver the goods/services specified in the strategy?
- Can we deal with the likely **responses that competitors** will make?
- Do we have access to **technology, materials and resources**?
- Do we have enough **time** to implement the strategy?

Strategies which do not make use of the existing competences, and which therefore call for new competences to be acquired, might not be feasible.

- Gaining competences via organic growth takes time
- Acquiring new competences can be costly

We look at budgets and financial resources in the next section.

1.4 Sustainability

Some organisations may feel it is appropriate to consider the longer term prospects for a strategy under a separate heading of **sustainability**. This indicates that a firm should aim to adopt strategies which will deliver a long-term competitive advantage.

2 Strategic management accounting, DCF and investment appraisal

FAST FORWARD

Decisions about investment can be illuminated by the use of relevant costs and discounting.

The principles of relevant costs for decision-making and the techniques of DCF should be familiar to you already. Remember that a cost that is relevant to one decision may not be relevant to another one. This is particularly true of opportunity costs.

Exam focus point

For strategic management accounting, you must be able to apply these principles and techniques to situations where the data is either subject to uncertainty in the estimates, or else is incomplete. State your assumptions clearly. In the context of strategic management accounting, as a general guideline, the following is suggested as an approach.

(a)　Recognise why the accounting information is needed – what are we trying to do?

(b)　Assess whether the data is incomplete. If so, make any suitable assumptions that might be necessary.

(c)　Recognise whether any estimated data is uncertain, and of dubious reliability. If possible, assess how variations in the estimates would affect your financial analysis and recommendation.

2.1 Example: strategic management accounting and DCF analysis

Booters plc is a company which specialises in purchasing and re-selling land with development potential. The following data is available.

Market value of agricultural land	£20,000 per acre
Market value of land that can be developed	£200,000 per acre
Maintenance cost of land, per acre	£2,500 pa
Booters plc's cost of capital	19%

Agricultural land that is held by Booters plc can be let to farmers on short term leases for £300 per acre per annum, but maintenance costs would be payable by Booters.

The company has now received invitations to bid for two properties.

Property 1. 1.5 acres of land near a planned major road. Some of the land is about to be made subject to a compulsory purchase order, for sale to the local authority for £25,000. The remaining land (0.8 of an acre) can be re-sold to a property developer for £190,000, but not until about five years' time.

Property 2. A country estate of 160 acres, of which 15 acres might be released for residential housing development at any time in the next four years. Development of the remaining 145 acres will not be allowed.

This land will be put up for auction, unless Booters plc agrees now to pay a price of £1,400,000 beforehand. If the land goes up for auction, it is believed that a local businessman might offer £1,600,000, but the reserve price will be only £900,000.

Required. In the case of each property, what should Booters bid for the property, if anything?

Discussion

In this example, the data is incomplete. Some of the missing items would be readily available in a real-life situation, but other data would be unobtainable, except as guesswork.

Property 1. Most of the data we need for a simple financial analysis exists, but the data does not state whether the land is agricultural land or not, and so whether it can be let out to a farmer.

Otherwise, we have a straightforward DCF analysis.

	Year	Value/Cost £	Discount factor 19%	Present value £
Sale value of land, subject to compulsory purchase order	0	25,000	1.000	25,000
Sale value of remaining land	5	190,000	0.419	79,610
Maintenance cost of land, assumed to be £2,500 × 0.8 pa	1-5	(2,000)	3.058	(6,116)
Maximum purchase price				98,494

If the land sold under the compulsory purchase order takes time to sell, say one year, the value of the land would be lower, with the £25,000 sale value having to be discounted by a factor of 0.840 and a maintenance cost of land to be included (0.7 acres × £2,500, as a year 1 cost).

A maximum price of £98,000 might be indicated.

Property 2. Here the data is incomplete and uncertain.

(a) How likely is it that the 15 acres will be released for housing development?
(b) When is it most likely to be released?
(c) Is it agricultural land, and so could it be leased out to tenant farmers?
(d) Would the unwanted 145 acres be saleable at agricultural land prices, and if so, when would Booters plc know which land it did not want? Have the 15 acres for re-development been specifically identified?
(e) If the land goes for auction, would a bid above the reserve price be likely?

It is only by recognising what data is missing or uncertain that we can begin to carry out a sensible financial analysis.

Here the following assumptions are made.

(a) The land is agricultural land.

(b) The 15 acres for redevelopment have not been identified specifically. The remaining 145 acres cannot be re-sold until the planning permission has been obtained on the other 15 acres.

(c) The 145 acres could then be resold at agricultural land prices.

Two further assumptions call for business judgement.

(a) The 15 acres will be released for residential housing. There is a risk, of course, that it won't be.

(b) The land will not be released for four more years. It could, of course, be sooner.

Now we can carry out a DCF analysis.

	Year	Value/cost £	Discount factor 19%	Present value £
Sales value of 15 acres (15 × £200,000)	4	3,000,000	0.499	1,497,000
Sales value of 145 acres (145 × £20,000)	4	2,900,000	0.499	1,447,100
Sub-letting of 160 acres at £300 per acre	1-4	48,000	2.639	126,672
Maintenance cost of 160 acres at £2,500 pa	1-4	(400,000)	2.639	(1,055,600)
Maximum value of the land				2,015,172

Since Booters plc has been offered the chance to buy the property prior to auction for £1,400,000, the key questions are as follows.

(a) Is buying the land too much of a risk? If the land is not released for development, the 15 acres would be sold for only £300,000, and the PV of this would be only around £150,000. The maximum value of the land would now be about £1,350,000 less, at approximately £671,000.

(b) If the risk is considered to be worth accepting, should a price of £1,400,000 be accepted, or is it worth trying to get the land for something near the reserve price of £900,000 and running the risk of having to outbid a rival, by offering as much as £1,600,000 or even more?

Point to note

> There is no clear answer to either question, but a decision has to be taken. This is what strategic management is about! Now try this exercise.

 Question   **Domestic gas**

Learning outcome C(vi)

A public company responsible for the supply of domestic gas has received several requests from prospective customers in the Matsfold area to be connected to the gas supply system. Matsfold, an area consisting of about 8,000 residential dwellings, does not currently have any connection to the gas mains, and the company is now trying to reach a decision whether or not to provide gas supplies to the area.

(a) New customers are each charged £300 for being connected to the system and having a meter installed.

(b) Charges per quarter are:

    (i) standing charge of £15 plus.

    (ii) a charge for gas consumed, at the rate of £500 per 1,000 metered units. The average domestic consumption is about 120 metered units per month.

(c) Supplies of gas cost the company £0.08 per metered unit. Wastage of 20% must be allowed for.

(d) A postal market research survey of the Matsfold area elicited a 50% response, and 90% of the respondents indicated their wish to be connected to a gas supply.

(e) The company's cost of capital is 17%.

Required. What is the maximum capital project cost that the company should be willing to incur to persuade it to provide gas supplies to the Matsfold area?

Answer

(a) The main area of uncertainty here is the number of customers who would actually wish to be connected to the gas supply.

(b) To start with, it is assumed that gas supplies can be provided fairly quickly (ie in year 0), but this assumption can be changed quite easily later on.

(c) Other assumptions

   (i) The company might seek a payback on its investment within a specific time horizon – say ten or 15 years. However, cash flows in perpetuity will be used here to assess the project financially.

   (ii) A cost of capital of 17% pa is equal to a cost of 4% per quarter. This quarterly cost will be used to evaluate the PV of future revenues.

   (iii) A PV of net benefit per customer will be calculated, before an assessment is made of the maximum acceptable project cost.

(d) Workings, per customer

	£
Quarterly standing charge	15.0
Quarterly revenue for gas consumed	
(120 units × 3 months × £500 ÷ 1,000)	180.0
Cost of gas, including wastage	
(120 units × 100/80 × 3 months × £0.08)	(36.0)
Net income per quarter	159.0

(e) Financial evaluation, per customer

	Year	Discount factor per qtr 4%	Cash flow £	Present value £
Connection charge	0	1.0	300	300
Quarterly net income	In perpetuity	1/0.04 = 25.0	159	3,975
NPV of all future net income, per customer				4,275

(f) Financial evaluation for the area

   (i) The key issue is how many customers will actually want connecting to the gas supply, and how long will it take to connect them?

   (ii) The postal survey, taking an optimistic viewpoint, might suggest demand from 90% of 8,000 dwellings – 7,200 dwellings.

   (iii) A more realistic estimate might be just 50% of this, or even less. The company's experience with similar projects in the past could provide data to help in reaching a realistic estimate about this. Without further information about the likely margin of error in the data from the postal survey, its reliability is hard to assess. After all, it is one thing to reply to a survey saying that you would like to be connected to the gas supply, but faced with a connection charge of £300, you might easily change your mind!

(g) The estimate of demand is crucial.

Possible demand (customers)		Maximum acceptable project cost £
3,000	(× £4,275)	12,825,000
5,000		21,375,000
7,000		29,925,000

As you can see, the potential variation in the figures is enormous. What would your judgement be, and how would you advise the company's senior management?

2.2 Target returns for new capital investments: the cost of capital

> **Cost of capital.** 'Minimum acceptable return on an investment, generally computed as a discount rate for use in investment appraisal exercises. The computation of the optimal cost of capital can be complex, and many ways of determining this opportunity cost have been suggested.'　　(CIMA *Official Terminology*)

Setting target returns for new capital investments could help to ensure that the future returns for the organisation and its shareholders are sufficient to allow a company to achieve its overall target return. In practice, things are not so simple.

(a)　The return on new capital investments is only one aspect of making an adequate return. For most companies, it is the **return on existing products** that is the major influence on profitability and return.

(b)　The actual return on capital is measured **retrospectively**, as ROI, profits, earnings per share or dividends plus capital growth. A DCF return, in contrast, is measured by future cash flows.

Many groups of companies have a corporate treasury function within the holding company, which controls the use of the group's internally-generated funds by means of a central 'banking system.' The holding company will 'loan' capital to subsidiary operating units and charge out the funds at the corporate cost of capital. The target DCF rate of return selected by an organisation might be based on the following.

(a)　The **weighted average cost of capital** (WACC of the organisation).

(b)　The **marginal cost of capital** – ie the cost of the extra capital required to finance a specific project.

(c)　The **opportunity cost** of the capital required to finance the project.

(d)　A cost of capital that is adjusted to allow for the **risk element** in the particular capital investment.

(e)　A return based on the **capital asset pricing model**.

2.3 Strategic value analysis

Ultimately, investment decisions are supposed to increase **shareholder value** (a measure of shareholders' wealth as reflected in the share price).

Strategic value analysis is an approach which measures the potential financial benefit or loss to shareholders from pursuing strategic options.

(a)　**Shareholder value analysis** suggests the following **'value drivers'** generate a company's future cash flows.

- Sales growth rate (percentage)
- Operating profit margin
- Cash tax rate
- Incremental fixed capital investment
- Incremental working capital investment
- Planning period
- Cost of capital

The resulting free cash flows over the planning period can be discounted at the cost of capital to get an estimated shareholder value from pursuing an option

(b)　**Economic value added** is a similar approach, structured in a different way. We look at these measures again in Part E of the Study Text in the context of performance measurement and control.

The model above can be used as a decision making tool. For example, moving into a new market might be associated with **sales growth**, but cash flows will be under pressure from incremental **fixed and working capital investment**.

2.4 Strategic problems in investment appraisal

FAST FORWARD

> Strategic decisions cannot be reduced entirely to computation. **Qualitative factors** must also be considered.

Key term

> **Strategic investment appraisal.** 'Method of investment appraisal which allows the inclusion of both financial and non-financial factors. Project benefits are appraised in terms of their contribution to the strategies of the organisation either by their financial contribution, for non-financial benefits, by the use of index numbers or other means. (CIMA *Official Terminology*)

It is not always easy, or even possible, to quantify some of the strategic issues which affect an investment decision. It is all very well to do DCF analysis on estimated future cash flows to come up with a net present value, or to work out a payback period. What is difficult to predict, however, are **trends in the industry** as a whole.

2.4.1 External orientation

As a firm's strategy is linked very much with its position in the market place, any investment appraisal of a project must take the broader strategic issues into account.

Two questions can be posed of a strategic investment therefore, in addition to financial evaluation.

(a)   Does a project generate value to **customers**, so that the cash generated will provide a return?

(b)   Will these cash flows be **sustained** in the light of the competitive environment?

Point to note

> Strategic investment decisions must be assessed with regard to their:
>
> - Immediate financial viability
> - Effect on competitive advantage in the light of environmental uncertainties

2.4.2 Procedure for strategic investment appraisal

The following ten steps for approaching strategic projects have been suggested.

1	Determine the investment project to be analysed.
2	Determine the strategic objectives for the project.
3	Determine alternative ways of achieving the same strategic objectives.
4	Analyse a small number of alternatives.
5	Try and determine what will happen if nothing is done (but this does not mean that you assume that competitors will do nothing).
6	Determine key internal and external assumptions.
7	Collect data on areas of greatest uncertainty.
8	Carry out sensitivity analysis tests.
9	Redefine the project on the basis of 8.
10	Expose key assumptions and debate them.

2.4.3 Investment decisions

There are a number of different types of spending which can be conceived as **strategic investment issues** even though not all of them are recorded as such in financial statements.

- Investing in brands and marketing
- Investing in corporate image
- R&D to create knowledge for future exploitation
- Information technology
- Acquisitions

2.4.4 Marketing expenditure

There is some justification for treating certain types of **marketing expenditure** as investment. Levels of marketing expenditure are often significant, and any marketing strategy will have to be evaluated accordingly. However, according to Keith Ward, 'levels of marketing expenditure…are often subjected to far less rigorous financial evaluations than smaller financial commitments on more tangible assets.'

Marketing expenditure can be evaluated using a variety of methods.

- Cash flow modelling with **NPV**
- Use of **non-financial measures** to benchmark spend (see Chapters 13-15 for more detail on performance measurement)
- **Modelling competitor responses**

We looked at marketing more closely in Chapter 5 when we studied the competitive environment. Here, we will consider the application of investment appraisal techniques to marketing expenditure.

Exam focus point

The November 2005 Section A mini-case offered 15 marks for a fairly simple DCF calculation that was complicated by a specific requirement to compute an equivalent annual value. This baffled a lot of students but is actually very simple. The point about the value of the equivalent annuity is that it is a series of identical cash flows at one year intervals. If the annual value is multiplied by the appropriate cumulative discount factor it produces a given present value. Therefore, if we have already calculated a net present value from a series of positive and negative cash flows, we can find the equivalent annuity by dividing the NPV by the appropriate cumulative discount factor.

3 Risk and cost behaviour

FAST FORWARD

Among the problems associated with strategic decision making is the lack of certainty associated with the forecasting techniques used. Whether or not probabilities may be assigned to outcomes, techniques exist for minimising the impact of this uncertainty, including CVP analysis.

Strategies deal with future events: the future cannot be predicted. An example would be the UK's departure from the exchange rate mechanism of the European Monetary System in September 1992, in contradiction to all prior statements by the government.

We can make a distinction between risk and uncertainty, but often the terms are used interchangeably.

(a) **Risk** is sometimes used to describe situations where outcomes are not known, but their probabilities can be estimated.

(b) **Uncertainty** is present when the outcome cannot be predicted or assigned probabilities.

3.1 Types of risk

Key term

Risk is taken to mean both general unquantifiable **uncertainty** (eg political risk) and **volatility**, often measured by standard deviation.

Risk	Comment
Physical risk	Earthquakes, fire, flooding, and equipment breakdown. In the long-term, climatic changes: global warming, drought (relevant to water firms).
Economic risk	Assumptions about the economic environment might turn out to be wrong. Not even the government forecasts are perfect.
Financial risk	This term has a specific technical meaning: **the risk to shareholders caused by debt finance**. The risk exists because the debt finance might prevent capital growth or the payment of dividends, particularly when trading is difficult. The converse is that when businesses buoyant, interest payments are easily covered and shareholders receive the benefit of the remaining profits.

Risk	Comment
Business risk	Lowering of entry barriers (eg new technology); changes in customer/supplier industries leading to changed relative power; new competitors and factors internal to the firm (eg its culture or technical systems); management misunderstanding of core competences; volatile cash flows; uncertain returns; changed investor perceptions increasing the required rate of return.
Political risk	Nationalisation, sanction, civil war, political instability, can all have an impact on the business.
Exchange risk	This is the risk that changes in exchange rates affect the value of a transaction in a currency, or how it is reported.

 Case Study

In 1995, Unilever launched Persil Power, a washing powder with a new ingredient. Disaster struck. Procter and Gamble, a competitor, demonstrated that in certain conditions the ingredient damaged clothes. P&G conducted an effective public relations war. Unilever withdrew the product.

In June 1998 the Swiss pharmaceuticals company Roche announced the withdrawal of its new heart drug Posicor because of adverse side affects. Its shares suffered on the market.

3.2 Who suffers risk?

Risk and return are related. An investor will want a higher return to compensate for the increased risk of a project.

For example, investors in a company in a low-risk business might be satisfied with a return of, say, 15%, whereas in a comparable high-risk business the required return might be a minimum of 25%.

There may be a **minimum return** that shareholders will accept, allowing for the risk of the investment.

Different stakeholders in a company or a decision have different attitudes to risk.

(a)　Shareholders are able to **diversify their portfolios**, so they can have shares in a number of firms, some offering high return for high risk, others offering a low return for a low risk.

(b)　Key decision makers are managers, and their perceptions of risk are likely to be quite different.

3.3 The management accountant and risk

3.3.1 Targets for risk

If the primary financial target can be converted into a target rate of return for individual capital projects, how can risk be expressed in practical terms for decision-makers?

(a)　A **premium** for risk can be added to the target DCF rate of return.

(b)　To protect cash flows, it might be made a condition of all new capital projects that the project should **pay back** within a certain period of time, say three to four years.

3.3.2 Risk appraisal in strategy evaluation

One of the problems arising when evaluating alternative strategies is the reliability of the data used.

(a)　Business planners frequently use various operational research techniques to measure the degree of uncertainty involved.

(b)　Also, there is the use of basic **probability theory** to express the likelihood of a forecast result occurring. This would evaluate the data given by informing the decision-maker that there is, for example, a 50% probability that an acceptable result will be achieved, a 25% chance that the worst result will occur and a 25% chance that the best possible result will occur. This evaluation of risk might help the executive to decide between alternative strategies, each with its own risk profile.

When evaluating a strategy, management should consider the following.

(a)   Whether an individual strategy involves **an unacceptable amount** of risk. If it does, it should be eliminated from further consideration in the planning process.

(b)   However, the risk of an individual strategy should also be considered in the context of the **overall portfolio** of investment strategies adopted by the company.

3.3.3 Risk and cost behaviour: operational gearing

CVP analysis (breakeven analysis) can be useful in strategic planning in order to assess what share of the market a company would need to achieve to break even or to achieve a target return with a particular strategy. For example, if a company is planning to make a new product for a particular market, and estimates of capital investment costs and fixed and variable running costs were fairly reliable, the company could assess the following for a number of different sales prices.

(a)   How many sales would be needed to break even each year, and so what market share would be needed.

(b)   How many sales would be needed over a given period (of say, three years) assuming a gradual increase in annual sales, in order to break even in DCF terms (ie achieve an NPV = 0). The required market share per year for each year of the project could then be assessed.

Key term

> **Cost-volume-profit analysis (CVP).** 'Study of the effects on future profit of changes in fixed cost, variable cost, sales price, quantity and mix.'   CIMA *Official Terminology*

A related risk is the **cost structure** of the business.

(a)   A **high level of fixed costs** means that large losses are made if sales are less than breakeven, but that once breakeven is achieved, larger profits follow.

(b)   A **high proportion of variable product costs** means that the total costs are always sensitive to actual production volumes. Losses are lower, but so are profits.

In other words, the business's **operational gearing** (the ratio of fixed to variable costs) is an important indicator of risk. Where there is a high proportion of fixed costs, a strategy might be more risky, although it promises a higher return. A high proportion of genuinely variable costs can mean more flexibility.

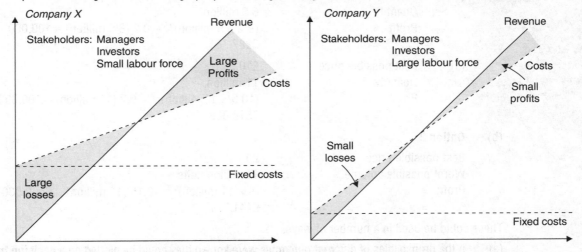

The two graphs have the same breakeven point, but X is much more sensitive to lower sales. It is more volatile. X promises higher profits, but risks higher losses than Y.

With any strategy there is a **stakeholder response risk**, an environmental factor which can intrude on the management accountant's cost behaviour diagrams. Bankers, employees and the government are all interested parties in a business. If a business pursues a particular strategy, this might antagonise the government of the country in which it is operating.

3.3.4 Probabilities and risk

Higher risks tend to be associated with higher returns. This is the principle underlying the Capital Asset Pricing Model, and we have already seen that the target DCF rate of return for capital expenditure projects may be varied according to the project's risk.

Some risks can be measured by probabilities.

(a)   An average expected profit or NPV can be measured as an **expected value** (EV) of the different probabilities.

(b)   Risk can be quantified as a **standard deviation of expected profit or NPV**.

3.4 Example: uncertainty about sales demand, costs and profits

A company is trying to make a strategic decision about whether to introduce a new production process. The process would reduce unit variable costs of production significantly but would increase fixed costs of production substantially. Forecast sales demand is uncertain, for a range of different selling prices. Non-production costs are also uncertain. The key information in the question could be reduced to the following.

(a)   **Option 1**. Keeping existing system

   (i)   Sales price could be anywhere in the range £9 – £10.5 per unit
   (ii)   Sales quantity could be anywhere in the range 8.5 million to 11 million units
   (iii)   Profits in £ would be $(PQ)^{0.8} - 0.2Q - 100,000$ where
           P = price
           Q = quantity sold

(b)   **Option 2**. Introduce new production system

   (i)   Sales price had to be £9 per unit or less
   (ii)   Sales quantity could be anywhere above 11 million units at the chosen price
   (iii)   Profit would be $(PQ)^{0.8} - 0.15Q - 400,000$

A suitable approach to tackling this problem would be to consider the profits that would be earned at a number of different price/quantity combinations, for both Options 1 and 2. A 'worst possible' and 'best possible' estimate could have been made, and the various possible outcomes analysed and discussed. Some figures are shown below, for illustration purposes.

(a)   **Option 1**

   (i)   Worse possible price   £9
           Quantity   8.5 million
           Profit = $(9 \times 8.5 \text{ million})^{0.8} - 0.2 (8.5 \text{ million}) - 100,000$
                   =   £227,351

   (ii)   Best possible price   £10.5
           Quantity   11 million
           Profit = $(10.5 \times 11 \text{ million})^{0.8} - 0.2 (11 \text{ million}) - 100,000$
                   =   £518,808

(b)   **Option 2**

        Best possible price   £9
        Worst possible volume   11 million units
        Profit = $(9 \times 11 \text{ million})^{0.8} - 0.15 (11 \text{ million}) - £400,000$
                =   £441,771

These could be used in a number of ways.

(a)   If the probabilities of different outcomes were known they could be plotted on a **decision tree**.

(b)   The outcomes might be used in a **decision matrix**, if they could be related to different sets of circumstances.

(c)   An **assessment** of risk might be carried out.

4 Decision techniques

FAST FORWARD

Decision-making processes can be supported by rational techniques, including decision trees, cost/benefit analysis, ranking and scoring, scenario building, decision matrices and sensitivity analysis.

This section describes a number of techniques to enable a systematic approach to be taken to certain strategic decisions.

4.1 Decision trees

Key term

Decision tree. 'Pictorial method of showing a sequence of interrelated decisions and their expected outcomes. Decision trees can incorporate both the probabilities of, and values of, expected outcomes, and are used in decision making.'   (CIMA *Official Terminology*)

Decision trees are a useful tool for helping managers choose between different courses of action. The tree structure allows them to lay out options and investigate the possible outcomes of choosing these option.

There are **two stages in preparing a decision tree.**

   (a)   **Drawing the tree itself**, to show all the choices and outcomes

   (b)   **Putting in the numbers:** the probabilities, outcome values and expected values (EVs).
         (Expected value is calculated as **probability × outcome**.) For example, if you have a 1% chance of winning £100, the expected value of the winning is £1.

The role of decision trees then in strategic planning is to assess which choices are **mutually exclusive**, and to try and give them some quantitative value. As such, they are useful in:

   •   Clarifying strategic decisions when they are complex
   •   Using risk (in probability terms) as an **input** to quantifying the decision options
   •   Ranking the relative costs and benefits of the options

4.2 Cost/benefit analysis

Cost/benefit analysis is a strategy evaluation technique often used in the public sector, where many of the costs and benefits of a project are intangible.

Key term

Cost/benefit analysis involves a comparison between the cost of the resources used, plus any other costs imposed by an activity (eg pollution, environmental damage) and the value of the financial and non-financial benefits derived.

In many public sector decisions, a cost/benefit analysis is conducted on the following basis.

   (a)   The project and its overall objectives are defined.

   (b)   The benefits, including social benefits, are analysed in detail. It is not always easy to put a value on social costs.

   (c)   The net benefits for the project are estimated, if possible. A road might reduce journey times, and so save money.

It can help businesses negotiate with public sector officials. For example, most large building projects have to get planning permission from the local authority. Local government officials will sometimes insist on certain social benefits to be included in a project.

4.3 Ranking and scoring

Ranking and scoring methods are less precise than decision trees. Some goals may be hard to quantify, and strategic decisions generally take more matters into account than can be dealt with by uncertain estimates of probability.

This is best illustrated by means of a simple example. The objectives are weighted in relative importance (so that minimising competitive threats is the most important).

	Objectives				
Strategic option	Growth in profit by over 10%	Reduce dependence on suppliers	Minimise competitive threats	Score	Rank
Do nothing	X	X	X	–	
Cut costs by subcontracting	✓	X	X	4	3rd
Expand product range	✓	X	✓	9	1st
Offer discounts to customers for fixed term contract	X	X	✓	5	2nd
Objective weighting	4	3	5		

In the example, expanding the product range would be chosen as the firm believes this will enhance profits and minimise competitive threats. Note that this is a deliberately simple example. In many cases, the strategies may not be mutually exclusive.

4.4 Scenarios

Scenario building is the process of identifying alternative futures. A strategy can be evaluated in terms of the various models of the future a company has. For example, Shell in the 1980s (quoted by Johnson and Scholes) developed three scenarios of UK economic activity and government policy to try and estimate the likely demand for oil.

4.5 Decision matrices

A **decision matrix** is a way of comparing outcomes with a variety of circumstances. Outcomes can be selected on a number of bases, and the decision matrix clarifies the choice.

When a decision has to be made, there will be a range of possible actions. Each action will have certain consequences, or **payoffs**. The payoff from any given action will depend on the circumstances (for example, high demand or low demand).

For a decision with these elements, a **payoff table** can be prepared. This is simply a table with rows for circumstances and columns for actions (or vice versa) and the payoffs in the cells of the table. Here is an example.

Payoff table for decision on level of advertising expenditure: payoffs in £'000 of profit after advertising expenditure

		Actions: expenditure		
		High	Medium	Low
Circumstances	I	+50	+30	+15
of the economy	II	+20	+25	+5
	III	−15	−10	−5

Having worked out the consequences of different actions under different circumstances, we need to select a criterion for making our decision. Two basic decision rules cater for optimists and pessimists respectively.

(a)   **Hope for the best**: the maximax rule can be applied in two equivalent ways:

(i)   Maximise the maximum profit

(ii)   Minimise the minimum costs or losses

Using this rule, we would decide on high expenditure as this offers the best of the favourable outcomes. Note that in this case, we are looking at economy condition 1, since this offers the highest profit: minimising cost or loss does not apply.

(b) **Expect the worst**: the minimax rule also has two equivalent versions:

(i) Maximise the minimum profit
(ii) Minimise the maximum costs or losses

Using this rule we examine economy condition 3 since this cause the greatest losses. Here we would choose low expenditure.

To consider only one payoff of each action may be thought unrealistic. The *Hurwicz* criterion seeks to remedy this by taking a **weighted average** of the best and worst payoffs of each action:

$$\text{Weighted payoff} = \alpha \times \text{worst payoff} \times (1 - \alpha) \times \text{best payoff}$$

α is a number between 0 and 1, sometimes called the **pessimism-optimism index**. The value chosen reflects one's attitude to the risk of poor payoffs and the chance of good payoffs. The action with the highest weighted payoff is selected.

Another possible approach is to consider the extent to which we might come to regret an action we had chosen. This is the **minimax regret** rule.

| Regret for any combination of action and circumstances | = | Payoff for best action in those circumstances | − | Payoff of the action actually taken in those circumstances |

To apply this rule it is necessary to calculate the regret for each cell for each course of action.

4.6 Sensitivity analysis

Key term

> **Sensitivity analysis** 'Modelling and risk assessment procedure in which changes are made to significant variables in order to determine the effect of these changes on the planned outcome. Particular attention is thereafter paid to variables identified as being of special significance.'   (CIMA *Official Terminology*)

Sensitivity analysis involves asking 'what if?' questions, and so it can be used for strategic planning. By changing the value of different variables in a decision model, a number of **different outcomes** will be produced. For example, wage increases can be altered to 10% from 5%; demand for a product can be reduced from 100,000 to 80,000, the introduction of new processing equipment can be deferred by six months, on the revised assumption that there will be delays, and so on.

A particularly powerful decision-related technique is to establish the percentage change in each assumption that would lead to a different decision. This can give a good indication of overall risk and also show which variables need the closest monitoring.

Chapter Roundup

- Strategic choices are evaluated according to their **suitability** (to the organisation and its current situation), their **feasibility** (eg in terms of usefulness or competences) and their **acceptability** (eg to relevant stakeholder groups).

- Decisions about investment can be illuminated by the use of relevant costs and discounting.

- Strategic decisions cannot be reduced entirely to computation. **Qualitative factors** must also be considered.

- Among the problems associated with strategic decision making is the lack of certainty associated with the forecasting techniques used. Whether or not probabilities may be assigned to outcomes, techniques exist for minimising the impact of this uncertainty, including CVP analysis.

- Decision-making processes can be supported by rational techniques, including decision trees, cost/benefit analysis, ranking and scoring, scenario building, decision matrices and sensitivity analysis.

Quick Quiz

1   What are the three criteria organisations should use for evaluating individual strategies?
2   What is strategic value analysis?
3   List the steps for analysing strategic investment projects
4   Identify some types of risk.
5   Explain the relationship between risk and operational gearing.
6   Define cost/benefit analysis.
7   How is 'expected value' calculated when preparing a decision tree?
8   What is being described here? 'Study of the effect on future profit of changes in fixed cost, variable cost, sales price, quantity and mix'.

1   Suitability, acceptability and feasibility

2   Strategic value analysis is an approach which measures the potential financial benefit or loss to shareholders from pursuing strategic options.

3
- Determine the investment project to be analysed.
- Determine the strategic objectives for the project.
- Determine alternative ways of achieving the same strategic objectives.
- Analyse a small number of alternatives.
- Try and determine what will happen if nothing is done (but this does not mean that you assume that competitors will do nothing).
- Determine key internal and external assumptions.
- Collect data on areas of greatest uncertainty.
- Carry out sensitivity analysis tests.
- Redefine the project on the basis of 8.
- Expose key assumptions and debate them.

4
- Physical
- Economic
- Financial
- Business
- Stakeholder response risk

5   The business's operational gearing (the ratio of fixed to variable costs) is an important indicator of risk. Where there is a high proportion of fixed costs, a strategy might be more risky, although it promises a higher return. A high proportion of genuinely variable costs can mean more flexibility.

6   Cost/benefit analysis involves a comparison between the cost of the resources used, plus any other costs imposed by an activity (eg pollution, environmental damage) and the value of the financial and non-financial benefits derived

7   Probability × outcome

8   Cost – volume profit analysis (CVP); also known as breakeven analysis

Now try the question below from the Exam Question Bank

Number	Level	Marks	Time
Q11	Intermediate	n/a	30 mins

Implementing strategy

Issues in strategic management

12

Introduction

In this chapter we draw together our coverage of certain discrete issues that require strategic management attention. Each is in itself a major business management activity.

Section 1 is about project management. Major projects both have impact at the strategic level and wide-ranging effects across the organisation. Senior management attention is required if they are to remain under control.

Lean systems are covered in Section 2. Most businesses attempt to control their costs, but the best results are achieved when a comprehensive, strategic view is taken.

Section 3 discusses the notion of change. Change management is an important strategic activity.

In Sections 4 and 5 we consider the strategic aspect of marketing, starting with the important distinction to be made between that and marketing's more routine, operational aspects.

Section 6 examines business process re-engineering. This is an innovative response to the challenge of established methods and can bring both cost savings and efficiency improvements.

In Section 7 we look at some new ideas in the field of organisation structure. Section 8 deals with the important topic of e-commerce.

Topic list	Learning outcomes	Syllabus references	Ability required
1 Managing projects	D(i)	D5	Evaluation
2 Lean systems	D(i)	D6	Evaluation
3 Change management	D(vi)	D7	Analysis
4 Marketing and strategy	D(i)	D8	Evaluation
5 Customer relationships	B(iv)	B4	Discussion
6 Re-engineering and innovation	C(v)	C10	Evaluation
7 Organisation structure	D(i)	–	Evaluation
8 E-commerce	D(v)	D9	Evaluation

1 Managing projects

FAST FORWARD

> The hierarchy of **project management** extends upwards beyond the project manager. More senior managers must provide strategic control. The main instrument for such control is the **project board**. PRINCE2 project management proceeds on the basis that a project is driven by its business case.

Knowledge brought forward

> The concepts and techniques of **project management**, including a discussion of the **PRINCE2** methodology, form part of the syllabus for Paper 5 **Integrated Management** and are examined in the BPP Study Text for that paper. It is not appropriate to discuss these matters further here and we will assume that you are familiar with them.
>
> If you are unsure about these matters, you should refer back to your BPP Study Text or Passcards for paper P5.

Nevertheless, project management is a major and growing matter of managerial concern and major projects have strategic impact. We must, therefore, give some consideration to the role and responsibilities of the senior manager with regard to projects and the management of project managers. We will make use of the PRINCE2 framework to illustrate this discussion, emphasising those **processes** and **components** that require senior management attention.

1.1 Management

An important advantage of PRINCE2 is that a clear **management structure** of roles and responsibilities within the system is defined; this may be adapted according to the skills available within the organisation and the nature of the project.

Management implies a structure of authority and accountability. PRINCE2 recognises **four layers of management responsibility**, though levels may be combined or eliminated if appropriate. A major project of strategic significance will be of interest to the organisation's **strategic apex**, which may appoint one of its members or form a **steering committee** to set policy to support business objectives. An **executive committee** below strategic apex level may have the job of translating policies into specific projects that support them.

The top level of management for an individual project is the **project board**. This provides overall guidance and must represent the business interests of the organisation. Two other constituencies are also represented.

(a)   The **senior user** represents the interests of those who are affected by the introduction of the new system and is accountable for the quality of the specification.

(b)   The **senior supplier/senior technical** person represents those charged with implementing the project. This role may be filled by an external prime contractor or a person within the organisation such as the purchasing officer or, in the case of an IT project, for example, the senior IT person appointed to the project.

Clearly, Chartered Management Accountants working in senior roles may well find themselves involved in project management at one of these levels.

1.2 Business case

It is a fundamental aspect of PRINCE2 that a project is **driven by its business case**; the continuing viability of the project is checked at regular intervals.

A business case is not something that is confined to commercial organisations; the term may be understood as meaning a reasoned account of what is to be achieved and why it will be of benefit. Occasions when the business case must be referred to should be specified at the outset; this is to ensure focus on what the project is really supposed to be about. The business case may require updating as the project progresses. It is a strategic management role to ensure that this principle is adhered to.

1.3 Control

The project board restricts authorisation to one project stage at a time and manages by exception.

1.4 Processes

PRINCE2 Processes are largely identifiable as approximately equivalent to stages of the **project lifecycle**, though they also relate to aspects of continuing project management activity. There are eight processes, several of which require senior management input.

- Directing a project
- Starting up a project
- Initiating a project
- Planning
- Controlling a stage
- Managing stage boundaries
- Managing product delivery
- Closing a project

Directing a project is the responsibility of the senior management team or project board. This process continues throughout the life of the project but is limited to **higher aspects of control and decision-making**.

Starting up a project is also a senior responsibility. It is a short scene-setting pre-project process concerned with fundamentals such as the project's aims and the appointment of the project board and project manager.

Controlling a stage includes a structure of reports and meetings.

(a) A **project initiation meeting** involving senior management agrees the scope and objectives of the project and gives approval for it to start.

(b) The completion of each project stage is marked by an **end stage assessment**, which includes reports from the project manager and the project assurance team to higher authority. The next stage does not commence until its plans have been reviewed and approved.

(c) **Mid stage assessments** are optional and may arise if, for example, a stage runs for a particularly long time or it is necessary to start a new stage before the current one is complete.

(d) **Highlight reports** are submitted regularly to the project board by the project manager. These reports are the main overall routine control mechanism and their frequency (often monthly) is agreed at project initiation. They are essentially progress reports and should include brief summaries of project schedule and budget status.

Closing a project is the process by which the project manager brings the project to a conclusion. It consists of checking and reporting on the extent that the project has been a success. The completion of the project is formally marked by the **project closure meeting**. This is held to ensure that all planned work has been carried out, including any approved variations to the plan, and that the work has been accepted.

2 Lean systems

FAST FORWARD

Business must respond to intensified competition, particularly from other countries, by improving its efficiency and reducing its costs.

Before the 1970s, barriers of communication and **geographical distance** limited the extent to which overseas organisations could compete in domestic markets. Cost increases could often be passed on to customers and so there were **few efforts to maximise efficiency and improve management practices**, or to reduce costs. **During the 1970s**, however, **overseas competitors** gained access to domestic markets by **establishing global networks for acquiring raw materials and distributing high-quality, low-priced goods**. To succeed, organisations had to compete against the best companies in the world.

Organisations need to be able to compete in today's fast-moving, sophisticated world markets. they need to be innovative and flexible and be able to deal with short product life cycles. They may want to reduce set-up times and inventories and have the greatest possible manufacturing flexibility. In addition, there is constant and unrelenting pressure to drive down costs. This has led to the development of **lean systems**, particularly in manufacturing.

2.1 Flexible manufacturing technology

Key term

> A **flexible manufacturing system** (**FMS**) is an 'integrated, computer-controlled production system which is capable of producing any of a range of parts, and of switching quickly and economically between them'.
> (CIMA *Official Terminology*)

A flexible manufacturing system (FMS) is a **highly-automated manufacturing system**, which is computer controlled and capable of producing a broad 'family' of parts in a flexible manner. **It is characterised by small batch production, the ability to change quickly from one job to another and very fast response times**, so that output can be produced quickly in response to specific orders that come in.

The point to note is that the **lean approach** is focused on a **production plan based on actual demand** rather than production being based on a plan which it is hoped demand will follow.

2.2 Just-In-Time (JIT) Systems

FAST FORWARD

> **JIT** aims for zero inventory and perfect quality and operates by demand-pull. It consists of **JIT purchasing** and **JIT production** and results in lower investment requirements, space savings, greater customer satisfaction and increased flexibility.

The 'Toyota system' commonly known as **Just in Time** is the archetypal lean manufacturing system. It draws its inspiration from the need to **eliminate waste**.

'Traditional' responses to the problems of improving manufacturing capacity and reducing unit costs of production might be described as follows.

- Longer production runs
- Economic batch quantities
- Fewer products in the product range
- More overtime
- Reduced time on preventive maintenance, to keep production flowing

In general terms, longer production runs and large batch sizes should mean less disruption, better capacity utilisation and lower unit costs. Just-in-time systems challenge such 'traditional' views of manufacture.

Key terms

> **Just-in-time** (JIT) is a 'system whose objective is to produce or to procure products or components as they are required by a customer or for use, rather than for stock.
> **Just-in-time system** is a ''pull' system, which responds to demand, in contrast to a 'push' system, in which stocks act as buffers between the different elements of the system, such as purchasing, production and sales'.
> **Just-in-time production** is 'a production system which is driven by demand for finished products, whereby each component on a production line is produced only when needed for the next stage'.
> **Just-in-time purchasing** is 'a purchasing system in which material purchases are contracted so that the receipt and usage of material, to the maximum extent possible, coincide'. (CIMA *Official Terminology*)

Although described as a technique in the *Official Terminology*, JIT is more of a **philosophy or approach to management** since it encompasses a **commitment to continuous improvement** and the **search for excellence** in the design and operation of the production management system.

JIT has the following **essential elements**.

Element	Detail
JIT purchasing	Parts and raw materials should be purchased as near as possible to the time they are needed, using **small frequent deliveries against bulk contracts**.
Close relationship with suppliers	In a JIT environment, the responsibility for the **quality of goods lies with the supplier**. A **long-term commitment** between supplier and customer should therefore be established: the supplier is guaranteed a demand for his products since he is the sole supplier and he is able to plan to meet the customer's production schedules. If an organisation has confidence that suppliers will deliver material of 100% quality, on time, so that there will be no rejects, returns and hence no consequent production delays, **usage of materials can be matched with delivery of materials and stocks can be kept at near zero levels**. Suppliers are also chosen because of their close proximity to an organisation's plant.
Uniform loading	All parts of the productive process should be operated at a speed which matches the rate at which the final product is demanded by the customer. Production runs will therefore be shorter and there will be smaller stocks of finished goods because output is being matched more closely to demand (and so storage costs will be reduced).
Set-up time reduction	Machinery set-ups are **non-value-added activities** (see below) which should be reduced or even eliminated.
Machine cells	Machines or workers should be **grouped by product or component** instead of by the type of work performed. The **non-value-added activity of materials movement** between operations is therefore **minimised by** eliminating space between work stations. Products can flow from machine to machine without having to wait for the next stage of processing or returning to stores. **Lead times and work in progress are thus reduced**.
Quality	Production management should seek to **eliminate scrap and defective units** during production, and to avoid the need for reworking of units since this stops the flow of production and leads to late deliveries to customers. Product quality and production quality are important 'drivers' in a JIT system.
Pull system (Kanban)	A Kanban, or signal, is used to ensure that products/ components are only produced when needed by the next process. Nothing is produced in anticipation of need, to then remain in stock, consuming resources.
Preventative maintenance	Production systems must be reliable and prompt, without unforeseen delays and breakdowns. Machinery must be kept fully maintained, and so preventative maintenance is an important aspect of production.
Employee involvement	Workers within each machine cell should be trained to operate each machine within that cell and to be able to perform routine preventative maintenance on the cell machines (ie to be **multiskilled and flexible**).

2.2.1 Value added

JIT aims to eliminate all **non-value-added costs**. Value is only added while a product is actually being processed. Whilst it is being inspected for quality, moving from one part of the factory to another, waiting for further processing and held in store, value is not being added. Non value-added activities (or **diversionary** activities) should therefore be eliminated.

'A **value-added** cost is incurred for an activity that cannot be eliminated without the customer's perceiving a deterioration in the performance, function, or other quality of a product. The cost of a picture tube in a television set is value-added.

The costs of those activities that can be eliminated without the customer's perceiving deterioration in the performance, function, or other quality of a product are non-value-added. The costs of handling the materials of a television set through successive stages of an assembly line may be non-value-added. Improvements in plant layout that reduce handling costs may be achieved without affecting the performance, function, or other quality of the television set.'

(Horngren)

Question

Value-added activity

Learning outcome D(i)

Which of the following is a value-added activity?

A   Setting up a machine so that it drills holes of a certain size
B   Repairing faulty production work
C   Painting a car, if the organisation manufactures cars
D   Storing materials

Answer

The correct answer is C.

The other activities are non-value-adding activities.

Case Study

The following extract from an article in the *Financial Times* illustrates how 'just-in-time' some manufacturing processes can be. The emphasis is BPP's.

'Just-in-time manufacturing is down to a fine art at *Nissan Motor Manufacturing (UK)*. **Stockholding of some components is just ten minutes** – and the holding of all parts bought in Europe is less than a day.

Nissan has moved beyond just-in-time to **synchronous supply** for some components, which means manufacturers deliver these components directly to the production line minutes before they are needed.

These manufacturers do not even receive an order to make a component until the car for which it is intended has started along the final assembly line. Seat manufacturer *Ikeda Hoover*, for example, has about 45 minutes to build seats to specification and deliver them to the assembly line a mile away. It delivers 12 sets of seats every 20 minutes and they are mounted in the right order on an overhead conveyor ready for fitting to the right car.

Nissan has **close relationships with this dozen or so suppliers** and deals exclusively with them in their component areas. It involves them and even their own suppliers in discussions about future needs and other issues. These companies have generally established their own manufacturing units close to the Nissan plant.

Other parts from further afield are collected from manufacturers by *Nissan* several times at fixed times. This is more efficient than having each supplier making individual haulage arrangements.'

2.2.2 Problems associated with JIT

JIT should not be seen as a panacea for all the endemic problems associated with Western manufacturing. It might not even be appropriate in all circumstances.

(a)   It is not always easy to predict patterns of demand.

(b)   JIT makes the organisation far more vulnerable to disruptions in the supply chain.

(c)   JIT, originated by Toyota, was designed at a time when all of Toyota's manufacturing was done within a 50 km radius of its headquarters. Wide geographical spread, however, makes this difficult.

 Case Study

- 'Just-in-time works well during normal business times. Companies that once kept months of safety stock now get by with days, or even hours of materials ... . But how about when your industry [high-tech] suddenly undergoes a tremendous boom, and demand far exceeds projections for parts? ... Just look at cell phones. The worldwide boom in cellular phone sales wasn't exactly a surprise – sales of these units have been on a fast climb for years. Yet one distributor reports a wait of 18 months to obtain high-frequency transistors for hand held devices.'

('Just in time, or just too late?', Doug Bartholomew, *Industry Week,* August 2000)

- The Kobe earthquake in Japan in 1995 severely disrupted industry in areas unaffected by the actual catastrophe. Plants that had not been hit by the earthquake were still forced to shut down production lines less than 24 hours after the earthquake struck because they held no buffer stocks which they could use to cover the shortfall caused by non delivery by the Kobe area suppliers.

- In October 1991 the workforce at the French state-owned car maker *Renault's* gear-box production plant at Cléon went on strike. The day afterwards a British plant had to cease production. Within two weeks *Renault* was losing 60% of its usual daily output. The weaknesses were due to the following.

    –   Sourcing components from one plant only

    –   Heavy dependence on in-house components

    –   Low inventory

    –   The fact '...that Japanese-style management techniques depend on stability in labour relations, something in short supply in the French public sector'.

(*Financial Times*, 31 October 1991)

 Question   JIT

Learning outcome D(i)

Batch sizes within a JIT manufacturing environment may well be smaller than those associated with traditional manufacturing systems.

What costs might be associated with this feature of JIT?

1   Increased set-up costs

2   Opportunity cost of lost production capacity as machinery and the workforce reorganise for a different product

3   Additional materials handling costs

4   Increased administrative costs

A   None of the above

B   1, 2, 3 and 4

C   1 only

D   2 and 3 only

Answer

The correct answer is B.

2.3 World class manufacturing (WCM)

> World class manufacturing (WCM) aims for high quality, fast production, and the flexibility to respond to customer needs.

World class manufacturing (WCM) is a term much in vogue at present. It was coined in the mid-1980s to **describe the fundamental changes taking place in manufacturing companies** we have been examining. WCM is a very broad term.

Key term

> The *Official Terminology's* definition of **world class manufacturing** is a 'position of international manufacturing excellence, achieved by developing a culture based on factors such as continuous improvement, problem prevention, zero defect tolerance, customer-driven JIT-based production and total quality management'.

In essence, however, WCM can be taken to have four key elements.

Key element	Description
A new approach to product quality	Instead of a policy of trying to detect defects or poor quality in production as and when they occur, WCM sets out to **identify the root causes of poor quality, eliminate them, and achieve zero defects, that is 100% quality**, thereby incorporating the principles of **TQM**.
Just-in-time manufacturing	See Section 4
Managing people	WCM aims to utilise the skills and abilities of the work force to the full. Employees are given **training** in a variety of skills, so that they can **switch from one task to another**. They are also given more responsibility for production scheduling and quality. A **team approach** is encouraged, with strong trust between management and workers.
Flexible approach to customer requirements	The WCM policy is to **develop close relationships** with customers in order to know what their requirements are, supply them on time, with short delivery lead times and change the product mix quickly and develop new products or modify existing products as customer needs change.

A WCM manufacturer will have a clear **manufacturing strategy** aimed at issues such as quality and reliability, short lead times (the time from start to finish of production), flexibility and customer satisfaction. But to compete, the world class manufacturer must appreciate that it is **not just in manufacturing that he must excel**. A **clear understanding** of the relationship between all of the factors which add value to an organisation's products (the **value chain**) is vital.

The value chain is made up of the following.

- Research and development
- Design
- Production
- Marketing

- Distribution
- Customer service
- Customers

It **starts externally** with suppliers, links them to the internal functions of R&D, design, production, marketing, distribution and customer service, and **ends externally** with suppliers.

To improve quality, reduce costs and increase innovation, the manufacturer must ensure that the **functions within the value chain are coordinated** within the overall organisational framework.

2.4 Manufacturing location

An important aspect of cost control has been the emergence of low-wage countries as preferred centres for manufacturing. This process has encouraged '**off-shoring**', particularly of unskilled and semi-skilled work; the economies of less-developed countries are helped to grow and costs are contained. The process has been going on for many years, especially in basic, highly competitive industries, such as textiles, footwear and consumer electronics, and it has been suggested that manufacturing in high wage western economies must inevitably decline.

 Case Study

The Financial Times reported in 2005 that the picture is more complex and indicated five strategic influences on decisions about the location of manufacturing.

(a) **Market location and shipping costs**. It makes sense to locate production of breakable, bulky and low value items close to major markets.

(b) **Customisation**. Where products are manufactured to specific user requirements, such as large commercial air conditioning systems, customer satisfaction is enhanced if supply chains are short and service is flexible.

(c) **Commercial confidentiality**. It is easier to preserve a competitive edge in technology if manufacturing is concentrated in a small number of secure sites. *Toyota* keeps it most advanced technology at home in Japan.

(d) **Automation**. Ease of automation of manufacturing processes can remove the cost advantage of off-shoring by cutting labour costs even in high-wage economies.

(e) **Competition**. Competition is often limited in highly specialised niche markets, especially where there is a dominant proprietary technology. This can reduce pressure to reduce costs, since low price is less of a selling advantage.

3 Change management

FAST FORWARD

Change is inevitable in most organisations and must be managed. It can be **incremental** or **transformational** and management may be **proactive** or **reactive**.

For many businesses, the development of an effective strategy requires a significant degree of organisational change; it is unusual to be able to trundle along happily doing the same things in the same way as they have been done in the past.

Like any other important business activity, change must be managed if it is to be effective and resources are not to be wasted. And strategic change must be managed in a strategic fashion.

Some change is **transformational**, that is, extensive and crucial to the organisation.

TRANSFORMATION

Organisational	*In the way the system operates*	*In employee consciousness*
Major changes in job definitions, and reporting lines, creation of new departments and elimination of old ones.	Major changes in communication patterns, working relationships and processes	Major changes in the way that things are viewed, involving shifts in attitudes, beliefs and myths

However, much change is incremental: there is steady development that may, over time, lead to the compete redesign of significant aspects of the organisation.

3.1 Strategic change

While change itself may be divided into two types, **incremental** and **transformational**, so too may the management approach to change be divided into **reactive** and **proactive**. *Johnson and Scholes* suggest the model of change shown below.

Nature of change

		Incremental	Transformational
Management role	Proactive	Tuning	Planned
	Reactive	Adaptation	Forced

The importance of the **proactive management** role is that it implies that organisational change may be undertaken *before* it is imposed by events. It may, in fact, result from the process of forecasting and be response to *expected developments*. The organisation that does not take a proactive stance in the matter of change is likely to find itself in the **forced** quadrant of the diagram. **Forced change** is likely to be both painful and fraught with risk.

The need for change can affect any aspect of the organisation. The creation of new products and services is an obvious area for change, as is the development of the processes by which they are created and delivered. However, change can also become necessary in the **supporting activities** and **linkages** of the **value chain**, since **core competences** can be developed in these areas.

Inevitably, it is in these more amorphous areas, where human behaviour is of vital importance, that the management of change becomes most important and most difficult.

3.2 Change and the individual

FAST FORWARD

Change can have a significant impact on people's circumstances and even health. They tend to oppose it and it must therefore be introduced carefully.

3.2.1 Effect of change on individuals

(a)   There may be **physiological changes** in a person's life, both as the natural product of ageing, and as the result of external factors (a change in the pattern of shift-working).

(b)   **Circumstantial changes** – living in a new house, establishing new relationships, working to new routines – will involve letting go of things, and learning new ways of doing things.

(c)   Change affects individuals **psychologically.**

(i)   **Disorientation** before new circumstances have been assimilated. A new set of models may have to be confronted, if the change involves a new roles set, new milieu, new relationships.

(ii)   **Uncertainty** may lead to **insecurity**, especially acute in changes involving work (staying in employment) and/or fast acclimatisation (a short learning curve may lead to feelings of incapacity).

(iii)   New expectations, challenges and pressures may generate **role stress** in which an individual feels discomfort in the role he or she plays.

(iv)   **Powerlessness**. Change can be particularly threatening if it is perceived as an outside force or agent against which the individual is powerless.

3.2.2 Resistance to change at work

Resisting change means attempting to preserve the existing state of affairs against pressure to alter it. Despite the possibly traumatic effects of change most people do *not* in fact resist it on these grounds alone. Many people long for change, and have a wealth of ideas about how it should be achieved.

3.2.3 Reactions to proposed change

(a) **Acceptance** whether enthusiastic espousal, co-operation, grudging co-operation or resignation

(b) **Indifference:** (usually where the change does not directly affect the individual) apathy, lack of interest, inaction

(c) **Passive resistance:** refusal to learn, working to rule; pleas of ignorance or defensiveness; procrastination

(d) **Active resistance:** deliberate 'spoiling', go-slows, deliberate errors, sabotage, absenteeism or strikes

Case Study

Whether caused by mergers and acquisitions or the market, change has been at the top of management consciousness in the public and private sectors for a decade. Yet it remains the case that many change programmes will be either a disaster or an expensive joke. A disaster because so often they destroy value, cause share prices to tumble, force talent to walk out of the door, spark destructive rumours in the press and wreck carefully constructed networks. A joke because so often nothing fundamental changes as executives mouth platitudes and make big announcements while everyone else lets them have their fun and carries on exactly as before.

Indeed, in many offices, resistance becomes one of the satisfactions of work. It is common enough to blame 'human forces' for the failure of these initiatives. People do not do what they should, they do not show enthusiasm in the right measure at the right time, they do not buy in. But Jeanie Daniel Duck, who as senior vice-president of The Boston Consulting Group carries a certain battle-bloodied authority about her subject, has taken the understanding of the dynamics of those forces several stages on while serving up a timely, well-judged argument that few executives will care for.

First, change is essentially an emotional proposition. Second, it is very difficult. Third, it involves personal change. Oh, and there's nothing touchy-feely about it, either. There is a kind of silent consensus in business that if anyone disagrees with a management strategy, they are negative, hostile freeloaders who would quarrel with the sun for shinning on them. Ms Duck is withering about such attitudes. Any business leader who seeks to blame failure on people deserves to fail. Managers can have all the commercial logic and strategic vision in the world but if they cannot get employees to understand what they are doing and why, and voluntarily elicit their excitement, forget it.

Stephen Overell, Financial Times, 2 May 2001

3.2.4 Technological change and the working environment

The consequences of **technological changes** are particularly felt in the world of work.

(a) Unskilled and **semi-skilled jobs** will be automated.

(b) **Degrading of old skills**. New skills will be needed, and there will be more pressure on managers to provide training or re-training for staff.

(c) As equipment becomes simpler to use, there could be opportunities for **greater flexibility** in manning, with one worker able to carry out more varied tasks.

(d) Since more jobs will be **part-time**, there will be less need for full-time employees.

(e) Better communications systems, portable computers etc reduce the need for people to work together in an office. There will be more **working at home.**

(f)   Working at home is likely to speed up the progression towards 'sub-contracting', and some managers might become self-employed **consultants**.

(g)   Improved information systems should help managers to **plan and control** work more effectively.

(h)   Better information systems open up opportunities for more **centralisation** of decision making by top management and a **reduced need** for **middle managers**.

3.3 Models of the change process

The **Lewin/Schein** approach to changing human behaviour has three stages: Unfreeze – change – refreeze. **Systems intervention strategy** is an intuitive method that may be implemented in three stages: diagnosis, design and implementation. The **champion of change model** uses an individual or group to lead the change process. Gemini 4Rs is based on reframing, restructuring, revitalising and renewal.

3.3.1 The change process

In the words of *John Hunt* (*Managing People at Work*): 'Learning also involves re-learning – not merely learning something new but trying to unlearn what is already known.' This is, in a nutshell, the thinking behind the *Lewin/Schein* three stage approach to changing human behaviour, which may be depicted as follows.

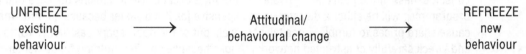

UNFREEZE existing behaviour $\longrightarrow$ Attitudinal/ behavioural change $\longrightarrow$ REFREEZE new behaviour

Step 1   **Unfreeze** is the most difficult stage of the process, concerned mainly with 'selling' the change, with giving individuals or groups a **motive** for changing their attitudes, values, behaviour, systems or structures.

(a)   If the need for change is immediate, clear and necessary for the survival of the individual or group, the unfreeze stage will be greatly accelerated.

(b)   Routine changes may be harder to sell if they are perceived to be unimportant and not survival-based.

(c)   Unfreezing processes need four things

(i)   A trigger (eg a crisis).

(ii)   Someone to challenge and expose the existing behaviour pattern, by providing data about its negative effects.

(iii)   The involvement of outsiders.

(iv)   Alterations to power structure.

Step 2   **Change** is mainly concerned with identifying what the new, desirable behaviour should be, communicating it and encouraging individuals and groups to adopt it. The new ideas must be shown to work.

Step 3   **Refreeze** is the final stage, implying consolidation or reinforcement of the new behaviour. Positive reinforcement (praise, reward) or negative reinforcement (sanctions applied to those who deviate from the new behaviour) may be used. HRM practice is particularly important here.

3.3.2 Systems intervention strategy

Systems intervention strategy (SIS) is a technique for bringing about change. It is a logical approach, not unlike the rational model of strategy. Like that model, it should be seen as **iterative** in nature: the complexity of human behaviour makes it necessary to revise and amend constantly.

SIS consists of three basic stages.

•   Diagnosis
•   Design
•   Implementation

Diagnosis. There are three main processes in the diagnosis stage.

- Analysis and description of the current situation
- Definition of objectives and constraints
- Formulation of measures to control progress

Design. In the design stage possible ways of achieving the desired results are examined in detail. Consideration is given to likelihood of success and the implications of each option for all parts of the organisation are considered.

Implementation. In the implementation stage the progress of the chosen option is managed and monitored against the specified control measures.

3.3.3 Champion of change model: the role of the change agent

The **champion of change model** recognises the importance of change being led by a **change agent**, who may be an individual or occasionally a group.

Step 1   **Senior management** are the **change strategists** and decide in broad terms what is to be done. There is a need for **powerful advocacy** for change at the strategic apex. This will only occur if senior management are themselves agreed on the need for change. This is a role requiring a clear **vision** of what the change is to achieve.

Step 2   They appoint a **change agent** to drive it through. Senior management has three roles.

- Supporting the change agent, if the change provokes conflict between the agent and interest groups in the organisation
- Reviewing and monitoring the progress of the change
- Endorsing and approving the changes, and ensuring that they are publicised

Step 3   The change agent has to **win the support of functional and operational managers,** who have to introduce and enforce the changes in their own departments. The champion of change has to provide advice and information, as well as evidence that the old ways are no longer acceptable.

Step 4   The change agent **galvanises managers into action** and gives them any necessary support. The managers ensure that the changes are implemented operationally, in the field. Where changes involve, say, a new approach to customer care, it is the workers who are responsible for ensuring the effectiveness of the change process.

It is important to realise that successful change is not something exclusively imposed from above. There is a sense in which middle and junior managers are **change recipients** in that they are required to implement new approaches and methods. However, they are themselves also **change agents** within their own spheres of responsibility. They must be committed parts of the change process if it is to succeed.

3.3.4 The Gemini 4Rs framework for planned strategic change

Management consultants *Gouillart and Kelly* describe a four-dimensional process for business transformation in their book 'Transforming the Organisation'. This approach aims to cover all the important components of the organisation's identity. Each of the four dimensions of the process has three components.

Reframing involves fundamental questions about what the organisation is and what it is for.

(a)   **Achieve mobilisation**: create the will and desire to change.
(b)   **Create the vision** of where the organisation is going.
(c)   **Build a measurement system** that will set targets and measure progress.

Restructuring is about the organisation's structure, but is also likely to involve cultural changes.

(a)   **Construct an economic model** to show in detail how value is created and where resources should be deployed.
(b)   **Align the physical infrastructure** with the overall plan.

(c)   **Redesign the work architecture** so that processes interact to create value.

Revitalising is the process of securing a good fit with the environment.

(a)   Achieve market focus.
(b)   Invent new businesses.
(c)   Change the rules of competition by exploiting technology.

Renewal ensures that the people in the organisation support the change process and acquire the necessary skills to contribute to it.

(a)   **Create a reward system** in order to motivate.
(b)   **Build individual learning**.
(c)   **Develop the organisation** and its adaptive capability.

3.4 Force field analysis

FAST FORWARD

The forces driving and restraining change may be analysed using **force field analysis**.

Current organisational practices and interest groups can embody a powerful inertia holding up the change process.

Kurt Lewin developed a simple technique of visualising the change process called **force field analysis**. In any group or organisational situation there is an interplay of driving and restraining forces. The balance between them keeps things as they are. The example below describes a public sector organisation whose management are introducing a performance review system.

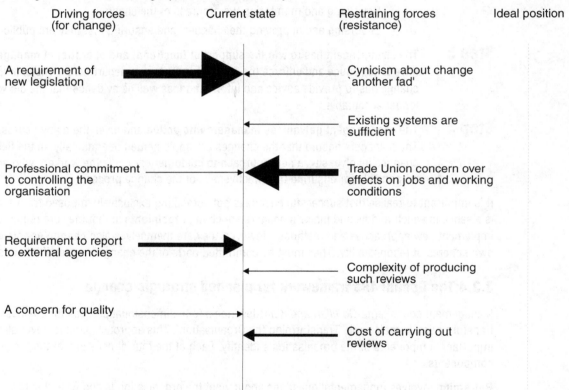

Forces can be impersonal (eg a new law, new technology), personal (the commitment of a new leader), institutional (trade union), or environmental (competitors). Lines of varying thickness to represent the probable strength of different forces.

Senior (drawing on the advice of *Carnall* and *Huczyuski and Buchanan*) suggests a practical route to applying the force field analysis idea.

(a)   Define the problem in terms of the current situation and the desired future state.

(b)   List the forces supporting and opposing the desired change and assess both the strength and the importance of each one.

(c)   Draw the force field diagram.

(d)   Decide how to strengthen or weaken the more important forces as appropriate and agree with those concerned. Weakening might be achieved by persuasion, participation, coercion or bargaining, while strengthening might be achieved by a marketing or education campaign, including the use of personal advocacy.

(e)   Identify the resources needed.

(f)   Make an action plan including event timing, milestones and responsibilities.

3.5 Overcoming resistance to change   11/07

> The management of change must include consideration of its **pace**, **manner** and **scope**.

When dealing with resistance to change, managers should consider three aspects of the change.

- Pace
- Manner
- Scope

3.5.1 Pace of change

The more gradual the change, the **more time** is available for questions to be asked, reassurances to be given and retraining (where necessary) embarked upon.

Presenting the individual concerned with a **fait accompli** ('Let's get it over with – they'll just have to get used to it!') may short-circuit resistance at the planning and immediate implementation stages. It may cause problems later.

3.5.2 The manner of change

The **manner** in which a change is put across is very important.

(a)   **Confront resistance.** Talking through areas of conflict may lead to useful insights and the adapting of the programme of change to advantage.

(b)   **Keep people informed.** Information should be sensible, clear, consistent and realistic: there is no point issuing information which will be seen as a blatant misrepresentation of the situation.

(c)   **Explanation.** The change can be sold to the people: people can be convinced that their attitudes and behaviours need changing.

(d)   **Skills training.** Learning programmes for any new skills or systems necessary will have to be designed according to the abilities and previous learning experience of the individuals concerned.

(e)   **Empathy.** Getting to know the people involved in and affected by changes enables their reactions to be anticipated.

(f)   The degree to which **consultation or participation** will be possible (or genuine) will depend on management's attitude towards the competence and trustworthiness of its workforce.

3.5.3 Styles of change management

Johnson, Scholes & Whittington identify five styles of change management.

- Education and communication
- Collaboration/participation
- Intervention
- Direction
- Coercion/edict

Education and communication

Education and communication is an approach based on persuasion: the reasons for change and the means by which it will be achieved are explained in detail to those affected by it. It is appropriate when change is **incremental**. This style is time-consuming, but can be useful if there has been misinformation in the past. However, it is a top-down approach and depends on a **willingness** to accept management's plans as appropriate. This may not, in fact, be present.

Collaboration / participation

Collaboration, or participation, brings those affected by strategic change into the change management process; for example drawing them into issue identification, prioritisation and the creation of new routines to implement newly established strategy. It may improve decision quality by bringing wider experience and knowledge to bear. However, it may be time-consuming and it will be **subject to the influence of the existing culture and paradigm**, which may limit its potential effectiveness.

Intervention

Intervention is undertaken by a **change agent** who delegates some aspects of the change process to teams or individuals, while providing guidance and retaining overall control. Delegated aspects can include both design and implementation activities. Final responsibility for achieving the necessary change remains with the change agent, but this kind of participation can build **commitment** and a **sense of ownership**.

Direction

Direction is a top-down style in which **managerial authority** is used to establish and implement a change programme based on a clear future strategy. It is thus suited to **transformational** rather than **incremental** change. It has the potential advantages of speed and clarity, but may lead to **resistance**. Its success depends in part on the adequacy of the proposed strategy: if this is inappropriate, the best managed of change programmes will not result in wider strategic success.

Coercion / edict

Coercion is an **extreme form of direction**, being based on the use of power to impose change. It is likely to provoke opposition but may be the best approach in times of confusion or crisis.

3.5.4 Scope of change

The **scope of change** should also be carefully reviewed.

(a)   **Total transformation** will create greater insecurity – but also greater excitement, if the organisation has the kind of innovative culture that can stand it – than moderate innovation.

(b)   There may be **hidden changes** to take into account: a change in technology may necessitate changes in work methods, which may in turn result in the breaking up of work groups.

(c)   Management should be aware of **how many different aspects** of their employees' lives they are proposing to alter – and therefore on how many fronts they are likely to encounter resistance.

 Case Study

The famous research by *Coch and French* into resistance to change in a pyjama factory provides evidence in favour of consultation. The company faced resistance to frequent changes to jobs and work methods necessitated by the product and production method development. This resistance showed in pay complaints, absenteeism and leaving, low efficiency (despite financial incentives), restriction of output and hostility to management. The main problem was that changes and transfers led to loss of status and earnings, through reduced efficiency ratings.

Coch and French designed an experiment in which changes were introduced in three production groups with different levels of participation.

(a)   The *non-participative group* was informed about the change but not involved in the decision-making. Resistance was immediate; conflict flared, efficiency remained low, and some members left.

(b) The *representative group* was given a hand in the change to the extent that after a preliminary meeting of explanation, representatives were given appropriate training and subsequently trained fellow members. The group was co-operative and submissive and efficiency rose rapidly.

(c) The *total participation group* also had a preliminary meeting, but all members then took part in the design and standard-setting for the new job. The group recovered its efficiency rating very rapidly, and to a level much higher than before the change, without conflict or resignations.

(d) The *non-participative members* were later re-grouped and followed the total participation procedure – with the beneficial results of the latter. Coch and French concluded that it was not the people or personality factors that mattered, but the *way in which change was implemented*.

Peter Honey (quoted by *Robinson* in *Managing after the Superlatives*) suggests that each of the sources of resistance to change identified below can be dealt with in a different way.

Cause	How to deal with it
Parochial self-interest	**Negotiation** (eg offer incentives to those resisting on grounds of self-interest).
Misunderstanding	This is best dealt with by **educating and reassuring** people. Trust has to be earned.
Different viewpoints of the situation	Change can be promoted through participation and by **involving potential resisters**.
Low tolerance of change	Force the change through and then **support** the new behaviours it requires. In short, people have to be encouraged (by carrot and stick methods) to adopt the new methods.

3.6 Managing conflict

FAST FORWARD

The introduction of change can easily lead to conflict, though it is not the only source of dissension. The management of conflict is an important aspect of change management, as well as being useful in other contexts.

3.6.1 Symptoms of conflict

- Poor communications
- Interpersonal friction
- Inter-group rivalry and jealousy
- Low morale and frustration
- Widespread use of arbitration and appeals to higher authority

3.6.2 Tactics of conflict

(a) **Withholding information** from another.

(b) **Distorting information**. This will enable the group or manager presenting the information to get their own way more easily.

(c) **Empire building**. A group (especially a specialist group such as accounting) which considers its influence to be neglected might seek to **impose rules, procedures,** restrictions or official requirements on other groups.

(d) **Informal organisation**. A manager might seek to by-pass formal channels of communication and decision-making by establishing informal contacts and friendships with people in a position of importance.

(e) **Fault-finding** in the work of other departments: department X might duplicate the work of department Y – hoping to prove department Y 'wrong' – and then report the fact to senior management.

3.6.3 Management responses to the handling of conflict

Not all of these are effective.

Response	Comment
Denial/withdrawal	If the conflict is very trivial, it may indeed blow over without an issue being made of it, but if the causes are not identified, the conflict may grow to unmanageable proportions.
Suppression	Smoothing over, to preserve working relationships despite minor conflicts.
Dominance	This creates all the lingering resentment and hostility of win-lose situations.
Compromise	Bargaining, negotiating, conciliating. To some extent, this will be inevitable in any organisation made up of different individuals. However, individuals tend to exaggerate their positions to allow for compromise, and compromise itself is seen to weaken the value of the decision, perhaps reducing commitment.
Integration/ collaboration	Emphasis must be put on the task, individuals must accept the need to modify their views for its sake, and group effort must be seen to be superior to individual effort.

Handy suggests two types of strategy which may be used to **turn conflict into competition or argument**, or to manage it in some other acceptable way.

(a)   **Environmental ('ecological') strategies** involve creating conditions in which individuals may be better able to **interact co-operatively** with each other. Such strategies involve:

   (i)   Agreement of **common objectives**
   (ii)   Reinforcing the **team nature** of organisational life, via culture
   (iii)   Providing **feedback** information on progress
   (iv)   Providing adequate co-ordination and communication **mechanisms**
   (v)   Sorting out territorial/role conflicts in the **organisational structure**

(b)   **Regulation strategies**. These are directed to control conflict.

   (i)   The provision of **arbitration** to settle disputes.
   (ii)   The establishment of **detailed rules and procedures**.
   (iii)   A liaison/co-ordination officer or **committee.**
   (iv)   Using **confrontation**, or inter-group meetings, to hammer out differences.
   (v)   **Separating** the conflicting individuals/departments.
   (vi)   **Ignoring the problem**, if it is genuinely likely to 'go away'.

3.6.4 Changes and external stakeholders

The company's relationship with its stakeholders and other aspects of its boundaries with the environment has been presented so far as a passive and reactive process. Management respond to stakeholder demands. However there can be a number of conflicts in the relationship.

Management (and other internal stakeholders) are in possession of a lot more information about the company than any other group. Management are therefore in a position to **mould the expectations** of some stakeholder groups, to direct their demands in certain directions. In other words, management can craft stakeholder expectations in a similar way to that in which they might craft strategy.

(a)   Customer expectations can be crafted by **clever marketing**. Also, the power of customers can be reduced by product differentiation, erecting barriers to entry, raising switching costs and so forth.

(b)   Suppliers and distributors can be managed in a number of ways. Drawing them into a **closer operating relationship** (eg joint product development, just-in-time systems) can be a way of managing the relationship and controlling their influence.

(c)   The public and the government can be **managed by advertising, public relations,** lobbying, and pre-empting legislation. Supermarkets, for example, sometimes promote healthy eating rather than protest about it.

(d)   Some companies deliberately **cultivate good relations with members of the investment community** (eg pension fund managers, analysts working for securities firms).

4 Marketing and strategy

4.1 The marketing mix

FAST FORWARD

> Much marketing management relates to the **marketing mix**. The basic mix consists of the four Ps: Product, price, promotion and place. For service organisations a further three Ps may be added to form the extended marketing mix: people, processes and physical evidence.

The marketing function aims to satisfy customer needs profitably through an appropriate **marketing mix.**

Key term

> **Marketing mix:** 'the set of controllable variables and their levels that the firm uses to influence the target market'. These are product, price, place and promotion and are sometimes known as the 4 Ps.

The design of the marketing mix will be decided on the basis of management intuition and judgement, together with information provided by marketing research (eg of the image of the product in the eyes of the customer, and the reasons which make customers buy a particular product).

Elements in the marketing mix partly act as substitutes for each other and they must be **integrated.** This is so the product can be positioned in the market to appeal to the customer. For example, a firm can raise the selling price of its products if it also raises product quality or advertising expenditure. Equally, a firm can perhaps reduce its sales promotion expenditure if it is successful in achieving a wider range and larger numbers of sales outlets for its product, etc.

4.1.1 Product

From the firm's point of view the product element of the marketing mix is what is being sold, whether it be widgets, power stations, haircuts, holidays or financial advice. From the customer's point of view, a **product is a solution to a problem or a package of benefits.** Product issues in the marketing mix will include such factors as:

- Design (size, shape)
- Features
- Quality and reliability
- After-sales service (if necessary)
- Packaging

Here are some **issues related to products.**

(a)   The **core product** is the most basic description of the product – a car is a means of personal transport. The **actual product** is the car itself, with all its physical features such as a powerful engine, comfortable seats and a sun roof. The **augmented product** is the car plus the benefits which come with it, such as delivery, servicing, warranties and credit facilities for buyers.

(b)   The **product range** consists of two dimensions.
  (i)   **Width**. A car maker may have products in all parts, known as segments, of the market: luxury cars, family cars, small cheap cars, and so on.
  (ii)   **Depth**. It may then offer a wide variety of options within each segment – a choice of engines, colours, accessories and so on.

(c)   **Benefits offered to the customer.** Customers differ in their attitudes towards new products and the benefits they offer.

4.1.2 Place

Place deals with how the product is distributed, and how it reaches its customers. We discussed aspects of distribution from an operational perspective in Chapter 8.

(a) **Channel**. Where are products sold? In supermarkets, corner shops? Which sales outlets will be chosen?

(b) **Logistics.** The location of warehouses and efficiency of the distribution system is also important. A customer might have to wait a long time if the warehouse is far away. Arguably, the **speed of delivery** is an important issue in **place**.

 Case Study

The selling of motor insurance in the UK has been revolutionised by Direct Line insurance, which sells over the phone, rather than through a network of high street brokers. Others have copied this approach.

A firm can distribute the product itself (direct distribution) or distribute it through intermediary organisations such as retailers, brokers etc. Key issues are:

(a) **Product push**: the firm directs its efforts to distributors to get them to stock the product.

(b) **Customer pull**: the firm persuades consumers to demand the product from retailers and distributors, effectively pulling the product through the chain.

4.1.3 Promotion

Many of the actual activities of the marketing department are related to **promotion**. Promotion is the element of the mix over which the marketing department generally has most control. A useful mnemonic is AIDA which summarises the aims of promotion.

*   Arouse **Attention**
*   Generate **Interest**
*   Inspire **Desire**
*   Initiate **Action** (ie buy the product)

Promotion in the marketing mix includes all marketing communications which let the public know of the product or service.

*   Advertising (newspapers, billboards, TV, radio, direct mail, internet)
*   Sales promotion (eg special displays in particular stores)
*   Direct selling by sales personnel.
*   Public relations

4.1.4 Price

The price element of the marketing mix is the only one which brings in revenue. Pricing was discussed at length in Chapter 9.

 Question

Two markets

Learning outcome D(i)

How might a manufacturer of chairs market to both the consumer market and the industrial market for office furniture?

The marketing mix selected for the consumer market might be low prices with attractive dealer discounts, sales largely through discount warehouses, modern design but fairly low quality and sales promotion relying on advertising by the retail outlets, together with personal selling by the manufacturing firm to the reseller. For the industrial market, the firm might develop a durable, robust product which sells at a higher price; selling may be by means of direct mail-shots, backed by personal visits from salespeople.

4.1.5 The extended marketing mix

People

The importance of employees in the marketing mix is particularly important in **service marketing**, because of the **inseparability** of the service from the service provider: the creation and consumption of the service generally happen at the same moment, at the interface between the server and the served. Front-line staff must be selected, trained and motivated with particular attention to customer care and public relations.

In the case of some services, the **physical presence** of people performing the service is a vital aspect of customer satisfaction. The staff involved are performing or producing a service, selling the service and also liaising with the customer to promote the service, gather information and respond to customer needs.

Processes

Efficient **processes** can become a marketing advantage in their own right. If an airline, for example, develops a sophisticated ticketing system, it can offer shorter waits at check-in or wider choice of flights through allied airlines. Efficient order processing not only increases customer satisfaction, but cuts down on the time it takes the organisation to complete a sale.

Issues to be considered include the following.

- Policies, particularly with regard to ethical dealings (a key issue for many consumers)
- Procedures, for efficiency and standardisation
- Automation and computerisation of processes
- Queuing and waiting times
- Information gathering, processing and communication times
- Capacity management, matching supply to demand in a timely and cost effective way
- Accessibility of facilities, premises, personnel and services

Such issues are particularly important in service marketing; because of the range of factors and people involved, it is difficult to standardise the service offered. Quality in particular specifications will vary with the circumstances and individuals.

Services are also innately **perishable**: their purchase may be put off, but they cannot be stored. This creates a need for process planning for efficient work.

Physical evidence

Services are **intangible**: there is no physical substance to them. This means that even when money has been spent on them the customer has no **evidence of ownership**. These factors make it difficult for consumers to perceive, evaluate and compare the qualities of service provision, and may therefore dampen the incentive to consume.

Issues of intangibility and ownership can be tackled by making available a physical symbol or representation of the service product or of ownership, and the benefits it confers. For example, tickets and programs relating to entertainment; and certificates of attainment in training are symbolic of the service received and a history of past positive experiences.

Physical evidence of service may also be incorporated into the design and specification of the service environment by designing premises to reflect the quality and type of service aspired to. Such environmental factors include finishing, decor, colour scheme, noise levels, background music, fragrance and general ambience.

4.1.6 The ideal marketing mix

The ideal marketing mix is one which holds a **proper balance** between each of these elements.

(a)   One marketing activity in the mix will not be fully effective unless proper attention is given to all the other activities. For example, if a company launches a costly promotion campaign which emphasises the superior quality of a product, the outlay on advertising, packaging and personal selling will be wasted if the quality does not live up to customer expectations.

(b)   A company might also place too much emphasis on one aspect of the marketing mix, and much of the effort and expenditure might not be justified for the additional returns it obtains. It might for example, place too much importance on price reductions to earn higher profits, when in fact a smaller price reduction and greater spending on sales promotion or product design might have a more profitable effect.

4.1.7 The product life cycle and the marketing mix

The product life cycle has implications for the marketing mix, which will differ according to each stage. We discuss this later in this section.

4.2 Strategy and market position

FAST FORWARD Strategy may be based to some extent on the company's market position, with different plans for followers, challengers and nichers.

In this section we will examine some of the options that apply most appropriately to the strategic management of individual products or brands. An appreciation of scale is important when considering strategy. The strategies we discuss below may be regarded as detailed strategy for a major global organisation. On the other hand, they may constitute the essence of corporate strategy for a smaller company.

Most of the material in this section is based on *Strategic Marketing Management* by *Wilson, Gilligan and Pearson*.

4.2.1 Strategies for market leaders

PIMS research has revealed the advantages of high market share and market leadership in particular. A company in this position may try to do three things.

(a)   **Expand the total market** by seeking increased usage levels; and new uses and users. These aims correspond to market penetration and market development.

(b)   **Protect the current market share**. The most common way of doing this is by means of continuous product innovation.

(c)   **Expand market share**. This may be pursued by enhancing the attractiveness of the product offering in almost any way, including increased promotion, aggressive pricing and improved distribution.

Military analogies have been used to describe defensive strategies for market leaders.

(a)   **Position defence** relies upon not changing anything. This does not work very well.

(b)   **Mobile defence** uses market broadening and diversification.

(c)   **Flanking defence** is needed to respond to attacks on **secondary markets** with growth potential.

(d)   **Contraction defence** involves withdrawal from vulnerable markets and those with low potential. It may amount to surrender.

(e)   **Pre-emptive defence** gathers information on potential attacks and then uses competitive advantage to strike first. Product innovation and aggressive promotion are important features.

(f)   **Counter-offensive** defence reacts to an attack in one of three ways.

(i)   Meeting it head on, for example entering a price war

(ii)   Exploiting a weakness in the attacker's strategy, perhaps by product innovation

(iii)   Attacking the attacker's base, perhaps by cutting price in its strongest market

4.2.2 Strategies for market challengers

The market challenger seeks to **build market share** in the hope of eventually overtaking the existing leader. However, this does not necessarily mean attacking the market leader head-on. This is a risky strategy in any case, because of the leader's resources in cash, promotion and innovation. Instead, the challenger may attack smaller regional firms or companies of similar size to itself that are vulnerable through lack of resources or poor management.

Military analogies have also been used to describe the challenger's attacking options.

(a)   The **head-on attack** matches the target's marketing mix in detail, product for product and so on. A limited frontal attack may concentrate on selected desirable customers.

(b)   The **flank attack** is mounted upon a market segment, geographic region or area of technology that the target has neglected.

(c)   The **encirclement attack** consists of as large number of simultaneous flank attacks as possible in order to overwhelm the target.

(d)   The **bypass attack** is indirect and unaggressive. It focuses on unrelated products, new geographic areas and technical leap-frogging to advance in the market.

(e)   **Guerilla attack** consists of a series of aggressive, short-term moves to demoralise, unbalance and destabilise the opponent. Tactics include drastic price cuts, poaching staff, political lobbying and short bursts of promotional activity.

 Case Study

Dolls

Between 2001 and 2004, *Mattel* lost 20% of its share of the worldwide fashion-doll segment to smaller rivals such as *MGA Entertainment*, creator of a hip new line of dolls called *Bratz*. MGA recognised what Mattel had failed to – that preteen girls were becoming more sophisticated and maturing more quickly. At younger ages, they were outgrowing *Barbie* and increasingly preferring dolls that looked like their teenage siblings and the pop stars they idolised. As the target market for Barbie narrowed from girls ages three to 11 to girls about three to five, the Bratz line cut rapidly into the seemingly unassailable Mattel franchise. Mattel finally moved to rescue Barbie's declining fortunes, launching a brand extension called *My Scene* that targeted older girls, and a line of hip dolls called *Flavas* to compete head-on with Bratz. But the damage was done. Barbie, queen of dolls for over 40 years, lost a fifth of her realm almost overnight – and Mattel didn't see it coming.

GS Day and PJH Schoemaker, Harvard Business Review, November 2005

4.2.3 Strategies for market followers

The market follower accepts the status quo and thus avoids the cost and risk associated with innovation in product, price or distribution strategy. Such a **me-too** strategy is based on the leader's approach. This can be both profitable and stable. However, to be consistently successful, such a strategy must not simply imitate. The follower should compete in the most appropriate segments, maintain its customer base and ensure that its turnover grows in line with the general expansion of the market. It should be aware that it may constitute an attractive target for market challengers. The follower must therefore control its costs and exploit appropriate opportunities.

4.2.4 Strategies for market nichers

Avoiding competition by **niching** is a profitable strategy for small firms generally and for larger organisations where competition is intense. The key to niching is **specialisation**, but there are other considerations.

(a)   The chosen market must have some growth potential while being uninteresting to major competitors.

(b)   The firm must be able to serve its customers sufficiently well to build up sufficient goodwill to fend off any attacks.

(c)   It must be possible to build up sufficient size to be profitable and purchase efficiently.

Serving a single niche can be risky: a sudden change in the market can lead to rapid decline. **Multiple niching** can overcome this problem.

4.3 Strategy and the product life cycle

We have already mentioned the relationship between the product life cycle and the marketing mix. There are also strategic implications.

4.3.1 The relevance of the product life cycle to strategic planning

In reviewing outputs, planners should assess, if possible:

(a)   The **stage of its life cycle** that any product has reached.

(b)   The **product's remaining life**, ie how much longer the product will contribute to profits.

(c)   How **urgent is the need to innovate**, to develop new and improved products? New and innovative products can lower entry barriers to existing industries and markets, especially if new technology is involved.

(d)   The interests of the company are best met with a balanced product portfolio. Managers therefore must plan when to introduce new products, how best to extend the life of mature ones and when to abandon those in decline.

There are difficulties with the product life cycle concept, however.

(a)   **Recognition**. How can managers recognise where a product stands in its life cycle?

(b)   **Not always true.** The S-shaped curve of a product life cycle does not always occur in practice. Some products have no maturity phase, and go straight from growth to decline. Some never decline if they are marketed competitively.

(c)   **Changeable**. Strategic decisions can change or extend a product's life cycle.

(d)   **Competition varies** in different industries. The financial markets are an example of markets where there is a tendency for competitors to copy the leader very quickly, so that competition has built up well ahead of demand.

4.3.2 The diffusion process and the life cycle

An important issue to planners is how quickly a new product will be adopted by the market. A number of factors influence the speed at which new ideas and product innovations will spread or be diffused through the marketplace.

*   The **complexity** of the new product
*   The relative **advantages** it offers
*   The degree to which the innovation fits into **existing patterns** of behaviour or needs
*   The **ability to try** the new product, such as samples, test drives or low value purchases entailing little risk
*   The ease with which the products benefits can be **communicated** to the potential customer

The **adoption process** refers to the stages a customer goes through before making a purchase decision. The five stages identifiable in most models of this process are these.

*   Awareness
*   Interest
*   Evaluation
*   Trial
*   Adoption

There can be a considerable time lag between awareness and adoption.

4.3.3 Diffusion and marketing strategy

Marketers usually want to ensure a rapid diffusion or rate of adoption for a new product. This allows them to gain a large share of the market prior to competitors responding. A **penetration policy** of low introductory pricing and promotions designed to facilitate trial is associated with such a strategy.

In some markets, particularly where R&D cost has been high, where the product involves 'new' technology or where it is protected from competition perhaps by patent, a **skimming policy** may be adopted. Here price is high representing very high unit profits. Sales can be increased in steps with price reductions, in line with available capacity or competitors responses.

4.3.4 Segmentation and the life cycle

Segmentation issues are relevant to the product life cycle.

(a)   At the introduction and growth stage, it may not be possible to segment the market as sales volumes are so small.

(b)   Rather more difficult decisions occur at the maturity and decline stages.

(i)   Do you find new segments in the market?

(ii)   Do you let the product die?

(iii)   Do you re-position the product, by technical modifications or other changes in the marketing mix to extend the life cycle?

Traditionally many firms have tended only to operate at home as long as performance there was satisfactory. Then, when domestic performance declined, they tried to close the gap by exporting. But this is possible only if the product is at different stages in its life cycle in different countries.

This type of strategy is now far less feasible, although not entirely impossible. The revolution in communications among countries during recent years has narrowed the time gap. As a result of these developments, **international marketing must consider many markets simultaneously**, with a view to implementing a global introduction.

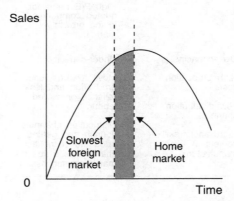

Where overseas markets or alternative market segments are similar, simultaneous product launches in different markets are necessary to ensure that the product is launched in all potential markets before rivals have time to pre-empt the firm.

		Phase of the product life cycle		
	Introduction	Growth	Maturity	Decline
1 Products	Initially, poor quality. Product design and development are a key to success. No standard product and frequent design changes (eg microcomputers in the early 1980s).	Competitors' products have marked quality differences and technical differences. Quality improves. Product reliability may be important.	Products become more standardised and differences between competing products less distinct.	Products even less differentiated. Quality becomes more variable.
2 Customers	Initial customers willing to pay high prices. Customers need to be convinced about buying.	Customers increase in number.	Mass market. Market saturation. Repeat-buying of products becomes significant. Brand image also important.	Customers are 'sophisticated' buyers of a product they understand well.
3 Promotion	High advertising and sales promotion costs. High prices possible.	High advertising costs in absolute terms, but falling as a % of sales. Prices falling.	Markets become segmented. Segmentation and extending the maturity phase of the life cycle can be key strategies.	Less money spent on advertising and sales promotion.
4 Competition	Few or no competitors.	More competitors enter the market. Barriers to entry can be important.	Competition at its keenest: on prices, branding, servicing customers, packaging etc.	Competitors gradually exit from the market. Exit barriers can be important.
5 Profit margins and pricing	High prices but losses due to high fixed costs.	High prices. High contribution margins, and increasing profit margins. High P/E ratios for quoted companies in the growth market.	Falling prices but good profit margins due to high sales volume. Higher prices in some market segments.	Still low prices but falling profits as sales volume falls, since total contribution falls towards the level of fixed costs. Some increase in prices may occur in
6 Manufacturing and distribution	Over-capacity. High production costs. Few distribution channels. High labour skill content in manufacture.	Under-capacity. Move towards mass production and less reliance on skilled labour. Distribution channels flourish and getting adequate distribution channels is a key to marketing success.	Optimum capacity. Low labour skills. Distribution channels fully developed, but less successful channels might be cut.	Over-capacity because mass production techniques are still used. Distribution channels dwindling.

4.4 Brands

 **FAST FORWARD**

> **Branding** removes anonymity and gives identification to a company and its goods and services.

4.4.1 Why brand?

Key term

> According to Kotler a **brand** is 'a name, term, sign, symbol or design or combination of them, intended to identify the goods or services of one seller or group of sellers and to differentiate them from those of competitors'.

Another way of considering this issue is the concept of **brand equity**. This is the asset that the marketer builds to ensure continuity of satisfaction for the customer and profit for the supplier. The 'asset' consists of consumer attitudes, distribution channels and other relationships.

The reasons for branding are as follows.

(a) It is a form of **product differentiation** that can make it possible to change premium prices.

(b) The more a product is similar to competing goods, the more branding is necessary to create a separate **product identity**.

(c) It leads to a more ready **acceptance** of a manufacturer's goods by wholesalers/retailers. The power of the retailer is reduced and it is easier to enter new markets.

(d) It facilitates **self-selection** of goods in self-service stores and also makes it easier for a manufacturer to obtain the optimum **display space** in shops and stores.

(e) It reduces the importance of **price differentials** between goods.

(f) **Brand loyalty** in customers gives a manufacturer more control over marketing strategy and his choice of channels of distribution.

(g) Strong brands form **barriers to entry**.

(h) Brands can have much **longer lifecycles** than products, especially when the technology is developing rapidly.

(i) Where products form a range and are marketing as such it is difficult to analyse revenues and marketing costs by product, service the availability of each product can influence sales of the others. Analysis of costs and revenues is simplified by the use of brands.

4.4.2 Branding strategies

Kotler has identified the following five strategies a company can use once it has established its brand(s):

(a) **Line extension** – an existing name is applied to new variants of existing products, for example Coca-cola launching Diet coke.

(b) **Brand extensions** – using an existing brand to launch a product in a new category, for example chocolate bars such Mars or Galaxy and Mars / Galaxy ice creams.

(c) **Multi-branding** – launching several brands in the same category, for example Kellogg's offers a breakfast cereals with their own brands – for example, All-bran, Cornflakes, Cocopops, Rice Krispies.

(d) **New Brands** – new products are launched under their own brand, for example Coke attempting to sell bottled water under the 'Dasani' brand.

(e) **Co-branding** – two brands are combined in an offer, for example Sony Playstations were offered in a package with Tomb Raider game.

The decision as to whether a brand name should be given to a range of products or whether products should be branded individually depends on quality factors.

(a) If the brand name is associated with quality, all goods in the range must be of that standard.

(b) If a company produces different quality (and price) goods for different market segments, it would be unwise to give the same brand name to the higher and the lower quality goods because this could deter buyers in the high quality/price market segment.

The **advantages of branding** include the following.

(a) Branding facilitates **memory recall**, thus contributing to self-selection and improving customer loyalty.

(b) In many **cultures** branding is preferred, particularly in the distribution channel.

(c) Branding is a way of obtaining **legal protection** for product features.

(d) It helps with **market segmentation**.

(e) It helps build a strong and positive **corporate image**, especially if the brand name used is the company name (eg Kelloggs, Heinz).

(f) It makes it easier to link **advertising** to other marketing communications programmes.

(g) **Display space** is more easily obtained and point-of-sale promotions are more practicable.

(h) If branding is successful, other **associated products** can be introduced.

(i) The need for expensive **personal selling**/persuasion may be reduced.

Branding is not always such a powerful technique in contexts where other agents of the marketing mix are more important.

Cement

In Europe and the USA, cement is a commodity delivered to construction companies. It is rarely a 'consumer' product. In Mexico, and other countries, cement is a consumer product. It is bought, in bags, by individual householders who may prefer to do their own building work. In such a country, branding is important. The Mexican firm, *Cemex*, which has acquired many local producers, actively pushes consumer branding of cement in some markets.

4.4.3 Brand management accounting and brand valuation

In an article in the February 2002 issue of *Financial Management,* Hart and Roslender link the tasks of brand management and marketing firmly with the accountant's role, as a new step in strategic management accounting.

Their research found a range of brand management accounting techniques in the companies they studied.

- Brand profit and loss accounts
- Brand contribution analyses
- Brand net cash flow projections and market valuations
- Brand marketing expenditure plans
- Brand performance information (such as measures of market share, brand awareness and customer loyalty)

Other approaches to valuing brands include the following.

(a) **How much the brand cost to create** (including any R&D costs associated with the brand).This can be inaccurate, as current values may not reflect historic cost.

(b) **Calculate the NPV of net earnings** attributable to the brand – a standard shareholder value approach (as discussed later in Chapter 15).

(c) **Market price of the brand**. How much could the brand be sold for on an open market? This again may be inaccurate because the value a potential buyer may be prepared to pay will not be the same as its value in the current portfolio.

(d) **Price premium** that the brand can command over an unbranded good in the marketplace.

4.4.4 Threats to brands

Established brands have seen their advantage eroded by two factors that both relate to the growth of major retail supermarket chains.

(a) **Generic products** appeal both to the cost-conscious and those who refuse to be impressed by brand values. Generic products are usually high volume commodity products such as basic foods and household goods.

(b) **Own label products** or store brands are capable of creating as much product differentiation as producers' brands. This is advantageous to the retailer because they can only be bought in their stores.

Producers can respond in several ways.

(a) Supplying the stores with their generic and own label goods. This allows the capture of at least some of the value created.

(b) Increased promotion

(c)   New products, for example Kelloggs extending their breakfast cereal range to include Nutrigrain cereal bars.

(d)   Emphasise that they do **not** produce generic and own label goods and that their products are therefore unique.

(e)   Create low-price **flanking brands** that can compete with generics

5 Customer relationships

FAST FORWARD

In recent times emphasis has increased on building and maintaining good long-term **relationships** with customers. This is because such relationships are more profitable than constantly searching for new customers owing to repeat purchasing, ease of service and so on.

The **stakeholder concept** suggests a **wider concern** than the traditional marketing approach of supplying goods and services which satisfy immediate needs. The supplier-customer relationship extends beyond the basic transaction. The customer needs to remain satisfied with his purchase and positive about his supplier long after the transaction has taken place. If his satisfaction is muted or grudging, future purchases may be reluctant or non-existent and he may advise others of his discontent. Customer tolerance in the UK is fairly high, but should not be taken for granted.

In deciding strategic direction and formulating marketing strategy, any company needs to address issues of customer care, because of:

(a)   **Legal** constraints

(b)   Industry **codes of conduct**

(c)   The recognition that keeping existing customers happy is cheaper than acquiring new ones

(d)   The **value chain**. Customer care is part of after-sales service and offers an opportunity for differentiation. It is also a valuable source of information.

Customer variation

Not all customers are the same. Some appear for a single cash transaction and are never seen again. Others make frequent, regular purchases in large volumes, using credit facilities and building up a major relationship. Yet another type of customer purchases infrequently but in transactions of high value, as, for instance, in property markets. This variation will exist to a greater or lesser extent in all industries, though each will have a smaller typical range of behaviour. However, even within a single business, customers will vary significantly in the frequency and volume of their purchases, their reasons for buying, their sensitivity to price changes, their reaction to promotion and their overall attitude to the supplier and the product. **Segmentation** of the customer base can have a major impact on profitability, perhaps by simply tailoring promotion to suit the most attractive group of customers.

Selling through intermediaries

Many businesses sell to intermediaries rather than to the end consumer. Some sell to both categories; they have to recognise that **the intermediary is just as much a customer as the eventual consumer**. Examples are manufacturers who maintain their own sales organisation but appoint agents in geographically remote areas and companies who combine autonomous operations with franchising. While it is reasonable to give the highest priority to the needs of the **ultimate consumer** and insist on some control over the activities of the intermediary, it must be recognised that he will only perform well **if his own needs are addressed**. For instance, a selling agent who has invested heavily in stock after being given exclusive rights in an area should be consulted before further demands are made on his cash flow by the launch of a new product.

5.1 Customer retention

Variation in customer behaviour was mentioned above. The most important aspect of this variation is whether or not the customer comes back for more. Customers should be seen as potentially providing a lifetime of purchases so that **the turnover from a single individual over time might be very large indeed**. It is widely accepted that there is a non-linear relationship between customer retention and profitability in that **a fairly small amount of repeat purchasing generates significant profit**. This is because it is far more expensive in promotion and overhead costs to convert a non-buyer into an occasional buyer than to turn an occasional buyer into a frequent buyer. The repeat buyer does not have to be persuaded to give the product a try or be tempted by special deals; he needs less attention from sales staff and already has his credit account set up. New customers usually have to be won from competitors.

The process of retaining customers for a lifetime is an important one and one in which integrated marketing communications has an important role to play. Instead of one-way communication aimed solely at gaining a sale it is necessary to develop an effective two-way communication process to turn a **prospect into a lifetime advocate**.

Today's highly competitive business environment means that customers are only retained if they are **very satisfied** with their purchasing experience. **Any lesser degree of satisfaction is likely to result in the loss of the customer**. Companies must be active in monitoring customer satisfaction **because very few will actually complain. They will simply depart**. Businesses which use intermediaries must be particularly active, since research shows that even when complaints are made, the principals hear about only a very small proportion of them.

 Case Study

Customer care

In the increasingly competitive service sector, it is no longer enough to promise customer satisfaction. Today, customer 'delight' is the stated aim for companies battling to retain and increase market share.

British Airways, which lists delighting customers among its new goals, says ensuring the safety of passengers and meeting all their needs drives everything it does. 'Other airlines fly the same routes using similar aircraft. What BA must do is provide a superior standard of efficiency, comfort and general service which persuades passengers to fly with us again and again,' says Mike Street, director of customer services at BA.

Kwik-Fit, the car repair group, is another company that has included customer delight in its mission statement. Its forecourt promises to deliver '100 per cent customer delight' in the supply and fitting of vehicle brakes, tyres and exhausts leaves little margin for mistakes – and none at all for making any customer unhappy. Staff attend courses at company-run centres covering 'all practical aspects of their work, customer care and general management techniques'. Commitment is encouraged by 'job security', opportunities for promotion and a reward package that includes profit-related pay and shares in the company.

Customer satisfaction is monitored via reply-paid questionnaires distributed after work is carried out and through a freephone helpline that is open 24 hours a day. Kwik-Fit also says its customer survey unit 'allows us to make contact with 5,000 customers a day, within 72 hours of their visit to a Kwik-Fit Centre'.

Financial Times

The most satisfactory way to retain customers is to offer them products which they perceive as providing superior benefits at any given price point. However, there are specific techniques which can increase customer retention. Loyalty schemes such as frequent flyer programmes, augment the product in the customer's eyes. The club concept, as used by *Sainsbury* and *Tesco*, offers small discounts on repeated purchases. The principal benefit of both these types of scheme, however, is the enhanced knowledge of the customer which they provide. Initial registration provides name, address and post code. Subsequent use of the loyalty card allows a detailed purchasing profile to be built up for individual customers. This enables highly targeted promotion and cross-selling later.

Research indicates that **the single largest reason why customers abandon a supplier is poor performance by front-line staff**. Any scheme for customer retention must address the need for careful selection and training of these staff. It is also a vital factor in **relationship marketing**.

Complaints

Complaints are among the best things that can happen to a company. They give managers the chance to rectify the situation over and above customer expectations; they give low cost feedback on how your products and services are perceived and handled properly, they create 'goodwill ambassadors' for your brand. In June, TMI, along with the Institute of Customer Service, the trade body, published research into how and why people in the UK complain and how they are dealt with. Among other findings, it confirmed the old management cliché that people tend not to complain they simply walk away. It is the expense of replacing customers that makes handling complaints well so cost-effective.

'We estimate that it costs five times as much to recruit a new customer as it does to keep an existing one,' says Julie Robinson, director of service delivery at *Virgin Atlantic*, the airline. 'As part of our staff training we need to show people that giving compensation when something goes wrong is not giving away the company's profits. Quite the opposite.' So what is the 'right' way to handle a complaint? Almost everyone agrees on step one: listen. 'You must listen to the customer,' says Ms Robinson, 'and not interrupt until you have under stood the problem.' But what then? Mr Brennan's company advocates an eight-step process. After saying 'thank you' comes explaining why you appreciate the complaint; apologising; promising you will do something about it straight away; asking for more information; correcting the mistake; checking customer satisfaction and, finally, preventing future mistakes. Mr Brennan is quick to point out the order of these steps. 'Many people ask for information first, such as name and address, making the customer feel as if they are somehow under suspicion. A complaint is a gift from a customer.'

This unexpected generosity from the woman at the counter is confirmed by Stephen Walker, head of customer service at *Marks and Spencer*, the retailer, a UK company that is almost synonymous with handling complaints effectively. 'The information people give you when they complain,' he says, 'is invaluable to the organisation. We run a central database where complaints are logged, from which we can feed information back to the relevant buyer and suppliers, often on the same day. Customers are looking for a quick resolution of the problem and an assurance that we will do what we can to ensure it doesn't happen again.' Managers of big companies can also use complaints to develop one-to-one relationships with customers. 'Complaints offer an excellent chance to deal with customers face to face,' says Mr Walker. 'If you take a complaint seriously, and deal with it in a generous way, you can buy them for life.'

David Baker, *Financial Times, 2 August 2000*

5.2 Relationship marketing   5/05

FAST FORWARD

There is a move away from transactions to **relationship marketing**. Firms aim to build loyalty, especially where switching costs are high and a lost customer is probably lost for a long time.

Key concept

Relationship marketing is defined very simply by *Grönroos* as the management of a firm's market relationships.

Much has been written in recent years on **relationship marketing**. *Gummesson* suggests it is a 'paradigm shift' requiring a **dramatic change** in marketing thinking and behaviour, not an add-on to traditional marketing.' In his book *Total Relationship Marketing*, he suggests that the core of marketing should no longer be the 4Ps, but 30Rs, which reflect the large number of complex relationships involved in business. *Kotler* says 'marketing can **make promises** but only the whole organisation can **deliver satisfaction**'. *Adcock* expands on this by remarking that relationship marketing can only exist when the marketing function fosters a **customer-oriented service culture** which supports the network of activities that deliver value to the customer.

Relationship marketing is thus as much about **attitudes** and **assumptions** as it is about techniques. The marketing function's task is to inculcate habits of behaviour at all levels and in all departments which will enhance and strengthen the alliance. It must be remembered, however, that the effort involved in long-term relationship building is more appropriate in some markets than in others. Where customers are purchasing intermittently and switching costs are low, there is always a chance of business. This tends to be the pattern in commodity markets. Here, it is reasonable to take a **transactions approach** to marketing and treat each sale as unique. A **relationship marketing approach** is more appropriate where switching costs are high and a lost customer is thus probably lost for a long time. Switching costs are raised by such factors as the need for training on systems, the need for a large common installed base, high capital cost and the incorporation of purchased items into the customer's own designs.

Meeting customer needs

The conceptual or philosophic nature of relationship marketing leads to a simple principle, that of **enhancing satisfaction by precision in meeting the needs of individual customers**. This depends on extensive two-way communication to establish and record the customer's characteristics and preferences and build a long-term relationship. *Adcock* mentions three important practical methods which contribute to this end.

- Building a customer database
- Developing customer-oriented service systems
- Extra direct contacts with customers

Use of technology

Modern **computer database systems** have enabled the rapid acquisition and retrieval of the individual customer's details, needs and preferences. Using this technology, relationship marketing enables telephone sales staff to greet the customer by name, know what he purchased last time, avoid taking his full delivery address, know what his credit status is and what he is likely to want. It enables new products to be developed that are precisely tailored to the customer's needs and new procedures to be established which enhance his satisfaction. It is the successor to **mass marketing**, which attempted to be customer-led but which could only supply a one-size-fits-all product. The end result of a relationship marketing approach is a mutually satisfactory relationship that continues indefinitely.

Customer care

Relationship marketing *extends* the principles of **customer care**. Customer care is about providing a product which is augmented by high quality of service, so that the customer is impressed during his transaction with the company. This can be done in ignorance of any detail of the customer other than those implicit in the immediate transaction. The customer is anonymous. **Relationship marketing is about having the customer come back for further transactions by ending the anonymity**. Adcock says 'To achieve results, it will be necessary to involve every department … in co-ordinated activity aimed at maximising customer satisfaction'. The culture must be right; the right people must be recruited and trained; the structure, technology and processes must all be right.

It is inevitable that **problems** will arise. A positive way of dealing with errors must be designed into the customer relationship. *W Edwards Deming*, the prominent writer on quality, tells us that front line sales people cannot usually deal with the causes of mistakes as they **are built into the products, systems and organisation structure**. It is therefore necessary for management to promote vertical and horizontal interaction in order to spur changes to eliminate the **sources** of mistakes.

It is inevitable that there will be multiple contacts between customer and supplier organisations. Each contact is an opportunity to enhance or to prejudice the relationship, so staff throughout the supplier organisation must be aware of their marketing responsibilities. Two way communication should be encouraged so that the relationship can grow and deepen. There is a link here to the database mentioned above: extra contacts provide more information. Confidential information must, of course, be treated with due respect.

Customer Loyalty

The problem with profitable customers is retaining them, because they will attract the attention of your competitors. Building customer relationships may be the answer to both types of problem.

Relationship marketing is grounded in the idea of establishing a learning relationship with customers. At the lower end, building a relationship can create cross-selling opportunities that may make the overall relationship profitable. For example, some retail banks have tried selling credit cards to less profitable customers. With valuable customers, customer relationship management may make them more loyal and willing to invest additional funds. In banking, these high-end relationships are often managed through private bankers, whose goals are not only to increase customer satisfaction and retention, but also to cross-sell and bring in investment.

In determining which customers are worth the cost of long-term relationships, it is useful to consider their lifetime value. This depends on:

- Current profitability computed at the customer level
- The propensity of those customers to stay loyal
- Expected revenues and costs of servicing such customers over the lifetime of the relationship

Building relationships makes most sense for customers whose lifetime value to the company is the highest. Thus, building relationships should focus on customers who are currently the most profitable, likely to be the most profitable in the future, or likely to remain with the company for the foreseeable future and have acceptable levels of profitability.

The goal of relationship management is to increase customer satisfaction and to minimise any problems. By engaging in 'smarter' relationships, a company can learn customers' preferences and develop trust. Every contact point with the customer can be seen as a chance to record information and learn preferences. Complaints and errors must be recorded, not just fixed and forgotten. Contact with customers in every medium, whether over the Internet, through a call centre, or through personal contact, is recorded and centralised.

Many companies are beginning to achieve this goal by using customer relationship management (CRM) software. Data, once collected an centralised, can be used to customise service. In addition, the database can be analysed to detect patterns that can suggest better ways to serve customers in general. A key aspect of this dialogue is to learn and record preferences. There are two ways to determine customers' preferences: transparently and collaboratively.

Discovering preferences transparently means that the marketer learns the customers' needs without actually involving them. For example, the Ritz Carlton Hotel makes a point of observing the choices that guests make and recording them. If a guest requests extra pillows, then extra pillows will be provided every time that person visits. At upmarket retailers, personal shoppers will record customers' preferences in sizes, styles, brands, colours and price ranges and notify them when new merchandise appears or help them choose accessories.

Barbara Kahn, *Financial Times, 9 October 2000*

5.3 Differences between transactional and relationship marketing

Transactional	Relationship
Importance of single sale	Importance of customer relation
Importance of product features	Importance of customer benefits
Short time scale	Longer time scale
Less emphasis on service	High customer service
Quality is concern of production	Quality is concern of all
Competitive commitment	High customer commitment
Persuasive communication	Regular communication

Marketing, Principles and Practice: Adcock, Bradfield, Halborg and Ross

Adcock *et al* point out that the most important issue in customer retention is focusing marketing effort on activities that promote a strong relationship rather than a single transaction.

By now you are familiar with the 4Ps of the basic marketing mix. **Relationship marketing** is highly dependent upon a fifth P: **people**. The features of the basic 4Ps must support the commitment to developing mutually beneficial customer relationships. The **behaviour of the people** involved in the customer relationship is even more important, because relationship marketing success depends on their motivation to achieve it. In turn, that motivation depends to a great extent upon the leadership exercised by marketing managers. It is not enough to expect self-motivation because *all* staff are involved, not just those with a sales role.

5.4 Implementing relationship marketing programmes

Kotler suggests five steps, suitable for business-to-business or service markets.

Step 1   Identify **key customers**: (see below)

Step 2   Assign a **relationship manager** to each

Step 3   Develop clear **job descriptions**

Step 4   Appoint a manager to supervise the relationship managers

Step 5   Develop long-term plans for developing **relationships**

5.4.1 Sustaining the relationship

(a)   Offer **superior customer value** by personalising the interaction, involving two-way communication. This is essential for service industries such as life assurance. Hotels have systems that remember guests' preferences.

(b)   Be trustworthy and **reliable**, for example by offering a replacement.

(c)   **Tighten the connection**. Once the relationship is established, it must be nurtured to make it harder for the customer to defect.

(d)   **Co-ordinating capabilities**. The more successful the relationship, the greater the risk of imitation.

Kotler's approach is suitable for B2B markets or personal services such as financial advice. Some firms, however, have sought through data mining techniques to get a long-term view of the customer.

Loyalty cards are designed to reward customers for repeat purchase. They:

- Collect information about customer purchasing habits, enabling targeted marketing communication
- Reward customers for repeat purchase, to encourage sales volumes

Loyalty schemes vary in the benefit they offer.

(a)   Recent UK research indicates that owners of 'loyalty' cards spend more, but they are not necessarily loyal.

(b)   Furthermore, most customers still shop around and have one or more loyalty cards.

(c)   **Loyalty cards may prove to be an expensive failure**. Safeway in the UK has abandoned its UK loyalty card, preferring to invest in other forms of promotional activity determined by stores individually.

5.4.2 Key accounts

So far we have considered the retention of customers as an unquestionably desirable objective. **However, for many businesses a degree of discretion will be advisable**. 'Key' does not mean large. A customer's **potential** is very important. The definition of a key account depends on the circumstances. Key account management is about managing the future.

Customers can be assessed for desirability according to such criteria as the profitability of their accounts; the prestige they confer; the amount of non-value adding administrative work they generate; the cost of the selling effort they absorb; the rate of growth of their accounts and, for industrial customers, of the turnover of their own businesses; their willingness to adopt new products; and their credit history. Such analyses will almost certainly conform to a *Pareto* distribution and show, for instance that 80% of profit comes from 20% of the customers, while a different 20% generate most of the credit control or administrative problems. Some businesses will be very aggressive about getting rid of their problem customers, but a more positive technique would be to concentrate effort on the most desirable ones. These are the **key accounts** and the company's relationship with them can be built up by appointing **key account managers**.

Key account management is often seen as a high level selling task, but should in fact be a business wide team effort about relationships and customer retention. It can be seen as a form of co-operation with the customer's supply chain management function. The key account manager's role is to integrate the efforts of the various parts of the organisation in order to deliver an enhanced service. This idea has long been used by advertising agencies and was successfully introduced into aerospace manufacturing over 40 years ago. It will be the key account manager's role to maintain communication with the customer, note any developments in his circumstances, deal with any problems arising in the relationship and develop the long-term business relationship.

The key account relationship may progress through several stages.

(a)   At first, there may be a typical **adversarial sales-purchasing relationship** with emphasis on price, delivery and so on. Attempts to widen contact with the customer organisation will be seen as a threat by its purchasing staff.

(b)   Later, the sales staff may be able to foster a mutual desire to increase understanding by wider contacts. Trust may increase.

(c)   A **mature partnership stage** may be reached in which there are contacts at all levels and information is shared. The key account manager becomes responsible for integrating the partnership business processes and contributing to the customer's supply chain management. High 'vendor ratings', stable quality, continuous improvement and fair pricing are taken for granted.

Exam focus point

Customer relationship management (CRM) was the subject of a Part B question in the draft specimen paper for this exam. The question called for a critical evaluation of CRM, illustrated by examples.

This hint from the Examiners about customer relationships was amplified in May 2005, when they offered six marks in Question 1 simply for a description of relationship marketing; they also offered a further nine marks in the next requirement of Question 1, which asked, in part, how to implement a scheme of relationship marketing.

6 Re-engineering and innovation   5/06

FAST FORWARD

As businesses, their markets and the wider environment develop and change with the passage of time, it is appropriate to reconsider the way they do things from time to time. **Business process re-engineering** is a useful approach based on challenging basic assumptions about business methods and even the objectives they are designed to achieve. IT can be very useful here, but simply to automate a process is not the same as re-engineering it.

In recent years the emphasis has been very much on the **use of information technology for competitive advantage**. An earlier trend (still relevant to many situations) involved focussing attention **inwards** to consider how **business processes** could be redesigned or re-engineered to improve efficiency.

The changes that may be made to processes may be classified as **automation**, **rationalisation** or **re-engineering**.

Key terms

Business automation is the use of computerised working methods to speed up the performance of existing tasks.
Business rationalisation is the streamlining of operating procedures to eliminate obvious inefficiencies. Rationalisation usually involves automation.

Automation and rationalisation are relatively the most common forms of organisational change. They usually offer modest returns and little risk. **Automation** usually involves assisting employees to carry out their duties more efficiently – for example introducing a computerised accounting package. **Rationalisation** involves not only the automation of a process but also efficient process design. For example, an automated banking system requires the standardisation of account number structure and standard rules for calculating daily account balances – in this situation automation encouraged a certain amount of rationalisation.

<table>
<tr><td>

Key term

</td><td>

Business process re-engineering is the 'selection of areas of business activity in which repeatable and repeated sets of activities are undertaken; and the development of improved understanding of how they operate and of the scope for radical redesign with a view to creating and delivering better customer value'.

(CIMA *Official Terminology*)

</td></tr>
</table>

Business process re-engineering involves fundamental changes in the way an organisation functions. For example, processes which were developed in a paper-intensive processing environment may not be suitable for an environment which is underpinned by IT.

The main writing on the subject is *Hammer and Champy's Reengineering the Corporation* (1993), from which the following is taken.

> **Business Process Re-engineering** is the fundamental rethinking and radical redesign of business processes to achieve dramatic improvements in critical contemporary measures of performance, such as cost, quality, service and speed.

The key words here are **'fundamental'**, **'radical'**, **'dramatic'** and **'process'**.

(a) **Fundamental** and **radical** indicate that BPR assumes nothing: it starts by asking basic questions such as 'why do we do what we do', without making any assumptions or looking back to what has always been done in the past.

(b) **'Dramatic'** means that BPR should achieve 'quantum leaps in performance', not just marginal, incremental improvements.

(c) **'Process'** is explained in the following paragraphs.

<table>
<tr><td>

Key term

</td><td>

A **process** is a collection of activities that takes one or more kinds of input and creates an output.

</td></tr>
</table>

For **example**, order fulfilment is a process that takes an order as its input and results in the delivery of the ordered goods. Part of this process is the manufacture of the goods, but under BPR the aim of manufacturing is **not merely to make** the goods. Manufacturing should aim to **deliver the goods that were ordered,** and any aspect of the manufacturing process that hinders this aim should be re-engineered. The first question to ask might be 'Do they need to be manufactured at all; should they be purchased from another organisation?'

A re-engineered process has certain **characteristics**.

- Often several jobs are **combined** into one
- Workers often **make decisions**
- The **steps** in the process are performed in **a logical order**
- **Work** is performed where it **makes most sense**
- Checks and controls may be reduced, and **quality 'built-in'**
- One manager provides a **single point of contact**
- The advantages of **centralised and decentralised** operations are combined

6.1 Example: BPR

This scenario is based on a problem at Ford.

A company employs 25 staff to perform the standard accounting task of matching goods received notes with orders and then with invoices. About 80% of their time is spent trying to find out why 20% of the set of three documents do not agree.

One way of improving the situation would have been to computerise the existing process to facilitate matching. This would have helped, but BPR went further: why accept any incorrect orders at all?

'What if all the orders are entered onto a computerised database? When goods arrive at the goods inwards department they either agree to goods that have been ordered or they don't. It's as simple as that. Goods that agree to an order are accepted and paid for. Goods that are not agreed are *sent back* to the supplier. There are no files of unmatched items and time is not wasted trying to sort out these files.'

(Alan Lewin, 'Business process re-engineering', *CIMA Student,* February 1996)

Lewin notes the gains for the company: less staff time wasted, quicker payment for suppliers, lower stocks, and lower investment in working capital.

6.2 Principles of BPR

Hammer presents **seven principles** for BPR.

(a)   Processes should be designed to achieve a desired customer-focused **outcome** rather than focusing on existing **tasks.**

(b)   Personnel who use the **output** from a process should **perform** the process. For example, a company could set up a database of approved suppliers; this would allow personnel who actually require supplies to order them themselves, perhaps using on-line technology, thereby eliminating the need for a separate purchasing function.

(c)   Information processing should be **included** in the work which **produces** the information. This eliminates the differentiation between information gathering and information processing.

(d)   **Geographically-dispersed** resources should be treated as if they are **centralised.** This allows the benefits of centralisation to be obtained, for example, economies of scale through central negotiation of supply contracts, without losing the benefits of decentralisation, such as flexibility and responsiveness.

(e)   Parallel activities should be **linked** rather than **integrated.** This would involve, for example, co-ordination between teams working on different aspects of a single process.

(f)   Workpeople should be **self-managing**, exercising greater autonomy over their work. The traditional distinction between workers and managers can be abolished: decision aids such as expert systems can be provided where they are required.

(g)   Information should be captured **once** at **source.** Electronic distribution of information makes this possible.

6.2.1 Is there a BPR methodology?

Davenport and *Short* prescribe a **five-step approach** to BPR.

Step 1   Develop the **business vision and process objectives**. BPR is driven by a business vision which implies specific business objectives such as cost reduction, time reduction, output quality improvement, Total Quality Management and empowerment.

Step 2   **Identify the processes** to be redesigned. Most firms use the 'high impact' approach, which focuses on the most important processes or those that conflict most with the business vision. Lesser number of firms use the Exhaustive approach that attempts to identify all the processes within an organisation and then prioritise them in order of redesign urgency.

Step 3   Understand and **measure the existing processes** – to ensure previous mistakes are not repeated and to provide a baseline for future improvements.

Step 4   **Identify change levers**. Awareness of IT capabilities could approve useful when designing processes.

Step 5   Design and **build a prototype** of the new process. The actual design should not be viewed as the end of the BPR process – it should be viewed as a prototype, with successive alterations. The use of a prototype enables the involvement of customers.

6.3 IT and BPR

Simply computerising existing ways of doing things does not mean a process has been re-engineered. Technology may be able to add value by re-designing business processes.

IT is not the solution in itself, it is an **enabler**. BPR uses IT to allow an organisation to do things that it is not doing already. For example, teleconferencing reduces the cost of travelling to meetings – a re-engineering approach takes the view that teleconferencing allows more frequent meetings.

As *Hammer* and *Champy* put it, 'It is this disruptive power of technology, its ability to break the rules that limit how we conduct our work, that makes it critical to companies looking for competitive advantage.'

Examples of how technology has changed the way work is conducted include:

(a) **Shared databases** allow information to be accessed simultaneously from many locations.

(b) **Expert systems** may allow non-specialists to do work that previously required an expert.

(c) **Telecommunications networks** mean that businesses can simultaneously reap the rewards of centralisation and decentralisation.

(d) **Decision support tools** allow decisions to be made by a larger number of staff.

(e) **Wireless** communication technology allows staff 'in the field' to send and receive information wherever they are.

(f) **Interactive websites** allow personalised contact with many customers (or at least the appearance of personalised contact).

(g) Automatic identification and **tracking technology** allows the whereabouts of objects or people to be monitored.

(h) High performance computing allows **instant** revision of plans rather than periodic updates.

6.4 Why focus on processes?

Many businesses recognise that value is delivered **through processes,** but still define themselves in terms of their functional roles. To properly harness the resources within a business a clear agreement of the management and implementation of processes is needed. **Without this focus** on processes:

(a) It is **unclear how value is achieved** or can continue to be achieved.

(b) The **effects of change** on the operation of the business are **hard to predict**.

(c) There is no basis to achieve **consistent** business improvement.

(d) **Knowledge is lost** as people move around or out of the business.

(e) Cross-functional interaction is not encouraged.

It is **difficult to align the strategy** of an organisation with the people, systems resources through which that strategy will be accomplished.

One way of portraying the relationship between organisation strategy, process, people and technology is shown below.

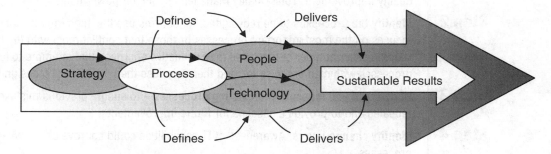

6.5 Redefining BPR

There are concerns that BPR has become misunderstood. According to an independent study of 100 European companies, BPR has become allied in managers' minds with narrow targets such as **reductions in staff numbers** and other **cost-cutting** measures.

6.5.1 Problems with BPR

In addition to the perception, referred to above, that BPR is mainly about reducing headcount, several other criticism have been levelled at the way the idea has been implemented.

(a) Any successful BPR programme is likely to result in significant **changes** that will affect staff widely. All the personal and management problems discussed earlier in this chapter will apply.

(b) BPR as practised is a kind of **scientific management**: a rational approach to **improving efficiency**. It neglects the direct link to **effectiveness** originally envisaged and may, by reducing the number of managers in an organisation, reduce innovation and creativity at the same time. *Hamel and Prahalad* call this process **hollowing out**.

(c) While BPR practice generally seeks to empower workers, it assumes they will work within structures and systems imposed by others. This places strict limits on the scope for releasing their potential with such modern ideas as **teamworking** and **coaching**.

(d) Established systems often have valuable but unrecognised features, particularly in the area of **control**. When a process is re-engineered from scratch, particularly when done with a view to cutting costs, such desirable features as segregation of duties and management supervision may be lost.

6.5.2 Beyond BPR

Champy suggests that management itself should be re-engineered. Managers are not used to thinking in systems terms, so, instead of looking at the **whole picture** (which might affect their own jobs), they tend to **seize on individual aspects** of the organisation.

It is argued that process re-engineering is really only a part of the **wider picture**. A report in the *Financial Times* (see below) on an unnamed company suggested four sets of changes as important to the transformation from a company which **satisfies** customers, to a company that **delights** them – and from a company which is **competent** to a company which is the **best** in its industry. Extracts from the report follow.

'... **first, breaking down barriers** between its different disciplinary specialists and national units by a series of procedural and structural steps, of which the re-engineering of cross-unit processes is only one;

second, developing an explicit set of values and behaviour guidelines which are subscribed to (or 'shared') by everyone in the organisation;

third, redefining the role of management in order to foster much more empowerment, responsibility and decisiveness at every level.

All this requires the creation of the **fourth factor: an unprecedented degree of openness** and trust among managers and employees'.

 Case Study

Workflow systems/process re-engineering

Work design, whether it is related to work in the factory or at the desk, is a process of arriving at the most **efficient** way of completing tasks and activities that minimises effort and reduces the possibility of mistakes. It is involved in increasing productivity and efficiency whilst maintaining or improving quality standards.

Today work design is often referred to as process re-engineering and has a bad press because the perceived outcome is reduced employee numbers or downsising. As we move increasingly to a computerised workplace the use of workflow systems is growing and changing the nature of work from one of social contact to service to the system.

A **workflow system** is a system that organises work and allocates it to particular workstations for the attention of the person operating the workstation. The system usually also incorporates a document-management facility. There are three main forms in which workflow systems operate. These are on the **casework basis**, the **flowline basis** or an **ad hoc basis**.

The **casework** basis functions by knowing the individual caseload of staff and directs existing cases to the appropriate caseworker and new cases or customers are allocated on the basis of equalising caseload.

The **flowline** approach allocates a small number of tasks to each operator and the case flows along the line from screen to screen. The **ad hoc** system works on the basis of equalising workload, regardless of who may have dealt with the case previously. The choice depends on the particular circumstances of the business and the approach taken to customer service.

Workflow management provides supervisors with information on screen about the workloads of individuals and information on their processing capabilities with statistics for average time taken to deal with a case, errors detected by the system as a percentage of cases, and so on. This information is intended to ensure that staff receive appropriate support and training, but can be and is used for bonus payments and league tables of performance.

In one organisation where workflow has been used in sales-order processing, the use of the management statistics has become quite draconian and the average period of employment of sales-order staff is three months.

The **advantages** and benefits of workflow systems come mainly from improvements in productivity and efficiency and better or speedier services to customers.

Offset against these benefits are the **disadvantages** stemming from the way that workflow systems are implemented and managed.

A list of the **benefits from the employer's point of view** would be:

- More efficient office procedures
- Providing workflow management
- Equalising of workloads
- Monitoring of operator performance
- Better security
- Ensuring work gets done when it should get done

The **dangers** lie in the segmentation or specialisation in a small number of tasks before passing the work on to the next person's screen, almost like a production line. This **de-skilling** of work increases boredom and leads to high staff turnover. It also reduces social contact to a minimum and the contact that does exist takes place via the system.

So far the casework approach, where staff deal with cases as a 'one stop shop', is the most empowering and beneficial for staff. The skills needed are high and there is a greater sense of completion and satisfaction for operators.

In the flowline approach people are demoralised at the repetitive nature of the work. Ad hoc approaches seem to fall between two stools – there is work satisfaction to a degree and no sense of continuing customer contact.

Adapted from: 'Computer talk' – Workflow systems Trevor Bentley – CIMA Articles database

6.6 Automate, informate, transformate

FAST FORWARD

The **automate, informate** and **transformate** framework is very similar to BPR's **automation, rationalisation** and **re-engineering**, as is **process innovation**, which focuses on the creation of new processes to achieve business objectives.

The implementation and development of information systems can impact upon an organisation in different ways. Automation, rationalisation and re-engineering provide one framework for analysing and explaining this impact. The writer *Zuboff* devised a similar framework, using the terms **automate**, **informate** and **transformate**. These terms are explained in the following table.

Stage/term	Comment
Automate	This involves the automation of repetitive manual tasks. Automate type changes typically take place during the initial introduction of information systems and information technology into an organisation. The new system replaces or speeds up previously manual tasks.
	(Corresponds to the automation stage in the **automation**, rationalisation, re-engineering framework.)
Informate	Some processes are redesigned to exploit the potential of information technology.
	Operating procedures are streamlined and the organisation infrastructure becomes more integrated, for example linking the order processing system with the stock control system.
	(Corresponds to the **rationalisation** stage in the automation, rationalisation, re-engineering framework.)
Transformate	Information systems and information technology are used to change the way the organisation operates and the way business is done. Systems are utilised that allow the organisation to conduct business in a way that was previously not possible.
	Transformate type changes may involve significant changes in organisation structure. This is a more risky strategy, which goes much further than rationalisation of processes. A traditional retail business moving to web-based e-commerce could be viewed as a fundamental change.
	Transformate type changes may bring competitive advantage.
	(Corresponds to the **re-engineering** stage in the automation, rationalisation, re-engineering framework.)

6.7 Process innovation

Davenport introduced the theory of Process Innovation (PI) in 1993.

Key term

Process innovation (PI) combines the adoption of a process view of the business with the application of innovation to key processes. What is new and distinctive about this combination is its enormous potential for helping any organisation achieve major reductions in process cost or time, or major improvements in flexibility, service levels, or other business objectives.

Process innovation is similar to BPR. PI does however focus to a greater extent on the **creation of new processes**. For this reason, PI is seen by some as being an even more radical approach. The role of IT in PI may be contrasted with its role in BPR. In the latter, as we have already explained, IT is normally an **enabler**, allowing the organisation to achieve its desired outcome in ways that were previously impossible. In PI, IT is often the **trigger for change**: new technology will not so much transfer existing processes as create the possibility of **completely new outcomes**.

Davenport identifies five steps of PI.

Step 1   Identify business areas or processes suitable for innovation.

Step 2   Identify the tools that can be used to innovate (change levers).

Step 3   Develop statements of purpose for the process ('process vision').

Step 4   Understand existing processes and prepare for new systems and processes.

Step 5   Design and prototype new processes.

Compare this procedure with that for BPR given in subsection 6.2.1.

Exam focus point

A question in the May 2006 exam examined the role of IT in Process innovation and Business process re-engineering.

It is important that you understand the differences between PI and BPR, and appreciate that while IT is often a change trigger for PI, it is usually an implementation tool for PR.

7 Organisation structure

You should already be reasonably familiar with basic ideas about how organisations are structured and managed from your studies for Paper 5, *Integrated Management*. The BPP Study Text for Paper 5 covers these matters in Chapters 1 and 2.

7.1 The traditional organisation and the management accountant

FAST FORWARD

The three essential aspects of the nature of organisations, social arrangements, agreed goals and controlled performance make it inevitable that an organisation's strategy, its structure and the work of the management accountant are intimately entwined. The **classical approach** is being replaced by more **flexible methods** as a result of the pressure from environmental developments, including **globalisation** and **developments in IS**.

Developing and managing an **efficient organisation** is an important aspect of **strategic implementation**: it is through the medium of the organisation that the chosen strategy is pursued and the one should be optimised to support the other. Indeed, as *Chandler* and others have shown, structure and strategy are intimately entwined. There is a similar intimate relationship between organisation structure and the management methods, culture and philosophy that make it work. Management accountants and their work are embedded in an organisational setting: inevitably, therefore, developments in either the way organisations are structured or the way management accountants do their work are bound to interact with one another.

Buchanan and Huczynski suggest that there are three essential aspects that define an organisation.

(a)   **Social arrangements**. Organisations are social arrangements. People, with all their behavioural complications, make up a major part of any organisation. Management accountants must always remember that the systems, procedures and rules that they design and operate will both affect and be affected by such matters as motivation, conflict and ambition.

(b)   **Collective goals**. Organisations pursue collective goals. The definition of those goals and the relative priority accorded to each requires management accounting input in such forms as cost estimates, project evaluation and budget preparation.

(c)   **Controlled performance**. Organisations are about controlled performance. This is obviously a major theme of the management accountant's role both in strategic management and more generally within the organisation.

In fact, a large part of the management accountant's work in the field of strategy will either influence or be influenced by organisation structure. Accountants are used to working within a rational, deterministic framework of rules and procedures that trace their roots back to the classical school of management theory, Carnegie's cost accounting methods and Scientific Management.

7.2 The changing business environment

Major environmental changes have affected many aspects of the way businesses and other organisations operate, including the way in which they are structured. Here are some examples.

(a)   Challenges in products and processes methods have come from new and innovative firms, particularly in the Far East.

(b)   There is mounting pressure for increased corporate social responsibility and for more attention to be paid to stakeholders other than owners.

(c)   The rapid development of IS has made revolutionised the way information (both external and internal) can be used for competitive advantage.

These changes mean that the classical model of the organisation is no longer necessarily the most appropriate.

7.3 Developments in organisation theory

FAST FORWARD

A number of writers on organisations and management have made similar recommendations about the need for **innovation**, **flexibility**, **communication**, **empowerment**, **leveraging of knowledge** and a **network approach to organising resources** both within the organisation and outside its boundaries.

7.3.1 Contingency theory

The contingency approach suggests that many aspects of the management of organisations, including the way they are structured, arise as a result of the varying influences to which they are subjected. Here are some possible influences on organisation structure.

Influence	Comment
Age	• The older the organisation, the more formalised its behaviour. Work is repeated, so is more easily formalised and standardised. • Organisation structure reflects the age of the **industry's** foundation.
Size, growth and degree of centralisation	The larger the organisation, the **more elaborate** its structure will be, the larger the average size of the units within it, the more formalised its behaviour (for consistency).
Co-ordination and leadership	Mutual adjustment, direct supervision and standardisation all have consequences for organisation structure.
Skills of managers and workers	Can people be left alone to do the job, or do they require close supervision?
Geographic dispersion	An organisation with several sites will have a different organisation structure from one located in one place.
Fashion and culture	Bureaucracies, for example, are deeply unfashionable, but they are often the best at doing certain kinds of work. Indeed, **Burns and Stalker**, who developed the concept of organic and mechanistic organisations held that neither type of organisation had any intrinsic merits, as the key variables were **product-markets** and **technology**.
Control and environment	The more an organisation is subject to **external control or influence**(eg by government, holding company) the more centralised and formalised its structure. The power needs of organisational members (to control others, or at least to control their own working conditions) can lead to centralisation.

Influence	Comment
Technology	• The stronger the technical system (ie the technology) the more formalised the work, and the more bureaucratic the structure of the operating core. • The more sophisticated the technology, the more elaborate and professional the support staff will be (eg specialists who understand it). • **Information technology** has a profound effect on organisation structure, especially with regard to delayering.
Strategy and the nature of work	Probably the most important influence of all: markets served, generic strategy, the nature of the product and distribution channel and many more strategic issues will affect structure, as remarked earlier.

7.3.2 Kanter

In her book *The Change Masters*, *Rosabeth Moss Kanter* identified two contrasting organisational responses to the problems produced by change and innovation.

(a)   The *segmentalist* approach is unable to create an integrated response to new problems because of its strongly compartmentalised, mechanistic structure and methods. Managers produce solutions to the aspects of the problem that concern their own responsibilities and no one takes an overview.

(b)   The *integrative* approach looks at the whole problem and is prepared to innovate to solve it, even to the extent of changing the organisation and the way it does things.

The integrative approach requires management to deploy three important sets of skills

(a)   **Power skills** are needed in order to persuade others to take risks.

(b)   **Problem management** skills focus on employee participation and working in teams.

(c)   **Change design and construction skills**.

Kanter makes recommendations for the managers of segmentalist organisations that wish to move to a more integrative style.

(a)   Encourage a **culture of pride** in the firms achievements

(b)   Improve **lateral communication**

(c)   Widen the **distribution of information** about company plans

(d)   Devolve and decentralise power as low down the hierarchy as possible, **delayering** where possible to reduce unnecessary layers of hierarchy.

7.3.3 Stacey: chaos theory

We discussed some of Stacey's ideas about organisations as the products of **complex responsive processes** in Chapter 1. This is, perhaps, the extreme view of the way organisations are evolving away from the classical model.

7.3.4 The third wave

It is now a commonplace to see the influence of advances in IS as creating a 'third wave' of economic development comparable to the development of agriculture and the industrial revolution. Whether or not a change of such magnitude is taking place, there is no doubt that there have been a number of very important IS based developments in the nature of work and the way it is organised.

(a)   **Mass customisation** of products *via* one-to-one marketing, web-based trading, the accumulation of customer information and the development of large **relationship marketing** databases.

(b)   **Disintermediation** is taking place both within organisations, as a result of delayering made possible by IS, and in the market place. Customers can deal direct with producers *via* their websites, or with a new kind of distributor typified by *Amazon*. **Network organisations** represent a mosaic of productive relationships that transcend older models based on the ownership of resources.

(c) **Network economies** arising from the number of devices in use are becoming more important than economies of scale, which depend on the number of items produced. As the take up of any device incorporating an aspect of communications increases, so the usefulness and hence the value of an individual device grows as well.

(d) The importance of the **service sector** and the **knowledge worker** is accelerating and the **leveraging of knowledge** itself is rising in importance as a business resource.

Hope and Hope identified 'the ten key issues of the management information wave'.

- **Strategy** should be innovative, based on core competences and organised using networks and alliances.
- **Customer value** should be based on product leadership, operational excellence or customer knowledge.
- **Knowledge management**: leverage human capital, market data and internal IS, to create competitive advantage.
- **Business organisation**: base on networks rather than hierarchies.
- **Market focus** should be on the best (most profitable) customers, not on volume.
- **Management accounting** should be relevant and empowering; managing the business, not just the numners.
- **Measurement and control** measures should not constrain innovation.
- **Shareholder value** depends on human capital, not physical assets.
- **Productivity** is about people's ability to create value, not utilising fixed assets.
- **Transformation**: abandon the classical approach and Scientific Management; embrace the third wave.

Ezzamel et al suggest the following characteristics of 'new wave management'.

- Flexible supervision and employee self-discipline
- Development of people
- Participative problem-solving
- Multi-functional teams
- Continuously evolving responsibilities and tasks

7.4 New structural models

New approaches to the structuring of organisations form part of the syllabus for Paper 5 and you should revise this topic from Chapter 2 of the BPP Study Text for that Paper. The new forms include **virtual**, **network**, and **shamrock** organisations. Typically these modern approaches feature loose, delayered, organic relationships, exploitation of IS by empowered knowledge workers and a flexible approach to mission and strategy. However, the shamrock organisation in particular, with its emphasis on core and peripheral workers is symptomatic of a new casualisation of labour, with implications for security and benefits at all levels.

Nonetheless, despite (or perhaps because of) this proliferation of new models of organisational structure, it is crucial that management adopt the most appropriate structure for the organisation they are running.

7.5 The new organisation and the management accountant

The new approaches will involve **management accountants in providing more information** to more people than previously, for decision making, for control and for reward and motivation.

The looser, more innovative ways of working mentioned above will be of particular significance to the management accountant. Here are some examples.

(a) All **traditional routines** in such areas as invoice processing will be challenged by, for instance, empowerment and network approaches.

(b) **Cost management**. Challenging traditional routines will also lead the management accountant to challenge all cost areas, to identify whether they add value or not. This means the accountant's role is no longer confined to **cost control**, but also extends to identifying opportunities for **cost reduction**.

(c) **Activity based management** of costs may come to prominence within an organisation, with cross-functional responsibility centres predominating. This is likely to require a **revision of budgetary control systems**.

(d) Functions, including some aspects of finance work, may be **outsourced** and **network structures** may be used both inside and outside the organisation: the accountant will have to provide and use control information in new ways.

(e) **Decisions** may be pushed down the hierarchy and out to the periphery, but they must still be made on sound grounds. Management accounting information will be more widely distributed, especially to **self-managing teams**, and there may be a requirement for control systems that will facilitate dispersed decision-making but prevent its abuse.

(f) **Flexible patterns of employment** may lead to increased staff turnover with consequent loss of experience and cultural control: this may increase the need for closer rather than looser control of the work of temporary staff and teleworkers.

(g) **Performance measurement**. Similarly, there may be a greater need for performance measurement for knowledge and contract workers. At the same time, normal cost accounting for labour will become more complicated as pay rates and the split into direct and indirect labour become more problematical.

(h) The overall system of control will depend on whether the organisation is one that depends on the knowledge and skills of its workforce, invests in and trusts them, or whether it uses flexible approaches to **exploit** them more effectively. A balance must be struck between empowerment and control.

(i) The problem of motivating and rewarding the creative individual will be complicated by the move to **team working**.

8 E-commerce

Very few businesses can afford to ignore the potential of the Internet for driving forward strategy and activity at all levels. Internet usage can range from use of email at one extreme to the almost entirely virtual business model represented by audio and video downloads at the other.

8.1 The Internet and e-commerce challenge traditional business thinking

There are several features of the Internet which make it radically different from what has gone before.

(a) It **challenges traditional business models** – because, for example, it enables product/service suppliers to interact directly with their customers, instead of using intermediaries (like retail shops, travel agents, insurance brokers, and conventional banks).

(b) Although the Internet is global in its operation, its benefits are not confined to large (or global) organisations. **Small companies** can move instantly into a global market place, either on their own initiative or as part of what is known as a 'consumer portal'.

(c) It offers a **new economics of information** – because, with the Internet, much information is free. Those with Internet access can view all the world's major newspapers and periodicals without charge.

(d)   It supplies an almost incredible **level of speed** of communication, giving virtually instant access to organisations, plus the capacity to complete purchasing transactions within seconds.

(e)   It has created **new and cheaper networks of communication** – between organisations and their customers (either individually or collectively), between customers themselves (through mutual support groups), and between organisations and their suppliers.

(f)   It stimulates the appearance of **new intermediaries** and the disappearance of some existing ones. Businesses are finding that they can cut out the middle man, with electronic banking, insurance, publishing and printing as primary examples.

(g)   It has led to **new business partnerships** through which small enterprises can gain access to customers on a scale which would have been viewed as impossible a few years ago.

(h)   Work is becoming **independent of location**. Clerical, administrative and knowledge work can be done at any location. This can reduce establishment and travelling costs, especially if people work at home, but the loss of personal interaction can affect **motivation** and **job satisfaction**.

(i)   The **nature of work** is changing since increased quantities of available data and more powerful methods of accessing analysing it mean that greater attention can be paid to customising product offerings to more precisely defined target segments.

 Case Study

A university can put its reading list on a website and students wishing to purchase any given book can click directly through to an online bookseller such as Amazon.com. The university gets a commission; the online bookseller gets increased business; the student gets a discount. Everyone benefits except the traditional bookshop.

(j)   It promotes **transparent pricing** – because potential customers can readily compare prices not only from suppliers within any given country, but also from suppliers across the world.

(k)   It facilitates **personalised attention** – even if such attention is actually administered through impersonal, yet highly sophisticated IT systems and customer database manipulation.

(l)   It provides sophisticated **market segmentation** opportunities. Approaching such segments may be one of the few ways in which e-commerce entrepreneurs can create **competitive advantage**.

(m)   The web can either be a **separate** or a **complementary** channel.

(n)   A new phenomenon is emerging called **dynamic pricing**. Companies can rapidly change their prices to reflect the current state of demand and supply.

These new trends are creating **pressure** for companies. The main threat facing companies is that **prices will be driven down by consumers' ability to shop around**.

8.2 Varieties of e-commerce

Both businesses and customers can originate e-commerce activity; thus there are four main categories: B2B, B2C, C2B and C2C. Channel structures are the means by which products and services are delivered to customers. Disintermediation removes intermediaries from supply channels while reintermediation establishes new ones. Countermediation is the creation of a new intermediary by an established company to compete *via* a business with established intermediaties.

E-commerce can be divided into four main categories.

B2B (Business-to-Business) – involves companies doing business with each other, as when manufacturers sell to distributors and wholesalers sell to retailers. Pricing is based on quantity of order and is often negotiable.

B2C (Business-to-Consumer) – involves businesses selling to the general public, typically through catalogues with **shopping cart software**.

C2B (Consumer-to-Business) – a consumer posts his project with a set budget online and within hours companies review the consumer's requirements and bid on the project. The consumer reviews the bids and selects the company that will complete the project.

C2C (Consumer-to-Consumer) – an excellent example of this is found at *eBay*, where consumers sell their goods and services to other consumers. Another technology that has emerged to support C2C activities is that of the payment intermediary *PayPal*. Instead of purchasing items directly from an unknown, un-trusted seller, the buyer can instead send the money to Pay Pal, who forward it to the vendor's account.

The transaction alternatives between businesses and consumers are shown in the matrix below:

		Delivery by	
		Business	Consumer
Exchange initiated by	Business	B2B Business models eg *VerticalNet.com*	B2C Business models eg *Amazon.com*
	Consumer	C2B Business models eg *Priceline.com*	C2C Business Models eg *eBay.com*

8.3 Market place channel structures

Channel structures are the means by which a manufacturer or selling organisation delivers products and services to its customers. The simplest channel structure is **direct**: the business deals directly with the customer without the assistance of any **intermediaries**. The more complex the channel structure, the more intermediaries (wholesalers and/or retailers) are used in the supply chain. Intermediaries offer a wide range of services and facilities: they include agents, traders, brokers, dealers, wholesalers/ distributors and providers of specialised information.

The main changes to channel structures facilitated through the Internet include **disintermediation** (direct selling), **reintermediation** (new intermediaries) and **countermediation** (the creation of a new intermediary by an established company)

8.3.1 Disintermediation

Disintermediation is the removal of intermediaries in a supply chain that formerly linked a company to its customers. Instead of going through traditional distribution channels, with intermediaries such as a distributor, wholesaler, broker or agent, companies may now deal with every customer directly via the Internet.

Examples

You can already bypass publishers to get a book printed at tiny cost through self-publishing sites such as *Lulu.com*. Gambling is being changed by online sites arranging bets directly between individuals, not through bookmakers, with *Betfair* being the market leader in this respect.

Disintemediation process

Disintermediation may be initiated by **consumers** because they are aware of **supply prices** direct from the manufacturer or wholesaler. Alternatively, it may be instigated by the author or creator of a work, such as *Steven King* selling his books directly to the public. There are also third party aggregators or buyer's clubs that link consumers with producers to obtain lower prices.

Reverse auction sites that allow consumers to specify an item they wish to purchase, allowing producers and others to bid on the item.

Traditional value chain in publishing

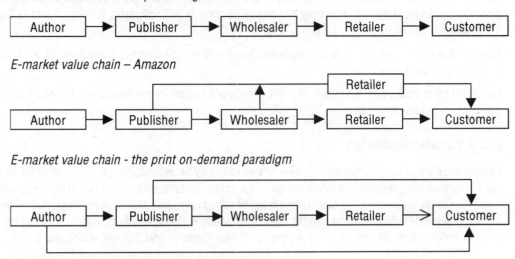

8.3.2 Reintermediation

Reintermediation is the establishment of new intermediary roles for traditional intermediaries that were disintermediated. In some cases, a new element of a supply chain simply replaces a single displaced element, such as Amazon.com replacing retailers. In other cases, a reintermediating entity replaces multiple supply chain elements. These new intermediaries do one of two things.

(a)   Provide customers with **new**, **important value-added services** not provided in the new direct customer-supplier relationship. An example is *Kelkoo* which is a shopping/price comparison search engine.

(b)   Provide customers with **more efficient means** of transacting business.

The ever-increasing number of 'hubs', 'portals', 'aggregators', 'clearinghouses' and 'exchanges' shows that entirely new ways of doing business are being created. Those organisations (or individuals) clever enough to recognise the opportunities provided by the Web and are reinventing themselves as 'cybermediaries' or 'infomediaries' – intermediaries offering value-added services to consumers and vendors over the Internet.

8.3.3 New types of intermediary

Search engines and directories – search engines, such as Google and *Alta Vista* provide search facilities based on data generated by software engines, that search the web. Directories such as Yahoo provide a general index of a large variety of different sites.

Search agents (Search bots) gather material from other sites. For example *Shopbot* searches across online shops.

Portals provide a gateway to the Web and may also offer **signposting**, selected **links** and other services to attract users. Internet Service Provider's (ISP) home pages such as www.AOL.com are an example of portals, and the large ISPs offer a wide range of added value services. Variations on the portal as gateway are: a horizontal portal or user customised gateway (eg *my Yahoo*); a vertical portal or special interest portal eg, *CNET* – a portal for users interested in developments in IT; and an enterprise information portal, which is an organisation's home page for employees, including corporate info and selected links.

'E-tailers' or consumer shopping sites such as Amazon. While starting as simply a bookshop on the web it has added a variety of products and types of services. By contrast, *Tesco* is an offline retailer which is offering web-based order and delivery services.

Auction sites such as eBay support online auctions.

Publisher web sites are traffic generators that offer content of interest to consumers.

Virtual resellers are intermediaries that exist to sell to consumers. They are able to obtain products directly from manufacturers, who may hesitate to go directly to consumers for fear of **alienating retailers** upon which they still largely depend.

Forums, **fan clubs**, and **user groups** can play a large role in facilitating customer-producer feedback and supporting market research.

Financial intermediaries. Any form of e-commerce will require some means of making or authorising payments from buyer to seller.

8.3.4 Countermediation

Countermediation is the creation of a new intermediary by an established company in order to compete *via* e-business with established intermediaries. Examples include *B&Q* setting up *diy.com* to help people who want to do their own DIY, *Boots* setting up *handbag.com*, and *Opodo.com* which has been set up by a collaboration of nine European airlines. Countermediation also refers to possible partnerships with another independent intermediary eg, mortgage broker *Charcol* and *Orange*, which was Freeserve.

 Case Study

Airlines. The impact of the Internet is seen clearly in the transportation industry. Airlines now have a more effective way of bypassing intermediaries (ie travel agents) because they can give their customers immediate access to flight reservation systems. *EasyJet*, was the first airline to have over half of its bookings made online.

Travel agents. The Internet has also produced a new set of online travel agents who have lower costs because of their ability to operate without a High Street branch network. Their low-cost structure makes them a particularly good choice for selling low margin, cheap tickets for flights, package holidays, cruises and so forth.

In 2004 *BA* stopped paying commission to travel agents for flight bookings, intending to move to an entirely Internet-based system for bookings. In 2005 the European industry saw significant consolidation when *Sabre Holdings*, the US owner of *Travelocity*, bought *Lastminute.com*.

Tesco is already the UK's largest Internet grocery business, but other companies are rapidly developing new initiatives. *Waitrose@work* allows people to order their groceries in the morning (typically through their employer's intranet communication system) and then have them delivered to the workplace in the afternoon: this approach achieves significant distribution economies of scale for Waitrose.

Financial services. The impact of the Internet is especially profound in the field of financial services. New intermediaries enable prospective customers to compare the interest rates and prices charged by different organisations for pensions, mortgages and other financial products. This means that the delivering companies are **losing control of the marketing** of their services, and there is a **downward pressure on prices**, especially for services which can legitimately be seen as mere commodities (eg house and contents insurance).

8.4 Disadvantages of e-commerce

FAST FORWARD

E-commerce presents completely new **problems** of management and organisation.

E-commerce involves an unusual mix of people – security people, web technology people, designers, marketing people – and this can be very difficult to manage. The e-business needs supervision by expensive specialists.

In spite of phenomenal growth the market is still fuzzy and undefined. Many e-businesses have only recently reported making any **profit**, the best-known example being **Amazon.com** the Internet book-seller.

Unless the e-business is one started completely from scratch, any new technology installed will **need to link up with existing business systems**, which could potentially take years of programming. Under-estimating the time and effort involved is a common obstacle.

The international availability of a website means that the **laws of all countries** that transactions may be conducted from have to be considered. The legal issues surrounding e-commerce are complex and still developing.

Case Study

For some the Internet is a necessary evil – others browse and surf the net with that obsessive drive that is peculiar to any new technology. But the Internet is not just any new technology. It is the most important communications development since the advent of the telephone, and like the telephone it has created its own culture and given birth to new businesses and new possibilities.

Early confusion about the Internet meant that many companies built their own websites after learning the rudiments of HTML. They had registered their company name and done everything by the book. The website went online and they all waited with bated breath. Nothing happened. No new business arrived and nothing changed, and they couldn't understand why.

E-commerce is a tidal wave; if you choose to participate you either 'sink or swim'. You must be daring enough in design to achieve something quite different from the ways things have been done in the past.

A website is a shopfront that must be located in the centre of town in the full gaze of everyone. A good one can make a small business as powerful and competitive as some of the largest players. It just needs flair and commitment to succeed. But to do so there are some measures that must be used. Marketing outside the web, in the press or even on the radio can alert the market to the website. The site itself should be properly identified by name, registered competently with the appropriate search engines and it must look good.

WEBSITE ESSENTIALS
• Integration with all company systems (ie back office)
• Speedy implementation
• Quick and easy updating by own staff to retain topicality
• Self producing audit records
• Promotion via the Internet
• Press and PR for website
• Attractive design but appropriate for the web
• Scope to interact with visitors
• Planned structure to include profitable business concept
• Control and maintenance by owner, without developer involvement

The appearance of a website is extremely important. Attractive and easy to fill interactive forms can lure a sales prospect into being a buyer. One has seconds in which to achieve this end. Too many graphics slow down the procedure. The experience of visiting and browsing through the shop and responding to the goods on offer must be clever, intriguing, quick and efficient. Millions of pounds worth of business is lost on the Internet every day as a result of so-called interactive websites that are difficult to operate and dull.

Adapted from *Management Accounting,* February 2000

8.5 The Internet in context

FAST FORWARD

> The **Internet** has the capacity to transform many businesses via the introduction of new technology and skills and, eventually, the re-positioning of the offering to fit the new market conditions.

Commentators highlight so-called 'megatrends' which, coupled with the Internet, are changing the face of organisations:

(a) New **distribution channels**, revolutionising sales and brand management.

(b) The continued **shift of power** towards the consumer.

(c) **Growing competition** locally, nationally, internationally and globally.

(d) An acceleration in the **pace of business**.

(e) The **transformation of companies** into 'extended enterprises' involving 'virtual teams of business, customer and supplier' working in collaborative partnerships.

(f) **Reduced importance of location**. The availability of internet connections is making the physical location where people work less important.

(g) A re-evaluation of how companies, their partners and competitors **add value** not only to themselves but in the wider environmental and social setting.

(h) Recognition of '**knowledge**' as a strategic asset.

Most observers and experts agree that a successful strategy for e-commerce cannot simply be bolted on to existing processes, systems, delivery routes and business models. Instead, management groups have, in effect, to start again, by asking themselves such **fundamental questions** as:

- What do customers want to buy from us?
- What business should we be in?
- What kind of partners might we need?
- What categories of customer do we want to attract and retain?

In turn, organisations can visualise the necessary changes at three interconnected levels.

Level 1 The simple **introduction of new technology** to connect electronically with employees, customers and suppliers (eg through an intranet, extranet or website).

Level 2 **Re-organisation** of the workforce, processes, systems and strategy – in order to make best use of the new technology.

Level 3 **Re-positioning** of the organisation to fit it into the emerging e-economy.

So far, very few companies have gone beyond levels (1) and (2). Instead, pure Internet businesses such as Amazon.com and AOL have emerged from these new rules: unburdened by physical assets, their competitive advantage lies in knowledge management and customer relationships.

 Case Study

Conventional thinking says that a company should pay no more to bring in a customer than the net present value of the stream of profits that the customer will subsequently generate. Yet in the e-commerce context, investors have often rewarded companies for customer acquisition without asking any questions about how quickly those customers may disappear. The evidence suggests that many 'dot.com' enterprises remain unable to achieve sustained profitability or indeed any profitability at all.

8.6 Building an e-commerce strategy

FAST FORWARD

> An e-commerce strategy, like any other strategy option, must be **suitable**, **acceptable** and **feasible**. It should work well with any existing operations; be acceptable to distributors in particular; and not make impractical demands for cash and skilled labour.

A **strategy for e-commerce**, while not necessarily constituting the organisation's overall strategy, is likely to have wide implications and to involve and affect more than one function or department within the organisation. It should, therefore, be considered at the highest level of management and it is particularly necessary that it should conform to the **standard criteria for strategic choice**: suitability, acceptability and feasibility.

8.6.1 Suitability

There are a few large organisations, such as Amazon, whose overall strategy is based on e-commerce. However, for most companies, e-commerce will be a **supplement to more traditional operations**, with the website forming a supplementary medium for communication and sales. It is important that the e-commerce strategy supports the overall strategy generally. One way of approaching this would be to consider the **extended marketing mix** and the need for **balance**, **consistency** and **mutual support** between the elements. A very simple example would consider the question of whether to confine the website to an essentially communications role, or to incorporate a fully featured on-line shopping facility. A specialist chain store dealing in, say, camping and outdoor equipment would expect to expand its market if it developed on-line shopping. On the other hand, a manufacturer of specialist luxury goods, such as the most expensive fountain pens, would probably have a policy of distributing through carefully selected retailers. It is unlikely that on-line shopping would appeal to the target market segment: they would probably enjoy the shopping experience and would want to try the products before they bought them.

8.6.2 Acceptability

The e-commerce strategy must be **acceptable to important stakeholders**. Distributors are particularly important here. Pursuing our luxury goods example we would expect that retailers chosen for their attractive premises, skilled and attentive staff and air of luxury would be unhappy to find their position usurped by a website.

8.6.3 Feasibility

Feasibility is a matter of **resources**. The fundamental resource is cash, but the availability of the **skilled labour** needed to establish and administer a website will be crucial to the e-commerce strategy. It may be appropriate to employ **specialist consultants** for these purposes.

Under this heading, we might identify the following points for consideration.

(a)   The first thing to do is to try to establish precise **objectives** for the new strategy element. It may not be possible to do this conclusively, and consideration of objectives may have to proceed alongside the processes outline below, all passing through several iterations.

(b)   An estimate and analysis of **costs** and **benefits** should be undertaken. This should cover all the possible options, such as what services are to be offered, whether a full catalogue is to be put online, whether Internet selling is envisaged, whether a search function is required and so on.

(c)   A detailed **budget** should be prepared, probably using estimates from the cost and benefit analysis. Where Internet selling is to be offered, pricing policy must be established: there is a theory that customers expect goods and services to be discounted when sold online, since they are aware that administrative costs are likely to be lower than in more traditional forms of distribution.

(d)   **Specific technical requirements**

 •   Web hosting software
 •   Server computers (more than one system to provide redundancy)

8.6.4 Launch

It may be appropriate to launch the website to a restricted number of potential customers in order to ensure that its functionality is satisfactory. This might be done on a regional basis, with promotion through appropriate press and TV channels. When a national launch is approved, it will be necessary to promote the website nationally and to ensure that the web address is included in all corporate stationery and display material.

Chapter Roundup

- The hierarchy of **project management** extends upwards beyond the project manager. More senior managers must provide strategic control. The main instrument for such control is the **project board**. PRINCE2 project management proceeds on the basis that a project is driven by its business case.

- Business must respond to intensified competition, particularly from other countries, by improving its efficiency and reducing its costs.

- **JIT** aims for zero inventory and perfect quality and operates by demand-pull. It consists of **JIT purchasing** and **JIT production** and results in lower investment requirements, space savings, greater customer satisfaction and increased flexibility.

- **World class manufacturing (WCM)** aims for high quality, fast production, and the flexibility to respond to customer needs.

- Change is inevitable in most organisations and must be managed. It can be **incremental** or **transformational** and management may be **proactive** or **reactive**.

- Change can have a significant impact on people's circumstances and even health. They tend to oppose it and it must there fore be introduced carefully.

- The **Lewin/Schein** approach to changing human behaviour has three stages: Unfreeze – change – refreeze. **Systems intervention strategy** is an intuitive method that may be implemented in three stages: diagnosis, design and implementation. The **champion of change model** uses an individual or group to lead the change process. Gemini 4Rs is based on reframing, restructuring, revitalising and renewal.

- The forces driving and restraining change may be analysed using **force field analysis**.

- The management of change must include consideration of its **pace**, **manner** and **scope**.

- The introduction of change can easily lead to conflict, though it is not the only source of dissension. The management of conflict is an important aspect of change management, as well as being useful in other contexts.

- Much marketing management relates to the **marketing mix**. The basic mix consists of the four Ps: Product, price, promotion and place. For service organisations a further three Ps may be added to form the extended marketing mix: people, processes and physical evidence.

- Strategy may be based to some extent on the company's market position, with different plans for followers, challengers and nichers.

- **Branding** removes anonymity and gives identification to a company and its goods and services.

- In recent times emphasis has increased on building and maintaining good long-term **relationships** with customers. This is because such relationships are more profitable than constantly searching for new customers owing to repeat purchasing, ease of service and so on.

- As businesses, their markets and the wider environment develop and change with the passage of time it is appropriate to reconsider the way they do things from time to time. **Business process re-engineering** is a useful approach based on challenging basic assumptions about business methods and even the objectives they are designed to achieve. IT can be very useful here, but simply to automate a process is not the same as re-engineering it.

- The **automate**, **informate** and **transformate** framework is very similar to BPR's **automation**, **rationalisation** and **re-engineering**, as is **process innovation**, which focuses on the creation of new processes to achieve business objectives.

- The three essential aspects of the nature of organisations, social arrangements, agreed goals and controlled performance make it inevitable that an organisation's strategy, its structure and the work of the management accountant are intimately entwined. The **classical approach** is being replaced by more **flexible methods** as a result of the pressure from environmental developments, including **globalisation** and **developments in IS**.

- A number of writers on organisations and management have made similar recommendations about the need for **innovation**, **flexibility**, **communication**, **empowerment**, **leveraging of knowledge** and a **network approach to organising resources** both within the organisation and outside its boundaries.

- The new approaches will involve **management accountants in providing more information** to more people than previously, for decision making, for control and for reward and motivation.

- **E-commerce** challenges traditional business models; makes global markets available to small businesses; transforms transparency of pricing; and offers new opportunities for market segmentation.

- Both businesses and customers can originate e-commerce activity; thus there are four main categories: B2B, B2C, C2B and C2C. Channel structures are the means by which products and services are delivered to customers. Disintermediation removes intermediaries from supply channels while reintermediation establishes new ones. Countermediation is the creation of a new intermediary by an established company to compete *via* a business with established intermediaties.

- E-commerce presents completely new **problems** of management and organisation.

- The **Internet** has the capacity to transform many businesses via the introduction of new technology and skills and, eventually, the re-positioning of the offering to fit the new market conditions.

- An e-commerce strategy, like any other strategy option, must be **suitable**, **acceptable** and **feasible**. It should work well with any existing operations; be acceptable to distributors in particular; and not make impractical demands for cash and skilled labour.

1   In PRINCE2, the continuing viability of a project is established by reference to:

   A   The senior user
   B   The business case
   C   The project board
   D   The most recent end stage assessment

2   Complete the gap in the sentence below using one of the expressions given in brackets.

   'In JIT manufacturing, ... is used to ensure that products or components are only produced when needed by the next process.'

   (uniform loading, a kanban system, employee involvement, a close relationship with suppliers)

3   Fill in the blanks in the diagram below.

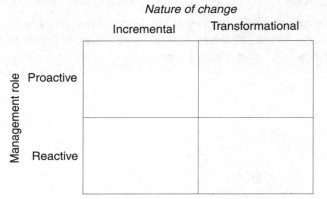

4   In the Lewin/Schein three stage change management model, what general principle does management use to embed the desirable new behaviour?

5   How may the nature and extent of a programme of change be best analysed in order to facilitate the effective management of resistance to change?

   A   Diagnosis, design, implementation
   B   Unfreeze, change, refreeze
   C   Pace, manner, scope
   D   Physiological, psychological, circumstantial

6   What are the 7Ps of the extended marketing mix?

7   What is multi-branding?

8   Which of the following is not a principle of BPR, according to *Hammer*?

   A   Information gathering should not be separated from information processing
   B   Work people should be self-managing as far as possible
   C   Processes should evolve from current methods
   D   Parallel activities should be linked rather than integrated

9   What are the four main categories of e-commerce?

1   B   A project can only be judged viable by reference to its business case.

2   A kanban system is used for this purpose.

3

Nature of change

		Incremental	Transformational
Management role	Proactive	Tuning	Planned
	Reactive	Adaptation	Forced

4   Reinforcement; both positive and negative

5   C   Diagnosis, design, implementation is a summary of the complete systems intervention strategy, while unfreeze, change, refreeze is the Lewin/Schein model of the complete change process. Option D is a checklist of the ways change can affect individuals and should certainly be considered when implementing a change programme. However, option C provides the best approach to planning for dealing with resistance to change.

6   Product, price, promotion, place, people, processes, physical evidence.

7   Using more than one brand name for similar goods.

8   C   It is fundamental to BPR that current methods should be examined most critically: the emphasis is always on the desired outcome rather than existing processes.

9   B2B; B2C; C2B; C2C.

Now try the question below from the Exam Question Bank

Number	Level	Marks	Time
Q12	Intermediate	n/a	30 mins

Measuring performance I

Introduction

Strategies can fail when they are **implemented. Feedback information** is needed. In the past, firms relied purely on financial measures, but this created some problems, particularly in relating the short term to the long term.

Performance measurement is all about **communicating the objectives** of the company and concentrating efforts towards them. **Strategic control** (Section 2) indicates the need for a review of strategic performance over a whole host of measures, as opposed to just the numbers, although many companies still use the traditional **budgetary control process** as the main basis for measuring performance (Section 3).

The aim of strategic control is to review **long term** indicators of the business. The **balanced scorecard** (Section 5) is one way by which **financial and non-financial** (strategic) performance can be measured. Other multidimensional models of performance, chiefly the **performance pyramid,** are described in Section 6.

At **operational level,** some useful indicators of performance are given for both service and manufacturing businesses (Sections 7 and 8).

Finally, this chapter considers the impact of both legal and voluntary **regulation** on corporate performance. Corporate codes, for example on ethical issues, are becoming a feature of business strategy.

Topic list	Learning outcomes	Syllabus references	Ability required
1 Control and performance measurement	D(i)	D1	Evaluation
2 Strategic control and critical success factors	D(i)	D11	Evaluation
3 Budgetary control systems	D(i)	D1	Evaluation
4 Performance measures: financial and non-financial	D(i)	D2	Evaluation
5 The balanced scorecard	D(ii)	D3	Evaluation
6 Other multidimensional measures of performance	D(ii)	D3	Evaluation
7 Performance: service departments and firms	D(iii)	D3	Evaluation
8 Performance: manufacturing	D(iii)	D3	Evaluation
9 Regulation and performance	C(vii)	D1, D2	Evaluation

1 Control and performance measurement

1.1 Control systems

FAST FORWARD

> All systems of control can be analysed using the **cybernetic model**. The essence of this model is the **feedback** of control action to the controlled process: the control action itself being generated from the comparison of actual results with what was planned.

You should be familiar with the way that control systems work from your studies for P5. However, we will revise the essentials here in order to set the scene for what follows.

1.1.1 Cybernetic control

To some extent, planning and controlling are two sides of a single coin, since a plan is of little value if it is not put into action, while a system of control can only be effective if the people running it know what it is they are trying to achieve.

In the cybernetic system, an objective is established: for the organisation, this might be the current year's budget. Actual achievement is measured, perhaps by means of monthly reports, and a process of comparison takes place. In the organisation, managers fulfil this role by comparing budget and actual figures. They then take control action to make up for any failure to achieve the plan This control action feeds back into the activity of the organisation and its effects should become apparent in the next monthly report. This **feedback loop** is the essence of any control system, though sometimes it may be difficult to discern its existence and operation.

Key terms

> **Feedback** occurs when the results (outputs) of a system are used to control it, by adjusting the input or behaviour of the system. Businesses use feedback information to control their performance.
>
> **Single loop feedback** results in the system's behaviour being altered to meet the plan.
>
> **Double loop feedback** can result in changes to the plan itself.

Emmanuel et al describe **four necessary conditions that must be satisfied before any process can be said to be controlled.** These will help us to put control into a wider context still.

(a)   **Objectives** for the process being controlled must exist, for without an aim or purpose control has no meaning.

(b)   The **output of** the process must be **measurable** in terms of the dimensions defined by the objectives.

(c)   A **predictive model** of the process being controlled is required so that causes for the non-attainment of objectives can be determined and proposed corrective actions evaluated.

(d)   There must be a **capability of taking action** so that deviations of attainment from objectives can be reduced.

It is important to understand that this concept of control involves more than just measuring results and taking corrective action. Control in the broad sense embraces **the formulation of objectives** – deciding what are the things that need to be done – as well as monitoring their attainment by way of feedback. Management accountants working in senior management will be major contributors to the objective-setting process for two reasons.

(a)   As *Drucker* pointed out, the most crucial aspect of management performance in business is economic success; that is, **financial targets are the vital ones**.

(b)   Targets are only useful if performance can be **measured**: performance measurement is a major aspect of management accountancy.

1.1.2 Control strategies

Ouchi identified **market**, **bureaucratic** and **clan** control strategies; their application is very much dependent on the control contingencies encountered.

William Ouchi identified three types of control strategy for organisations. They are all capable of analysis as cybernetic control systems.

- **Market** control
- **Bureaucratic** control
- **Clan** control

To these we add **personal centralised** control, described by *Child*. This is the type of control that is based on hierarchical relationships, where decisions are taken by superiors who then supervise their implementation.

Market control

Market control is the use of the **price mechanism and related performance measures** internally and externally, to control organisational behaviour. It is used in loose organisational firms such as consortia and alliances and in the construction industry when sub-contractors are employed.

At **divisional level**, market control can also be used, although this is sometimes problematic. It is only relevant if there are separate divisions, which are established as **profit centres, or investment centres**.

Such control systems are only effective where it is possible to price the output of a division effectively and where there is **external competition as a reference**.

Bureaucratic control

Bureaucratic control uses rules and reports to maintain control. Control is based on the principles of scientific management – specialisation of work, simplification of work methods, and standardisation of procedures.

Four main mechanisms are used: standard operating procedures, statistical reports, budgets, and appraisal.

Clan control

Clan control is based on **corporate culture** and depends on three principal organisational characteristics.

(a) Shared **values and traditions**.

(b) It is assumed that those who are hired are committed to the organisation and its customers. In other words, they share the same **assumptions** as management.

(c) Creating a sense of **common purpose**. Employees develop a strong personal identification with the goals of the organisation.

1.2 Performance measurement   5/07

Performance measurement aims to establish how well something or somebody is doing in relation to previous or expected activity or in comparison with another thing or body. It aims to:

- **Communicate** the objectives of the company
- **Concentrate efforts** towards those objectives
- **Produce feedback** for comparison with the plan

Key term

Performance measurement is the 'process of assessing the proficiency with which a reporting entity succeeds, by the economic acquisition of resources and their efficient and effective development, in achieving its objectives. Performance measures may be based on non-financial as well as on financial information.'

(CIMA *Official Terminology*)

1.2.1 The purpose of performance measurement

Performance measurement has become such an accepted part of business life that sometimes we lose sight of its purpose.

(a) Performance measurement is part of the overall cybernetic (or feedback) control system, providing the essential **feedback** spur to any necessary control action.

(b) It is a major input into communications to **stakeholder groups**, including the widening field of corporate reporting.

(c) It is intimately linked to **incentives** and **performance management** systems, providing evidence of results against agreed objectives.

(d) Motivation may be enhanced since managers will seek to achieve satisfactory performance in areas that are measured.

Neely summarised the purpose of performance measurement in his 'Four CPs of Performance Measurement':

(a) **Check position** – how well are we doing?

(b) **Communicate position** – to stakeholders so that they know how the business is performing

(c) **Confirm priorities** – setting targeted for business and developing action plans to help achieve them

(d) **Compel progress** – measuring performance is a strong driver for change, especially if it is linked to reward.

 Case Study

In 2004 the Economist Intelligence Unit and Marakon Associates, a consultancy organisation, surveyed 197 companies with turnover exceeding US$500m. The survey revealed some disturbing facts.

- Less than 15% of companies compare performance with their SBU's prior year strategic plans.
- Actual performance in terns of return on capital is rarely as good as was projected.
- Financial forecasts generally are unreliable.
- As a result, the strategic apex has no idea whether underperformance is caused by poor planning, poor execution, both or neither.

Harvard Business Review, July-August 2005

1.2.2 Approaches to performance measurement

An important aspect of the management accountant's role is to help implement and control strategies through performance measurement.

There are a number of key areas to consider when determining the approach to adopt towards performance evaluation in a given set of circumstances.

Area to consider	Comments
What is evaluated?	Some approaches concentrate on the performance of the organisation as a whole, while others look at strategic business units, divisions, functions or the individual.
Who wants the evaluation?	Some approaches are based on the viewpoint of a single interest group such as investors. Others take in the views of various interest groups (for example employees).
What are the objectives of the organisation?	Is there a single goal or many goals? Are the goals short or long term?
Are quantitative measures or	Quantitative measures (eg ROI or number of rejects) may not seem

Area to consider	Comments
qualitative measures appropriate?	relevant but qualitative measures (eg customer satisfaction) are sometimes perceived to be too subjective.
What targets are used to assess performance?	Measures are meaningless unless they are compared against something. Common sources of comparison are historic figures, standards/budgets, similar external activities, similar internal activities, indices and trends over time.

Question
Project leadership

Learning outcome D(i)

How could product leadership be measured, besides considering market share?

Answer

Qualitative measures ought to be available in the form of reviews by consumer magazines, newspapers, and trade press, awards, endorsement by public figures, and direct comment from customers.

2 Strategic control and critical success factors

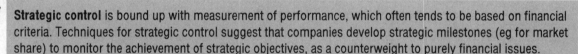

Strategic control is bound up with measurement of performance, which often tends to be based on financial criteria. Techniques for strategic control suggest that companies develop strategic milestones (eg for market share) to monitor the achievement of strategic objectives, as a counterweight to purely financial issues.

Critical success factors are the few key areas where things must go right for the organisation to flourish.

We introduced the idea of critical success factors earlier in this Study Text when discussing strategy for information systems and technology. Here, we consider their use as an impact to strategic control.

Michael Goold and *John J Quinn* write: 'Most companies take pride in fostering a performance-driven culture that emphasises profitability as the key goal for business management ... [but] ... too much emphasis on budgetary control and short-term profit can disguise strategic problems.'

2.1 Gaps and false alarms

Many firms have spent time measuring the wrong things – the trick is to remove 'false alarms' from performance measures and replace them with measures that fill gaps in coverage. **Gaps** (important areas which are neglected) include:

- New product introduction
- Customer satisfaction
- Employee involvement

In *Management Accounting* (May 1995), *Robert Booth* identified the following problems.

- Short-term measures predominate over long-term measures
- Financial proxies (eg EPS) predominate over reality
- Efficiency takes precedence over effectiveness
- Economy takes precedence over efficiency
- Individual department performance measures take precedence over how departments are linked together to satisfy the customers

2.2 Strategic control systems

Formal systems of strategic control are rare, although more companies are adopting them.

(a) The formal process begins with a **strategy review**, perhaps each year. The key assumptions on which the strategy is based must be monitored.

(b) **Milestones of performance** both of a quantitative and qualitative nature are developed.

(c) **Strategic budgets** indicate the resources to be spent on strategic targets.

Informal systems of strategic control. Many companies do not 'define explicit strategic objectives or milestones that are regularly and formally monitored as part of the ongoing management control process'.

- Informality promotes flexibility
- Formal systems can become over-bureaucratic
- Openness of communication is necessary
- A narrow focus on individual strategic objectives can blind managers to wider issues

The characteristics of strategic control systems can be measured on two axes: how formal is the process and how many milestones are identified for performance? Goold and Quinn recommend the following guidelines.

(a) **Linkages**. If there are important linkages among business units, the formality of the process should be low, to avoid undermining co-operation.

(b) **Diversity**. If there is a great deal of diversity, it is doubtful whether any overall strategic control system is appropriate.

(c) **Risk**. Firms whose strategic stance depends on high risk decisions which could destroy the company as a whole need strategic control systems which have a large number of performance criteria so that problems will be easily detected.

(d) **Change**. Fashion-goods manufacturers must respond to relatively high levels of environmental turbulence, and have to react quickly.

(e) **Competitive advantage**. For control purposes, it is useful to distinguish between two types of business.

　　(i) Businesses with few sources of competitive advantage. In this case, perhaps market share or quality is the source of success.

　　(ii) Businesses with many sources of advantage. In this case, success over a wider number of areas is necessary. The greatest dangers in this sort of business are misdirected effort and high cost.

The introduction of a formal or semi-formal strategic control system to monitor a firm's strategic position has certain advantages.

- Realism in planning
- The encouragement of higher performance standards
- More motivation for business units
- More timely intervention by senior management

2.3 Critical success factors and key performance indicators

We discussed critical success factors (CSF) earlier in this Study Text in Chapter 3 when we were considering business objectives. Where the CSF approach is used, it will be appropriate to establish one or more **key performance indicators** (KPI) for each CSF.

Some KPIs which cover both **financial and non-financial criteria** are outlined below.

Sphere of activity	Key performance indicators
Marketing	Sales volume Market share Gross margins

Sphere of activity	Key performance indicators
Production	Capacity utilisation Quality standards
Logistics	Capacity utilisation Level of service

Some criteria which are regularly used in choosing between alternative plans for specific elements of the marketing mix are outlined below.

Activity	Key performance indicators
New product development	Trial rate Repurchase rate
Sales programmes	Contribution by region, salesperson Controllable margin as percentage of sales Number of new accounts Travel costs
Advertising programmes	Awareness levels Attribute ratings Cost levels
Pricing programmes	Price relative to industry average Price elasticity of demand
Distribution programmes	Number of distributors carrying the product

2.4 The product life cycle and control systems

We examined the implications of the product life cycle (PLC) for the marketing mix in Chapter 12. *Ward* suggests that the PLC is also relevant to the design and operation of control systems and performance measurement.

	Introduction	Growth	Maturity	Decline
Information needed	The environment Potential market size and buyer value	Market growth Market share Marketing effectiveness Competitor information and effectiveness of marketing	Competitors' costs Limiting factor	Rate of decline When to exit Realisable asset values
Critical success factors	Time to develop and launch	Growth in share Sustainable competitive advantage	Contribution per unit of limiting factor Customer retention rates	None
Performance measures	Evaluate using DCF of life-cycle cash flows Lead indicators of market success, eg advertising effectiveness, distributor acceptance	DCF evaluation of marketing costs Specific marketing objectives Market share	ROI Profit margin Operating cash flow Market share	Free cash flow compared with opportunity costs of assets used

Note Ward's emphasis on external measures relating to customers and competitors and the way that conventional financial measures such as ROI do not appear until the maturity phase.

2.5 Stakeholder interest performance measures

We discussed measures of performance relevant to stakeholders other than shareholders in Chapter 3.

3 Budgetary control systems

FAST FORWARD

Budgetary control systems are subject to some criticism, but are still used by many companies to compel planning, co-ordinate activities and motivate employees, as well as to evaluate performance. Deviations from the plan are corrected via **control action.**

Key term

Budgetary control is the process whereby the 'master budget, devolved to responsibility centres, allows continuous monitoring of actual results versus budget, either to secure by individual action the budget objectives or to provide a basis for budget revision'.   (CIMA *Official Terminology*)

A budget is a **plan expressed in monetary terms.** It is prepared and approved prior to the budget period and may show income, expenditure and capital to be employed.

Purpose of budgets

- To compel planning
- To co-ordinate activities
- To communicate ideas
- To provide a framework for responsibility accounting
- To motivate employees and management
- To evaluate performance

Negative effects of budgets include

- No incentive as the budget is unrealistic
- A manager may add 10% to his expenditure budget to ensure that he can meet the figure
- Manager achieves target but does no more
- A manager may go on a 'spending spree'
- Draws attention away from the longer term consequences

Problems with budgetary control

- The managers who set the budgets are often not responsible for attaining them.
- The goals of the organisation as a whole, expressed in the budget, may not coincide with the personal aspirations of the individual managers.
- Control is applied at different stages by different people.

How to improve behavioural aspects of budgetary control

- Develop a working relationship with operational managers
- Keeping accounting jargon to a minimum
- Making reports clear and to the point
- Providing control and information with a minimum of delay
- Ensuring actual costs are recorded accurately
- Allow for participation in the budgetary process

Limitations to the effectiveness of participation

- Some people prefer tough management
- A manager may build slack into his won budget
- Management feels that they have little scope to influence the final outcome

3.1 Activity based budgeting (ABB)

> **Activity-based budgeting** is a 'method of budgeting based on an activity framework and utilising cost driver data in the budget setting and variance feedback processes'. (CIMA *Official Terminology*)

ABB focuses on what the organisation actually does (its objectives) rather than on the resources it buys to do it.

If the objective of a production department is produce quality output, the techniques of ABB will focus on the activities rather than inputs.

Key features of ABB include:

- It links strategic planning with operational decisions/control
- It embodies the total quality management (TQM) philosophy
- It seeks to detect and eliminate non value adding activities

3.2 Continuous rolling budget

> **Rolling/continuous budget** is a 'budget continuously updated by adding a further accounting period (month or quarter) when the earliest accounting period has expired. Its use is particularly beneficial where future costs and/or activities cannot be forecast accurately.' (CIMA *Official Terminology*)

3.2.1 Operating a rolling budget

- 12 month budget prepared – first quarter meticulously
- At the end of the first quarter the actuals are compared to budget
- Update the budgets for the next quarter with more detail

3.2.2 Advantages

- The company has a budget 12 months into the future
- Management are more accountable due to continuous review
- Budgets are more realistic and up to date
- New goals are communicated quicker

3.2.3 Disadvantages

- There is a lot of time and resource involved in the continuous updating of budgets
- Motivation to achieve the original budget is reduced

3.3 Zero based budgeting (ZBB)

> **Zero based budgeting** is a 'method of budgeting that requires all costs to be specifically justified by the benefits expected'. (CIMA *Official Terminology*)

Zero-based budgeting (ZBB) was developed as a means of **controlling public expenditure**. Government departments are happy to spend all the money they can lay theirs hands on and usually have ambitious plans available to soak up any funds that become available. The traditional approach to public sector budgeting is to plan to fund whatever was done in the preceding period, with an allowance for inflation. The ZBB approach is to **demand fresh justification for all activities each year**.

3.3.1 Operating a zero based budget

- The budget for the next period is initially set at zero
- The choices are listed in accordance with cost benefit analysis
- The available resources are allocated based on ranking

3.3.2 Advantages of ZBB

- It can identify and remove inefficient or obsolete operations
- It can result in a more efficient allocation of resources
- It involves widespread participation
- It responds to changes in the environment

3.3.3 Disadvantages

- There is a large volume of paperwork
- There may be a lack of necessary skills in the management team
- It may emphasise short term benefits and ignore long term goals

3.4 Criticisms of traditional budgeting

According to an article in *CIMA Insider* in February 2001, 'traditional budgets hold companies back, restrict staff creativity and prevent them from responding to customers'. Jeremy Hope and Robin Fraser quote a 1998 survey which found that 88% of respondents were dissatisfied with the budgeting model. They also quote research which came up with some surprising statistics.

(a)   78% of companies do not change their budget during the annual cycle. Managers tend to 'manage around' their budgets.

(b)   60% do not link strategy and budgeting.

(c)   85% of management teams spend less than one hour a month discussing strategy.

Budgets tend to focus upon financial outputs rather than quantitative performance measures, and are not linked to employee performance. Hope and Fraser believe that organisational and behavioural changes are required, and they link these with the new business environment to suggest 'a management model that really supports strategy'. We summarise this in the table below.

Change in environment	How to succeed?	Key success factors	'Budget barriers'
• **Rising uncertainty**	• Cope with uncertainty by adapting quickly	• Devolve authority • Fast information • Strategy an adaptive process	• Too many rules • Restricted information flows • Fixed cycles are difficult to change
• **Importance of intellectual capital**	• Find (and retain) good people	• Recruit and develop good staff and set up a fair reward system	• Budgets tend to ignore people and lead to 'management by fear' and a cost-cutting mentality
• **Increasing pace of innovation**	• Create an innovative climate	• Share knowledge • See the business as a series of investments, not just components of a budget	• Central planning and bureaucracy encourage short-termism, and stifle creativity
• **Falling prices and costs**	• Operate with low costs	• Adopt a low cost network structure • Challenge costs • Align resources and costs with strategy	• Budgets prevent costs being challenged, they simply become 'entitlements'

Change in environment	How to succeed?	Key success factors	'Budget barriers'
• **Declining customer loyalty**	• Attract and keep the right customers	• Set up strong customer relationships • Establish a customer-facing strategy	• Budgeted sales targets and product focus tends to ignore customer needs
• **More demanding shareholders**	• Create consistent shareholder value	• Take a long term view of value creation • Base controls on performance	• Budgets tend to focus on the short term, with no future view

 Case Study

According to Hope and Fraser, 'giving managers control of their actions and using a few simple measures, based on key value drivers and geared to beating the competition, is all that most cases require'.

Challenging costs is inevitably part of such a process. Swedish bank Handelsbanken is a key exponent. Its low costs are the product of several factors, according to EVP finance Sven Grevelius.

(a) Small head office staff

(b) People in regions and branches are self sufficient and are measured by competitive results, which has produced an attitude keen to weed out unwarranted expenses

(c) Lower credit losses because front line staff feel more concerned to make sure that the information on which they base lending decisions is correct

(d) Central services and costs are negotiated rather than allocated

(e) Internet technology is used to reduce costs, with the benefit accruing to the customer's own branch

'Devolving responsibility for results, turning cost centres into profit centres; squeezing central costs, using technology and ... eradicating the budgeting "cost entitlement" mentality are just some of the actions we have taken to place costs under constant pressure,' says Grevelius.

4 Performance measures: financial and non-financial

5/07, 11/05

FAST FORWARD

Performance measures must be relevant to both a clear objective and to operational methods and their production must be cost-effective.

4.1 Deciding what measures to use

Clearly different measures are appropriate for different businesses. Determining which measures are used in a particular case will require **preliminary investigations** along the following lines.

(a) The **objectives/mission** of the organisation must be **clearly formulated** so that when the factors critical to the success of the mission have been identified they can be translated into performance indicators.

(b) **Measures** must be **relevant** to the way the organisation operates. Managers themselves must believe the indicators are useful.

(c) **The costs and benefits of providing resources** (people, equipment and time to collect and analyse information) to produce a performance indicator must be carefully **weighed up**.

4.2 Financial modelling and performance measurement

> Profitability, activity and productivity are the basic material of performance measurement, but measures cannot be established in isolation for the strategy plans and tasks of the organisation.

Financial modelling might assist in performance evaluation in the following ways.

(a) **Identifying the variables** involved in performing tasks and the relationships between them. This is necessary so that the model can be built in the first place. Model building therefore shows what should be measured, helps to explain how a particular level of performance can be achieved, and identifies factors in performance that the organisation cannot expect to control.

(b) **Setting targets for future performance**. The most obvious example of this is the budgetary control system described above.

(c) **Monitoring actual performance**. A flexible budget is a good example of a financial model that is used in this way.

(d) **Co-ordinating long-term strategic plans with short term operational actions.** Modelling can reflect the dynamic nature of the real world and evaluate how likely it is that short-term actions will achieve the longer-term plan, given new conditions.

4.3 Profitability, activity and productivity

In general, there are three possible **points of reference for measurement**.

(a) **Profitability**

Profit has two components: **cost and income**. All parts of an organisation and all activities within it incur costs, and so their success needs to be judged in relation to cost. Only some parts of an organisation receive income, and their success should be judged in terms of both cost and income.

(b) **Activity**

All parts of an organisation are also engaged in activities (activities cause costs). Activity measures could include the following.

(i)   Number of orders received from customers, a measure of the effectiveness of marketing
(ii) Number of machine breakdowns attended to by the repairs and maintenance department

Each of these items could be measured in terms of **physical numbers**, **monetary value**, or **time spent**.

(c) **Productivity**

This is the quantity of the product or service produced in relation to the resources put in, for example so many units produced per hour or per employee. It defines how efficiently resources are being used.

The **dividing line between productivity and activity is thin**, because every activity could be said to have some 'product', or if not can be measured in terms of lost units of product or service.

Question	Invoicing

Learning outcome D(i)

An invoicing assistant works in a department with three colleagues. She is paid £8,000 per annum. The department typically handles 10,000 invoices per week.

One morning she spends half an hour on the phone to her grandfather, who lives in Australia, at the company's expense. The cost of the call proves to be £32.

Required

From this scenario identify as many different performance measures as possible, explaining what each is intended to measure. Make any further assumptions you wish.

Invoices per employee per week: 2,500 (activity)
Staff cost per invoice: £0.06 (cost/profitability)
Invoices per hour: 2,500/(7 × 5) = 71.4 (productivity)
Cost of idle time: £32 + £2.14 = £34.14 (cost/profitability)

You may have thought of other measures and probably have slight rounding differences.

4.4 Financial performance measures

Financial measures (or **monetary measures**) are very familiar to you. Here are some examples, accompanied by comments from a single page of the *Financial Times*.

Measure	Comment
Profit	The commonest measure of all. Profit maximisation is usually cited as the main objective of most business organisations: 'ICI increased pre-tax profits to £233m'; 'General Motors... yesterday reported better-than-expected first-quarter net income of $513 (£333m) ...
Revenue	'The US businesses contributed £113.9m of total group turnover of £409m'.
Costs	'Sterling's fall benefited pre-tax profits by about £50m while savings from the cost-cutting programme were running at around £100m a quarter'; 'The group interest charge rose from £48m to £61m'.
Share price	'The group's shares rose 31p to 1278p despite the market's fall'.
Cash flow	'Cash flow was also continuing to improve, with cash and marketable securities totalling $8.4bn on March 31, up from $8bn at December 31'.

The important point to note here is that the monetary amounts stated **are only given meaning in relation to something else**. Profits are higher than last year's; cashflow has improved compared with last quarter's.

We can generalise the above and give a list of yard-sticks against which financial results are usually placed so as to become measures.

- **Budgeted** sales, costs and profits
- **Standards** in a standard costing system
- The **trend** over time (last year/this year, say)
- The **results of other parts** of the business
- The **results of other businesses**
- The **economy** in general
- **Future potential** (eg a new business in terms of nearness to breaking even)

Question

Profit

Learning outcome D(i)

Choose the appropriate word(s) in the following statements and decide whether each correct statement is an advantage or a disadvantage of the use of the profit measure.

(a)   Management theory suggests that there is an advantage/there is no advantage in having a single objective.

(b)   Encourages/does not encourage short-termism.

(c)   Profit is always/not always a simple concept.

(d)   Profit makes quantitative analysis possible/impossible.

(e)   Non-financial factors are not important/are important in long-term performance measurement.

(f)   Profit is a broad/narrow performance measure.

(g) Profit fails to allow for/enables decentralisation.

(h) Profit is/is not the sole short-term objective of a firm.

(i) Profit motivates/does not motivate cost centre managers.

(j) Profit enable/does not enable unlike units to be compared.

(k) Profit motivates and educates managers/does not motivate and educate managers.

(l) Profit is always/not always an effective measure for controlling managerial performance.

(m) Profit should be/should not be related to risk, as well as to capital employed.

Answer

Advantages

(a) Management theory suggests that there is an advantage in having a single objective.

(d) Profit makes quantitative analysis possible.

(f) Profit is a broad performance measure.

(g) Profit enables decentralisation.

(j) Profit enables unlike units to be compared.

(k) Profit motivates and educates managers.

Disadvantages

(b) Profit encourages short-termism.

(c) Profit is not always a simple concept.

(e) Non-financial factors are important in long-term performance measurement.

(h) Profit is not the sole short-term objective of a firm.

(i) Profit does not motivate cost centre managers.

(l) Profit is not always an effective measure for controlling managerial performance.

(m) Profit should be related to risk, as well as to capital employed.

4.5 The profit measure

Profit has both advantages and disadvantages as a measure of performance, as outlined in an article in the August 1998 *CIMA Student*.

Advantages	Comment
Single criterion	Easier to manage, as the sole concern is the effect on the bottom line
Analysis has a clear objective: ie the effect on future profits.	Easier than cost/benefit analysis, for example
A broad performance measure that incorporates all other measures	'If it does not affect profit it can be ignored.'
Enables decentralisation	Managers have the delegated powers to achieve divisional (and therefore group) profit.
Profitability measures (eg ROI) can compare all profit-making operations even if they are not alike.	This ignores the balance between risk and return.
Management motivation and education	Bonuses based on simple profit targets are easy to understand.

Disadvantages	Comment
Encourages **short-termism** and focus on the annual cycle, at the expense of long term performance	Examples: cutting discretionary revenue investments, manipulating of accounting rules, building up stocks

Disadvantages	Comment
Profit differs from **economic income**.	
A firm has to satisfy **stakeholders** other than shareholders, such as the government and the local community.	This may include environmental/ethical performance measures.
Liquidity is at least as important as profit.	Most business failures derive from liquidity crises.
Profit should be related to **risk**, not just capital employed.	Rarely done
Profits can **fluctuate** in times of rapid change.	For example, as a result of exchange rate volatility
Profit measures cannot easily be used to motivate **cost centre** managers.	They do not control profit.
Not useful for new businesses	Most startups will be unprofitable for at least two years.
Easily manipulated	Especially over a single period: think back to your cost accounting studies and the effect of stock changes on profit under absorption costing, for example
Pure profit based measures do not consider **capital spending**.	Growth in asset levels can be uncontrolled; alternatively, productive capacity may be allowed to decline.

4.5.1 Ratios

Ratios are a **useful** way of measuring performance for a number of reasons.

(a)   It is easier to look at **changes over time** by comparing ratios in one time period with the corresponding ratios for periods in the past.

(b)   Ratios are often **easier to understand** than absolute measures of physical quantities or money values. For example, it is easier to understand that 'productivity in March was 94%' than 'there was an adverse labour efficiency variance in March of £3,600'.

(c)   Ratios relate one item to another, and so help to **put performance into context**. For example the profit/sales ratio sets profit in the context of how much has been earned per £1 of sales, and so shows how wide or narrow profit margins are.

(d)   Ratios can be **used as targets**. In particular, targets can be set for ROI, profit/sales, asset turnover, capacity fill and productivity. Managers will then take decisions which will enable them to achieve their targets.

(e)   Ratios provide a way of **summarising an organisation's results**, and **comparing them with similar organisations**.

4.5.2 Percentages

A percentage expresses one number as a proportion of another and gives meaning to absolute numbers.

Example	Comment
Market share	A company may aim to achieve a 25% share of the total market for its product, and measure both its marketing department and the quality of the product against this.
Capacity levels	These are usually measured in percentages. 'Factory A is working at 20% below full capacity' is an example which indicates relative inefficiency.
Wastage	This is sometimes expressed in percentage terms. 'Normal loss' may be 10%, a measure of inefficiency.

Example	Comment
Staff turnover	This is often measured in this way. In the catering industry for example, staff turnover is typically greater than 100%, and so a hotel with a lower percentage could take this as an indicator both of the experience of its staff and of how well it is treating them.

4.6 Quantitative and qualitative performance measures

It is possible to distinguish between **quantitative information**, which is **capable of being expressed in numbers**, and **qualitative information**, which **can only be expressed in numerical terms with difficulty**.

An example of a quantitative performance measure is 'You have been late for work twice this week and it's only Tuesday!'. An example of a qualitative performance measure is 'My bed is very comfortable'.

The first measure is likely to find its way into a staff appraisal report. The second would feature in a bed manufacturer's customer satisfaction survey. Both are indicators of whether their subjects are doing as good a job as they are required to do.

Qualitative measures are by nature **subjective and judgmental** but this does not mean that they are not valuable. They are especially valuable when they are derived from several different sources because then they can be expressed in a mixture of quantitative and qualitative terms which is more meaningful overall: 'seven out of ten customers think our beds are very comfortable' is a quantitative measure of customer satisfaction as well as a **qualitative** measure of the perceived performance of the beds.

4.7 Measuring performance in the new business environment

FAST FORWARD

Growing dissatisfaction with financial performance measures has led to other measures being developed, based on **operational performance**.

In the June 1998 edition of *Management Accounting*, Jeremy Hope and Robin Fraser argued that if organisations are serious about gaining real benefits from decentralisation and empowerment, they need to **change the way in which they set targets, measure performance and design reward systems.** (The emphasis and heading are BPP's.)

Targets and responsibilities

'The SBU [strategic business unit] manager is once again asked for a **'stretch target'**. However, under this management model [suggested by Hope and Fraser] she knows that 'stretch' really means her best shot with **full support** from the centre (including investment funds and improvement programmes) and a sympathetic hearing should she fail to get all of the way. Moreover, she alone carries the **responsibility** for achieving these targets. There is neither any micro-management from above, nor any monthly 'actual versus budget' reports. **Targets are both strategic and financial**, and they are underpinned by clear action plans that cascade down the organisation, building **ownership and commitment at every level**. Monthly reports comprise a **balanced scorecard set** of graphs, charts and trends that track progress (eg financial, customer satisfaction, speed, quality, service, and employee satisfaction) **compared with** last year and with other **SBUs within the group** and, where possible, with **competitors**. Quarterly **rolling forecasts** (broad-brush numbers only) are also prepared to help manage production scheduling and cash requirements but they are not part of the measurement and reward process.

Performance review

Of course, if there is a significant blip in performance (and the fast/open information system would flag this immediately), then a performance review would be signalled. Such reviews focus on the effectiveness of action plans and what further improvements need to be made and maybe even whether the targets (and measures) themselves are still appropriate.'

There are a number of reasons why this approach is **successful**.

(a)   Managers are not punished for failing to reach the full target.

(b) The use of the balanced scorecard ensures that all key perspectives are considered.

(c) Because managers set their own targets and plan the changes needed to achieve them, real ownership and commitment are built. Feedback and learning takes place as a result of the tracking of action plans. (Contrast this with numerical variances that tell managers nothing about what to do differently in the future).

(d) Beating internal and external competitors is a constant spur to better performance.

(e) Managers share in an bonus pool that is based on share price or long-term performance against a basket of competitors. Resource and knowledge sharing is therefore encouraged.

4.8 Non-financial performance measures

It is worth remembering that performance measures can be both financial and non financial.

Key term

> **Non-financial performance measures** are 'measures of performance based on non-financial information which may originate in and be used by operating departments to monitor and control their activities without any accounting input. Non-financial performance measures may give a more timely indication of the levels of performance achieved than financial measures do, and may be less susceptible to distortion by factors such as uncontrollable variations in the effect of market forces on operations.'
>
> (CIMA *Official Terminology*)

Here are some examples of non-financial performance measures.

Areas assessed	Performance measure
Service quality	Number of complaints
	Proportion of repeat bookings
	Customer waiting time
	On-time deliveries
Production performance	Set-up times
	Number of suppliers
	Days' inventory in hand
	Output per employee
	Material yield percentage
	Schedule adherence
	Proportion of output requiring rework
	Manufacturing lead times
Marketing effectiveness	Trend in market share
	Sales volume growth
	Customer visits per salesperson
	Client contact hours per salesperson
	Sales volume forecast v actual
	Number of customers
	Customer survey response information
Personnel	Number of complaints received
	Staff turnover
	Days lost through absenteeism
	Days lost through accidents/sickness
	Training time per employee

Question

Learning outcome D(i)

Draw up a list of performance criteria for a hotel.

Answer

Financial performance: profit and loss per department, variance analysis (eg expenditure on wages, power, catering, bedrooms and so on).

Competitive performance: market share (room occupied on a total percentage of rooms available locally); competitor occupancy; competitor prices; bookings; vacant rooms as a proportion of the total attitudes of particular market segments.

Resource utilisation: rooms occupied/rooms available service quality measure: complaints, room checks.

Quality of service: Complaints, results of questionnaires

The beauty of non-financial performance measures is that **anything can be compared if it is meaningful to do so**. The measures should be tailored to the circumstances so that, for example, number of coffee breaks per 20 pages of Study Text might indicate to you how hard you are studying!

4.8.1 The advantages and disadvantages of non-financial measures

Unlike traditional variance reports, they can be provided **quickly** for managers, per shift or on a daily or hourly basis as required. They are likely to be **easy to calculate**, and **easier for non-financial managers to understand** and therefore to use effectively.

There are problems associated with choosing the measures and there is a danger that **too many such measures could be reported**, overloading managers with information that is not truly useful, or that sends conflicting signals. There is clearly a need for the information provider to work more closely with the managers who will be using the information to make sure that their needs are properly understood.

Research on more than 3,000 companies in Europe and North America has shown that the strongest drivers of competitive achievement are the intangible factors, especially **intellectual property, innovation** and **quality.** Non-financial measures have been at the forefront of an increasing trend towards **customer focus** (such as TQM), **process re-engineering** programmes and the creation of **internal markets** within organisations.

Arguably, non-financial measures are **less likely to be manipulated** than traditional profit-related measures and they should, therefore, **offer a means of counteracting short-termism**, since short-term profit at any expense is rarely an advisable goal.

Remember

> The ultimate goal of commercial organisations in the long run is likely to remain the maximisation of profit, and so the **financial aspect cannot be ignored**.

A further danger is that they might lead managers to pursue detailed operational goals and become blind to the overall strategy in which those goals are set. A combination of financial and non–financial measures is likely to be most successful.

4.8.2 The performance measurement manifesto

Eccles argues that financial measures alone are inadequate for monitoring the progress of business strategies based on creating customer value, satisfaction and quality, partly because they are **historical** in nature and partly they cannot measure current progress with such strategies directly. He also notes the impulse to **short-termism** given by such measures. There is a need for a performance measurement system that includes both financial and non-financial measures. The measures chosen must be **integrated**, so that the potential for discarding non-financial measures that conflict with the financial ones is limited.

Eccles says that the development of a good system of performance measurement requires activity in five areas.

(a) The **information architecture** must be developed. This requires the identification of performance measures that relate to strategy and the gradual, iterative development of systems to capture the required data.

(b) An appropriate **information technology strategy** must be established.

(c) The company's **incentives system** must be aligned with its performance measures. Eccles proposes that qualitative factors should be addressed by the incentive system.

(d) **External influences** must be acknowledged and used. For example, benchmarking against other organisations may be used, while providers of capital should be persuaded to accept the validity of non-financial measures.

(e) **Manage the implementation** of the four areas above by appointing a person to be responsible overall as well as department agents.

4.9 Value for money (VFM) audits

Value for money audits can be seen as being of particular relevance in not-for-profit organisations. Such an audit focuses on **economy, efficiency** and **effectiveness.** These measures may be in conflict with each other. To take the example of higher education, larger class sizes may be **economical** in their use of teaching resources, but are not necessarily **effective** in creating the best learning environment.

 Case Study

A recent study by the Public Management Foundation has found that public sector managers are concerned largely with 'making a difference' in the community. Improving services and increasing the satisfaction of those using them were the two most important goals.

While the introduction of private sector management techniques in the 1980s has served to sharpen the attention given to financial performance, public sector managers rated the value of financial management lower than service improvement.

5 The balanced scorecard   Pilot paper, 11/06

FAST FORWARD

An approach that tries to integrate the different measures of performance is the **balanced scorecard**, where key linkages between operating and financial performance are brought to light. This offers four perspectives

- Financial
- Customer
- Innovation and learning
- Internal business

A theme so far has been that financial measurements do not capture all the strategic realities of the business, but it is possible to go too far in this direction. A failure to attend to the 'numbers' can rapidly lead to a failure of the business.

 Case Study

The fall from grace of Digital Equipment, in the past second only to IBM in the world computer rankings, was examined in a *Financial Times* article. The downfall is blamed on Digital's failure to keep up with the development of the PC, but also on the company's culture.

The company was founded on brilliant creativity, but was insufficiently focused on the bottom line. Outside the finance department, monetary issues were considered vulgar and organisational structure was chaotic. Costs were not a core part of important decisions – 'if expenditure was higher than budget, the problem was simply a bad budget'. Ultimately the low-price world of lean competitors took its toll, leading to huge losses.

Financial measurements do not capture all the strategic realities of a business. A technique which has been developed to integrate the various features (financial and non-financial) of corporate success is *Kaplan and Norton's* **balanced scorecard**.

Key term

> The **balanced scorecard** approach is 'an approach to the provision of information to management to assist strategic policy formulation and achievement. It emphasises the need to provide the user with a set of information which addresses all relevant areas of performance in an objective and unbiased fashion. The information provided may include both financial and non-financial elements, and cover areas such as profitability, customer satisfaction, internal efficiency and innovation.' (CIMA *Official Terminology*)

The balanced scorecard seeks to translate mission and strategy into objectives and measures, and focuses on **four different perspectives**, as follows.

The balanced scorecard

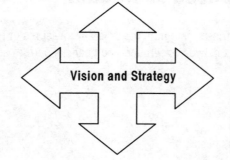

Financial Perspective

How should we create value for our shareholders to succeed financially? (covers traditional measures such as growth, profitability and shareholder value, with measures set through talking directly to the shareholders)

Customer Perspective

To achieve our vision, how should we appear to our customers? What do new and existing customers value from us? (cost, quality, reliability etc)

Vision and Strategy

Internal Business Process

What business processes what must we excel at to achieve financial and customer objectives?

Innovation and Learning Perspective

How can we continue to create value and maintain the company's competitive position through improvement and change? (acquisition of new skills; development of new products)

Performance targets are set once the key areas for improvement have been identified, and the balanced scorecard is the **main monthly report**.

The scorecard is **balanced** in the sense that managers are required to think in terms of all four perspectives, to **prevent improvements being made in one area at the expense of another.**

Broadbent and Cullen identify the following **important features** of this approach.

- It looks at both **internal and external matters** concerning the organisation
- It is related to the key elements of a company's strategy
- Financial and non-financial measures are linked together

5.1 Problems

As with all techniques, problems can arise when it is applied.

Problem	Explanation
Conflicting measures	Some measures in the scorecard such as research funding and cost reduction may naturally conflict. It is often difficult to determine the balance which will achieve the best results.
Selecting measures	Not only do appropriate measures have to be devised but the number of measures used must be agreed. Care must be taken that the impact of the results is not lost in a sea of information. The innovation and learning perspective is, perhaps, the most difficult to measure directly, since much development of human capital will not feed directly into such crude measures as rate of new product launches or even training hours undertaken. It will, rather, improve economy and effectiveness and support the achievement of customer perspective measures.
Expertise	Measurement is only useful if it initiates appropriate action. Non-financial managers may have difficulty with the usual profit measures. With more measures to consider this problem will be compounded.
Interpretation	Even a financially-trained manager may have difficulty in putting the figures into an overall perspective.

The scorecard should be used **flexibly.** The process of deciding **what to measure** forces a business to clarify its strategy. For example, a manufacturing company may find that 50% – 60% of costs are represented by bought-in components, so measurements relating to suppliers could usefully be added to the scorecard. These could include payment terms, lead times, or quality considerations.

5.2 Linkages

Disappointing results might result from a **failure to view all the measures as a whole**. For example, increasing productivity means that fewer employees are needed for a given level of output. Excess capacity can be created by quality improvements. However these improvements have to be exploited (eg by increasing sales). The **financial element** of the balanced scorecard 'reminds executives that improved quality, response time, productivity or new products, benefit the company only when they are translated into improved financial results', or if they enable the firm to obtain a sustainable competitive advantage.

5.3 The vertical vector

Kaplan and Norton's original perspectives may be viewed as hierarchical in nature, with a **vertical vector** running through the measures adopted.

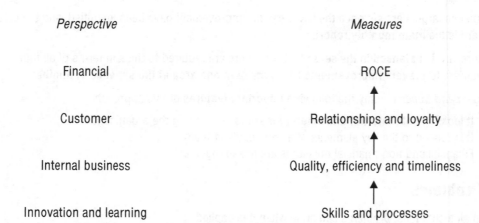

Perspective	Measures
Financial	ROCE
Customer	Relationships and loyalty
Internal business	Quality, efficiency and timeliness
Innovation and learning	Skills and processes

The balanced scorecard only measures performance. It does not indicate that the strategy is the right one. 'A failure to convert improved operational performance into improved financial performance should send executives back to their drawing boards to rethink the company's strategy or its implementation plans.'

5.4 Implementing the balanced scorecard

The introduction and practical use of the balanced scorecard is likely to be subject to all the problems associated with balancing long-term strategic progress against the management of short-term tactical imperatives. Kaplan and Norton recognise this and recommend an iterative, four-stage approach to the practical problems involved.

(a) **Translating the vision**: the organisation's mission must be expressed in a way that has to be clear operational meaning for each employee.

(b) **Communicating and linking**: the next stage is to link the vision or mission to departmental and individual objectives, including those that transcend traditional short-term financial goals.

(c) **Business planning**: the scorecard is used to prioritise objectives and allocate resources in order to make the best progress towards strategic goals.

(d) **Feedback and learning**: the organisation learns to use feedback on performance to promote progress against all four perspectives.

5.5 Example

An example of how a balanced scorecard might appear is offered below.

Balanced Scorecard

Financial Perspective

GOALS	MEASURES
Survive	Cash flow
Succeed	Monthly sales growth and operating income by division
Prosper	Increase market share and ROI

Customer Perspective

GOALS	MEASURES
New products	Parcentage of sales from new products
Responsive supply	On-time delivery (defined by customer)
Preferred supplier	Share off key accounts' purchases
	Ranking by key accounts
Customer partnership	Number of cooperative engineering efforts

Internal Business Perspective

GOALS	MEASURES
Technology capability	Manufacturing configuration vs competition
Manufacturing excellence	Cycle time Unit cost Yield
Design productivity	Silicon efficiency Engineering efficiency
New product introduction	Actual introduction schedule vs plan

Innovation and Learning Perspective

GOALS	MEASURES
Technology leadership	Time to develop next generation products
Manufacturing learning	Process time to maturity
Product focus	Percentage of products that equate to 80% sales
Time to market	New product introduction vs competition

 Case Study

An oil company (quoted by Kaplan and Norton, *Harvard Business Review*) ties:

- 60% of its executives' bonuses to their achievement of ambitious financial targets on ROI, profitability, cash flow and operating cost
- 40% on indicators of customer satisfaction, retailer satisfaction, employee satisfaction and environmental responsibility

5.6 Using the balanced scorecard

(a) Like all performance measurement schemes, the balanced scorecard can influence behaviour among managers to conform to that required by the strategy. Because of its comprehensive nature, it can be used as a wide-ranging driver of organisational change.

(b) The scorecard emphasises **processes** rather than **departments**. It can support a competence-based approach to strategy, but this can be confusing for managers and may make it difficult to gain their support.

(c) Deciding just what to measure can be especially difficult, especially since the scorecard **vertical vector** lays emphasis on customer reaction. This is not to discount the importance of meeting customer expectations, purely to emphasise the difficulty of establishing what they are.

A word of warning

Kaplan and Norton never intended the balanced scorecard to replace all other performance measurement systems a business may use. They acknowledge that financial measures and financial results remain important, but suggest business can use the BSC to help deliver strategic goods.

6 Other multidimensional measures of performance

FAST FORWARD

The **performance pyramid** derives from the idea that an organisation operates at different levels, each of which has different (but supporting) concerns.

6.1 Performance across a range of dimensions

There have been a number of ideas concerning the measurement of performance across a range of dimensions. For example, as long ago as 1952 General Electric undertook a measurements project which concluded that there were eight key results areas (or critical success factors).

- Profitability
- Market position
- Productivity
- Product leadership
- Personnel development
- Employee attitudes
- Public responsibility
- Short v long term balance

6.2 The performance pyramid

The **performance pyramid** derives from the idea that an organisation operates at different levels, each of which has different concerns (which should nevertheless support each other in achieving business objectives). They therefore require different performance measures.

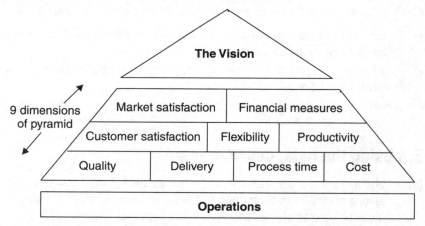

Note: When looking at any appraisal of costs it is crucial to understand the **processes driving** the costs rather then simply looking at them as figures in the management accounts.

(a)   At **corporate level** the vision is developed and financial and market objectives are set in accordance with it.

(b)   At **strategic business unit** level, strategies are developed to achieve these financial and market objectives.

(i) **Customer satisfaction** is defined as meeting customer expectations

(ii) **Flexibility** indicates responsiveness of the business operating system as a whole

(iii) **Productivity** refers to the management of resources such as labour and time

(c) These in turn are supported by more specific **operational** criteria.

(i) **Quality** of the product or service, consistency of product and fit for the purpose

(ii) **Delivery** of the product or service, ie the method of distribution, its speed and ease of management

(iii) **Cycle time** of all processes from cash collection to order processing to recruitment

(iv) **Cost** (or waste) meaning the elimination of all non value added activities

The pyramid highlights the links running between the **vision for the company** and **functional objectives**. It hopes to ensure not only goal congruence but also a consistency of performance across all business areas, and a balanced approach.

7 Performance: service departments and firms

FAST FORWARD

Performance is more difficult to measure where there is no physical product. Services are intangible, they are consumed at the same time as they are produced and they cannot be stored. This leads to measures of performance based on output productivity and effectiveness.

7.1 Service departments

Measuring performance in a service department will focus management attention on matters such as the following.

- How the service department is using up resources of the organisation
- What its resources are costing
- Whether the department should be capable of improved efficiency and lower costs

The principles of control theory still apply, so that a system of performance evaluation for service departments or selling activities needs:

(a) A **budget, standard or target** for the department to work towards

(b) A system of **measuring actual performance** and comparing it against the budget, standard or target

(c) A system for deciding when **control action** ought to be considered

7.1.1 Setting a standard, budget or target

A standard, budget or target can be set for a service department in a number of ways.

(a) There might be a budgeted expenditure limit for the department.

(b) **Standard performance measures** might be established as targets for efficiency. Standard performance measures are possible where the department carries out routine activities for much of its work.

(c) Targets or standards might be set for the **quality of the service**.

(i) To provide training to employees up to a quantifiable standard

(ii) To respond to requests for help within a specified number of minutes, hours or days

(iii) To respond to materials requisitions within a specified period of time

(d) To perform a **targeted quantity of work** with a budgeted number of staff.

(e) **To meet schedules for completing certain work**.

(i) Scheduled dates for completion of each stage in a product development project in the R&D department

(ii) Scheduled dates for the DP department to complete each stage of a new computer project

(f)   **To make a profit**. A service department might be designated as a profit centre. It would charge other departments for the services it provides at a 'commercial' transfer price rate, and it would be expected to earn a 'profit' on the work it does.

7.1.2 Standards for cost or efficiency

Two methods of setting a standard measure of performance in a service department are:

- Standard cost per unit of activity
- Standard quantity of 'output' per unit of resource used up

With both methods, there has to be a measurable quantity or volume of activity in the department. Both types of standard can be employed within a control system, and they are not mutually exclusive.

Examples of standard measures of performance in service departments might be as follows.

(a)   In the accounts receivable section of an accounts department, for example, the volume of activity could be measured by:

(i)   Number or value of invoices issued
(ii)   Number or value of payments received
(iii)   The number or value of bad debts

A budget for the section could then establish a standard cost per invoice issued, or a standard cost per £1 received or receivable, or a standard % of bad debts. In addition, there could be standards for the number or value of invoices issued per man/day.

(b)   In a sales department, activity could be measured by the number and value of orders taken, the number of customer visits, or the number of miles travelled by sales representatives. There could be a standard cost per customer visit, a standard cost per £1 of sales, and so on. Alternatively, standards could be set for the amount of work done per unit of resource consumed, and in a sales department, such standards include:

(i)   Standard number of customer visits per salesperson per day
(ii)   Standard number and value of sales per customer visit
(iii)   Standard number of miles travelled per £1 of sales

(c)   In a transport department, activity could be measured in tonne/miles (tonnes of goods delivered and miles travelled) and standards could be established for:

(i)   Cost per tonne/mile
(ii)   Drivers' hours per tonne/mile
(iii)   Miles per gallon consumed

7.1.3 Measuring and evaluating performance

Once a target, budget or standard has been set, we have a basis for evaluating performance, by comparing actual results against the target.

7.1.4 Indices of 'output' in a service department

Standards for work done in a service department could be expressed as an index. For example, suppose that in a sales department, there is a standard target for sales representatives to make 25 customer visits per month each. The budget for May 19X5 might be for ten sales representatives to make 250 customer visits in total. Actual results in May might be that nine sales representatives made 234 visits in total.

Performance could then be measured as:

Budget   100   (Standard = index 100)

Actual   104 $\left(\dfrac{234}{9 \times 25} \times 100 \right)$

This shows that 'productivity' per sales representative was actually 4% over budget.

Advantages of indices are as follows.

(a) They are easily understood.

(b) Once established, they can be used to evaluate:

    (i) Actual results in a period against the standard

    (ii) Trends in productivity over time

(c) They can incorporate a 'basket' of different types of job. In the example of customer visits by sales representatives, not all customer visits are the same. Travelling time to some customers will be longer than to others, and some customers will take longer to deal with than others. With indexing, weightings can be given to different types of visit.

7.1.5 Selecting measures of performance

Key item(s) of performance to be measured should be identified. Examples include return, growth, productivity, market share, and cost control.

(a) Return can be measured as ROI, RI, profit and so on.

(b) Growth can be measured by sales growth, profit growth, investment spending, capacity fill and so on.

(c) Productivity measures can be applied to machinery as well as labour.

(d) Market position and status, or quality of product/service, could be measured by market research, or through customer responses and complaints.

(e) Cost control involves identifying the nature of the costs that ought to be controlled and comparing actual spending with budget.

This can be applied to the finance function.

(a) **Define the boundaries** of the finance function. Does it include data processing, for example, or stock control or treasury management?

(b) **Define formal objectives** for the function as a whole, and then for each main section, for supervisory and managerial staff and for the operation of systems (for example payroll).

(c) Ascertain what **activities** each section does (or should do) to achieve its objectives.

(d) **Identify appropriate measures**, on the basis of the objectives and activities identified. The 'pyramid' approach should be used, with successively more detailed information for successively junior levels of staff.

(e) Select suitable **bases of comparison**. Possibilities are time, budgets, standards or targets, intra-group comparison, or intra-organisational comparison, if verifiably comparable data is available.

7.2 Types of service organisation

Lin Fitzgerald et al, identify three different types of service organisation, as follows.

(a) **Professional services**, for example a management consultancy. Such services are characterised as being highly adaptable to individual customer needs, dependent upon staff/customer contact, people-based and relying on short chains of command and highly autonomous employees.

(b) **Mass services**, for example rail travel. These involve little customisation and limited customer contact, they are predominantly equipment-based and require defined tasks and set procedures to be performed with little exercise of judgement.

(c) **Service shops**, for example, a bank. These fall between the above extremes in terms of customisation, customer contact, people/equipment and levels of staff discretion.

7.3 Results and determinants

The results and determinants framework may be used for measuring service provision.

Fitzgerald *et al* advocate the use of a range of performance measures covering six 'dimensions' in what is known as the **results and determinants framework**.

(a) **Results**

    (i)   **Competitive performance**, focusing on factors such as sales growth and market share.

    (ii)   **Financial performance**, concentrating on profitability, liquidity, capital structure and market ratios.

(b) **Determinants** (of those results)

    (i)   **Quality of service** looks at matters like reliability, courtesy, competence and availability. These can be measured by customer satisfaction surveys.

    (ii)   **Flexibility** is an apt heading for assessing the organisation's ability to deliver at the right speed, to respond to precise customer specifications, and to cope with fluctuations in demand.

    (iii)   **Resource utilisation** considers how efficiently resources are being utilised. This can be problematic because of the complexity of the inputs to a service and the outputs from it and because some of the inputs are supplied by the customer.

    (iv)   **Innovation** is assessed in terms of both the innovation process and the success of individual innovations. Individual innovations can be measured in terms of whether they have improved the organisation's ability to meet the other five performance criteria.

8 Performance: manufacturing

A wide range of measures exists for measuring manufacturing performance. They range from simple cost/output efficiency measures to more complex ideas relating to quality and innovation.

A number of performance indicators can be used to assess operations. They are particularly relevant to the internal business and customer perspectives of the balanced scorecard.

- Quality
- Number of customer complaints and warranty claims
- Lead times
- Rework
- Delivery to time
- Non-productive hours
- System (machine) down time

These indicators can also be expressed in the form of ratios or percentages for comparative purposes. Like physical measures, they can be produced quickly and trends can be identified and acted upon rapidly. Examples of useful ratios might be as follows.

(a) **Machine down time: total machine hours**. This ratio could be used to monitor machine availability and can provide a measure of machine usage and efficiency.

(b) **Component rejects: component purchases**. This ratio could be used to control the quality of components purchased from an external supplier. This measure can be used to monitor the performance of new suppliers.

(c) **Deliveries late: deliveries on schedule**. This ratio could be applied to sales made to customers as well as to receipts from suppliers.

(d) **Customer rejects/returns: total sales**. This ratio helps to monitor customer satisfaction, providing a check on the efficiency of quality control procedures.

(e) **Value added time: production cycle time**. Value added time is the direct production time during which the product is being made and value is therefore being added.

8.1 Advanced manufacturing technology

The advent of **advanced manufacturing technology (AMT)** has meant that many organisations will need to modify their performance measures so that the information they provide will be useful in controlling operations in the new manufacturing environment.

8.2 Performance measurement for manufacturing

Performance measurement in manufacturing is increasingly using non-financial measures. Malcolm Smith identifies four over-arching measures for manufacturing environments.

- **Cost**: cost behaviour
- **Quality**: factors inhibiting performance
- **Time**: bottlenecks, inertia
- **Innovation**: new product flexibility

8.2.1 Cost

Possible non-financial or part-financial indicators are as follows.

Area	Measure
Quantity of raw material inputs	Actual v target number
Equipment productivity	Actual v standard units
Maintenance efforts	No. of production units lost through maintenance No. of production units lost through failure No. of failures prior to schedule
Overtime costs	Overtime hours/total hours
Product complexity	No. of component parts
Quantity of output	Actual v target completion
Product obsolescence	% shrinkage
Employees	% staff turnover
Employee productivity	direct labour hours per unit
Customer focus	% service calls; % claims

8.2.2 Quality

Integrating quality into a performance measurement system suggests attention to the following items.

Area	Measure
Quality of purchased components	Zero defects
Equipment failure	Downtime/total time
Maintenance effort	Breakdown maintenance/total maintenance
Waste	% defects; % scrap; % rework
Quality of output	% yield
Safety	Serious industrial injury rate
Reliability	% warranty claims
Quality commitment	% dependence on post-inspection % conformance to quality standards
Employee morale	% absenteeism
Leadership impact	% cancelled meetings
Customer awareness	% repeat orders; number of complaints

> **Total quality management (TQM)** is an 'integrated and comprehensive system of planning and controlling all business functions so that products or services are produced which meet or exceed customer expectations. TQM is a philosophy of business behaviour, embracing principles such as employee involvement, continuous improvement at all levels and customer focus, as well as being a collection of related techniques aimed at improving quality such as full documentation of activities, clear goal-setting and performance measurement from the customer perspective.' (CIMA *Official Terminology*)

8.2.3 Time

A truly just-in-time system is an ideal to which many manufacturing firms are striving. Time-based competition is also important for new product development, deliveries etc. The management accounting focus might be on throughput, bottlenecks, customer feedback and distribution.

Area	Measure
Equipment failure	Time between failures
Maintenance effort	Time spent on repeat work
Throughput	Processing time/total time per unit
Production flexibility	Set-up time
Availability	% stockouts
Labour effectiveness	Standard hours achieved / total hours worked
Customer impact	No. of overdue deliveries Mean delivery delay

8.2.4 Innovation

Performance indicators for innovation can support the 'innovation and learning' perspective on the balanced scorecard. Some possible suggestions are outlined below.

Area	Measure
The ability to introduce new products	% product obsolescence Number of new products launched Number of patents secured Time to launch new products
Flexibility to accommodate change	Number of new processes implemented Number of new process modifications
Reputation for innovation	Media recognition for leadership Expert assessment of competence Demonstrable competitive advantage

8.3 Activity based measures of performance

Many writers have seen the potential of the activity-based approach to management accounting to provide new performance indicators. For example, if the number of purchase requisitions is a cost driver for a number of purchasing, receiving and accounting activities then it would be possible to compare the resources which ought to be employed to process a given number of requisitions with the resources actually employed.

8.4 Use of experience curves

As we have seen in Chapter 9, the **experience curve** can be used in strategic control of costs. It suggests that as output increases, the cost per unit of output falls. To recap, this results from:

(a) **Economies of scale** – in other words an increased volume of production leads to lower unit costs, as the firm approaches full capacity.

(b) A genuine **'learning effect'** as the workforce becomes familiar with the job and learns to carry out the task more efficiently. As a process is repeated, it is likely that costs will reduce due to **efficiency, discounts** and **reduced waste**.

(c) **Technological improvements**.

8.5 Target costing

This brings us on to **target costing**, an approach used in Japan. This is based on the principle that a product must have a target price that will succeed in winning a target share of the market.

When a product is first manufactured, the **target cost** will usually be well below the current cost, which is determined by current technology and processes, and experience effects. Management then sets benchmarks for improvement towards the target costs, by improving technologies and processes.

Target costing is thus in effect a process of establishing what the cost of the product should be over the entire **product life cycle**.

(a) In the short run, because of development costs and the learning time needed, costs are likely to exceed price.

(b) In the longer term, costs should come down (eg because of the experience curve) to their target level.

9 Regulation and performance

Modern society is very concerned to define for itself what is and what is not 'acceptable'. Businesses are taking this concern on board, and both **legal** and **voluntary** regulations will affect company performance.

9.1 Organisational guidelines and corporate codes

Organisations are coming under increasing pressure from a number of **sources** to behave more ethically.

- **Government**
- UK and European **legislation**
- **Treaty obligations** (such as the *Kyoto protocol*)
- **Consumers**
- **Employers**
- **Pressure groups**

These sources of pressure expect an ethical attitude towards the following.

- **Stakeholders** (employees, customers, competitors, suppliers and society at large)
- **Animals**
- **Green issues** (such as pollution and the need for recycling)
- **The disadvantaged**
- Dealings with **unethical companies or countries**

Reidenbach and Robin usefully distinguish between **five different attitudes to corporate ethics**. The following is an adapted version of a report in the *Financial Times*.

(a) **Amoral organisations**

Such organisations are prepared to **condone any actions that contribute to the corporate aims** (generally the owner's short-term greed).

(b) **Legalistic organisations**

Such organisations **obey the letter of the law but not necessarily the spirit of it**, if that conflicts with economic performance. Ethical matters will be ignored until they become a problem.

(c)   **Responsive companies**

These organisations take the view – perhaps cynically, perhaps not – that there is **something to be gained from ethical behaviour.** It might be recognised, for example, that an enlightened attitude towards staff welfare enabled the company to attract and retain higher calibre staff.

(d)   **Emerging ethical (or 'ethically engaged') organisations**

They take an **active** (rather than a reactive) **interest in ethical issues**.

(e)   **Ethical organisations**

These organisations have a **'total ethical profile'**: a philosophy that informs everything that the company does and a commitment on the part of everyone to carefully selected core values.

9.2 Corporate codes and corporate culture

 Case Study

British Airways was caught in 1993 waging a 'dirty tricks' campaign against its competitor *Virgin Atlantic*. British Airways maintained that the offending actions (essentially, the poaching of Virgin's customers) were those of a small group of employees who overstepped the bounds of 'proper' behaviour in their eagerness to foster the interests of their employer.

An alternative view digs a little deeper. Some observers believed that the real villain of the piece was British Airways' abrasive corporate culture, inspired by the then chairman of BA, Lord King.

One of BA's responses to its defeat in the courts against Virgin and the bad publicity arising from the case was to introduce a code of ethics.

Many commentators would argue that the introduction of a code of ethics is **inadequate** on its own. To be effective a code needs to be accompanied by **positive attempts to foster guiding values, aspirations and patterns of thinking that support ethically sound behaviour** – in short a **change of culture**.

9.2.1 Company code of conduct

A corporate code typically contains a series of statements setting out the company's values and explaining how it sees its responsibilities towards stakeholders.

9.2.2 The impact of a corporate code

A code of conduct can set out the company's expectations, and in principle a code such as that outlined above addresses many of the problems that the organisations may experience. However, **merely issuing a code is not enough**.

(a)   The **commitment of senior management** to the code needs to be real, and it needs to be very clearly communicated to all staff. Staff need to be persuaded that expectations really have changed.

(b)   Measures need to be taken to **discourage previous behaviours** that conflict with the code.

(c)   **Staff need to understand** that it is in the **organisation's best interests** to change behaviour, and become committed to the same ideals.

(d)   Some employees – including very able ones – may find it very difficult to buy into a code that they **perceive may limit their own earnings** and/or restrict their freedom to do their job.

(e)   In addition to a general statement of ethical conduct, **more detailed statements** (codes of practice) will be needed to set out formal procedures that must be followed.

9.3 Green and social issues and the management accountant

Management Accounting has seen a number of articles on green and social issues and their impact on management accountants.

Martin Bennett and Peter James ('The green bottom line: management accounting for environmental improvement and business benefit', November 1998) looked at the **ways in which a company's concern for the environment can impact on its performance.**

(a) **Short-term savings** through waste minimisation and energy efficiency schemes can be substantial.

(b) **Pressures on businesses** for environmental action are increasing.

(c) Companies with poor environmental performance may face **increased cost of capital** because investors and lenders demand a higher risk premium.

(d) There are a growing number of **energy and environmental taxes**, such as the UK's landfill tax.

(e) Accidents and long-term environmental effects can result in **large financial liabilities**.

(f) **Pressure group campaigns** can cause damage to reputation and/or additional costs.

(g) Environmental legislation may cause the **'sunsetting'** of products and opportunities for **'sunrise' replacements**.

(h) The cost of processing input which becomes **waste** is equivalent to 5-10% of some organisation's turnover.

(i) The phasing out of CFCs has led to markets for alternative products.

They go on to suggest six main ways in which business and environmental benefits can be achieved.

(a) **Integrating the environment into capital expenditure decisions** (by considering environmental opposition to projects which could affect cash flows, for example)

(b) **Understanding and managing environmental costs**. Environmental costs are often 'hidden' in overheads and environmental and energy costs are often not allocated to the relevant budgets.

(c) **Introducing waste minimisation schemes**

(d) **Understanding and managing life cycle costs.** For many products, the greatest environmental impact occurs upstream (such as mining raw materials) or downstream from production (such as energy to operate equipment). This has led to producers being made responsible for dealing with the disposal of products such as cars, and government and third party measures to influence raw material choices. Organisations therefore need to identify, control and make provision for environmental life cycle costs and work with suppliers and customers to identify environmental cost reduction opportunities.

(e) **Measuring environmental performance.** Business is under increasing pressure to measure all aspects of environmental performance, both for statutory disclosure reasons and due to demands for more environmental data from customers.

(f) **Involving management accountants in a strategic approach to environment-related management accounting and performance evaluation.** A 'green accounting team' incorporating the key functions should analyse the strategic picture and identify opportunities for practical initiatives. It should analyse the short-, medium– and long-term impact of possible changes in the following.

   (i) **Government policies**, such as on transport
   (ii) Legislation and regulation
   (iii) Supply conditions, such as fewer landfill sites
   (iv) Market conditions, such as changing customer views
   (v) Social attitudes, such as to factory farming
   (vi) Competitor strategies

Possible action includes the following.

   (i) Designating an **'environmental champion'** within the strategic planning or accounting function to ensure that environmental considerations are fully considered.

   (ii) Assessing whether **new data sources** are needed to collect more and better data

   (iii) Making **comparisons** between sites/offices to highlight poor performance and generate peer pressure for action

   (iv) Developing **checklists** for internal auditors

   Such analysis and action should help organisations to better understand present and future environmental costs and benefits.

Corporate social accounting is the 'reporting of the social and environmental impact of an entity's activities upon those who are directly associated with the entity (for instance, employees, customers, suppliers) or those who are in any way affected by the activities of the entity, as well as an assessment of the cost of compliance with relevant regulations in this area'. (CIMA *Official Terminology*)

Lynne Paine (*Harvard Business Review*, March-April 1994) suggests that ethical decisions are becoming more important, as penalties, in the US at least, for companies which break the law are become tougher. Paine suggests that there are two approaches to the management of ethics in organisations:

(a) A **compliance-based** approach is primarily designed to ensure that the company and its personnel act within the letter of the law. Mere compliance is not an adequate means for addressing the full range of ethical issues that arise every day. This is especially the case in the UK, where **voluntary codes** of conduct and self-regulating institutes are perhaps more prevalent than the US.

(b) An **integrity-based approach** combines a concern for the law with an emphasis on managerial responsibility for ethical behaviour … . When integrated into the day-to-day operations of an organisation, such strategies can help prevent damaging ethical lapses.

Chapter Roundup

- All systems of control can be analysed using the **cybernetic model**. The essence of this model is the **feedback** of control action to the controlled process: the control action itself being generated from the comparison of actual results with what was planned.

- Ouchi identified **market**, **bureaucratic** and **clan** control strategies; their application is very much dependent on the control contingencies encountered.

- **Performance measurement** aims to establish how well something or somebody is doing in relation to previous or expected activity or in comparison with another thing or body. These measurer's
    - **Communicate** the objectives of the company
    - **Concentrate efforts** towards those objectives
    - **Produce feedback** for comparison with the plan

- **Strategic control** is bound up with measurement of performance, which is often based on financial criteria. Techniques for strategic control suggest that companies develop strategic milestones (eg for market share) to monitor the achievement of strategic objectives, as a balance to purely financial issues.

- **Critical success factors** are the few key areas where things must go right for the organisation to flourish.

- **Budgetary control systems** are subject to some criticism, but are still used by many companies to compel planning, co-ordinate activities and motivate employees, as well as to evaluate performance. Deviations from the plan are corrected via **control action.**

- Performance measures must be cost-effective, and relevant to both a clear objective and to operational methods

- Profitability, activity and productivity are the basic material of performance measurement, but measures cannot be established in isolation for the strategy plans and tasks of the organisation.

- Growing dissatisfaction with financial performance measures has led to other measures being developed, based on **operational performance.**

- An approach that tries to integrate the different measures of performance is the **balanced scorecard**, where key linkages between operating and financial performance are brought to light. This offers four perspectives:
    - Financial
    - Customer
    - Innovation and learning
    - Internal business

- The **performance pyramid** derives from the idea that an organisation operates at different levels, each of which has different (but supporting) concerns.

- Performance is more difficult to measure where there is no physical product. Services are intangible, they are consumed at the same time as they are produced and they cannot be stored. This leads to measures of performance based on output productivity and effectiveness.

- The results and determinants framework may be used for measuring service provision.

- A wide range of measures exists for measuring manufacturing performance. They range from simple cost/ output efficiency measures to more complex ideas relating to quality and innovation.

- Modern society is very concerned to define for itself what is and what is not 'acceptable'. Businesses are taking this concern on board, and both **legal** and **voluntary** regulations will affect company performance.

1   **Fill in the blanks** in the statements below, using the words in the box.

The aims of performance measurement are as follows

- (1) .... the (2) .... of the company
- Concentrating (3) .... towards objectives
- Part of the (4) .... process where (5) .... is compared with the (6) ....

• plan	• objectives	• control
• feedback	• efforts	• communicating

2   What is an example of a critical success factor for the production function?

3   Which of the following is a perceived disadvantage of zero based budgeting (ZBB)?

A   There are no incentives as the budget is often unrealistic

B   The managers who set the budgets are not responsible for attaining them

C   Too many people are involved

D   It may emphasise short term benefits rather than long term goals

4   'In general, there are three possible points of reference for measurement'. What are they?

....

....

....

5   Give some examples of non-financial performance measures that can be applied to an assessment of marketing effectiveness.

6   What are the four perspectives on the balanced scorecard?

....

....

....

....

7   What are the specific operational criteria contained in the performance pyramid?

8   What have been seen as the four 'over-arching' measures for manufacturing environments?

9   **Fill in the blanks** in the statements below, using the words in the box.

A corporate (1) ....   typically contains   a series of (2) .... setting out the company's (3) .... and explaining how it sees its (4) .... towards (5) ....

• stakeholders	• code	• statements
• responsibilities	• values	

10   What are some of the disadvantages of using profit as a performance measure?

Answers to Quick Quiz

1   (1) Communicating (2) objectives (3) efforts (4) control (5) feedback (6) plan

2   Quality standards / capacity utilisation

3   D

4   Profitability
    Activity
    Productivity

5   Trend in market share   Sales volume growth
    Customer visits per salesperson   Client contact hours per salesperson
    Sales volume forecast v actual   Number of customers
    Customer survey response information

6   Customer
    Internal business processes
    Innovation/learning
    Financial

7   Quality   Delivery
    Process time   Cost

8   Cost   Quality
    Time   Innovation

9   (1) code (2) statements (3) values (4) responsibilities (5) stakeholders

10 Encourages short-termism and focus on the annual cycle, at the expense of long term performance

    Profit differs from economic income

    A firm has to satisfy stakeholders other than shareholders, such as the government and the local community

    Liquidity is at least as important as profit

    Profit should be related to risk, not just capital employed

    Profits can fluctuate in times of rapid change, eg exchange rates

    Profits measures cannot easily be used to motivate cost centre managers

Now try the question below from the Exam Question Bank

Number	Level	Marks	Time
Q13	Examination	25	45 mins

Measuring performance II

Introduction

In this chapter we concentrate on the **financial perspective** area of the balanced scorecard. Financial measures of performance are those you will be most likely to have a hand in.

The material in this chapter should not present you with too many problems. There are no techniques or concepts that you have not encountered earlier in your studies. The point is that management accounting and financial measures can be flexibly applied.

In this chapter we review the performance of **investment** decisions and we also look at **contribution analysis** and **variance analysis** (Sections 2 and 3). This should be mostly revision for you. In Sections 4-5 we discuss appraisal of particular **business units and divisions**, and we look at the **relationships** between them (Section 7).

Although this chapter is in many respects concerned with **control**, we examine in detail why some 'control' measures can have a dysfunctional impact on strategic decision-making.

A general theme of this chapter is that accounting measures such as ROI must be used with some care, because:

- They reflect **organisation structure**, rather than business processes
- They are easily **manipulated** by accountants and managers
- They are rendered uncertain by **inflation** (Section 1)

Topic list	Learning outcomes	Syllabus references	Ability required
1 Inflation	D (iii)	D 1	Evaluation
2 Using NPVs to control strategic investments	C(i)	C2, C3, C8, C9	Evaluation
3 Using contribution margin as a measure of performance	D(i)	D 1	Evaluation
4 Divisional performance: return on investment (ROI)	D(i), D(iii)	D 4	Evaluation
5 Divisional performance: residual income (RI)	D(i), D(iii)	D 4	Evaluation
6 Comparing profit centre performance	D(i), D(iii)	D 4	Evaluation
7 Interfirm comparisons and performance ratios	D(i)	D 4	Evaluation

1 Inflation

FAST FORWARD

> **Inflation** makes it harder to compare performance over time, as it affects accounting values, and hence measures of performance. It affects base line and comparative figures.

When an organisation prepares its strategic plans, it will probably build some assumptions about the rate of inflation into the plan itself.

1.1 The consequences of inflation

The problem for performance measurement is to decide what the actual effect of inflation has been, how this compares with the plan, and what significance this might have for performance measures and control action.

(a) If a company operates in a competitive market, where customers resist price increases, it may be unable to pass on all its cost increases to the customer, and so the effect of inflation would be to reduce its profitability.

(b) If a company exports goods overseas, domestic price inflation will push up the cost of its goods to foreign buyers unless the exchange rate were to fall to compensate for the rate of inflation.

1.2 Controlling inflation

Inflationary pressures on costs ought to be kept as much under control as possible.

- Given anticipated material cost increases is there scope through exercising 'buyer power' over suppliers to keep them below the rate of inflation?
- Is the material being effectively used?
- Labour pay agreements should be competitive but kept as low as possible.
- Labour efficiency must match the competition.
- Expenses should be rigorously controlled.
- The timing of price increases should be monitored carefully.

1.3 Performance measurement and inflation

You should already know the argument that a major problem with the historical cost convention is that it can report that an organisation is making a profit, when it has in fact suffered a fall in its operating capacity. In other words, inflation can conceal poor performance.

There are five consequences of historical cost accounting which, because of price inflation, reduce the reliability of the information given in company accounts.

- Non-current asset values and depreciation.
- Cost of sales.
- Increase in working capital needed to support normal trading operations.
- Borrowing benefits.
- Comparability of figures from year to year (and also between one company and another).

1.4 Trends: comparability of figures over time

One method of measuring performance is to look at trends over a period of time; for example, the trend over a number of years in dividend per share, EPS, and sales volume (in £s). An estimate of whether there has been 'real' growth in dividends, earnings or sales can be made simply by 'taking away' an estimate of the inflationary element in the growth. For example, given the following figures:

	1	2	3
Earnings per share	40p	45p	55p
Retail price index	100	105	112

the rate of 'real' growth in EPS could be estimated approximately as follows.

(a)   Year 2 compared with Year 1

    (i)   Total increase $\dfrac{45p}{40p}$ = 1.125

    (ii)   Increase in RPI $\dfrac{105}{100}$ = 1.05

    (iii)   'Real' increase $\dfrac{1.125}{1.05}$ = 1.071 ie 7.1%

(b)   Year 3 compared with Year 2

    (i)   Total increase $\dfrac{55p}{45p}$ = 1.222

    (ii)   Increase in RPI $\dfrac{112}{105}$ = 1.067

    (iii)   'Real' increase $\dfrac{1.222}{1.067}$ = 1.145 ie 14.5%

1.5 Ratios for control

When ratio measurements are used as targets for control, they may be unaffected by inflation, because both sides of the ratio might be equally inflated.

(a)   Accounting return on capital employed, ie:

$$\frac{\text{Profit}}{\text{Capital employed}}$$

If both profit and capital employed are equally affected by inflationary increases, the ROI ratio would be unaffected. However, if capital employed is not subject to the same inflationary increases as profit, trends in ROI would be misleading.

(b)   Similarly, the profit/sales ratio would be unaffected as a control measure by inflation, provided that profits and sales were equally boosted by inflationary increases.

(c)   The same argument would apply to a number of other ratios, such as asset turnover, average receivables payment period, inventory turnover, gearing ratio, and the current ratio etc.

2 Using NPVs to control strategic investments

FAST FORWARD

Discounted cash flows can be used to assess the performance of capital investment projects, by comparing anticipated and actual cash flows, discounted in an appropriate way. It is probably a lot harder, although not impossible, to apply these to profit centres.

The easiest form of strategic decision to control relates to **capital expenditure**, such as investment in machinery.

2.1 The control of capital expenditure

Key term

Capital projects involve 'any long term commitments of funds undertaken now in anticipation of a potential inflow of funds at some time in the future.'   (Hartley).

Once a project is given the go-ahead, with a spending ceiling of £x, the progress of the project should be monitored. Although **direct expenditure** can be monitored, it is not always easy to identify **additional indirect expenditures** and extra **working capital investment** as a direct cause of the project.

Assume a firm has a level of sales of £1,000,000 pa. It has a choice of two investments. Both involve saving costs, but neither will have an effect on sales revenue. Project A involves developing an exclusive distribution system, and has a positive NPV of £50,000. Project B involves investing in new production equipment and has an NPV of £100,000. Normally project B would be chosen, as it has the higher NPV, but if you were told that:

(a)   A new competitor had entered the market, threatening sales revenue by an undefined amount

(b)   Project A would raise barriers to entry

you might prefer Project A, as it has additional benefits in **protecting revenue**.

With long-term planning, capital expenditure decisions should be based on an evaluation of future cash flows, discounted at an appropriate cost of capital to an NPV.

2.2 Cash flows and NPVs for strategic control: shareholder wealth

Control at a strategic level should be based on measurements of **cash flows**, ie actual cash flows for the period just ended and revised forecasts of future cash flows. Since the objective of a company might be to maximise the wealth of its shareholders, a control technique based on the measurement of cash flows and their NPV could be a very useful technique to apply.

A numerical example might help to illustrate this point.

Suppose that ABC Ltd agrees to a strategic plan from 1 January 20X1 as follows.

Year	20X1	20X2	20X3	20X4	20X5	Total
Planned net cash inflow (£'000)	200	300	300	400	500	1,700
NPV at cost of capital 15%	174	227	197	229	249	1,076

Now suppose that ABC Ltd reviews its position one year later.

(a)   It can measure its actual total cash flow in 20X1 – roughly speaking, this will be the funds generated from operations minus tax paid and minus expenditure on fixed assets and plus/minus changes in working capital.

(b)   It can revise its forecast for the next few years.

We will assume that there has been no change in the cost of capital. Control information at the end of 20X1 might be as follows.

Year	20X1 (actual)	20X2 (forecast)	20X3	20X4	20X5	Total
Net cash inflow (£'000)	180	260	280	400	540	1,660
NPV at cost of capital 15%	180	226	212	263	309	1,190

A control summary comparing the situation at the start of 20X1 and the situation one year later would now be as follows.

	£'000
Expected NPV as at 1.1.20X1	1,076
Uplift by cost of capital 15%	161
	1,237
Expected NPV as at 1.1.20X2	1,190
Variance	47 (A)

The control information shows that by the end of 20X1, ABC Ltd shows signs of not achieving the strategic targets it set itself at the start of 20X1. This is partly because actual cash flows in 20X1 fell short of target by (200-180) £20,000, but also because the revised forecast for the future is not as good now either. In total, the company has a lower NPV by £47,000.

The reasons for the failure to achieve target should be investigated. Possible reasons include the following.

- A higher-than-expected pay award to employees, which will have repercussions for the future as well as in 20X1
- An increase in the rate of tax on profits
- A serious delay in the implementation of some major new projects
- The slower-than-expected growth of an important new market

Do not be surprised if calculations are required in the exam: this is a management accounting subject. If calculations are required you will inevitably have to use or comment on them in support of an argument.

NPV calculations rely on obtaining information about actual and forecast cash flows. In practice, it is not often easy to identify the attributable cash flows for individual capital projects or individual profit centres, and so other financial measures of performance have to be applied. These are now described.

3 Using contribution margin as a measure of performance

The basic concept of **contribution** can be used strategically if questions about strategic factors are examined in its light. It is also appropriate for SBU performance measurement.

Contribution margin can be defined as 'the difference between sales volume and the variable cost of those sales, expressed either in absolute terms or as a contribution per unit.'

The contribution per unit is 'often related to a key or limiting factor to give a sum required to cover fixed overhead and profit, such as contribution per machine hour, per direct labour hour or per kilo of scarce raw material.'

(a) A **contribution centre** is a profit centre where expenditure is calculated on a marginal cost basis.

(b) **Contribution per unit of limiting factor** is a measurement for optimising the use of scarce resources.

Contribution margins are also used for measuring performance in terms of **breakeven analysis**.

3.1 Contribution and strategic decisions

3.1.1 Product market issues

Consider, for example, a situation where an automobile manufacturer wishes to launch a new model, the success of which is crucial to corporate survival. Fixed costs are the capital required to develop the vehicle and tool up, which will appear in the breakeven equation as depreciation, development costs and operational fixed costs. Variable costs will have been identified and reliable sales forecasts will have been obtained. From this data, two figures can be computed.

(a) The number of vehicles required to **break even**.

(b) The number of vehicles required to generate **adequate returns** over the life of the model or the investment, and, significantly, what this represents in terms of market penetration and market share.

Johnson and Scholes argue that breakeven analysis has a useful role to play in appraising and controlling strategy. Questions can be asked based on the breakeven model.

- What is the **probability** of achieving the desired levels of market penetration?
- Do the **conditions in the market** lend themselves to achieving that desired penetration?
- Will the **competitors** allow a profitable entry?

- Are the **cost and quality** assumptions feasible?
- Are the **funds available**, not just to complete the development but to establish the production capacity and skilled manpower to achieve the desired penetration?

3.1.2 Exit

Firms with high exit barriers may use contribution as the main tool for decision making. Ward cites the example of a coal mine, as to the type of decisions taken. High exit barriers result from:

- The actual costs of closure, redundancy and so on
- The cost of re-opening the mine, if demand for coal and prices picks up
- Costs which will not be avoided by the closure

3.2 Applying contribution margin accounting to divisional performance measurement

A danger with contribution margin analysis is that firms in a competitive industry might be tempted to sell at prices which cover marginal costs, but fail to earn an adequate return on **sunk fixed costs**.

Applying the principle that managers should only be made accountable for costs and revenues which they are in a position to control directly, it follows that short-term controls for profit centres should focus largely on contribution margins, because in the short run, only revenues and variable costs tend to be **controllable**.

However, some directly attributable fixed costs might also be controllable in the short term, or at least might be avoidable if the scale of business operations were to be reduced significantly. Fixed costs can therefore be classified as follows.

(a) Costs which are **directly attributable** to a particular activity, and which tend to rise or fall in steps as the scale of activities is increased or lowered.

(b) **Unavoidable costs**. Many fixed costs are committed, or not directly attributable to any particular activity.

One way of measuring profit for an investment centre or a profit centre is as follows.

	£
Sales revenue	X
less Variable cost of sales	(X)
equals Contribution	X
less Directly attributable fixed costs (avoidable/controllable)	(X)
equals Gross profit	X
less Share of unavoidable (committed*/uncontrollable*) fixed costs	(X)
equals Net profit	X

(* in the short term. In the long term, all fixed cost items should be controllable and 'variable'.)

4 Divisional performance: return on investment (ROI)

ROI is based on **organisation structure**, not business processes, and is only suitable to products at the mature phase of the life cycle.

Many large firms are organised into **strategic business units** (SBUs).

Key term

A **strategic business unit (SBU)** is a 'section, usually a division, within a larger business organisation, that has a significant degree of autonomy, typically being responsible for developing and marketing its own products or services'.
(CIMA *Official Terminology*)

A typical SBU is a division of the organisation 'where managers have control over their own resources, and discretion overt the deployment of resources within specified boundaries'.
(Ward)

FAST FORWARD

The performance of these business units is complicated by the degree of autonomy their managers enjoy.

We have covered DCF and contribution margin accounting first of all for these reasons.

(a)   Both techniques are in theory applicable to controlling and assessing strategies and can be applied to **divisional performance measurement**

(b)   DCF addresses the issue in terms of **cash flows**

In practice, many firms use more 'traditional' accounting based measures, such as return on investment (ROI). First some definitions.

Key terms

Return on capital employed (ROCE)

$$\frac{\text{Profit before interest and tax} \times 100}{\text{Average capital employed}}$$

Indicates the productivity of capital employed. The denominator is normally calculated as the average of the capital employed at the beginning and end of the year. Problems of seasonality, new capital introduced or other factors may necessitate taking the average of a number of periods within the year.

Return on investment (ROI)

$$\frac{\text{Profit before interest and tax} \times 100}{\text{Operations management capital employed}}$$

Often used to assess managers' performance. Managers are responsible for all assets (normally defined as non-current assets plus net current assets).
(CIMA *Official Terminology*)

ROI is normally used to apply to investment centres or profit centres. These normally reflect the existing organisation structure of the business.

ROI shows how much profit in accounting terms has been made in relation to the amount of capital invested. For example, suppose that a company has two investment centres A and B, which show results for the year as follows:

	A	B
Profit after depreciation, before tax and interest	£60,000	£30,000
Assets generating income	£400,000	£120,000
ROI	15%	25%

Investment centre A has made double the profits of investment centre B, and in terms of profits alone has therefore been more 'successful'. However, B has earned a much higher ROI. This suggests that B has been a more successful investment than A.

The main reasons for the widespread use as a measure of ROI as a performance indicator are these.

(a)   **Financial reporting**. It ties in directly with the accounting process, and is identifiable from the profit and loss account and the balance sheet, the firm's most important communications media with investors.

(b)   **Aggregation**. ROI is a very convenient method of measuring the performance for a division or company as an entire unit.

4.1 Measurement problems: non-current assets

The problems with ROI relate to accurate measurement.

4.1.1 Net assets

It is probably most common to use **return on net assets**. There are two main problems.

(a)   If an investment centre maintains the same annual profit, and keeps the same assets without a policy of regular non-current asset replacement, its ROI will increase year by year as the assets get older. This can give a false impression of improving 'real' performance over time.

(b)   It is not easy to **compare fairly** the performance of one investment centre with another. Non-current assets may be of different ages or may be depreciated in different ways.

4.1.2 Return on gross assets

(a)   **Advantage**. Ignoring depreciation removes the problem of ROI increasing over time as fixed assets get older and get depreciated.

(b)   **Disadvantages**.
(i)   Measuring ROI as return on gross assets ignores the **age factor**. Older non-current assets usually cost more to repair and maintain. An investment centre with old assets may therefore have its profitability reduced by repair costs.

(ii)   **Inflation and technological change** alter the cost of non-current assets. If one investment centre has fixed assets bought ten years ago with a gross cost of £1 million, and another investment centre, in the same area of business operations, has fixed assets bought very recently for £1 million, the quantity and technological character of the fixed assets of the two investment centres are likely to be very different.

4.1.3 ROI: replacement cost

The view that ROI should be measured in terms of **replacement cost** (either net or gross) is connected to the arguments in favour of **current cost accounting**. In a period of price inflation, ROI based on historical costs is difficult to interpret because it will become higher as assets get older, by virtue of the fact that profits will be measured in current-year money.

4.1.4 Measurement problems: what are 'assets' anyway?

Prudence and other accounting principles require that items such as research and development should only be carried forward as an investment in special circumstances.

Many 'costs' do have the effect of enhancing the long-term revenue-earning capacity of the business. A good example is **brands**: many firms have capitalised brands for this reason. For decision-making and control purposes, the expenditure on brands might be better treated as an investment.

4.1.5 The target return for a group of companies

If a group of companies sets a target return for the group as a whole, or if a company sets a target return for each SBU, it might be company policy that no investment project should go ahead in any subsidiary or investment centre unless the project promises to earn at least the target return. For example, it might be group policy that:

(a)   There should be no new investment by any subsidiary in the group unless it is expected to earn at least a 15% return.

(b)   Similarly, no fixed asset should be disposed of if the asset is currently earning a return in excess of 15% of its disposal value.

(c)   Investments which promise a return of 15% or more ought to be undertaken.

Problems with such a policy are these.

(a)   Investments are appraised by DCF whereas actual performance will probably be measured on the basis of ROI.

(b)   The target return makes no allowance for the different risk of each investment centre.

(c)   In a conglomerate an identical target return may be unsuitable to many businesses in a group.

4.2 Example: the problem with setting a target ROI

Suppose that an investment in a fixed asset would cost £100,000 and make a profit of £11,000 pa after depreciation. The asset would be depreciated by £25,000 pa for four years. It is group policy that investments must show a minimum return of 15%.

The DCF net present value of this investment would just about be positive, and so the investment ought to be approved if group policy is adhered to.

Year	Cash flow (profit before dep'n) £	Discount factor 15%	Present value £
0	(100,000)	1.000	(100,000)
1	36,000	0.870	31,320
2	36,000	0.756	27,216
3	36,000	0.658	23,688
4	36,000	0.572	20,592
		NPV	2,816

However, if the investment is measured year by year according to the accounting ROI it has earned, we find that its return is less than 15% in year 1, but more than 15% in years 2, 3 and 4.

Year	Profit £	Net book value of equipment (mid-year value) £	ROCE
1	11,000	87,500	12.6%
2	11,000	62,500	17.6%
3	11,000	37,500	29.3%
4	11,000	12,500	88.0%

In view of the low accounting ROI in year 1, should the investment be undertaken or not?

(a)   Strictly speaking, investment decisions should be based on IRR, and should not be guided by short term accounting ROI.

(b)   Even if accounting ROI is used as a guideline for investment decisions, ROI should be looked at over the full life of the investment, not just in the short term. In the short term (in the first year or so of a project's life) the accounting ROI is likely to be low because the net book value of the asset will still be high.

In our example, it is conceivable that the group's management might disapprove of the project because of its low accounting ROI in year 1. This approach is short-termist, but it nevertheless can make some sense to a company or group of companies which has to show a satisfactory profit and ROI in its published accounts each year, to keep its shareholders satisfied with performance.

4.3 Possible behavioural implications of ROI: short-termism and lack of goal congruence

Since managers will be judged on the basis of the ROI that their centre earns each year, they are likely to be motivated into taking those decisions which increase their centre's short-term ROI. An investment might be desirable from the group's point of view, but would not be in the individual investment centre's 'best interest' to undertake. Thus there is a lack of **goal congruence**.

In the short term, a desire to increase ROI might lead to projects being taken on without due regard to their risk.

Any decisions which benefit the company in the long term but which reduce the ROI in the immediate short term would reflect badly on the manager's reported performance.

Question
Manipulation

Learning outcome D(iii)

Describe any methods you can think of (and their implications) which managers would use to manipulate the return on investment figures, if ROI was calculated as:

$$\text{Return on total assets} = \frac{\text{Profit before interest, tax, depreciation}}{\text{Gross fixed assets} + \text{total current assets}}$$

Answer

(a) Keep gross assets to a minimum
  (i) Avoid capital expenditure
  (ii) Acquire all assets on operating leases
(b) Manipulate current assets
  (i) Factor debtors (ie sell the debts)
  (ii) Introduce over-generous settlement discounts, set not by the prevailing interest rate (the true cost) but by divisional ROI targets to encourage early payment.
  (iii) Sell all inventories before the balance sheet date and repurchase them immediately after.
  (iv) Refuse credit.
(c) Manipulate the return by investing in projects with higher long-term risk even if they offered better short-term profits.

Compare these measures to the balanced scorecard: clearly they cause dysfunctional behaviour in customer relations and in internal processes (eg inventory management). Too much effort is devoted to manipulating the figures, not improving the business.

(Note. This exercise is based on an example cited by *Ward* in *Strategic Management Accounting*.)

4.4 ROI, strategy and product-market issues

4.4.1 ROI reflects organisation structure, not business processes

ROI is based on the existing organisation structure of a business.

(a) Business process re-engineering suggests that many organisation structures are badly designed in themselves.
(b) The use of ROI in a responsibility accounting framework perpetuates the bad effects of the existing organisation structure.
(c) All investment projects may involve the co-operation of many departments in a business, along the whole extent of the value chain.

4.4.2 Product life cycle: ROI is not suitable to all phases

Product-market issues are also relevant. ROI is suited to the **mature phase**, when the market is established. ROI is also best suited to cash cows on the BCG matrix.

4.4.3 ROI aggregates all products in a portfolio

We have seen that many firms have a **portfolio of products** in different stages of the life cycle – in fact this is necessary for the firm's long term survival. ROI does not suggest the right strategic action to be taken with regard to new products or declining products, rising stars, question marks or dogs.

5 Divisional performance: residual income (RI)

FAST FORWARD

Residual income (RI) gets round some of the problems of ROI, by deducting from profit an imputed interest charge for the use of assets.

An alternative way of measuring the performance of an investment centre, instead of using ROI, is residual income (RI).

Key term

> **Residual income** is 'profit minus a charge for capital employed in the period'.
>
> (CIMA *Official Terminology*)

RI is calculated as 'Earnings before interest and tax – (invested capital x imputed rate).'

The imputed cost of capital might be the organisation's cost of borrowing or its weighted average cost of capital. Alternatively, the cost of capital can be adjusted to allow for the risk characteristics of each investment centre, with a higher imputed interest rate being applied to higher risk centres.

5.1 The advantages and weaknesses of RI compared with ROI

The advantages of using RI are as follows.

(a)   Residual income will increase when:
  (i)   Investments earning above the cost of capital are undertaken
  (ii)   Investments earning below the cost of capital are eliminated

(b)   Residual income is more flexible since a different cost of capital can be applied to investments with different risk characteristics.

The weakness of RI is that it does not facilitate comparisons between investment centres nor does it relate the size of a centre's income to the size of the investment, other than indirectly through the interest charge.

5.1.1 RI versus ROI: marginally profitable investments

Residual income will increase if a new investment is undertaken which earns a profit in excess of the imputed interest charge on the value of the asset acquired. When a manager is judged by ROI, a marginally profitable investment would be less likely to be undertaken because it would reduce the average ROI earned by the centre as a whole.

Residual income does not always point to the right decision, because notional interest on accounting capital employed is not the same as IRR on cash investment. However, residual income is more likely than ROI to improve when managers make correct investment/divestment decisions, and so is probably a 'safer' basis than ROI on which to measure performance.

5.2 Example: ROI versus residual income

Suppose that Department H has the following profit, assets employed and an imputed interest charge of 12% on operating assets.

		Department H
	£	£
Operating profit	30,000	
Operating assets		100,000
Imputed interest (12%)	12,000	
Return on investment		30%
Residual income	18,000	

Suppose now that an additional investment of £10,000 is proposed, which will increase operating income in Department H by £1,400. The effect of the investment would be:

	£	£
Total operating income	31,400	
Total operating assets		110,000
Imputed interest (12%)	13,200	
Return on investment		28.5%
Residual income	18,200	

If the Department H manager is made responsible for the department's performance, he would resist the new investment if he were to be judged on ROI, but would welcome the investment if he were judged according to RI, since there would be a marginal increase of £200 in residual income from the investment, but a fall of 1.5% in ROI.

The marginal investment offers a return of 14% (£1,400 on an investment of £10,000) which is above the 'cut-off rate' of 12%. Since the original return on investment was 30%, the marginal investment will reduce the overall divisional performance. Indeed, any marginal investment offering an accounting rate of return of less than 30% in the year would reduce the overall performance.

Residual income should not be used as a means of making asset purchasing decisions; nevertheless, it may be a useful alternative to ROI where there is a conflict between purchase decisions indicated by a positive NPV in discounted cash flow, and the resulting reduction in divisional ROI which 'reflects badly' on management performance.

5.3 NPV, residual income, and annuity depreciation

Another approach to measuring divisional performance, which attempts to achieve consistency with the NPV rule, is to treat divisions as lessees of assets owned by head office. For each asset that it uses, the division will receive an annual **finance lease charge** for the life of the asset, which is calculated from:

- The cost/estimated residual value of the asset
- The asset's expected life
- A target cost of capital for the division

6 Comparing profit centre performance

FAST FORWARD

Profit centres are often compared. Problems arise when managers are judged on matters they cannot control. A variety of measures involving **contribution** are used to isolate controllable costs.

Problems in measuring **divisional performance** include allocation of head office costs, and different asset valuations.

When departments within an organisation are set up as profit centres, their performance will be judged on the profit they earn. The performance of profit centres might be compared on the basis of profit/sales ratios, contribution earned per unit of scarce resource, or profit growth rates.

6.1 Dysfunctional decisions and goal congruence

A profit centre manager might take decisions that will improve his own centre's performance at the expense of other parts of the business.

- Profit centre managers tend to put their own profit performance above everything else.
- Profit centres are not isolated entities, but related divisions within a single organisation.

Question

Learning outcome D (iii)

What are the likely behavioural consequences of a head office continually imposing its own decisions on divisions?

Answer

Decentralisation recognises that those closest to a job are the best equipped to say how it should be done and that people tend to perform to a higher standard if they are given responsibility. Centrally imposed decisions are likely to make managers feel that they do not really have any authority and therefore that they cannot be held responsible for performance. They will therefore make less effort to perform well.

6.2 Comparing profit centre performance

Shillinglaw suggested that four profit concepts could be used to measure and report divisional profit internally within a company. Each has its own purpose.

(a) **Contribution**

(b) **'Controllable profit'** – contribution minus all the division's fixed costs controllable by the manager.

(c) **Controllable margin** – controllable profit minus all other costs directly traceable to the division.

(d) **Net profit or net contribution**, less a share of service centre costs and general management overhead. However, 'net profit' is the least useful of the four, because the allocation of general overhead costs must inevitably be largely arbitrary.

6.2.1 Contribution

A principle of responsibility accounting is that profit centre managers should only be held accountable for those revenues and costs that they are in a position to control. Increases in production volume, within the relevant range of output, will raise profit by the amount of increase in contribution.

A divisional performance statement based on contribution might appear as follows.

	Division A	Division B	Total
	£'000	£'000	£'000
Sales	80	100	180
Less variable costs	60	50	110
Contribution	20	50	70
Less fixed costs			50
Profit			20

(a) Divisional performance can be improved by increasing the sales price, or volume of sales, or reducing the unit variable cost.

(b) The relative profitability of divisions A and B could be compared by means of their C/S ratios (in this example, 25% and 50% respectively).

(c) If there is a production limiting factor, performance could also be measured in terms of contribution per unit of limiting factor. In our example, if there is a shortage of cash for working capital acting as a restriction on output, and if divisions A and B use £2,500 and £8,000 in working capital respectively, the contribution per £1 of working capital employed would be £8 for division A and £6.25 for division B (so that a transfer of some production resources from B to A might be profitable under these circumstances).

6.2.2 Controllable profit

One drawback to using contribution alone as a measure of divisional performance is that although it indicates the short-term controllable results of the division, it gives no indication as **to longer-term underlying profitability**.

In the following example, closure of division X might be justified, since there would be a net saving in annual running costs of £5,000.

	Division X	Division Y	Total
	£'000	£'000	£'000
Sales	70	120	190
Less variable costs	50	80	130
Contribution	20	40	60
Less directly attributable fixed costs	25	25	50
Profit of the division	(5)	15	10
Less fixed costs (general)			8
Company profit			2

6.2.3 Controllable margin

A further refinement of this approach to profit centre accounting is to make a distinction between fixed costs over which the centre manager has short-run discretionary control, for example advertising costs and sales promotion expenditures, and fixed costs over which the manager has no personal control, such as his own salary, or depreciation of assets.

		Division X	Division Y	Total
		£'000	£'000	£'000
	Sales	70	120	190
	Less variable costs	50	80	130
(1)	Contribution	20	40	60
	Less fixed costs directly attributable to the manager's discretionary control	8	20	28
(2)	Profit attributable to the manager	12	20	32
	Less fixed costs directly attributable to the profit centre, outside the manager's control	17	5	22
(3)	Profit attributable to the profit centre	(5)	15	10
	Shared fixed costs			8
	Company profit			2

6.2.4 Net profit: after charging a proportion of shared fixed costs

An argument against measuring profit on the basis of contribution less directly attributable fixed costs is that no one is made responsible for earning a sufficiently large profit to ensure that shared fixed costs are covered, and that the organisation as a whole is profitable.

6.2.5 The problems of absorption costing

Absorption costing systems are perhaps the 'traditional' method of accounting for divisional performance, but they have some serious drawbacks.

(a) **They are not a method of responsibility accounting**, in that managers cannot control the general fixed costs charged to their division, and are not properly responsible for them.

(b) **The method of apportioning fixed costs can vary**, according to the basis chosen.

Residual income and interdepartmental comparisons.

With a residual income method of reporting divisional profits, four different 'profit' figures can be identified, as follows. It is quite possible that divisions will do better or worse, in comparative terms, according to which measure is used.

		Division A	
		£'000	£'000
Sales:	external		310
	internal transfers		210
			520
Variable costs of goods sold internally and externally		220	
Variable divisional expenses		20	
			240
(1)	**Controllable contribution**		280
Controllable divisional overhead			90
(2)	**Controllable profit**		190
Depreciation and other expenses on controllable fixed assets (eg lease costs)		50	
Interest on controllable fixed assets		15	
			65
(3)	**Controllable residual income**		125
Depreciation and other expenses on non-controllable fixed assets		20	
Allocated central expenses		40	
Interest on non-controllable fixed assets		10	
			70
(4)	**Net residual income**		55

6.3 Head office as a profit centre or investment centre: charging for services

One way of improving the responsibility accounting system might be to establish head office as a profit centre or investment centre in its own right.

6.4 Service departments

Just as it is important in measuring production performance to distinguish between fixed and variable costs, between directly attributable costs and shared general overheads and between controllable and uncontrollable costs, so too should these distinctions be made for service department costs.

(a) The department might incur costs that are variable with the volume of activity in the department. Variable costs should be identified, and control reporting should compare actual costs with a flexed budget.

(b) The department's directly attributable fixed costs should be identified, because these are the running costs that would be saved if the department were to be closed down.

6.5 Making non-current assets controllable

Non-current assets are 'controllable' by a divisional manager if he or she has the authority to purchase or dispose of assets. But suppose that a division has non-current assets that are temporarily surplus to requirements. Unless the divisional manager disposes of the asset, which might be inappropriate because the asset might be needed at some time in the future, the division's short term ROI or residual income will be reduced because of the surplus 'controllable' non-current assets. One method, used by some firms, of overcoming this problem of 'controllability' of non-current assets is to establish a head office 'pool' of non-current assets. Divisional managers can obtain non-current assets from this pool when they are needed, and return them when they become surplus to requirements.

6.6 Added value

Key term

> Although added value can be measured in different ways, the broad concept is that **added value** equals sales minus the costs of materials and bought-in services.

Managers are then made responsible for the following.

(a) Total value added earned.

(b) The way in which value added is divided between labour costs, non-current asset depreciation, profit.

(c) Value added earned per unit of key resource (per machine hour, say, or direct labour hour).

Division B

	£'000	£'000
Sales		400
Materials	160	
Bought-in services	80	
		240
Value added		160
Direct labour	70	
Indirect labour	50	
Depreciation	30	
		150
Profit		10

7 Interfirm comparisons and performance ratios

As well as comparing profit centres within a group, comparisons are also made between **companies in an industry**. Problems include a lack of information and different accounting polices. As well as monitoring performance from the investor's point of view, such schemes can be used in **competitive analysis. Ratio analysis** might be useful in this context.

Interfirm comparisons are comparisons of the performance of different companies, subsidiaries or investment centres.

7.1 The purpose of interfirm comparisons

(a) One company can compare its performance against another, as part of **competitive analysis or benchmarking**.

(b) **Senior management** can compare the performance of different subsidiary companies within their group.

(c) **Investors** can compare different firms in an industry.

(d) A company's **status** as a potential takeover target, or as a potential takeover threat, can be evaluated.

A financial comparison between rival public limited companies might cover:

- The best profits record (ROI, growth in profits and EPS)
- The best financial structure (financial gearing, debt ratio, interest cover)
- The 'best quality' profits or best growth prospects (P/E ratio comparison)
- The best cash flow position

7.2 Which firms should be compared with each other?

It is unrealistic to assume that all firms ought to be able to earn comparable ROI.

- Some industries are more profitable than others
- Some companies need a big investment in non-current assets

There are a number of basic requirements for an interfirm comparison to be successful.

(a) The companies compared must all belong to a **similar industry** to enable comparison.

(b) Reports might be given in the form of lists of **ratios**. If ratios are to be helpful for control purposes, comparisons should be limited to companies of roughly the same size.

(c) The results of each of the participants must be adjusted so that, as far as possible, the same **accounting policies** are used for each.

7.3 Performance ratios

Ratios are useful in that they provide a means of comparison of actual results:

- With a budget, or desired target
- With ratios of previous years' results, in order to detect trends
- With ratios of other companies or divisions
- With industry or governmental indices.

7.3.1 Ratios from financial statements

You should be familiar with the balance sheet and profit and loss account ratios.

(a) **Income statement ratios** include profit margin (profit/sales) which can be analysed as follows, in a hierarchy of subsidiary ratios.

(i) $\dfrac{\text{Production cost of sales}}{\text{Sales}}$ which can be broken down into:

(1) $\dfrac{\text{Material costs}}{\text{sales value of production}}$ or $\dfrac{\text{Material costs}}{\text{total costs of production}}$

(2) $\dfrac{\text{Works labour cost}}{\text{sales value of production}}$ or $\dfrac{\text{Labour costs}}{\text{total cost of production}}$

(3) $\dfrac{\text{Production overheads}}{\text{sales value of production}}$ or $\dfrac{\text{Production overheads}}{\text{total costs of production}}$

(ii) $\dfrac{\text{Distribution and marketing costs}}{\text{Sales}}$

(iii) $\dfrac{\text{Administrative costs}}{\text{Sales}}$

(b) **Statement of financial position ratios** include the following, broken down further.

(i) **Asset turnover** (sales/capital employed), which can be analysed by class of asset (eg sales/non-current assets).

(ii) **Working capital ratios** covering liquidity (eg current ratio, current assets/current liabilities) and turnover periods for receivables, payables and inventory (eg credit period taken by credit customers).

(iii) Gearing ratios covering borrowings.

Question
Strategic significance

Learning outcome D(i)

What might be the strategic significance of the following, when compared to the industry average?

(a) A high non-current asset turnover.
(b) High gearing
(c) Far higher non-current assets but lower labour costs.

Answer

(a) The firm is using capital efficiently – or is operating at high capacity.
(b) The firm has to reach a high profit level to pay its lenders – it might have less flexibility in pricing than competitors.

(c)   This might imply that the firm is more capital-intensive, in other words that perhaps it has invested in technology rather than labour. Given the high level of fixed costs which can be deduced from this, the firm might have to price aggressively to maintain market share.

Question   Subsidiaries

Learning outcome D(i)

Calculate and compare the ROI, asset utilisation and profitability of the two subsidiaries whose results are shown below.

	A Ltd	B Ltd
	£	£
Capital employed	300,000	800,000
Net profit	60,000	120,000
Sales	1,250,000	2,400,000

Answer

	A Ltd	B Ltd

ROI

$$\frac{£60,000}{£300,000} \times 100\% = 20\% \qquad\qquad \frac{£120,000}{£800,000} \times 100\% = 15\%$$

Asset turnover

$$\frac{£1,250,000}{£300,000} = 4.17 \text{ times} \qquad\qquad \frac{£2,400,000}{£800.000} = 3 \text{ times}$$

Profit/sales ratio

$$\frac{£60,000}{£1,250,000} \times 100\% = 4.8\% \qquad\qquad \frac{£120,000}{£2,400,000} \times 100\% = 5\%$$

A Ltd has a higher ROI than B Ltd. This is because, although it earned a lower net profit per £1 of sales (4.8p compared with 5p) its capital employed generated more sales turnover, and its asset turnover was nearly 40% higher, at 4.17 times compared with 3 times for B Ltd.

7.4 The calculation of return on investment in interfirm comparisons

There are several issues to consider when deciding how to measure both the return and the capital employed.

7.4.1 Return

Definition of return. Return might be taken as profit after tax. However, when interfirm comparisons are being made, this would be unsuitable, for two reasons.

(a)   The **tax rate** applicable to one company's profits may be different from the tax rate applicable to another's.

(b)   One company might be financed largely by borrowing, receiving tax relief on interest payments. Another company might be entirely equity financed.

Measuring return (profit). When there is a comparison between the results of subsidiaries within the same group or the results of investment centres within a single company, there may be a problem with **transfer prices**.

7.4.2 Capital employed/investment

Should assets be valued on the basis of historical cost, replacement cost, disposal value, current value or some other similar inflation-adjusted basis?

(a) Historical cost has the severe drawback that in a period of inflation, the balance sheet value of older non-current assets can fall below their 'realistic' current value, and so the measurement of ROI will give a misleading (excessively high) percentage return.

(b) Depreciation charges against non-current assets might also fail to reflect the loss of value from using the assets during the period, when historical cost accounting is used.

(c) Replacement cost or current cost might be difficult to estimate whereas historical cost is a readily-known value.

(d) Disposal value is only useful when the non-current assets are readily marketable (eg property) but in such cases a target return on disposal value represents an opportunity cost of the investment.

7.4.3 The accounting policies of different companies

Typical differences in accounting policies and asset acquisition methods between one firm and another are these.

- The assumed life of non-current assets
- The method of depreciation used
- Accounting for intangible non-current assets, such as development costs and goodwill
- Inventory valuation methods
- Renting accommodation instead of buying the freehold or leasehold
- Purchasing operating non-current assets or leasing/renting them

Chapter Roundup

- **Inflation** makes it harder to compare performance over time, as it affects accounting values, and hence measures of performance. It affects base line and comparative figures.

- **Discounted cash flows** can be used to assess the performance of capital investment projects, by comparing anticipated and actual cash flows, discounted in an appropriate way. It is probably a lot harder, although not impossible, to apply these to profit centres.

- The basic concept of **contribution** can be used strategically if questions about strategic factors are examined in its light. It is also appropriate for SBU performance measurement.

- **Profit centre organisation** reflects the structure of authority in the organisation, and managers are made accountable and rewarded on the basis of profit centre results.

- **Return on investment (ROI)** is a convenient measure, which ties in easily with the firm's accounts. However, there are measurement and valuation problems, especially in relation to non-current assets. These can encourage managers to take decisions which are not in the firm's best long-term interest. ROI does not easily account for risk.

- ROI is based on **organisation structure**, not business processes, and is only suitable to products at the mature phase of the life cycle.

- The performance of these business units is complicated by the degree of autonomy their managers enjoy.

- **Residual income** (RI) gets round some of the problems of ROI, by deducting from profit an imputed interest charge for the use of assets.

- **Profit centres** are often compared. Problems arise when managers are judged on matters they cannot control. A variety of measures involving **contribution** are used to isolate controllable costs.

- Problems in measuring **divisional performance** include allocation of head office costs, and different asset valuations.

- As well as comparing profit centres within a group, comparisons are also made between **companies in an industry**. Problems include a lack of information and different accounting polices. As well as monitoring performance from the investor's point of view, such schemes can be used in **competitive analysis. Ratio analysis** might be useful in this context.

Quick Quiz

1　Control of a strategic level should be based on measurements of ....

2　Define 'contribution margin'.

3　What is the main problem associated with ROI as a performance measure?

4　ROI is a form of ROCE.

☐　True

☐　False

5　Residual income (RI) is a measure of the centre's profits after deducting a notional or imputed .... cost.

6　What do you understand by the term 'divisional autonomy'?

7　What are 'controllable profit' and 'controllable margin'?

8　Give a broad definition of 'added value'.

9　In what way can inflation conceal poor performance?

10　A division with capital employed of £400,000 currently earns a ROI of 22%. It can make an additional investment of £50,000 for a 5 year life with nil residual value. The average net profit from this investment would be £12,000 after depreciation. The division's cost of capital is 14%. Calculate the residual income before and after the investment.

Answers to quick quiz

1　Cash flows

2　Contribution margin can be defined as 'the difference between sales volume and the variable cost of those sales, expressed either in absolute terms or as a contribution per unit.'

3　It is mainly to do with the problem of accurate measurement of the value of the assets used to produce the return. For example, it is probably most common to use return on net assets. Inflation and technological change alter the cost of fixed assets, so that it becomes difficult to compare the performance of different divisions.

4　True

5　Interest

6　The term refers to the right of a division to govern itself, that is, the freedom to make decisions without consulting a higher authority first and without interference from a higher body.

7　Controllable profit – contribution minus all the division's fixed costs controllable by the manager.

　Controllable margin – controllable profit minus all other costs directly traceable to the division.

8　Added value equals sales minus the costs of materials and bought-in-services

9　An organisation may be making a profit, but have suffered a fall in its operating capacity. Using the historical cost accounting convention, a company might have assets in its balance sheet valued on the basis of costs dating back 5, 10, 20, 30, or even 40 years or more. The costs of these assets would not be comparable with each other, partly because of technological developments over time, but largely because of inflation.

10

	Before investment £	After investment £
Divisional profit	88,000	100,000
Imputed interest		
(400,000 × 0.14)	56,000	
(450,000 × 0.14)		63,000
Residual income	32,000	37,000

Now try the question below from the Exam Question Bank

Number	Level	Marks	Time
Q14	Examination	25	45 mins

15

Strategic control

Introduction

This final chapter of the Study Text describes some more themes in **controlling performance** with the ultimate aim of increasing **shareholder value**. Many large firms are organised into strategic business units, and multinational firms in particular have specific management problems in relation to setting **objectives** and **performance assessment** (Section 2).

Transfer prices (Section 3) are a way of promoting divisional autonomy, but the transfer price needs to be fair, neutral and administratively simple. Otherwise, prices may be set in such a way as to improve the results of one subsidiary at the expense of another.

Turning away from the performance of the **managed unit**, in Section 4 we look at rewarding **managerial performance** itself. In this section we describe **agency theory**. A typical plc has a large number of **owners** (or principals) who have no real idea what their **agents** (the directors/managers) are doing.

Rewarding managers for their performance is a method of **control** in the sense that managers will have some **incentive** to achieve the organisation's objectives if they can see a reward (large bonus, share options) at the end of it.

We conclude the chapter with a look at an important analysis of the various ways in which the strategic apex may elect to exert control.

Topic list	Learning outcomes	Syllabus references	Ability required
1 Achieving success for the shareholder	D(i)	D1	Evaluation
2 International subsidiaries	D(i)	D4	Evaluation
3 Transfer pricing	D(iii)	D4	Comprehension
4 Managerial performance: agency theory and reward systems	D(i), D(iii)	D1, D4	Comprehension
5 Strategic management styles	D(i)	D1	Evaluation

1 Achieving success for the shareholder

FAST FORWARD

A management team is required by an **organisation's shareholders** to **maximise the value of their investment** in the organisation and a plethora of performance indicators is used to assess whether or not the management team is fulfilling this duty.

1.1 Shareholder value

A management team is required by an **organisation's shareholders** to **maximise the value of their investment** in the organisation and a plethora of performance indicators is used to assess whether or not the management team is fulfilling this duty.

The majority of these **performance measures** are based on the information contained in the organisation's published accounts. Not only do these indicators often give **conflicting messages**, they can be easily **manipulated** and often provide **misleading** information. Earnings per share, for example, is reduced by capital-building investments in research and development and in marketing.

What is more, the **financial statements** themselves **do not provide a clear picture of whether or not shareholder value is being created or destroyed.** The **profit and loss account**, for example, indicates the quantity but not the quality of earnings and it does not distinguish between earnings derived from operating assets as opposed to non-operating assets. Moreover, **it ignores the cost of equity financing** and only takes into account the costs of debt financing, thereby penalising organisations which choose a mix of debt and equity finance. Neither does the cashflow statement provide particularly appropriate information. Cashflows can be large and positive if an organisation underspends on maintenance and undertakes little capital investment in an attempt to increase short-term profits at the expense of long-term success. On the other hand, an organisation can have large negative cashflows for several years and still be profitable.

The use of a **shareholder value approach** to performance measurement involves moving the focus of attention away from simply looking at short-term profits to a **longer-term view of value creation**, the motivation being that it will help the business stay ahead in an increasingly competitive world.

Exam focus point

> Shareholder value may be increased by merging with another company. This was the topic of a question in Section A of the May 2001 paper under the old syllabus.

But what is meant by shareholder value? Quite simply, **shareholder value is in the eye of the shareholder:** different shareholders will value different aspects of performance.

- Financial returns in the short-term
- Short-term capital gains
- Long-term returns or capital gains
- Stability and security
- Achievements in products produced or services provided
- Ethical standards

(It is unlikely that the last two alone make a company valuable to an investor.)

These factors and others will all be reflected in a company's share price, but stock markets are notoriously fickle and tend to have a short-term outlook.

1.1.1 Shareholder value analysis

Wider share ownership and more knowledgeable investors are forcing companies to understand the techniques by which their companies are being judged. The terminology **shareholder value** is used widely to describe a range of shareholder focussed performance indicators developed by various consultancies.

One approach is **shareholder value analysis (SVA)**, devised by *Alfred Rappaport* (*Creating Shareholder Value,* 1986) and the subject of articles in *Management Accounting*. SVA is also referred to as **value based management**.

> **Shareholder value** is the 'total return to the shareholders in terms of both dividends and share price growth, calculated as the present value of future free cash flows of the business discounted at the weighted average cost of the capital of the business less the market value of its debt'.
>
> (CIMA *Official Terminology*)

Shareholder value = (business value − debt)

Where business value is calculated as the PV of free cashflows from operations plus the value of any marketable assets held.

The value of a corporation can be established by developing a future **cash flow forecast** and converting it into a present value. The total value of the business is then found by taking away the value of any debt and adding any value from external investments. Dividing the result by the number of shares gives the **shareholder value per share**. This technique has been used extensively in acquisition situations and is often known as **cash flow return on investment (CFROI)**.

1.1.2 Drivers of shareholder value

Rappaport proposes that this **single figure value** for a business be calculated by **reference to seven 'value drivers'**, which drive the generation of **cash.**

(a)   **Sales growth rate**: an increase in profitable sales should increase free cash flow.

(b)   **Operating profit margin**: the higher the margin on sales, the better.

(c)   **Cash tax rate**: the higher the tax, the more of the shareholders' value the government takes.

(d)   **Fixed capital investment rate**: cash invested in non-current assets reduces free cash flows even though it may lead to growth.

(e)   **Working capital investment rate**: a similar principle applies.

(f)   **The planning period**: the further into the future a firm can reasonably forecast its cash flows, the greater the PV and hence the business value.

(g)   **Cost of capital**: PV obviously depends on the discount rate employed.

According to Johnson and Scholes, applying SVA requires a whole new mindset, termed **value based management**. Central to this way of thinking is the identification of the cash generators of the business, or **value drivers**, examples of which are listed above. These will be both external and internal. For example, **competitive rivalry** is a major external value driver because of its direct impact on margins.

All the consultants who have followed Rappaport's ideas work from the same principles.

(a)   **Profit** has become discredited as a performance measure.

(b)   The traditional cost of capital used in the P&L, interest, is inadequate. A composite measure taking into account the complex **capital structure** of a business is needed.

(c)   What really needs to be measured is **how well the business is performing for the shareholders.**

> The November 2001 exam contained a question on using SVA to determine product and service development. The examiner commented on the 'abject lack of understanding of the concept of SVA'. This is just as relevant to the new syllabus exam.

1.2 How does business strategy promote increased shareholder value?

A diagram helps to show how strategy drives the business towards increased shareholder value, which for many businesses is the primary objective of strategy.

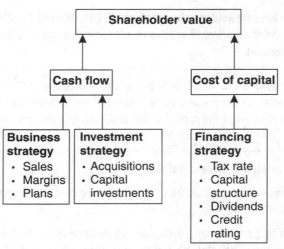

Shareholder value
├── Cash flow
│   ├── **Business strategy**
│   │   · Sales
│   │   · Margins
│   │   · Plans
│   └── **Investment strategy**
│   · Acquisitions
│   · Capital investments
└── Cost of capital
    └── **Financing strategy**
        · Tax rate
        · Capital structure
        · Dividends
        · Credit rating

(Adapted from CIMA Insider, March 2001)

The adoption of a value based approach to managing an enterprise has wide-ranging implications.

Culture: shareholder value must be accepted as the purpose for which the organisation exists. This may have greatest impact at the **strategic apex**, whose members may have had their own, different ideas on this subject; however, the importance of creating shareholder value must be emphasised in all parts of the business.

Nevertheless it is crucial that management do not overlook underlying business processes in the quest for value based metrics. Core business processes (for example, quality management, innovation, and customer service) should still be monitored alongside value based metrics.

Relations with the market: shareholder value should be reflected in share price. The company's senior managers must **communicate effectively with the market** so that their value-creating policies are incorporated into the share price. However, they must not be tempted to manipulate the market: this may be a difficult area to manage, given that executive rewards should reflect the share price. One way in which management should look to communicate performance to the market is through the use of performance indicators. These metrics should then, in turn, form the basis of the performance targets for divisional managers to achieve.

Strategic choices: the maximisation of shareholder value must be the object of all strategic choices. This will affect such matters as **resource allocation** and HR policies and will have particular relevance to the evaluation of expensive projects such as acquisitions and major new product development.

 Case Study

The Kingfisher group has announced that it is demerging its electrical division, in a bid to boost shareholder value by transforming it into a specialist DIY group. Sir Geoff Mulcahy, who is standing down as chief executive, said that the benefits of having a clear and focused DIY management outweighed the benefits of keeping the divisions together. He hopes that a standalone electrical business will be given a better rating by investors.

 Case Study

'For the last 15 years or so [shareholder value] ... has been the mantra for those who believe that companies should be run for the exclusive benefit of shareholders, with the interest of management aligned to shareholders through the use of stock options and similar equity-linked incentive schemes' (Edward Chancellor, *'Perverse Incentives'*, June 2002).

Chancellor believes that this idea should now come under closer scrutiny in the wake of the Enron collapse and other accounting scandals. Managers have often been guilty of earnings manipulation, inflating the share price and enriching themselves through the exercise of share options at the expense of shareholders. At Global Crossing, the telecoms firm, managers received billions of dollars in stock option profits while investors were left with worthless shares.

The shareholder value doctrine depends upon the efficient market hypothesis, which claims that a company's share price and market value is the same as its intrinsic value. The boom and bust in the 'dotcom' sector shows that shares may sometimes be over or under-valued, at least in the short run. Markets are constantly testing and discarding new ideas, so what may seem like a good idea one day is terrible the next. To quote again from Chancellor, 'Notable examples include the tens of billions of euros spent by European telecoms companies on licences to operate third generation mobile phone systems. Never mind that the technology was untried and the demand for the services unproven, the market was indicating that the money was well spent.'

1.3 Economic value management

FAST FORWARD

Economic value management hinges in the idea of an **economic profit,** which is derived after adjusting traditional accounting profits for the write offs that are made for **value building expenditures** such as training and advertising. By adding such expenditures back to accounting profit, better comparison can be made between companies.

Key term

Economic value added (EVA)™ 'A measure which approximates a company's profit. Traditional financial statements are translated into EVA statements by reversing distortions in operating performance created by accounting rules and by charging operating profit for all of the capital employed. For example, written-off goodwill is capitalised, as are extraordinary losses and the present value of operating leases. Extraordinary gains reduce capital.'

Stern Stewart

EVA = Adjusted profits* after tax – (Adjusted invested capital × WACC)

* Stern Stewart calls this net operating profit after tax (NOPAT).

Economic value management hinges on the calculation of **economic profit (EP).** A comparison of economic profit with required return results in a figure for **economic value added or destroyed**. The calculation of EP requires several **adjustments** to be made to traditionally-reported accounting profits. These adjustments are made to **avoid the immediate write-off of value-building expenditure** such as research and development expenditure, advertising expenditure or the purchase of goodwill.

The adjustments are intended to produce a figure for capital employed which is a more accurate reflection of the **base upon which shareholders expect their returns to accrue** and to provide a profit after tax figure which is a more realistic measure of the **actual cash yield generated** for shareholders from recurring business activities.

EVA theory says that in order to add economic value, a project or business unit must deliver more net operating profit, after all taxes and costs, than it costs to have access to the total capital used to generate that profit.

1.3.1 Principles of EVA

The principles of EVA, devised by the US consultants Stern Stewart, are:

- Investment leads to assets regardless of accounting treatments
- Assets once created cannot be diminished by accounting action

Such an approach contrasts favourably with information based on traditional accounting concepts and conventions. The prudence concept, for example, requires revenue expenditure (such as maintenance expenditure on plant and machinery) to be written off to the profit and loss account in the accounting period in which it is incurred. This is to reflect the fact that such expenditure may have no long-term benefits. It is therefore not very surprising that if management are assessed using performance measures calculated using traditional accounting policies, they are unwilling to invest in or spend money on activities which immediately reduce current year's profit.

It is claimed that EP provides the basis for a useful management performance appraisal measure because **while EP increases, so does the market value added (MVA) for a company and shareholder value**.

1.3.2 Benefits of economic value added

(a) **Net present value**

Economic value added focuses on the **long-term net present value of a company.** Managerial performance will be improved by investing in positive NPV projects, not investing in negative NPV projects and lowering the cost of capital.

(b) **Financing**

By including a financing element, the **cost of capital** is emphasised, and hence managers must have regard for **careful investment** and **control of working capital.** If managers choose negative NPV projects, the imputed capital charge will ultimately be greater than earnings.

(c) **Cash flows**

The adjustments within the model mean that economic value added should be based on **cash flows** rather than accounting data and hence it may be **less distorted** by the **accounting policies** chosen.

(d) **Clarity of measure**

Economic value added is a **monetary figure** rather than a ratio, and one that can be easily **linked to financial objectives**.

1.3.3 Drawbacks of economic value added

(a) **Failure to measure short-term position**

Economic value added does **not measure NPV** in the short-term. Projects with good long-term NPV, but large initial cash investments or poor initial returns, may be rejected by managers who are being judged on their **short-term performance.**

(b) **Use of historical accounts**

Economic value added is based on historical accounts which may be of **limited use** as a guide to the future. In practice also the influences of accounting policies on the starting profit figure may not be completely negated by the adjustments made to it in the economic value added model.

(c) **Other value drivers**

Other value drivers such as non-capitalised goodwill may be important despite being **excluded from the accounts**.

(d) **Adjustments**

Making the necessary adjustments can be **problematic** as sometimes a large number of adjustments are required.

(e) **Cost of capital**

The cost of capital used is calculated by the **capital asset pricing model,** and is therefore based upon the **assumptions** of that model such as **no change in risk.**

(f) **Inter-company comparisons**

Companies which are larger in size may have larger economic value added figures for this reason. Allowance for relative size must be made when inter-company comparisons are performed.

1.4 Example on EVA

Recommend which plc, X or Y, to invest funds in. Justify your decision.

Profit and loss account for the previous year (£m's)

	X	Y
Sales	26.0	62.0
Cost of sales	18.0	47.0
Gross profit	8.0	15.0
Production overheads	1.2	2.4
Advertising	0.6	2.0
Depreciation	1.1	1.6
Training	0.1	1.8
R & D	0.6	2.0
Bad debt expense	0.2	0.3
PBIT	4.2	4.9
Investment base	26.5	40.6

Solution

Traditional ROI techniques would give X plc 15.8% and Y plc 12.1%, and therefore choose X plc for investment. However this ignores the fact that Y is more heavily involved in developing the long term future of its company by spending on training, advertising and R & D. These items, under EVA, would be added back to obtain a comparison using operational expenses.

Adjusted ROI	X	Y
Original profit	4.2	4.9
Training	0.1	1.8
Advertising	0.6	2.0
R & D	0.6	2.0
New profit	5.5	10.7
New ROI	20.8%	26.4%

There is still a lack of information here to make a final decision, although the original analysis and decision to invest in X plc has been considerably refined. Business risk, market dynamics, previous year's results, competitor comparisons, and investment portfolio issues will all affect the analysis.

'**Economic value added** is the best indicator of business performance. When it is projected for future years and discounted to the present value, it represents the net present value of all past and future investments and cash flows. Therefore, by making increases in EP a priority, the economic value added of a company will increase, which will, in turn, lead to increases in a company's market value (and therefore its share price).'

(John Mayfield, 'Economic value management: the route to shareholder value', *Management Accounting*, September 1997)

1.5 Market value added (MVA)

Market value added (MVA) is the difference between the market value of a company and the economic book value of capital employed.

This might be thought of as being related to EVA, being the net present value created for shareholders over the life of the company. The difference is that EVA is essentially **historic**, while MVA is assumed (under the efficient market hypothesis) to be the market's assessment of the firm's ability to add value **in the future**. It is thus very similar to Rappaport's idea of business value and his list of **value drivers** is relevant. The idea of market valuation, however, brings into play all the variables that affect market expectations, such as the firm's ability to win the trust of investors and investors' understanding of the business.

Market value added is 'the difference between a company's market value (derived from share price) and its economic book value (the amount of capital that shareholders and debt holders have committed to the firm throughout its existence, including any retained earnings)'.　　　　　　(CIMA *Official Terminology*)

Put another way, MVA is 'the difference between what investors put into the company as capital and what they could get out by selling at today's market price' (Al Ehrbar). In theory, **MVA is the present value of all future EVAs**. However, **market sentiment** will always affect the share price too.

The difficulty with this measure is that while capital employed (monies invested by shareholders in the company) represents investments made in the **past**, market value is the present value of **future** cash flows. So what does MVA (ie, the difference between these two) really represent? In addition, shareholders are buying and selling shares all the time – there must be as many measures of MVA for a company as there are individual shareholders.

1.6 Total shareholder return (TSR)

Total shareholder return (TSR) is the total percentage return to shareholders over a given period.

Total shareholder return is defined as the **total percentage return to shareholders over a period** using the formula

$$\frac{\text{Dividend per share} + \text{Movement in share price}}{\text{Share price at the start of the period}}$$

This measure is very simple to calculate, and can be used to compare performance of similar companies. As with MVA, however, it is not immune to market sentiment.

Case Study

Nokia, the Finnish mobile phone company, produced a total shareholder return (TSR) of 1,660 per cent over the years 1996-2001, putting it top of a recent FT European performance league table. In late 2000 it commanded 35 per cent of global mobile unit sales.

Characteristics of companies in the league table with high TSRs include:

- Strong management and clear strategy
- Strong communication with investors, customers and staff
- Ability to innovate (in technology, product design, customer service)
- Successful international expansion

2 International subsidiaries

The task of setting objectives within a **multinational** is complex, and several problems must be resolved. For example, setting up systems of **performance measurement** will need to consider:

- realistic **standards** country to country
- **controllability** of cash flows
- **currency conversion**

The task of setting objectives within a multinational is complex, and several problems must be resolved.

A question may require consideration of particular difficulties with performance measurement when plant and marketing operations are in various parts of the world.

(a) **Capital structure**. Where foreign subsidiaries are financed partly by loans, the differing rates of interest in each country might affect the relative profitability of subsidiaries.

(b) **Cost structure**. Overseas subsidiaries may have a different operational gearing.

(c) **Accounting policies**. In each country, the subsidiary may adopt a different rate of depreciation so that profits and asset values are not comparable. Profits can be transformed into losses by accounting policies.

(d) **Government policy**. There will be differences in the levels of grants or concessions from the national government and in the rate of taxation and interest.

(e) **Transfer prices** for goods and services between the subsidiaries may be set in such a way as to improve the results of one subsidiary (or head office) at the expense of another (eg if goods are transferred from a subsidiary to head office at cost, the subsidiary will get no profit and the head office will obtain the goods at a low price).

(f) **Workforce**. A justification for expanding into developing countries is to take advantage of lower wages.

(g) **Exchange rate fluctuations** may turn profits into losses and vice versa.

(h) **Risk**. Some overseas operations may be a greater risk than others so that higher returns may be required from them.

(i) **Life cycle**. The same product may be at different stages in its product life cycle in each country, as we have seen.

(j) **Transport**. If a subsidiary in, say, the United Kingdom is performing much worse, and incurring higher unit costs of production than a comparable subsidiary in, say, Germany, it may still be uneconomic to switch production from the United Kingdom to Germany because the extra costs of transport to the UK may exceed the savings in the costs of production.

(k) **Domestic competition**. The market of the overseas subsidiary may face a unique configuration of Porter's five forces.

(l) **Different economic conditions**.

Increasing demands that larger accompanies adopt the principles of **corporate social responsibility** complicate the problem of controlling the activities of foreign subsidiaries. The corporate **mission statement** can be useful here, if it incorporates the aspirations and standards promoted by all stakeholder groups, not just those of shareholders. Such a mission statement can be incorporated into divisional performance measurement schemes that can also reflect the particular national and industrial circumstances of each division.

2.1 International comparisons

If the firms or subsidiaries being compared operate in different countries there will be certain problems for performance measurement.

(a) **Realistic standards**. It may be difficult to establish realistic standards for each different country. Performance standards should take account of local conditions, considering local opportunities as well as any restrictions on the activities of an operating unit in a particular country.

(b) **Controllable cash flows**. Care must be taken to determine which cash flows are controllable and to separate these from those outside the control of local management. In particular the distortions caused by local taxation laws should be eliminated.

(c) **Currency conversion**. Considerable friction and difficulty in measuring performance can be caused by the use of inappropriate currency conversion rates.

(d) **Basis for comparison**. Following on from the problem of setting realistic standards of performance, central management must exercise care when attempting to compare performance between the different countries.

Normal procedures may have to be adjusted.

(a) **Reports**

    (i) **Standardised** to allow comparative analysis between subsidiaries

    (ii) Use an agreed **common language** and currency

(iii)   **Frequent** as necessary to allow proper management

(iv)   Cover all the **information needs** of headquarters

(b)   **Meetings**

Gatherings between HQ executives and subsidiary management allow for more intensive information exchange and monitoring; and minimise misunderstandings. They do however take up time and resources, and are generally not as regular as reports.

(c)   **Information technology**

Information technology makes it much easier for marketing and financial performance to be monitored closely, given the speed of transmission of e-mail and Internet communications.

Meetings can even be conducted by video-conferencing – this might prove cheaper than flying.

(d)   **Control of intermediaries**

The problem with controlling 'outsiders' is that there is no control by **ownership**. In the final analysis **negative controls** such as legal pressures or threats to discontinue relationships can be used, resulting perhaps in loss of business. The best control is through good selection and by making it clear to intermediaries that their interests and the company's coincide.

2.2 Exchange rates and transfer pricing

The most obvious problem is the exchange rate, but Ward argues that this may not be serious.

(a)   A firm which makes an investment in a factory intends to use the factory, not sell it. So whilst changes in exchange rates alter the value of the original investment this does not matter so much in the long term, providing that the subsidiary is making a profit at the same rate, in local terms.

(b)   This might seem a rather dangerous assertion; however, it is sometimes asserted that long-term differences in rates of exchange result from inflation.

In practice many companies have to budget for exchange rate changes which affect their plans. A firm can lock itself into particular exchange rate by hedging or other financing. Jaguar used this when, as an independent British company, most of its sales were in the US. Hedging instruments were used to protect its profits from any fall. As well as operational issues, such as the acquisition of funds, hedging contracts etc, there is the obviously vexed problem of performance assessment.

It might be helpful to illustrate this with a question.

| Question | Overcapacity |

Learning outcome D(i)

Enharmonic Changes Ltd is a company with two European factories: at Sharp in the UK and at Pflatte in South Africa. The company is facing overcapacity at Sharp even though it is the most productive plant. The company makes *Andantes*. The relative performance of each factory at rates of £1= 200 Yen and 14 Yen = 1 South Africa Rand (ZAR) is as follows.

	Sharp		*Pflatte*	
	£	Yen equiv (200Y: £1)	South African rands	Yen equiv (14Y: 1 ZAR)
Selling price	100	20,000	2,000	28,000
Cost of production	75	15,000	1,600	22,400
Gross profit	25	5,000	400	5,600
Margin		25%		20%

In Japanese Yen terms, the UK factory has a higher margin, but the actual profits from making and selling Andantes in South Africa are higher than in the UK.

(a)   However, given the overcapacity in the UK, and given transportation cost at £10 per andante from the UK to South Africa, should the UK factory be used as a sole source for the South African plant? Assume that the Pflatte pays Sharp in sterling for the Andantes. Assume that profits are remitted to

Japan in South African rands. Assume the £: Yen and ZAR: Yen relationships are as above, but that £: ZAR rates are as follows

(i)   £1 = 20 ZAR.
(ii)   £1 = 15 ZAR.

(b)   What would be the position if Andantes were shipped over directly, and Pflatte did *not* pay Sharp any money for the components?

Answer

(a)   (i)   Pflatte sources from the UK (£1 = 20 ZAR)

		Pflatte	
	£	ZAR	Yen equivalent
Selling price	–	2,000	28,000
Sourcing cost from UK	75 × 20	(1,500)	(21,000)
Transport from UK	10 × 20	(200)	(2,800)
Gross profit margin		300	4,200
Margin			15%

(ii)   Pflatte sourcing from the UK (£1 =15 ZAR)

	£	ZAR	Yen equivalent
Selling price (ZAR)		2,000	28,000
Sourcing cost from UK	75 × 15	(1,125)	(15,750)
Transport from UK	10 × 15	(150)	(2,100)
Gross profit margin		725	10,150
Margin			36.2%

(b)

	£	ZAR	Yen
Revenue	–	2,000	28,000
Cost (UK)	(75)	–	15,000
Transport	(10)	–	2,000
Profit/(loss)	(85)	2,000	11,000

Tutorial note

Further permutations can be tried. For example the relative exchange rates between £ and Yen, and ZAR and Yen would also affect the decision. So, even though greater Yen profit is made by Pflatte, the differences in production costs can, at *some* rates of exchange, make it easier for Pflatte merely to sell andantes imported from Sharp. In option (b), no currency changes hands between Pflatte and Sharp, but at prevailing rates of exchange, it is still better for Pflatte to sell andantes made at Sharp than to make them itself.

There are particular problems in the management of overseas subsidiaries.

(a)   How much **control**? There is always a tension between autonomy and centralisation.

(b)   **Staffing**. Expatriate managers are often expensive. Housing costs, school fees etc often have to be paid. In addition there are cultural problems in adjusting to the country and the way of doing business.

3 Transfer pricing   11/05

FAST FORWARD

Transfer pricing is used to encourage optimal performance by keeping track of costs incurred throughout a business. Ideally, prices should be set by reference to the **external market**, but where this is not possible transfer prices will have to be **negotiated**, or head office might **impose** a transfer price.

> **Transfer price** is the 'price at which goods or services are transferred between different units in the same company. May be set on a number of bases, such as marginal cost, full cost, market price or negotiation. For the transfer of goods between units in different countries, tax implications mean that the respective governments have to accept the method used. They are likely to insist on *arm's-length transfer prices*.'
>
> (CIMA *Official Terminology*)

Where there are **transfers of goods or services between divisions**, the transfers could be made 'free' to the division receiving the benefit. For example, if a garage and car showroom has two divisions, one for car repairs and servicing and the other for sales, the servicing division will be required to service cars before they are sold. The servicing division could do its work for the car sales division without making any record of the work done. However, unless the cost or value of such work is recorded, management cannot keep a check on the amount of resources (such as labour time) being used up on new car servicing. It is necessary for control purposes that some record of the inter-divisional services should be kept. Inter-divisional work can be given a cost or charge: a **transfer price**.

Transfer prices are a way of promoting **divisional autonomy**, ideally without prejudicing the measurement of **divisional performance** or discouraging overall **corporate profit maximisation**. The management accountant therefore has to devise a method of transfer pricing which meets three criteria.

- Equity (provides a fair measure of divisional performance)
- Neutrality (avoids the distortion of business decision making)
- Administrative simplicity

The transfer price should provide an **'artificial' selling price** that enables the transferring division to earn a return for its efforts, and the receiving division to incur a cost for benefits received, and should be set at a level that enables profit centre performance to be measured 'commercially'. This means that the transfer price should be a **fair commercial price**.

3.1 Transfer pricing with constant unit variable costs and sales prices

An ideal transfer price should reflect **opportunity cost**.

Where a **perfect external market price exists** and unit variable costs and sales prices are constant, the opportunity cost of transfer will be one or other of the following

- External market price
- External market price less savings in selling costs

3.2 Example: transferring goods at market price

A company has two profit centres, A and B. Centre A sells half of its output on the open market and transfers the other half to B. Costs and external revenues in a period are as follows.

	A	B	Total
	£	£	£
External sales	8,000	24,000	32,000
Costs of production	12,000	10,000	22,000
Company profit			10,000

Required

What are the consequences of setting a transfer price at market price?

If the transfer price is at market price, A would be happy to sell the output to B for £8,000, which is what A would get by selling it externally.

	A		B		Total
	£	£	£	£	£
Market sales		8,000		24,000	32,000
Transfer sales		8,000		–	
		16,000		24,000	
Transfer costs			8,000		
Own costs	12,000		10,000		22,000
		12,000		18,000	
Profit		4,000		6,000	10,000

The consequences, therefore, are as follows.

(a) **A earns the same profit** on transfers as on external sales. B must pay a commercial price for transferred goods.

(b) A will be indifferent about selling externally or transferring goods to B because the profit is the same on both types of transaction. B can therefore ask for and obtain as many units as it wants from A.

3.3 Adjusted market price

Internal transfers in practice are often cheaper than external sales, with savings in selling and administration costs, bad debt risks and possibly transport/delivery costs. It would seem reasonable for the buying division to expect a **discount** on the external market price.

If profit centres are established, however, and unit variable costs and sales prices are constant, there are two possibilities.

(a) Where the supplying division has spare capacity the ideal transfer price will simply be the **standard variable cost of production.**

(b) When there is a scarce production resource, the ideal transfer price will be the variable cost of production plus the contribution forgone by using the scarce resource instead of putting it to its most profitable alternative use.

3.4 Cost-based approaches to transfer pricing

Cost-based approaches to transfer pricing are often used in practice, because there is often no external market for the product that is being transferred or because, although there is an external market, it is an imperfect one because there is only limited external demand.

3.4.1 Transfer prices based on full cost

Under this approach the full standard cost (including fixed overheads absorbed) that is incurred by the supplying division in making the product is charged to the receiving division. If a **full cost plus** approach is used, a profit margin is also included in this transfer price.

A company has 2 profit centres, A and B. Centre A can only sell half of its maximum output externally because of limited demand. It transfers the other half of its output to B which also faces limited demand. Costs and revenues in a period are as follows.

	A	B	Total
	£	£	£
External sales	8,000	24,000	32,000
Costs of production in the division	12,000	10,000	22,000
(Loss)/Profit	(4,000)	14,000	10,000

If the transfer price is at full cost, A in our example would have 'sales' to B of £6,000 (ie half of its total costs of production). This would be a cost to B, as follows.

	A		B		Company as a whole
	£	£	£	£	£
Open market sales		8,000		24,000	32,000
Transfer sales		6,000		–	
Total sales, inc transfers		14,000		24,000	
Transfer costs			6,000		
Own costs	12,000		10,000		22,000
Total costs, inc transfers		12,000		16,000	
Profit		2,000		8,000	10,000

The transfer sales of A are self-cancelling with the transfer costs of B so that total profits are unaffected. The transfer price simply spreads the total profit of £10,000 between A and B. Division A makes no profit on its work and using this method, would prefer to sell its output on the open market if it could.

3.4.2 Transfer prices based on full cost plus

If the transfers are at cost plus a margin of, say, 25%, A's sales to B would be £7,500.

	A		B		Total
	£	£	£	£	£
Open market sales		8,000		24,000	32,000
Transfer sales		7,500		–	
		15,500		24,000	
Transfer costs			7,500		
Own costs	12,000		10,000		22,000
		12,000		17,500	
Profit		3,500		6,500	10,000

Compared to a transfer price at cost, A gains some profit at the expense of B. However, A makes a bigger profit on external sales in this case because the profit mark-up of 25% is less than the profit mark-up on open market sales, which is (£8,000 – 6,000)/£6,000 = 33%. The transfer price does not give A fair revenue or charge B a reasonable cost, and so their profit performance is distorted. It would seem to give A an incentive to sell more goods externally and transfer less to B. This may or may not be in the best interests of the company as a whole.

Division A's total costs of £12,000 will include an element of fixed costs. Half of division A's total costs are transferred to division B. However from the point of view of division B the cost is entirely variable.

Suppose that the cost per unit to A is £15 and that this includes a fixed element of £6, while division B's own costs are £25 per unit, including a fixed element of £10. The total variable cost is really £9 + £15 = £24, but from division B's point of view the variable cost is £15 + £15 = £30. This means that division B will be unwilling to sell the final product for less than £30, whereas any price above £24 would make a contribution.

3.4.3 Transfer prices based on variable cost

A variable cost approach entails charging the variable cost that has been incurred by the supplying division to the receiving division. As above, we shall suppose that A's cost per unit is £15, of which £6 is fixed and £9 variable.

	A		B		Company as a whole
	£	£	£	£	£ £
Market sales		8,000		24,000	32,000
Transfer sales at variable cost		3,600		–	
$\left(£9/£15 \times 6,000\right)$					
		11,600		24,000	
Transfer costs			3,600		
Own variable costs	7,200		6,000		13,200
Own fixed costs	4,800		4,000		8,800
Total costs and transfers		12,000		13,600	22,000
(Loss)/Profit		(400)		10,400	10,000

The problem is that with a transfer price at variable cost the supplying division does not cover its fixed costs.

3.5 Transfer prices based on opportunity costs

It has been suggested that transfer prices can be set using the following rule.

Transfer price per unit = **standard variable cost** in the producing division plus the opportunity cost to the organisation of supplying the unit internally.

The opportunity cost will be one of the following.

(a) The maximum **contribution foregone** by the supplying division in transferring internally rather than selling externally

(b) The **contribution foregone** by not using the same facilities in the producing division for their next best alternative use

(c) If there is no external market for the item being transferred, and no alternative uses for the division's facilities, the transfer price = standard variable cost of production.

(d) If there is an external market for the item being transferred and no alternative use for the facilities, the transfer price = the market price.

3.6 Transfer pricing when unit variable costs and sales prices are not constant

When unit variable costs and/or unit selling prices are not constant there will be a profit-maximising level of output and the ideal transfer price will only be found by careful analysis and sensible negotiation.

(a) The starting point should be to establish the output and sales quantities that will optimise the profits of the company or group as a whole.

(b) The next step is to establish the transfer price at which both profit centres, the supply division and the buying division, would maximise their profits at this company-optimising output level.

(c) There may be a range of prices within which both profit centres can agree on the output level that would maximise their individual profits and the profits of the company as a whole. Any price within the range would then be 'ideal'.

3.7 Problems in transfer pricing

(a) If transfer prices are set at **full cost** the transferring division makes no profit.

(b) If **full cost plus** is used the problem is how to set the margin at a level that all parties perceive as being fair.

(c) If **variable cost** is used the transferring division does not cover its fixed costs but two-part prices (the variable cost transfer price plus a fixed annual fee) might be used to overcome this.

(d) Transfer prices based on **standard cost** are fairer than transfer prices based on actual costs because if actual costs are used the transferring division has no incentive to control its costs: it can pass on its inefficiencies to the receiving division.

(e) On the other hand, standards may become out of date so it is advisable to have an agreement to revise them periodically.

3.8 Negotiated transfer prices   11/05

When authority is decentralised to the extent that divisional managers negotiate transfer prices with each other, the agreed price may be finalised from a mixture of accounting arithmetic, politics and compromise.

Inter-departmental disputes about transfer prices are likely to arise and these may need the intervention of head office to settle the problem.

(a) **Head office imposition**. Head office management may impose a price which maximises the profit of the company as a whole.

(b) On the other hand, head office management might restrict its intervention to the task of **keeping negotiations in progress** until a transfer price is eventually settled.

Where **negotiation** is necessary there should be an understanding of the 'risk/return' profile. *Tomkins* suggests the following methodology, which head office can apply when mediating in disputes.

(a) **Identify the outer bounds of the transfer price**. In other words, at what transfer price does the buying division end up earning the entire group profit, and at what transfer price does the selling division earn the entire group profit?

(b) **Variability**. At each transfer price, compare each division's expected profits and the variability of the profits.

(c) Incorporate **risk attitudes** in a fair transfer price, so that the profit-share between divisions takes the riskiness of the project into consideration.

Exam focus point

A question in the November 2005 exam illustrates the most likely way that the topic of transfer prices will be examined. It is highly unlikely that you will be asked to compute a transfer price, or even to discuss the various methods. It is far more likely that a question will test your understanding of the basic issues: fairness, autonomy, motivation, risk and so on.

3.9 International transfer prices

When firms transfer goods and services *internally*, but also *internationally*, the transfer price mechanism allows them to **move value from one country to another** without actually engaging in trade. Bearing in mind the difficulty discussed above of establishing the level at which a transfer price should be set, we may say that a 'low' price effectively moves value into the receiving country, while a 'high' one moves it into the transferring country.

3.9.1 Using transfer prices

This ability to decide in which country value (and particularly *profit*) is created is extremely useful.

(a) It can be used to **manage taxation**.
 (i) Profit can be minimised in states with high profits taxes.
 (ii) Selling prices can be minimised in states with high levels of irrecoverable VAT (and similar taxes).
 (iii) The value imported into countries with high tariff levels can be minimised.

(b) It can be used to **move profits to the home country** from states with restrictions on repatriation of profits or on currency exchange.

(c) It can be used strategically.
 (i) It can **disguise the attractiveness** of an operation to competitors by reducing profits.

(ii)   It can enable a **low-price strategy aimed at driving out competition** without arousing the suspicions of the local tax authorities by declaring a very low level of profit. However, this course of action is likely to lead to accusations of dumping.

3.9.2 Centrally determined transfer prices and strategy

These considerations produce pressure for multinational companies to set their transfer prices centrally. There are, however, other important strategic considerations relating to this approach.

(a)   **Autonomy**. Centrally determined transfer prices can seriously affect the ability of national managers to **influence the performance of their divisions**. This can affect their overall motivation, encourage them to seek ways around the restrictions imposed and make it more difficult to assess their overall performance.

(b)   **Transaction cost economics**. Transaction cost theory is dealt with in Paper 5 but it is also relevant to Paper 6. In terms of transaction cost economics, a centrally determined, non-market based transfer price makes an implicit assumption that the **hierarchy solution** is the best one. However, there may not have been any actual consideration of the market alternative. A resource or competence based approach to strategy would immediately challenge this and call for detailed consideration of the benefit a market based approach. The crucial question is whether the business should actually be operating any given national subsidiary at all, or whether its services should be bought in.

3.10 The Eccles matrix

R J Eccles suggested that the method of setting transfer prices should reflect the organisation's **degree of diversification** and its **degree of vertical integration**.

(a)   Where both diversification and integration are low, as, for example, in the relationship between two shops in a retail chain, a transfer price may not even be required , but if it is, it can be set collaboratively.

(b)   Where diversification is low, but vertical integration is high, as in the relationship between two different stages of product assembly, co-operation is important, so the transfer price should be negotiated: it should probably be set at full cost so that resource allocation is appropriate and the supplying division's costs are covered.

(c)   Where diversification is high and integration is low, as in the now unfashionable diversified conglomerate, transfers are likely to be uncommon and should be at market price, as is the rest of each subsidiary's trade.

(d)   Nevertheless, where diversification and integration are both high, as may be the case when there is extensive trade along a supply chain combined with similarly extensive market-based exchanges, once again, the transfer price should be set collaboratively.

4 Managerial performance: agency theory and reward systems

4.1 Agency theory

Where the management of a business is separated from its ownership by the employment of professional managers, the managers may be considered to be the agents of the owners. **Agency theory** is concerned to analyse the way agents may be expected to behave and how they can be motivated to promote their principals' interest.

Few large businesses are managed by their owners. In the case of larger companies, the shareholders are numerous and unlikely to wish to take part in the management of the company, viewing it simply as a vehicle for investment. Even where ownership is concentrated, large companies tend to be managed mostly by professional managers who have little ownership interest, if any. This **separation of ownership**

from control has been a feature of business for over a century and brings with it a recurring problem: the business should be managed so as to promote the economic interest of the shareholders as a body, but the power to manage lies in the hands of people who may use it to promote their own interests. How can the managers be made to favour the interest of the owners rather than their own?

Principle – agent relationship

This problem is not confined to the management of companies: it is the general problem of the **agency relationship** and occurs whenever one person (the **principal**) gives another (the **agent**) power to deal with his affairs. The relationship between principal and agent has been subjected to some quite abstruse economic and mathematical analysis; this area of study is called **agency theory**. It proceeds on the basis that principals and agents are rational utility maximisers. *Wilson and Chua*, explain what this means for agents in *Managerial Accounting: Method and Meaning* (1993) as follows.

- They behave rationally in seeking to maximise their own utility
- They seek financial and non-financial rewards
- They tend to be risk-averse and, hence, reluctant to innovate
- Their individual interests will not always coincide with those of their principals
- They prefer leisure to hard work

Key term

> **Agency theory** is a 'hypothesis that attempts to explain elements of organisational behaviour through an understanding of the relationships between principals (such as shareholders) and agents (such as entity managers and accountants). A conflict may exist between the actions undertaken by agents in furtherance of their own self-interest, and those required to promote the interests of the principals. Within the hierarchy of entities, the same goal incongruence may arise when divisional managers promote their own self-interest over those of other divisions and of the entity generally.'   (CIMA *Official Terminology*)

Two important concepts are used to explain the things that can go wrong in the agency relationship: **adverse selection** and **moral hazard**.

Key term

> **Adverse selection** is the making of poor choices. It occurs perhaps most often because the chooser lacks the information necessary to make a good choice.

Adverse selection can be exacerbated in the agency relationship when the agent has an incentive to withhold information from the principal, thus creating **information asymmetry**. We see this in two important instances.

(a) **Appointment of the agent**: the principal attempts to appoint a competent and trustworthy agent, but potential agents thus have an incentive to conceal any evidence there may be that they are incompetent or untrustworthy.

(b) **Assessing the agent's performance**: the principal desires to reward the agent according to the standard of his performance, but the agent controls or is able to influence the information the principal uses to assess that performance.

Key term

> **Moral hazard** arises whenever people are protected from the adverse consequences of their actions; they have no incentive to exercise correct judgement and are free to act in an irresponsible manner.

To protect a person from the adverse consequences of his behaviour is to encourage irresponsibility, hence the moral dimension of the concept.

Moral hazard is not confined to principal-agent relationships. It occurs in banking, for example, when government guarantee schemes allow bankers to make injudicious loans. It is also an important argument against debt forgiveness for impoverished countries: poor countries that currently manage to pay their debts would have no incentive to do so if debt forgiveness became a general policy. Their hard-won credit status could disappear, undermining the structure of private investment in those countries, with inevitable undesirable results for their economic development.

In the agency relationship, we are concerned with the use the agent makes of the authority with which he has been entrusted. Moral hazard will exist unless at least part of the agent's remuneration is contingent upon his making responsible use of his authority.

4.2 Agency theory and the business organisation

Agency theory is clearly relevant to the modern business organisation. The directors are the agents of the shareholders, employed to manage the business in the shareholders' interest. To do this they are given considerable power over the resources of the business. How can the shareholders be sure that they will not abuse this trust?

To a lesser extent, agency theory also applies within the organisation. The directors cannot do everything: they must employ subordinate managers to put their plans into action. How can the directors be sure that those subordinates are not abusing their trust? This aspect of the problem is particularly relevant to the new organisational structures and practices discussed in Chapter 12. These rely to an increasing extent on the initiative, skills, creativity and enthusiasm of quite junior members of the organisation, since this is what creates competitive advantage. They also depend on both motivating and empowering these employees. Therefore, the issue of trust comes to prominence.

Agency theory is thus very relevant to the fields of both performance measurement and executive compensation. **Moral hazard** can be reduced by making the rewards paid to the directors and managers contingent upon their satisfactory performance: the information asymmetry that leads to **adverse selection** can be reduced by making proper information about that performance available to the shareholders (in the case of the directors) and to the directors (in the case of the subordinate managers).

Unfortunately, the existence of **uncontrollable factors** undermines this neat prescription. It is difficult to devise performance measures that relate specifically to a manager so as to be able to judge his or her performance as a manager. As soon as the issue of **ability as a manager** arises it is necessary to **consider him in relation to his area of responsibility**. If we want to know how good a manager is at marketing the only information there is to go on is the marketing performance of his division (which may or may not be traceable to his own efforts).

4.2.1 Uncontrollable factors

> **FAST FORWARD**
>
> **Managerial performance** should be assessed on those items that are directly **controllable** by the manager in question.

It is generally considered to be unreasonable to assess managers' performance in relation to matters that are beyond their control. Therefore **management performance measures** should **only include those items that are directly controllable by the manager** in question.

There are different degrees of controllability.

(a) A divisional manager may have no control over the level of head office costs. It may seem unfair that X division, say, is allocated 10% of £1m = £100,000, when it is actually demands made by division Y that caused costs to be that high rather than £500,000 (10% × £500,000 = £50,000).

However, X division does have control over the relative demands it places on head office. If it placed fewer demands perhaps its percentage contribution could fall, say, to 5%.

(b) Likewise a division may not have control over the overall level of a group's interest charge, which will depend on the source of funds and on other division's activities. However, it may have control over its working capital requirements and perhaps over capital expenditure.

Special attention is required to the problems of segregating managerial performance from the economic performance of the managed unit. The distinction is very important. *Horngren* provides a good illustration.

'The most **skilful divisional manager is often put in charge of the sickest division in an attempt to change its fortunes**. Such an attempt may take years, not months. Furthermore the manager's efforts may merely result in bringing the division up to a minimum acceptable ROI. The division may continue to be a poor profit performer in comparison with other divisions. If top management relied solely on the absolute

ROI to judge management, the skilful manager would be foolish to accept such a trouble-shooting assignment.'

4.2.2 Key issues

Key issues in agency theory are **attitudes to risk** and the **observability of effort**.

(a) Conventional management accounting assumes that principals protect agents from risk – it only makes managers responsible for things they can control. Agency theory suggests that if principals are risk averse then they should share the risk with agents and this can increase the utility of both parties. Making a large part of an executive's potential reward subject to some profit target is a simple example of such a contract.

(b) The principal may find it difficult to observe the agent's efforts. Alternatively the principal may not be able to evaluate the effort because he does not possess the information on which the decision to expend that much effort was based.

The **relevance of agency theory to control** issues is made clear in an article in *CIMA Student,* by J G Williams: 'Corporate governance: aims and developments' (February 1996). The point is that a **typical plc has a large number of owners (shareholders) who have no real idea what their agents (the directors) are doing.**

'Agency theory gives a clear structure to the problems of a relationship between shareholders (principals) and directors (their agents) where the principals have the problem of motivating and controlling their agents to act in their interest.

- Supervision is impracticable. It is impossible to see what the agents are doing, and what effort they are making.

- The agents have superior knowledge of the situation and potential profits, and the agents may be motivated to act in their own interests rather than those of the shareholders.'

4.2.3 Limitations of agency theory

Many of the assumptions of agency theory are open to question, however. *Wilson and Chua* describe the **limitations** of agency theory as follows.

'Firstly, it is essentially a two-person analysis and, although it may be possible to extend it to a whole hierarchical organization, this has yet to be done. Secondly, it is a single period model which neglects the potential impact of a continuing employment relationship. Finally, the descriptive validity of the utility maximizing assumptions is open to question.'

In the context of agency theory, some writers (including *Emmanuel et al*) refer to the contract between the organisation and the manager, meaning not only the legal employment contract, but the understanding between the two parties that is enforced by the organisation's administrative processes and by the forces of the labour market (how easy it is for managers to move elsewhere and for organisations to find replacements).

The relevance of this to the role of the management accountant is that the needs of outsiders to the management team (the shareholders) must be taken into account, especially with regards to any risky decisions which may not yield a satisfactory return.

4.3 Possible management performance measures

In the light of the above the following can be suggested.

(a) **Subjective measures may** be used, for example ranking performance on a scale of 1 to 5. This approach is used in the civil service. It is obviously highly imprecise but if properly done it should avoid the problems that arise when a good manager is hampered by a poor division.

(b) **The judgement of outsiders can** be regarded as a measure of managerial performance. This may be difficult to implement for many companies but the method is used. A company might, for example, design a share option scheme so that directors could only exercise their options if the share price outperformed the FT-SE 100 index over, say, five years.

(c) **Upward appraisal** is used by some businesses. This involves staff giving their opinions on the performance of their managers.

(d) **Accounting measures** can be used, but must be tailored according to what or whom is being judged.

(e) **Non-financial measures** may include market share measurements or a variety of other qualitative criteria.

4.4 Rewarding managers

Rewarding managers for their performance is a method of **control**, although money is not the only type of reward they may seek. Managers may also look for power, status and responsibility.

Rewarding managers for their performance is a method of control in the sense that it is **assumed that attempts will be made to achieve the organisation's objectives in return for rewards.** This, in turn, **derives from motivation theory,** which suggests that people have wants or desired outcomes and modify their behaviour accordingly.

4.4.1 What type of reward?

Money is not the only type of reward that managers might seek. Emmanuel *et al* cite Vancil's **categorisation of rewards** into three types.

- The **pleasure** that is derived from **managing one's own entity**
- The **power and status** that accompanies the position of being manager
- Rewards in the form of **money** or with **a monetary value**

4.4.2 How to link performance and rewards

A good reward system should have the following characteristics.

(a) It should **offer real incentives**, sufficiently high after tax to make extraordinary effort worthwhile.

(b) It should **relate payments to criteria over which the individual has control** (otherwise he will feel helpless to ensure his reward, and the expectancy element in motivation will be lacking).

(c) It should **make clear the basis on which payments are calculated**, and all the conditions that apply, so that individuals can make the calculation of whether the reward is worth the extra level of effort.

(d) It should be **flexible** enough to reward different levels of achievement in proportion, and with provision for regular review and adaptation to the changing needs of the organisation.

(e) It should be **cost effective** for the organisation.

4.4.3 Lower cut-off point

Emmanuel *et al* suggest that a **linear link** is the most common method of linking performance and reward, but with a lower cut-off point because organisations **do not want mediocre performance to be rewarded.**

4.4.4 Upper cut-off point

Most schemes also have upper cut-off points, for a variety of reasons.

(a) A fear that the high bonuses that would be paid might not be deserved because of:
- A windfall gain
- Increased current period reported profit at the expense of the long term
- A faulty plan design (the fear is greatest when the plan is new)

(b) A desire not to encourage unsustainably high growth and profitability.

(c) A desire not to pay lower-level managers more than upper-level managers earn (vertical compensation equity).

(d) A desire to keep total compensation consistent over time, so that managers are able to sustain their lifestyle.

(e) A desire to adhere to standard corporate and industry practices.

(Emmanuel et al)

4.4.5 Common types of scheme

There are three common types of scheme.

(a) Under a **profit-related pay scheme**, pay (or part of it) is related to results achieved (performance to defined standards in key tasks, according to plan). A form of **management by objectives** will probably be applied (see Chapter 12).

(b) **Profit-sharing schemes** offer managers bonuses, perhaps in the form of shares in the company, related directly to profits.

(c) **Group incentive schemes** typically offer a bonus for a group (equally, or proportionately to the earnings or status of individuals) which achieves or exceeds specified targets.

Incentive and recognition schemes are **increasingly focused not on cash**, but on non-cash awards, such as gifts and travel vouchers. These are cheaper for the organisation, especially as they are regarded as 'won' rather than deserved by right.

Schemes should of course be **tailored to suit the circumstances**. A bonus scheme for part-time non-executive directors remunerated by fees under contract for a fixed term of years should ensure that they take a longer-term view of the organisation in the interests of shareholders.

4.5 Problems with incentive schemes

 FAST FORWARD

Incentive schemes have their problems, including those relating to timescale, measurement and motivation.

4.5.1 Short-termism

Exam focus point

There is an implicit assumption in the paragraphs above that short-termism should be avoided if possible. There may be occasions when short termism is to be encouraged, and this could be the topic of an exam question.

There are a number of problems associated with measures specifically designed to avoid short-termism.

(a) The link between current expenditure or savings and long-term effect may not be clear.

(b) There is a danger that over-investment for the future may have such an adverse impact on present performance that the future envisaged is impossible to achieve.

(c) Incentive schemes for long-term achievements may not motivate since effort and reward are too distant in time from each other (or managers may not think that they will be around that long!).

The incentive systems of 30 UK, US and German companies were examined (in a study by J Cotes et al, Management Accounting Research) to see if there existed any bias towards the short or long term.

(a) In all companies, some measure of **profitability** was a primary corporate objective, measured as return on investment, earnings per share or some equivalent measure.

(b) **Marketing objectives** (eg sales growth, market share) came next, although German and US companies placed greater emphasis on these than UK firms.

Short-termist incentive schemes might include the following.

- **Share options**
- Bottom line profits in absolute terms
- Returns on assets – easily manipulated
- Residual income

Long-termist schemes are based perhaps on marketing/sales objectives, profit margin, and other measures related to **management by objectives**.

When should short-termism be **encouraged**? One way of answering this question is to be bloody-minded and make a case for **never** encouraging short-termism. A short-term approach may be appropriate in certain circumstances however.

- In **highly uncertain and changeable situations**, for example in the fashion industry
- When a short-term approach is **consistent with long-term goals** (for instance a business may make do with old, inefficient plant, awaiting the availability of a new technology)
- When **stakeholders also take a short-term view**
- When **competitors** do likewise
- Under **financial constraints** or difficulties such as workflow problems or insolvency
- Some organisations have **duties to maintain a certain financial position**

4.5.2 Problems of measurement

Clearly the way in which measurements are taken could seriously affect the reward a manager receives. There are three main issues.

(a) It is **questionable** whether any performance measures or set of measures can provide a **comprehensive assessment** of what a single person achieves for the organisation. There will always be the old chestnut of **lack of goal congruence,** employees being committed to what is measured, rather than the objectives of the organisation.

(b) Particularly where performance has to be measured by **non financial performance measures** (such as in the public sector), the results are formed from **subjective judgement.**

(c) It is difficult to **segregate the controllable component** of performance from the uncontrollable component.

4.5.3 Problems of motivation

Schemes will only work if **rewards** seem both **desirable and achievable.**

(a) **Money is not the only motivator** – different individuals value different types of reward. Some people may be in a job because it offers **'job for life'** security and a pension; although current working practices have made this less common it is still true in areas of the public sector and large 'institutionalised' companies. **Personal objectives** may also be important; public sector nurses or teachers may feel they are following a vocation regardless of the rewards offered.

(b) When an individual's work performance is dependent on work done by other people (and much work involves co-operation and interdependence with others), an **individual bonus scheme is not always effective**, since **individual performance can be impaired by what other people have done.**

(c) There is evidence that the **effectiveness** of incentive schemes **wears off over time**, as acceptable 'norms' of working are re-established.

(d) The **value of a reward may be affected by factors beyond the organisation's control.** For example a reward such as a company car (associated with achieving a certain status) may be so highly taxed that managers do not consider the effort of achieving the reward to be worthwhile.

4.5.4 Particular problems in the public sector

In addition to the general problems outlined above, performance-related reward schemes in the public sector have particular problems.

(a) **Timescale.** Many projects (for example, environmental programmes) can only be assessed for effectiveness in the longer term.

(b) **The political dimension.** A senior manager in the public sector may be set a goal which is highly undesirable from the point of view of opposition parties: if a change of power is imminent, might the manager later be rewarded for **not** achieving it!

5 Strategic management styles 11/07

> Goold and Campbell identified three major approaches to running divisionalised conglomerates: **strategic planning**, **strategic control** and **financial control**.

The **role of the corporate centre** in a divisionalised company has been the subject of much theory and research. Indeed, the diversified conglomerate itself has itself been challenged as a form of economic organisation. There are **three generally accepted possible roles for the centre**.

- Determination of overall strategy and the allocation of resources
- Controlling divisional performance
- Provision of central services

All three of these roles have been subject to debate.

Centralised determination of strategy has been challenged as inappropriate in a diversified conglomerate. Similarly, **resource allocation**, it has been suggested, is the proper role of **capital markets**; and the rigour of the vetting carried out by central staff has been questioned.

Controlling divisional performance is subject to all the arguments for and against decentralisation already discussed. The ability of the centre to prevent **strategic drift** has been questioned, though the radical market alternative can only work in drastic ways, such as takeover.

Centralised provision of certain **services**, such as legal and HR departments, is promoted as enhancing efficiency through the attainment of economies of scale. However, it is also suggested that many of these services can be contracted for locally at no greater cost and with the advantage of precluding any tendency to empire-building at the centre.

5.1 Research

Goold and Campbell researched the role of the centre in 16 British-based conglomerates. They concentrated on the first two roles summarised above, which they referred to as **planning influence** and **control influence**. The variation in these roles allowed the identification of eight distinct **strategic management styles**.

Planning influence was exercised in a variety of ways, but a fairly smooth spectrum of styles was observable, ranging from minimal, where the centre is little more than a holding company, to highly centralised, where the managers in the business units have responsibility only for operational decisions.

Control influence was exercised by the agreement of **objectives**, the monitoring of **results** and the deployment of **pressures and incentives**. This gave rise to three distinct categories of control influence: **flexible strategic**, **tight strategic** and **tight financial**.

Of the eight strategic management styles they defined, Goold and Campbell found that three of them were particularly common; each was associated with one of the three **control influence** categories mentioned above and with a different degree of **planning influence**.

5.2 Strategic management styles

5.2.1 Strategic planning

The strategic planning management style is associated with the flexible strategic type of control influence and a fairly high degree of central planning influence. The **centre establishes extensive planning processes** through which it works with business unit managers to make substantial contributions to strategic thinking, often with a unifying overall corporate strategy. Performance targets are set in broad terms, with an **emphasis on longer-term strategic objectives**. Such organisations build linked international businesses in core areas. Business units tend to follow bold strategies and often achieve above industry average **growth** and **profitability**.

5.2.2 Strategic control

The strategic control management style involves a **fairly low degree of planning influence** but uses **tight strategic control**. The centre prefers to leave the planning initiative to the business unit managers, though it will review their plans for acceptability. **Firm targets are set** for a range of performance indicators and performance is judged against them. The centre concentrates on rationalising the portfolio. Such companies achieve **good profits** but are **less successful at achieving growth**.

5.2.3 Financial control

The centre exercises influence almost entirely through the budget process. It takes little interest in business unit strategy and controls through profit targets. Careers are at stake if budgets are missed. Strategies are **cautious** and rarely global. Business unit managers tend to sacrifice market share to achieve high profits. As a result, these companies produce **excellent profits**, but **growth comes mainly from acquisitions**.

Exam focus point

> The November 2007 question contained a question looking at the impact of an acquisition on strategic management styles. The examiner noted, however, that candidates often displayed a lack of knowledge of this syllabus area, with some confusing strategic planning with the rational planning model. Be aware that strategic planning is a specific management style not a generic term.

Question
Head office

Learning outcome D(i)

XYZ has over 500 profit centres (ranging from baggage handling equipment to stockings) and revenues of £7bn. Head office staff amount to 47. Each profit centre must provide the following.

(a)   The *annual profit plan*. This is agreed in detail every year, after close negotiation. It is regarded as a commitment to a preordained level of performance.

(b)   A *monthly management report*, which is extremely detailed (17 pages). Working capital is outlined in detail. Provisions (the easiest way to manipulate accounts) are highlighted.

Is XYZ a strategic planner, a strategic controller or a financial controller?

Answer

Financial controller.

5.3 Influences on the choice of planning organisation

(a)   Highly diversified groups are much more difficult to control from the centre, and a **financial controller** system would probably be suitable.

(b)   When **big capital investments** are planned, head office should be involved in the decision.

(c)   When **cash flow** is tight, other strategies must be sacrificed to the paramount concern for short term survival and attention to cash flow.

(d)   Organisations in a single industry which is fairly stable would perhaps be more efficiently managed by a hierarchical, centralised management system, structured perhaps on a functional basis (production, marketing etc).

(e)   Top management might prefer one approach.

- A management team is required by an **organisation's shareholders** to **maximise the value of their investment** in the organisation and a plethora of performance indicators is used to assess whether or not the management team is fulfilling this duty.

- **Economic value** management hinges in the idea of an **economic profit,** which is derived after adjusting traditional accounting profits for the write offs that are made for **value building expenditures** such as training and advertising. By adding such expenditures back to accounting profit, better comparison can be made between companies.

- **Market value added** (MVA) is the difference between the market value of a company and the economic book value of capital employed.

- The task of setting objectives within a **multinational** is complex, and several problems must be resolved. For example, setting up systems of **performance measurement** will need to consider:
    - realistic **standards** country to country
    - **controllability** of cash flows
    - **currency conversion**

- **Transfer pricing** is used to encourage optimal performance by keeping track of costs incurred throughout a business. Ideally, prices should be set by reference to the **external market**, but where this is not possible transfer prices will have to be **negotiated**, or head office might **impose** a transfer price.

- Where the management of a business is separated from its ownership by the employment of professional managers, the managers may be considered to be the agents of the owners. **Agency theory** is concerned to analyse the way agents may be expected to behave and how they can be motivated to promote their principals' interest.

- **Managerial performance** should be assessed on those items that are directly **controllable** by the manager in question.

- **Rewarding managers** for their performance is a method of **control**, although money is not the only type of reward they may seek. Managers may also look for power, status and responsibility.

- Incentive schemes have their problems, including those relating to timescale, measurement and motivation.

- Goold and Campbell identified three major approaches to running divisionalised conglomerates: **strategic planning**, **strategic control** and **financial control**.

1   Profits can be transformed into losses by accounting policies.

    ☐   True

    ☐   False

2   How might controllable cash flows vary between international subsidiaries?

3   When setting transfer prices, the management accountant has to devise a method which meets these three criteria:

    ....

    ....

    ....

4   A transfer price should be
    (i)   An 'artificial' selling price
    (ii)   A fair commercial price

    A   (i) only
    B   (ii) only
    C   both (i) and (ii)
    D   neither (i) nor (ii)

5   How can the important distinction between managerial performance, and the economic performance of the managed unit, be illustrated?

6   Who is the principal and who is the agent in a company?

7   How can management by objectives be regarded as a system of control?

8   Define 'shareholder value analysis'.

9   Which of Goold and Campbell's strategic management styles is associated with a fairly low degree of planning influence from the corporate centre but tight strategic control?

10   What are the three generally accepted roles for the corporate centre in running divisionalised conglomerates?

1   True

2   Local tax rates may differ

3   Equity or fairness
    Neutrality
    Administrative simplicity

4   C

5   The most skilful divisional manager is often put in charge of the sickest division in an attempt to change its fortunes. Such an attempt may take years, not months.

6   Principal = shareholder   or   Principal = board
    Agent = manager/director   Agent = subordinate manager

7   Managers are required to specifically state the objectives that they expect to attain. Actual results can then be measured against these objectives.

8   Shareholder value analysis is an approach to financial management which focuses on the creation of economic value for shareholders, as measured by share price performance and flow of dividends.

9   Strategic control

10 Determination of overall strategy and the allocation of resources; Controlling divisional performance; Provision of central services

Now try the question below from the Exam Question Bank

Number	Level	Marks	Time
Q15	Examination	50	90 mins

We have analysed the requirements of question 15 in some detail, as it is a detailed case-study scenario and requires careful reading.

Appendix:
Mathematical tables

Tables

Area under the normal curve

This table gives the area under the normal curve between the mean and the point Z standard deviations above the mean. The corresponding area for deviations below the mean can be found by symmetry.

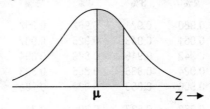

$Z = \dfrac{(x-\mu)}{\sigma}$	0.00	0.01	0.02	0.03	0.04	0.05	0.06	0.07	0.08	0.09
0.0	.0000	.0040	.0080	.0120	.0160	.0199	.0239	.0279	.0319	.0359
0.1	.0398	.0438	.0478	.0517	.0557	.0596	.0636	.0675	.0714	.0753
0.2	.0793	.0832	.0871	.0910	.0948	.0987	.1026	.1064	.1103	.1141
0.3	.1179	.1217	.1255	.1293	.1331	.1368	.1406	.1443	.1480	.1517
0.4	.1554	.1591	.1628	.1664	.1700	.1736	.1772	.1808	.1844	.1879
0.5	.1915	.1950	.1985	.2019	.2054	.2088	.2123	.2157	.2190	.2224
0.6	.2257	.2291	.2324	.2357	.2389	.2422	.2454	.2486	.2517	.2549
0.7	.2580	.2611	.2642	.2673	.2704	.2734	.2764	.2794	.2823	.2852
0.8	.2881	.2910	.2939	.2967	.2995	.3023	.3051	.3078	.3106	.3133
0.9	.3159	.3186	.3212	.3238	.3264	.3289	.3315	.3340	.3365	.3389
1.0	.3413	.3438	.3461	.3485	.3508	.3531	.3554	.3577	.3599	.3621
1.1	.3643	.3665	.3686	.3708	.3729	.3749	.3770	.3790	.3810	.3830
1.2	.3849	.3869	.3888	.3907	.3925	.3944	.3962	.3980	.3997	.4015
1.3	.4032	.4049	.4066	.4082	.4099	.4115	.4131	.4147	.4162	.4177
1.4	.4192	.4207	.4222	.4236	.4251	.4265	.4279	.4292	.4306	.4319
1.5	.4332	.4345	.4357	.4370	.4382	.4394	.4406	.4418	.4429	.4441
1.6	.4452	.4463	.4474	.4484	.4495	.4505	.4515	.4525	.4535	.4545
1.7	.4554	.4564	.4573	.4582	.4591	.4599	.4608	.4616	.4625	.4633
1.8	.4641	.4649	.4656	.4664	.4671	.4678	.4686	.4693	.4699	.4706
1.9	.4713	.4719	.4726	.4732	.4738	.4744	.4750	.4756	.4761	.4767
2.0	.4772	.4778	.4783	.4788	.4793	.4798	.4803	.4808	.4812	.4817
2.1	.4821	.4826	.4830	.4834	.4838	.4842	.4846	.4850	.4854	.4857
2.2	.4861	.4864	.4868	.4871	.4875	.4878	.4881	.4884	.4887	.4890
2.3	.4893	.4896	.4898	.4901	.4904	.4906	.4909	.4911	.4913	.4916
2.4	.4918	.4920	.4922	.4925	.4927	.4929	.4931	.4932	.4934	.4936
2.5	.4938	.4940	.4941	.4943	.4945	.4946	.4948	.4949	.4951	.4952
2.6	.4953	.4955	.4956	.4957	.4959	.4960	.4961	.4962	.4963	.4964
2.7	.4965	.4966	.4967	.4968	.4969	.4970	.4971	.4972	.4973	.4974
2.8	.4974	.4975	.4976	.4977	.4977	.4978	.4979	.4979	.4980	.4981
2.9	.4981	.4982	.4982	.4983	.4984	.4984	.4985	.4985	.4986	.4986
3.0	.49865	.4987	.4987	.4988	.4988	.4989	.4989	.4989	.4990	.4990
3.1	.49903	.4991	.4991	.4991	.4992	.4992	.4992	.4992	.4993	.4993
3.2	.49931	.4993	.4994	.4994	.4994	.4994	.4994	.4995	.4995	.4995
3.3	.49952	.4995	.4995	.4996	.4996	.4996	.4996	.4996	.4996	.4997
3.4	.49966	.4997	.4997	.4997	.4997	.4997	.4997	.4997	.4997	.4998
3.5	.49977									

Present value table

Present value of £1 ie $(1+r)^{-n}$ where r = interest rate, n = number of periods until payment or receipt

Periods	Interest rates (r)									
(n)	1%	2%	3%	4%	5%	6%	7%	8%	9%	10%
1	0.990	0.980	0.971	0.962	0.952	0.943	0.935	0.926	0.917	0.909
2	0.980	0.961	0.943	0.925	0.907	0.890	0.873	0.857	0.842	0.826
3	0.971	0.942	0.915	0.889	0.864	0.840	0.816	0.794	0.772	0.751
4	0.961	0.924	0.888	0.855	0.823	0.792	0.763	0.735	0.708	0.683
5	0.951	0.906	0.863	0.822	0.784	0.747	0.713	0.681	0.650	0.621
6	0.942	0.888	0.837	0.790	0.746	0.705	0.666	0.630	0.596	0.564
7	0.933	0.871	0.813	0.760	0.711	0.665	0.623	0.583	0.547	0.513
8	0.923	0.853	0.789	0.731	0.677	0.627	0.582	0.540	0.502	0.467
9	0.914	0.837	0.766	0.703	0.645	0.592	0.544	0.500	0.460	0.424
10	0.905	0.820	0.744	0.676	0.614	0.558	0.508	0.463	0.422	0.386
11	0.896	0.804	0.722	0.650	0.585	0.527	0.475	0.429	0.388	0.350
12	0.887	0.788	0.701	0.625	0.557	0.497	0.444	0.397	0.356	0.319
13	0.879	0.773	0.681	0.601	0.530	0.469	0.415	0.368	0.326	0.290
14	0.870	0.758	0.661	0.577	0.505	0.442	0.388	0.340	0.299	0.263
15	0.861	0.743	0.642	0.555	0.481	0.417	0.362	0.315	0.275	0.239
16	0.853	0.728	0.623	0.534	0.458	0.394	0.339	0.292	0.252	0.218
17	0.844	0.714	0.605	0.513	0.436	0.371	0.317	0.270	0.231	0.198
18	0.836	0.700	0.587	0.494	0.416	0.350	0.296	0.250	0.212	0.180
19	0.828	0.686	0.570	0.475	0.396	0.331	0.277	0.232	0.194	0.164
20	0.820	0.673	0.554	0.456	0.377	0.312	0.258	0.215	0.178	0.149

Periods	Interest rates (r)									
(n)	11%	12%	13%	14%	15%	16%	17%	18%	19%	20%
1	0.901	0.893	0.885	0.877	0.870	0.862	0.855	0.847	0.840	0.833
2	0.812	0.797	0.783	0.769	0.756	0.743	0.731	0.718	0.706	0.694
3	0.731	0.712	0.693	0.675	0.658	0.641	0.624	0.609	0.593	0.579
4	0.659	0.636	0.613	0.592	0.572	0.552	0.534	0.516	0.499	0.482
5	0.593	0.567	0.543	0.519	0.497	0.476	0.456	0.437	0.419	0.402
6	0.535	0.507	0.480	0.456	0.432	0.410	0.390	0.370	0.352	0.335
7	0.482	0.452	0.425	0.400	0.376	0.354	0.333	0.314	0.296	0.279
8	0.434	0.404	0.376	0.351	0.327	0.305	0.285	0.266	0.249	0.233
9	0.391	0.361	0.333	0.308	0.284	0.263	0.243	0.225	0.209	0.194
10	0.352	0.322	0.295	0.270	0.247	0.227	0.208	0.191	0.176	0.162
11	0.317	0.287	0.261	0.237	0.215	0.195	0.178	0.162	0.148	0.135
12	0.286	0.257	0.231	0.208	0.187	0.168	0.152	0.137	0.124	0.112
13	0.258	0.229	0.204	0.182	0.163	0.145	0.130	0.116	0.104	0.093
14	0.232	0.205	0.181	0.160	0.141	0.125	0.111	0.099	0.088	0.078
15	0.209	0.183	0.160	0.140	0.123	0.108	0.095	0.084	0.074	0.065
16	0.188	0.163	0.141	0.123	0.107	0.093	0.081	0.071	0.062	0.054
17	0.170	0.146	0.125	0.108	0.093	0.080	0.069	0.060	0.052	0.045
18	0.153	0.130	0.111	0.095	0.081	0.069	0.059	0.051	0.044	0.038
19	0.138	0.116	0.098	0.083	0.070	0.060	0.051	0.043	0.037	0.031
20	0.124	0.104	0.087	0.073	0.061	0.051	0.043	0.037	0.031	0.026

Cumulative present value table

This table shows the present value of £1 per annum, receivable or payable at the end of each year for n years. $\dfrac{1-(1+r)^{-n}}{r}$

Periods					Interest rates (r)					
(n)	1%	2%	3%	4%	5%	6%	7%	8%	9%	10%
1	0.990	0.980	0.971	0.962	0.952	0.943	0.935	0.926	0.917	0.909
2	1.970	1.942	1.913	1.886	1.859	1.833	1.808	1.783	1.759	1.736
3	2.941	2.884	2.829	2.775	2.723	2.673	2.624	2.577	2.531	2.487
4	3.902	3.808	3.717	3.630	3.546	3.465	3.387	3.312	3.240	3.170
5	4.853	4.713	4.580	4.452	4.329	4.212	4.100	3.993	3.890	3.791
6	5.795	5.601	5.417	5.242	5.076	4.917	4.767	4.623	4.486	4.355
7	6.728	6.472	6.230	6.002	5.786	5.582	5.389	5.206	5.033	4.868
8	7.652	7.325	7.020	6.733	6.463	6.210	5.971	5.747	5.535	5.335
9	8.566	8.162	7.786	7.435	7.108	6.802	6.515	6.247	5.995	5.759
10	9.471	8.983	8.530	8.111	7.722	7.360	7.024	6.710	6.418	6.145
11	10.368	9.787	9.253	8.760	8.306	7.887	7.499	7.139	6.805	6.495
12	11.255	10.575	9.954	9.385	8.863	8.384	7.943	7.536	7.161	6.814
13	12.134	11.348	10.635	9.986	9.394	8.853	8.358	7.904	7.487	7.103
14	13.004	12.106	11.296	10.563	9.899	9.295	8.745	8.244	7.786	7.367
15	13.865	12.849	11.938	11.118	10.380	9.712	9.108	8.559	8.061	7.606
16	14.718	13.578	12.561	11.652	10.838	10.106	9.447	8.851	8.313	7.824
17	15.562	14.292	13.166	12.166	11.274	10.477	9.763	9.122	8.544	8.022
18	16.398	14.992	13.754	12.659	11.690	10.828	10.059	9.372	8.756	8.201
19	17.226	15.679	14.324	13.134	12.085	11.158	10.336	9.604	8.950	8.365
20	18.046	16.351	14.878	13.590	12.462	11.470	10.594	9.818	9.129	8.514

Periods					Interest rates (r)					
(n)	11%	12%	13%	14%	15%	16%	17%	18%	19%	20%
1	0.901	0.893	0.885	0.877	0.870	0.862	0.855	0.847	0.840	0.833
2	1.713	1.690	1.668	1.647	1.626	1.605	1.585	1.566	1.547	1.528
3	2.444	2.402	2.361	2.322	2.283	2.246	2.210	2.174	2.140	2.106
4	3.102	3.037	2.974	2.914	2.855	2.798	2.743	2.690	2.639	2.589
5	3.696	3.605	3.517	3.433	3.352	3.274	3.199	3.127	3.058	2.991
6	4.231	4.111	3.998	3.889	3.784	3.685	3.589	3.498	3.410	3.326
7	4.712	4.564	4.423	4.288	4.160	4.039	3.922	3.812	3.706	3.605
8	5.146	4.968	4.799	4.639	4.487	4.344	4.207	4.078	3.954	3.837
9	5.537	5.328	5.132	4.946	4.772	4.607	4.451	4.303	4.163	4.031
10	5.889	5.650	5.426	5.216	5.019	4.833	4.659	4.494	4.339	4.192
11	6.207	5.938	5.687	5.453	5.234	5.029	4.836	4.656	4.486	4.327
12	6.492	6.194	5.918	5.660	5.421	5.197	4.988	4.793	4.611	4.439
13	6.750	6.424	6.122	5.842	5.583	5.342	5.118	4.910	4.715	4.533
14	6.982	6.628	6.302	6.002	5.724	5.468	5.229	5.008	4.802	4.611
15	7.191	6.811	6.462	6.142	5.847	5.575	5.324	5.092	4.876	4.675
16	7.379	6.974	6.604	6.265	5.954	5.668	5.405	5.162	4.938	4.730
17	7.549	7.120	6.729	6.373	6.047	5.749	5.475	5.222	4.990	4.775
18	7.702	7.250	6.840	6.467	6.128	5.818	5.534	5.273	5.033	4.812
19	7.839	7.366	6.938	6.550	6.198	5.877	5.584	5.316	5.070	4.843
20	7.963	7.469	7.025	6.623	6.259	5.929	5.628	5.353	5.101	4.870

Exam question and answer bank

What the examiner means

The table below has been prepared by CIMA to help you interpret exam questions.

Learning objective	Verbs used	Definition
1 Knowledge What you are expected to know	• List • State • Define	• Make a list of • Express, fully or clearly, the details of/facts of • Give the exact meaning of
2 Comprehension What you are expected to understand	• Describe • Distinguish • Explain • Identify • Illustrate	• Communicate the key features of • Highlight the differences between • Make clear or intelligible/state the meaning of • Recognise, establish or select after consideration • Use an example to describe or explain something
3 Application How you are expected to apply your knowledge	• Apply • Calculate/ compute • Demonstrate • Prepare • Reconcile • Solve • Tabulate	• Put to practical use • Ascertain or reckon mathematically • Prove with certainty or to exhibit by practical means • Make or get ready for use • Make or prove consistent/compatible • Find an answer to • Arrange in a table
4 Analysis How you are expected to analyse the detail of what you have learned	• Analyse • Categorise • Compare and contrast • Construct • Discuss • Interpret • Produce	• Examine in detail the structure of • Place into a defined class or division • Show the similarities and/or differences between • Build up or compile • Examine in detail by argument • Translate into intelligible or familiar terms • Create or bring into existence
5 Evaluation How you are expected to use your learning to evaluate, make decisions or recommendations	• Advise • Evaluate • Recommend	• Counsel, inform or notify • Appraise or assess the value of • Advise on a course of action

1 Four Star Products

Four Star Products plc is a major manufacturing organisation with a range of consumer products. Founded over seventy years ago and run for many years by the founder and his family, the company was rather traditional in its strategy, tending to stick to the hardware and other household goods that it understood. A formal system of strategic planning was introduced in 1962 and remains in place today, with a 47 person strong planning department reporting to a Planning Director.

Since a financial crisis in 1994, the dominance of the founding family has been diluted by banker power and the appointment from outside of a new CEO, a new CFO and three non-executive directors. The CEO has a reputation for turning companies around and his strategy has been to move into the IT and telecommunications sectors in force. He has made little use of the work of the planning department, preferring to commission research externally. Unfortunately, the recent collapse of the Internet bubble and fall in interest in IT and telecomms shares has led to Four Star suffering significant losses and a fall in its share price. One of the CEO's plans for cost reduction is to abolish the planning department.

Required

(a)   Is the CEO justified in his attitude towards the planning department?

(b)   Explain how the formal planning process is intended to deal with events such as the collapse of the Internet business model.

Approaching the question

You must learn to read question settings critically. Look for hints and keywords and ask questions of the information given to you. This is illustrated here.

Four Star Products plc is a major manufacturing organisation with a range of consumer

> How quickly does the market move? Is rapid introduction of new products required?

products. Founded over seventy years ago and run for many years by the founder and his

family, the company was rather traditional in its strategy, tending to stick to the hardware and

> Culture? Flexibility? Innovation?

other household goods that it understood. A formal system of strategic planning was

introduced in 1962 and remains in place today, with a 47 person strong planning department

> Rational model

reporting to a Planning Director.

> That is a lot of people and likely to be a major overhead

Since a financial crisis in 1994, the dominance of the founding family has been diluted by

> Concern for financial performance

banker power and the appointment from outside of a new CEO, a new CFO and three non-

executive directors. The CEO has a reputation for turning companies around and his strategy

> Change of sector – how practical?

has been to move into the IT and telecommunications sectors in force. He has made little use

of the work of the planning department, preferring to commission research externally.

> Why?

Unfortunately, the recent collapse of the Internet bubble and fall in interest in IT and telecomms

shares has led to Four Star suffering significant losses and a fall in its share price. One of the

CEO's plans for cost reduction is to abolish the planning department.

> Requirement for cost reduction

2 IT strategy

45 mins

Learning outcome B(vi)

Explain *five* reasons why it is essential for a modern organisation to have an IT strategy.

Illustrate your answer with examples of these reasons drawn from your own knowledge and experience.

(25 marks)

3 Management and social responsibility

45 mins

Learning outcome B(iii)

In what respects may the need to exercise social responsibility shape the relationship of management to stakeholders?

(25 marks)

Approaching the answer

This is a difficult question, mainly because it seems very short, and possibly even a bit vague, and you may wonder how you can plan and write for 45 minutes on this topic. Thinking about the requirement should throw up several issues for you to consider. Let's look at it again.

In what respects may the need to exercise social responsibility shape the relationship of management to stakeholders?

> Who are the stakeholders likely to be affected?
>
> Not just talking about shareholders!

> Why is there ever a need to exercise social responsibility?

> What is social responsibility? A minefield! Different stakeholders define it in different terms. (But have a definition in your mind)

> What is the usual relationship between managers and stakeholders? Why are such relationships important?

Answer plan

Organise the things that you have noticed and your points arising into a coherent answer plan. Not all of the points may need to go into your answer, so spend some time thinking them through and prioritising them.

Definition of social responsibility – not just environmentalism, but also social issues. Organisation must be aware of wider society. This will sometimes have to override commercial pressures. There are costs and benefits.

Where are the limits? The world as a whole? Argument that businesses discharge some responsibility simply by creating wealth and paying taxes.

Pressures come from stakeholders – managers don't do it under their own steam.

Stakeholder analysis (for each one, describe the relationship, and their particular interest in social responsibility)

(a) **Employees** – paid workers, but also members of society. Legal regulations such as health and safety

(b) **Customers** – paying for goods and services. Can put pressure on products to set new standards eg 'dolphin friendly' tuna fishing

(c) **Suppliers** – may impose restrictions

(d) **Professional bodies** – ethical standards for management to follow

(e) **Elected authorities** – can affect management in a number of ways (legislation, public opinion, influence over commercial organisations)

(f) **Shareholders** – profit! Might not appreciate resources being used on worthy projects that earn no money.

BPP LEARNING MEDIA

Management issues – they need to weigh up the conflicting demands

(a)   Monitoring the expectations people have of the organisation

(b)   Achieving good publicity

(c)   Selecting socially responsible activities.

    (i)   Ensuring core activities are conducted in a socially responsible way

    (ii)   Supporting activities which are for public welfare (eg charitable donations)

(d)   Clearly knowing the minimum acceptable standards. Is it worth going further?

4 Development agencies

45 mins

Learning outcome B(i)

A leading manufacturer of personal computers has set up its manufacturing operation in a region of the country which has seen a decline of its traditional industries, lower prosperity and higher unemployment than the rest of the country. Its decision was seen as a success for the Regional Development Agency, which had been hoping to attract such companies to the region.

Required

(a)   What do you think would be the objectives of a Regional Development Agency (RDA), and how might its objectives and those of a manufacturer of high technology items be expected to coincide in the matter of choosing a location for the European manufacturing base?   **(10 marks)**

(b)   Describe the environmental factors which you think might be influential in encouraging a high-tech manufacturer to locate its operations in an under-developed or declining region, and how the RDA might have tried to exploit these influences.   **(15 marks)**

(Total = 25 marks)

5 U plc

45 mins

Learning outcome A(v)

The management accountant of U plc has evaluated the activities of two of its important competitors. Within their industry the three firms together share some 60% of the market supplying public authorities. It is suggested that the three firms' financial results can be represented as follows.

	Variable costs/ turnover	Operating profit/ turnover	Operating profit/ capital employed
A Limited	40%	10%	22½%
U plc	30%	7½%	15%
Z plc	25%	15%	20%

A Limited is thought to enjoy a 25% share of the market, Z plc some 20% and U plc 15%. It is also significant that U plc's price/earnings ratio is reported as 10.4 whereas shares in Z plc are fetching 17.3 times current earnings. This confirms the directors' belief that U plc's attempts to improve market share by promotional advertising and exhibition activity have been less effective than had been hoped for.

Senior sales personnel have argued that buyers' search costs are such that once a satisfactory vendor rating has been arrived at, it is difficult to persuade authorities to change their suppliers. It has also become apparent that several customers are merely using U plc's fine pricing to prise additional discounts from their regular supplier. This has had the effect of reducing competitors' return on capital employed below what would otherwise be regarded as reasonable.

Alternative marketing strategies have been proposed – one is that U plc should increase its prices in line with competition so that at least 12½% is earned on turnover. If, as is believed, customers will not readily change their suppliers, it is assumed that improved returns will become available to U plc. This would also bring U plc's variable costs' ratio more into line with those of Z plc.

An alternative argument is that U plc is out-of-date in its production procedures and that the difficulties arise mainly because its capital equipment cannot be adapted to product development sufficiently quickly.

A Limited may use less capital-intensive production methods but it compensates for this by being able to adapt more readily to changes required by its customers.

Required

(a) Evaluate U plc's existing and the two proposed marketing strategies in terms of the likely effects on the company's financial results. **(9 marks)**

(b) Recommend whether an offer by U plc of three of its shares for every two held in Z plc would be in the interest of the present shareholders of U plc. **(8 marks)**

(c) Explain what further growth could be reasonably expected by U plc's shareholders were the merger to come about. **(8 marks)**

(Total = 25 marks)

6 Marketing orientation

Learning outcome B(iv)

(a) Organisations which claim to be 'market orientated' attempt to define the nature of the business in which they are operating. Discuss the relevance of such a definition to an organisation which has its objective stated other than in profit terms. **(13 marks)**

(b) In what ways does organisational buyer behaviour differ from consumer buyer behaviour? **(12 marks)**

(Total = 25 marks)

7 Torodial Tooling   30 mins

Learning outcome C(vi)

Toroidal Tooling manufactures a range of highly specialised cutting tools for the engineering industry. It also acts as exclusive UK selling agent for three complementary product ranges manufactured overseas. Toroidal tooling has been in the machine tool industry for 107 years and is still largely family owned. Perhaps as a result, it is rather sleepy and vulnerable to competition from the major global players. Recently, Toroidal has seen its annual turnover stagnate at about £27M and is aware that its competitors are cutting deep into its market. Profitability is falling.

Toroidal has never had a very sophisticated accounting system, so its knowledge of its costs is rudimentary. However, its salespeople have good knowledge of the market and they suggest that prices are not the most important consideration among customers. Delivery, after sales service and product reliability seem to be more important. Toroidal's product reliability is generally good, but it is often late with deliveries and customers complain that they can rarely obtain accurate information on the progress of their orders. The sales force also note that the overall product range contains several important gaps that are not compensated for by overlaps elsewhere. The overlaps are caused by Toroidal's well-established agency policy of accepting their overseas principals' complete product ranges. There are four basic sales categories: buffing and polishing wheels; grinding wheels; taps and dies; and high speed steel cutting tools. Within each of these main categories, however, there are up to seven distinct product groups and five brand names.

Required

The Managing Director of Toroidal has asked your advice about two principal areas of concern.

(a) With regard to the company's product portfolio, explain a technique that could be used to assess the commercial value of the various product groups.

(b) With regard to the company's business systems, explain a technique that could be used to provide a broad overview of the way it operates.

8 Contract catering

Learning outcome A(iii), A(iv)

Contract caterers are firms which supply food and drink to the employees of 'client firms'. Client firms might prefer to hire contract caterers instead of employing their own in-house catering staff.

The following data describes past trends and current developments in the contract catering industry.

(i)   The early growth in contract catering was largely concentrated among companies employing between 100 and 1,500 people, of which there are about 22,000 in the UK. The 'average' current value of a catering contract is about £10,000 pa, which represents the provision of roughly 200 meals a day. About one-third of UK companies employing between 100 and 1,500 people use contract caterers. The rest prefer to provide their own in-house catering.

Organisations employing more than 1,500 people will normally be able to provide in-house catering more cheaply than the cost of contract catering.

(ii)   Cook-chill catering has been developing in recent years. This is a process whereby contract caterers cook food in a central production unit and then blast-chill the food. The food is then distributed to the locations where it will be eaten and is regenerated in special ovens which heat the food quickly and without drying. In January 1987, a report by the London Food Commission made some warnings about the safety and quality of blast-chilled food.

(iii)   There has been a significant shift over recent years towards consumer preference for vegetarian or other health foods. For example, a survey of students' eating habits found that 18% were either vegetarian or sought to avoid eating meat.

(iv)   Crown immunity has been removed from hospitals, so that hospitals may now be liable for prosecution over inadequate hygiene standards in catering, in just the same way as cafes and restaurants in the private sector.

(v)   Technological developments in automatic vending machines include vending machines allied to a microwave oven, controlled by a microprocessor, and able to accept plastic cards as payment instead of cash.

(vi)   In the City of London, lunch time used to be regarded as the end of the effective working day, and many City managers had long and expensive lunches in City restaurants. Lunchtime has now changed its character, and has become a short break before the opening of the US financial markets.

Required

(a)   Using the data given, analyse the threats and opportunities facing the various segments of the contract catering industry, and suggest how contract catering firms may choose to develop their products or markets in response to these opportunities or threats.   **(20 marks)**

(b)   Suppose that a client firm of a contract caterer is dissatisfied with the increasing costs of contract catering, and wishes to monitor the costs of the service. Recommend two performance measurements, any one of which might provide a suitable basis for setting a target and monitoring the actual costs of the service.   **(5 marks)**

(Total = 25 marks)

9 Product market strategy

Learning outcome C(i), C(ii)

It has been stated that an industry or a market segment within an industry goes through four basic phases of development. These four phases – introduction, growth, maturity and decline – each has an implication for an organisation's development of growth and divestment strategies.

The following brief profiles relate to four commercial organisations, each of which operate in different industries.

- **Company A**. Established in the last year and manufactures state of the art door locks which replace the need for a key with computer image recognition of fingerprint patterns.
- **Company B**. A biotechnological product manufacturer established for three years and engaged in the rapidly expanding animal feedstuffs market.
- **Company C**. A confectionery manufacturer which has been established for many years and is now experiencing low sales growth but high market share in a long established industry.
- **Company D**. A retailing organisation which has been very profitable but is now experiencing a loss of market share with a consequent overall reduction in turnover.

Required

(a)   Explain

(i)   The concept of the industry life cycle, and

(ii)   The phase of development in which each of the industries served by the four companies is positioned. **(7 marks)**

(b)   Discuss how Ansoff's product market growth vector matrix may be applied by the firms in developing their growth and divestment strategies. **(18 marks)**

(Total = 25 marks)

10 Grier and Box plc

45 mins

Learning outcome C(i)

Grier and Box plc is a manufacturing company that has emerged from economic recession to earn a profit before interest and tax of £14.8 million last year. The company has six operating divisions, and the results for last year were as follows.

	Electrical equipment £m	Fluid controls £m	Metals £m	Division Industrial services £m	Bathroom accessories £m	Tubes £m	Total £m
Sales	40.0	25.2	17.1	33.7	7.0	6.0	129.0
Cost of sales							
Materials	34.7	20.3	8.0	14.7	4.5	1.5	83.7
Salaries and wages	1.2	1.8	2.1	3.0	1.0	2.4	11.5
Other costs	2.1	1.9	4.0	8.0	1.0	2.0	19.0
	38.0	24.0	14.1	25.7	6.5	5.9	114.2
Profit before interest and tax	2.0	1.2	3.0	8.0	0.5	0.1	14.8
Market share	40%	27%	30%	25%	8%	3%	

The company's summarised balance sheet as at the end of last year was:

	£m	£m
Net fixed assets		65.0
Current assets	35.0	
Current liabilities	20.0	
Net current assets		15.0
		80.0
Loan capital		48.0
		32.0
Share capital		10.0
Reserves		22.0
		32.0

Required

You are asked to comment on each of the following matters that have been raised by the company's managing director.

(a)   He believes that some of the product divisions manufacture too many low value-added items which require huge working capital investments.

From the data given, which product divisions are these, and what are the implications of low value-added items for financial returns and profitability?   **(8 marks)**

(b)   He wishes to make a strategic decision about the long-term viability of both the bathroom accessories division and the tubes division.

(i)   The bathroom accessories division produces bathroom fittings, which are sold to a manufacturer of bathroom ceramics (baths and washbasins etc). The division is still profitable, but there are indications that the manufacturers of bathroom ceramics are beginning to produce their own bathroom accessories, and market a total 'package' to their own customers.

(ii)   The tubes division is barely profitable and would need considerable capital expenditure to improve efficiency and make it more competitive.

What are the arguments for selling off these divisions now, even though both are profitable?   **(6 marks)**

(c)   The company needs to reduce its financial gearing, which is too high. However, the company also needs to spend large sums of capital for equipment replacement and modernisation programmes, investments in new projects and new product developments. All capital investment projects should have a target payback period.

(i)   Discuss the factors which should influence how long the payback period should be for:

(1)   equipment replacement programmes

(2)   new development projects

(ii)   Discuss the relative importance of the strategic aim of reducing gearing and the aim to continue to invest in modernisation programmes.   **(5 marks)**

(d)   The company is about to introduce a decentralisation programme, in which decision making is pushed as far down the line as possible and head office staff is cut from 56 in number to just 20. The managing director believes that control can be exercised from head office by having a regular reporting system. 'There is much more attention in my mind to looking at ratios and questioning deviations from budget.'

What are the main dangers of relying on ratio analysis and budgetary control for co-ordination and control of the group?   **(6 marks)**

(Total = 25 marks)

11 FG plc   **27 mins**

Learning outcome C(vi)

Following a review of its plans for expansion, FG plc carried out an assessment of its plant utilisation. The company is considering sub-contracting the work of those departments where plant utilisation is poor. The resources thus released could then be used to increase production capacity in those departments where shortages currently occur.

The following information is available.

(a)   Disposal of under-utilised plant is estimated to provide £100,000 net of demolition costs. This work is expected to take six months from the date of the decision.

(b)   Installation of the additional production equipment to overcome the current shortages will take two years. Stage payments will need to be made to specialist plant suppliers as follows.

	£
From the date of decision	
6 months	50,000
12 months	75,000
18 months	157,000
2 years	370,500
30 months	472,500

(c)   The net cash inflow from the additional production would amount to:

in year 3 from the date of the decision, to £450,000
in year 4 from the date of the decision, to £650,000
in year 5 from the date of the decision, to £700,000
After year 5 some undefined benefits may accrue.

(d)   The company's marginal cost of capital after allowing for taxation is at present 16% per annum. Were the project to be financed from borrowed funds it is thought that future borrowings would cost the company an additional 2% per annum.

Required

(a)   Provide a financial analysis of the proposal in order to determine whether the company should be advised to proceed with its implementation.   **(6 marks)**

(b)   Comment on factors significant for this decision which have not been provided in the information given.   **(5 marks)**

(c)   Comment on the helpfulness of an internal rate of return calculation to evaluate this proposal.

(4 marks)

(Total = 15 marks)

12 Simon Clark

Learning outcome D(vi)

Simon Clark is Head of the Department of Business at a local public sector college which provides professional training on a part-time basis for students who are already in employment. The students are mainly studying for professional qualifications in either accountancy, marketing or personnel. A number of students are also studying for general management qualifications. Increasingly this college is experiencing competition from a newly established private sector organisation. This private sector organisation is able to deliver programmes more efficiently and effectively than the older established college because of its more flexible work contracts and working practices. The traditional method of tuition has been on a part-time day release basis (one day or one half-day a week) away from work, studying within the college. With local companies becoming more reluctant to give their staff time off on a regular basis to study, Simon is proposing that more of the training should be carried out on a distance-learning basis, often being supplemented by taught weekend programmes. This will involve the staff in writing study materials and working weekends.

Simon's college has a teaching staff who, in recent years, have had to adapt to new situations including organisational structure changes and syllabus changes. However they are most unhappy about the current proposals which could result in their conditions of service worsening. They are reluctant to work on a weekend basis without additional payments. This would make the college uncompetitive. The private sector college, although it employs high quality staff, is able to absorb the high costs by employing lecturers on a freelance basis and by having larger class sizes, the students being drawn from a larger catchment area. Simon is becoming frustrated by his staff's apparent opposition to accept the proposed changes, and he is contemplating what to do next.

Required

Simon has arranged a meeting with his staff to discuss weekend working and study material production.

(a)   Identify and discuss the different tactics which Simon could make use of in dealing with this conflict.

(b) Discuss how Simon might encourage his staff to be more supportive of the proposed change in work practice.

13 Management accounting information

45 mins

Learning outcome D(iii)

It has been said that management accounting has traditionally been concerned with providing information for decision making and controlling costs. It has often been criticised for not providing sufficient relevant information to management because it tends to impose general techniques as a solutions in situations which demand custom-designed (directly applicable) methods and specific information.

Required

(a) Discuss the validity of this criticism of management accounting. **(13 marks)**

To be relevant to the needs of the organisation, management accounting systems need to be designed to accommodate its specific requirements taking account of the circumstances of its particular business environment. One such circumstance may be the change in traditional working patterns. For example, it can no longer be assumed that all employees will be located on the organisation's premises in carrying out their duties. Some are likely to provide their services from remote locations.

(b) Compare the approach to providing relevant management accounting information for strategic decision making purposes in

   (i) a manufacturing organisation which employs staff on site, with

   (ii) a service organisation which employs contractors. The contractors mainly work from home to provide technical solutions for customers engaged in large scale building projects.

(12 marks)

(Total = 25 marks)

14 Nominee holdings

45 mins

Learning outcome D(i), D(iii)

Nominee Holdings plc, an investment conglomerate, co-ordinates the capital expenditure proposals of its subsidiaries by:

(a) Allowing each company to pledge its asset base as loan security where value is likely to be added to the equity provided the parent's resources are in no way jeopardised (eg by having to give any form of guarantee)

(b) Ranking applications from subsidiaries for reinvestment of operating profits according to the premium available over the group's average cost of capital and their accord with its medium-term strategy.

Outline investment plans have been submitted for approval as follows.

	Dairy-P Ltd	Keen Casements	Flexi-Carbon Ltd
Project cost *	£150,000	£65,000	£125,000
(standard deviation)	£41,000	0 (ie firm)	£15,000
Profitability index (using DCF 19.5%)	1.41	1.28	1.35
Current Asset ratio (of project proposal)	1.70	0.65	1.21
Mortgage debentures outstanding	£200,000	nil	£150,000
Rate of interest	10%	–	15%
Second mortgage debentures outstanding	£50,000	nil	nil
Rate of interest	17%	–	–
Fixed assets at current valuation	£400,000	£15,000	£250,000

* mean of pessimistic, most likely and optimistic

The subsidiary companies are not aware of the parent company's directors' unhappiness about the future of Dairy-P Ltd. The parent board expects the European Union to continue inflating the cost of that company's inputs and is investigating the feasibility of moving the processing facilities to Greece as that country integrates its economy into the European Union. Nominee Holdings plc's cash and short-term deposits earn on average only 5% pa and amount to some 20% of the company's net worth according to its management accounts, which price non-monetary assets at replacement cost.

Required

(a)   Put forward appropriate recommendations for Nominee Holdings plc's directors to consider.

(15 marks)

(b)   Explain how divisional performance should be measured in the interest of the group's shareholders.

(5 marks)

(c)   Propose the means of charge-out that would be appropriate for the parent company to debit subsidiaries for their capital employed.

(5 marks)

(Total = 25 marks)

15 The S group

90 mins

Learning outcome D(iii)

Company development

The headquarters of the S Group is located in K, a country which has experienced rapid economic growth in recent years.

S itself has been established for over 100 years. Two brothers first started trading in K and developed the group, which is now a highly profitable international conglomerate company. Its diverse business activities range from capital goods manufacture, through materials handling to operation of airlines and banking. Some of its activities involve the transfer of partly completed goods between manufacturing and assembly plants located in different countries. The group operates a divisional structure.

Economic circumstances

Over the last three years the region of the world in which K is located has been subject to serious economic difficulties. K itself has not been affected as much as some of its neighbours, owing to the fact that its independent currency is pegged to the US dollar.

There has been much activity and intervention by the monetary authorities in K to protect the value of the currency, and this has proved to be largely successful, despite the intense pressure exerted by foreign speculators. Nevertheless, the effects of the regional economic difficulties are being felt. This is exemplified by the recent emergence of unemployment after a period of 30 years of full employment and a dramatic fall in property prices.

Organisational economic objectives

Fifty five per cent of S's holding company shares are held within the families of the original founders. The remaining forty five per cent of the shares are mainly held by international banks and other financial institutions located all over the world. These institutional shareholders maintain constant pressure on the directors to improve earnings per share and increase dividend payments. The directors have stated that their main objective is to increase shareholder value. In satisfying the requirements of the shareholders the directors are conscious of the need for improved efficiency in the group's operations. Consequently, the holding company's board of directors carefully scrutinises the activities of the constituent subsidiary companies within the group.

Divisional performance measurement

S has always applied a traditional form of measurement to assess the performance of the group's subsidiaries. It uses return on capital employed (ROCE) and defines this as:

$$\frac{\text{Profit before interest and tax}}{\text{Average capital employed}} \times 100$$

(The capital employed value is the average of that shown at the beginning and end of the year.)

The performance of the divisional managers is strictly monitored on this basis and their remuneration increases if they achieve growth in their ROCE, which is measured annually. Inevitably, the divisional managers strive to improve their performance as measured by this method.

The Agricultural Equipment (AE) Division

The AE division, which is not located in K, assembles components into a single product. It receives the components from other subsidiaries in the group which are situated in other countries. The group as a whole has been able to benefit from economies of scale, as a result of other subsidiary divisions, which have long experience in manufacturing, supplying AE. Following assembly, AE ships the product to various customers throughout the world. The geographical location of the country in which AE is situated enables the product to be easily exported, but the division is subject to high levels of corporation tax.

The transfer prices of the components transferred to AE are set centrally by group head office located in K. The divisional manager of AE has no influence over them at all. The group head office may vary the transfer prices during the financial year.

Comparative results for the AE division over the last two years (translated into K's currency) are as follows:

	Last year		Previous year	
	K$m	K$m	K$m	K$m
Sales		800		750
Components	600		400	
Assembly costs	100		75	
		700		475
Gross profit		100		275
AE Division Head Office (all fixed)		75		75
Net profit before interest and tax		25		200
Average capital employed		2,020		2,000

Selling prices over the two years remained stable.

It may be assumed that the variable costs of the supplying division, relating to the transferred components, were neutral in respect of AE division's profitability over the two years.

The budgeted and actual selling price per unit was K$50,000 in each of the two years. The budgeted production and sales level for each year was 18,000 units. it can be assumed that there were no opening and closing stocks for finished goods or work in progress in either of the years.

The budgeted cost per unit for each of the last two years was as follows:

	Last year	Previous year
	K$	K$
Assembly	6,000	5,000
Components transferred	35,000	25,000
	41,000	30,000

It can be assumed that there was no change in the currency exchange rate between the AE division's host country and K$ in the last two years. There have been discussions at S Group headquarters regarding the deteriorating performance of AE and there is growing pressure to close it down. The AE divisional manager believes there is little he can do in the circumstances, where he only controls a small proportion of the total costs of the division.

Potential for growth in AE division

Despite the reduced profitability in the last financial year, the divisional manager of AE believes there is potential for growth. He has put forward plans to group headquarters to take over a competitor company in the country in which the division is situated. This would result in an increase for the division in world wide market share and provide the capacity to increase the range of agricultural equipment supplied in accordance with the divisional manager's perception of demand. To do this AE will need to obtain funds which will be secured against group assets.

Required

(a) State the sources from which the board of directors of S may obtain information relating to the group's business environment and how it might use that information for strategic management purposes. Explain how the board of directors might assure itself of the quality of that information for strategic management purposes. (You are not required to consider the ecological environment in answering this question.) **(12 marks)**

(b) Making use of the information contained in the case, produce a critical appraisal of the method applied by S Group's directors to assess the performance of the AE division. **(16 marks)**

(c) Discuss the factors which should be taken into consideration by the directors of S in deciding whether the strategic development proposals put forward by AE's divisional manager should be pursued. **(10 marks)**

(d) Assume that the AE division makes the acquisition as proposed by its divisional manager. Recommend how S Group's directors should improve the methods of measuring the performance of the AE division in order to assess its contribution to the group's strategic requirement to increase shareholder value. **(12 marks)**

(Total = 50 marks)

Approaching the answer

You should read through the requirement before working through and annotating the question as we have, so that you are aware of what things you are looking for. We have also prepared a précis of the case, which follows this annotated version, summarising the key issues.

Company development

The headquarters of the S Group is located in K, a country which has experienced rapid economic growth in recent years.

> Turbulent environment? Unstable? Good infrastructure? Or boom then bust?

> Long established indicates a certain stability

S itself has been established for over 100 years. Two brothers first started trading in K and

> Big numbers, although an unfashionable business model now

developed the group, which is now a highly profitable international conglomerate company. Its diverse business activities range from capital goods manufacture, through materials handling to operation of airlines and banking. Some of its activities involve the transfer of partly completed goods between manufacturing and assembly plants located in different countries.

> Products and services – marketing/ branding issues?

> Transfer pricing issues

The group operates a divisional structure.

> Performance assessment

Economic circumstances

Over the last three years the region of the world in which K is located has been subject to serious

> Will foreign exchange policy become an issue?

economic difficulties. K itself has not been affected as much as some of its neighbours, owing to the fact that its independent currency is pegged to the US dollar.

Economic environment could become unfavourable

There has been much activity and intervention by the monetary authorities in K to protect the value of the currency, and this has proved to be largely successful, despite the intense pressure exerted by foreign speculators. Nevertheless, the effects of the regional economic difficulties are being felt. This is exemplified by the recent emergence of unemployment after a period of 30 years of full employment and a dramatic fall in property prices.

Organisational economic objectives

Could this imply conservative management and resistance to change?

Global profile

Fifty five per cent of S's holding company shares are held within the families of the original founders. The remaining forty five per cent of the shares are mainly held by international banks and other financial institutions located all over the world. These institutional shareholders maintain constant pressure on the directors to improve earnings per share and increase dividend payments.

Stakeholder analysis – short term interests?

As would generally be expected).

The directors have stated that their main objective is to increase shareholder value. In satisfying the requirements of the shareholders the directors are conscious of the need for improved efficiency in the group's operations. Consequently, the holding company's board of directors carefully scrutinises the activities of the constituent subsidiary companies within the group.

Tight central control?

What does 'efficiency' mean? Cost control?

Divisional performance measurement

S has always applied a traditional form of measurement to assess the performance of the group's subsidiaries. It uses return on capital employed (ROCE) and defines this as:

Advantages and disadvantages of this as a measure

$$\frac{\text{Profit before interest and tax}}{\text{Average capital employed}} \times 100$$

Note this for your calculations!

(The capital employed value is the average of that shown at the beginning and end of the year.)

Possible disadvantages here – disincentive to invest and thereby increase capital employed, for example

The performance of the divisional managers is strictly monitored on this basis and their remuneration increases if they achieve growth in their ROCE, which is measured annually.

Inevitably, the divisional managers strive to improve their performance as measured by this method.

The Agricultural Equipment (AE) Division

The AE division, which is not located in K, assembles components into a single product. It receives the components from other subsidiaries in the group which are situated in other countries. The group as a whole has been able to benefit from economies of scale, as a result of other subsidiary divisions, which have long experience in manufacturing, supplying AE. Following assembly, AE ships the product to various customers throughout the world. The geographical location of the country in which AE is situated enables the product to be easily exported, but the division is subject to high levels of corporation tax.

Interest from the tax authorities in the transfer pricing, as a method of reducing profits?

The transfer prices of the components transferred to AE are set centrally by group head office located in K. The divisional manager of AE has no influence over them at all. The group head office may vary the transfer prices during the financial year.

Comparative results for the AE division over the last two years (translated into K's currency) are as follows:

These numbers are vital for answering part (b)

No incentive to manage his costs as he does not control them, yet he is judged on them via ROCE!

| | Last year | | Previous year | |
	K$m	K$m	K$m	K$m
Sales		800		750
Components	600		400	
Assembly costs	100		75	
		700		475
Gross profit		100		275
AE Division Head Office (all fixed)		75		75
Net profit before interest and tax		25		200
Average capital employed		2,020		2,000

Selling prices over the two years remained stable.

It may be assumed that the variable costs of the supplying division, relating to the transferred components, were neutral in respect of AE division's profitability over the two years.

The budgeted and actual selling price per unit was K$50,000 in each of the two years. The budgeted production and sales level for each year was 18,000 units. It can be assumed that there were no opening and closing stocks for finished goods or work in progress in either of the years.

What does this mean? Basically that the big increase in costs is not due to higher costs of the supplying division being passed on, but rather due to higher transfer prices. Is using ROCE in such circumstances a fair performance measure? There must be a better one!

The budgeted cost per unit for each of the last two years was as follows:

| | Last year | Previous year |
	K$	K$
Assembly	6,000	5,000
Components transferred	35,000	25,000
	41,000	30,000

It can be assumed that there was no change in the currency exchange rate between the AE division's host country and K$ in the last two years. There have been discussions at S Group headquarters regarding the deteriorating performance of AE and there is growing pressure to close it down. The AE divisional manager believes there is little he can do in the circumstances, where he only controls a small proportion of the total costs of the division.

Is it really deteriorating?

Potential for growth in AE division

Despite the reduced profitability in the last financial year, the divisional manager of AE believes there is potential for growth. He has put forward plans to group headquarters to take over a competitor company in the country in which the division is situated. This would result in an increase for the division in world wide market share and provide the capacity to increase the range of agricultural equipment supplied, in accordance with the divisional manager's perception of demand. To do this, AE will need to obtain funds which will be secured against group assets.

Increased sales, profits, contribution to shareholder value

Cost of those funds?

But is this perception realistic?

Overall précis of the case

S Group, **highly profitable international conglomerate**, established for over 100 years. Located in K, a country which has experienced rapid economic growth (currency pegged to the US$), although the region it is in has been subject to difficulties recently: unemployment and falling property prices.

Business activities: capital goods manufacture, materials handling, operation of airlines, banking. Some **transfer of goods** between plants in different countries. The group operates a **divisional structure**.

Shareholders: 55% families of the original founders, 45% held by worldwide financial institutions who press for improved **EPS** and increased **dividends**. Main **objective** of group is to **increase shareholder value**. Subsidiaries' activities closely scrutinised by centre.

Uses **ROCE** for performance measurement and for influencing manager remuneration, defined as:

$$\frac{\text{Profit before interest and tax}}{\text{Average capital employed}} \times 100$$

The **AE division** (not located in K) assembles components which it receives from other subsidiaries in other countries, and then ships the completed capital goods to customers. Group benefits from economies of scale. AE is subject to high levels of corporation tax.

Transfer prices of the components are set **centrally**. Divisional manager of AE has no influence.

(**Results** for the AE division are as in the tables above).

There have been discussions at head office regarding the **deteriorating performance** of AE, with pressure to close it down. AE divisional manager only controls a small proportion of his total costs, but remains committed – has put forward plans for **acquisition** of a domestic competitor to increase both AE's **global market share** and its **product range**, to be **financed** by funds secured against group assets.

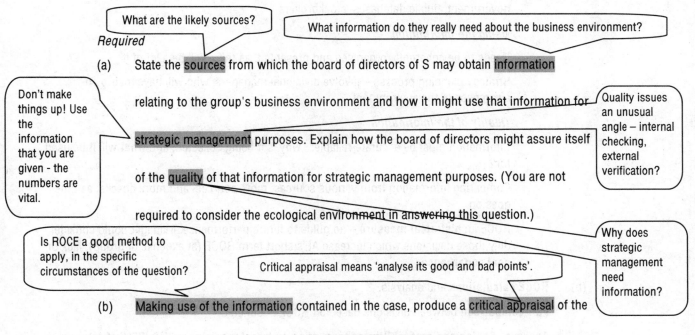

What are the likely sources?

What information do they really need about the business environment?

Required

(a)   State the sources from which the board of directors of S may obtain information

Don't make things up! Use the information that you are given - the numbers are vital.

relating to the group's business environment and how it might use that information for

Quality issues an unusual angle – internal checking, external verification?

strategic management purposes. Explain how the board of directors might assure itself

of the quality of that information for strategic management purposes. (You are not

required to consider the ecological environment in answering this question.)

Why does strategic management need information?

Is ROCE a good method to apply, in the specific circumstances of the question?

Critical appraisal means 'analyse its good and bad points'.

(b)   Making use of the information contained in the case, produce a critical appraisal of the

method applied by S Group's directors to assess the performance of the AE division.

No need to make any recommendations yourself!

(c) Discuss the factors which should be taken into consideration by the directors of S in deciding whether the strategic development proposals put forward by AE's divisional manager should be pursued.

Discuss – this is easiest if you categorise the factors. Which ones are more important?

Financial and non-financial is a useful basis upon which to structure your discussion.

It is irrelevant if you think it is a bad idea!

(d) Assume that the AE division makes the acquisition as proposed by its divisional manager. Recommend how S Group's directors should improve the methods of measuring the performance of the AE division in order to assess its contribution to the group's strategic requirement to increase shareholder value.

Recommend new divisional performance assessment methods – and give reasons.

Define shareholder value.

Indicate how appropriate your recommendation is to the need to monitor contributions towards shareholder value: ease of measurement, validity of calculations, fairness to the division…

Answer plan

Think about the points you want to make, and prioritise them.

Importance of understanding the environment/trends – define **strategic intelligence**

(**Maintain a database** – financial/non-financial indicators).

(a) *Sources of environmental information*

(i) **Internal sources** – staff, stakeholders

Importance of management information system – info on sales, costs, market share

(ii) **External sources** – media, consultants, academic/trade journals, trade bodies, Internet, government, public databases, stockbrokers

Using the information

Needs to be coherently organised and presented, as there will be a lot of it.

Strategy planning process – involve divisional managers, who will have their own awareness of the environment

Quality of the information

Information must be accurate/reliable: **why** is it being collected, and **what** will it be used for?

Comparing information from various sources: more sources, and more checks, as time goes on.

ROCE an **historical measure** – no guide to future performance. Manager could consider only those decisions which increase AE's short term ROCE (at expense of group): lack of **goal congruence.**

(b) **ROCE calculations** and analysis.

Fair comparison between divisions based on ROCE is difficult.

Analysis of **sales and profitability**, concentrating on **transfer pricing policy** (75% of sales value last year/53% in previous year).

Conclusion that the performance of AE is being assessed on factors beyond its control, using an unsatisfactory measure.

(c) Key objective: **increase shareholder value.** Does acquisition fit in with the overall **strategic direction** of the group? Must understand reasons for it – do they balance the level of **risk**?

Possible problems/issues to consider:

(i) **Costs**
(ii) Customers reaction/ market research
(iii) Incompatibilities
(iv) Lack of information

Refer to the analysis in part (b) – AE is actually profitable, so should it risk that with this venture?

Non financial factors too – such as problems of **implementation** /human resources issues.

(d) **Performance measurement** should become more **forward looking.** Balance long v. short term.

Shareholder value analysis – definition

Factors to focus on re the AE division (Rappaport's value drivers):

(i) **Market share** forecasts and trends
(ii) Investment in **working capital**
(iii) **Cash flows**
(iv) **Corporation tax planning**
(v) **Cost of funding** (incremental value of the acquisition must exceed the cost of capital)

Economic value management – definition

Applied to the AE division – adjust for the transfer price.

1 Four Star Products

Part (a)

> **Tutorial note**. This is a relatively simple question to start this subject with. It will give you good practice at marshalling your knowledge and presenting it in a way that is related to the scenario, both of which are essential skills for this subject.
>
> Do not worry if you reach a different conclusion from the one in the suggested solution, or even no conclusion at all. It is very important to understand that there are few absolutely correct answers to questions in strategic management. Success does not just depend on learning. You must be familiar with the material, certainly, but you must also be able to apply it to an infinite variety of problems.
>
> What is important in questions of this type is that you offer reasoning that is both theoretically sound and relevant to the setting.

Answer plan

NB Q not so much about the planning department as about what it does. Therefore answer requires critique of formal planning approach.

Against

- Difficulty of forecasting discontinuities
- Linear approach – annual cycle
- Isolation of planners from operations
- Politics
- Implementation
- Learning

For

- Systematic approach
- Sets targets
- Co-ordination of objectives, departments, activities
- Organised attention to environment

Criticisms of the rational model concern both the theory behind it and how it has worked in practice. Empirical studies have not proved that formal planning processes contribute to success.

Planning theory assumes that the development of the business environment can be forecast, and to some extent controlled. In conditions of stability, forecasting and extrapolation make sense. But forecasting cannot cope with sudden **discontinuities** and **shocks**, such as the change from mainframe computing to PCs, which nearly destroyed IBM.

Part of the problem is the **linear approach** sometimes adopted, using an annual cycle. Unfortunately, strategically significant events outside the organisation are rarely synchronised with the annual planning cycle. Four Star's financial crisis in the early 1990s is, perhaps, an example.

Another problem is that formal planning can **discourage strategic thinking** among operational managers. Once a plan is locked in place, people are unwilling to question it. The internal significance of the chosen performance indicators leads managers to focus on fulfilling the plan rather than concentrating on developments in the environment. Strategy becomes something for specialists.

A complementary problem arises when the planners are separated from the operational managers; the implication is that the planners do not really need day-to-day knowledge of the product or market. However, small-scale developments can have important strategic influence and should not be ignored.

The rational model by definition assumes that an **objective approach** prevails. Unfortunately, no account is taken of the essentially political processes that determine many plans. There also problems of implementation. Managers are not all-knowing, and there are limits to the extent to which they can control the actual behaviour of the organisation. This places limits upon what can be achieved. Discovering strengths and weaknesses is a learning process. Implementing a strategy is necessary for learning – to see if it works.

On the other hand, we can discern an important role for **formal planning activities**. Apart from anything else, a desire to do things in a systematic way naturally leads to rational planning; deciding what to do, and when and how it should be done. Such an approach can make management control more effective by developing detailed and explicit targets. This shows managers at all levels where they fit in and forces them to confront the company's expectations of them

The development of a plan for a large organisation such as Four Star includes an important element of **co-ordination**. Long-term, medium-term and short-term objectives, plans and controls must be made consistent with one another. Similarly, the activities of the different business functions must be directed towards a common goal.

Also, companies cannot remain static: they have to cope with and exploit changes in the **environment**. It is clear from the CEO's use of external agencies and his new strategy for Four Star that he understands this. We may speculate that he is not so much an enemy of strategic planning as much as he is unimpressed with the performance of the Four Star planning department.

Part (b)

> **Tutorial note**. This part of the question is fairly unusual in that there is pretty much a single correct approach to a good answer; that is, this question is about the environmental analysis aspect of the rational planning model and not very much else will do. However, notice that a good answer will point out the weakness of the forecasting process: the future is essentially unknowable and the danger of detailed research is that we forget this and come to believe that we do indeed know just what is going to happen.

Answer plan

- Nature of environmental analysis
- The environment – divisions
- Desk research
- Market research
- Informal research
- Technical nature of Internet boom
- Importance of judgement
- Relationship of formal planning to strategic decision making-support

Environmental analysis is a fundamental part of strategic business management. The aim of the analysis is to identify opportunities and threats and to assess their significance. The environment itself may be divided both according to its proximity to the organisation and according to its inherent features. Thus, the task environment, dealing with suppliers, customers, competitors and so on, may be differentiated from the wider, general environment and, indeed, from the global physical environment. The general, or macro, environment is often analysed under such headings as political, economic, social and technological.

The work of analysis can be carried on to a great extent by **desk research**. This may be quite adequate for keeping abreast of the more general aspects of the macro environment, and even for some parts of the task environment, such as changing labour costs and the fortunes of competitors. However, more complex and expensive methods, such as market research surveys may be required for some aspects of the task environment, and more intuitive ones, such as personal contact between senior managers for others.

In the case of the Internet business model, which was given enormous publicity, it should have been easy to obtain a full understanding of both principle and technique by the methods outlined above. The problem with the collapse of confidence in the model was that foretelling was very much a matter of **judgement**. Extremely large sums of money were invested on quite rational grounds and very few commentators took a pessimistic view.

This is not a failure of the formal planning process as such, but rather a failure of strategic judgement at the highest levels of the organisations concerned. Planning techniques cannot foretell exactly what the future holds, let alone control it. Their purpose is to support those who must take strategic decisions, not to replace them.

2 IT strategy

> **Tutorial note**. This question refers to an 'IT strategy' rather than an 'IS/IT strategy'. This should not have prevented you from including material relating to information systems that utilise IT in your answer.
>
> In a question such as this ensure you structure your answer clearly – dealing with each of the five reasons you provide separately and providing sufficient information, including an example, to earn five marks for each reason.

Reasons for having an IT strategy

In this answer we identify five reasons for developing an IT strategy, using the example of a typical small firm offering domestic services such as plumbing and electrical work. For convenience we shall refer to this firm as **EG Ltd**.

(1) **Rationalising the existing investment in IT**

Because of the benefits it offers (speed, accuracy, and so on) IT has become a **key component of most aspects of modern businesses**. Most organisations have reached the stage in their IT maturity whereby IT has been used to automate tasks previously performed manually or by obsolete technology. Most organisations could **not now conceivably disinvest in IT**, and return to traditional methods of getting work done.

However, it is common in organisations, from small to large, for IT to have been **introduced piecemeal** to address specific requirements without due regard having been paid to the way that the individual systems **work together and communicate**.

Adoption of a strategy is therefore necessary to guide the direction and scope of the **whole** IT development of a firm allowing it to match the **resources available** to the changing **environment** and enable the firm to meet its **primary business objectives**. All of these matters – overall use of resources, environmental issues and overall objectives – are key issues in the formulation of business strategies.

The next stage of IT development is to **exploit the utmost that IT has to offer** by **re-engineering the processes** with the aid of IT rather than just automating current processes.

Example

EG Ltd originally invested in stand-alone PCs for basic administrative tasks such as writing letters to customers and keeping accounts. None of its systems were fully integrated, and much work still involves inefficiencies such as re-inputting of data, or manual searches for information that is held in computerised form but is not accessible by a computer search.

An organisation-wide strategy needs to be formulated if the various systems are to be brought together, enabling further gains, for instance, automatic generation of letters to debtors, proper accessible databases of customers, suppliers, materials, staff resources.

(2) **Beating competitors and enhancing relationships**

The **traditional** view of IT's role in competitive strategy is largely **reactive** – that is, a response to existing competitive strategy and business process, but not a critical factor in **shaping** that strategy and process.

A more sensible approach is to position IT in a **pro-active** role where the competitive strategy is not viewed as given, but rather as something that should be challenged, extended and perhaps modified, in light of **emerging technologies and applications**.

The perspective of IT strictly as a **support** function in competitive strategy is increasingly out-dated. Firms are now seeking ways to exploit IT to transform their basic businesses, **enhance their relationships** with suppliers and customers, and **create new market opportunities**.

Today, successful competitive strategy and corporate results are likely to focus on a small number of performance attributes including **speed, flexibility, quality** and **scale**. All four areas are **profoundly affected** by an organisation's **effective use of IT** to facilitate, enhance and accelerate strategic execution.

Example

EG Ltd's original investment in IT was made partly **because their competitors and suppliers** were clearly investing in such systems too, and EG's manually-produced communications with the outside world made the entire firm **look old-fashioned and inefficient**.

Greater use of technologies now available, or becoming available, could enable EG Ltd to **surpass** many competitors and **deal much more effectively** with suppliers and customers. For instance, **computerised scheduling and booking systems** could enable EG to respond more quickly to urgent call-outs and **make and honour promises** to customers about when work will be done and how long it will take (something at which the industry in general is notoriously bad). **EDI links** to suppliers could greatly simplify ordering and administration for both parties. A good **website** could generate a great deal of new business.

(3) **Getting the systems that are really needed**

In the past many organisations have found that information systems have failed to deliver expected benefits for reasons such as the following.

(i) There is no **commitment by the top management** of an organisation. IT strategy invariably involves some degree of **change**, and, unless top management is behind the strategy, its implementation can prove to be impossible.

(ii) The **users and providers of IT** in the organisation have not been fully enough involved. If new systems are simply imposed on such people and they are given no chance to explain their **real needs** there is a strong chance that the system will not reflect their needs.

The process of going through the planning stage in itself is extremely valuable as it provides a mechanism not only for determining what needs to be done but, if properly handled, it also ensures that the result is **achieved by consensus of all interested parties.** This means that the plan is far more likely to be put into effect satisfactorily. The formulation of an **IT strategy** should then result in a clear and **generally understood and agreed** document which sets out the relative priorities of each approved project together with the identification and allocation of the appropriate **resources, approval and delivery** dates, arrangements for **testing and training, and** so on.

Example

EG Ltd originally acquired computers in cases where the manager of a function wanted one and had sufficient influence in the organisation to obtain funding. Other managers were either not interested or did not have the influence. Users, therefore, either had computers imposed on them or were deprived of them.

A **culture change** is needed: those who are opposed to computerisation or simply lack enthusiasm need to be persuaded of the benefits.

(4) **Continually improving the management of the organisation**

IT brings **ongoing** revolution in the way information is created, used and presented to management. After the strategy has been developed, it must be regarded as a living entity that the organisation needs to review on a regular and systematic basis as circumstances change.

Any strategic view of IT must take technical developments into account. For instance the **Internet** and **Intranet** popularity has forced many managers to rethink the direction of applications and infrastructure investments. The most popular applications use web publishing for existing documents, web forms for transaction entry or web-to-database links to access corporate data.

Example

EG Ltd could benefit from introducing an Intranet in ways such as the following.

(i)   An organisation-wide phone directory that is always up-to-date, containing internal numbers and frequently used external numbers.

(ii) Sales information including price lists for jobs, staff availability for urgent call-outs, and supplier and competitor information, including links to suppliers' and competitors' web sites.

(iii) A technical database for staff such as plumbers and electricians showing how various jobs are done, how the latest tools and materials should be used, legal and safety requirements and so on.

(5) **Obtaining synergies and economies of scale**

If IT is not integrated to corporate strategy a business is almost certain to be **spending too much,** if only because a sizeable percentage will be **spent on the wrong things**. If this goes unchecked there is very little chance that the company will realise the economies of scale and informational synergies that the business needs.

A company's IT architecture comprises **five different component architectures**: applications, technology, data, methods and management practices, and **spending needs to keep these architectures in balance**. For instance, if a large amount is spent on new technologies, but **nothing on training and data conversion** then at best there will be a lag before the new facilities are exploited to the full. The benefits of the IT expenditure might be delayed until the skills of users are available to produce them.

Example

EG Ltd is typical in that it has only computerised its administration so far: it has not considered benefits that could arise from using technology in **other areas of its business**, such as mobile phones and portable PCs for staff such as plumbers and electricians to use on site.

3 Management and social responsibility

> Start off with a definition, and try to come up with an example

Social responsibility is a hard term to define, but many would say it means acting with regard to social welfare. No organisation would ever admit to be socially irresponsible. Organisations claim to act responsibly on social issues, whether this means using social issues in a marketing campaign (such as 'Computers for Schools' vouchers handed out by supermarkets), or the widespread claims of **environmentalism** (claimed by many organisations, from petrol companies to 'dolphin-friendly' tuna fleets).

> As we said, this area is a minefield! Try not to be too controversial with opinions or political allegiances. Refer instead to the obvious difficulties faced by an organisation charged with corporate social responsibility

In brief, for an organisation to act with social responsibility, it should align its goals with those of the wider society in which it is a part. However, the **purpose and direction of society**, not to mention its goals, are generally political decisions, rather than obviously commercial ones. Any company these days has to overcome an almost inbuilt public distrust and cynicism about corporate objectives. Many simply will not believe that a company is operating other than purely for the benefit of its shareholders and senior managers. Recent scandals such as Enron have not helped.

Moreover, is the wider society limited to the national economy or the world as a whole? The consequences of a **global corporation** acting with 'social responsibility' in one society may cause it to act without social responsibility in another (eg shipping hazardous waste from a country with tough environmental legislation, to one with few controls).

So we can see that in multinational corporations, the exercise of social responsibility is distributed over several countries, but again, management will only let it override commercial objectives if it either is part of the inbuilt culture of the firm, or if the voice of public opinion in the market is strong. An example is the use of rainforest hardwoods: some consumer organisations are suggesting boycotting these products.

A business almost certainly has objectives, which, in the long term, it can claim will enhance social welfare - the creation of wealth as a result of business activities is felt to be of benefit to society as a whole.

Refer to the specifics of the manager's role, as this is what the question is asking. It is pressure from stakeholders that we are really concerned with

What are their concerns?

Show some awareness of current workplace issues – social changes and the law are fruitful areas for discussion. (You do not need detailed knowledge of employment legislation)

For each stakeholder that you note in your answer, explain the relevance of social responsibility for them. Give examples where you can

The managers of organisations which seek to be socially responsible rarely start off with a theoretical notion of social responsibility which they then seek to implement. Rather, organisations which act responsibly do so in response to **pressures from their various stakeholders**. Some of these pressures are outlined below.

Make sure that you know who the relevant stakeholders are!

Employees

Employees are stakeholders. Their relationship is twofold. Firstly, it is their labour which keeps the organisation in operational existence, despite the impact of technology. Secondly, as citizens they are members of the wider society in which the organisation operates.

Employees value certainty and regularity of wages, in other words that the employing organisation will honour the contract of employment. Secondly, to act with social responsibility implies a concern and respect for safety in the workplace, whether this be equipment, buildings, or hours worked. (It is believed that repetitive strain injury arises from too much uninterrupted time at the word processor.)

Social responsibility towards workers can also include a coherent career and training structure so that people can better themselves. It is believed that an economy's productivity is affected by the level of workforce skill, and so training is both beneficial for the trainee and for the company as a whole.

Other aspects include adapting to other pressures on employee's lifestyles. Workplace crèches, for example, are of great assistance to great numbers of working women, but employers are unlikely to introduce them if there is no commercial benefit.

Management has a certain amount of discretion, but this is circumscribed by law. Health and safety for example is subject of regulation, as it was felt that commercial imperatives would not justify the expense, and that employers are not necessarily altruistic. Other benefits are won as the result of the relationship between management and organised labour.

So, the exercise of social responsibility towards the workforce is constrained by the law, by organised labour, and in some instances by the recognition that social responsibility can be of benefit in encouraging employee loyalty and skill.

Customers

Customers are stakeholders in that they pay for the organisation's output of goods and services. They generally want quality products for as low a price as possible, but it can get more complex than that. In some consumer goods sectors, public attitudes – with some direction from government and lobby groups – have made the environmental impact of an organisation's activities open to public comment. This has led suppliers to reduce CFCs in aerosol cans, and to introduce ranges of goods which are supposed to be friendly to the environment.

Suppliers

Social responsibility towards suppliers may include the simple procedure of paying them on time. Many small businesses fail, and people lose their jobs, because of liquidity issues connected with late payment by business customers.

A supplier may also make restrictions on the end-use of products a condition of sale. For example, a supplier of high-technology items may require that these are not re-exported to the enemies of the nation where the supplier is based.

Professional bodies

Control is exercised over certain members of management by their membership of professional bodies, which have standards of ethics and conduct

Elected authorities

Society's elected political representatives can affect management in a number of ways, by legislation as has already been mentioned, by influencing the climate of public opinion, or by trying to persuade commercial organisations to follow a particular line or policy. An example is business sponsorship of the arts in the UK. The tenor of government policy was to reduce government funding and to encourage commercial organisations to avail themselves of the marketing opportunities thereby provided.

For example, if a firm bids for a contract from a local authority, contract compliance (by which the contract is only awarded to a firm which operates an equal opportunities policy) could affect the actions of management.

Elected authorities can also compel social authority by legislation (eg anti-pollution legislation), 'contract compliance' rules, or even taxation. Company reporting requirements might include a 'social audit'.

Shareholders

The main interest of shareholders is profit, and they might have objections to money being spent on projects which are socially responsible, as such profits reduce the return on the investment. As many shareholders are large institutions like pension funds, their duties can be adversely affected by the use of organisational resources on activities which do not make a profit.

It is possible that some shareholders, and other commentators, would assert that the creation of wealth is the only desirable social objective, and anything which intervenes in this objective is damaging in the long run.

Management options

> Now go back to considerations of management – there are costs and benefits to be weighed up

Social responsibility has costs and benefits for an organisation, and management have to weigh up the **conflicting demands** of different stakeholders. With this must be balanced the duty of managing the business so that the most **effective use is made of the resources** allocated for the purpose. In the context of social responsibility, this can involve the following initiatives.

> What can managers do to take note of social responsibility issues, while continuing in their general duty of managing the resources available to them?

> There is a fine line to tread – it's possible to do too much!

(a) Monitoring the **expectations** people have of the organisation, as an enterprise which trumpets its environmental friendliness will be expected to live up to its claims in all areas.

(b) Achieving maximum **good publicity** for any project.

(c) Selecting **appropriate socially responsible activities**.

    (i) Ensuring that the firm's **core activities** are conducted in a socially responsible way

    (ii) **Subsidising, supporting or sponsoring** those activities which are for public welfare (eg charitable donations)

(d) Clearly distinguishing between what are the **minimum acceptable standards** in a particular situation, and what are **additional** to them.

(e) Reporting the **social audit** has been suggested as a means to monitor the wider record of companies and their responsibilities (eg number of industrial accidents).

4 Development agencies

Tutorial note. This is a tricky question on the environment, which concentrates on the "P" of the PEST framework (the political/legal environment). A variety of incentives, funded by national governments, exist for locating capacity in a particular area. Think of the reasons why this might be, and do not let the specific language of the question (the Acronym 'RDA', for example) put you off providing a sensible answer. There are clues in the question scenario as to the issues involved.

In part (a) set out the objectives of the RDA, then those of the computer manufacturer, followed by your analysis of how they may be expected to coincide.

For part (b) we have offered six influential environmental factors, which would be enough to earn the 15 marks on offer, provided there is adequate explanation of the points given and they are not merely listed. Think of the important supporting factors for a business when setting up anywhere. They can be grouped into the following broad areas:

- Customers and markets
- Suppliers
- Competitors
- Labour and physical resources
- Finance

(a)   The objective of a Regional Development Agency is to promote industrial and commercial growth and development in an underdeveloped or declining region, with a view to bringing more employment and economic wealth to relatively underdeveloped areas of the country.

The objective of the computer manufacturer would be primarily a financial one, to seek certain financial returns for its shareholders. The strategic decision to set up a computer manufacturing operation in Europe would seem to indicate the following about the manufacturer.

- Expects increasing sales in Europe
- Wishes to locate a manufacturing plant close to its European markets

The objective of the RDA and the objective of the computer manufacturer would coincide if a location in the region is the best location commercially for the manufacturer. The RDA should therefore have done its best to achieve the following.

- Bring the commercial advantages of the region to the manufacturer's attention
- Offer some commercial incentive itself, if possible
- Offer assistance to the manufacturer in identifying suitable sites

(b)   The environmental factors might have been as follows.

(i)   The availability of components supplies

A computer manufacturer will want supplies of components from external suppliers, and is likely to want the bulk of its supplies to be provided from local sources. Many components will be custom made for the specific manufacturer.

The RDA should have been able to:

(1)   Obtain a list of the components that the manufacturer would want to buy locally

(2)   race local suppliers able to supply the components and who would provide price quotations for them

(3)   Provide this supplier and price information to the manufacturer.

(ii)   Other high-tech manufacturers in the area

The existence of other high-tech manufacturers in the region would be an indication that there are good component suppliers in the region and that other environmental factors might be conducive to small computer manufacture in the area.

(iii)   Proximity to markets

A manufacturing base should be fairly close to its major markets, so as to minimise distribution costs (provided, of course, that manufacturing costs are not so high in the area as to outweigh the advantages of proximity to markets). Geographical distance need not be a problem if there are efficient transport links.

(iv)   Productivity

An important factor in keeping down manufacturing costs is productivity, especially amongst skilled workers. A reputation in high-tech industries for highly productive staff and good labour relations would be an advantage for the region.

(v)   The availability of a good site

The site wanted by the computer manufacturer would presumably be close to a good transport system and a prestige location, to suit the corporate image of a major computer manufacturer. One of the key tasks of the RDA would be to help the manufacturer to locate such a site.

(vi) **Financial incentives**

The government (through the RDA) could offer certain financial incentives to encourage a manufacturer to set up operations in the region. The most obvious of these would be a cash grant, in the form perhaps of a regional development grant and selective regional assistance.

Financial incentives will therefore be a 'sweetener' for the computer manufacturer.

5 U plc

Tutorial note. The answer to part (a) examines the three strategies in turn.

(i) Existing promotional advertising and exhibitions
(ii) Raise prices
(iii) Adapting production procedures

It looks at the potential risks and benefits of each, keeping in mind the objective of increasing market share, turnover and margins, and comes up with a conclusion.

Other points to note are

- The reaction of A Ltd and Z plc to any strategy change of U plc
- The cost of the different options for U plc
- The timescale needed to introduce major changes
- The high investment risk in a major spending programme
- Balancing long-term and short-term benefits for U plc

It is not clear from the question whether the 'alternative' marketing strategies are mutually exclusive, or whether they should be considered in combination. This solution tries to adopt the view that the strategies could be considered either in isolation or in combination.

Part (b) concludes that the offer described would not be good enough for acceptance by Z. Simple manipulation of the figures given in the question, with a basic assumption about turnover levels, shows that Z is a far stronger company. The question does ask whether it would be in the interest of U plc shareholders, so make sure that your answer includes reference to this (even though such a deal would be highly unlikely to take place!)

In part (c) do not forget to mention the benefits of operating synergy (in addition to increased turnover, profit and ROCE). Marketing and production operations, for example, could be combined.

(a) **Existing strategy**

The existing strategy of attempting to **boost market share** by **promotional** advertising and exhibitions has not shown any success to date. It is difficult to relate advertising expenditure directly to higher sales, and it is possible that U plc's market share will improve in the course of time if advertising and exhibition displays are continued.

On the other hand, there may be a weakness in the nature of the advertising campaign – ie what is the objective of the campaign? – and the product might not be one which can be exhibited with any great success. The **reluctance of customers to switch** to a new supplier indicates that advertising might not be an effective marketing strategy at all.

Unless the promotional advertising and exhibitions can be expected to increase sales, or prevent a fall in sales, the expenditure involved in the current strategy will result in a lower **profit/turnover ratio** and lower **profit/capital employed ratio** than would otherwise be achievable.

Strategy to raise prices

The strategy to raise prices so as to achieve a minimum profit/sales ratio of 12½%, compared with the current 7½%, implies **price rises** of at least 5%. If the strategy were successful, profits would be about two-thirds higher, and so the profit/capital employed figure would also rise by about two-thirds to 25%. With an unchanged P/E ratio the **share price** of U plc shares would also rise by two-thirds.

Another advantage of this strategy, compared with the current one, is that the company would make savings in advertising and promotion costs.

The major drawback to this strategy is that U plc's current **low price strategy**, whilst not winning any new customers because of the reluctance of customers to change supplier, could mean that higher prices will result in some loss of business. If the demand for U plc's product is **inelastic**, the financial benefits of a price rise would exceed the drawback of some loss of market share. However, if demand at higher prices shows a **high elasticity**, (which is sometimes the case in oligopoly markets) the loss of sales and market share could be considerable, in which case the higher-price strategy would **fail to achieve the objective** of a 12½% profit/sales ratio.

Adopting production procedures

The third marketing strategy of adapting **production procedures** so as to become more flexible, **responsive to customer demands** and capable of faster **product development**, would presumably have the objective of increasing market share. A Ltd, which has the greatest flexibility of the three companies, has the biggest market share but also the highest variable costs. This strategy, were it successful, might eventually succeed in improving U plc's results so as to become comparable to A Ltd's. However, it is not clear how easily U plc could switch to a strategy of greater flexibility, and what this might involve in terms of scrapping existing capital equipment and converting to a less capital-intensive system of operating.

The third strategy would take longer to implement than the other two, and so its benefits would be longer in coming. It would also be the highest-risk strategy of the three, if a large amount of **capital expenditure** were involved.

The choice of strategy must also take account of **competitors'** reactions. Presumably they have already reacted to the current strategy. A price increase by U plc should not be a direct threat to the others. A change in production methods, though, would be more threatening, and Z plc and A Ltd might take counter-measures of some kind.

Of the three strategies, a strategy of increasing prices might seem to offer the best immediate prospects of improved financial results, but the consequences of higher prices on sales volume ought to be investigated closely before such a strategy is adopted. The strategy of adapting production procedures might offer the best long-term prospects, but it is a high-risk strategy, especially if competitors take successful counter-measures.

(b) It is assumed that the three companies specialise in the single market and that their financial results do not include results from any other trading activities.

A 'takeover' of Z plc by U plc would then appear to be an unusual suggestion, and one that would be most unlikely to succeed.

Suppose, for the purpose of illustration, that the total market were worth £10 million in sales turnover. The results of U plc and Z plc could then be compared as follows:

	Turnover £m		Profit £		Capital employed £	P/E ratio	Market capitalisation £m
U plc	1.5	(7.5%)	112,500	(÷ 15%)	750,000	10.4	1.17
Z plc	2.0	(15%)	300,000	(÷ 20%)	1,500,000	17.3	5.19
			412,500		2,250,000		

On the basis of the figures, it would seem that Z plc has twice the **capital employed** of U plc and over four times the current **market capitalisation**. An offer of only three shares in U plc for two shares in Z plc would be impossibly low.

The offer would be in the interests of U plc shareholders, were it to succeed, because the **ROCE** of the new company would be higher (about 18.3% on the basis of the figures above). Since U plc would be offering three of its shares (currently priced on a P/E of 10.4) for two shares in Z plc (currently on a P/E of 17.3) there would also be a small improvement in the **EPS** for U plc shareholders. This in turn would result in a higher share price, even if the P/E ratio of the new company remained at 10.4.

In order to afford the takeover, U plc would almost certainly have to **issue new shares**, and **control** of the company would be affected. This might not be in the interest of existing shareholders, especially any major shareholder in the company.

As indicated earlier, however, this is not an offer that Z's board of directors or shareholders should wish to accept.

(c)   The growth that might be expected would be as follows:

(i)   Without synergy and without growth, the combined company's **profits and ROCE** would be higher than for U plc on its own.

(ii)   The combined **market share** of the merged company would start at 35%. If the sales turnover of the total market is rising annually, the company's **turnover** would also increase. This should result in a higher total **contribution** and **operating profit**, a higher **profit/sales ratio** and a higher **ROCE**.

(iii)   The combined company might hope to succeed in improving its results through **synergy**.

(1)   **Marketing operations** could be combined, with some savings in costs. There would also be the possibility of more effective sales and promotional activities, resulting in new clients and a bigger market share.

(2)   **Production operations** might be rationalised with some savings in **capital equipment**. This would improve the profit/capital employed ratio and the ROCE.

(3)   There might be some synergy with **R&D activities**, enabling the combined company to develop **new products** more successfully, thus rivalling A Ltd in this respect and so perhaps winning some customers from A Ltd.

6 Marketing orientation

Tutorial note. The essence of a market orientation is to find out what the customer needs and attempt to satisfy those needs, rather than to devise a product or service and then offer it for use.

A non-profit organisation will have 'customers' too. Our answer to part (a) indicates that a bit of re-thinking can help any organisation to focus its effort on its customers. We include three examples. You may have thought of others.

Part (b) is a straightforward examination of the differences between consumer and industrial marketing. It is worth learning these differences, but the concept of the DMU is the most important element to mention.

(a)   **Marketing orientation'** is a management philosophy which holds that the key task of an organisation is to identify the needs and wants of **customers** in a **target market**, and to adapt the organisation to satisfying them **effectively and efficiently**. An organisation whose objective is to make profits would be market-oriented in order to satisfy customers and thereby be more profitable than it could by means of any other policy.

An organisation which does not have a profit objective may be a charity, an organisation formed to promote a cause (for example a political party) or an organisation which is established to provide a certain non-commercial service (for example a club or a government department). These organisations still have 'target markets' and 'customers' with needs to satisfy, and therefore a market-oriented approach by the management of the organisation is a feasible proposition.

An initial **definition of the nature of the business** in which an organisation operates is useful because it helps the business to focus on the interests of the consumer. For example, as profit-making organisations, Hollywood film companies eventually realised that they were not film-makers but firms in the entertainment market. As a result, instead of competing unsuccessfully with television, they switched profitably into the production of television programmes.

A similar exercise might help **non-profit-motivated organisations** to re-assess their future. For example, the fire department of a local authority might redefine its purpose from fighting fires to 'being in the business of minimising injury and damage through fire or other accidents'. This redefinition, if it is in keeping with the needs of customers, would extend the activities of the department to fire prevention, rescuing victims from accidents etc.

Another example might be a public swimming pool, which defines its business, not as providing a facility for swimming but as swimming for general recreation and life protection. In this way, the pool's management might extend its activities into swimming classes, life-saving classes, opening a swimming club for sports competition etc.

As a final example, a charitable organisation might define itself, not in terms of raising funds and providing food to help a starving population in an overseas country, (product or service orientation) but in terms of the business of providing for the health and security of the population in the short term and for the improvement of the population's well-being in the longer term (ie market orientation). In this way the charity's management might actively seek ways, not only of providing food and medical supplies, but also of providing funds for education and investment in agricultural machinery, or even an infrastructure of roads and communications for the country concerned.

(b)   An understanding of who buys your product, how they buy it and what influences the buying process is fundamental to establishing marketing strategy for both **consumer** and **industrial** marketing managers. There is, however, general agreement that there are certain features in **organisational buying** that are not found in consumer markets and that these features have implications for sales strategy. These are as follows.

(i)   **Fewer potential organisational buyers**. Often 80% of output is sold to relatively few organisations. In consumer selling, the presence of intermediaries (ie wholesalers/retailers) can mean there are relatively few direct buyers, although the ultimate number of end consumers can amount to millions.

(ii)   **Organisational buyers are more rational.** Although people buying for organisations are only human and may, as individuals, prefer the colour of a particular product, on the whole the buying behaviour is more rational. Economic criteria tend to be used. Also, the buying decision has to be justified to other parts of the organisation.

(iii)   **Organisational buying may be to satisfy specific requirements.** Often buyers determine product specifications and so the seller must tailor the product to meet them. In consumer marketing, products are rarely geared to individual customers.

(iv)   **Reciprocal buying may be important.** For example, a company supplying business documentation (eg invoices) to a chain of garages may only get the business if they have all their company cars serviced there.

(v)   **Organisational buying can be more risky.** Often the contract is agreed before the product is made. Technical problems could arise later which could make the product uneconomic to produce. In addition, very large sums of money are often involved, such as with the purchase of a new computer system.

(vi)   **Organisational buying is usually more complex than consumer buying.** Many people could potentially get involved – engineers, directors, marketing people. It may therefore be necessary to sell as a team. The main way in which the decision making process varies is that a **group** of people, rather than an individual consumer, will normally be involved. This is known as the Decision Making Unit (DMU). The DMU is usually made up of:

•   Users (often initiators, for example production)
•   Deciders (those with authority, for example directors)
•   Influencers (marketing, research and development, other managers)
•   Buyers (who execute the purchase)
•   Gatekeepers (for example, secretaries, receptionists)

(vii)   **Organisational buying has a different buying motive** or need. Consumer buying is usually for personal consumption whereas industrial buying is not. The development of formal specifications and the review of potential supplier proposals, together with the development of an order routine, make the process more formal and tangible.

7 Toroidal Tooling

Part (a)

Portfolio analysis examines the current status of the organisation's products and their markets. A variety of techniques may be used, including the product lifecycle concept, the GE business screen and the Shell matrix. One of the best established is the BCG matrix

The Boston Consulting Group (BCG) developed a matrix based on empirical research that assesses a company's products in terms of potential cash generation and cash expenditure requirements. Products (or even complete product divisions) are categorised in terms of market growth rate and relative market share.

(a) Assessing rate of market growth as high or low depends on the conditions in the market. No single percentage rate can be set, since new markets may grow explosively while mature ones grow hardly at all. Toroidal's sales force seems to be well informed about its market and its collective judgement will be useful here.

(b) Relative market share is assessed as a ratio: it is market share compared with the market share of the largest competitor. Thus a relative market share greater than unity indicates that the product or SBU is the market leader. It has been established empirically that market leaders tend to be more profitable than their competitors. This is felt to be due largely to economies of scale. Obtaining this information requires Toroidal to do some desk research in industry publications: their marketing staff are probably best placed to do this.

The matrix offers guidance as to appropriate strategy for each category of product.

Four major strategies can be pursued with respect to products, market segments and, indeed, SBUs.

(a) **Build**. A build strategy forgoes short term earnings and profits in order to increase market share.

(b) **Hold**. A hold strategy seeks to maintain the current position.

(c) **Harvest**. A harvesting strategy seeks short-term earning and profits at the expense of long-term development.

(d) **Divest**. Divestment reduces negative cash flow and releases resources for use elsewhere.

		Market share	
		High	Low
Market growth	High	Stars	Question marks
	Low	Cash cows	Dogs

(a) **Stars**. In the short term, these require capital expenditure in excess of the cash they generate, in order to maintain their market position, but promise high returns in the future. Strategy: build.

(b) In due course, stars will become **cash cows**. Cash cows need very little capital expenditure and generate high levels of cash income. Cash cows can be used to finance the stars. Strategy: hold or harvest if weak.

(c)   **Question marks**. Do the products justify considerable capital expenditure in the hope of increasing their market share, or should they be allowed to die quietly as they are squeezed out of the expanding market by rival products? Strategy: build or harvest.

(d)   **Dogs** may be ex-cash cows that have now fallen on hard times. Although they will show only a modest net cash outflow, or even a modest net cash inflow, they are cash traps which tie up funds and provide a poor return on investment. However, they may have a useful role, either to complete a product range or to keep competitors out. Strategy: divest or hold.

Toroidal has a wide range of products and product groups. It may be advisable to preface the portfolio analysis exercise with an assessment of the appropriateness of the existing classification. This might save a great deal of work in those areas where brand ranges overlap.

Part (b)

The value chain model of corporate activities, developed by Michael Porter, offers a bird's eye view of the firm and what it does. Competitive advantage, says Porter, arises out of the way in which firms organise and perform value activities. These are the means by which a firm creates value in its products

Activities incur costs, and, in combination with other activities, provide a product or service which earns revenue.

Porter grouped the various activities of an organisation into what he calls a value chain, which is illustrated below.

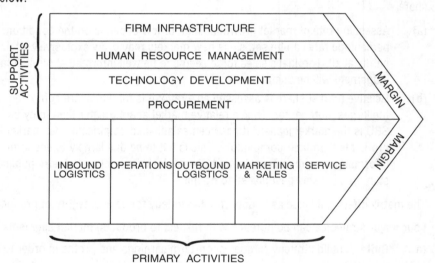

The margin is the excess the customer is prepared to pay over the cost to the firm of obtaining resource inputs and providing value activities. It represents the value created by the value activities themselves and by the management of the linkages between them.

Primary activities are directly related to production, sales, marketing, delivery and service.

(a)   Inbound logistics includes receiving, handling and storing inputs to the production system: warehousing, transport, stock control and so on. Toroidal's apparent poor performance in meeting orders promptly is a weakness that would be highlighted here.

(b)   Operations convert resource inputs into a final product. Resource inputs are not only materials. People are a resource especially in service industries. Toroidal has two kind of operations: manufacturing its own products and dealing those produced by its agency principals. This area will therefore bear close examination in case the two types of operation come into conflict, for example over stock holding and packing (which take us into the next activity).

(c)   Outbound logistics includes storing the product and its distribution to customers: packaging, testing, delivery and so on.

(d)   Marketing and sales activities include informing customers about the product, persuading them to buy it, and enabling them to do so: advertising, promotion and so on. There is much scope for thought here, concerning the multiplicity of brands that Toroidal deals in.

(e)   After sales service includes installing products, repairing them, upgrading them, providing spare parts and so forth. Clearly, Toroidal has problems in this area.

Support activities provide purchased inputs, human resources, technology and infrastructural functions to support the primary activities.

(a)   Procurement acquires the resource inputs to the primary activities (eg purchase of materials, subcomponents equipment).

(b)   Technology development includes such activities as product design, improving processes and resource utilisation.

(c)   Human resource management activities include recruiting, training, developing and rewarding people.

(d)   Management planning activities include planning, finance and quality control. Porter believes that these activities are crucially important to an organisation's strategic capability in all primary activities.

Linkages connect the activities of the value chain.

(a)   Activities in the value chain affect one another. For example, more costly product design or better quality production might reduce the need for after-sales service.

(b)   Linkages require co-ordination. For example, Just In Time requires smooth functioning of operations, outbound logistics and service activities such as installation.

The variety of Toroidal's products, brands and business relationships may make the management of linkages a fruitful area for investigation.

8 Contract catering

> **Tutorial note.** Part (a) of this question is all about converting threats into opportunities. The answer has been structured around the points (i) to (vi) outlined in the question data. The threats (and the opportunities they could create) are then set out. For example, the 'threat' of increasing vegetarianism and health consciousness can be converted into an opportunity to expand the product ranges offered.
>
> Increasing food regulation could also bring opportunities to service markets now wary of being caught in violation of the rules.
>
> In part (b) we have come up with two simple cost measures as required by the question. You may have thought of others. The important thing is to have come up with examples that can represent a *target* to work towards. They should not be over-complicated.

(a)   **Threats and opportunities** (numbers refer to factors identified in question)

(i)   It would seem that most large organisations should be able to provide their own in-house catering more cheaply. Even so, there might be possible clients amongst larger firms, and a contract caterer with sufficient resources to service a large client might see an opportunity in a direct marketing approach to these firms.

The sales and profit potential for contract catering to smaller firms is not clear from the data given in the question. This potential market segment might be profitable as developments in cook-chill catering and automatic vending machines continue.

(ii)   Cook-chill catering appears to bring both opportunities and threats to the market. The **cost advantages** of producing food in a central production unit will include:

–   Saving in kitchen space at distribution points
–   Less capital expenditure on catering equipment
–   Lower maintenance costs
–   Fewer catering staff

Cook-chill food can be prepared during normal working hours and, on re-heating, served up at any time of the day. This should reduce labour costs of overtime working in cases where food has to be provided to shift workers or at odd times of the day.

However, the **safety aspect** of cook-chill foods should be considered, and any firm which invests in cook-chill production methods will find itself liable to its customers and their employees, especially in cases where there is inadequate management and operational controls over the chilling, re-heating or shelf life of the food. There is an opportunity here to improve customer service and client satisfaction (and hence return business) by strict adherence to safety standards that go beyond the minimum required by law.

(iii) The growing preference for health foods suggests that there will be continuing opportunities to develop new or more **varied ranges** of foods in a catering service. The corresponding threat of this development is that any contract catering firm which does not offer vegetarian meals or other health food might eventually find that it loses some customers.

(iv) The removal of Crown immunity from hospitals is likely to make hospitals much more wary about preparing food for patients, or washing up crockery and cutlery by 'traditional' domestic methods. In many hospitals there could be a switch to using 'disposable' food products and disposable plates and cups etc – for example, cook-chill foods, supplied perhaps by contract caterers.

The drawback for firms in this sector will be the need for hospitals to keep their costs under control, so that they are unlikely to buy disposable food products from caterers unless at a low price.

(v) Vending machines linked to a microwave oven can provide a round-the-clock food and drinks service offering a wide range of products. Plastic cards used as 'payment' have the advantage that machines do not have to be continually emptied of money.

Provided that vending machines are clean, efficient and provide a varied product range, there is likely to be a growth market in the vending machine market sector. Many people are fairly casual about eating, and might prefer a vending machine service to a sit-down three course meal in the works canteen or office cafeteria.

(vi) Changing work habits in the City of London creates threats for city restaurateurs who might lose lunchtime business. Restaurants might however be able to attract more evening business, as City workers finally end their day in the early to late evening.

The changing habits might also create opportunities for contract caterers to provide palatable food which can be served quickly to City workers in their work premises during a short lunch break.

Many City firms might increasingly award contracts to such caterers and so this market segment should provide opportunities for rapid growth.

(b) It is assumed that the contract caterer's customers will subsidise the cost of the meals to their employees, so that the meals are sold below cost. Two possible measures of performance.

(i) The **food cost recovery rate** as a percentage of contractor's charges. For example, if meals cost the employer £10,000 and employees pay £3,000 in meal prices, the food cost recovery rate would be 30%. Actual results would be compared against a target food cost recovery rate.

(ii) The **cost per employee** of the catering service. Actual cost would be compared against a target.

9 Product market strategy

Tutorial note. This question requires practical application of two syllabus models to various companies in different industries, and as such it is typical of questions at this level. You must be able to analyse the information presented, in this case identifying the phase of development reached by each industry, then applying Ansoff's matrix. You may have been distracted by the phrase 'industry' life cycle, but this is no different in principle to the product life cycle with which you should be familiar. Being able to tie the industries in question to the respective life cycle phases in part (a) should cause few problems, and indeed is not worth too many marks.

Part (b) is more challenging. We have opened our answer with a diagram to link the narrative to, as it makes the answer easier to follow. You may have done the same, as it helps to focus the mind!

In summary, our conclusions for part (b) were broadly as follows

	Key feature	Option
• Company A	Innovation	Product development
• Company B	Growing market	Product development and/or market penetration
• Company C	Mature market	Market development
• Company D	Weak position, with sales down	Divestment to free resources before fighting on where possible

(a)   (i)   The **industry life cycle** reflects the fact that the profitability and sales of an industry can be expected to change over time. It is an attempt to recognise distinct stages in an industry's sales history. The classic **life cycle pattern** is commonly described by a curve as follows.

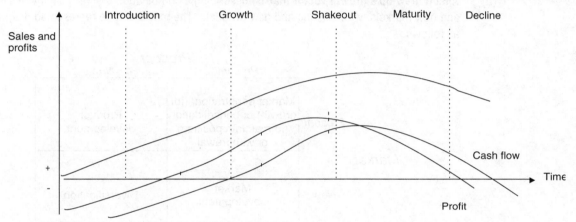

Introduction

(1) A new industry product takes time to find acceptance by would-be purchasers and there is a slow growth in sales. Unit costs are high because of low output and expensive sales promotion.

(2) There may be early teething troubles with technology.

(3) The industry for the time being is a loss-maker.

Growth

(1) With market acceptance, sales will eventually rise more sharply, and profits will rise.

(2) Competitors are attracted. As sales and production rise, unit costs fall.

Maturity

(1) The rate of sales growth slows down and the industry reaches a period of maturity which is probably the longest period of a successful industry's life. Innovation may have slowed down by this stage.

(2) Most products on the market will be at the mature stage of their life. Profits are good.

Decline

(1) Sales will begin to decline so that there is over-capacity of production in the industry. Severe competition occurs, profits fall and some producers leave the market.

(2)   The remaining producers seek means of prolonging product life by modification and searching for new market segments. Many producers are reluctant to leave the market, although some inevitably do because of market fragmentation and falling profits.

(ii)   The industries in which each of the companies appear to be operating are as follows.

(1)   **Company A**. This is operating in the introductory phase of what is a very new innovation, but this innovation is located within a very old industry.

(2)   **Company B**. This is positioned in a rapidly expanding and relatively young industry, experiencing a growth phase.

(3)   **Company C**. This company is in a mature industry, as witnessed by the low growth but high market share. Profits are likely to be good.

(4)   **Company D**. While the retailing industry itself is not in decline, this company appears to be, as it is losing ground to competitors in what is a highly competitive industry. The competitors may be larger companies able to compete more effectively on marketing mix issues such as price.

(b)   **Ansoff** drew up a **growth vector matrix**, describing a combination of a firm's activities in current and new markets, with existing and new products. The matrix can be represented diagrammatically as follows.

		Product	
		Present	New
Market	Present	Market penetration; (for growth) or consolidation (to maintain position) or withdrawal	Product development
	New	Market development	Diversification

Company A is involved with launching a very **innovative** product to revolutionise an existing market (home security). Such product development forces competitors to innovate and may provide initial barriers to entry, with newcomers to the industry being discouraged. This will give Company A the chance to build up rapid **market penetration**, but as competitors enter the market, it must make sure that it keeps household and commercial customers interested via constant innovation. The drawback to this is the related **expense and risk**. Company A must also make sure that it has enough resources to satisfy demand so that competitors cannot poach market share.

Product improvements will be necessary to sustain the market, so Company A must make sure that enough resources are given to **research and development** of new technologies (and hence new products) in its field, as well as to maintaining sufficient production capacity to satisfy current demand.

Company B is engaged in a rapidly expanding market that is likely to attract many **competitors** keen for their own share of the market and profits. The growth strategy is limited to the current agricultural market, so referring to the Ansoff matrix above, the company is going to be mainly concerned with **market penetration** and **product development**, with an emphasis on the latter to make life more difficult for new competitors. By investing in product development, the company will see a necessary expansion in its R&D facility. To keep the new products and the company itself in the public eye, it may need to invest more in **marketing** and **promotion.**

With **market penetration**, the company will aim to achieve the following.

•   Maintain or increase its **share** of the current market with its current products, for example through competitive pricing, advertising, sales promotion and quality control

•   Secure **dominance** of the market and drive out competitors

- Increase **usage by existing and new customers**. The customer base is likely to be expanding

Company C is in the **mature phase** of its life cycle. As the current market is mature, the company can achieve growth via the investigation of **new markets**. Referring to the Ansoff matrix, this means pursuing a strategy of **market development.** Seeing as the current market is mature, with satisfied customers and little innovation, there is small scope for market development, unless it is via short term aggressive tactics such as cuts in prices.

Selling current products to new markets is likely to be more successful, and may include one or more of the following strategies.

- New **geographical areas** and export markets
- **Different package sizes** for food and other domestic items
- **New distribution channels** to attract new customers
- **Differential pricing policies** to attract different types of customer and create new market segments
- **Mass marketing techniques** that encourage customers to switch brands

The company may also investigate the possibility of developing **new products** to make up for those that are in the **decline phase** of the life cycle. This may lead to the creation of more **cash cows**.

Company D is in a difficult position, with a weak position in a well established market. It needs to undertake some rigorous **analysis of costs**. A strategy of **divestment** may be advised to enable it to reduce costs and concentrate on more profitable areas of activity. **Resource limitations** mean that less profitable outlets or products may have to be abandoned. This could involve analysis of individual contributions, perhaps using **direct product profitability** techniques.

The market has become less attractive and Company D needs to assess its image and profitability. It is likely that customers have become more discerning on price, as has happened in the UK retailing sector in the past few years. When some product areas have been divested, the company may find that it has the **resources** to pursue strategies of **market penetration** for some products and **new product development** to improve its image with customers.

A strategy of **total withdrawal**, and **diversification** into wholly new industries is not seen as appropriate for any of the companies described in the question. It could not be recommended because of the attendant **risks**.

Company D does need to be careful, and it is facing the most difficult situation of all the companies that have been described. As **Johnson and Scholes** point out, it is one thing to eliminate unprofitable products but will there be sufficient growth potential among the products that remain in the product range?

In addition, new products require some initial **capital expenditure**. Retained profits are by far the most significant source of new funds for companies. A company investing in the medium to long term which does not have enough **current income from existing products** will go into liquidation, in spite of its future prospects.

10 Grier and Box plc

(a) **Value added** is 'the increase in realisable value resulting from an alteration in form, location or availability of a product or service, excluding the cost of purchased materials or services' (CIMA). In a simplified definition, value added is measured as **sales minus materials costs.**

Division	Value added £m	Value added/sales ratio
Electrical equipment	5.3	13.25%
Fluid controls	4.9	19.44%
Metals	9.1	53.22%
Industrial services	19.0	56.38%
Bathroom accessories	2.5	35.71%
Tubes	4.5	75.00%

The MD would appear to be referring to the electrical equipment and fluid controls divisions, whose value added is only about 13% and 19% of sales value respectively. The implications of making and selling low value added items are the following.

    (i)   **Profit/sales ratios** will be small because materials costs are a large proportion of total sales value. For electrical equipment, this was 5% last year, ignoring interest on capital, and for fluid controls, it was 4.8%.

    (ii)   Attempts to **improve efficiency and reduce labour costs** will therefore have only a small effect on profit/sales ratios.

    (iii)   Improving **profitability** will rely largely on reducing materials costs or increasing sales.

    (iv)   A very **large increase in sales** would be needed to earn a sizeable increase in profits.

    (v)   The **working capital investment** in the products will be high, because of the high materials cost of production.

    (vi)   For reasons (i) and (v), **ROCE** will be low.

(b) The fundamental question in both cases is whether each business can make an effective **contribution** to the company in the future. Both divisions are currently earning profits, but if they are unlikely to contribute significantly to the group in future the following will occur.

    (i)   Any capital invested in the division will be tied up, earning relatively low returns.

(ii)   It is therefore be more appropriate to sell the businesses now, to obtain a reasonable price whilst they are profitable, and to use the revenue earned from the sales to invest in projects that would earn a better return.

The bathroom accessories division faces the prospect of having to compete in its market with companies which are currently its customers. The threat of backward vertical integration by manufacturers of bathroom ceramics suggests that the division:

(i)   Might struggle to retain its market share
(ii)   Might even lose market share

The long-term prospects for profit and sales growth are therefore poor.

The tubes division has a very small share of its market. It is doubtful whether the capital investment needed to improve efficiency would be justified (although a DCF evaluation should be made) and in view of the very small market share, the long term prospects for the product are probably poor.

In terms of **BCG classification**, tubes and bathroom accessories are probably **'dog'** products for the company and should be sold off.

(c)   (i)   **Capital expenditure on replacement equipment** to manufacture well-established products should have a **short payback period**, because the products ought to be earning good profits and cash inflows. A payback period of about 2 – 3 years might be suitable.

Capital expenditure on new development projects will be **high risk spending** and so should perhaps be evaluated at a higher DCF cost of capital. However, new projects take time to become established, and so their payback period will be longer than for equipment replacement projects.

A suitable payback period would depend on the nature of the business and the 'normal' time for new projects to become established in the marketplace.

(ii)   If the company wishes to **reduce its gearing**, which is currently high at 60%, a suitable balance should be made in the company's strategic plans between using cash inflows to **reduce borrowing** and using cash inflows to **invest** in modernisation programmes.

Manufacturing companies must remain efficient to be competitive and profitable, and effective modernisation programmes should be an essential feature of their strategic plans. There is no reason why Grier and Box plc cannot use its earnings partly to repay debt and partly for new investments.

The need to reduce gearing from 60% is a valid **strategic aim**. Taking the company's average interest cost of debt is 10%, then the current level of debt would be £4.8m per annum which gives the company an interest cover of only (14.8 ÷ 4.8) 3.1 times.

(d)   There are several main **dangers**.

(i)   The **reporting system**, using performance ratios and budget variances, might be inadequate. It must be capable of providing regular and up-to-date reports which:

(1)   Report key performance measures
(2)   Draw management attention to significant divergences between actual and plan.

(ii)   The **budget** itself might be built on incorrect assumptions and so budget **variances** might be misleading and incorrect.

(iii)   Budgets get **out of date**. There would probably need to be an additional system whereby revised forecasts are prepared, perhaps every three months, and actual results compared against the revised forecast in reports to head office.

(iv)   There has to be a **retained authority** for head office staff to insist on control measures being taken by line managers, when they consider that actual performance indicates a need for **control action**.

11 FG plc

(a) A discount rate of 18% will be used since this gives the worst possible outcome. It is assumed that the cash flows are given net of taxation.

Year	Cash inflow £'000	Cash outflow £'000	Net cash flow £'000	18% discount factor	Present value £
1	100	(125.0)	(25.0)	0.847	(21,175)
2	–	(527.5)	(527.5)	0.718	(378,745)
3	450	(472.5)	(22.5)	0.609	(13,702)
4	650	–	650.0	0.516	335,400
5	700	–	700.0	0.437	305,900
			Net present value		227,678

The project produces a net present value of almost £230,000. It pays back during the fourth year, probably towards the end of the year if the cash inflow occurs evenly.

The project therefore seems viable despite the conservative views taken on cash flows and should proceed. However management should be aware of the following points arising from the information supplied.

(i) The **payback period** is very long and this increases the risk associated with the project.

(ii) There is no information as to how the **net cash inflow** from the additional production has been derived. If it has been assumed that all output can be sold at current prices then this may be over-optimistic.

(iii) If the project were to be financed from borrowed funds this may cause an unacceptable increase in the company's **gearing**.

(iv) The project may produce a higher NPV than shown because of the undefined benefits which may accrue after year 5.

(b) Other factors to be considered include the following.

(i) **Reliability of the plant suppliers**. The project has a long payback period therefore any delay could be critical and would increase the risk substantially. The contract should include penalty clauses to protect FG from the cost of delays, or more than one supplier could be used.

(ii) **Disruption caused by building work**. This may cause lost production in other departments if their activities are disturbed.

(iii) **Staff redeployment**. It may be necessary to make staff redundant or to retrain them, both of which have inherent cost implications.

(iv) **Use of sub-contractors**. FG's customers may not be happy to hear that a third party is now manufacturing the product. It will probably depend on the importance of the product to the customer. FG must have adequate control over the quality and reliability of supply and must instigate appropriate quality control procedures. Clarification is also needed on stock policy – would finished stocks be held by the sub-contractor, and if so, what are the cash flow implications for FG?

(c) The **internal rate of return** (IRR) suffers from a number of **interpretation problems**, particularly with this project. The forecast cash flows are non-conventional in that they do not become positive until year 4. These non-conventional cash flows will result in more than one IRR for the project, which would be difficult for management to interpret.

Another problem with both the IRR and the NPV is that they do not take account of **risk**.

For this simple accept/reject decision, the **large NPV** combined with a consideration of the **qualitative factors** should provide enough information for managers to make their decision.

12 Simon Clark

Part (a)

> **Tutorial note.** This is a very easy question if you have studied your BPP Study Text conscientiously, since the suggested solution follows closely the relevant paragraph in Chapter 12. However, as always, knowing the theory is not enough; it must be related to the setting, as we relate it in our answer below.
>
> You could use Lewin's models to approach this question and you would be awarded appropriate marks so long as you demonstrated the pressures and influences on Simon Clark and integrated your answers with the case scenario.

Simon has a range of possible responses to his problem of potential conflict with his staff.

Deny problem exists

Some essentially trivial problems blow over without particular management effort. This type of problem can be ignored. If Simon feels that this is the case here, he can effectively deny that a problem exists and withdraw from considering it further. However, the proposed changes would require very important changes to working practices at the college and conditions of service and the staff are 'most unhappy'. It seems unlikely that denial and withdrawal would be a satisfactory response, since teaching as an occupation is particularly demanding of individual motivation.

Smoothing over disputes

A more active policy would be to suppress the problem by smoothing over any overt disputes, if possible, in order to preserve working relationships. This approach is unlikely to produce the changes evidently required at the College, so Simon may have to combine it with a certain amount of coercion, imposing necessary changes unilaterally. This is a recipe for continuing dispute and the lingering hostility of 'win-lose' situations. The effect on motivation is likely to be even more dire than a policy of denial and withdrawal. Indeed, the teaching staff may retaliate by withdrawing their co-operation and working to rule.

Compromise and negotiation

A more positive approach for Simon to take would involve a willingness to make compromises *via* a process of bargaining, negotiation and conciliation. It is likely that there is some room for manoeuvre in the matter of weekend working, perhaps by offering time off *in lieu*. The staff are no doubt well aware of the potential threat to their interests from the private college and may be prepared to adjust their initial position.

Integration and collaboration

This approach may, perhaps, be extended into a more sophisticated process of integration and collaboration, in which a continuing dialogue can establish both common ground and general agreement as to what is necessary for the achievement of the overall task. To achieve this, Simon must overcome his frustration and attempt to bring the staff into full participation in the changes that affect them.

Part (b)

> **Tutorial note**. Generating support is an important aspect of change management generally. This question is about one department in quite a small organisation, so more complex change management strategies, such as the Gemini 4Rs and the Systems Intervention Strategy are probably over complex. We are concerned here with management techniques that would be useful to the head of a single department in such an organization.
>
> This is essentially a problem of practical leadership. Some aspects of the solution, such as providing resources, are easy both to specify and to implement. Other, less concrete, measures related to human behaviour, such as the importance of communication are less easy to describe and, indeed, to perform. Do not shy away from these less material things and do cover them in as precise a way as you can. It is very easy to be vague and woolly about such matters. Try to be definite. For example, don't just say 'communicate' say 'hold a meeting' as well.

It seems likely from the staff's initial reaction to Simon's proposals that he has not given sufficient thought to enlisting their support. This may reflect his managerial technique, or lack of it. If he is to succeed with his plan to change the way things are done, he will have to improve the way he deals with his staff in both material and intangible ways.

Improve communications

The highest priority is to improve his overall relations with the staff. He must make more effective communication a continuing personal target in order to improve motivation and mutual understanding. He must ensure that the staff see him as approachable and sympathetic to their concerns, within the limitations set by reality.

Improve understanding

Simon Clark should ensure that his staff understand that his proposals are a response to a serious commercial threat that affects them all and not an arbitrary decision. He should point out the potential effects upon them of failing to respond to the commercial competition and the opportunities and rewards that success will bring. He should encourage the staff to think for themselves about the situation the college is in, invite them to debate it among themselves and make alternative proposals if they can. Such participation, even if it does not produce any feasible new ideas, will make whatever solution is eventually decided upon more acceptable.

However, Simon must not abdicate responsibility. It is his role to make the final decision and to implement it. There are several measures he can take to promote acceptance of change.

Promote acceptance of change

He may be able to **enlist the support of more senior staff** who have the respect of their peers as change agents. Their role would be to lend their credibility to the new arrangements, to assist with its planning and implementation and to provide practical day-to-day leadership in the context of change.

He should **support positive responses** to change with praise and reward and deal firmly with negative behaviour such as murmuring and absenteeism.

The need for change has been forced upon the College and the Department and it may be that time and resources are limited. However, Simon's aim should be to introduce change at a measured pace and avoid the rush and panic that is sure to upset the staff and provoke hostility.

Similarly, he should make a case for the provision of resources to the change process, so that for instance, some promotions might result, or working conditions be improved. Quite small enhancements such as decorating the staff common room or providing a new photocopier would help to present the change in a positive light.

13 Management accounting information

Tutorial note. This is a familiar topic for examination questions at this level. The relevance of management accounting information has troubled academics and practitioners alike, and has been influential in the development of new techniques (such as ABC or the balanced scorecard) over the past decade or so, in an effort to make management accounting seem more relevant to modern business.

The question is broken down into two parts. The first requires an analysis of the validity of the criticism that management accounting information is irrelevant for decision making. The second part asks you to think about the provision of management accounting information in two different types of organisation.

Our answer to the first part takes the stance that while new techniques are available, many firms do not sufficiently tailor their information collection to specific decisions, and need to develop systems to make sure that they are able to undertake financial analysis, planning and control. No one solution will suit all businesses.

Our answer to the second part considers issues of financial v non-financial information, organisational structure and performance measurement. These will vary between the two organisations concerned.

(a) In 1987 **Kaplan and Johnson** wrote a stinging critique of the management accounting profession in *Relevance Lost*. Seeing the challenge facing management accountants as being one of providing more **relevant** information for decision making, they argued that traditional management accounting systems may not always provide this. Management accounting information is often biased towards the **past** rather than the future, and management accounting systems do not always detect **strategic issues**.

Decision making is a **forward** and **outward** looking process, and management accounting information has been too inward looking and directed largely towards **financial reporting**. Historical costs are necessary to report to shareholders, but the classifications of transactions for reporting purposes are not necessarily relevant to decision making.

Internal vs external focus

Much management accounting information is devised for **internal consumption**. However, strategic management involves looking at the **external environment**, and strategy is pursued in relation to **competitors**. Their actions need to be understood and quantified to be able to devise appropriate response activity.

Some management accounting techniques such as **variance analysis** are seen as too simplistic and largely irrelevant for decision making in a 21st century business. Modern business is embracing new ways of working, including **outsourcing** and **homeworking**, and there is constant pressure to improve quality and service and reduce costs. Some techniques such as **activity based costing** have been developed which are designed to take specific business processes and cost drivers into account when measuring profitability and performance. Techniques such as **customer account profitability and direct product profitability** attempt to replace general analysis with specifics, but in general many firms continue to use old costing systems which are too general in their application to be able to support specific strategic decisions.

It could be argued, that the production of more relevant costs does not necessarily make the management accountant a strategic partner for the chief executive overnight. Management accountants do however need to tackle this issue of the relevance of the information they provide for **strategy formulation** and **control decisions** at higher levels in the organisation. Strategic plans may cover a long period into the future, and often involve big changes and new ventures. How can the management accountant support such developments?

CIMA has defined **'strategic management accounting'** as 'a form of management accounting in which emphasis is placed on information which relates to factors external to the firm, as well as to non-financial information and internally generated information.' Ward suggests that the role of the strategic management accountant can be analysed as being split between **financial analysis,**

financial planning and **financial control**. These roles encompass the current **position** of the business, its **goals** and **objectives** and its **feedback** mechanisms, which compare planned with actual performance. They may involve obtaining information from other **functions** in the organisation, such as production, distribution or marketing.

Contingency theory is a theory that has been developed which states that there is no universally applicable best practice in the design of control systems such as management accounting systems. Specific **business** and **environmental** factors will influence the operation of the system, such as organisational structure, technology and the market. The management accountant needs to analyse and present information which takes these specifics into account.

(b)   Both types of organisation are going to be interested in the provision of a range of both **financial** and **non-financial information.** On the financial side, both organisations will be interested in measures such as cost control, contribution, profits, return on investment, cash flow measures, liquidity, competitiveness and market share. Non-financial measures will include issues such as product or service quality, levels of innovation, customer satisfaction and flexibility in meeting customer needs quickly.

The main distinction between the two companies is in **organisational structure**. One of the companies operates from one site. Usual methods of cost collection, reporting and profitability analysis will be able to be employed. The other is highly fragmented and so information collection may require more detailed systems and closer monitoring of the operatives working from home.

Performance appraisal of staff will be easier for the manufacturing company, and it may be that the staff identify with the company more strongly and are more motivated to achieve **company objectives**, both because they are contracted employees in the traditional sense and because they work together at one site each day. The homeworking contractors may have less sense of such loyalty and could be motivated mainly by considerations such as adding to their own stock of experience and their hourly rate.

The homeworkers are also likely to be working on their own individual projects or tasks, and could all be facing different problems and issues in the effective performance of their work. The standard management accounting system will not necessarily recognise this. It is also possible that they are being paid at different rates according to their experience (this is less likely to be sustainable in a one-site company), making comparisons of individual profitability more complex.

Many organisations operate with off-site employees, and it is becoming increasingly common to employ **outworkers** as traditional working methods are replaced. Standard reports on activities and profitability, both historical and future, are still capable of being produced despite the fact that off-site employees are now more common. The **collection** of such information may be more complicated, but advances in **technology** and computer links should enable information to be logged from remote sites all over the world if necessary.

This scenario provides an example of how management accounting systems need to be **adapted** to organisational realities. Some techniques may be consistently applied in all organisations (measuring employee productivity, for example) while others will be adapted. The one-site company may find it easier than the fragmented one to establish, define (and therefore control) meaningful **cost centres**. Individual **contract profitability** should be easily measurable by both companies, regardless of staff location, although comparing the costs of off-site employees may need to take pay rate differentials into account, as mentioned above.

Measures such as **return on investment** will be more easily defined in the manufacturing company because it is likely to have significant investment in plant and equipment. For the service company on the other hand, the chief asset is its body of professional staff, which may have a high turnover and which is less capable of being assessed in this way. As ROI is normally used to apply to investment centres or profit centres it generally reflects the **organisation structure** of the business. As mentioned previously, such centres are more likely to be a feature of the site-based company.

14 Nominee holdings

> **Tutorial note.** This is a question which includes elements of financial management and management accounting (DCF, performance measurement). Indeed, the DCF rate of return or 'charge out' rate for capital is relevant to quantifying a company's long-term objectives.
>
> The need to balance risk and return is an idea strongly suggested by the data in the question, and this touches on the overall objectives of the group. Sources of finance and gearing have to be considered, and these are problems of financial strategy as well as financial management.
>
> The possible closure of a subsidiary is also a feature of the question, with emphasis on the strategic planning considerations.
>
> It is necessary for some assumptions to be made.
>
> It is not clear whether the project cost is the cost of the initial fixed asset expenditure, or whether it also includes the required investment in working capital.
>
> It is also not clear what is meant by a 'current asset ratio'. If the question intended this to be the current ratio – ie the ratio of current assets to current liabilities, a current ratio of over 1 would indicate that some investment in working capital would be needed in addition to the fixed asset expenditure. A current ratio of less than 1 would indicate that current liabilities would help to finance the fixed assets.

(a)   To: directors of Nominee Holdings

Recommendations to consider

(i)   Three subsidiaries have submitted capital expenditure proposals, all of which would probably add value to the holding company's equity. The nature of the projects should be studied, to ensure that each project is in accord with the group's medium-term strategy. In the case of the Dairy-P project, this might not be so, since the group's strategy might favour a move of processing facilities to Greece. Clearly, if it is the group's intention to close down Dairy-P, the Dairy-P project should not be approved.

(ii)   The holding company's cash and short-term deposits amount to some 20% of its net worth, which is a very high proportion. The company is cash rich. However, its return on its cash and short-term deposits is exceedingly low, at 5%. This poor return compares most unfavourably with the company's average cost of capital (19.5%) and mortgage debenture nominal rates of interest (10% – 17%).

The holding company ought to investigate its cash management, with a view to:

(1)   Improving the return to much more than 5%.

(2)   Using some cash to finance investments by subsidiaries. It is an unsatisfactory situation when the holding company employs its assets to earn 5% whilst subsidiaries are having to borrow at 10% – 17% gross (6.5% – 11% net of tax relief, taking the rate of corporation tax to be 35%) to finance new projects.

(3)   Using some surplus cash to buy back and cancel some ordinary shares in the company. Authority for the company to purchase its own shares would have to be obtained from the shareholders in general meeting.

(iii)   Subsidiaries are required to justify projects financially, using DCF and the group's weighted average cost of capital, on the grounds that each project holds prospects of a positive NPV. The group should re-assess whether the weighted average cost of capital ought to be used. (Further recommendations about this are given in part (c)).

(iv)   **Dairy-P Ltd project**
This is a risky project. The estimated PV of benefits is (£150,000 × 1.41) = £211,500 and the NPV is £61,500. However, the project cost of £150,000 has a standard deviation of £41,000 and so if the actual project cost turns out to be 1.5 standard deviations above the mean, the project's NPV would be negative.

Assuming a normal distribution for project costs, the probability of a negative NPV would be (0.5 − 0.4332) = 0.0668, or 6.68%.

Dairy-P's fixed assets are currently valued at £400,000, and it is not stated how many of these assets provide the security for the first and second mortgage debentures, totalling £250,000. If the project were to go ahead, costing £150,000 in fixed assets plus the need for some working capital investment, Dairy-P might not be able to raise the finance by borrowing without a guarantee being given to the lender from Nominee Holdings. This appears to be unacceptable to the group. Dairy-P would therefore need finance from the cash resources of the holding company.

In view of the uncertain future of Dairy-P anyway, this project appears to be too risky, and incapable of attracting suitable finance at an acceptable rate of interest. Unless the group decides not to switch operations to Greece, and to risk some of its own cash in the project, the Dairy-P Ltd proposal should be turned down.

(v) **Keen Casements project**

This is a fairly small project, which promises to earn an NPV of (0.28 × £65,000) £18,200 on an investment of £65,000.

There is a problem, however, with financing the project. The subsidiary has no loan capital outstanding, but if it had to finance the project by borrowing, it is unlikely that fixed assets worth £15,000 plus the fixed assets bought for the project (up to £65,000) would provide adequate security. Indeed, if the subsidiary has a bank overdraft as part of its negative net current assets (current ratio = 0.65) the bank might already have a fixed and floating charge over the existing assets.

It is assumed that the management of Keen Casements has the ability to invest successfully in a project costing over 400% more than the value of its entire fixed assets at current valuation.

(vi) **Flexi-Carbon project**

This project involves some risk. The estimated NPV is (0.35 × £125,000) £43,750. The standard deviation of the project cost is £15,000, and so the actual cost would have to be 2.92 standard deviations above the mean before the NPV became negative. The probability that this would occur is negligible - (0.5 − 0.4983) = 0.0017 or 0.17%, assuming that the potential project cost is normally distributed.

Flexi-Carbon's gearing level is already quite high. It has fixed assets currently valued at £250,000, a fairly low current ratio (1.21 for the proposed project) and yet mortgage debenture borrowings of £150,000. Further borrowing from external lenders would be difficult, and as with the Keen Casements project, it is doubtful whether the subsidiary could raise the finance unless the holding company itself provided the funds, or at least a guarantee for further borrowing.

(vii) In conclusion, it is recommended that the holding company should finance all (or most) of the Keen Casements and Flexi-Carbon projects, provided that they are in accord with the group's medium-term strategy.

In contrast, the Dairy-P project is more risky, and Dairy-P's future is uncertain. The expectation of higher input costs and the possibility of moving operations to Greece are two aspects of the same problem. If the Dairy-P project is rejected, the group's directors should perhaps initiate discussions with the subsidiary's board about Dairy-P's problems and future.

(b) **Divisional performance** should be measured in such a way as to indicate what sort of return each subsidiary is making on the **shareholders'** investment. Shareholders themselves are likely to be interested in the performance of the group as a whole, measured in terms of return on shareholders' capital, earnings per share, dividend yield, and growth in earnings and dividends.

These performance ratios cannot be used for subsidiaries in the group, and so an alternative measure has to be selected, which compares the return from the subsidiary with the value of the investment in the subsidiary.

Two performance measures could be used which provide a suitable indication of performance from the point of view of the group's shareholders.

(i) **Return on capital employed**, which from the shareholders' point of view would be:

$$\frac{\text{profit after interest}}{\text{net assets at current valuation minus long - term liabilities (eg long - term borrowings)}}$$

(ii) Alternatively, **residual income** could be used. This can be measured as:

| profit before interest (controllable by the subsidiary's management) |

minus | a notional interest charge on the controllable investments of the subsidiary |

equals | residual income. |

Each subsidiary would be able to increase its residual income if it earned an **incremental profit in excess of the notional interest charge on its incremental investments** – ie in effect, if it added to the value of the group's equity.

(c) It is assumed that the rate of charge-out should apply to the reinvestment of operating profits of the group.

It seems that at the moment the subsidiaries are expected to earn a return on their investments in excess of the group's weighted average cost of capital (WACC), in other words the return that the market expects (currently 19.5%). This is not satisfactory, for two separate reasons.

(i) The WACC is not the group's marginal cost of extra capital. Decisions ought to be made on an **incremental** principle, so that if the incremental return from a project exceeds its incremental costs, allowing for the incremental cost of the capital needed to finance it, the project should go ahead. In the case of Nominee Holdings, a cash rich company, the marginal cost of capital at the moment would appear to be the opportunity cost of the cash and short-term investments, which is only 5%.

(ii) Each subsidiary is likely to have different **risk characteristics**. Investments in some subsidiaries will be more risky than investments in others. Investments that are more risky should be expected to promise a higher return, if the principle of the Capital Asset Pricing Model is applied, and arguably, each subsidiary ought to be set its own **target rate** of **return** to allow for its particular risk characteristics.

If the 'risk free' rate of return is taken as 5% – ie the return earned by the group's cash resources, a suitable premium over this rate might be worked out for each subsidiary.

15 The S group

Why is it important to have good information, and where will it be needed?

(a) A key task in the strategic management of any company is a willingness and an ability to understand the environment and anticipate future trends. Information will be required at both strategic and operational level. This is known as **strategic intelligence**, which can be defined as what a company needs to know about its business environment in order to be able to anticipate change and come up with appropriate strategies for the future.

> Use the question wording to break your answer in this part down to:
> - Sources of information
> - Using the information
> - Quality of the information

> Define strategic intelligence

There are many sources of environmental information.

> Broadly, there are internal and external sources for a company to choose from

Internal sources, or sources relatively close to the company, may include the sales force. It deals with the customers and so is in a position to obtain customer and competitor information. Stakeholders in the business such as employees, management and shareholders will influence the business and so are also a good source of internal information. It will be appropriate to set up a **database** for this information, containing both financial and non-financial indicators.

The **management information system** may generate information about the environment as well as information on sales, costs, market share and profitability.

> Think of plenty of examples to use in your answer, guided of course by the number of marks that are available

External sources of information are various. The media (newspapers, periodicals and television) offer many types of environmental information covering all kinds of environmental issues: social, political, economic and technological. Export consultants might specialise in dealing with particular countries (possibly relevant to a multinational like the S Group thinking about new markets), and academic or trade journals will give information about a wide variety of relevant issues to a particular industry. The S Group is likely to subscribe to some of these. As a large multinational, it may be represented on a trade body (an example is the British Retail Consortium in the UK) where it can meet competitors and discuss issues of interest. The **Internet** is also a fruitful source of information.

The **government** and public **databases** can be a source of statistical data, maybe relating to the money supply, the trade balance and so forth. Stockbrokers provide investment reports which often contain detailed analysis of industries and countries, and specialist consultancy firms can provide information. Universities and academic journals publish research results, with projects often being sponsored by large companies like the S Group.

Using the information

> The key to using information and being confident about its quality is being absolutely sure what the information is to be used for. This will influence its presentation

The information can be used in **devising appropriate strategies** for the future direction of the business environment. It is easy to be overwhelmed by the volume of relevant environmental information on offer and the variety of data that could be used, so S must make sure that the information it collects is collated and presented in a **coherent** fashion. This will enable the directors of S to assess the current position of the company and decide upon future strategies appropriate to the business environment.

Assuming that a company the size of S has some kind of **strategic planning function**, then it must make sure that the strategy planning process involves the divisional managers, who will be able to see that the business environment (of which they will be keenly aware) is being taken account of in strategy formulation.

Quality of the information

To be relevant and useful for decision making, the information gathered by S, both internal and external, must be **accurate** and **reliable**. A key priority is an understanding of **why** the information is being collected, and **what** it will be used for. This will indicate the level of detail required.

> **Departmental specialists will be very important in ensuring accuracy**

To be sure of the reliability and accuracy of internal information, **specialists** from the relevant company departments may be required to give assurances on the accuracy of information provided by their systems. Staff 'on the ground', such as the sales staff mentioned earlier, will have a far better knowledge of individual markets and competition activity than strategy setters higher up in the organisation.

> **Important to note that information sources are not static, they will change and evolve with time**

Databases must be used with care as they can rapidly go out of date and must be regularly maintained. S should assure itself of the quality of data from both its internal and external databases. Comparing information from various sources can provide checks as to accuracy. As time goes on and S develops more and more **information sources**, it is likely that these sources will fluctuate in number as the less reliable sources are replaced with more accurate ones, and new methods of collecting information are devised.

(b) ### ROCE

By using return on capital employed (ROCE) as a performance measure, S is using an **historical measure** which is no guide to future performance and shows a lack of a forward looking perspective. **Past results** are not necessarily an indication of **future profitability**. Since the manager of AE is judged on this basis, he may be tempted into decisions which increase AE's short term ROCE. An investment might be desirable from the group's point of view, but would not be in the individual manager's interest to undertake. Thus there is a lack of **goal congruence**. A desire to increase ROCE might lead to projects being taken on without due regard to their **risk**.

> **This part brings in performance appraisal, and you are required to assess the method by which one of the company divisions is measured. Our answer considers ROCE and its limitations, and includes some basic numerical analysis**

If we look at ROCE for the AE division for last year and the previous year, we can see that it has decreased from 10% to 1.24%. This has very little to do with an increase in average capital employed (which has only increased by 1.1% over the year) and everything to do with an erosion in gross profit from 36.7% to 12.5% (see below).

> **Numerical analysis**

The tiny increase in capital employed probably reflects the fact that there is little incentive for the manager to invest (assuming the investment decision is his to take) because any decisions which reduce ROCE in the short term will reflect badly on his reported performance. It is difficult to comment further on this small increase in capital employed, as no information is given in the scenario.

> **Further limitations of ROCE**

A **fair comparison** between different divisions using ROCE is not easily achieved. Fixed assets may be of different ages or may be depreciated in different ways. If a division maintains the same annual profit, and keeps the same assets without a policy of replacement, its ROCE will increase year by year as the assets get older. This can give a false impression of improving 'real' performance over time.

Sales and profitability

> **You will need to consider the sales and profitability of the division, and the importance of transfer pricing issues. Some basic number work should be included to support your analysis**

AE has suffered a reduction in gross profit from $275m to $100m, a decrease of 64%. Head office fixed costs remained constant, but budgeted costs per unit increased from 63% of sales value to 87.5%. This can be attributed to **transfer pricing policy** (see below).

Despite this, it can be demonstrated that the performance of the division last year was an improvement on the previous year in terms of **sales**.

	Last year	*Previous year*
Budgeted sales	K$900m	K$900m
Actual sales	K$800m	K$750m
Increase on previous year	6.67%	–
Actual volumes	16,000 units	15,000 units
% short of revenue target	11.1%	16.7%
Contribution volume variance	K$18m (A)	K$60m (A)

Assembly costs increased by 33.3% across the year, which is surprising given the much smaller increase in sales revenue, and the fact that the budgeted increase was 20%. No more information is given on assembly costs to enable further comment, although the divisional manager should certainly examine these costs as they fall under his control.

The **contribution volume variance** is calculated by multiplying the shortfall in unit sales volume from budget by the budgeted contribution per unit. Performance by this measure appears to be much better than the previous year, but it is probably unwise to read too much into this figure as the unit cost structures in both years are so different, with the budgeted contribution being dramatically reduced last year (from $20,000 to $9,000) after the rise in components transfer costs (which are in any case beyond the control of the divisional manager).

Transfer pricing policy

> It should not be difficult to agree with our conclusion that the transfer pricing policy is punitive. Why do you think such a policy has been imposed upon AE?

This is the area of prime concern as regards impact on AE division profitability. Transfer costs have risen to 75% of sales value last year, which compares with 53% in the previous year. They were budgeted at 70% of selling price (50% in the previous year). Total components costs have increased by 50% over the year, with sales up only around 7%.

Questions need to be asked about how the transfer price is being set. If the transferring division is inefficient, it is transferring those inefficiencies to AE, and AE's profitability is being severely affected. Alternatively the head office of S, under pressure to increase returns to its shareholders, may be deliberately imposing a large transfer price in order to cut AE division profits and **minimise its tax** bill in what is a high rate regime. This is likely to be investigated by tax authorities, especially since there has been a big year-on-year increase.

Either way, the performance of AE is being assessed on factors beyond its control. From the figures given in the question, the transfer pricing policy has contributed to 86% of the division's unit costs and is therefore a highly significant factor in assessing its performance. The board must consider AE's longer term potential for adding to shareholder value. Assessing its performance using ROCE alone, especially when that return is rendered artificially low by high transfer prices, will be to ignore its future profit potential.

(c)

> This part of the question requires consideration of a strategic development proposal. Key issues to consider are goal congruence, strategic 'fit' and the level of risk involved

The key objective of the board of S is to **increase shareholder value** and it must ensure that the AE divisional manager's plans fit in with the overall **strategic direction** of the group. Some acquisitions are driven by the personal goals of the acquiring company's managers. Again, the issue of **goal congruence** needs to be addressed. If it is true that the acquisition will enable AE division to increase market share then the board should give the proposal serious consideration.

It is important for the company to understand its reasons for acquisition, and that these reasons should be valid in terms of its strategic plan. The acquisition may give the AE division a new product range, heightened market presence and enable it to consolidate its distribution process, for example. However, the board of S must consider the level of **risk** involved. Acquiring companies in overseas markets is risky.

The divisional manager of AE is likely to believe, seeing as his division is under threat of closure, that the **opportunities** offered by the acquisition cannot be found within AE itself. However, acquisitions do have associated problems and the board of S may have to consider the following issues.

> Acquisitions do have their problems and our answer includes a consideration of some of these

(i)   **Cost.** The deal may be too expensive, or resisted by the target company. The necessary funds may have to be diverted from other group operations. Advice fees (bankers, corporate financiers) may be high.

(ii)   The **customers** of the target company may go elsewhere and the promised market share fail to materialise. Has enough **market research** been carried out?

(iii)   **Incompatibility**. In general, the problems of assimilating new products, customers, suppliers, markets, employees and different management systems might create problems of 'overload' for AE.

(iv)   **Lack of information**. Will the improvements in market share really be achieved? How strong is the competition? Does the AE division have the skills and experience to see the plan through? It has failed to achieve its own turnover targets, so can it manage those of an entirely new company?

> You might want to refer back to part (b) and reinforce the point that AE is not doing as badly as the initial analysis suggested

Following the analysis presented in part (b), it should be clear to the directors of S that the AE division is improving its performance, despite the transfer pricing policy. This profitability may be jeopardised by the acquisition.

Aside from financial factors such as **expected costs and revenues** (which S must be fully satisfied on if it is to commit funds which could, after all, be deployed elsewhere in the group), the group should bear in mind **non-financial factors** regarding the takeover.

> Remember that the issues to consider are not always financial ones!

Some major problems of **implementation** may arise relating to human resources and personnel issues, such as morale, performance assessment and culture. If key managers or personnel leave, the business will suffer and future development of the new entity (maybe into more new markets) may be compromised.

This acquisition may well be an opportunity not to be missed, but S must make sure that this is indeed the case and that **market development** is likely to flow from it.

> This is a basic necessity

(d)   **Performance measurement** should become more **forward looking** than merely placing a reliance on historical measures such as ROCE. In this way the future of the AE division can be planned with more clarity, and its contribution to increasing shareholder value will be considered over the longer term, although this may clash with some investors who are looking for a **short term return.**

> This revisits the ground covered in part (b) and asks for better ways of measuring the contribution of the AE division.

As an increase in shareholder value is a key objective of the business, performance indicators will be required to assess whether or not the management team is fulfilling this duty. The use of what is known as a **shareholder value approach** to performance measurement involves moving the focus of attention away from simply looking at short term profits to a longer term view of **value creation**, the motivation being that it will help the business stay ahead in an increasingly competitive market. The success (or otherwise) of the new AE division will contribute to the determination of shareholder value.

Shareholder value analysis

> Our answer examines SVA and EVA approaches

This is defined as 'an approach to financial management which focuses on the creation of economic value for shareholders, as measured by share price performance and flow of dividends'. The main premise is that a business is worth the net present value of its **future cash flows**, and these are driven by the following factors: sales growth, operating margin, fixed capital investment, working capital investment, cash taxes, the planning period and the cost of capital.

It follows that these are therefore the factors that the directors of S need to focus on when measuring the performance of the AE division.

When looking at future sales growth and margin, the directors will want to see whether the divisional manager's forecasts of increased **market share** have been realised, but will also need to extrapolate **forecast trends** in the market. This may include a consideration of new products.

Investment in both fixed and working capital will be required if growth is to be **sustained**. Forecast cash flows may need to be revised if growth and return to shareholders is to be achieved. Additional funding may be required.

> Evidence of wider commercial thinking

The level of **corporation tax** borne by the AE division has been high in the past. S has sought to mitigate its effects via its transfer pricing policy, but this may not be viable in the longer term (the policy is onerous, as we saw in part (b)) and S may need to look again at **tax planning** for the division.

> Show that you understand how SVA is applied

The cost of funding the project is fundamental to its success in increasing shareholder value. If the **incremental value** of the acquisition is in excess of the **cost of capital**, then **shareholder value** will be added. The cost of capital should be minimised, and any changes to it reflected in revised NPV calculations.

Economic value management

This is another form of strategic value analysis and hinges on the calculation of **economic profit (EP).** The calculation of EP requires several **adjustments** to be made to **traditionally reported accounting profits**. These are intended to produce a figure for capital employed which is a more accurate reflection of the base upon which shareholders except their returns to accrue, and to provide a figure which is a more realistic measure of the **actual cash generated** for shareholders from recurring business activities.

In the case of the AE division, adjustments could be made to take the transfer price items out of the calculation and apply a **notional cost of capital** to the adjusted profit. This would eliminate the somewhat artificial (and high) transfer price from the consideration of the **economic value added** by the division. The figures would read as follows.

		Last year K$m	Previous year K$m
Sales		800	750
Division costs	– assembly	(100)	(75)
	– head office	(75)	(75)
Cost of capital (say 12%)		(242)	(240)
EVA		383	360

This analysis can be carried further and presented in terms of future expectations for the new division. This will enable future performance to be planned and any action taken that may be necessary to ensure that the acquisition continues to deliver acceptable results.

> With more forward looking information, it will be easier for the S group to plan future divisional performance

Index

Note: **Key Terms** and their references are given in **bold**

Notes

Review Form & Free Prize Draw – Paper P6 Business Strategy (5/08)

All original review forms from the entire BPP range, completed with genuine comments, will be entered into one of two draws on 31 January 2009 and 31 July 2009. The names on the first four forms picked out on each occasion will be sent a cheque for £50.

Name: _____ Address: _____

_____

_____

How have you used this Interactive Text?
(Tick one box only)

☐ Home study (book only)

☐ On a course: college _____

☐ With 'correspondence' package

☐ Other _____

Why did you decide to purchase this Interactive Text? *(Tick one box only)*

☐ Have used BPP Texts in the past

☐ Recommendation by friend/colleague

☐ Recommendation by a lecturer at college

☐ Saw information on BPP website

☐ Saw advertising

☐ Other _____

During the past six months do you recall seeing/receiving any of the following?
(Tick as many boxes as are relevant)

☐ Our advertisement in *Financial Management*

☐ Our advertisement in *Pass*

☐ Our advertisement in *PQ*

☐ Our brochure with a letter through the post

☐ Our website www.bpp.com

Which (if any) aspects of our advertising do you find useful?
(Tick as many boxes as are relevant)

☐ Prices and publication dates of new editions

☐ Information on Text content

☐ Facility to order books off-the-page

☐ None of the above

Which BPP products have you used?

Text	☑	Success CD	☐	Learn Online	☐
Kit	☐	i-Learn	☐	Home Study Package	☐
Passcard	☐	i-Pass	☐	Home Study PLUS	☐

Your ratings, comments and suggestions would be appreciated on the following areas.

	Very useful	Useful	Not useful
Introductory section	☐	☐	☐
Chapter introductions	☐	☐	☐
Key terms	☐	☐	☐
Quality of explanations	☐	☐	☐
Case studies and other examples	☐	☐	☐
Exam focus points	☐	☐	☐
Questions and answers in each chapter	☐	☐	☐
Fast forwards and chapter roundups	☐	☐	☐
Quick quizzes	☐	☐	☐
Question Bank	☐	☐	☐
Answer Bank	☐	☐	☐
OT Bank	☐	☐	☐
Index	☐	☐	☐

	Excellent	Good	Adeqate	Poor
Overall opinion of this Study Text	☐	☐	☐	☐

Do you intend to continue using BPP products?   Yes ☐   No ☐

On the reverse of this page are noted particular areas of the text about which we would welcome your feedback. The BPP Learning Media author of this edition can be e-mailed at: adrianthomas@bpp.com

Please return this form to: Nick Weller, CIMA Publishing Manager, BPP Learning Media Ltd, FREEPOST, London, W12 8BR

Review Form & Free Prize Draw (continued)

TELL US WHAT YOU THINK

Please note any further comments and suggestions/errors below

Free Prize Draw Rules

1   Closing date for 31 January 2009 draw is 31 December 2008. Closing date for 31 July 2009 draw is 30 June 2009.

2   Restricted to entries with UK and Eire addresses only. BPP Learning Media Ltd employees, their families and business associates are excluded.

3   No purchase necessary. Entry forms are available upon request from BPP Learning Media Ltd. No more than one entry per title, per person. Draw restricted to persons aged 16 and over.

4   Winners will be notified by post and receive their cheques not later than 6 weeks after the relevant draw date.

5   The decision of the promoter in all matters is final and binding. No correspondence will be entered into.